History of West Africa

VOLUME ONE

Edited by
J. F. A. Ajayi
Professor of History, University of Ibadan

and

Michael Crowder
Professor of History, Abdullahi Bayero College, Ahmadu Bello University

Longman

Longman Group Limited
London

Associated companies, branches and representatives throughout the world

First published 1971

ISBN 0 582 64518 2 *cased*
ISBN 0 582 64551 4 *paper*

Printed in Great Britain by J. W. Arrowsmith Ltd., Bristol

Contents

Acknowledgements

The publishers are grateful to the following for permission to reproduce photographs:

G. E. Connah, p. 56; Thurstan Shaw, p. 56; Ivor Wilks, p. 363

Maps by Leo Vernon

Publisher's note

Collation of a symposium work such as this involves accepting the contributions from authors at different times relating to their own writing programmes at the time of commission. As a result the work of some contributors was submitted at a much earlier date than that of others. Professor Thurstan Shaw particularly wishes it to be pointed out that his chapter was written in 1966.

Notes on contributors

R. A. Adeleye, PH.D. (Ibadan) is lecturer in history at the University of Ibadan. He specialises in Islamic movements in the Western Sudan, and in addition to articles in various journals he has published *Power and Diplomacy in Northern Nigeria 1800–1906* (1971).

I. A. Akinjogbin, PH.D. (London) is Professor of History at the University of Ife. His field of historical studies is Yorubaland and Dahomey and he has collected extensive oral traditions in both areas. Publications include *Dahomey and its Neighbours* (1963), *Ewi Iwoyi* (1969) and articles in *The Journal of African History, The Journal of the Historical Society of Nigeria, Odu* and others.

E. J. Alagoa, PH.D. (Wisconsin) is Senior Research Fellow at the Institute of African Studies, University of Ibadan. His speciality is the use of oral tradition in historical reconstruction, and his publications include *The Small Brave City-State: a history of Nembe-Brass in the Niger Delta* (1964) and articles in *The Journal of the Historical Society of Nigeria, The Journal of African History, Africa, Tarikh* and others.

Philip D. Curtin, PH.D. (Harvard) is Professor of History at the University of Wisconsin. Publications include *The Atlantic Slave Trade: A Census* (1969), *Africa Remembered* (1967), *The Image of Africa* (1964), *Two Jamaicas* (1955) and articles in *The Journal of African Studies, African Studies Bulletin* and others.

Robin Horton, B.A. (Oxon.) is Professorial Fellow in the Faculty of Social Science, University of Ife. Widely known for his work on the interpretation of West African religions, particularly of the Kalabari-Ịjọ, his publications include articles in *Africa, The Journal of the Royal Anthropological Institute* and *Man*.

John Hunwick, B.A. (London) is Associate Professor in the Department of History at the University of Ghana. He was previously on the staff of the University of Ibadan where he founded the Department of Arabic and Islamic Studies, and his research and publications are concerned mainly with the history of Muslim West Africa and the growth and development of Islam there.

Nehemia Levtzion, Ph.D. (London) is Senior Lecturer in African History and Chairman of the African Studies Department at the Hebrew University of Jerusalem. Publications include *Muslims and Chiefs in West Africa: a study of Islam in the Middle Volta Basin in the pre-colonial period* (1968) and articles in *The Journal of African History, Asian and African Studies* and others.

A. L. Mabogunje, Ph.D. (London) is Professor of Geography and former Dean of the Faculty of Social Sciences at the University of Ibadan. He specialises in urbanisation in Africa and his publications include *Yoruba Towns* (1962), *The City of Ibadan* (1967) and *Urbanisation in Nigeria* (1969).

Thurstan Shaw, M.A., Ph.D., (Cantab.) F.S.A. is Research Professor of Archaeology in the University of Ibadan and Vice-President of the Pan-african Congress on Prehistory and the Study of the Quaternary. Publications include *Excavation at Dawu* (1961), *Archaeology and Nigeria* (1964) and *Igbo-Ukwu* (1970).

Abdullahi Smith, M.A. (Cantab.) is Professor of History at Ahmadu Bello University and Vice-President of the Historical Society of Nigeria. He is widely recognised as a leading authority on the history of the Islamic States of West Africa.

J. Suret-Canale, Professeur agrégé de Géographie (France) and Docteur ès sciences historiques (U.S.S.R.), is carrying out research at the Centre National de la Recherche Scientifique and is co-director of the Centre d'Etudes et de Recherches Marxistes in Paris. Publications include *Afrique Noire* (2 vols) and *La République de Guinée.*

Ivor Wilks, M.A. (Wales), Ph.D. (Cantab.) is Professor of African History, Northwestern University. He taught at the University of Ghana from 1953 to 1966 and has worked on a wide range of topics in the history of Ghana and adjacent countries. Recently he has been concerned with the development of the Asante state, and its relations with the peoples to the north. His publications include *The Northern Factor in Ashanti History* (1961); articles in *The Journal of African History, Transactions of the Historical Society of Ghana, Africa,* and others; and contributions to various collected papers on Africa.

John Ralph Willis, Ph.D. (London) is Professor of African History at the University of California, Berkeley. His interest has focused on the evolution of Islamic institutions and the growth of Islamic culture in Africa and publications include 'Jihad fi sabil Allah, its Doctrinal Basis in Islam, and some Aspects of its Evolution in Nineteenth Century West Africa' (in *The Journal of African History*, 1967). He has a keen interest in the availability of historical source material and has done much to assist in the reprinting of many rare contemporary books and documents in African history.

The Editors:

J. F. A. Ajayi, B.A., Ph.D., is Professor of History at the University of Ibadan and was a Fellow of the Center for Advanced Study in the Behavioral Sciences at Stanford 1970–1971. His publications include *Milestones in Nigerian History* (1962), *Yoruba Warfare in the nineteenth century* (with R. S. Smith), *Christian Missions in Nigeria 1841–1891* (1965) and articles in *The Journal of the Historical Society of Nigeria, Tarikh* and others. He has also edited (with I. Espie) *A Thousand Years of West African History* (1965) and is general editor of the Ibadan History Series. In recent years he has become the principal spokesman for the Ibadan approach to African history, which he himself did much to pioneer.

Michael Crowder, M.A., is Professor of History at Abdullahi Bayero College of Ahmadu Bello University and former Director of the Institute of African Studies at the University of Ife. His historical writing includes *The Story of Nigeria* (1962), *Senegal: A Study in French Assimilation Policy* (1962), *West Africa under Colonial Rule* (1969) and many articles, introductions to symposia and school history texts. He is currently engaged in research in Borgu on the western border of Nigeria. In addition Michael Crowder has a wide interest in African studies and in the development of African arts and has organised many conferences, symposia and festivals, including the First International Congress of Africanists, the proceedings of which he edited jointly with Professor Lalage Bown.

List of maps

Introduction

J. F. A. AJAYI AND MICHAEL CROWDER

The aim of the editors of the two volume *History of West Africa* is to provide a lucid, scholarly and authoritative synthesis of West African history that can serve as a basic university textbook, as a work of reference for teachers, and a general background for all those interested in West African studies. Because of the great variety of written and oral sources in many languages, the wide range of scholarly work in learned journals, as well as the wide gaps in our current knowledge of West African history, synthesis at this level is still very difficult for the individual historian to attempt. We have therefore called upon the services of scholars noted for their knowledge of particular areas and periods of West African history.

In doing this, we have not been unaware of the difficulties involved in asking over thirty scholars trained in different disciplines and writing in different places to tell different parts of a connected but often controversial story. In this first volume, apart from three introductory chapters on the lands and peoples of West Africa, the archaeology of West Africa and the process of state formation, our approach has been regional and we have varied the regions so as to encourage different perspectives on the complex story. Repetitions and apparent contradictions are inherent in such an approach. Yet, in spite of this and of the large number of authors contributing, we have been impressed, as editors, by the extent to which a coherent picture has emerged about the West African past.

In this first volume, the major emphasis has been on the theme of state formation in West Africa. We believe that the different chapters have substantially advanced our understanding of the processes involved whether in societies which had no centralised administration or in those which already had rudimentary state organisations, whether in the savannah, the forest, or on the coast. We hope that the new insights provided here in the interaction between land tenure, agriculture and other economic activities on the one hand, and state formation on the other, will stimulate further research especially in the area of social and economic history which, as far as West Africa is concerned, has tended to lag so far behind studies in its political history.

Any one who has ever planned a collaborative history on this scale will be aware of the many hazards involved. There are many problems that can be anticipated and accordingly provided for. But there are many that are unexpected. In our case, the Nigerian Civil War occasioned delays and changes of authors for both volumes, often at short notice. This has left those authors who met our original deadline in risk of being out of date even before publication in view of the amount of new material that appears every year on West African history. The death of one of our contributors, the distinguished anthropologist, Dr R. E. Bradbury, when we were already anxious to go to press, is the cause of the one major gap in this book, that on the history of the Yoruba and Edo-speaking peoples before 1500. We are hopeful that this volume will be of sufficient merit and usefulness to justify future editions and we have accordingly commissioned another author to write this chapter. We have been acutely aware of the rapid changes that have taken place in our knowledge of West African history in the little more than five years since we planned this history and invited our authors to contribute to it. The scholarly study of West African history is still in its infancy and we feel it our duty in each succeeding edition to take account of new material and new scholars so that this history can continue to be as authoritative as possible.

One basic editorial point has to be brought to the notice of our readers. We abandoned the attempt to standardise the spelling of personal and place names since there is as yet little agreement on the orthography of these names and many of our authors are firm in their adherence to their chosen orthography. We hope this will not confuse our readers, and our indexer has been assiduous in ensuring that variant spellings of a particular name or place are indexed together. We also hope that this problem of orthography will point to the urgency of establishing standard, universally accepted spellings for personal and place names in African history and geography.

Chapter XI of this volume was originally written in French and we owe the excellent translation to Dr Joan White. We owe a great debt of gratitude for valuable advice received from the many readers we consulted on different chapters, particularly from Prof. Abdullahi Smith on chapters of the Sudanic region.

Finally, this history could not have been published without the support of the University of Ibadan, in particular its Department of History and its secretarial staff; Fourah Bay College of Sierra Leone, in particular its Institute of African Studies and its secretarial staff; the University of Ife, in particular its Institute of African Studies and its secretarial staff; and the Center for Advanced Study in the Behavioral Sciences, Stanford, California, and its secretarial staff. To the Vice-Chancellors of the three universities and the Director of the Center, we wish to express our sincere thanks.

J. F. Ade. Ajayi
University of Ibadan

Michael Crowder
University of Ife
January 1971

CHAPTER 1

The land and peoples of West Africa

AKIN MABOGUNJE

The history of West Africa is the long story of human movements, incursions, displacements, intermixtures or successions of peoples, and of the impact of these on the beliefs, attitudes and social organisation of the various peoples who today inhabit this great area. Without a geographical basis, such a story would be, in the words of Heylyn 'like a dead carkasse having neither life nor motion at all'.[1] Its people, the makers of history, would seem to be walking on air. Moreover, as Michelet said, 'the land too must not be looked upon only as the scene of action. Its influence appears in a hundred ways, such as in the food and the climate. As the nest, so is the bird. As the country, so are the men'.[2]

In spite of the deterministic undertone of Michelet's statement, there is no doubt that much in the history of West Africa becomes understandable when set against the background of the character of the land on which the events took place. For while human ingenuity and resourcefulness are not space-bound, their manifestation and development are often conditioned by the nature of the local material with which they have to work. The result is a close interaction between the people and their land, between the course of history and the elements of environment.

HEAT, RAIN AND WIND

The West African environment is characterised by broad, extensive east-west belts which contrast sharply from south to north. Both the longitudinal extent and the latitudinal diversity are the product of its climates. The climates, in turn, are caused by the geographical location of West Africa and by the seasonal migration and pulsation of two air-masses. West Africa extends roughly from 5° to 25° north latitude and from 17° west to 15° east longitude. In all, it covers some 2.4 million square miles, or nearly five-sixths of the area of the United States. From its western to its eastern

1 Peter Heylyn, *Microcosmus, or a Little Description of the World*, London, 1621, p. 11.
2 Jules Michelet, *Histoire de France*, Paris, 1869, 3rd edn. (preface).

extremities the distance is some 1,750 miles, nearly the same as that between London and Moscow. Its north-south distance is over 1,350 miles, about that from Rome to Oslo. Given its latitudinal position between the Equator and the Tropic of Cancer, West Africa is an area of perpetually high temperature throughout the year. While this means that plant and animal life cannot be retarded because of an insufficiency of heat and light, it makes the availability of moisture a serious problem, and so the rôle of the air-masses becomes of vital importance.

The more widespread of the two is the tropical continental air-mass. This is a warm, dry and dusty air-mass formed over the Sahara desert and known, when on the move, as the Harmattan. At its maximum extent in January it covers the whole of West Africa as far as the Atlantic Ocean. Alternating seasonally with it is the tropical maritime air-mass formed over the southern Atlantic Ocean. This is a warm and humid air-mass which extends in July and August over West Africa to about latitude 21° north. Much of the rainfall in West Africa derives from convectional activities within this air-mass. However, for such convectional activities to give rise to rain, the depth of the tropical maritime air-mass over an area must be at least 3,000 feet.[3] This depth in turn is governed by the height of the front separating the tropical maritime and tropical continental air-masses. This front is known as the Inter-tropical Front (ITF) or sometimes as the Inter-tropical Convergence Zone (ITCZ).

During the period from January to July this front moves progressively inland and allows a sufficient depth of humid air to form over most of West Africa, bringing rain to large parts of the region. From July to December the front retreats southwards, and though rain continues to fall in the southern parts, the north now becomes completely dry, being under the influence of the continental air-mass from the Sahara. Thus we have the well-known seasonal pattern of rainfall distribution in West Africa. In the south rain falls virtually throughout the year but with a tendency towards two seasons, one lasting from March to July, the other from September to December. There is a relatively long dry season of between two to three months from December to March and a short one in August. Total annual rainfall is usually over fifty inches, reaching well over a hundred inches along parts of the coast. As we go north, the rain period becomes concentrated into one season varying from seven to four months while the dry season becomes correspondingly more severe. Total annual rainfall also drops to below fifty and at the Sahara border to less than ten inches.

The air-masses whose vertical convectional movements determine these weather conditions also have a horizontal component in the winds. These winds in the north tend to blow from the north-east. In the south their initial direction is from the south-east, but on crossing the Equator they are

3 R. J. Harrison Church, *West Africa*, 5th edn., London, 1966, p. 22.

forced to veer to the right and so become south-west in direction. Highly regular in their flow, they are known as trade winds, but they have played very little part in the history of West Africa compared with their rôle in East Africa. There, the winds were of crucial importance for sailing boats coming from the shores of India and the Middle East to trade on the East African coastland. West Africa, on the other hand, lies on the offshore side of the north-east trades. While sailing boats from Europe from the time of Christopher Columbus came as far south as the Canary Islands in the hope of being speeded on their voyage to North America by the north-east trades, there was no wind to blow them in the opposite direction within the latitudes of West Africa. Besides, the coast of West Africa is not far from the doldrums of the equatorial low pressure belt. This belt moves north and south each year with the apparent motion of the sun. When the doldrums lie close to the West African coast from about April to September little wind blows, and sailing boats, like that of Coleridge's *Ancient Mariner*, were held up for days waiting for a gust of wind to blow their vessels out of the area.[4]

FORESTS AND GRASSLANDS

This north-south movement of the wind and rainfall belts underlines the latitudinal diversity which is so striking in the geography of West Africa, and which is clearly reflected in the vegetational zoning in the area. The vegetation of West Africa varies from forest in the south through extensive grassland area to desert country in the north (Fig. 1.1). Each vegetation belt extends from east to west, giving a longitudinal spaciousness which has been of great significance in the history of the area.

The forest regions of the south vary from mangrove through freshwater swamps to lowland rain forest. The lowland rain forest is easily the most extensive of them all, reaching inland for about two hundred miles from the coast. It stretches across West Africa from present-day Sierra Leone in the west to the foot of the Cameroon mountains in the east. The only notable break is in the Accra corridor where grassland conditions extend to the coast. The tropical rain and swamp forests in their natural state constitute very dense vegetation and are very humid, with rather subdued light. Their trees grow to some two hundred feet in height and have a girth of over three feet. More typical are their huge buttresses growing from some feet above the base of the trunk.

These characteristics of the tropical rain and swamp forest inhibit dense human settlement. Perhaps in the early stages of human evolution the presence of numerous small game might have supported small groups of hunting, fishing and gathering communities. The difficulty of clearing the humid and dense vegetation with fire must have discouraged agricultural

4 J. W. Blake, *European Beginnings in West Africa, 1454–1578,* London, 1937, p. 14.

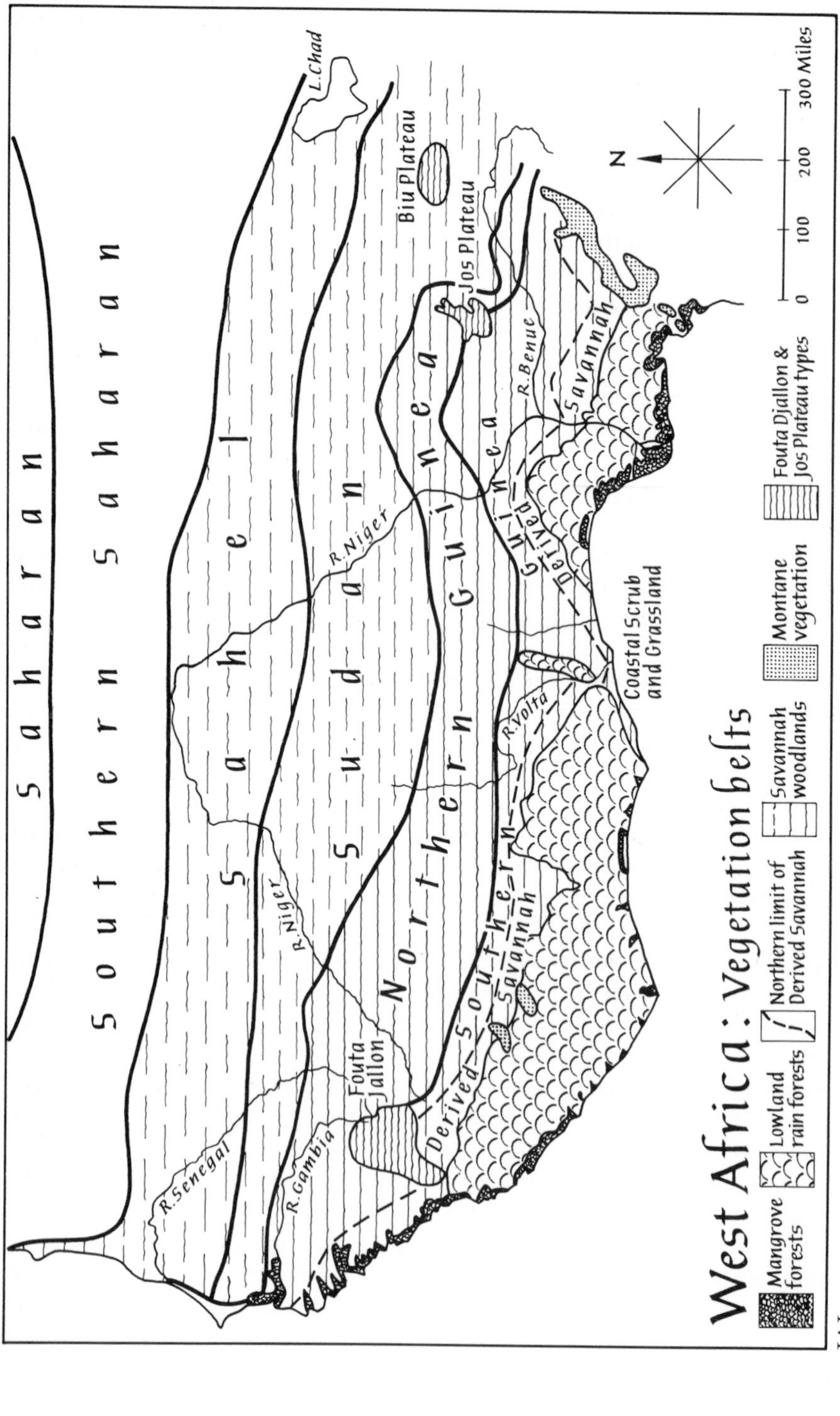
West Africa : Vegetation belts
Saharan
Southern Saharan
Sahel
Sudan
Northern Guinea
Southern Guinea Savannah
Derived Savannah
Derived Guinea Savannah
L.Chad
Biu Plateau
Jos Plateau
R.Benue
R.Niger
R.Niger
R.Volta
R.Senegal
R.Gambia
Fouta Jallon
Coastal Scrub and Grassland
N
0
100
200
300 Miles
Mangrove forests
Lowland rain forests
Northern limit of Derived Savannah
Savannah woodlands
Montane vegetation
Fouta Djallon & Jos Plateau types

1:1

settlement. Indeed it is generally believed that, save for the guinea-yam and oil palm, no major cultivated plants were domesticated in this area.[5] Most of its present wealth in this respect is derived from crops introduced from Asia and America within historical times.

Even today large stretches of the forest belt in Sierra Leone, Liberia, Ivory Coast, Ghana and Nigeria still carry very little population. Paradoxically, some of the most densely settled areas in West Africa today are also to be found in this belt. Many of the more important of these human groups, however, have traditions of having moved in, generally from the north, and of having displaced or absorbed less organised and more primitive aboriginal people. We are thus led to conclude that in the early periods of West African history the rôle of the forest areas has been that of a refugee zone, providing, albeit temporarily, some degree of security from the aggressiveness of stronger, better organised groups in the grassland region to the north.

Grasses cover more than three-quarters of the area of West Africa, but they are not of uniform character, richness or height. In general the grasses grow shorter the further north one goes. In the southern parts they average between five and ten feet and are interspersed by clumps of broad-leaved, short-boled deciduous trees which in places reach as much as fifty feet in height. This is the Guinea savannah, much of which is noted for the prevalence of the tsetse-fly. Much of the Guinea savannah is broken up and the characteristic plains of the land farther north are here replaced by sloping and elevated features such as the Adamawa Highlands, the Jos Plateau, the Atacora Mountains, the Banfora Scarps and the valleys of numerous major streams. Moreover, the balance between the wet and dry seasons has encouraged the development and widespread exposure of infertile, hard lateritic crusts. For these reasons the Guinea savannah is a sparsely populated area. Its broken and rough topography has inhibited the ease of movement of horse-riding invaders so that in parts this region too has served as a refugee zone for weaker, less organised and more primitive groups in West Africa. Driven to the hill-tops or cut off within broad valley slopes, these small groups or fragments of groups have continued to chart their own independent cultural existence, oblivious of, and forgotten by, the world. Today, nowhere else in West Africa is such extreme ethnic and linguistic fragmentation found as in the Guinea savannah region. Of the 434 ethnic groups within Nigeria, for instance, nearly 300 are found within this grassland zone. Most of them number less than 50,000 people and only two groups number over 100,000.

North of the Guinea savannah are the Sudan and the Sahel savannah—areas of generally lower rainfall and shorter grasses. Annual rainfall in the Sudan savannah averages between twenty and forty inches, most of it

5 G. P. Murdock, *Africa, its Peoples and their Culture History*, New York, 1959, p. 66.

coming within four to five months of the year. In the Sahel, average rainfall is between ten and thirty inches and its concentration is between three to four months of the year. In consequence, the grasses are below five feet in height and tend to be feathery. Broad-leaved trees are rarely found and are replaced by shorter, thorny trees with small widely spaced leaves. Murdock believes that the origin of agriculture in Negro Africa must be looked for in this area. He ascribes its introduction to the Mande people who live in the extreme western part of the Sudan grassland around the headwaters of the Niger River.[6] According to him, the major crops domesticated here include the pearl millet, the sorghum, cow-pea, bambara groundnut, calabash and cotton, all of which even today still dominate agricultural production in this area. From this nucleus the crops were diffused eastward until they met the Malaysian complex of food crops coming in from the east.

The Sudan-Sahel grassland country has other significance in West African history. Developed on an extensive, open, level pediplain of the interior plateau of the African continent, it gives a broad vista of land, broken here and there only by the occasional bare rock inselbergs. The expansiveness is tempting and throughout history has served to beckon man to roam and survey the land beyond the next dome hill, to capture it for his own, and to leave on it the imprint of his activities. Ellen Semple's assertion that the statesman of the plain is a nature-made imperialist who nurses wide territorial policies and draws his frontiers for the future might well apply here. To him 'far-flung battle line' is significant only as a means 'to secure a far-flung boundary line'.[7]

Movement and fusion have thus characterised human activities in the Sudan-Sahel savannah. This has been aided in particular by the relative absence of the tsetse-fly and the greater possibility of rearing animals, especially the larger livestock such as cattle, donkeys, horses and camels. These are man's major beasts of burden. These animals are believed to have been introduced into the African continent from Asia by way of Egypt, and all except the camel, which first appeared in Greco-Roman times, arrived along with agriculture in the early Neolithic period.[8] The horse and the camel were the prized animals of the conquering nomad and the means of welding large areas of the Sudan together in one form of political relation or another. But it was cattle and the smaller livestock which ensured sufficient concentration of population to make such political relationships meaningful. Through the meat they provided, and especially through their manure, these animals made agriculture in parts of the Sudan savannah rise to a relatively high level of productivity by the time

6 Ibid.

7 E. C. Semple, *Influences of the Geographic Environment*, New York, 1911, pp. 482–3.

8 R. H. Dyson, 'Archaeology and the domestication of animals in the Old World', *American Anthropologist*, 1953, pp. 661–73.

of ancient Ghana. The surplus production of the dense rural population led to the emergence in this area of numerous urban centres trading across the Sahara with North Africa and Europe during this period.

THE CHANGING ENVIRONMENT

There has been considerable speculation as to whether the climate and vegetation of West Africa have remained stable throughout historical times or whether in fact the desiccating climate of the Sahara has not gradually been extending its way southward. There is sufficiently conclusive evidence that, in prehistoric times, in a period known to geologists as the quaternary, the Sahara was much wetter than it is today and its vegetation was more steppe than desert. Some of the best evidence for this includes the vast complex system of valleys cut deeply into its rocks, as well as the remains of fauna whose normal habitat is known to be more humid than the present desert conditions would permit.[9] This humid cycle in the climate of the Sahara was associated on a global scale with the end of the Ice Age in Europe and a gradual northward shift of climatic belts so that in Africa a belt of dryness came to replace the steppe conditions of the past. But while there is general agreement about this particular change of climate during the quaternary, attempts to extrapolate the trend as having continued into historic times must be viewed with considerable suspicion.[10] Some of the arguments put forward in support of this extrapolation include the Romans' replacement of the elephant by the camel during the fourth century A.D. as well as the ruins of the Roman agricultural economy in the northern margin of the Sahara and its replacement by the pastoral nomadic economy of the Arabs and Berbers. At the southern margin of the desert, the activation of dormant sand-dunes earlier in this century also seemed to lend credibility to this speculation.

None of the arguments, however, can stand up to rigorous examination. The Tunisian Department of Agriculture in the 1920s demonstrated beyond doubt that, with proper management, the rich olive harvests of Roman times could be duplicated today. And Gautier quotes Gsell as saying that 'most of the springs which supplied the Roman settlements are still in existence. Has their volume diminished in the last fifteen centuries? . . . Such rare statements as we have permit us to believe that, in some places at least, this volume has not been modified.'[11]

With regard to the introduction of the camel, it has been suggested that there is no need to postulate a climatic crisis to explain the introduction into an area of an animal more fleet-footed and dependable than others before it.

9 E. F. Gautier, *Sahara, the Great Desert*, trans. D. F. Mayhew, New York, 1935, pp. 56–61.
10 E. P. Stebbing, 'The encroaching Sahara: the threat to the West African Colonies', *Geographical Review*, lxxxv, 6, 1935, pp. 506–24; and *The Creeping Desert in the Sudan and Elsewhere in Africa*, Khartoum, 1953, p. 165.
11 Gautier, *Sahara*, p. 96.

No such crisis has been suggested for the introduction by the Spaniards of horses and cattle into the Americas in the fifteenth and sixteenth centuries.

As for the activation of dormant sand-dunes which Stebbing regards as indicative of a southern extension of the Sahara, there is now enough evidence to ascribe this phenomenon to other causes. Stebbing called attention to the rapid drying out of Lake Chad, a universal lowering of the water table in the area and a consequent reactivation of former sand-dunes.[12] An Anglo-French Commission set up in 1937 to investigate these matters disproved many of Stebbing's conclusions. However, the Commission emphasised the increasing deterioration of the environment by wind and water due to the action of man. It urged, among other things, protection of headwaters, preservation of forests and contour farming.

What emerges from these controversies is the major fact that throughout history human activities have been a most potent factor of environmental modification. In West Africa evidence of this abounds both at the margin and within the vegetation belts. Marginal modification is more commonly the product of deterioration of environment, internal modification may be due to a conscious decision to encourage the cultivation of particular crops. Environmental deterioration is found not only on the margin of the desert and the grassland but also of the grassland and the forest. Both overgrazing and overcultivation can give rise to deterioration of grassland into deserts. An example of this is ancient Ghana. The core of the former empire is now desert, environmental deterioration having set in with the Almoravides Conquest. More recently, the concentration of too many Fulani herdsmen and their cattle at the few water points in the Sahel savannah during the dry season leads to the destruction of the grass cover and the exposure of the sand to the action of wind and rain. Ridge cultivation down the slopes, especially in areas of relatively dense population, helps to concentrate rain water when it comes and facilitates rapid erosion. In either case, the grass vegetation can no longer take root and the condition continues to degenerate until remedial intervention by man is undertaken.

In the case of the forest-grassland margin, the age-old system of land preparation by annual bush-firing has had the effect of killing the forest trees, which are not fire-tolerant, and has favoured the invasion of grasses, especially the tough, spiky *imperata cylindrica.*

Fire-tolerant savannah trees colonise these grasslands and help to simulate a savannah environment in areas which otherwise would be forests. The antiquity of bush-firing is documented by Hanno on his voyage to the West African Coast some 2,500 years ago and its widespread use today points to its having increased in importance over time. More recently, its effect has been accentuated under the impact of rapidly growing population

12 Stebbing, *The Forests of West Africa and the Sahara,* London, 1937, pp. 22–36; see also L. D. Stamp, 'The southern margin of the Sahara: comments on some recent studies on the question of desiccation', *Geog. Rev.*, XXX, no. 2, 1940, pp. 297–300.

and the shortening of the fallow period.

Vegetal modifications have not all been inimical to the best interest of man. Over large areas of forest land, secondary regrowths in which the oil palm dominates provide valuable products for both domestic use and international commerce. Such spectacular transformations of the primeval forests are recorded in the Ibo country of Nigeria as well as in southern Dahomey, Togoland and parts of Sierra Leone. Elsewhere the transformation has resulted from the clearing of the forest by man and its replacement by such tree crops as cocoa, kola and rubber.

Changes in environment may significantly affect the course of history. Because of the relationship between vegetation and climate, there is considerable concern as to the effects any modification, whether natural or man-made, may have on the latter. Aubreville, for instance, considers that the rain forests of West Africa are responsible for replenishing the south-westerly winds with moisture without which the savannahs would have less rain, lower relative humidity and a shorter rainy season—all of which would have adverse effects on human occupation of the area and lead to movements of far-reaching import.[13]

THE STABLE FOUNDATIONS

Unlike the climate and vegetation, the relief and structure of West Africa have shown greater stability. The two most striking facts about the relief are the generally low elevation of between six and sixteen hundred feet and the wide, monotonous, level surface. The low elevation is in part responsible for the generally high temperatures. Compared with the higher plateaux of East and Southern Africa, West Africa is so monotonously hot as to be unsuited for European colonisation. Today, the number of Europeans living there is less than 100,000. Their small number means the absence of a settler problem which, elsewhere on the continent, has bedevilled the struggle of the Africans for self-determination. However, even within West Africa, there are a few isolated plateaux and highlands such as the Fouta Jallon mountains, the Guinea Highlands, the Jos Plateau, the Adamawa, Bamenda and Cameroon Mountains which are generally above 4,000 feet and, in consequence, have much lower temperatures throughout the year (Fig. 1.2). They are free of the debilitating tsetse-fly and, with their grassy cover, have attracted to their heights peoples like the Fulani herdsmen and, in the colonial period, Europeans looking for hill stations to which they could retire during the hottest parts of the year.

The wide, interior grassy plains have been shown to have great historical significance for the movements and migrations of peoples in West Africa. These plains are the products of millennia of erosion by the numerous rivers that drain the area of West Africa, the most important being the Niger, Benue, Volta, Senegal and Gambia. The Niger is the third longest river in

13 A. Aubreville, *Climats, forêts désertification de l'Afrique tropicale,* Paris, 1949, pp. 333–8.

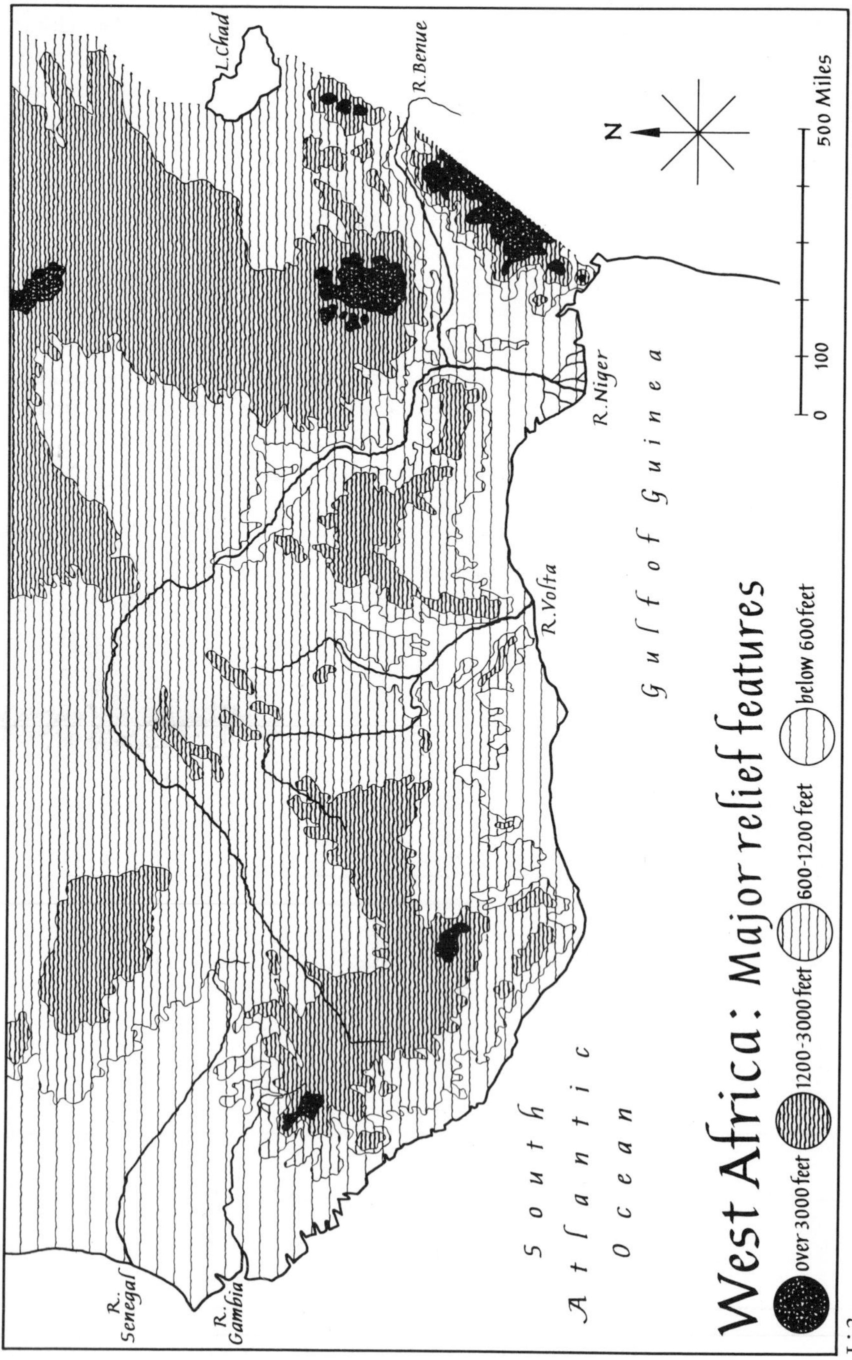
West Africa: Major relief features
over 3000 feet
1200-3000 feet
600-1200 feet
below 600 feet
South Atlantic Ocean
Gulf of Guinea
R. Senegal
R. Gambia
R. Volta
R. Niger
R. Benue
L. Chad
N
0
100
500 Miles

1:2

Africa with a length of 2,600 miles and a course which takes it through all the varied environments of West Africa. It rises on the north-facing slopes of the Fouta Jallon and, after flowing northwards towards the desert, describes an arc between Timbuktu and Gao, and then flows southward through grassland and forest country to reach the sea in one of the most impressive deltas in the world.

In spite of their length and number, the rivers of West Africa have not been very significant as lines of human movement. The existence of falls and rapids along their courses, the presence of delta-swamps and sand-bars at their mouths, and the high seasonality of their flow have made it difficult for vessels of sizeable tonnage to sail any distance on the rivers. Indeed, it has been claimed that these characteristics of the rivers have been a major factor in keeping Africa a 'dark continent' until recently. Today, human ingenuity is coping with most of these problems. The sand-bars are being dredged to facilitate easy entry of vessels, the river flow is being controlled to extend the range of navigability, and the falls and rapids are being dammed to produce the electricity so vital for modern economic development.

The West African coastline was also initially repellent to human contacts from across the seas. For hundreds of miles, its surf-beaten shores show no indentation or natural harbours where ships may berth. The only exception was at the mouth of the River Rokel in Sierra Leone where Freetown was established early in the nineteenth century. Portions of the coast had lagoons which could have provided safe haven for ships, but their entrances were obstructed by shallow sand-bars. These obstacles necessitated the construction of artificial harbours at Takoradi, Tema and Cotonou, and of artificial lagoon entrances at Abidjan and Lagos.

In terms of structure, West Africa shows a basic distinction between old, crystalline, metamorphic rocks of the basement complex and relatively young sedimentary rocks (Fig. 1.3). The basement complex rocks occupy over a third of the area of West Africa and form part of the vast continental foundations. Although they are all known to be pre-Cambrian in age, precise dating has been possible only of a few. Within West Africa, these rocks occur in two major blocks. The western and larger of the two blocks extends from Sierra Leone and Guinea eastward to Upper Volta and western Ghana. The eastern block covers Togoland, Dahomey and most of northern and western Nigeria. The western block is particularly rich in such minerals as gold, diamonds, haematite iron-ore, chrome and manganese ore; the eastern is rich in tin and probably in uranium.

Surrounding these older rocks are sedimentary rocks of various ages. These are largely sandstone, limestone and shale. The sandstone deposits, especially those of paleozoic age, have tended to exercise a negative influence on human settlement as they drain too quickly and create serious problems of water supply. Large areas of Mali and Ghana where they occur have some of the lowest densities of population in West Africa today.

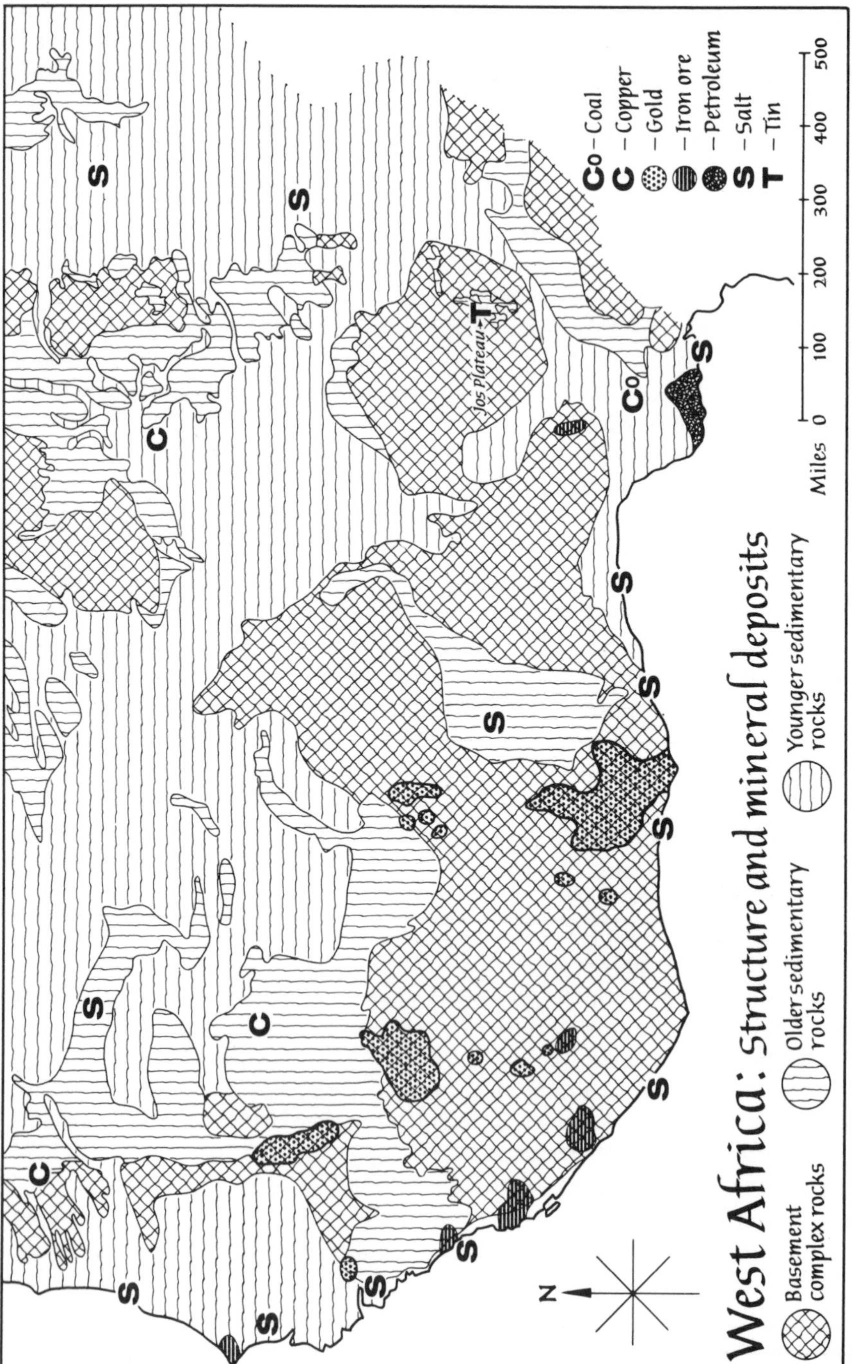
West Africa: Structure and mineral deposits
Basement complex rocks
Older sedimentary rocks
Younger sedimentary rocks
Co – Coal
C – Copper
– Gold
– Iron ore
– Petroleum
S – Salt
T – Tin
Jos Plateau
N
Miles 0 100 200 300 400 500

I:3

Younger sandstone deposits of cretaceous and later age have embedded in them seams of sub-bituminous coal as well as various oil-bearing formations. This is especially true of the area of the Niger delta in eastern Nigeria. These fuel minerals have in recent times been of considerable importance for the economic development of those parts of West Africa where they are found.

Over both the metamorphic and sedimentary rocks, age-long weathering by climatic elements has led to the formation of a surface layer of ferruginous lateritic material. This material is found either in the form of crusts with a thickness of as much as thirty feet or in the form of blocks and pebbles. Most ferruginous laterites have too low an iron content to be of interest to modern large-scale industrial concerns but in the past their significance was considerably greater. Indeed, much in the history of West Africa is related to the ability of various groups to smelt local iron ore and to fashion from it implements of agriculture or warfare.

The origin of iron metallurgy in West Africa is still a matter of some controversy among archaeologists.[14] Some have suggested diffusion from the ancient kingdom of Meroë (or Cush) which flourished for nearly a thousand years in the area of the great bend of the Nile, south of Dongola. Others have suggested ancient Carthage. More recently, there has been suggestion of independent invention within West Africa. At any rate, what is clear is the antiquity of the knowledge of iron-working. Davidson has suggested that the possession of this knowledge has been of critical importance for various conquering groups who have sought to organise the peoples of West Africa into kingdoms and empires. The knowledge of iron-working was crucial for the spread and practice of agriculture among the Negroes. Important centres of ancient working are revealed by huge deposits of slag heaps. Examples of such deposits have been found in the lower Ivory Coast, especially along the Sassandra river, at Bahali in the Chad Republic and at Koulikoro in the present Republic of Mali. Some indication of the pre-European skill at iron-mining in West Africa can be had from a description by Ewart in 1890 of an iron ore mine near Ajilete in the Egbado Division of Western Nigeria. The mine, according to him, consisted of 'a large number of holes eight feet in diameter, now filled up, but formerly sunk to a depth of fifty to sixty feet, out of which excellent iron ore was taken and used for axes, hoes and so on'.[15]

Although iron ore has been of considerable importance for human development in West Africa, gold has been probably of greater historical significance. This mineral is found in pre-Cambrian metamorphic rocks of both the Birimian and the Tarkwaian series. These rocks occur as bankets or conglomerate reefs such as have made the Rand region of South Africa

14 See Thurstan Shaw, ch. 2, p. 69 below.
15 Report of a Visit to Ilaro by Major W. H. Ewart, C.O. 806/334, no. 40, encl. 1, 28 Aug. 1890.

famous. However, a large part of the gold that provided important articles of trade in the period of the great Sudanic empires came from alluvial deposits in the valleys of rivers flowing over these rock formations. Some of the best known areas of alluvial gold workings are thus in the Galam, Bambuk and Boure region between the upper reaches of the Senegal and Niger Rivers, areas which have been identified with the Wangara of medieval documents. Other areas of historical importance include the Lobi area along the Black Volta River in south-western Ivory Coast and the south-western areas of modern Ghana. Gold from these areas was traded with Europe and North Africa through the intermediary of Berber merchants across the desert. Indeed, according to Mauny, the Sudan was probably one of the principal providers of gold to the European world through the Middle Ages, until the discovery of America.[16]

Throughout this period and right up to the late nineteenth century, an important item of barter for gold in West Africa was salt. According to El Bekri, an Arab geographer of the eleventh century, the Ferawi, one of the gold-producing tribes of the forest region of West Africa, were so much in need of salt that they were willing to exchange the one for an equal weight of the other.[17] Much of this salt was in the form of rock salt or natron found in the Sahara desert and in those parts of West Africa bordering on the deserts. There have been workings for centuries at Trarza and Idjil in Mauritania and at Taoudeni in present-day Mali. Saline earths were probably dug around Lake Chad and probably along the dallols or seasonal streams running from the Sahara to the Niger. There is evidence that salt was also distilled from sea water all along the West African coast.

Minerals of minor historical significance in West Africa include copper and tin. Both metals are on the whole rare there and it has been suggested that their relative scarcity has been responsible for West Africa having no developed example of Bronze Age civilisation. The main example of ancient copper mining comes from western Mauritania, near Akjoujt, where Moroccan influence cannot be ruled out. Akjoujt is today a major centre for mining copper, much of which is exported to France. Some smaller examples have been traced at Gaoua in the Upper Volta. Otherwise, copper seems to have been mainly imported in small quantities into West Africa. Tin-mining appeared to have been practised on the Jos Plateau well before the arrival of the Europeans. An important centre for its smelting was Liruein-Delma from where it was distributed in the form of thin rods or 'straws'. Today some 10,000 tons of this mineral are exported annually from the Jos Plateau and provide valuable foreign exchange for the Nigerian economy.

16 Raymond Mauny, *Tableau géographique de l'Ouest Africain au moyen âge,* Dakar, 1961, p. 301.
17 El Bekri, *Description de l'Afrique septentrionale*, trad. de Slane, Algiers, 1913, pp. 327–31; see also E. W. Bovill, *The Golden Trade of the Moors*, London, 1958, p. 84.

These five minerals, but especially iron ore, gold and salt, were the most important historically in West Africa. They provided the implements of war and of agriculture, the precious articles of long-distance commerce, the medium of exchange for high-valued commodities, major alimentary and medicinal salts, and articles of ornament and finery. But of all the minerals and metals, it was the use of iron and the control of the gold trade that provided the basis for the major events of history. As Davidson has emphasised:

> 'Behind the obscurities of early West Africa history, one may reasonably detect iron-smelting and international trade (in gold) as underlying factors which had decisive influence in the hands of men who practised them. Practical and military concentration became possible and at least for those who would rule, desirable. Alliances of interest emerged, became fused into centres of power, acquired geographical identity, and reappeared as territorial states'.[18]

These developments initially took place among peoples within the grassland areas of West Africa and were largely responsible for the emergence of large, fairly well organised human groups within this zone.

PEOPLES AND CULTURES

Unlike in East and Central Africa, there have been no spectacular archaeological finds which might illuminate the history of early man or men-like apes in West Africa. There is, however, a growing body of archaeological evidence of the settlement of the area from the early paleolithic or old Stone Age period. There is no reason to doubt that from that time on the dominant racial group in West Africa has been negroid with slight incursions of members of the caucasoid race. Negroid occupation, in fact, extended over a large part of the present-day Sahara desert and it has been suggested that many of the rock-paintings in that area were due to animal-rearing Negroes whose descendants are still to be found even today in the desert.[19]

The empire-builders of the grassland zone

In terms of historical significance we distinguish between savannah and forest Negroes. The former, in general, tend to be tall in stature and dark brown in skin colour. Some of the best known among them include the Soninke, the Malinke, the Bambara, the Mossi, the Songhai, the Hausa and the Kanuri (Fig. 1.4). The Soninke, Malinke and Bambara belong to a

18 Basil Davidson, *Old Africa Rediscovered*, London, 1964, p. 84.
19 Mauny, *op. cit.*, p. 444.

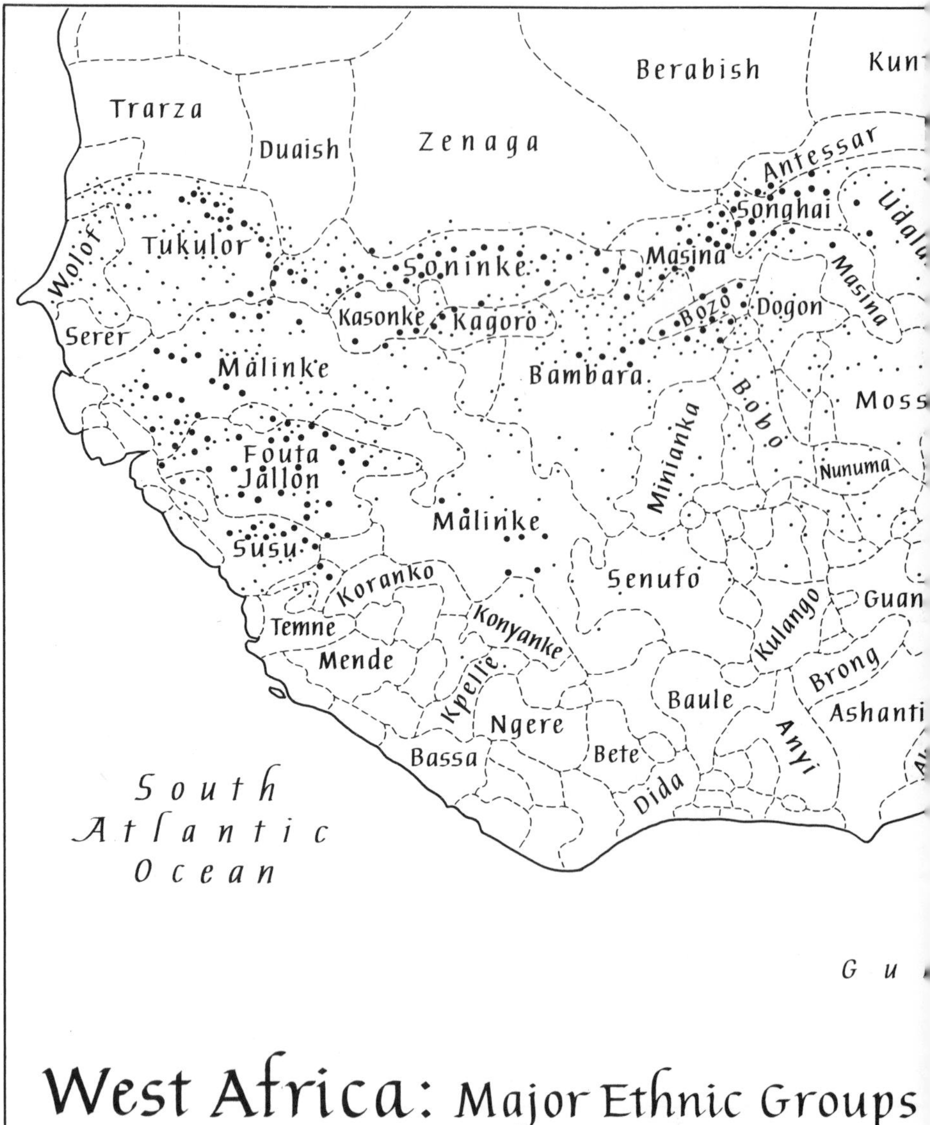
Berabish
Trarza
Duaish
Zenaga
Antessar
Songhai
Wolof
Tukulor
Soninke
Masina
Masina
Kasonke
Kagoro
Bozo
Dogon
Serer
Malinke
Bambara
Bobo
Minianka
Fouta
Jallon
Nununa
Malinke
Susu
Senufo
Koranko
Kulango
Guan
Konyanke
Temne
Mende
Brong
Kpelle
Baule
Ashanti
Ngere
Anyi
Bassa
Bete
Dida
South
Atlantic
Ocean
West Africa: Major Ethnic Groups
FULANI
Aristocrats
Nomad and Semi-Nomads

1:4

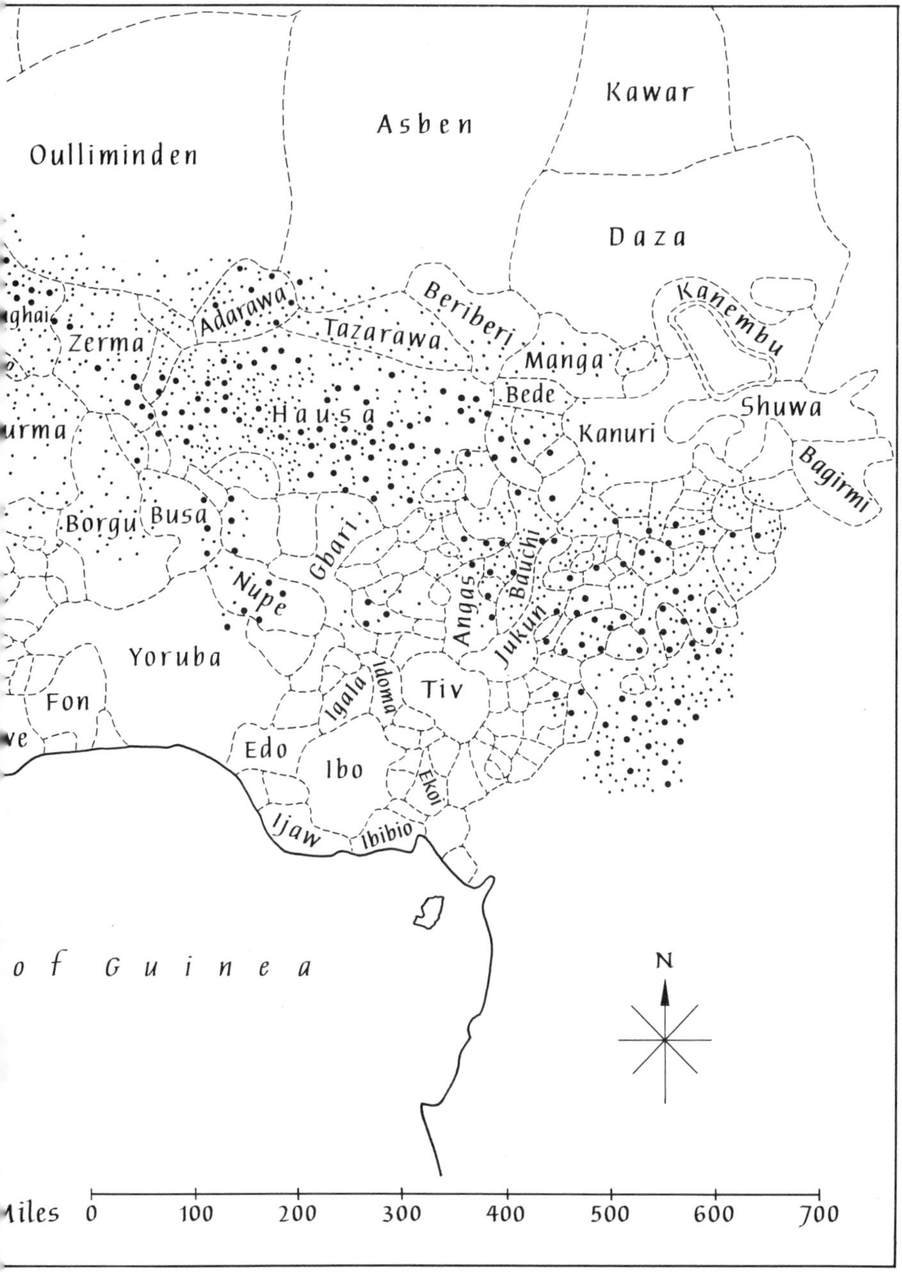
Oulliminden
Asben
Kawar
Daza
Kanembu
Beriberi
Adarawa
Tazarawa
Manga
Zerma
Bede
Hausa
Shuwa
Kanuri
Bagirmi
Borgu
Busa
Gbari
Nupe
Bauchi
Angas
Jukun
Yoruba
Fon
Igala
Idoma
Tiv
Edo
Ibo
Ekoi
Ijaw
Ibibio
of Guinea
N
Miles 0 100 200 300 400 500 600 700

group which are commonly referred to as Mandingoes or Mande-speaking.[20] They are significant in West African history as the group which established some of the ancient West African empires. Murdock ascribes to them the invention of agriculture in the Sudan. The early economic development of these peoples gave them considerable advantage over other peoples and provided the basis for their commercial activities with the Arabs of North Africa. The Soninke who occupied territory close to the edge of the Sahara desert were already organised into the powerful ancient empire of Ghana when the Arabs first appeared in the Sudan. They had evolved complex political institutions which enabled them to weld together numerous smaller groups over an extensive area of the Sudan between the Atlantic and the River Niger and reaching northward into Mauritania. Today the Soninke are highly Islamised. They number less than half a million but are considerably intermixed with other groups such as the Malinke and the Bambara.

The Malinke are a much larger group than the Soninke, numbering almost a million. They, too, by the eleventh century had established a small state on the River Niger which came to be known as Mali. This state grew rapidly in the thirteenth century, occupying large parts of the former empire of Ghana. At its apogee it dominated most of West Africa from the edge of the tropical rainforest in the south, to Senegal in the north-west and Air in the north-east. In spite of the early acceptance of Islam among this group, the majority of the Malinke remain pagan to this day.

The Bambara or Baumana number about a million and, like the Malinke, have been little affected by Islam. They retain their animistic beliefs and ancestor worship except for the small group or caste of fishermen on the River Niger who are largely Muslims and are known as the Somono.

All the Mandingo groups are generally tall and slender in build, with finer features, fuller beard and lighter skin colour than the neighbouring populations. Among them agriculture remains of primary importance and some irrigation is practised. Although animals, including cattle, are kept, just as with the Hausa of Nigeria, this is more often for prestige than for economic reasons. Their typical mode of spatial organisation is in compact permanent villages or towns which are sometimes fortified by an encircling palisade. Each village or each quarter in a town is composed of members of an exogamous lineage. In each community until the colonial period, religious and temporal power was usually combined in one individual known as the *dugutigi*, or 'master of the land'.[21] Traditionally, he was the descendant of the first settler, though in the case of recent migration he could be selected by the community. He was the high priest of the village and remained supreme in all matters concerning the allotment of land as well as in spiritual affairs. Social organisation among the Mandingoes takes the

20 Murdock, *op. cit.*, pp. 64–77 refers to them as the Nuclear Mande.
21 C. G. Seligman, *Races of Africa*, London, 1957, p. 57.

form of age grades of both sexes as well as secret societies, which are particularly composed of elderly men.

West of the Mandingo area and extending to the Atlantic Ocean are various groups, notably the Tukulor, the Wolof and the Serer, whom Murdock refers to as Senegambian. The Tukulor are a Negro group who today occupy the middle Senegal region. From about the seventh century A.D. onwards their territory appears to have covered much of present-day Mauritania and was organised into a powerful state independent of the Soninke Empire of Ghana. However, in the eleventh century, incursions of Berbers who were expanding southward from Morocco under Arab pressure from the rear forced most Tukulor out of this area. More than this, it led to considerable miscegenation between the two groups so that today the Tukulor are regarded as a people of 'two-colours'—the negroid and caucasoid Tukulors.

The Tukulor, however, are clearly Negroes who had accepted Islam by the eleventh century and vigorously engaged in proselytising activities, especially among their close neighbours, the Wolof and the Serer. All three groups show their exposure to Berber influence by their having integrated the milking of cattle with their farming system. The basic unit of their spatial organisation is that of the extended family compound, consisting of a cluster of huts arranged, usually in a circle, round an open space and often surrounded by a fence. Sometimes, especially among the Wolof, these compounds adjoin closely to form compact villages. The Serer live in semi-dispersed hamlets, and, among some of them, no government was recognised beyond the level of local headmen and councils of elders. The Wolof and Tukulor, on the other hand, evolved more complex political organisations. Each state of the Wolof was ruled by a paramount chief whose person was taboo and who had certain of the attributes of a divine king. Their society was characterised by an extreme social stratification, some ten castes being distinguished below the monarchy. These include a landed aristocracy, a hereditary military class, members of craft guilds, free peasants, hereditary house servants, and slaves. The Wolof number about a million while the Serer are about half a million.

East of the Mandingoes and largely within the great bend of the River Niger live the Songhai who, like the Soninke and Malinke, dominated large parts of the western Sudan from the thirteenth century to the end of the sixteenth. The empire they founded extended, at the height of its power in the early sixteenth century, from close to the Atlantic in the west to include most of the Hausa states of Northern Nigeria in the east. Despite the fall of the empire in 1596, the Songhai dominion persisted until the nineteenth century among the two million people who constituted the Songhai nation. Like their neighbours to the west, the Songhai have been exposed to considerable North African influence. This is shown in the strong influence of Islam, the widespread practice of irrigation, the occasional appearance of the shaduf, the use of animal manure as fertiliser and the milking of cattle. Although dependent on agriculture, the Songhai from their famous cities of Timbuktu and Gao have for centuries been engaged in long-distance trade within and beyond the Sudan. They are essentially Negroes although they have miscegenated with Tuaregs and Fulas.

South of the Songhai, in the headwaters region of the Volta river, are found numerous small ethnic groups, the largest and most important of which are the Mossi. Although organised into two powerful federated states—Wagadugu and Yatenga—the Mossi have played a comparatively limited rôle in the great historical events that swept across the Sudan from A.D. 1000. On the other hand, their kingdom seems to have served as a buffer, protecting their smaller and weaker southern neighbours from exposure to these events. Even the impact of Islam was, until the nineteenth century, slight and sporadic. Murdock suggests that the Mossi culture reflects fairly closely the Mandingo culture before the empire-building career of the latter and their contact with the Berbers and Arabs from the north.[22]

Political organisation among the Mossi was derived largely from a religious conception centred on the deification of the earth and of their ancestors. Each local community had a ritual headman charged with the responsibility of maintaining good relations with the earth and thus ensuring the welfare of the people. The local communities or villages were organised into districts under numerous appointive chiefs, who were commonly eunuchs and whose major task was to collect regular taxes and special duties. The districts were grouped into five provinces, each under a governor appointed by the monarch or *Mogho-Naba* who maintained an elaborate court at Wagadugu. The Mossi are an agricultural people but with cattle playing a very limited rôle in their economy.

East of the Mossi is the country of the Hausa. Though essentially Negro and culturally homogenous, the Hausa are not a homogenous ethnic group. Indeed, the word is mainly of linguistic significance, denoting all those people of the Western and Central Sudan who speak the Hausa language as their mother-tongue. According to tradition, the Hausa are all descendants of one Bayajidda (Abuyazidu), son of Abdullahi, king of Baghdad. The latter, after quarrelling with his father, journeyed to Bornu and thence to Daura where he slew a snake that used to prevent the local people from drawing water from a well. The Queen of Daura then married Bayajidda and had a son called Bawo. When his father died, Bawo ascended his throne and had six sons who became the kings of Kano, Zazzau (Zaria), Gobir, Katsina, Rano and Biram. Together with Daura, these states were known as the 'Hausa Bakwai' or the seven Hausa states in contradistinction to the 'Banza Bakwai' or the seven bastard 'Hausa' states which were probably states under Hausa influence. The latter group included Zamfara, Yauri,

22 Murdock, *op. cit.*, p. 78.

Gwari, Nupe, Kororofa (Jukun) and Yoruba. Largely because of the lack of a central authority, the Hausa were never a conquering group but had been subjected to external domination at various times. In the fourteenth century, according to the *Kano Chronicle*, Islam was introduced from Mali, though it also appears to have come in from Bornu at an earlier stage. In the early sixteenth century Hausa formed for a short while part of the Songhai empire, though they also paid tribute to the king of Bornu. Then early in the nineteenth century they were conquered by the Fulani and organised into the present emirates.

The Hausa, apart from being excellent farmers and rearers of stock, are enterprising traders and skilful artisans. They had developed a variety of industries producing in particular textiles and leatherwork which formed important articles of trade with North Africa and other parts of the Sudan in the Middle Ages. Leo Africanus wrote in 1510 about Hausaland that 'here were great stores of artificers and linen weavers; and such shoes made as the ancient Romans were wont to wear, the greatest part whereof is carried to Timbuktu and Gao'.[23]

Islam pervades the social and cultural aspects of Hausa life, although its influence has been minimal among such Hausa-speaking tribes as the Maguzawa and Abagwariga. Islamic influence has been most pronounced in political ideas and organisation and in the legal system. The prevailing pattern of settlement is the dispersed hamlet, although the medieval trade of the area encouraged the flowering of numerous towns many of which such as Kano, Katsina and Zaria, have survived to the present.

Further east are the Kanuri, the Kanembu and the Baghirmi who occupy the Chad Basin. These Negro groups are believed to have been affected culturally by North African groups—the Kanuri by the Arabs and the Kanembu by the Berbers.[24] North African influence, however, is more clearly evident in the degree to which these groups have become Islamised. Islam penetrated this area as early as the eleventh century, though its spread into the highland areas occupied by the Baghirmi and other smaller groups has been limited.

Complex political organisation among the Kanuri, Kanembu and Baghirmi pre-dates the coming of Islam. As early as the eighth century the Sef dynasty had established a hegemony over the area, first in Kanem and later in Bornu. This dynasty lasted for over a thousand years until 1846 when it was defeated by Wadai. It is perhaps the longest dynastic reign on record in the world. Just as with the Hausa, much of the social organisation of the Kanuri, Kanembu and Baghirmi has been influenced by Islam. Their economy is similar to that of the Hausa though groups on Lake Chad practise fishing and cultivate some rice. Age-long participation in trans-

23 Leo Africanus, *The History and Description of Africa*, trans. J. Pory (1600), London, 1896, iii, p. 828.
24 Seligman, *op. cit.*, p. 54.

Saharan trade is reflected here, too, in the existence of towns dating from before the fifteenth century. These towns suffered greater destruction in the nineteenth century than was the case in Hausaland. The Kanuri, Kanembu and Baghirmi today number about three million.

South of the Kanuri are numerous small ethnic groups, the largest among whom include the Jukun and the Tiv. In spite of their small size, the historical rôle of these two groups has been significant. Both the Jukun and the Tiv are largely pagan. The Jukun had by the sixteenth century evolved a complex state known as Kororofa, based on the belief in a semi-divine king, which in the seventeenth century made extensive conquests in the Hausa country. The Tiv, on the other hand, are not known to have evolved any political organisation above the lineage. Their lineage system is peculiar and is based on the principle of segmental opposition. In face of a common enemy, the lineages could and did unite, but only for so long as there was danger. They are a vigorous and warlike people and, with the Jukun, number nearly two million. The two groups are found within the Benue river valley, although Murdock classifies them with the 'Plateau Nigerians'. He also asserts that part of the historical significance of the 'Plateau Nigerians' was their mediating the diffusion of Malaysian food plants from the east to the Guinea Coast as well as their being progenitors of the Bantu tribes who penetrated the equatorial rain forest and ultimately most of the southern third of the African continent.[25]

The forest dwellers

As pointed out earlier, whereas the savannah areas of West Africa have encouraged the movement and fusion of people, the forest areas have served as a refugee zone for numerous small and relatively weak groups. Today this region is characterised by extreme ethnic fragmentation, no less than five hundred ethnic groups having been identified. Some of these groups, especially in the eastern half of the forest belt, are of such size or historical importance that they deserve to be treated in some detail. These include the Ibo, the Edo, the Yoruba, the Nupe, the Fon and the Ashanti. Further west are the Kru, the Kpelle, the Temne and the Mende. Linguistically all these groups belong to Greenberg's Kwa division of the Niger-Congo group. Their economy depends largely on the yam and oil palm in the east and on rice in the west. Many other crops in the area are believed to have been introduced either from Asia or from America. None of the groups keeps more than a few cattle and there is no tradition of milking.

Politically, a number of the more important groups had evolved relatively highly organised nation-states before the advent of the Europeans. Of the six important groups mentioned above as occupying the eastern forest area, only the Ibo had no centralised political organisation above the

25 Murdock, *op. cit.*, p. 90; see also Thurstan Shaw, ch. 2, p. 74, below.

level of the local headman and council of elders. The Ibo occupy the south-eastern part of Nigeria and number some eight million today. Some form of supracommunal religio-political organisation was provided through the agents of the Aro-Chuku Oracle, which was the final arbiter for all inter-tribal strife. Age grade organisation was of particular importance and provided the framework for the administration of individual communities.

By contrast to the Ibo, as early as the twelfth century the Edo of Benin had established a nation-state which conquered and subjugated most of the neighbouring groups by the sixteenth century. The administrative organisation was of a hierarchical type with the Oba or king at the top, who had exclusive right of life and death over his subjects. The kingdom, for administrative purposes, was divided into a number of tribute units or fiefs, comprising variously single villages, groups of villages and chieftaincies. These were confided to fief-holders responsible for their daily administration. The king was assisted in the government of the kingdom by seven hereditary nobles, the Uzama, and two other groups of non-hereditary chiefs. Benin kingdom was one of the earliest African states to come into contact with the Europeans. Indeed, for some time from the end of the fifteenth century, Portuguese missionaries were busy there proselytising the Catholic religion. Their influence, however, did not last long and until recently the Edo religious beliefs centred on a High God with numerous lesser gods and quasi-mythological deified heroes. These beliefs underlie the splendid works of art that have made Benin famous. The ruling family in Benin, though not the generality of the people, claim consanguinary relation with the Ife dynasty of Yorubaland.

The Yoruba people are found west of the Edo, especially in what is now Western Nigeria. Their traditional territory extends to include the south-western part of Northern Nigeria and the south-eastern part of Dahomey. In all, they number about thirteen million people. Although occupying large areas of forest country, the Yoruba were originally a grassland people. With their common religious centre at Ile-Ife and their belief in common descent from Oduduwa, the Yoruba are distinguished by a high degree of cultural homogeneity. Political organisation was based on the existence of kingdoms, each under an Oba or divine king ruling with the aid of the Ogboni society, an elaborate military system, and age grade organisations. All these were conducive to the security of life and property and no doubt contributed to the creation of the numerous large towns that have distinguished the Yoruba from many other Negro peoples. Trading also played an important part in the urban tradition among this people. Their religious beliefs are of great complexity as they include both an elaborate ancestor cult and the worship of a Sky-God, Olorun, and of lesser gods such as Shango, the God of Thunder. Islam has made great progress among the Yoruba but since the 1840s this has been paralleled by the activities of Christian missionaries.

The Nupe are to be found north of the Yoruba country within the broad river valley of the Niger. They are a mixed Muslim-pagan group with a Hausa-like political and economic system. The Etsu Ede is regarded as the founder of the dynasty. The Etsu was an absolute ruler who had an administrative machinery which featured four chiefs as well as palace personalities such as the sister of the monarch. The Nupe kingdom was divided into two regions—one, the domain of the king, the other the domains of his vassals. Political organisation was less centralised than that of the neighbouring Yoruba or Hausa, but Nupe artistic production in copper, glass, textile and hide is still some of the best on the continent. The guild system was also well developed and is in many respects comparable to that of medieval Europe. The Nupe kingdom was first heard of in about the tenth century, but it seems that by the thirteenth century it had been gradually displaced southwards under frequent attacks by the Hausa state of Katsina. The Nupe seem for much of their history to have been in a state of vassalage to either the Hausa or the Yoruba, though on occasion they took the offensive against the Oyo-Yoruba, destroying their capital. Islam was introduced to the area in about 1750 soon after which its dynasty was replaced by a Fulani emir. The Nupe today number a million people.

The Fon occupied much of the southern Dahomey forest and had come into the limelight by the early eighteenth century when they established their famed kingdom of Dahomey. The Fon monarch was an absolute ruler, who ruled the country through an administrative hierarchy of provincial governors, district chiefs and local headmen who were responsible for tax collection. At the capital city of Abomey, the ruler maintained an elaborate court with palace ministers of both sexes. The power of the state and the lucrative trade in slaves were both maintained by a large standing army whose shock troops were the redoubtable Amazons, a corps of some 2,500 female soldiers. For a century and a half after 1730 the Fon kingdom prospered extraordinarily through the conquest of a series of petty coastal states and a virtual monopoly of all external trade on the Slave Coast. The Fon have remained largely pagan, though French influence has encouraged some to turn to Catholicism. They number today over a million people.

West of the Fon, the other group of note are the Ashanti who are typical in every respect of the Akan-speaking peoples and differ from the others only in the exceptional degree to which they have developed the characteristic Akan political institutions. The basis of Akan social organisation is the rule of matrilineal descent. Every freeborn Akan, whatever his tribe, belongs to one of eight exogamous matrilineal clans, each associated with a totemic animal connected with the first emergence of the clan female ancestor on earth. All political offices, from the kingship down, are hereditary in particular lineages of the community in which the office is exercised. Thus, the kingship is vested in a lineage of the Oyoko clan domiciled in Kumasi. Land and other property rights are generally vested in segments of these local lineages.

Political organisation among the Ashanti was decentralised. The Asantehene was a paramount ruler over what was in essence a confederation of provincial chiefs from whom he received financial levies and occasional tributes. The chiefs in their turn exercised authority over sub-chiefs and headmen of villages under their jurisdiction. Besides ruling as suzerain, the king himself exercised the functions of a provincial chief so far as the affairs of the capital and the villages dependent on it were concerned. The king was not an absolute ruler but was controlled to a certain extent by a council comprising the queen mother, chiefs of the most important provinces, and the general of the army. The symbol of national solidarity was the famous 'Golden Stool' which came into being during the time of Osei Tutu (1700–30), the fourth known king of the Ashanti and the founder of the Empire. The Ashanti religion acknowledges a belief in an Earth Spirit as well as in a Supreme God of the firmament who is, however, so remote from human affairs as not to attract worship and propitiation from men. These are reserved for lesser gods as well as for the ancestor spirits. The Ashanti today number nearly two million.

In the forest areas west of the Bandama River are numerous small tribes who exhibit cultures far less complex than those we have so far considered but who reveal an appreciable measure of cultural homogeneity. This cultural homogeneity has presumably resulted from contacts and borrowing within the area. For once these groups were isolated within the tropical forest zone, they seemed to have remained relatively unaffected by subsequent cultural advances in the Western Sudan. All the tribes of the area are negroid and most are pagan. Conversion to Islam has been going on although at a relatively slow pace. The economy is based primarily on subsistence agriculture and fishing and is distinguished from that of areas east of the Bandama river by the emphasis on rice cultivation. Political organisation was of the very simplest, authority nowhere transcending that of the headman and a council of elders at the local level. Among most groups, the headman commonly had a special ritual relationship to the land and was usually responsible for its administration. Secret societies, one for the males, called *Poro*, and another for the females, known either as *Sande* or *Bundu*, have sometimes exercised political and judicial influence beyond the village level, although their major rôle is in the religious activities connected with initiation ceremonies at puberty.

Of the numerous small tribes in this area, perhaps four are worthy of special mention. These are the Kru, the Kpelle, the Mende and the Temne. The Kru number over a million and are found in Liberia and the Ivory Coast. The coastal Kru have long been noted as brave and skilful sailors and fishermen and are to be found on almost every ship trading on the Guinea Coast. They are divided into small commonwealths, each with an hereditary chief, and have a well marked system of age grades. The Kpelle number nearly half a million and are to be found in Liberia and the neighbouring parts of Guinea. The Mende number over a million and form with the Temne the bulk of the interior population of Sierra Leone. The Temne are slightly less numerous and are found mainly in the northern half of the country.

The Fulani and others

Scattered throughout the Western Sudan from Senegal in the west to the Cameroons in the east are the Fulani (Fellata, Fula, Peul), who may be described as a caucasoid group with strong negroid intermixture. They number well over six million but for the most part are found living as ethnic minorities among such populous groups as the Soninke, Malinke, Bambara, Hausa and Mossi. Others are dispersed among the many smaller tribes of the Voltaic and Plateau Nigerian group. Only in a few discontinuous districts do they constitute the dominant element in the population. These include from west to east, the Senegal valley, Fouta Toro, Fouta Jallon, Kita, Masina, Liptako, Sokoto, Bauchi and Adamawa.

The origin of the Fulani has been a matter of considerable conjecture. Greenberg, for instance, has questioned their hamitic origin on the grounds that they speak a nigritic language closely related to those of the Serer and Wolof of the Senegambia.[26] Following on this, Murdock suggests that the ancestral Fulani came from the middle Senegal area and are the product of intermixture between the Tukulor in this area and incoming Berbers from the north.[27] The Berber incursion dated from the eleventh century and initially took the form of aggressive invasion. Later, they resorted to economic penetration, infiltrating with their herds into areas, especially in Fouta Toro, relatively unsuited to agriculture. In the resulting mixture, economic and demographic factors produced a new ethnic group among both the sedentary tillers and townspeople in the middle Senegal valley, namely, the pastoral and the sedentary Fulani.

The expansion of the pastoral Fulani dates from the twelfth and thirteenth centuries when they spread eastward across the Sudan, taking over at first only lands ill-suited to agriculture. For this reason, their expansion caused no alarm to their neighbours who, in fact, welcomed them for the manure their cattle provided on the fields and for the milk and butter which could be exchanged for agricultural products. Few of the pastoral Fulani were Muslim so that religion was not a point of sharp difference with their neighbours. Even when they were Muslim, the pastoral Fulani were generally of a tolerant disposition. However, they were invariably accompanied in their migration by some of their sedentary and more negroid

26 J. H. Greenberg, 'Studies in African linguistic classification', *Southwestern Journal of Anthropology*, v, 1949, pp. 190–8.
27 Murdock, *op. cit.*, pp. 415–16.

kinsmen. These were usually better educated, more sophisticated in political matters, and less tolerant of the infidel. It is this group which fostered the political interest of the whole group by military aggression often in the form of a *jihād* or holy war. It was in this way that the Fulani have become politically dominant in areas such as the Fouta Jallon, Masina, the Hausa country and the Nupe country.

The Fulani political system depended on a complex military organisation and was buttressed by Islamic teachings on the relation between conquerors and the conquered. Lands seized from conquered people became state property. Enemies who submitted voluntarily and accepted Islam escaped enslavement. Others were reduced to serfdom and required to labour on the lands owned by the state. Usually, in conquered territories which were already well organised, Fulani emirs simply replaced the traditional ruler and the subservience of the territory was ensured through an elaborate and effective system of tax collection. This is best seen in the emirates of Northern Nigeria where virtually all the rulers are today of Fulani descent.

Of the other non-negroid groups who are to be found in West Africa, the most important are the Shuwa Arabs of Bornu. Numbering nearly a quarter of a million, the Shuwa are largely pastoral. In the past they constituted the most important element in the Bornu army, and among them whole troops of horsemen were protected by chain armour which is said to reflect the influence of the Crusades. The Shuwa claim descent from Mohammed and are known to have been in this area from about the fifteenth century.

THE MOVEMENT SOUTH

It is evident from the above that the historical centre of population concentration in West Africa was the savannah area. It was here that conditions were most favourable for the development both of crop cultivation and animal husbandry. It was here that contacts with North Africa through the Sahara had stimulated the extensive growth of commercial activities and craft production and encouraged the flowering of numerous urban centres. And it was here that, given the nature of the environment, Negro Africa succeeded in giving rise to many of its famed empires, each of which at various times provided the 'peace' necessary for the pursuit of economic activities over large areas of the continent.

By contrast, the forest region had no such advantage. Although crop cultivation was practised, the environment was hostile to the rearing of livestock except for small animals. Trade activities, where they existed, had to depend on footpaths and human porterage—a fact which greatly limited the scope and volume of trade even among noted traders such as the Yoruba. Urban development was also for this reason greatly circumscribed, the Yoruba being again the striking exception. Generally, mobility was restricted by the absence of draft animals and this probably was one of the major reasons for the small scale of social and political organisation within the forest areas generally.

One of the most striking facts of West African history has been the persistence in various forms of a general movement of population into these forest regions. In ancient times, as already emphasised, this southward movement was an involuntary act by smaller and weaker tribal groups in the face of aggressive incursions of stronger immigrant communities. There has been no conclusive explanation as to the background of these movements from the north. The early Arab geographers treated the movement as the south-westward continuation from the east of the dispersal of people after the Great Flood of biblical mythology. Wahb ibn Munabeh, writing in 738, asserted that the descendants of Kush, who was the son of Ham and the grandson of Noah, include the people of the Sudan. El Masudi, the greatest of the medieval Arab geographers, wrote in the same vein two hundred years later in A.D. 947. According to him 'when the descendants of Noah spread across the earth, the sons of Kush, the son of Canaan, travelled towards the west and crossed the Nile. There they separated. Some of them, the Nubians and the Beja and the Zanj, turned to the rightward, between the east and the west; but the others, very numerous, marched toward the setting sun.'[28]

There has also been suggested a northern source for these movements in ancient times. This was based on the idea of a period of renewed desiccation of the Sahara towards the end of the Roman period, as a result of which camels were introduced into the Sahara. Although the idea of renewed desiccation is now no longer accepted, there is no doubt that the introduction of the camel did mark a turning point in the history of the Sahara and the areas around it. This animal, introduced by the Romans to facilitate development of their North African colonial territories, came to give the local nomadic Berbers, and later Arabs, considerable range of movement and power. Gradually, these people established an overlordship over the desert and became a definite menace not only to Roman supremacy in the north but also much later to the established Negro empires in the south. Their activities over the centuries probably constituted the great 'push factor' in the generally southerly mass migration of people in historic times.

By the beginning of the modern period, however, the Europeans were to insert a positive 'pull element' into these southern forest areas. At first, their rôle was that of slave traders. Their insatiable demand for slaves reverberated for some four centuries throughout the area of West Africa. There is enough evidence to show that the slaves involved were not just from the immediate coastal regions but also from far inland. Captain John Adams, for instance, had observed that 'slaves of the Hausa nation are brought to Ardrah (Porto Novo) by Oyo traders, and then sold either to

28 El Masudi, *Les prairies d'or*, texte et trad. C. Barbier de Meynard et Pavet de Courtelle, Paris, 9 vols, 1861–77.

Europeans or black traders belonging to Lagos and Badagry. Their attenuated bodies on their first arrival proves their journey to have been long, tedious and exhausting'.[29]

Large areas of the Guinea savannah throughout West Africa carry today relatively sparse population and constitute what is now generally known as the Middle Belt. This area, as pointed out earlier, is also characterised by the presence of numerous small ethnic groups with relatively simple social organisation. It has been suggested that this latter fact encouraged better organised groups to the north and south to prey on them for their supply of slaves. This progressive depopulation led to a general decline in density below the critical limits necessary to keep the tsetse-fly at bay.[30] The result was a major colonisation by this fly which has tended to encourage further depopulation. From this point of view, the Middle Belt has been described as the most indelible imprint in West Africa of four centuries of the trans-Atlantic slave trade.

However, this southward movement that began with the slave trade was continued in the era of legitimate commerce by the various European nations which carved up West Africa into spheres of trading, and later of political influence. Their colonial activities, especially in the field of sanitation, health and education, served to increase total population and the average expectation of life everywhere in West Africa. By emphasising agricultural production for export in their territories they further stimulated the southward or coastward shift of population. By the end of the colonial era in West Africa, the French had come to distinguish between an external and an internal sector in West Africa—a distinction with very close parallels in the British colonial territories.[31] The external sector comprised largely the forest belt within a distance of 150 to 200 miles of the coast where was concentrated most of the production for export, over eighty per cent of total purchasing power, most of the development in trade, transportation, education and health, and where an increasing majority of the total West African population was to be found. The internal sector lies inland 200 miles and beyond and is mainly in the grassland zone. Here, the primary producer received low returns for his produce because of the further cost which had to be incurred to transport this to the coast. And yet, he had to pay infinitely higher prices for the imported, manufactured articles which he was increasingly consuming and which had to be brought to him from the coast. In short, the people in the internal sector suffered the dual disadvantage of low returns for their exertions and high costs for their needs. It is thus no wonder that many in these areas earned more by moving further

29 Captain John Adams, *Sketches taken during Ten Voyages to Africa Between the Years 1786 and 1800*, London, 1823, p. 23.

30 Harrison Church, *op. cit.*, 5th edn., London, 1966, p. 164. Church gives critical limits as about twelve persons per square mile in country of few streams, or seventy per square mile where there are many streams.

31 J. Richard-Molard, *Afrique occidentale française*, Paris, 1956, pp. 187–8.

south to work. This meant a gradual deterioration of economic conditions in the interior region of West Africa and an increasing shift of population into the coastal, forested region to the south.

CONCLUSION: NEW DIFFUSION FROM THE SOUTH

This survey of the land and people of West Africa has tried to emphasise the geographical basis of the constant movement of population which seems to characterise much of West African history. It suggests that most historical movements of the past have been influenced by various 'push' factors emanating from the international relations of West Africa with peoples of northern and Saharan Africa. Evidence of these push factors include the prehistoric legends of migration from the north and north-east, the nature of political organisation in the early empires, the orientation of trading activities in the medieval period, and, most important of all, the spread of Islam and Islamic ideas. But it was not climate or any prehistorical crisis in the grassland areas that propelled these movements. It is true that the grassland facilitated the mobility and fusion of people more than the forest; also that these areas witnessed some of the greatest essays in empire building in West Africa before the modern period. But these were acts resulting from human decisions. All that can be ascribed to the physical environment is that it was permissive of these acts and gave locational advantages to peoples in the grassland right up to the colonial era.

The activities of the European colonial powers were, in a sense, a reversal of the traditional order of importance, for they gave new historical significance to the coastal forested areas of West Africa. Modern political movements in the present century have all had their roots in the rapidly growing urban centres in the forest zone. Of the thirteen new nation-states of West Africa, only three, Niger, Mali and Upper Volta, have no extension to the coast and these are among the poorest states in the sub-continent (Fig. 1.5). Of those with coastal extension, all without exception have their capital city on the coast. These capital cities have invariably combined with their political function other activities such as that of being chief port and major industrial centre of their country.

The result is that almost everywhere these port-capital cities have been the fastest growing centres in their respective country, attracting a disproportionately large percentage of the total population. Dakar in Senegal, for instance, had in 1960 a population of nearly half a million, which is about twenty per cent of the total population of the country. Freetown and its suburbs had in 1963 a population of about 200,000, which is nearly ten per cent of the total population of Sierra Leone. Accra Capital District had in 1960 a population of nearly half a million, or over seven per cent of the total population of Ghana.

These capital cities of West Africa are clearly the premier cities in their respective countries. They represent the culmination of national life, the

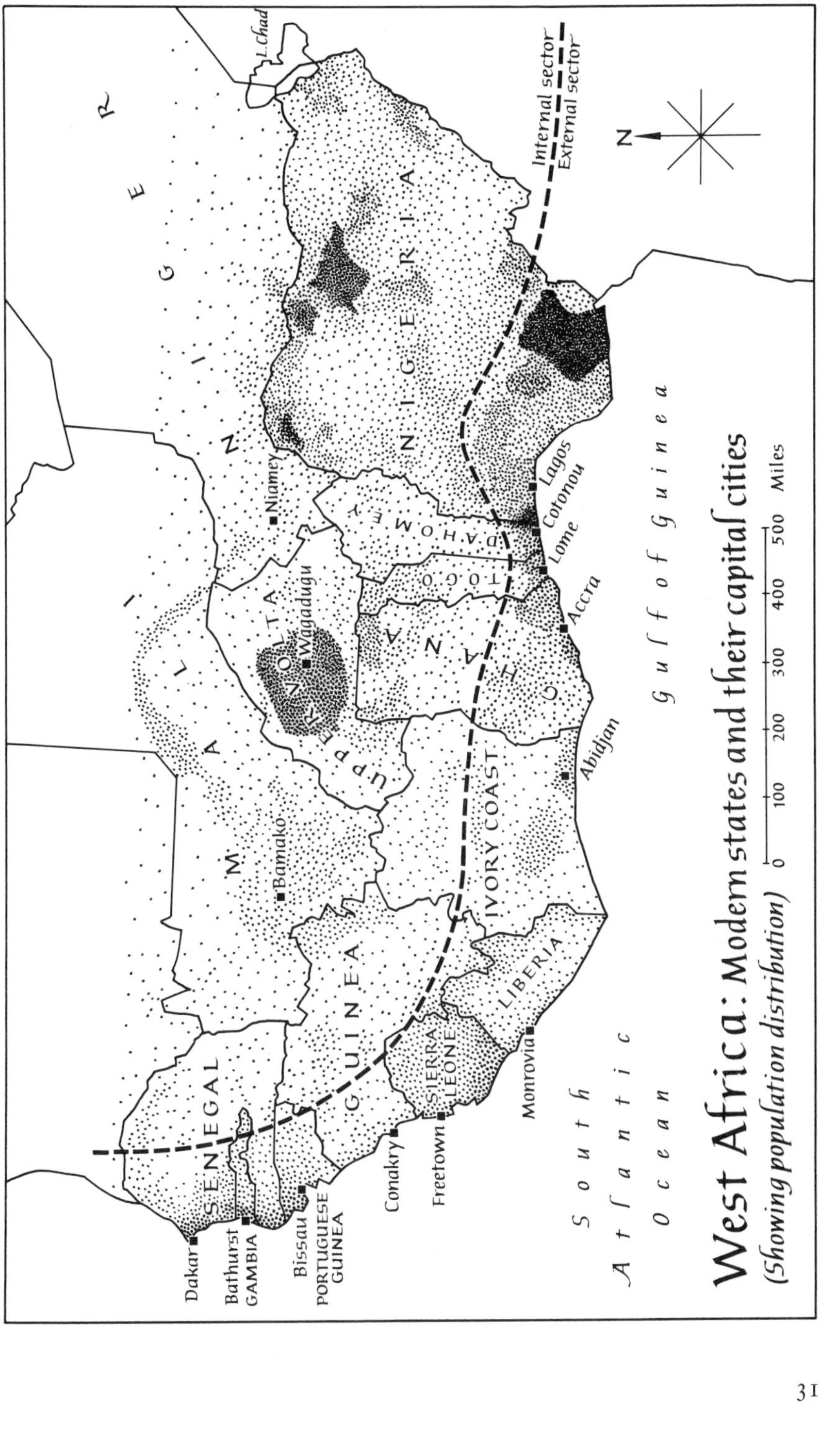

West Africa: Modern states and their capital cities
(Showing population distribution)

1:5

super-eminent market of the country and the destination of an unending stream of the young and ambitious in search of fame and fortune. Jefferson, however, emphasised that distinct primacy for such cities will develop only as the feeling of common nationality gets stronger in all parts of the country, although he admits that general education and easy communication are also important factors in this respect.[32] There is no doubt that in most West African countries today, the most crucial problem is how to encourage this feeling of common nationality. It has been emphasised that the southward movement of the last few centuries, especially its urban component to the capital cities in particular, is a step in this direction. In short, if the governments of the various countries can so organise the development of their land and peoples as to accelerate the movement into the cities, they may succeed in creating out of the welter of tribes nation-states whose glory and importance may yet surpass those of the various empires that emerged in West Africa in the distant past.

32 Mark Jefferson, 'The law of the primate city', *Geog. Rev.*, xxix, 2, 1939, pp. 226–32.

CHAPTER 2

*The prehistory of West Africa**

THURSTAN SHAW

In the present chapter 'prehistory' is used to indicate the period for which there are no written records or reliable oral sources, and for which therefore our knowledge is entirely derived from archaeology. The length of this period varies in different parts of the world, since written records begin at different dates. The same is true within West Africa. For the purposes of the present study, little will be said about this period after A.D. 1000, even though in many areas of West Africa knowledge of much of this period is almost entirely dependent upon archaeological methods.

'West Africa' is taken to mean the basins of the Senegal and Niger river systems and all land southward of them to the Atlantic Ocean, together with an area around Lake Chad.

It is really premature to attempt to write a chapter on the prehistory of West Africa. The data to write this properly are not yet available, and no amount of speculation will make up for the hard facts that are not there. There are a number of interesting detailed pieces of information but they are too few to link up—they tend to be isolated in space and time. Only the steady accumulations of further archaeological research in West Africa can cure this situation—and this is a slow and expensive business.

ENVIRONMENT

The geographical facts described in Chapter I are essential to an understanding of the prehistory of West Africa. A warning was given there against an excessively environmentalist interpretation of human history—but it should be remembered that when men only have a primitive technology and economy they are much more the creatures of their environment and much more subject to its dictates than people in highly developed civilisations with an advanced technology and a complex economy.

Between the utter dependence on environment of the animals who

*Written in 1966

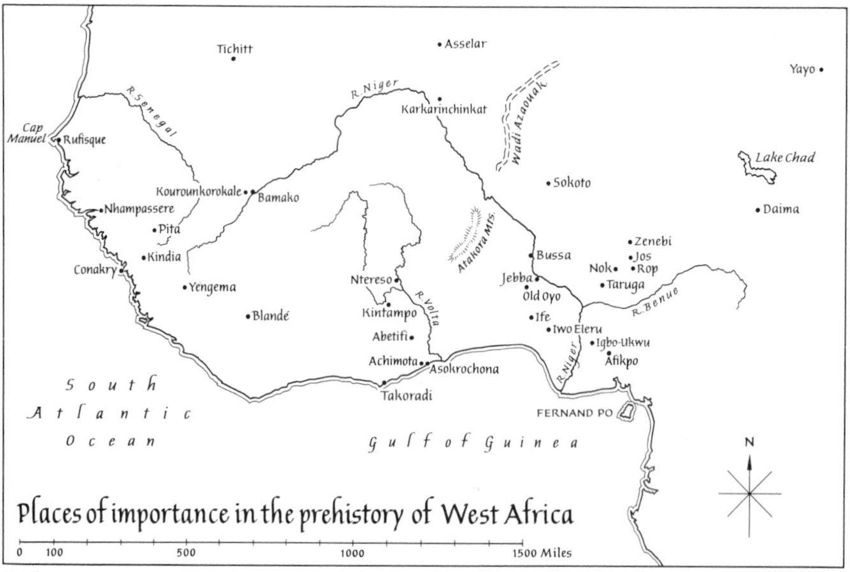

Places of importance in the prehistory of West Africa

2:1

were man's most recent and most direct ancestors, and the independence of environment enjoyed by modern man, there is a long story, more than a million years in duration. The growth in independence of environment was exceedingly slow at first, and only reaches its final accelerating phase in historical times. One of the most far-reaching tools which man invented and one which made possible an unprecedented increase in control of environment was that of writing, and this took place less than 6,000 years ago. In considering the life of peoples without writing, therefore, more attention has to be paid to factors of geographical environment than during the historical period.

The most salient of the basic geographical facts of West Africa described in Chapter I is the succession of vegetational zones running east and west, with the tropical rain-forest on the coast at the south, the wide savannah belt north of this, giving way to the sahel zone which itself merges into the Sahara desert to the north; but in addition the features which make irregularities in this general pattern are important.

CLIMATE

Forest, savannah and sahel provide very different environments for human beings to live in, but it cannot be assumed that what is now savannah or desert has always been so. There have been fluctuations of world climate over the past million years or more, and these have affected the distribution of vegetation zones. Climatic changes are important in the prehistoric record in two ways. The first is that they may represent changes in the environment in which man lived in a given area, and are therefore important for the interpretation of his way of life. Secondly, these climatic changes help us to date different phases of man's development—not in terms of absolute years, but relatively.

DATING

This mention of relative dating raises the whole question of archaeological methods of dating. Historians, particularly, accustomed to accurate dates in years, should be well aware of the limitations of archaeological methods of dating.

There are two kinds of archaeological dating—one 'relative', the other 'absolute'. As the name 'relative' implies, this kind of date simply states that B was before C but after A. The most important of the 'absolute' methods of dating is by means of radiocarbon. There are known and measurable sources of error in this, so that results are expressed as a statistical probability. Thus no radiocarbon date should be quoted without its standard error.

THE DEVELOPMENT OF EARLY MAN

There was a time when there was much popular talk about the search for 'the missing link' between man and monkeys, following a common misunderstanding of Darwin's propounding of the mechanisms of evolution. But there is no one 'missing link', nor did Darwin declare that man was descended from monkeys. What he did say was that man and the anthropoid apes, and ultimately the monkeys too, all had a common ancestry; and what we have now is evidence—not for one 'missing link'—but for a number of intermediate forms, which is what is to be expected from a proper understanding of biological evolution.[1]

The earliest sub-men at the beginning of the Pleistocene period walked on two feet, not on all fours, and were greatly differentiated from the apes and well on the way to becoming human beings. This is the genus *Australopithecus*, of which there were two main species; one was small (about four feet tall), light-boned and agile, with a full forehead and a smooth cranium, robust jaws and large teeth but without protruding canines, and appears to have been a meat-eater; the other species was bigger, heavy-boned and thick-skulled, with a sloping forehead, heavy supra-orbital ridges and a crest along the top of the skull, relatively small canine and incisor teeth but heavy, square grinding molars, and was apparently a vegetarian. Fossil remains of these Austrolopithecines have been found in eastern and southern Africa, dating back more than a million years. Their cranial capacity had not advanced very much beyond the maximum so far

1 L. S. B. Leakey, 'The evolution of man in the African continent', *Tarikh*, i, 3, London, 1966, pp. 1–11. D. R. Hughes and D. R. Brothwell, 'The earliest populations of man in Europe, W. Asia and N. Africa', in *The Cambridge Ancient History*, i, Cambridge, 1966. B. G. Campbell, *The Nomenclature of the Hominidae*, Occasional paper no. 22, Royal Anthropological Institute, London, 1965. S. L. Washburn, ed., *Classification and Human Evolution*, London, 1964.

recorded for gorillas (about 550 cc). No remains of this type have been found in West Africa.

The upright gait was of enormous importance, as this freed the hands for grasping and carrying. Quite apart from the tool-using and tool-making potential this represents, it allowed a great extension of the period of the infant's dependence on the mother, as she could carry it around with her with greater ease than any other animal. The freeing of the hands may also have allowed the reduction of the snout, since the jaws were not so necessary for gripping, which in turn allowed an increase in the size of the brain case.[2]

The genus *Homo* is first recognised in the primitive species *Homo erectus*, of which specimens have been found in Africa, Asia and Europe. Their cranial capacity ranges from 850 cc to 1300 cc, which is thus greater than that of any of the Australopithecines but still less than that of modern man. Early forms of this species are known from eastern and southern Africa, from Java, and there is one specimen from the borders of West Africa. It consists of the cranio-facial portion of a skull, and it was found in the upper sandy layer of the cliff of Angamma, 11 km north of the western wells of Yayo, some 200 km west-south-west of Largeau in the Republic of Chad.

The deposit in which it was situated consists of a lacustrine formation made up of a vertical series of sand layers, either loose or solidified into compact lenses. At first the skull was regarded as that of an Australopithecine, and the presence in the deposit of a very archaic type of elephant was taken to indicate the possibility of a lower Villafranchian age.[3] Later it came to be regarded as belonging to that subspecies of *Homo erectus* known as *Homo habilis*,[4] and the deposit to be of uppermost Villafranchian age. This puts it at the end of the Lower Pleistocene and the beginning of the Middle Pleistocene. M. Coppens, whose wife found it, named it *Tchadanthropus uxoris*, but this name has been stated to be invalid according to the principles of the International Code of Zoological Nomenclature.[5] A later form of *Homo erectus* is known from Ternifine, in Algeria (called by its finder *Atlanthropus mauritanicus*).[6]

It is still a matter of controversy whether *Australopithecus* was ancestral

2 C. F. Hockett and R. Ascher, 'The Human Revolution', *Current Anthropology*, v, 3, 1964, pp. 135–68.

3 Y. Coppens, 'Découverte d'un Australopithéciné dans le Villafranchien du Tchad', *Comptes Rendus Hebdomadaires des Séances de l'Academie de Science,* Paris, vol. 252, 1961, pp. 3851–2.

4 Coppens, 'L'Hominien du Tchad', *Actas del V Congresso Panafricano de Prehistoria y de Estudio del Cuaternario*, Tenerife, 1965, i, pp. 329–30. Coppens, 'L'Hominien du Tchad', *C. R. Hebd. Séanc. Acad. Scie.,* Paris, vol. 260, 1965, pp. 2869–71. H. B. S. Cooke, 'Tentative Correlation of Major Pleistocene Deposits in Africa', in *The Origin of Man*, ed. Paul L. Devore, Transcript of a Wenner-Gren Symposium, Chicago, 1965.

5 Campbell, *op. cit.*, p. 9.

6 C. Arambourg, 'Aperçu sur les Résultats des Fouilles du Gisement de Ternifine', *Actas del V Congresso Panafricano de Prehistoria y de Estudio del Cuaternario,* Tenerife, 1966, i, pp. 129–36.

to *Homo erectus* or whether the earliest forms of the latter overlapped with the former, which later died out. The evidence from Olduvai suggests overlapping.

Although the process itself was undoubtedly complex and the partial nature of our evidence inevitably makes its interpretation complex also, the additional data which have come to hand in the last twenty years have immeasurably clarified the story of man's evolution. It is a pity that some historians do not have sufficient perspective to appreciate its significance.[7] Philosophically speaking, a knowledge of this story may have more to contribute to an understanding of the human situation than the so-called 'lessons of history'.

STONE TOOLS

Evidence from Olduvai also suggests that it was *Homo erectus* who was responsible for making the earliest and simplest types of stone tools.

These are known as Oldowan, from Bed I of Olduvai Gorge in Tanganyika. They consist of pebbles flaked by percussion to form crude chopping and cutting tools varying in size from the dimensions of a table-tennis ball to that of a grapefruit.[8] Such tools are found in many places in Africa, and there is little doubt that their makers spread over the open savannah and bushy grasslands of almost the whole continent of Africa. At some localities, for example at Ain Hanech in Algeria, a high percentage of the tools are multifaceted (i.e. polyhedral); possibly these were used as missile stones for killing game rather than for cutting and chopping up the carcasses.[9]

Examples of pebble tools, and even of Ain Hanech type polyhedrals, are known from a number of places in West Africa.[10] The trouble is that although many of them conform in shape and style to the earliest known kinds of stone tools, pebble tools of this kind had a long history and are *also* sometimes found in later cultures. So we can only be sure that they really do belong to this very early period if they are independently dated, by being found *in situ* in deposits which can be dated either relatively or absolutely. This is the case at Olduvai and Ain Hanech, where the palaeontological evidence indicates a Villafranchian fauna, thus placing the deposits in the Lower Pleistocene. Unfortunately the damp conditions of so much of West Africa militate against the preservation of palaeontological evi-

7 J. Anene, 'Africa in perspective', *The Historia*, Ibadan, xi, 1, Ibadan, 1965, p. 9. A. Roe, 'Psychological Definitions of Man', in Washburn, ed., *Classification and Human Evolution*, London, 1964, p. 330.

8 L. S. B. Leakey, *Olduvai Gorge, A Report on the Evolution of the Handaxe Culture in Beds I-IV*, Cambridge, 1951, p. 34.

9. C. Arambourg, 'Traces possibles d'une industrie primitive dans un niveau Villafranchien de l'Afrique du Nord', *Bulletin de la société préhistorique française*, xlvii, 1950.

10 O. Davies, *Archaeology in Ghana*, Edinburgh, 1961, pp. 1-4 and *The Quaternary in the Coastlands of Guinea*, Glasgow, 1964, pp. 83-91. R. C. Soper, 'The Stone Age in Northern Nigeria', *Journal of the Historical Society of Nigeria*, iii, 2, 1965, p. 177.

dence, and there are no stone implements in our West African area that have been dated by this means. There is an example of palaeontological material of Pleistocene age which was recovered in Bornu in north-eastern Nigeria, in the digging of a well: this consisted of bones of a fossilised specimen of *Hippopotamus imaguncula* from a depth of 58 m.[11] This is very tantalising, because it suggests that there is palaeontological material of Pleistocene age there—and as likely as not archaeological material as well—but it lies under a mantle of later drift of great thickness.

CLIMATIC CHANGE IN WEST AFRICA

This poverty of palaeontological evidence in West Africa—especially when compared to north, east and south Africa—takes away one of the most useful kinds of relative dating for the Pleistocene period. What other evidence for climatic changes are there in West Africa, which are likely to be useful in giving us some relative dating of human cultures?

The principal source of evidence comes from raised shore lines and river terraces, giving indications of changes of climate or of alterations in sea-level resulting from glacial and inter-glacial periods. Work in East Africa led to the belief, first of all, in two major pluvial periods there,[12] then to four pluvials (called Kageran, Kamasian, Kanjeran and Gamblian) followed by two post-pluvial wet stages (called Makalian and Nakuran).[13] The interpretation of the evidence is an involved business, and opinion changed at one time to a belief in three major East African pluvials,[14] while more recently it has been stated that the only unequivocal evidence is for the last, or Gamblian, pluvial.[15] The situation is complicated in the East African area because it has been one of tectonic activity, which can produce evidence, in the form of raised shorelines on inland lakes, resembling evidence of climatic change. At one time the East African system of four pluvials and two post-pluvial wet phases was not only regarded as established but as having validity over most of sub-Saharan Africa. Neither of these propositions is now tenable. All one can say is that there have been changes in Africa during the Pleistocene, but great caution should be exercised in correlating these in widely separated parts of the continent without independent evidence. Even the term 'pluvial' is used vaguely to bracket different types of phenomena together, e.g. increase in total annual rain-

11 C. M. Tattam, 'A Review of Nigerian stratigraphy', *Annual Report of the Geological Survey of Nigeria, 1943*, Lagos, 1944, p. 39.

12 E. J. Wayland, 'Rifts, rivers and rains and early man in Uganda', *Journal of the Royal Anthropological Institute*, lxiv, 1934, pp. 332–52.

13 L. S. B. Leakey, 'The Lower Limits of the Pleistocene in Africa', *Report XVIII, International Geology Congress* (London 1948), 1950, pt. 9, pp. 62–5.

14 G. C. Simpson, 'Further studies in World Climate', *Quarterly Journal of the Royal Meteorological Society*, lxxxiii, 1957, pp. 459–85.

15 R. F. Flint, 'On the Basis of Pleistocene Correlation in East Africa', *Geological Magazine*, xcvi, 1959, pp. 265–84.

fall, increase in seasonal rainfall only, or even an increase in humidity without an increase in precipitation; often unknown factors of temperature differences may also have affected the situation. Reference has already been made above to the difficulties in elucidating the relationships between African pluvials and the northern sequence of glaciations; very complex questions of meteorology are involved. Nevertheless, progressive efforts have been made in this direction.[16] The truth seems to be that the various phenomena indicating wetter or drier periods in different latitudes are not *independently* dated with sufficient accuracy to permit of precise correlation. This is a pity because changes in the Sahara may have occasioned population movements which had repercussions further south.

On the theoretical side of this question we are not even sure of the source of greater rainfall than at present in the Sahara. Some have supposed that it was the result of a moving northwards of all the climatic belts during an interglacial period when the northern ice-sheets and the anticyclonic systems associated with them retreated towards the poles; thus a Saharan wet period would correspond to a northern interglacial.[17] Others attribute greater rainfall in the Sahara to a greater precipitation on the southern slopes of the Atlas mountains and on the Hoggar and Tibesti massifs as the result of the moving southwards of the temperature belt of westerly winds during a glacial maximum in Europe; this produced inland lakes in the present Sahara which further attracted rainfall. Yet others believe that the dry belt contracted during the glacial-pluvial sequence as a result of the increased precipitation from both rainfall systems to north and south.[18]

On the coast of Ghana, old shorelines at different heights above sea level almost certainly represent times when the worldwide sea level was higher than at present as the result of the melting of the polar ice-caps in interglacial periods, rather than being the consequence of tectonic movement of the land in relation to sea level. These old shorelines were first noted by members of the Gold Coast Geological Survey[19] and have sub-

16 Cooke, 'The problem of Quaternary Glacio-pluvial correlation in East and Southern Africa', *Proceedings of the Pan-African Congress on Prehistory* (3rd, Livingstone, 1955), London, 1957, pp. 51–5; J. D. Clark, 'Carbon 14 chronology in Africa south of the Sahara', *Proc. Pan-Afr. Congr. Prehist.* (4th, Leopoldville, 1959), Tervuren, 1962, ii, pp. 301–13. E. A. Bernard, 'Les climats d'insolation des latitudes tropicales au Quaternaire', *Bull. Acad. Roy. Sci. Colon.* (N.S.), v, 2, 1959, pp. 344–64; K. P. Oakley, *Man the Toolmaker*, London, 1963, pp. 81–90; H. Faure and H. J. Hugot, 'Chronologie absolue du Quaternaire en Afrique de l'Ouest', *Bulletin de l'Institut Français de l'Afrique Noire,* xxviii, A, 1966, pp. 384–7.

17 L. Balout, *Préhistoire de l'Afrique du Nord* (Arts et Métiers Graphiques), Paris, 1955.

18 J. Büdel, 'Die "periglazial"—Morphologische Wirkungen des Eiszeitklimas auf der ganzen Erde', *Erdkunde*, vii, 1953, p. 249.

19 A. E. Kitson, 'The Gold Coast: some considerations of its structure, people and natural history', *Geographical Journal*, xlviii, 1916, pp. 370–1; N. R. Junner, 'River and beach terraces and peneplain residuals', *Gold Coast Geological Survey, Annual Report 1938–39*, p. 22. 'Geology of the Gold Coast and Western Togoland', *Gold Cst. Geol. Surv. Bull.*, xi, 1940, pp. 33–6.

sequently been studied in greater detail by others,[20] who do not always agree on their interpretation. Comparable high sea levels have been recognised along the shores of the North Sea, in the Mediterranean and along the Moroccan coast, and characteristic local names given to them.

Much of the coast of West Africa outside Ghana is low-lying so that it is difficult to trace the old shorelines. Around Dakar raised beaches have been recognised, but the fact that the area was one of Pleistocene volcanic activity has made interpretation difficult.[21] Higher sea levels than the present have been recognised elsewhere in Senegal[22] and in Mauretania.[23] Four high shorelines have been recorded from Sierra Leone,[24] but their levels do not seem to correspond very well with those in Ghana.

In low-lying coastal areas, such as those along the Nigerian coast, at the time when the raised beaches were being formed along the Ghana coast, the sea transgressed inland to a corresponding height. Another factor here is the tremendous weight of sediments brought down into the Niger delta, which has the effect of slowly depressing the land. Since the last marine transgression it has been estimated that approximately 350 cubic miles of sediments have accumulated. This equals a depth of 50 ft over an area of 40,000 square miles.[25] During this period of relative deepening of the sea, there have been two standstills, marked by submerged coral banks and radiocarbon-dated as terminating at about 1900 B.C. and 900 B.C.

There is plenty of evidence for a higher and larger Lake Chad in the past. It is marked by the Bama ridge, upon which Maiduguri itself stands, which here runs northwest as far as Gashua and southeast beyond Bongor; both ends of this stretch then swing round to the north-east running up to enclose Largeau and the whole of the Bodélé depression and the Bahr-el-Ghazal. This ancient lake stood at a height of 332 m above sea level, compared with the present height of Lake Chad of 280 m. It had an area four times the size of Lake Victoria. Quite what it means in terms of climate it is difficult to be sure, because practically all the water which at present maintains Lake Chad comes from the tropical rain forest area by the Logone/Shari river system. At the time of Palaeochad, as the huge ancient lake has been called, it seems almost certain that there was not only a bigger

20 W. Brückner, 'The mantle rock ("Laterite") of the Gold Coast and its origin', *Geol. Rundsh.*, xliii, 1954, pp. 307–27. O. Davies, 'The raised beaches of the Gold Coast and their associated archaeological material', *Quaternaria*, iii, 1956, pp. 91–3: and *The Quaternary in the Coastlands of Guinea*, pp. 22–44.

21 H. Hubert and A. Lenoble, 'Notes géologiques sur Dakar', *Bulletin du Comité d'Etudes Historiques et Scientifiques de l'Afrique Occidentale Française*, ix, 1926, pp. 185–224. R. Corbeil, R. Mauny and J. Charbonnier, 'Préhistoire et Protohistoire de la presqu'île du Cap-Vert et de l'extrême ouest Sénégalais', *Bull. I.F.A.N.*, 1948.

22 J. Tricart, 'Carte géomorphologique du delta du Sénégal', *Bulletin de l'Association Géographique Français*, nos. 251–2, 1955, pp. 98–117.

23 G. Lecointre, *Libyca*, v, 1957.

24 Dixey, *Transactions of the Geological Society of South Africa*, xxii, 1919.

25 J. R. L. Allen and J. W. Wells, 'Holocene coral banks and subsidence in the Niger Delta', *Journal of Geology*, lxx, 1962, pp. 381–97.

contribution from the Jos Plateau than the seasonal river which is all it contributes at present, but that it was also the catchment area for a lot of precipitation running off the Tibesti and Ennedi massifs. In addition there is likely to have been less loss through evaporation; the very extent of a body of water this size would have made considerable local modification of the climate of the area surrounding it. It is likely that the great lake overflowed to the southwards and drained down the Benue. It has been calculated that the lake must have been receiving at least sixteen times the volume of water that it does today.

The Bama ridge, marking the south-western edge of the old lake, is regarded by those who have studied it as being a lagoon bar rather than the actual shoreline, which lay a little further to the southwest.[26] It is calculated that it took about 6,000 years to form. Such a constant high lake level cannot have occurred more recently than the last full pluvial (the 'Gamblian' in East Africa), perhaps during the period 40,000 to 25,000 years ago.

There is another, lower ridge known as the Ngelewa ridge, which runs much nearer the present lake shoreline and rises about 7 m above the present lake level. It may represent a period of stability during the retreat of Palaeochad towards the present area of the lake.

Terraces of river gravel on the sides of valleys above the present flood plain level are also indicators of climate, and ones which, like raised beaches, can be tied in to stages of human development if stone tools are incorporated in them and found actually in position. Both in the case of raised beaches and terraces a careful distinction has to be made between fresh and rolled specimens. A specimen that is fresh and has sharp edges must be contemporary with the formation of the deposit, whereas one that has been rolled may be contemporary with the deposit or it may have been incorporated from older material.

There are terraces on the R. Senegal[27] and in Guinée[28] but the only areas in West Africa where they have been systematically studied together with any associated stone artifacts is Nigeria and Ghana, especially the latter.[29] Davies recognises three terraces, High, Middle and Low, but does not anywhere adduce any evidence of any sunk channels. Naturally at different points along the courses of rivers and in different topographies absolute vertical heights above present river level may vary within limits for what was originally one terrace. Because of difficulties occasioned by topography and vegetation, two terraces may seem to merge with each other or be indistinguishable. But, very roughly, the High Terrace in Ghana is usually

26 A. T. Grove and R. A. Pullan, 'Some aspects of the Palaeogeography of the Chad Basin' in F. Howell, J. D. Clark and F. Bourlière, ed., *African Ecology and Human Evolution*, London, 1964, pp. 230–45.
27 Davies, *The Quaternary . . .*, p. 63.
28 Maignien, 'Le cuirassement des Sols en Guinée', *Mém. Serve. Carte, Géol. Als-Lorr. 16.*
29 Davies, *The Quaternary . . .*, pp. 45–68.

TABLE 2.2 (After Davies)

Climate	Shoreline	Terrace	Stone implements (West Africa)	Approximate date B.C.
	Beach III	Middle	Late Chellean	After 390,000
Kamasian II Pluvial			Early-Middle Acheulian	Before 39,000
	Beach IV		Late Acheulian	55,000
Inter-pluvial		Low Terrace	Early Sangoan	41,000
Gamblian Pluvial	Beach V		Developed Sangoan	40,000–30,000
Post-pluvial I		Upper Shoreline	Guinea Aterian	25,000–10,000
Sub-pluvial I				10,000–1,300
Post-pluvial II			Middle Stone Age	
Sub-pluvial II				
Makalian	Beach VI			
Post-pluvial III			Mesolithic	
Sub-pluvial III			Neolithic	900–present.

found at heights of 30–35 m above present river level, the Middle Terrace from 19–25 m, and the Low Terrace at 8–10 m.

As the result of his study of the evidence from Ghana and neighbouring regions, and comparing this with evidence from other parts of the Old World, Davies has suggested that the climatic stages listed in the first column of Figure 2.2 can be observed, and offers the accompanying correlation with shorelines, terraces, types of stone implements and very approximate dates.

More will be said presently about the names given to the different industries of stone implements.

Recent industrial work[30] has considerably increased our knowledge of the history of the Niger-Benue river system during Pleistocene times. It has been shown that it was only during the Pleistocene that the Nigerian Niger captured the waters of the Mali Niger, which probably as late as penultimate pluvial times drained into the Timbuctoo lake. A buried channel also exists; on the Benue at Makurdi at a depth of 80 m below present river level and 20 m below present sea level; at Jebba at a depth of more than 25 m below present sea level; while near Onitsha and Yola it lies at an even greater depth than this. This sunk channel probably represents the level at which the river was running at the time of the last major glaciation in the northern hemisphere when so much ocean water was

30 C. Voute, 'Geological and morphological evolution of the Niger and Benue valleys', *Proc. pan-Afr. Congr. Prehist.* (4th, Leopoldville, 1959), Tervuren, 1962, i, pp. 189–207.

locked up in ice that world sea levels were much lower. River terraces have been shown to exist between Jebba and Awuru at a height of 6–21 m and 25–36 m and in the Onitsha/Asaba area at heights of 22–24 m, 30–35 m, 50 m and 100–110 m. Voute did not consider it possible in the then state of knowledge to correlate the events of the Niger–Benue basin with the African stratigraphical sequence established with the aid of industrial complexes of stone tools. However, Sangoan implements have been found *in situ*, both rolled and unrolled, in terrace gravel 18 m above the present Niger floodplain level at Jebba[31] and at a height of 10 m above the River Haderi on the surface of a deposit of rubble and pebbles attributed by the finder to the Kamasian pluvial.[32] It would seem that the gravel at 18 m above the floodplain at Jebba was graded to the Pre-Gamblian high sea level, and such an interpluvial period for early Sangoan times would fit with its known age in other parts of Africa.

The Pleistocene geology of the Jos Plateau has been studied, where the different infills of older channels have been related to three cycles of erosion and deposition, tentatively equated to the East African Kamasian II, Gamblian and Nakuran phases.[33] Nearer the edge of the plateau, the first cycle seems to manifest itself in terrace gravel some 11 m above the present level of the Forom River.

Study of soils and soil profiles can also give information on past climates, and these have been studied in West Africa.[34] The formation of hard lateritic concretions should be indicative of a certain type of climatic condition, but unfortunately the experts are not agreed as to what this condition is. It has been suggested that the interpluvial periods before the last two main pluvials (Pre-Gamblian and Pre-Kanjeran or Pre-Kamasian II) were sufficiently arid in the latitudes concerned to cause the Sahara to extend south of the most northerly reaches of the Senegal and Niger rivers.[35] At some time in the past dune conditions extended much further south than at present in Northern Nigeria,[36] indicating a rainfall of less than 6 inches (150 mm) a year in areas that now receive about 34 inches (860 mm). These fossil dunes are not dated but they are perhaps best regarded as being Pre-Gamblian in age. The reason may not have been a shifting of climatic belts as such, but an indirect result of a low sea level at a time of

31 Soper, *op. cit.*, p. 186.

32 O. Davies, 'The Old Stone Age between the Volta and the Niger', *Bull. I.F.A.N.*, xix, 1957, pp. 592–616.

33 G. Bond, 'A preliminary account of the Pleistocene geology of the Plateau tin fields region of Northern Nigeria', *Proceedings of the third International West African Conference (Ibadan, 1949)*, Lagos 1956, pp. 189–202.

34 R. Mauny, 'Afrique occidentale française: la préhistoire', *Encylopédie de l'Empire français, Encyclopédie coloniale et maritime*, Paris, 1949, pp. 3–34. J. W. du Preez, 'Origin, classification and distribution of Nigerian laterites', *Proc. 3rd. Intern. W. Afr. Conf. (Ibadan, 1949)*, pp. 223–34. Brückner, *op. cit.* Davies, *The Quaternary* . . ., pp. 69–82.

35 H. Alimen, *The Prehistory of Africa*, London, 1957, p. 137.

36 Grove and Pullan, *op. cit.*, pp. 218–41.

great glaciation in northern Europe. The monsoon clouds, which account for the bulk of the precipitation in the rain forest area, drop their rain for a certain distance inland from the coast and then become exhausted; if the coast was further to the south, monsoon rains would not reach so far north. At the other extreme, it has been stated that at the Gamblian maximum the forest extended to 11° N,[37] and that around 2000 B.C. the northerly limit of the rain forest extended as far north as the present 30-inch isohyet.[38] It will be appreciated that an understanding of these changes in environment is essential for correct appreciation of the circumstances in which prehistoric man lived. It is unfortunate that as yet we do not have more certain knowledge about them.

THE STONE AGE

The pebble tools and flakes of 'Oldowan' type made and used by a subspecies of *Homo erectus* over a million years ago have already been mentioned. Although some pebble-tools in West Africa almost certainly belong to the period of man's earliest activity, there are none which can be said to be as unequivocally dated by stratigraphy and absolute dating methods as those at Olduvai Gorge. Some specimens have been found which do seem to be satisfactorily embedded in gravels, but then the gravels themselves are not assignable to an absolutely certain date.

The period of prehistory from the first emergence of man until the discovery of metal is usually called the 'Stone Age'. This is a convenient term which has been in long use, and resulted from the fact that the commonest and most durable of man's artifacts to survive from this immensely long period of time, approaching two million years, are made of stone. But stone was not the only material of which man made use, nor even, probably, the first. Bone and horn and wood were undoubtedly used, but they survive from such remote periods much less commonly; most kinds of stone are almost indestructible.

There is a considerable difficulty in writing at this particular juncture over the terminology to be employed for the different stages of the Stone Age in West Africa, as this is undergoing international revision. Because the European scheme did not fit what was found in Africa, the following was adopted by the Third pan-African Congress on Prehistory.[39] Earlier Stone Age, First Intermediate, Middle Stone Age, Second Intermediate, Later Stone Age. The 'Earlier Stone Age' in this scheme is largely synchronous with the Lower Palaeolithic of Europe, but thereafter the correspondences become less and less. For the last ten years the African scheme

37 Davies, *The Quaternary . . .*, p. 110.
38 O. Davies, 'The Neolithic revolution in tropical Africa', *Transactions of the Historical Society of Ghana*, iv, 1960, p. 16.
39 J. D. Clark ed., *Proc. pan-Afr. Congr. Prehist.* (3rd, Livingstone, 1955), London, 1957, p. xxxiii.

has had considerable usefulness, but it is now in need of modification.[40] For the purposes of the present chapter, however, the scheme of African terminology printed above will be used, although it is realised that it is likely soon to be out of date. It is one of those unfortunate timings which cannot be avoided.

THE EARLIER STONE AGE

The beginning of this includes the 'Oldowan' industrial complex, with pebble tools and simple flakes, about which enough has been said already. The rest of the Earlier Stone Age is often referred to as 'the handaxe' culture. Although a handaxe is not really an axe at all, it has become accepted as a term used to describe an ovate or pointed tool carefully flaked over both faces whose precise use cannot be known for certain, but which was well adapted to a variety of cutting or digging or piercing operations—rather like the modern pen-knife.

The best stratified sequence in Africa of the handaxe culture (called, from the first recognised find places in France, 'Chelles-Acheul' or 'Acheulian') comes from the Olduvai Gorge, where eleven stages have been recognised, the earliest itself appearing to develop out of earlier pebble tools of Oldowan type.[41] Five stages have been recognised in the Vaal river gravels of South Africa.[42] Acheulian industries are found all over Africa, in the unglaciated parts of Europe, in south-west Asia and southern India; northern India and the rest of Asia seem to have been occupied at this time by people who did not share the handaxe tradition but favoured instead their own kinds of chopping tools. The makers of both were probably subspecies of *Homo erectus*, but whereas the famous 'Peking man' of Choukoutien was found associated with the Far Eastern type of tool assemblage, no unequivocal association of handaxes with *Homo erectus* has yet been discovered. The time from the earliest kinds of handaxes to the most evolved represents a very long period of time indeed, perhaps beginning 400,000 years ago and lasting until about 60,000 years ago. Since this particular tradition of stone tools lasted such an immense length of time and technical innovation and change was infrequent, there was time for the different developments within it to be widely diffused over the whole area of the tradition. This is why there is a greater homogeneity over this wide area of the Old World during this time than in any of the later cultures.

There are local variations in the Acheulian and it survived later in some areas than in others, but the general pattern is remarkably similar. Its beginning is associated with the second of the great glaciations in Europe and it lasted into the last inter-glacial period. In Africa north of the equator

40 T. Shaw, *The West African Archaeological Newsletter*, no. 5, Ibadan, 1966, pp. 39–53.
41 Leakey, *Olduvai Gorge*, 1951.
42 C. Van Riet Lowe, 'The Vaal River chronology', *South African Archaeological Bulletin*, vii, no. 28, 1952, pp. 135–49.

it is noteworthy that the early type handaxes (formerly called 'Chellean') are absent in the Sahara, perhaps indicating an arid period there, possibly during the penultimate interglacial. Early handaxes have been claimed for Senegal,[43] Guinée,[44] Mauretania[45] and Ghana, where they are said to be stratigraphically established in a rolled condition in the Middle Terrace.[46] The area of their distribution has been mapped,[47] and this is said to indicate a colonisation from the River Niger along the Atakora Chain and the Togo hills.

The later stages of the Acheulian are marked by beautiful handaxes made by a more advanced technique. In Africa north of the equator their occurrence is widespread and prolific all over an area north of latitude 16° N. Perhaps this fact is to be correlated with the penultimate glacial period in northern Europe, resulting in much more plentiful rainfall over the northern part of the Sahara desert, which was contracted southwards to the area between 16° N and the northern limit of monsoon rainfall—which may have been some way south of where it is now, at a time of low sea level created by the glacial period (see above, p. 39).

During the Pleistocene period, there is evidence for the presence in what is now the Sahara of large animals such as elephant, rhinoceros, hippopotamus and giraffe, all the way from the northern limit of their present habitat right up to the Mediterranean coast.[48]

Acheulian implements, in addition to various forms of handaxe, include a broad-bladed cutting or chopping tool known as a 'cleaver', scrapers, and tools made on flakes, as well as stone balls which some people believe were used as 'bolas' stones—that is, three of them used tied together, each one fastened to the end of a thong knotted in the middle. Such a contraption, when whirled around and then thrown at a running animal, would tangle itself around its legs and bring it down. For Acheulian man was a well-organised hunter, and it has been demonstrated that a handaxe is a good tool for skinning a carcase; he was able to take on bigger and more powerful game than Oldowan man, who, although omnivorous and not just a vegetarian, was probably confined to small and 'slow' game, or the younger of larger animals, for his meat.

43 R. Corbeil, 'Mise en évidence d'industries lithiques anciennes dans l'extrême ouest Sénégalais', *Comptes Rendus de la Conférence Internationale d'Africainistes de l'Ouest I,* 1951, ii, pp. 387-90.
44 P. Créach, 'Sur quelques nouveaux sites et nouvelles industries préhistoriques d'Afrique Occidentale Française', *C. R Conf. Int. Afr. de l'Ouest I,* 1951, ii, pp. 397-430.
45 R. Mauny, 'Contribution à l'étude du Paléolithique de Mauritanie', *Proc. Afr. Congr. Prehist.* (2nd, Algiers, 1952), Paris 1955, pp. 461-79.
46 Davies, *The Quaternary . . .*, pp. 86-91.
47 O. Davies, 'The distribution of Old Stone Age material in Guinea, *Bull. I.F.A.N.,* xxi, sér. B, 1959, pp. 1-2.
48 R. Mauny, 'Répartition de la grande "faune éthiopienne" du Nord-Ouest Africain du Paléolithique à nos jours', *Proc. pan-Afr. Congr. Prehist.* (3rd, Livingstone, 1955), London, 1957, pp. 102-5.

It seems that in West Africa the high ground of the Jos Plateau in Nigeria was a moist area at a time when the northern Sahara was wet enough for Acheulian man to inhabit it comfortably, but when the desert belt extended southwards from 16° N to a point a good deal further south than it does now. Thus the Jos Plateau and the high ground to the north of it formed a sort of promontory of habitable land projecting southwards from Aïr and the main Saharan Acheulian area north of 16° N. For nowhere in West Africa is such good Acheulian material found as on the Jos Plateau, where it occurs in the basal gravels infilling channels which were probably cut by a major pluvial—which should be the penultimate one (the 'Kanjeran' or 'Kamasian II') and the infilling gravels therefore represent aggradation during the drier, succeeding pre-Gamblian inter-pluvial. There is a radiocarbon date of 'more than 39,000 years before the present'[49] for material associated with Acheulian tools in this basal gravel. This does not tell us very much, but it is the oldest radiocarbon date so far for West Africa. It compares with a date of 57,300 ± 300 years before the present for Late Acheulian in northern Zambia.

Nearer the edge of the Plateau, Acheulian material is derived from the terrace gravel above the Forom River, assigned to the penultimate major pluvial (see above p. 43). This Acheulian material of northern Nigeria and its geological provenance has received a fair amount of study.[50] It was at first regarded as belonging to the later stages of the handaxe sequence[51] and Davies regarded it as corresponding typologically to the later stages in East and South Africa,[52] although the absence of forms typical of the last stage was noted. However, the most recent study[53] has shown that there are considerable differences between the collections from different sites on the Jos Plateau and at the most northerly bend of the Gongola river, and that in at least one of them the pointed 'ficron' types occur, which are regarded as belonging to the latest phases of the Acheulian sequence. Accordingly it is probably best to regard this northern Nigerian Acheulian material as spanning a long period, not from the earliest Acheulian times but perhaps from towards the end of the penultimate pluvial and extending for a long time into the succeeding pre-Gamblian inter-pluvial. It has been noted that elsewhere in Africa, Acheulian man favoured open or lightly wooded savannah grasslands[54] and this seems to have been his habitat in northern Nigeria.

49 G. W. Barendson, E. S. Deevey and L. J. Gralenski, 'Yale natural radiocarbon measurements III', *Science*, cxxvi, no. 3279, pp. 916–17.

50 H. J. Braunholtz, 'Stone implements of Palaeolithic and Neolithic types from Nigeria', *Geological Survey of Nigeria, Occasional Paper no. 4*, 1926. B. E. B. Fagg, 'An outline of the Stone Age of the plateau minesfield', *Proc. 3rd Intern. W. Afr. Conf.* (Ibadan, 1949), Lagos, 1956, pp. 203–22.

51 Bond, *op. cit.*, p. 198.

52 Davies, 'The Old Stone Age . . .', *loc. cit.*, p. 594.

53 Soper, *op. cit.*, pp. 178–84.

54 Clark, *The Prehistory of Southern Africa*, Harmondsworth, 1959.

At a time when Acheulian man favoured the Jos Plateau, it is likely that parts of the Fouta Djallon massif may also have been suitable for human occupation—but in this case there was not the same 'bridge' across the desert belt from the main Acheulian occupation area north of 16° N. But neither has there been tin-mining on an extensive scale in the Fouta Djallon as there has been on the Jos Plateau—and if it had not been for the exposures made in the course of tin-mining it is doubtful whether we should know anything about the Acheulian occupation in the area. So much is archaeology dependent upon chance finds, and commercial or governmental enterprise of a non-archaeological character, for its initial discoveries. For the same reason the greatest caution should be exercised in equating the distribution of known finds with the real distribution, especially at a stage of knowledge such as has been reached in West Africa at the moment, when information is far from complete.

There was, perhaps, another route southwards from the area north of 16° N which Acheulian man favoured. There is a vast, fossilised valley system rising on the southern slopes of the Ahaggar in the Sahara, known under the name of the Azaouak in its main course and debouching into the Niger through the Dallol Bosso a hundred miles downstream from Niamey. If it is correct that this system was active at the time Acheulian man found a favourable habitat north of 16° N, it would have provided a less inhospitable route through the surrounding arid country, and led directly, across the River Niger, to the northern end of the Atakora chain of mountains where higher rainfall would again make life possible. At any rate, the distribution of Acheulian material along this chain of hills, continued in the Togo hills towards southeastern Ghana[55] suggests this route. But the penetration does not seem to have been very strong, no Acheulian material is firmly established stratigraphically in the area, and with small collections and individual pieces it is often very difficult on typology alone to assign them with certainty to the Acheulian period, since so many of the forms overlap or are similar to those used in the succeeding Sangoan period. The same can be said of the rather scattered and sporadic finds of artifacts that look as if they might be Acheulian in the rest of the savannah areas of West Africa.[56]

THE FIRST INTERMEDIATE PERIOD OF THE AFRICAN STONE AGE

This is the rather unsatisfactory name which was given to the stage between the Earlier Stone Age and the Middle Stone Age, partly because these two periods were well recognised in East and South Africa and the industries which occur in the time between them were in some senses regarded as transitional. In West Africa the period is represented by the industrial

55 Davies, 'The distribution of Old Stone Age material', *loc. cit.*, p. 105, fig. 2; and *The Quaternary* . . . , p. 91.
56 Davies, *The Quaternary* . . . , pp. 91–4.

complex known as the Sangoan, named after Sango Bay on the western shores of Lake Victoria where it was first recognised.

Although many of the pick and handaxe forms survive from the Acheulian, as well as flake tools, stone balls are rare and the cleaver disappears and is replaced by a much greater emphasis on picks, often of a rather heavy and massive form; choppers, often made of flaked pebbles, also occur. The distribution of Sangoan man's assemblages tends to follow woodland areas rather than the more open country favoured by his Acheulian predecessors, and it is often riverine also; but it does not seem to extend into the real tropical rainforest area. A likely interpretation of these facts taken together is that Sangoan man liked to be where he could find edible tubers and dig them up with his stone picks; hunting probably still played a part in the economy, and the stone picks may also have been used for digging animal traps. It looks as if this period belongs to a time when the northern hemisphere rainbelts had retreated northwards in the last inter-glacial period making most of the Sahara into desert again; perhaps this was why Sangoan man seems to have favoured the river valleys or well-watered hills. There is evidence to connect Sangoan man with the time of the formation of the Low Terraces on the rivers, and these are also to be connected with Beach V and the raised sea level of a warmer interval which occurred in the course of the last main glacial period in northern Europe. On the other hand in central Africa the Sangoan seems to be associated with the arid pre-Gamblian period and the beginning of the Gamblian pluvial.

The Sangoan probably began about 50,000 B.C. It seems to have spread out from a dispersal focus in the area of east and central Africa, and to have reached right down into Natal. Spreading westwards it is doubtful whether it ever really penetrated the true equatorial forest of the Congo, but it certainly flourished in the woodland areas to the south of it; it seems probable that it also diffused westwards from the Great Lakes area, passing north of the Congo rainforest. Sangoan man may have entered West Africa down the Benue Valley, passing up the Niger to northern Dahomey and thence southwards along the Atakora and Togo mountains along the route which may have been followed by Acheulian man before him. Dispersal along these routes is likely to have been assisted because the Sangoan industrial complex may represent a need to adapt to more wooded country in an increasingly arid period,[57] and this would have been a need felt at such a time by all members of the older Acheulian tradition. It seems likely that Sangoan man had the use of fire.[58]

In West Africa, at any rate, there seems to be a new pattern of settlement, with a rather more southerly distribution than in Acheulian times. An

57 Clark, *The Prehistory of Southern Africa*, p. 149.

58 K. P. Oakley, 'Earliest use of fire', *Proc. pan-Afr. Congr. Prehist.* (3rd, Livingstone, 1955), London, 1957, pp. 385–6.

industry from Cap Manuel at Dakar, which was formerly regarded as being Neolithic[59] is now considered to belong to the Sangoan industrial complex,[60] or perhaps to a somewhat later development from it. The same can be said of some material collected near Bamako.[61] In Nigeria, Sangoan material is found particularly in the stretch of country south of the Jos Plateau and north of the tropical rainforest, associated with river valleys, and in fact well stratified in terrace gravels at heights of 10–20 m above modern river level.[62] An industry from the Niger valley near Bussa, which consists mostly of worked pebbles and is without picks, is regarded on geological grounds as nevertheless being contemporary with the Sangoan, such a local variant being partly dictated perhaps by the character of the raw material. The same may be said for a collection of industries in the area of the upper Sokoto River, but which might be better regarded as degenerate Acheulian rather than as Sangoan.[63] A spread of Sangoan material down the Atakora-Togo chain and into southern Ghana has been reported.[64] Sangoan material is rare in northern Ghana but fairly widespread in southern Ghana, even in areas now heavily forested. It has been assumed that this indicates a less dense vegetation cover there during an arid period and this may prove to be correct; but although it is true that the Sangoan is a woodland rather than a forest culture, it is an a priori assumption that the equatorial forest was never penetrable by primitive man.

THE MIDDLE STONE AGE

This is the name given, first of all in southern Africa, to a group of industrial complexes, apparently associated with the later part of the Gamblian pluvial, after about 30,000 B.C. These industries show greater localisation and specialisation than before, and there are more regional variants. It seems possible that some of these industries, in particular that called the Lupemban and located in the more woodland areas surrounding the Congo equatorial forest, may have evolved out of a late and developed Sangoan. Some of the Sangoan forms survive in the shape of picks and even an occasional handaxe, but the tendency is for tools to become smaller and to be better made by a bifacial flaking technique. In the area south of the Congo forest true axes appear for the first time, made by detaching flakes from both sides of a parent core, and therefore sometimes called 'core-axes'; other forms of small axes and chisels were also made suggesting a

59 Corbeil, Mauny and Charbonnier, *op. cit.*, p. 413. R. Richard, 'Contribution à l'étude du gisement néolithique guinéen du Cap Manuel à Dakar', *Bull. I.F.A.N.*, xiv, 1952, pp. 247–58. Mauny, 'Review of R. Richard's "Le Toumbien du Cap Manuel Est"', *Bull. I.F.A.N.*, B, xx, 1958, p. 645.

60 Davies, *The Quaternary* . . . , p. 115. H. J. Hugot, 'Etat des recherches préhistoriques dans l'Afrique de l'Ouest, 1964–1965', *West African Archaeological Newsletter*, i, 1964, p. 5.

61 Davies, *The Quaternary* . . . , pp. 113–14.

62 Davies, 'The Old Stone Age . . .', *loc. cit.* Soper, *op. cit.*, pp. 184–6.

63 Soper, *op. cit.*, pp. 186–8.

64 Davies, *The Quaternary* . . . , pp. 98, 100.

development of wood-working techniques. Lanceolate points of very fine workmanship appear and it is difficult to resist the belief that these were hafted and used as spears. In the more open parts of southern and eastern Africa the Lupemban was not present, but the Middle Stone Age was represented by quite a large number of regional industrial complexes which all tended to be characterised by various forms of lance or spear point suggesting that hunting was an important part of the economy. Another new technique of stone-working also developed at this time, in which the core was carefully prepared to shape ready to receive one final, decisive blow to detach a flake or blade of a predetermined shape or character.

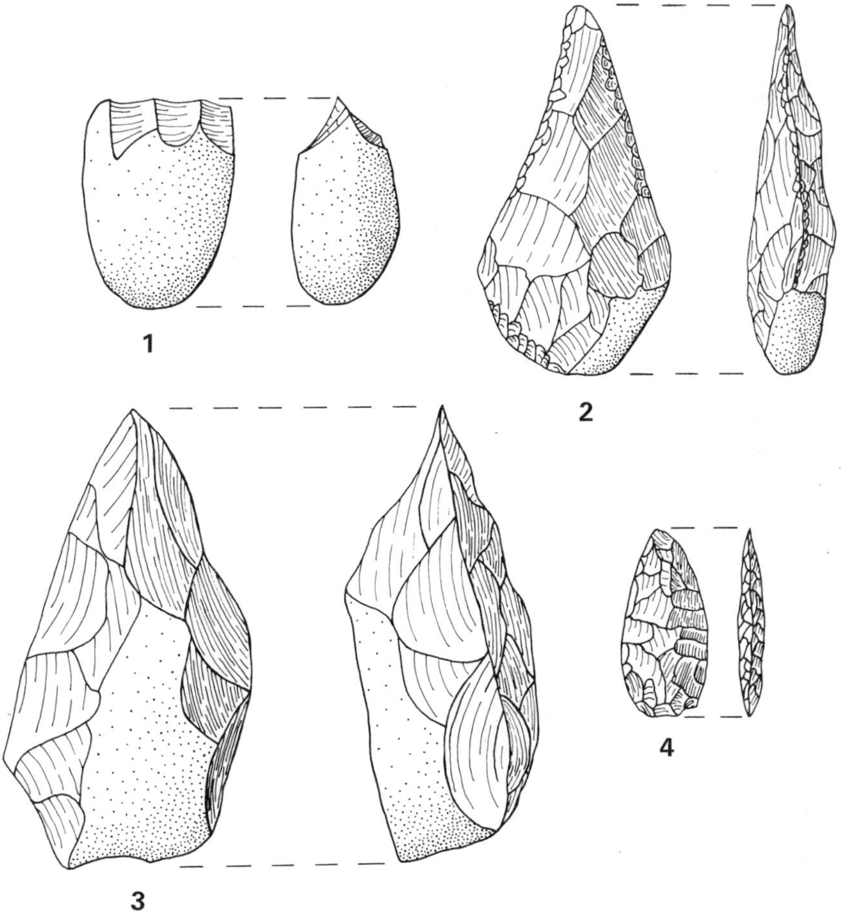

1 Oldowan type pebble-tool 2 Acheulian hand-axe 3 Sangoan pick 4 Middle Stone Age type point (After S. G. H. Daniels and G. E. Connah: half natural size)

In West Africa, industries belonging to the Middle Stone Age have been identified with much less certainty and clarity than in east and south Africa, but what there is seems to be closer to the Lupemban than to anything else. Rare specimens of Lupemban type have been found in Ghana,[65] and in Nigeria (seen in the collections of the University of Nsukka, found on the surface in the Afikpo area) but none have been found which give a satisfactory stratigraphical indication of their date. On the Jos Plateau and in the Lirue Hills to the north of it, considerable collections of material characterised by 'faceted butts', have been made from three stratified sites which have been classified as belonging to the Middle Stone Age.[66] However, they do not all have the indications of belonging to a woodland, Lupemban type of industrial complex, like the few Ghana specimens, but rather to have affinities with 'Middle Palaeolithic' types of industries in northern Africa. Perhaps this indicates that the Jos Plateau was once again a southward-projecting promontory of the North African cultural province during a wetter period, as it had been in Acheulian times, it being noteworthy that during the intervening arid period Sangoan material is conspicuously absent on the Plateau. There is a radiocarbon date from a piece of wood from the deposits at Zenebi, one of the alluvial sites producing Middle Stone Age material from Northern Nigeria, of 3485 ± 110 B.C., but the precise position of this piece of wood in relation to the stone artifacts is unrecorded, and the date is a good deal younger than would be expected for an industry of this type.

One industrial complex belonging to the end of Middle Palaeolithic times in Algeria and extending southwards some way into the desert is the Aterian, characterised by tanged points. Davies sees an extension of this industry into West Africa and calls it the Guinea Aterian,[67] but the evidence adduced is not very convincing and is doubted by many workers.[68] Davies also considers that industries from Bamako and Dakar, assigned by French workers to the Neolithic, are Sangoan or Middle Stone Age.[69] There certainly are a number of rather nondescript industries recorded from southern Ghana which appear by typology to belong to an undifferentiated Middle Stone Age family, or perhaps to the succeeding 'Second Intermediate' phase.[70]

Whereas we do not know anything about the physical characteristics of Sangoan man, Middle Stone Age man either qualified as *Homo sapiens* or was not far off it. The species known as *Homo rhodesiensis*, from Broken Hill, was associated with an early Middle Stone Age industry. The other

65 Davies, *The Quaternary* . . . , pp. 108–13.
66 Soper, *op. cit.*, pp. 188–90.
67 Davies, *The Quaternary* . . . , pp. 116–23.
68 H. J. Hugot, 'Limites Meridionales de l'Atérien', *Actas del V Congresso Panafricano de Prehistoria y de Estudio del Cuaternario*, Tenerife, 1966, pp. 95–106.
69 Davies, *The Quaternary* . . . , pp. 113–16.
70 Ibid, pp. 124–42.

human type which has been recognised in Africa at this time is the Proto-Bushman or Boskopoid (named after Boskop in the Transvaal, where the first specimen was discovered).

THE SECOND INTERMEDIATE PERIOD OF THE AFRICAN STONE AGE

This so-called 'Second Intermediate' period of the African Stone Age is in an unsatisfactory state, as what was regarded as the characteristic transitional 'Magosian' industry in East Africa, has been shown at the type site of Magosi, in Uganda, to be a mixture of distinct earlier and later industries.[71] In any case industries clearly belonging to this period have not been identified in West Africa. We are confined to a number of surface finds, which make up a rather heterogeneous collection with nothing very characteristic to distinguish them.[72] In Ghana many finds assigned to the period have been made on the inner silt terraces of the rivers, and in one cliff site an industry has been related to the sequence of eustatic sea levels.[73] The trouble with nondescript surface material is that much of it may well belong to the time of the Second Intermediate, while some of it may be later and belong to the Later Stone Age, but not have associated with it, at the particular place of finding, the material which would label it as such.

THE LATER STONE AGE

All over Africa in the Later Stone Age there came into being a full flowering of that development of very small carefully made implements called microliths.[74] So characteristic is this, and it represents such a change from the practice of earlier times, that it has been called 'the microlithic revolution'. It was really only the logical outcome of 'the hafting revolution', which made it possible. In many ways these very small stone implements, and the vast quantities of waste resulting from their manufacture, are much less attractive than the stone tools and weapons of earlier periods. But this impression of a rather mean and poverty-stricken standard of workmanship is probably quite erroneous, because in the archaeological record we only have a part of the total material culture preserved. It seems likely that these microlith users were craftsmen of a high order in exploiting their environment to make objects of wood and other organic materials which have only rarely survived.[75] Had we been able to see the composite implements, knives and arrowheads of which the microliths were only part,

71 M. Posnansky, 'Recent excavations at Magosi, Uganda: a preliminary report', *Man*, lxiii, 1963, p. 133.
72 Davies, *The Quaternary . . .*, pp. 151–82.
73 *Ibid.*, pp. 156–8.
74 B. Allchin, *The Stone-tipped Arrow*, London, 1966.
75 C. Gabel, *Stone Age Hunters of the Kafue*, Boston, 1965. B. H. Fagan and F. L. Van Noten, 'Wooden implements from late Stone Age sites at Gwisho Hot-springs, Lochinvar, Zambia', *Proc. Prehist. Soc.*, xxxii, 1966, pp. 246–61.

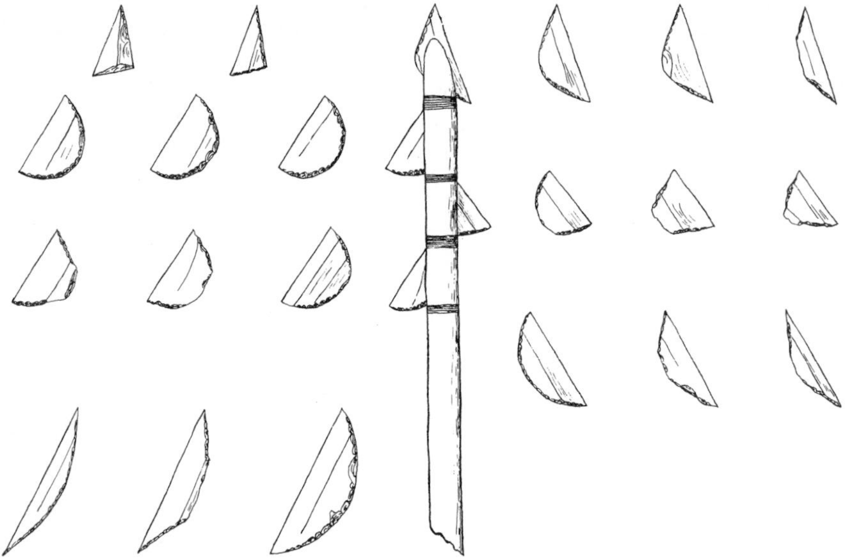

Late Stone Age microliths, showing probable manner of hafting as arrow points and arrow barbs (After Thurstan Shaw: natural size)

delicately and skilfully slotted into wooden holders and held in place by binding or mastic, they might have aroused our admiration.

Compared with the earlier periods of the Stone Age, the pace of cultural change was now quickening, although it remained very slow by modern standards. We can recognise cultural changes in terms of a thousand years instead of merely in terms of ten thousand or more. There are also more regional variants, as the world probably became more populated, and as increasing control over environment resulted in even more specific adaptations to different environments. This can be seen in the differentiation of the Later Stone Age cultures in east and south and north Africa, such as the Smithfield covering the greater part of the Republic of South Africa, the Nachikufan in north-eastern Zambia, the Wilton in large parts of the remaining areas of southern Africa and in East Africa, the Tshitolian which succeeds the Lupembo-Tshitolian in northern Angola and southern Congo, and the Iberomaurusian in the northern Maghreb.

The earliest radiocarbon dates in southern Africa for the beginning of this period are from Kamusongolwa[76] in Zambia and Matjes River in Cape Province,[77] which produced dates in the eleventh and ninth millennium B.C. respectively. There are a number of dates for the north African Iberomaurusian from the eleventh to the ninth millennium B.C.[78] In some places recognisably Wilton industries survived until the introduction of iron.

76 S. G. H. Daniels, 'The Later Stone Age', *Tarikh,* i, no. 3, London, 1966, p. 24.
77 Clark, *The Prehistory of Southern Africa,* p. 188.
78 J. Tixier, *Typologie de l'Epipaléolithique du Maghreb,* Paris, 1963, p. 22.

Once again the story is less well documented in West Africa than in other parts of the continent. There is now, however, dated and stratified evidence from Nigeria which belongs to this period, although only a brief notice of it has so far been published.[79] At a rock shelter called Iwo Eleru, fifteen miles from Akure, excavation revealed a Stone Age occupation culminating at the top in ground stone axes and pottery, overlying an apparently long period of occupation which produced a microlithic industry in which segments and chisel-ended blades or arrowheads, comparable to those in the Tshitolian, were greatly outnumbered by cores and waste flakes. The remains of a human skeleton, which belongs to the Stone Age layer and is not a later intrusion, was found between two rocks at the bottom of the deposit. Bone rarely survives in the humid acid soils of the more southerly parts of West Africa, and in this case it had been partially preserved by being under the driest part of the great rock overhang. Charcoal from around the skeleton was radiocarbon-dated to B.C. 9250 ± 200, and there was a date of B.C. 7200 ± 150 from another part of the deposit.

At the beginning of Late Stone Age times, not only was *Homo sapiens* fully evolved, and had in fact differentiated into the various subspecies regarded as the five or six main 'races' of mankind, but in addition the 'alternative' species of *Homo*—*Homo rhodesiensis* in sub-Saharan Africa and *Homo neanderthalensis* in Europe, North Africa and Asia—had become extinct.

The Upper Palaeolithic skeletons of Grimaldi (in southern France) are no longer considered to show negroid characteristics, and the earliest negroid skeletons so far recognised are those excavated at Khartoum and associated with a Later Stone Age industry.[80] There is no direct dating for these finds; their excavator posits a date of about 8000 B.C. but others would reduce this by two or three thousand years; the people concerned used pottery. A famous skeleton from Asselar, of negroid type, found in Mali about a hundred miles north of the central Niger bend, has been radiocarbon-dated to the end of the fifth millennium B.C. This is not inconsistent with the belief that Nilo-Sudanic negroids were responsible for the spread westwards across the Sahara of neolithic techniques and ways of living.[81]

Unfortunately there were no artifacts associated with this skeleton. The skeletal material of this period from southern Africa is Boskopoid (Proto-Bushman) and that of East Africa is either the same, or, in more numerous

79 T. Shaw, 'Excavations at Iwo Eleru, 1965', *W. Afr. Archaeol. Newsl.,* Ibadan, no. 3, 1965, pp. 15–16.
80 A. J. Arkell, *Early Khartoum*, Oxford, 1949.
81 L. C. Briggs, 'The Stone Age Races of Northwest Africa', *Bull. Am. Sch. Prehist. Res.*, Peabody Museum, Bull. 18, Massachusetts, 1955; 'Living Tribes of the Sahara and the Problem of their Prehistoric Origin, *Proc. pan-Afr. Congr. Prehist.* (3rd, Livingstone, 1955), London, 1957, pp. 195–9.

The Rock Shelter of Iwo Eleru. In the depths of the forest some fifteen miles from Akure, in Western Nigeria, the site is being cleared preparatory to excavation.

cases, characteristic of light-skinned Caucasoids. It is perhaps at first surprising that there are no traces of negroid features in East Africa even as late as 950 B.C.[82] But this fits in well with what we now believe to be the history of the spread of the Bantu-speaking users of iron subsequent to such a date (see below, p. 74).

At the moment of writing it is not possible to pronounce with much assurance upon the ethnic affinities of the Iwo Eleru skeleton, as the necessary detailed examination has not been completed, and in any case part of the facial skeleton—which is the thinnest part and the first to decay—is missing; this is very tantalising as it is one of the most diagnostic parts of a skull. However, it seems that its affinities are negroid.

The wear on the teeth is most peculiar. It is not the result of artificial filing but simply results from excessive attrition in use. The occlusal sur-

82 S. Cole, *The Prehistory of Eastern Africa*, London, 1964, p. 338.

faces of the teeth are worn down obliquely right to the gums, often only leaving sharp crescents of enamel which is all that is left after the rest of the crown has been sheared away. This unusual type of wear applies to the front teeth as well as to the back, and the oblique slopes go in different directions on different teeth. The most closely comparable wear on teeth which has been reported were in skeletons from the two earliest industrial complexes recognised in the long sequence of pre-Columbian occupations excavated in the Tehuacan valley in southern Mexico. These two phases are dated to the period between 9000 and 1500 B.C. before agriculture was established, and it is believed that the peculiar type of tooth wear was 'the result of pulling sand-covered fibrous plant material obliquely through the teeth to strip off the fleshy more edible parts. With advanced attrition of these anterior teeth, the opening of their pulp chambers, and subsequent tooth loss, the changing occlusal relationships became the secondary cause of the unusual wear pattern.'[83] The succeeding phase in the Tehuacan valley, dated to 1500–900 B.C., saw the beginnings of agriculture, and skeletons from this period show a quite different kind of tooth wear, with the molar teeth much abraded, but worn down flat, probably as the result of the incorporation in the meal of fine grit derived from the stone grain-rubbing equipment.

The type of wear found on the Iwo Eleru skeleton, then, appears to be characteristic of people in a pre-agricultural stage of existence in an area where fibrous tropical tubers were being eaten without the assistance of a pestle and mortar. This fits in with the stage of development one might expect to have been reached at a time in the tenth millennium B.C., the date provided by carbon 14.

The apparent absence at Iwo Eleru of the pestle and mortar and of any kind of agriculture is to be expected at this date. But to understand the succeeding stages of the Later Stone Age in West Africa, it is necessary to understand the story of the beginnings of agriculture in the Old World, and how this affected northern Africa and the area now occupied by the Sahara desert.

The beginnings of the cultivation of cereals and the domestication of animals took place in the area of the hilly flanks of the Fertile Crescent, that is, in northern Iraq, Iran, southern Anatolia and Palestine,[84] starting in the ninth millennium B.C. So radical was the change from a food-gathering existence to a food-producing economy that it was some years ago christened 'the Neolithic revolution', because it took place in the 'Neolithic' or New Stone Age. This change still remains a revolutionary one in essence,

83 J. E. Anderson, 'Human skeletons of Tehuacan', *Science,* cxlviii, 1965, pp. 496–7.

84 R. J. Braidwood, 'Near Eastern Prehistory', *Science,* cxxvii, 1958, pp. 1419–30. Braidwood and B. Howe, *Prehistoric Investigations in Iraqi Kurdistan*, Chicago, 1960. R. Solecki, 'Prehistory in Shanidar Valley, Northern Iraq', *Science*, cxxxix, 1963, pp. 179–93. D. W. Phillipson, 'The change from hunting and gathering to pastoralism and agriculture in Africa' *Tarikh,* i, no. 3, 1966, pp. 36–7.

but more recent work has shown that it was a much more long-drawn-out process than was at first thought. For North Africa a definition has been given that to qualify for the term Neolithic, one of the following must be present: (1) the grinding or polishing of stone axes or adzes, (2) bifacially-flaked arrowheads, (3) pottery, and (4) agriculture and the domestication of animals.[85] According to this definition it is possible to have a 'neolithic' without one, two or three of these elements, because, although taken together they constitute the 'Neolithic Revolution', the different elements were not adopted simultaneously everywhere.

Several things ultimately followed from the fundamental change to food-producing in the Neolithic revolution. It became possible for human groups to inhabit the same spots permanently, instead of in most cases being driven by the need to follow wild game and forage for wild products; the earliest true villages and permanent settlements are the result. It became possible for the first time to accumulate a surplus stock of goods—the granary came into being; for the first time it was possible to accumulate wealth. From this it followed that a greater specialisation in occupations became possible, as soon as one man was able to produce more food than was necessary for himself and his family; thus began the division of labour. The assured food supply also meant that a great increase in population became possible. The increased number of people living in a comparatively restricted area meant that social control needed to be more centralised, and because the mysteriously unpredictable fertility of the land, believed to be dependent on the favour of unseen powers, was all important, this was of paramount concern in any system of social sanctions set up. Here, perhaps, we can see the genesis of earth cults and of the idea of the divine king. Furthermore, all these developments, which constituted or flowed from the Neolithic revolution, formed the necessary foundations from which the next major change sprang, the 'urban revolution'.

The food-producing revolution, which was initiated in the hilly flanks of the Fertile Crescent, later moved into the great river valleys nearby and the innovation was introduced into their fertile plains. This seems to have happened in the fifth millennium B.C. in Egypt, where Neolithic communities are well documented from then until towards the end of the fourth millennium B.C., when this predynastic period ends and the Egyptian Old Kingdom begins. During the fourth millennium B.C. the Neolithic inhabitants of Esh Shaheinab, near Khartoum, kept domesticated goats[86] and the practice of agriculture spread into the central Sahara.[87] It must be

85 Balout, *op. cit.*, p. 450.

86 A. J. Arkell, *Shaheinab*, Oxford, 1953.

87 G. Delibrias and H. J. Hugot, 'Datations par le méthode dite du C 14 du Néolithique de l'Adrar Bous (Tenereen)', *Missions Berliet Ténéré—Tchad*, Paris, 1962, pp. 71–2. Hugot, 'Recherches préhistoriques dans l'Ahaggar Nord-Occidental', *Mem. du C.R.A.P.E.*, i, Paris, 1963, pp. 73–168. J. D. Clark, 'Radiocarbon dating and the spread of farming economy', *Antiquity*, xxxix, no. 153, 1965, pp. 45–8.

remembered that the climate of the Sahara was very much wetter during the fifth and fourth millennia B.C. than it is now. This may be part of the same meteorological phenomenon which produced the Makalian wet phase in East Africa. The evidence of geology and geomorphology suggests that it was getting wetter in the Sahara from about 6000 B.C. onwards, and that it was wetter still from 5000–3000 B.C.[88] This was an incident that was fairly insignificant geologically, but was humanly of great importance—just as, in the contrary direction, the subsequent desiccation was—because the changes crossed the threshold of conditions conducive to human occupation. In the third millennium B.C. a comparatively small decrease in rainfall initiated the final desiccation of the Sahara to bring it to the state we know it in today. Evidence from fossil pollen indicates that from about 6000 B.C. there was a vegetation of Mediterranean type in the central Sahara, with Aleppo pine, cypress and juniper, and in the mountains cedars, oaks, walnut trees and heaths. After 2800 B.C. this Mediterranean flora disappeared, to be replaced with *Acacia* vegetation. Records from the Sixth Dynasty in Egypt indicate that it was at this time, about 2500 B.C., that the desert moved up to the Nile valley.

A natural effect of this drying up of the Sahara was that its peoples tended to move out into peripheral regions where there was more water to support life. The later part of the third millennium B.C. is marked by the incursion into the Nile valley from the desert of the people known to archaeologists as the 'C group', and this was very likely a manifestation of increasing desiccation in the Sahara.

During the moister period before 2800 B.C. evidence of Neolithic peoples is abundant in the Sahara. It seems likely that the food-producing idea spread westwards from the Nile valley in the middle of the fourth millennium B.C. over what was then favourable terrain for the purpose. This is strongly suggested by similarities between the 'wavy-line' and 'dotted wavy-line' pottery of the Khartoum area and pottery found on Neolithic sites across the Sahara as far as the Hoggar.[89] The Neolithic industrial assemblages are not identical and a number of regional variants of the Sahara Neolithic have been recognised,[90] but they are characterised by an extraordinary number and proliferation of bifacial arrowheads, suggesting that hunting over the Sahara steppes, which at the time probably abounded in game, was still an important source of food supply. Pastoralism was

88 K. W. Butzer, 'Late glacial and postglacial climatic variation in the Near East', *Erdkunde*, ix, 1957, pp. 21–35; and 'Les changements climatiques dans les régions arides depuis le Pliocène', *Histoire de l'utilisation des terres arides,* U.N.E.S.C.O., 1961, pp. 35–64. P. Quezel and C. Martinez, 'Premiers résultats de l'analyse palynolgigue de sédiments recueillis au Sahara méridional à l'occasion de la Mission Berliet Ténéré—Tchad', in *Missions Berliet Ténéré—Tchad,* Paris, 1962, pp. 313–27. Th. Monod, 'The late Tertiary and Pleistocene in the Sahara' in C. Howell and F. Bourlière, *African Ecology and Human Evolution*, London, 1964, pp. 117–229.

89 Hugot, p. 185, 1963.

90 Alimen, *op. cit.*, pp. 161–79.

probably more important than agriculture, and it is believed that the numerous bovidian rock paintings and engravings in the Sahara belong to this period. Between 11° and 20° North it is possible in the southern Sahara to recognise a lacustrine facies of the Neolithic, characterised by bone fish-hooks and harpoons, belonging to people for whom fishing played an important part in the economy.[91] In the Maghreb, the Iberomaurusian industrial complex (see above, p. 54) had been succeeded by a more highly specialised one called the Capsian (after Ghafsa, in Tunisia), which, although retaining much of the Iberomaurusian microlithic element, also developed a propensity for burins and parallel-sided blades. When Neolithic ideas reached the area, some of the already existing Capsian elements persisted, in fusing with the new ideas, so that the resulting complex has been called the 'Neolithic of Capsian tradition'.

It is necessary to keep in mind the picture described above of what was happening in North Africa and in the area of the present Sahara during the last five millennia B.C. in order to understand what happened in the West African area to the south of it. At the moment of writing there is great difficulty in interpreting our scanty evidence, because we have no satisfactory radiocarbon datings of archaeological material between the eighth millennium and the last half of the first millennium B.C., and we do not even have satisfactory excavation reports of any well-stratified sites of clearly differing industrial complexes to give us even relative dating. Furthermore, over such a large area as West Africa there undoubtedly developed quite a large number of regional variants, so that when one observes differences between industrial complexes in different areas clearly belonging somewhere in these seven millennia it is often difficult to know whether to interpret the differences as being due to differences of time or to differences of place.

Probably the first archaeological sites to be excavated in West Africa, which yielded material belonging somewhere in the Later Stone Age, are a number of caves and rock shelters in Guinée, some of which were dug into over sixty years ago.[92] There was one site near Conakry, a group

91 T. Monod and R. Mauny, 'Découverte de nouveaux instruments en os dans l'Ouest Africain', *Proc. pan-Afr. Congr. Prehist.* (3rd, Livingstone, 1955), pp. 242–47.

92 E. T. Hamy, 'La grotte de Kakimbon à Rotoma près de Konakry', *Comptes Rendus du Congrès International d'Anthropologie et d'Archéologie Préhistorique,* sess. xii, 1900. P. Guebhard, 'Trois abris sous roche fouillés dans le Fouta-Djallon', *Bulletin Géogr. hist. descr.*, no. 3, 1907, pp. 408–20. Guebhard, 'Stations préhistoriques au Fouta-Djallon', *Comptes Rendus du Congrès Préhistorique de Beauvais,* 1909, pp. 281–9. L. Desplagnes, 'L'archéologie préhistorique en Guinée Française', *Bulletin de la Société Géogr. Comm. Bordeaux,* 1907. E. Hue, 'L'Age de la pierre à Fouta-Djallon', *Bull. Soc. Préhist. Fr.*, ii, 1912. R. Hubert, 'Objets anciens de l'Afrique occidentale', *Bull. Com. Etud. Hist. Scient. A.O.F.*, v, 1922, pp. 382–99. H. Breuil, 'L'Afrique', *Cahiers d'Art,* Paris, 1931. R. Delcroix and R. Vaufrey, 'Le Toumbien de Guinée Française', *L'Anthropologie*, xlix, 1939, pp. 265–312. T. Shaw, 'Report on excavations carried out in the cave known as "Bosumpra" at Abetifi, Kwahu, Gold Coast Colony', *Proc. prehist. soc.*, x, 1944, pp. 54–5.

around Kindia, and a group further inland still, in the Fouta Djallon around Pita. Unfortunately the way this important material is published makes it difficult to assess, and when one studies such of the material as is accessible and is not stored away in packing cases in Paris, lack of detailed stratigraphical notes from the original excavations makes it difficult to be certain of the associations; sometimes one wonders whether material from more than one stratigraphical layer is included in a single collection. Furthermore, the industries from these Guinée caves and rock shelters are far from identical and the differences seem to be genuine, even allowing for differences in material used. In some of them there are bifacial pieces which recall forms earlier than the Later Stone Age, perhaps of Lupemban style, but these do not seem to have been established as stratigraphically earlier than the rest of the material, and if this is the true situation it may represent a fusion of older and younger traditions. But without satisfactory stratigraphical separation, it may be difficult to distinguish between a Lupemban-style core axe and a later one, or even a rough-out for a ground stone-axe.

These implements have been regarded by some as hoes, and therefore as evidence of agriculture, and the flat, broad type (limande hoe) peculiar to Ghana, as regional variants, perhaps influenced by the nature of their quartzitic material.[93] The trouble with the latter is that they have not been published with any clear associations or with any real indication of date, relative or absolute. The majority of the Guinée sites produced microliths, ground stone axes and grinding stones, and some of them had pottery, although in the Grotte de Kakimbon pottery is said to occur only in the upper level.[94] On the other hand one site (Bandé Bokhon) has produced a large blade industry, which also contains burins, more truly reminiscent of the North African Capsian (not published but observed by the author in the Musée de l'Homme, Paris). Unfortunately no bone remains were preserved in these Guinée sites, so as yet we remain tantalisingly ignorant about the makers of the industries, as well as about their date and their relationships to their antecedents, or to the influences which may have penetrated from the outside and from what direction.

Excavations in the rock shelter of Blandè, in extreme south-east Guinée, near the borders of Ivory Coast and Sierra Leone, had important results, for they revealed an industry with ground stone axes and pottery together with large bifacial tools reminiscent of the Kindia and Fouta Djallon caves, but without a microlithic element.[95] This recalls the situation at the Grotte

93 Davies, *The Quaternary . . .*, pp. 203–30.
94 Hamy, *op. cit.*
95 B. Holas, 'Notes préliminaires sur les fouilles de la grotte de Blandè', *Bull. I.F.A.N.*, xii, 1950, pp. 999–1006; and 'Note complémentaire sur l'abri sous roche de Blandè', *Bull. I.F.A.N.*, xiv, 1952, pp. 1341–52. Holas and Mauny, 'Nouvelles fouilles à l'abri sous roche de Blandè (Guinée)', *Bull. I.F.A.N.*, xv, 1953, pp. 1605–17.

de Kakimbon, near Conakry. One has to be careful here because these Guinée industries may have been affected by the raw material they were using, but it seems unlikely that this can account for the absence at Blandè of microliths, as the presence of quartz was reported, commonly used for microliths elsewhere in West Africa; and the microlithic technique was applied to other kinds of stone as well in some of the Guinée caves. Furthermore a recently excavated cave at Yengema, in Sierra Leone, has confirmed the presence of an industry with ground stone axes and pottery but no microliths.[96] So it does look as if people with a Lupemban tradition of stone working (such as may be present at Cap Manuel (Dakar) and at Bamako) may have moved southwards at the time of the desiccation of the Sahara and the centrifugal movements of peoples from it consequent upon this; this may have been towards the end of the second millennium B.C. At some point, whether before they moved south, or as a result of later contact, these people adopted pottery and the technique of making ground stone axes from Sahara Neolithic people when the latter moved south into contact with them. This would suggest that the microlithic elements, present in the Kindia and Fouta Djallon rock shelters, arrived in this western part of West Africa later, and never penetrated as far south as Conakry and Blandè. Possibly even a genuinely 'Neolithic of Capsian tradition' affected the occupants of the cave of Bandé Bokhon, while the Rufisque industry, once regarded as 'Neolithic of Capsian tradition'[97] has since been declared not to be.[98] Unfortunately this industry is only a surface collection from two sites near Rufisque, but apart from being made of a pleasant-looking flint, is really little different from other West African microlithic industries.

There has in general been too ready a tendency to dub the Later Stone Age industrial complexes of West Africa which contain microliths as 'Neolithic of Capsian tradition'.[99] The correctness of this ascription has been questioned[100] and in any case it seems that the Later Stone Age industries of West Africa had their own microlithic continuum, particularly perhaps in the more easterly half of the area. It seems that it was *onto* this that 'Neolithic' elements of pottery and ground stone axes were grafted—not that Neolithic influences brought in microliths along with the ground stone axes. In other words, the process was very similar to that which produced the 'Neolithic of Capsian tradition' in the area of its occurrence, but the traditions absorbed in West Africa were indigenous and

96 Reported by Professor Carleton Coon at the Premier Colloque International d'Archéologie Africaine at Fort Lamy, 1966.

97 R. Vaufey, 'Le Néolithique de tradition capsienne au Sénégal', *Rivista di scienze preistoriche*, i, 1946.

98 Hugot, 'Etat des recherches préhistoriques dans l'Afrique de l'Ouest . . .', *loc. cit.*

99 Vaufrey, *op. cit.*; Alimen, *op. cit.*, pp. 229–33; Davies, *The Quaternary* . . . , p. 236.

100 H. J. Hugot, 'Essai sur les armatives de pointes de flèches du Sahara', *Libyca*, v, 1957, pp. 89–236; and 'Etat des recherches . . .', pp. 4–6.

not indebted to the Capsian, which is an industrial complex confined to north-west Africa.

It seems that we can see this indigenous microlithic tradition at Mejiro Cave, Old Oyo,[101] the lower levels at Iwo Eleru and in the lower layer of Rop.[102] In all of these was abundant microlithic material but without associated pottery or ground stone axes.

Davies has suggested a date of about 500 B.C. for the introduction of stone hoes and ground stone axes, but admits his dating is tentative.[103] He regards the introduction of pottery and small ground stone axes as late in the Neolithic period and to be subsequent to his 'Hoe-Cultures';[104] this may well be correct but at the moment it is not firmly supported by stratigraphical evidence. Similarly Davies may be correct in his identification of a Neolithic industrial complex which he calls the 'Kintampo-Culture', whose distribution is in the lower valley of the Black Volta and the Accra plains; it is characterised by the presence of so-called terracotta 'cigars'.[105] This is a misleading name for these objects which are not cigar-shaped, save only in section when viewed sideways. They were better called 'hatched rubbers', even if this does beg the question of their function. They are up to 22 cm in length, are commonly of soft sandstone, are of truncated 'bull roarer' shape but with a lenticular transverse section, and have their surface scored over with sets of parallel grooves, usually at right-angles to each other. An abrasive material was chosen and then made more abrasive by scoring the surface. Their form and appearance strongly suggest a rubbing or smoothing function, and many of those examined by the author show signs of having been worn down on the middle of the flat surface, some all over. Therefore it is better to regard them as rubbers of some kind, perhaps for smoothing pottery in the course of its manufacture,[106] perhaps for grating some not very hard kind of food such as yams. Since some of them have holes, as if for suspension (although no string-wear was observed) perhaps they were portable hones, for sharpening hardwood or bamboo knives; it seems a less likely probability that they were used for sharpening ground stone axes. Some of them show deeper grooves of the 'bead-polisher' variety; known for their abrasive properties, it would occur naturally to people to use them for this purpose—especially, perhaps, broken pieces. It seems unnecessary to call them musical instruments or

101 F. Willett, 'The microlithic industry from Old Oyo, Western Nigeria', *Proc. pan-Afr. Congr. Prehist.* (4th, Leopoldville, 1959), Tervuren, 1962, ii, pp. 261–72.
102 B. E. B. Fagg, 'Preliminary report on a microlithic industry at Rop Rock Shelter, Northern Nigeria', *Proc. Prehist. Soc.* x, 1944, pp. 68–9. E. Eyo, '1964 excavations at Rop Rock Shelter', *W. Afr. Archaeol. Newsl.*, Ibadan, no. 3, 1965, pp. 5–13.
103 Davies, 'The Neolithic revolution . . .', loc. cit., p. 16.
104 Davies, *The Quaternary* . . ., p. 245.
105 O. Davies, 'Neolithic cultures of Ghana', *Proc. pan-Afr. Congr. Prehist.* (4th, Leopoldville, 1959), Tervuren, 1962, ii, pp. 291–301; and *The Quaternary* . . ., pp. 239–47.
106 J. Anquandah, 'Ghana's terra-cotta cigars', *Ghana Notes and Queries*, no. 7, 1966, p. 26.

sweat-removers, and to be the last refuge of despair to say they are 'ritual objects'. Whether their presence among surface collections of other material of generally 'Neolithic' character warrants the creation of a special culture name is open to question, especially since, as far as can be ascertained, their only occurrences in excavated deposits, at Ntereso and Christian's Village, showed them to be associated with assemblages of considerably 'mixed' character.

The site of Ntereso is a remarkable one; it is unique, and puzzling. It is situated west of Tamale, in Ghana, just north of latitude 9° N. The significance of this is that it has produced arrowheads of unquestionably Saharan Neolithic type, far to the south of their main distribution, which does not normally extend to the south of 14° N; there are also bone fish-hooks and harpoons. The site was discovered as the result of making a borrow pit for road material, and was subsequently excavated, but the full report on this excavation has not yet been published. For the excavator, in spite of the Saharan Neolithic material, regarded the site as an Iron Age one, with the Neolithic elements as survivals.[107] The bottom layer is said to consist of filled-in water-holes, down to a depth of 8 ft, with material in them a little earlier than the rest; bone objects were plentiful and there was no iron. In Period II, there was a little iron and some bone objects; in Period III, there was iron and a few bone objects. Period II had the remains of rectangular houses which were burnt down before the Period III material was stratified over them. The Saharan type stone arrowheads persisted throughout, although the wide, hollow-based type were more numerous in the lowest level, and it was only this level which produced bone harpoons and fish-hooks. There appeared to be continuity in the pottery. A few micro-tranchet arrowheads 'occurred'.[108] Two radiocarbon dates from Ntereso have been published; 1240 ± 120 B.C. for the last phase of Level I, and 1630 ± 130 B.C. for Level III, but the excavator says that the last date for an iron-using culture is unacceptable. He therefore accepts the first date and infers from 'the probable duration of the site' that 'iron was known in Ghana at the latest before 1000 B.C.'[109] This inference is not acceptable to other archaeologists.

THE FOOD PRODUCING REVOLUTION

It was mentioned above that the revolutionary change from hunting and gathering to food production can be traced in south-west Asia back to the ninth millennium B.C. and that it seems to have reached the Nile valley area by the fifth millennium B.C. We also saw that the movement continued

107 Davies, *The Quaternary . . .*, p. 244.
108 O. Davies, 'The invasion of Ghana from the Sahara in the Early Iron Age', *Actas del V Congresso Panafricano de Prehistoria y de Estudio de Cuaternario*, Santa Cruz de Tenerife, 1966, pp. 27–42.
109 O. Davies, 'Comments on the Iron Age in sub-Saharan Africa', *Current Anthropology*, vii, 4, 1966, pp. 470–1.

westward into the then favourable parts of the Sahara; that Neolithic industrial assemblages are widely spread in this area; and that hunting and fishing remained important in the economy, although flocks and herds were now kept. From the Hoggar (Meniet) and Mauretania (Tichit) there is fossil pollen evidence for the cultivation of cereal crops, as well as field systems at Tichit.[110] There was no evidence of cereal cultivation at Esh Shaheinab, near Khartoum, although domesticated goats were kept and there is evidence of the use of nuts from the oil palm, *Elaeis guineensis*. As Esh Shaheinab is north of where such palms can now grow, this is taken by some as further evidence of wetter climate then, by others of palm nuts having been transported some distance. The point is that the temperate cereal crops of wheat and barley seem to have spread westwards and southwards from Egypt with difficulty, if at all; and needing winter rainfall they would in any case sooner or later have come up against a climatic frontier which they could not pass. They are grown on the Ethiopian high plateau, perhaps introduced there by people from Nubia at the time of the drying out of the Sahara in the second half of the third millennium B.C.; but wheat and barley did not spread more widely because they are unsuitable in the tropical savannah region without irrigation.[111] If it had not been for the combination of this climatic barrier *and* the desiccation of the Sahara at a crucial time, sub-Saharan Africa might not have become so cut off from subsequent developments as it was. On the other hand there were wild grasses in the sudanic climatic belt which have been domesticated and have given rise to the tropical cereals which we know as the sorghums and millets.

It is a fascinating question—to which archaeology is still seeking the answer—where and when this domestication took place, perhaps as the result of stimulus from people outside the area familiar with the cultivation of the more northerly cereals. It has been suggested that the people of the Stone Bowl culture of East Africa were cultivating guinea corn and millet in the second half of the second millennium B.C. *Digitaria* (acha, fonio, hungry rice) and *Oryza glaberrima* (African rice) seem to have been domesticated in the more northerly part of our West African area and to have become staples in this region, but not to have spread further east and south. A high antiquity for an independent invention of agriculture in the Upper Niger area has been suggested,[112] but the largely botanical evidence on which this idea rests has been discountenanced by botanists.[113] In the more

110 H. J. Hugot, 'Archaeology in Senegal, Mali, Mauretania and Guinea', *W. Afr. Archaeol. Newsl.*, Ibadan, no. 5, 1966, pp. 36–8.
111 J. D. Clark, 'The spread of food production in sub-Saharan Africa', *Journal of African History*, iii, no. 2, 1962, pp. 211–28.
112 R. Portères, 'Vieilles agricultures de l'Afrique intertropicale', *L'Agronomie Tropicale*, v, 1950, pp. 489–507. G. P. Murdock, *Africa, its Peoples and their Culture History*, New York, 1959.
113 H. C. Baker, 'Comments on the thesis that there was a major centre of plant domestication near the headwaters of the River Niger', *J.A.H.*, iii, 1962, pp. 229–33.

southerly parts of West Africa where forest conditions prevail, it is likely that yam cultivation began. It has been supposed that the bifacial tools, or 'hoes', of some facies of the West African Later Stone Age indicate the digging up of yams, either wild or cultivated. Although Asiatic species of yam (such as *Dioscorea alata*, the water yam) were later introduced into Africa, probably on the East African coast about the fifth century A.D., there are species of yam in West Africa (such as *Dioscorea cayanensis*) which were indigenously domesticated. When this took place we do not know, but it could easily have been fairly early in the West African Later Stone Age, and independent of the later stimulus from food-producers to the north and east. For once Later Stone Age people had discovered that there were yams to be dug up in forested areas, it is likely they would have been transported to a semi-permanent 'home' such as a rock shelter, tops would be cut off and thrown away outside and later be observed to have produced more yams. The absence of stone hoes does not necessarily imply the absence of agriculture; the earliest levels of food-producing Jericho yielded very few, while many African tribes have practised agriculture by means of digging sticks. The wear on the teeth of the Iwo Eleru skeleton is explained as the result of tearing at sand-covered tubers such as yams. This is likely to have taken place in the area of junction of the woodland savannah and the rain-forest, because the yam requires trees to grow up but is killed in dense forest from lack of sunlight. Its natural habitat, therefore, is the forest margins, gallery forests along streams, or in clearings in the forest.[114]

It has been mentioned that the Neolithic inhabitants of the Sahara may have been hunters and pastoralists rather than sedentary agriculturalists. Domesticated long- and short-horned cattle, sheep and goats were introduced from south-west Asia into Egypt about 5000 B.C., into the Hoggar soon after 4000 B.C., the Khartoum area about 3000 B.C., the Sudan belt generally about 2000 B.C.[115] Some believe that the humpless cattle spread across the Sahara area from east to west, others from west to east.[116] It is possible that the spread was from Egypt westwards along the north African littoral and down into the Hoggar through Fezzan, and thence eastwards through Tibesti, Ennedi, Dafur and Kordofan to the upper Nile valley area. Much of the evidence comes from rock paintings, which are difficult to date and therefore difficult to interpret. It looks as if many of these rock paintings and engravings in the Sahara were done by nomadic hunting peoples, disturbed by the agricultural, cattle-herding people who were portrayed as being of negroid type. Rock paintings of humpless cattle have

114 I. H. Burkill, 'Notes on the Genus Dioscorea in the Belgian Congo', *Bull. Jard. Dot. Etat Brux.*, xv, 1939, p. 345.
115 Clark, 'Carbon 14 chronology . . .' *loc. cit.*, 1962.
116 C. K. Cooke, 'The Rock Paintings and Engravings of Africa', *Tarikh* i, 3, 1966, pp. 45–66.

been reported from Northern Nigeria, but it is impossible to date them, although it is not unreasonable to suppose that they have a very considerable antiquity and go back to a time before the introduction of the humped variety.[117] Compared with the Sahara, rock paintings and engravings are not common in West Africa.[118] Associated with some rock paintings there are rock gongs and rock slides, some of which may have a considerable antiquity also, but it is difficult to tell in any particular case, as the use of some has continued up to today.[119] The humped cattle, on the other hand, appear to have been introduced into Africa at a later date via the Horn and to have been diffused into the rest of the continent and down the Nile into Egypt from there. It seems likely that domesticated sheep, goats and cattle were introduced into our West African area during the second and first millennium B.C. following the general displacement of peoples having domesticated animals, as a result of the drying-up of the Sahara. But at present we have no direct evidence about this from West Africa at all, as we have no osteological evidence of incontestably domesticated animals belonging to this period. Nor do we know what effect may have been caused as a result of immigrant cattle coming into the areas of the tsetse fly, nor do we know where the tsetse belts lay at the time, for these are known to move.[120]

THE URBAN REVOLUTION

From the beginning of the third millennium B.C. there flourished in north-eastern Africa for nearly 3,000 years one of the world's great early civilisations, that of Ancient Egypt. This was essentially a Bronze Age civilisation, and it was the discovery and use of metal which made possible so many of its achievements. But this was only one of the developments which ultimately followed from the foundations laid by the Neolithic revolution described above, and this second great change in the way of living has been called 'the urban revolution'. For it resulted in the development of cities and city-states, which, by the very derivation of the word, constitutes the attainment of 'civilisation'.

The urban revolution was, in a sense, the continuation of trends already observable as a result of the Neolithic revolution—larger and larger populations able to remain settled in one place, greater and greater accumulations of wealth, more and more centralised control. All these things were accelerated by the effect of agricultural communities settling in the great river valleys bordering on the hilly areas where the Neolithic revolution initially took place—the Indus, the Tigris-Euphrates and the Nile.

117 Fagg, 'The Rock Gong Complex Today and in Prehistoric Times', *J.H.S.N.*, i, no. 1, 1956, pp. 27–42.
118 Mauny, 'Gravures, peintures et inscriptions rupestres de l'Ouest Africain', *Init. afr.* no. 11, Dakar 1954.
119 Fagg, 'The Rock Gong Complex . . .', pp. 203–22.
120 K. M. Buchanan and J. C. Pugh, *Land and People in Nigeria*, London, 1958, pp. 47–50.

In this situation were invented writing, a knowledge of the calendar and of mathematics; trade developed with areas outside the river valleys for things not produced in them; and the use of metal for tools and weapons was discovered. The metal was copper, later allied with tin to make bronze. (Iron was only discovered in the later part of the second millennium B.C.) Another invention was that of the wheel, developed both for pottery making and for vehicles. All these innovations came to fruition in the third and second millenia B.C.

It was pointed out above that it was from 3000 B.C. onwards that the final desiccation of the Sahara set in. Herein lies the misfortune of Africa. In 3000 B.C. the benefits of the Neolithic revolution had reached both Britain and the central Sahara, and Bronze Age civilisation was just beginning in Egypt. But with the drying out of the Sahara after 3000 B.C. this became an increasingly impenetrable barrier until the camel became common there 3,000 years later. It may be that the Sahara was never a completely insuperable obstacle and that at times it was a highway for human movement,[121] but at this crucial period when the developments of the urban revolution were taking place in south-western Asia and the adjacent north-eastern corner of Africa, a barrier came down to the south of it, effectively sealing off the rest of Africa from these fertilising innovations. Europe was not so unlucky; no barrier came down between the Fertile Crescent and the Mediterranean onto which it abutted—so that it was possible for the Minoan and Mycenean civilisations to develop in the eastern Mediterranean, and subsequently that of the classical world. The European barbarians may have overrun this classical civilisation in the end, but they learnt its arts and it is from the cross-fertilisation of the two that European civilisation arose.

Thus while copper and bronze metallurgy reached Britain by the first half of the second millennium B.C., followed later by the wheel, and later still by iron, sub-Saharan Africa missed out copper and bronze metallurgy and the wheel, and only picked up its contacts again, as it were, when it took to the use of iron. It is no reflection on Africans that their ancestors had no Bronze Age; nor is it either failure, perversity or prejudice on the part of archaeologists not to have found what does not exist.[122] There are some indications that copper or bronze objects did find their way in a faint trickle into the area of Mauretania, probably southwards from Morocco, perhaps round about the middle of the first millennium B.C.,[123] but south of this the metal to supersede stone was iron.

121 M. Herskovits, *The Human Factor in Changing Africa,* London, 1962.
122 Anene, 'Africa in perspective', *loc. cit.*, p. 11.
123 R. Mauny, 'Un âge du cuivre au Sahara occidental?' *Bull. I.F.A.N.*, xiii, 1951, pp. 168–80.

THE COMING OF IRON TO WEST AFRICA

This introduction of iron into sub-Saharan Africa was a big event, of great importance for the whole continent. Not only did its superiority to copper and bronze give its possessors far greater control of their environment, but it also seems to be associated with the spread of Bantu-speaking peoples and the practice of agriculture. The evidence available at present suggests that the earliest area in sub-Saharan Africa where iron-working was practised was West Africa, and that the eastern end of this region was the first dispersal point for the Bantu languages.

Apart from the very early date claimed for iron-working at Ntereso (see above, p. 64)—a date earlier than anywhere else in Africa, including Egypt—the earliest evidence of iron-smelting comes from the complex which produces also the famous Nok terracotta figurines. Nok is the name of a small village at the southern end of Zaria Province in Nigeria, west of the Jos Plateau, which, being the place where these figurines were first discovered in the course of tin-mining, has given its name to the culture, according to accepted archaeological practice.

Most of the finds of Nok type have been revealed in alluvial tin-mining deposits.[124] A radiocarbon date of A.D. 200 $\pm$ 50 was obtained from wood in black clay overlying the sand and gravel of the youngest alluvial body, which contained the Nok cultural material.[125] Therefore the Nok material is likely to be older than this date. Radiocarbon dates for pieces of carbonised wood from the sand overlying the basal gravel of the youngest alluvial body gave a date of B.C. 900 $\pm$ 70; two pieces from the figurine horizon giving dates of B.C. 2100 $\pm$ 140 and B.C. 3600 $\pm$ 65 have been dismissed as impossibly early and representing material sludged in from an older deposit.[126] It was therefore suggested that the Nok culture belonged to the period between 500 B.C. and A.D. 200.[127] Confirmation of this has come more recently from a site at Taruga, where Nok style figurine material was associated with iron-smelting furnaces, yielding a date of B.C. 280 $\pm$ 120[128] which seems to contradict Davies's assertion that the Nok terracottas must date to the first two centuries A.D.[129] The terracotta figurine material includes life-size human heads and remains of torsos and kneeling figures up to two-thirds life size; there are also models of animals. The human figures show features very characteristic of African sculpture, in the disproportionate size and care in execution of the head, feet and

124 Fagg, 'An Outline of the Stone Age of the Plateau Minefield', *Proc. 3rd. Intern. W. Af. Conf.* (Ibadan, 1949), Lagos, 1956, pp. 203–22.

125 Barendson, Deevey and Gralenski, *op. cit.*

126 Fagg, 'The Nok culture in prehistory', *J.H.S.N.*, i, no. 4, 1959, p. 291.

127 Fagg, 'The Nok terra-cottas in West African Art History, *Proc. pan-Afr. Congr. Prehist.* (4th, Leopoldville, 1959), Tervuren, 1962, ii, p. 445.

128 Fagg, 'Radiocarbon dating of the Nok culture, Northern Nigeria', *Nature*, ccv, no. 4967, 1965, p. 212.

129 Davies, *The Quaternary* . . . , p. 248.

hands, compared with the rest of the body. Many figures are shown with deformities. The modelling is done with exquisite sensitiveness and a high degree of artistic craftsmanship. The style is very characteristic, particularly in the treatment of the eyes.

In the alluvial deposits where the majority of Nok figurines have been found, there also occur small stone arrow-points and barbs,[130] flat stone hoes and small ground stone axes, indented or 'dimpled' hammer-stones, perhaps for cracking nuts, pottery, quartz ear-, nose- and lip-plugs, iron-slag, iron-smelting tuyères, pieces of preserved furnace-wall, and cowrie-form tin beads almost certainly from the same horizon—but none of these have ever been published. Because of these associations the Nok culture has been regarded as transitional from the use of stone to the use of iron, when the latter was scarce and valuable but when stone was still used for some things. However, because of the nature of the alluvial deposits this view has been questioned and it has been suggested that the Nok culture was fully iron-using.[131] Since no Stone Age material has been found in the excavations of the Nok iron-smelting site of Taruga, nor at the only other known non-alluvial Nok site to be investigated at Katsina Ala, this view seems confirmed. The distribution of Nok material hitherto found extends in an oval-shaped area running north-west and south-east between the Jos Plateau and the reach of the River Niger downstream from Yelwa to the confluence, and extending across the Benue at its south-eastern end; but it is unlikely that we have as yet a true picture of its full distribution—although in view of the amount of tin-mining on the Jos Plateau it can be taken as reasonably certain that, had it been present there, it would have been discovered by now.

Thus the remarkable artistic makers of the Nok figurines, clearly negroids, are (if we except Ntereso) the earliest known makers of iron in sub-Saharan Africa. The question is—how did they come to be makers of iron?

Cases of independent invention are known, but are rare, and therefore have to be well documented before they can be accepted. Independent invention of the art of iron-smelting in West Africa has recently been suggested by an archaeologist working in Ghana (see above, p. 64), but this was only to account for radiocarbon dates alleged to be associated with ironwork of before 1000 B.C., 400 years before iron was commonly used in ancient Egypt. This is a hypothesis which will have to be taken seriously if there is more unequivocal evidence in the same area for iron-working at such an early date. The metallurgy of iron is more difficult than that of copper and bronze; iron does not occur in a natural state in the same way as copper and gold; in the ancient world of the Middle East it required the experience of some 3,000 years of copper and bronze metallurgy before

130 Fagg, 'An Outline of the Stone Age . . .', *loc. cit.*
131 Shaw, 'Field research in Nigerian archaeology', *J.H.S.N.*, ii, no. 4, 1963, p. 455.

iron was discovered. If an acceptable area of iron-working at a date prior to the Nok culture can be found from which the latter could have learnt the art, diffusion seems the better explanation.

There are two candidates which have been put forward as centres from which a knowledge of iron-working spread into sub-Saharan Africa. One is Meroe, in Sudan, and the other is ancient Carthage.[132]

The Negro kingdom of Kush flourished for nearly 1,000 years in the area of the great bend of the Nile south of Dongola, on the stretch of the river which contains the fourth and the fifth cataracts. Meroe is the name of the later, more southerly capital, after the earlier and more northerly one, Napata, had ceased to be the capital. Kush was semi-Egyptianised, and one of its rulers conquered Egypt in 751 B.C. and founded the Egyptian Twenty-fifth Dynasty. In some Meroitic sculpture one can see a mixture of Egyptian and negroid features and the essentially African characteristic of making the head large in proportion to the body—which is observable in the Nok terracottas. A hundred years later Kush lost Egypt to the invading Assyrians; later still the capital was moved from Napata to Meroe, which became a flourishing commercial centre—especially in the production of iron. There is abundant evidence at Meroe for a large scale iron-smelting industry, seen in large piles of slag—which made one commentator call Meroe 'the Birmingham of Africa'.[133] Unfortunately none of the iron-smelting industry is as yet very precisely dated, but it probably began in the fourth century B.C.[134] The kingdom of Kush came to an end early in the fourth century A.D. when it was conquered by the Axumites from Ethiopia.

Naturally Meroe has been put forward as the source from which sub-Saharan Africa learnt the art of smelting iron. At one time it was suggested that this was the result of the break-up of the Kushite kingdom in the fourth century A.D., but the radiocarbon dates for Nok show this to be too late; and it is too late also for the dates which have been obtained for the beginning of the Iron Age in the Zambia-Rhodesia area.[135] It is likely that a good deal of Meroitic iron found its way down the Nile to Egypt, where both iron ore and fuel for smelting were much scarcer; but with a well-established iron-smelting industry, it would be surprising if iron objects were not traded southwards and westwards; and where iron objects had led the way, it is possible that a knowledge of iron-smelting might follow if circumstances were favourable. In this way, a knowledge of iron-smelting may have travelled westwards through Kordofan and Darfur to north-eastern

132 H. Sassoon, 'Early sources of iron in Africa', *S. Afr. arch. Bull.*, xviii, no. 72, 1963, pp. 176–80.
133 A. H. Sayce, 'Second interim report on the excavations at Meroe in Ethiopia. II The historical results', *Bulletin of the American Anthropological Association*, iv, 1912, pp. 53–65.
134 A. J. Arkell, 'The Iron Age in the Sudan', *Curr. Anthrop.*, vii, no. 4, 1966, pp. 451–2.
135 Fagan, 'The Iron Age of Zambia', *ibid.*, vii, no. 4, 1966, pp. 453–62.
R. Summers, 'The Iron Age of Southern Rhodesia', *ibid.*, vii, pp. 453–62.

Nigeria, where we find it established a couple of centuries before Christ. The dates fit; and iron-smelting sites, although as yet undated, are reported from Ennedi[136] and in the Djourab[137] At the stratified occupation mound of Daima, just south of Lake Chad, iron makes its first appearance at a point approximately midway between a radiocarbon date in the late Stone Age level of 450±95 B.C. and a date 3 m higher up in the mound of A.D. 450±70.[138] (But see Editor's note at end of chapter.)

The other route for the introduction of a knowledge of iron-working into West Africa which has been put forward is from the north. It is likely that a knowledge of iron metallurgy and a general use of iron tools and weapons reached the Maghreb before it reached Egypt. For this was the area which came under the influence of Carthage, founded according to tradition in 814 B.C.,[139] a date not inconsistent with the archaeological evidence,[140] by trading and colonising Phoenicians who themselves in their homeland were much closer to earlier centres of iron-working in Syria, and the original invention area of the Armenian mountains. Carthage carried on a lively trade with the Berber peoples of her hinterland, who were likely first to have received iron objects, and later to have learnt the craft for themselves. It is claimed that among the Berber and Tibbu the word for iron can be derived from the Phoenician word, while in the Negro areas of West Africa the number of different words in the different languages indicates that a knowledge of iron has existed for a long time, long enough for this differentiation to have taken place.[141] In the Western Sahara there are rock engravings of horse-drawn vehicles, which trace out a route more or less parallel to the Atlantic seaboard but some distance inland from it, from Tlemcen through Aouineght to Adrar and Amazmaz, where it turns east towards the Middle Niger bend.[142] Whereas in Fezzan and Tassili the horse-drawn vehicle was introduced around 1000 B.C., it is believed that this extreme western route was probably developed, under Carthaginian influence, not before the seventh century B.C.

At the moment there is not enough dated evidence to decide between these two possibilities. Both Carthage and Meroe may have been centres for the dispersal of a knowledge of iron-working in Africa. But precisely when and by what routes this took place we do not know.

Once iron became plentiful it must have given its wielders a much greater mastery over their environment, and those who understood the

136 A. J. Arkell, *Wanyanga*, London, 1964, p. 15.
137 P. Huard, 'Introduction et diffusion du fer au Tchad', *J.A.H.*, viii, 3, 1966, pp. 377–404.
138 G. E. Connah, 'Radiocarbon dates for Daima', *W. Afr. Archaeol. Newsl.*, no. 6, 1967.
139 B. H. Warmington, *Carthage*, London, 1960, p. 20.
140 D. Harden, *The Phoenicians*, London, 1962, p. 34.
141 R. Mauny, 'Essai sur l'histoire des métaux en Afrique occidentale', *Bull. I.F.A.N.*, xiv, 1952, pp. 574–83.
142 R. Mauny, 'Une route préhistorique à travers le Sahara', *Bull. I.F.A.N.*, ix, 1947, pp. 341–57.

The main trench through Daima Mound, N.E. Bornu. The accumulation of occupation layers can be clearly seen; these begin early in the sixth century B.C. at the bottom and extend to the eleventh century A.D. near the top.

secrets of its working must have been regarded with awe. In sub-Saharan Africa other than West Africa, the spread of iron has been linked to the diffusion of the practice of agriculture and to the spread of the Bantu languages. For a long time the close-relatedness of all the Bantu languages has been recognised by linguists, and it has been believed that the initial spread of these languages over most of Africa south of 4° N began no more than two or three thousand years ago. One linguistic authority has placed the 'homeland' of the Bantu-speaking peoples in south-eastern Nigeria and Cameroun, whence they spread eastwards and southwards to fill up most of the rest of sub-Saharan Africa,[143] overrunning or driving into the less desirable parts of the continent, such as the Kalahari desert, the Hottentots and Bushmen who were still in a Later Stone Age stage of technology. As has been observed, such a dramatic overrunning of a continent needs a powerful dynamic to explain it. It has been suggested that this was the possession of the iron spear, and the picture has been drawn of small groups establishing their leadership and then language as fabulous hunters and meat-providers.[144] This may have had something to do with it, but the iron-bladed spear, except when allied to the horse, is not necessarily a more effective hunting weapon than the poisoned arrow, even if it may be a more effective fighting weapon. Is it not more likely, in the conditions of African vegetation, that, allied to the practice of agriculture, the dynamic was provided by the iron axe, the iron slashing knife or matchet, and the iron hoe?

Another linguistic authority declared that the Bantu 'homeland' was a belt of country running roughly east and west across Africa and centred on Katanga.[145] An attempt has now been made to reconcile the two views by accepting the priority of the south-eastern Nigeria/Cameroun area as the initial centre of dispersal, and then positing a quick 'dash' to the Katanga area, whence the population explosion resulting from the combination of agriculture and iron technology carried the Bantu into the remaining areas of their present distribution.[146] It is an attractive theory, but the 'quick dash' from Nigeria to Katanga, although not impossible, requires some explaining and at present lacks archaeological confirmation.

Returning to West Africa, it has already been observed that Nok figurine-makers were smelting iron to the south and west of the Jos Plateau by about the third century B.C., but there is no evidence of them after A.D. 200. What happened to them? Where did they go, or who supplanted them? We simply do not know as yet. With one exception, the 1,000 years which

143 J. H. Greenberg, *Studies in African Linguistic Classification*, New Haven, 1955.
144 C. Wrigley, 'Speculations on the economic prehistory of Africa', *J.A.H.*, i, no. 2, 1960, pp. 189–203.
145 M. Guthrie, 'Some developments in the pre-history of the Bantu languages', *J.A.H.*, iii, 1962, pp. 273–82.
146 R. Oliver, 'Bantu Genesis', *African Affairs*, lxv, no. 260, 1966, pp. 245–58.

follow the Nok culture and bring us into the protohistoric period when written records begin is extraordinarily blank, rather like the hiatus that used to exist between the Palaeolithic and the Neolithic before the connecting Mesolithic was discovered and recognised. It is a crucial period in the past of West Africa, because it must have been the formative period for those urban developments, states and political organisations which were in existence in West Africa by the time the European voyagers reached the west coast. The very fact that these were able to come into existence demonstrated the spread and effectiveness of iron technology allied to agriculture. Of course it is almost certain that this spread was uneven, and from the radiocarbon date of 25 ± 120 B.C. for the skeleton excavated in the upper microlithic layer at the Rop rock shelter on the Jos Plateau (see above, p. 63), it can be seen that in these hills a stone-using way of life, perhaps still largely a hunting economy, persisted long after the Nok iron-smelters were established in the plains below. The same thing happened in southern Africa, where the Bushmen hunter-gatherers continued to use stone, probably for more than 1,500 years, after the neighbouring Bantu agriculturalists started using iron.

Although it is not known for certain what happened to the Nok figurine-makers after the second century A.D., nevertheless there are certain characteristics in the terracotta figurines of Ife, in Western Nigeria, which point to the possibility of some continuity of artistic tradition.[147] These terracottas and the stone sculptures of Ife may be older than the famous brass heads, but in any case all efforts to obtain archaeological dating for any of the latter have so far proved unsuccessful. Some have suggested a date as early as the eleventh century A.D., or even earlier.[148] We do not know at what date or from where the technique of brass-casting was introduced into West Africa. That it was introduced from elsewhere and was not an independent invention can be taken as virtually certain, since the technique is complicated but had been known in Mesopotamia since the end of the fourth millennium B.C., and in Egypt since the second.[149] The technique employed was that known as *cire perdue*, or lost wax, in which a model is first made in wax of the object it is desired to create in brass. The wax model has a rod of wax sticking out of it, to form a pouring funnel in the mould, and the whole, except for the end of the wax rod, is then covered in clay. After this has dried, the wax model and the clay investiture are heated, when the wax melts and runs out, leaving a hollow space surrounded by a baked clay mould. Molten brass is then poured into the hole in the mould, which cools and sets in the shape of the interior hollow. The clay mould is then broken off the casting, to reveal the brass object inside.

147 F. Willett, 'Ife and its archaeology', *J.A.H.*, i, no. 2, 1960, pp. 231–48. Fagg, 'The Nok Terracottas . . .', pp. 447–8.
148 P. Dark, 'Benin, West African kingdom', *Discovery*, xviii, no. 5, 1957, p. 206.
149 M. E. L. Mallowan, 'The Amuq Plain', *Antiquity*, xxxvii, 1963, p. 190.

There is a tradition of such brass-casting which runs right through West Africa, especially along the northern part of the high forest belt, from the Ivory Coast to Cameroun—Baoule, Ashanti, Dahomey, Ife, Benin, Igbo-Ukwu, Bamenda. The fact that brass casting runs especially through this particular belt of country in West Africa is probably not to be explained so much in direct relation to the vegetation as to the fact that it was in this zone, at the meeting point of two ecological systems, that there were provided the requisite conditions for the growth of centralisation of political power and commercial wealth or both. In this situation objects of brass were luxury goods, only produced for royal courts or socially important people. In the auriferous areas of the western part of this belt the technique has also been used for making objects of gold. It is possible—but only a matter of speculation—that the technique was first used for gold, and only later transferred to brass—since the introduction of the technique is probably to be associated with the opening up of trans-Saharan caravan routes by the Arabs, as a result of which sub-Saharan West Africa came into closer contact with the Arab world; and the commodity which may have been one of the first to attract Arab trade—even if through intermediaries—was West African gold.[150] It is likely that the rise of the ancient kingdom of Mali was due to its advantageous situation in this respect. However, it seems more likely that the technique of *cire perdue* casting was introduced as a technique for brass-casting, and only locally adapted to the making of objects in gold. Perhaps we have a hint concerning the introduction of the technique of brass-casting in the finding in Ghana of locally made bronze copies of Byzantine lamps of fifth to seventh century style.[151] It may be possible eventually to throw light on the source of the raw material used by analysing the precise metal content of groups of West African bronzes and brasses.[152]

The oldest dating evidence we have for any West African bronzes comes from a non-auriferous area, at Igbo-Ukwu in Eastern Nigeria. The site was first discovered accidentally, as is the case with so many initial archaeological discoveries, when a man was digging a water-cistern.[153] A number of bronze vessels came to light, of very fine workmanship and of an artistic style quite unlike that of either Ife of Benin. Subsequently the site was excavated and another one discovered nearby.[154] The first proved to be

150 E. W. Bovill, *The Golden Trade of the Moors*, London, 1958, p. 67.

151 A. J. Arkell, 'Gold Coast copies of 5th–7th century bronze lamps', *Antiquity*, xxiv, 1950, pp. 38–40.

152 Shaw, 'Spectrographic analyses of the Igbo and other Nigerian bronzes', *Archaeometry*, iix, 1965, pp. 86–95.

153 G. I. Jones, 'Ibo bronzes from the Awka Division', *Nigerian Field*, viii, no. 4, 1939, pp. 164–7. J. O. Field, 'Bronze castings found at Igbo, Southern Nigeria', *Man*, xl, 1940, pp. 1–60.

154 Shaw, 'Excavations at Igbo-Ukwu, Eastern Nigeria: an interim report', *Man*, lx, no. 210, 1960, pp. 161–4.

the remains of a treasure house or shrine where sacred vessels and regalia were kept, the second a burial chamber of an important personage, perhaps a priest-king. In both sites further remarkable bronzes were found, and a third excavation discovered a pit which also contained bronzes of the same style.[155] Wood from a stool in the burial chamber was radiocarbon-dated to A.D. 840±145 and charcoal from the pit to 850±120. Unfortunately these finds stand rather on their own at the moment, and what is needed is to find and excavate other sites of the same period in adjacent areas.

Here it is necessary to leave this outline summary of the rather disjointed information about the prehistory of West Africa, which is all we have at the moment, and let the story be taken up by the historian[156] and the archaeology of the protohistoric period.

155 Shaw, 'Further excavations at Igbo-Ukwu', *Man*, xlv, no. 217, 1965, pp. 181–4.
156 C. C. Ifemesia, 'The peoples of West Africa around A.D. 1000', *J.F.A.*, Ajayi and I. Espie, ed., *A Thousand Years of West African History*, Ibadan, 1965, pp. 39–54.
Editor's note. For more up-to-date information relating to page 72, the reader is referred to an article by Thurstan Shaw, 'On Radiocarbon Chronology of the Iron Age in Sub-Saharan Africa' in *Current Anthropology*, x, 1969, pp. 226–231.

CHAPTER 3

Stateless societies in the history of West Africa

ROBIN HORTON

A DEFINITION OF 'STATELESS'

In dealing with a topic of this kind, it is important that we should start by being clear about the kind of society we are discussing. For purposes of convenience, I propose the following four-point definition:

1. In a stateless society, there is little concentration of authority. It is difficult to point to any individual or limited group of men as the ruler or rulers of the society.
2. Such authority rôles as exist affect a rather limited sector of the lives of those subject to them.
3. The wielding of authority as a specialised, full-time occupation is virtually unknown.
4. The unit within which people feel an obligation to settle their disputes according to agreed rules and without resort to force tends to be relatively small.

This definition, obviously, refers to an ideal type of society—to one pole of a classificatory continuum. In West African reality, some societies (e.g. Tiv, Lodagaa and most Ibo) fall very near this pole, and we have no hesitation in labelling them stateless. Others (e.g. some of the Liberian and Cross River groups) are nearer the middle of the continuum, and here we are more hesitant in our labelling. When we are talking of 'stateless societies', then, we are using an artificial and approximate categorisation. But the label is nonetheless a useful one, and, with this caveat in mind, we shall procede to use it.

DIFFICULTIES OF WRITING A HISTORY OF STATELESS SOCIETIES

It is not for nothing that I have entitled this chapter 'Stateless societies in the History of West Africa' rather than 'A history of stateless societies in West Africa'. For in the present state of our techniques, the difficulties of writing a 'history' of the same kind as you will find in the chapters of this book which deal with the great pre-colonial states are virtually insuperable.

In the first place, there are scarcely any contemporary written records covering the stateless societies in pre-colonial times. Pre-colonial Arab and European visitors to West Africa tended to be concerned with commerce, and so gravitated to the great states which were the centres of such commerce. Even where they were professional historians, the visitors tended to gravitate to those groups which were, in an obvious sense, 'making history'; and that, again, meant the great states. Since the doings of the stateless populations had relatively little impact on the life of the states, the visiting chroniclers heard very little about them and so had very little to record about them.

Secondly, although the stateless societies possess considerable oral traditions relating to their past, the difficulties of using such traditions are immense. Apart from anything else, their coverage is nothing like as deep, as rich, or as continuous as is that of the traditions of the great states. An obvious reason for this defect is the absence of the specialist historians who are to be found in the courts of most of the states. And there are yet other reasons connected with the nature of the social structures of these societies. Hence even if we did feel able to take the oral traditions of the stateless societies at their face value, they would not give us the sort of solid 200, 500, or 1,000 year coverage available to students of some of the great states.

Then again, of course, we *cannot* take oral traditions at their face value. Written records, it is true, can be suspect for all sorts of reasons. But at least what has been written down on a piece of paper does not change itself spontaneously so that when someone looks at it five years later it says something different. Yet this is precisely what *does* happen to things written on the human memory.

Frankly, we have not yet begun to perfect a methodology which will enable us to allow for these changes and so get back somewhere near to the historical events that originally inspired the traditions. True, one often hears great faith expressed in the collection of all variant versions of a tradition—the idea being that having collected these, one can then extract a common denominator which will be an approximation to historical fact. Now if any serious use is to be made of oral tradition, the collection of all variant versions is obviously an essential preliminary. This granted, there really is no reason why the common denominator should be any nearer historical truth than are the variants. An example drawn from my own fieldwork will bring this home. There is a village in the Niger Delta from which I have collected four or five variant oral traditions of origin. The common denominator remaining after mutually exclusive variants have been eliminated is an assertion that the village was founded by seven men who came down from the sky. Enough said, I think!

The reader should not infer that I am ruling out oral tradition as a source for historical reconstruction. Far from it. Indeed, one of my personal research commitments is to the collection and use of oral tradition in the eastern Niger Delta, for just this purpose.[1] The point I am trying to make is that we are not likely to get much further if we try to use oral tradition by itself—juggling with variant versions and so on. My own feeling is that real progress will be made when we are in a position to consider the indications of oral tradition alongside those of linguistic maps, culture trait maps, and the results of archaeological work on the sizing, dating and pottery-typing of abandoned settlements. Now the linguistic mapping of West Africa is going on apace. But cultural trait-mapping in this area has scarcely begun; and archaeological work is in its infancy.[2] So the resources for writing a 'history of stateless societies', comparable to the various histories of states which you will find later in this book, simply do not exist.

If we cannot at present write a 'history of' stateless societies, what then can we do with them? Well, we can say something about the present distribution of such societies. We can outline the main varieties of socio-political organisation to be found among them. And we can perhaps suggest something about the conditions of formation and persistence of these different varieties. If nothing else, this should help to extend the reader's idea of the diversity of societies which the agents of colonial rule had to face when they started to parcel up Africa into its present-day states. Seen in this light, the present essay points forward to later chapters on modern history which deal with such topics as the establishment of indirect rule and the significance of ethnic differences in modern national politics.

But our sketch of the stateless societies may also be relevant to an earlier period of West African history—the period of formation of the many states whose chronicles are written fully elsewhere in this book. Rich as they are, the sources for the histories of these states all too seldom take us back to a detailed account of their actual formation. Any questions about this must therefore be tackled by an indirect route. What I hope to show toward the end of this essay is that, with a little ingenuity, we can use our knowledge of the stateless societies to make at least some intelligent guesses about the origins of the states.

THE PRESENT-DAY DISTRIBUTION OF STATELESS SOCIETIES

It is difficult to make any valid general statement about the distribution of stateless societies in West Africa. For these societies are scattered about in

1 A sober attempt to work out ways of inferring from oral traditional evidence to historical reality is in fact one of the priority commitments of the Institute of African Studies at Ibadan University. The Institute's pilot scheme is focused on the Niger Delta area; but we hope that solutions to problems in this particular area will have a relevance for historical work using non-written sources in other parts of the continent.

2 On this, see a recent history of Africa which contends that the spade of the archaeologist 'has thus far lifted perhaps an ounce of earth on the Niger for every ton carefully sifted on the Nile'. G. P. Murdock, *Africa, Its Peoples and Their Culture History*, New York, 1959.

the interstices of the great states in a manner which does not correspond at all with geographical, vegetational or even linguistic zones. Perhaps the nearest thing to a valid generalisation would be the suggestion that they are mostly found away from the great long-distance trade routes and trade junctions. Indeed this fact, as we shall see later, has probably been a condition of their survival in stateless form.

Let me give a brief inventory of the main areas of concentration of these societies, moving from east to west. First, there is the great quadrilateral whose corners are formed by the Jos Plateau, the Forcados Estuary, the Cameroon Mountain, and the Mambila Plateau. Though there have been and still are some notable states in this area (e.g. Jukun and Igala), there are probably twenty million people living here in essentially stateless conditions. Prominent among them are most of the Ibo groups, the Ibibio, the Ijo, the Tiv, the Idoma, the Birom, the Angass, the Yako, the Mbembe and the Ekoi. Moving further west we find numerous pockets of stateless peoples in the area north of the Volta headwaters and south of the Niger bend. Prominent among these are the Lodagaa, the Lowiili, the Bobo, the Dogon, the Konkomba and the Birifor. Again, there are considerable concentrations of stateless peoples in the western Ivory Coast, and in the Liberian and Guinean hinterlands. Examples are the Bete, Kissi, Dan, Gagu and Kru peoples. In this south-western area, in fact, there are many groups that seem to hover on the borders of statelessness and state organisation. This is true of such peoples as the Bassa, the Grebo, the Mano and the Koranko. Finally, scattered throughout the length and breadth of the West African savannah, there are the five to seven million Fulani pastoralists.

Altogether, there are probably some thirty-five million West Africans living under essentially stateless conditions. This is a good many fewer than one might suppose from listening to the anthropologists, who are inclined to a romantic fascination with societies organised on principles diametrically opposite to those which prevail in their own. But it is also a good many more than one might gather from listening to the historians, who tend to ignore the stateless societies because they cannot readily bring their traditional techniques to bear on them.

VARIETIES OF STATELESS SOCIAL ORGANISATION

In what follows, I shall try to give an account of the principal varieties of stateless social organisation as they flourished at the beginning of the colonial era. Though indigenous organisation has in most cases been modified by the impact of colonial and post-colonial rule, I shall, for the sake of convenience, couch my description and analysis in what is commonly known as the 'ethnographic present'.

In giving this account, I shall stress the influence of ecological and demographic factors on social forms. These are not the only relevant factors; but they do appear to be of decisive importance.

I must emphasise that my account is both provisional and approximate. Provisional, because the ethnography of the area is still very uneven in character. Approximate, first because I have made a deliberate selection from the totality of relevant causal factors, and second because I have concentrated my attention on the most widely-distributed organisational variants. Nonetheless, the picture presented gives a reasonable synthesis of the facts as we know them to date, and raises numerous points for further testing and research.[3]

In consonance with my emphasis on ecology, I shall deal first with the agriculturalists, and then with the pastoralists.

THE AGRICULTURALISTS

The bulk of the stateless population of West Africa is made up of sedentary farmers. In the savannah these farmers are mostly concerned with grain crops, whilst in the forest, the emphasis is on root crops.

Despite the difference in their crops, savannah and forest farmers face much the same basic ecological and demographic conditions. Important among such conditions are:

a) An ecology based on subsistence agriculture,[4] with a poorly developed exchange and monetary sector.
b) Long-term utilisation of fixed tracts of land, rather than rapidly shifting settlement.[5]
c) Land in somewhat limited supply relative to population.
d) Although the basic unit of production is the compound family, several key operations of the agricultural cycle require the coopting by the family of much larger groups—say twenty to fifty men.
e) Communication is largely pedestrian.

From these conditions flow two sets of consequences which have a profound effect on the pattern of social organisation. First, there are the consequences relating to labour recruitment. In a subsistence economy with a poorly developed exchange and monetary sector, hiring of labour for large-scale agricultural operations is an option that does not arise. With

3 Much of what follows in this section is an elaboration of suggestions made by Daryll Forde in 'The anthropological approach to social science', *Advancement of Science*, iv, no. 15, 1947. One of the most fruitful of these suggestions concerns the radically different social situations which prevail in areas of dispersed and of compact settlement. This line of thought, as far as I am aware, has not been followed up by subsequent writers. But as I hope to show in the present chapter, it gives us a valuable key to understanding variation in stateless social organisation.

4 By 'subsistence agriculture', we mean a system of agriculture in which the bulk of the product is consumed by the producer.

5 It is true that the Tiv, among whom lineage organisation assumes an importance greater than can be seen anywhere else in West Africa, are a people in a state of intermittent migration. Even with a Tiv domestic group, however, cultivation rotates round a roughly fixed area for the few years of its stay in any particular locality.

hiring ruled out, reciprocal aid is the only possibility. And where communication is pedestrian the most convenient partners in any reciprocal aid agreement are neighbours. In these circumstances the group of neighbouring compound families is apt to develop strong cohesion.

Secondly, there are the consequences relating to acquisition of land, the basic means of livelihood. Once again, in a mainly subsistence economy, buying of land is an option that does not arise. With buying ruled out and a relatively limited supply, inheritance would seem to be the principal channel for orderly access to this essential resource. This means a strong tendency for up-and-coming young men to settle down with their close maternal or paternal seniors, according to which rule of inheritance is involved.[6] If this settling down with closely related seniors takes place consistently over several generations, and if the population is increasing, the core of the cohesive neighbourhood group will inevitably come to be a considerable number of close male kinsmen, related through whatever line determines the inheritance of land. Where the pressure on land is at all great, of course, the younger generation may be neither willing nor able to spend their days helping their seniors on their farms and waiting to take over when they die. Rather, they will try to expand onto new land. Even where this happens the tendency will be for them to settle down as close as possible to their erstwhile neighbours and to those from whom they hope to inherit. They will settle as close as possible to the former because these are people with whom they have already established ties of cooperation, and so will still be the partners of choice in large-scale operations on new land. They will settle as close as possible to those from whom they hope to inherit, with an eye to the time when they will be working both newly acquired and inherited land. Even where there is expansion, then, the neighbourhood group will still tend to be based on a body of close male kinsmen related through the line of land inheritance. And from this situation, it is but a short step to make kinship in the relevant line the guiding principle in the organisation and recruitment of the local group.

Once established as a guiding principle, the lineage idiom becomes a powerful force in its own right, a force capable of surviving to some extent the conditions that brought it into being. The reasons for this are much the same as those that lead tidy-minded anthropologists to spend so much of their time and energy studying lineage organisation. To put it briefly, the genealogical idiom provides men with a social calculus which

6 In the present essay, I have tended to ignore the difference between matrilineal and patrilineal reckoning. In fact, West Africa is a largely patrilineal region; and even in areas where this is not the case (e.g. Akan country), matrilineal reckoning is used in such a way that the core of the lineage is still a co-residential group of males related through the line of land inheritance. Perhaps the most significant difference between the West African matrilineage and its patrilineal counterpart lies in the weaker allegiance of its members. This is the product of strong ties to the father and his lineage which go with a tendency toward virilocal marriage combined with avunculocal residence for adult males.

is probably unique in its exactness, neatness and fineness of discrimination. Armed with an all-embracing genealogy a man can read off the degrees and kinds of his obligations to his fellows with an unrivalled ease and precision. A society that has once known the conveniences of genealogical reckoning does not lightly drop them. Throughout West Africa, indeed, the lineage appears as the basic building block of stateless agricultural society. Sometimes it dominates the social organisation. And even where other elements have come to prominence, they are, as we shall see, profoundly affected by having to coexist with it.

So much for the universality of the lineage. We must now turn our attention to the equally important fact that the scale and scope of lineage organisation varies greatly from one people to another. Thus on the one hand there are populations like those of the central Ibo and the Tiv, in which single genealogies embrace thousands or even hundreds of thousands of people, and in which the lineage idiom provides the dominant principle of social organisation. On the other hand, there are populations in which single genealogies embrace hundreds or mere scores of people, and in which other principles of social organisation operate above the level of the lineages, or even alongside them. Prominent among the latter are most of the Cross River peoples, the more easterly Ibo groups[7] and the Idoma in Nigeria; many groups around the Volta headwaters; and most of the stateless peoples of the western Ivory Coast and the Liberian-Guinean hinterland. This variation in the status of the lineage principle gives us the basis for a threefold social typology.

The Segmentary Lineage Systems (Type 1)

The term 'segmentary lineage system' is properly applied where a society is organised from top to bottom in terms of a single, embracing genealogical scheme, and where this scheme provides the sole or the dominant principle of social organisation. Now of the various types of stateless social organisation, it is the segmentary lineage system that seems to have taken up quite the largest space in the literature. Indeed, despite numerous caveats,[8] one still finds a number of general discussions in which it is treated as the veritable archetype of stateless organisation.[9] When one has combed the

7 The only monograph which has yet appeared on the social organisation of a particular Ibo community is M. M. Green, *Ibo Village Affairs*, London, 1947. There are, however, one or two useful general surveys; e.g. C. K. Meek, *Law and Authority in a Nigerian Tribe*, London, 1937; and D. Forde and G. I. Jones, *The Ibo and Ibibio Speaking Peoples* (Ethnographic Survey of Africa), London, 1950. The literature that has appeared so far indicates an intriguing variety of social organisation within the broad boundaries of the Ibo cultural area. When data on settlement patterns become available, this variety will make the Ibo an interesting test case for the hypothesis proposed in the present chapter.
8 See, for instance, Paula Brown, 'Patterns of authority in West Africa', *Africa*, xxi, 4, 1951.
9 The most recent example is Paul Bohannan's otherwise excellent *African Outline*, London, 1966 (see chap. 12, pp. 181–5).

West African ethnographic literature, one begins to find this rather surprising. For the segmentary lineage system turns out to be quite the rarest of the three types of organisation with which we shall be dealing in this essay. In fact, apart from the Tiv and certain Ibo groups, it appears to have no other representatives among West African farmers.[10]

The relative rarity of the 'pure type' segmentary lineage system is in fact not hard to understand. For the essence of this system is a thoroughgoing correspondence between genealogical, social and spatial distance. Close lineal kin are close neighbours and close social partners. More distant lineal kin are more distant neighbours and more distant social partners. Yet more distant lineal kin are yet more distant neighbours and yet more distant social partners. And so on up to the limits of the field covered by the lineage genealogy.

Now it is evident that this correspondence can only be maintained in certain rather special and rarely fulfilled conditions.

First, there must, at some stage in the development of this type of organisation, be a population steadily expanding by birth, to provide some basis in reality for the development of a massive genealogical scheme. Secondly, there must be a readily accessible supply of extra land, distributed fairly evenly round the domains of this population. The land supply must be such that each segment of the population can push sideways and outwards as it expands in numbers, whilst remaining in the same position relative to other segments; for only thus can the correspondence between genealogical, spatial and social relationships be preserved through the process of population growth.

Thirdly and most crucially, there must be a dispersed settlement pattern with fairly even density: myriads of scattered homesteads rather than a few large, compact villages. Such a pattern, it seems, can only prevail where the organisational demands of small-scale agriculture do not have to be weighed against those of defence against aggression. For while the former dictate that each small producing unit sit in the middle of its farm, the latter dictate that people should forgo proximity to their plots and band together in large, compact aggregates.

It may not be immediately evident to the reader why this third condition is so crucial for the development of an all-embracing genealogical framework. The important thing to see here is that the genealogy is a calculus, and that like other types of calculus, it has certain distinctive formal features which make it appropriate to some types of social situation but inappropriate to others. For it so happens that the kind of social situation

10 For a general outline of the Tiv segmentary lineage organisation, see Paul and Laura Bohannan, *The Tiv of Central Nigeria* (Ethnographic Survey of Africa), London, 1953; also Laura Bohannan, 'Political aspects of Tiv social organisation', in *Tribes Without Rulers*, ed., J. Middleton and D. Tait, London, 1959. For an outline of a central Ibo segmentary lineage organisation, see Green, *op. cit.*

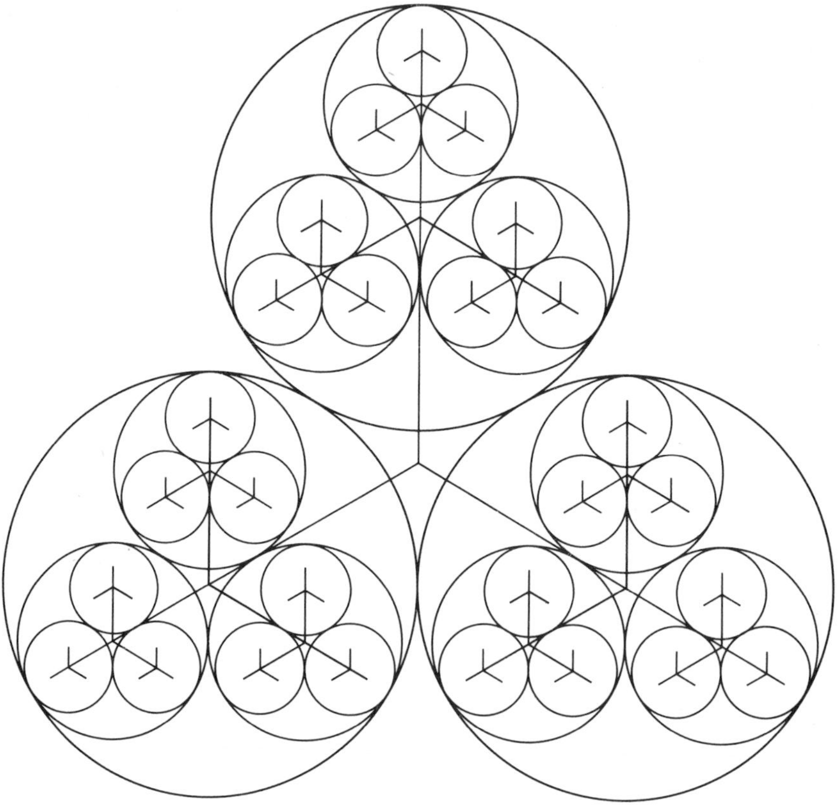

3.1 'Nesting series' of groupings characteristic of evenly dispersed settlement pattern. Note that lines connecting centres of groups could be equally well taken to represent genealogical links or schematised communication paths. This brings out vividly the element of isomorphism.

that goes with subsistence agriculture and an evenly dispersed settlement pattern is one to which the genealogical calculus is particularly appropriate. Let me elaborate. When the lineage idiom is used to define the unity of successively larger aggregates of people, there is an even progression in the number of genealogical links involved. Application of the idiom to a large aggregate of people thus creates the implication of a field in which, as the size of the group increases, there is, in some sense or other, a steady increase in the distance between its components. Genealogical reckoning is therefore particularly appropriate to social fields whose characteristics are in some way isomorphic to this implied situation.

Now, as we noted earlier, the prevailing conditions of subsistence agriculture plus pedestrian communication make spatial distance one of the most important determinants of social distance. Other things being equal, the closest neighbours are closest bound by ties of mutual cooperation and solidarity, whilst more distant neighbours are bound by looser ties, and yet more distant neighbours by yet looser ties. When there is an evenly dispersed settlement pattern, then, an even progression in the size of grouping goes with an even progression in the average spatial distance between the centres of sub-groups, and hence with an even progression in the social distance between sub-groups. Where, on the other hand, there are large, compact settlements separated by unpopulated areas, the situation is quite different. A progressive increase in size no longer goes with an even increase in spatial and hence in social distance. Whereas the first type of social field is clearly isomorphic to the situation implied by the lineage genealogy, the second is as clearly anisomorphic. So genealogical reckoning is appropriate to the first, inappropriate to the second (see Figs. 3.1 and 3.2).

These preconditions of the 'pure type' segmentary lineage organisation are fulfilled *par excellence* in the case of the Tiv, though a little less well in the case of the central Ibo groups. Both Tiv and central Ibo have expanding populations. Tiv, till very recently, have had just the sort of peripheral land supply cited as necessary for maintaining the genealogical/spatial/social correspondence. The central Ibo almost certainly had it earlier; and though it has now disappeared, it is compensated for by extensive seasonal labour migration and the adoption of non-agricultural jobs abroad. Finally, both Tiv and central Ibo were peoples expanding against very little effective resistance. They were therefore able to pay more attention to the demands of efficient agriculture than to those of efficient defence, and so lived in evenly scattered homesteads rather than in large, compact villages.

In saying that these two populations provide examples of 'pure type' segmentary lineage systems, I am perhaps exaggerating. For in West Africa at least, the conditions sufficient for the achievement of the type are never completely fulfilled, and there are consequently no societies which attain a perfect correspondence between genealogical, spatial and social distance. What we can say of Tiv, and to a lesser extent of some of the central Ibo, is that they give as good an approximation as any to such correspondence, and that they appear to be striving continually to attain the ideal. Thus in both these populations, small local inequalities of density and land supply often force individuals and small groups to leave their closest lineage kin and try their luck with remoter lineal relatives living some distance away. Such individuals and groups often turn to segments where they are closely related through the maternal line; and when they first settle down in their new homes they are regarded as somewhat marginal 'sister's sons' and 'daughter's sons'. With the passing of a generation or two, the hosts come inexorably to talk of these maternal links as patrilineal links; and correspondence between genealogical, spatial and social distance is thus restored. Once the principle of genealogical reckoning is established, it acquires a force of its own. And it is this that enables it to overcome a very considerable incidence of the sort of anomalies just

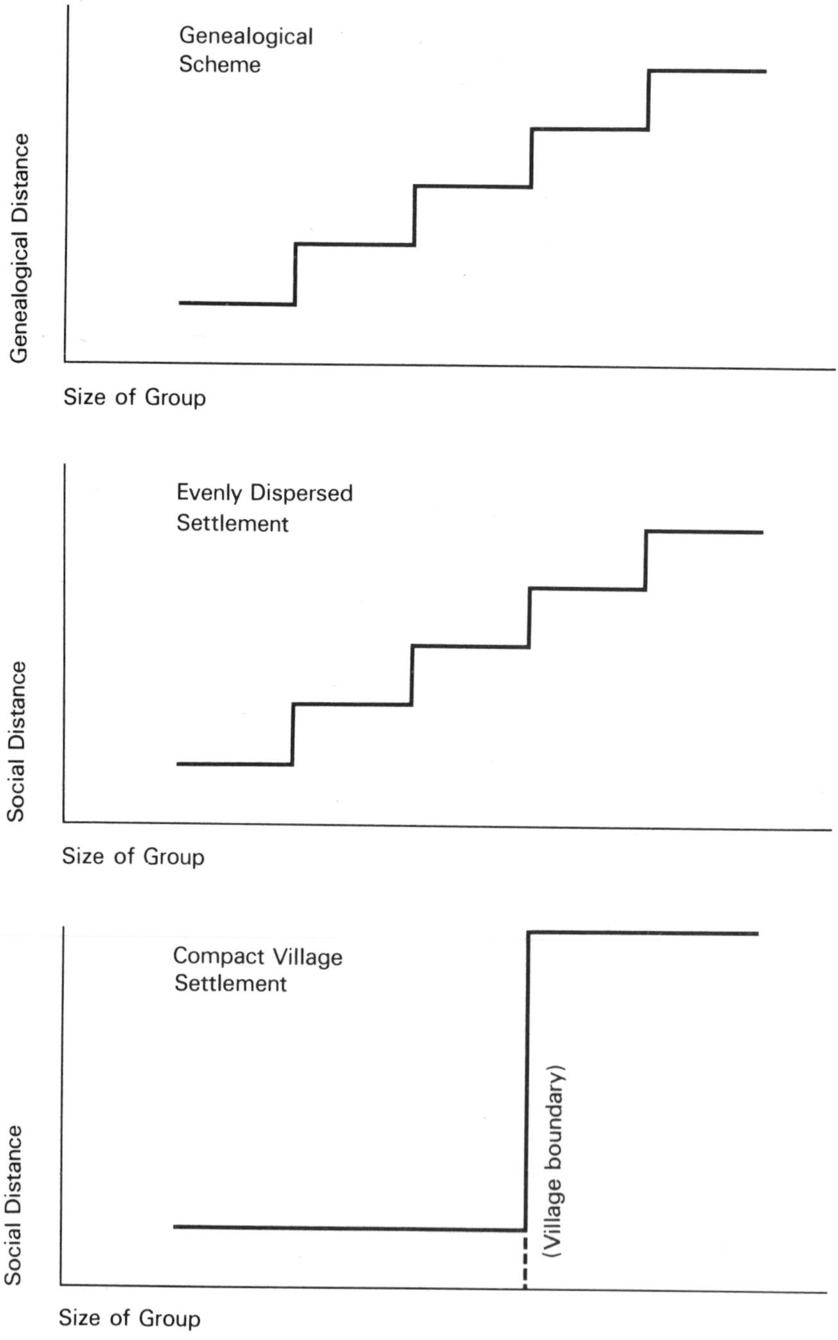

3.2 Genealogical/spatial/social relations

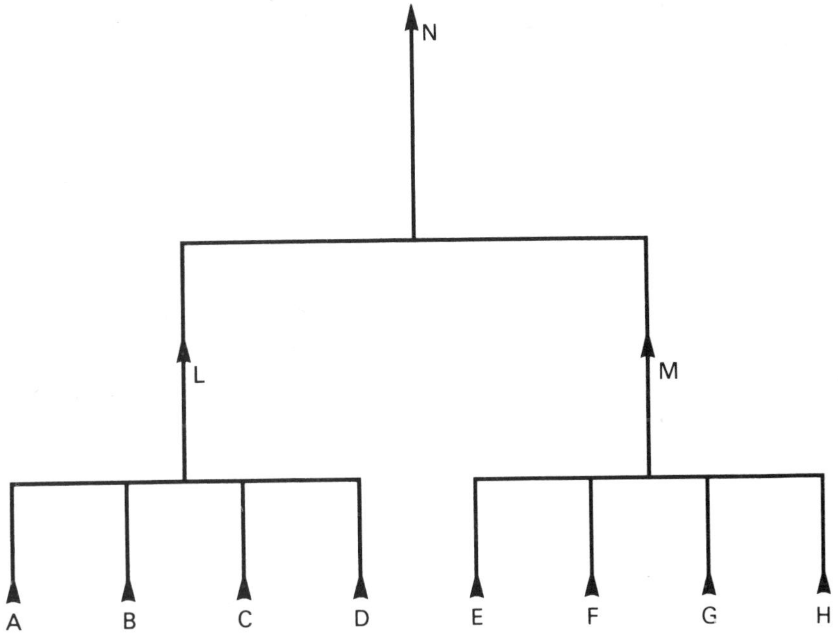

3.3 Lineage and political groups.

mentioned. There are, of course, limits to the rate of incidence of anomalies that can be coped with. But we shall leave till the next section any consideration of what happens when these limits are reached.

So much for the conditions in which these 'pure type' segmentary lineage systems flourish. Let us now turn to consider the salient features of their social organisation. Three of these are worth special note: the relativity of political grouping, the equivalence of segments, and the predominance of leadership over authority.

a) *The relativity of political grouping.* A remarkable feature of both Tiv and central Ibo social organisations is that what appears in some contexts to be a series of autonomous political units becomes in other contexts a single larger unit. In turn, this larger unit, though in some contexts it forms part of a series of autonomous units of comparable size, in other contexts combines with them to form a still larger unit. And so on until a level of concerted action involving several thousand people is reached.

The processes involved here can best be illustrated by reference to Fig. 3.3. In the absence of any external pressures, the small lineage segments A, B, C, D will act as autonomous and mutually competitive units. But if someone from the genealogically and spatially more distant unit E attacks a member of D or tries to appropriate his farm plots, A, B, C, D will unite into the larger lineage L and act in concert against E. When this happens, E will call upon F, G, H; and these will join with it to form the larger lineage M, which will then become locked in combat with L. However, if members of L are threatened by a more distant group, M will join with L, and form the still larger lineage N to deal with the offenders. When conflict subsides, the reverse process will take place. The larger groupings will disband rapidly, and the effective level of political integration will return to that represented by the small lineage segments A, B, C, D, E, F, G, H.

An important implication of all this is that from the point of view of the individual, there is no fixed point which he regards as the focus of his political allegience and of his legal obligations. The focus of allegiance and obligation is very largely relative to context.

Such relativity of political grouping, allegiance and obligation is obviously encouraged, if not produced, by the genealogical framework which serves to organise these societies. For genealogical reckoning draws heavily on the images and emotions of family life for its persuasive power; and one of the fundamental images of family life the world over is that of the bickering brothers who only unite when one or all of them is challenged by an outsider.[11] In the genealogical scheme, this image exerts its influence at each successive level, from the lowest to the highest. For at each successive level, the eponymous ancestors of the lineage segments are 'brothers', whose fate in life is to bicker and compete until an outsider comes to unite them—and then to return to their bickering when the outsider has gone.

But if the genealogical framework has contributed greatly to the relativity of political grouping, so too have those more basic ecological and demographic factors which are behind the prominence of genealogical reckoning itself. As we saw earlier, a subsistence agricultural economy combined with an evenly-dispersed settlement pattern makes for a series of 'circles of cooperation' in which social distance between sub-groups increases evenly and gradually as a function of group size. From the point of view of the individual, such a situation means that he can have no fixed 'in-groups' and 'out-groups', but only a field of social relations within which 'in-ness' declines gradually from centre to periphery. When this is so, the question of where he places his political allegiance can only be relative to the question of who opposes him. From the point of view of the system as a whole, such a situation means that no particular level of political cleavage is of outstanding significance vis-à-vis all other levels. Here again, relativity of political grouping must follow.

b) *The equivalence of segments.* At each level in the segmentary structure of Tiv and central Ibo social organisations, the segments that combine

11 See Bohannan and Bohannan, *The Tiv . . .*; L. Bohannan, 'Political aspects . . .'; and P. Bohannan, *African Outline*.

under pressure to form a single larger unit are conceived as strictly equivalent to one another. They are equals and they are rivals. This principle is so strongly entrenched that if it is threatened by the undue growth of one segment relative to its coordinates, this segment will divide, and its two offspring will be elevated fairly rapidly to the same level in the structure as was formerly occupied by their parent.

Let me illustrate this with reference to Fig. 3.4. A, B, C, D, E, F, G are names of segments. They are also the names of the founding ancestors of these segments. B and C are segments that normally unite under pressure to form the larger unit A. They are therefore equivalent. D and E are sub-segments of B, F and G sub-segments of C, D and E, F and G are also therefore equivalent. Now B grows so disproportionately that the population of each of its subsegments D and E is roughly equal to the population of C. As a result, B splits, and its name disappears from the scheme of reckoning. D and E replace B as 'brothers' of C. Equivalence is thus restored in demographic and political fact as well as in genealogical ideal.

The stress on the equivalence of segments is clearly another feature of these societies that owes much to the dominance of the genealogical calculus. For in genealogical terms, all those segments that combine under pressure into a single larger unit are 'sons' of a single 'father'. They are therefore in a symmetrical relation both to the larger unit and to each other. As with relativity of political grouping, however, we can also see the equivalence of segments as related to basic ecological and demographic factors. We can see it as related to the fact that, whatever the level selected for attention, all segments at that level have identical relations to the land they farm on. We can also see it as related to the fact that, under conditions of evenly dispersed settlement, groups of the same size must have roughly the same degree of social cohesion.

c) *Predominance of leadership over authority.* Tiv, and to a lesser extent central Ibo, are remarkable for the stress they lay upon leadership of the group against others, as opposed to authority exerted in the group's internal affairs.

Authority is not entirely absent. In both Tiv and Ibo populations, it is found at the lower levels of social organisation. Among Tiv, elders head groups of twenty to fifty people. Within these groups they preside over the administration of justice, the settlement of disputes, and the organisation of communal activities. Among the central Ibo, such groups tend to be a little larger. Above these lower levels, elders in authority tend to give way increasingly to men who represent their groups vis-à-vis others, or lead them against others. Thus where there are disputes between coordinate segments at higher levels of social organisation we find assemblies convened to resolve them. Characteristically, these assemblies do not consist of people in authority over the wider group which includes both parties to the dispute, for such people do not exist. Rather they consist of representatives of both sides who argue until a compromise is reached, or lead their groups into war if a compromise is not reached.

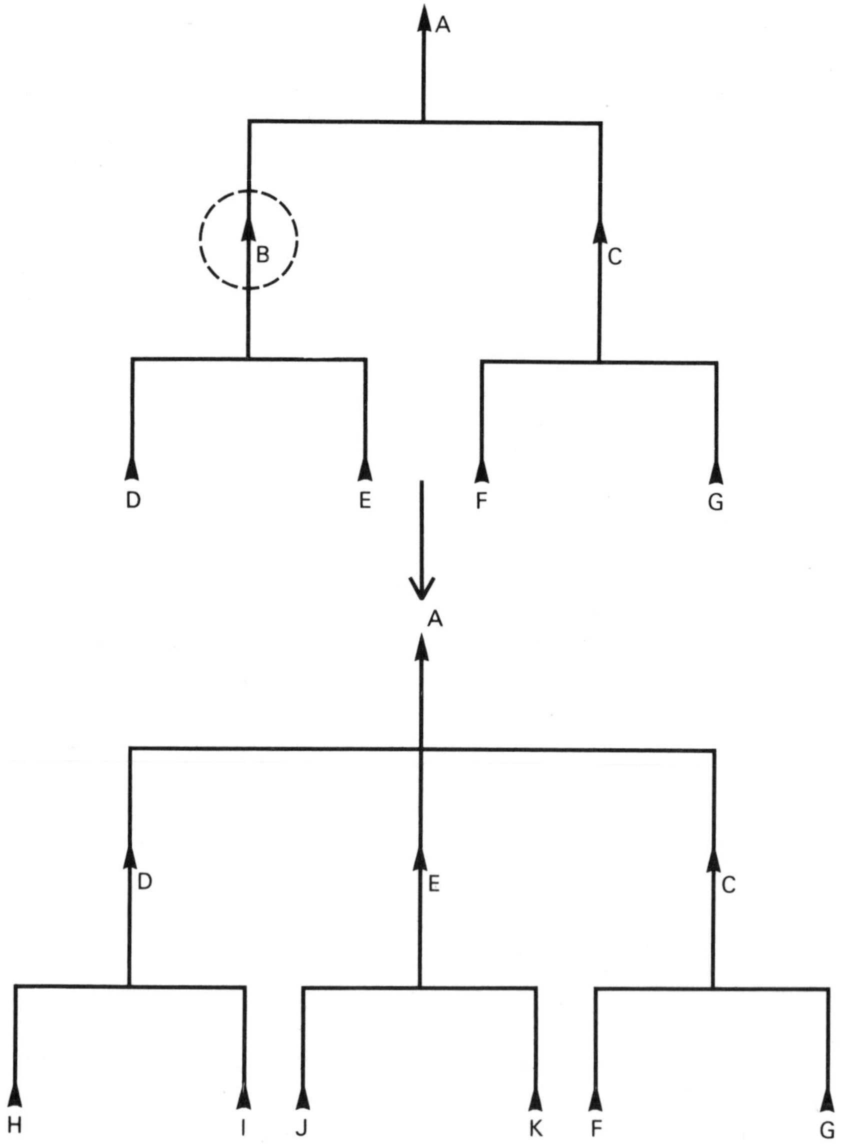

3.4 Readjustment of genealogy as a result of demographic imbalance.

Men who represent groups or lead them against others find themselves in a peculiar position when confrontation or conflict comes to an end. For, as we saw earlier, as soon as a large segment drops out of conflict, it tends to fall apart into its component units, and these in turn tend to fall apart into their component units—and so on until a low level of grouping is reached. In these circumstances the leader no longer has a group to take charge of. If he tries to exert influence over the people he led into the conflict situation he is likely to be accused of interfering in other people's affairs. For as soon as the segment he led has ceased effective existence, he is seen as belonging merely to one of its several component units. And the principle of strict equivalence between coordinate units and their personnel excludes him from any right to concern himself with the affairs of units other than his own.[12]

The predominance of leadership over authority, and the transience even of leadership, can therefore be seen as a necessary outcome of the relativity of political grouping and the equivalence of segments.

Such, then, are the 'pure type' segmentary lineage systems. They are paradoxical structures, as remarkable for the way in which they discourage the growth of internal differentiation and authority, as for the way in which, in the face of external threat, they permit the mobilisation of large numbers of men under powerful leaders. We shall have more to say about these characteristics when we discuss the question of state formation toward the end of this chapter. And they will come into the limelight again in later chapters which consider the eras of colonial rule and of the modern nation-states. Meanwhile, however, let us turn our attention to other, less highly publicised, forms of stateless social organisation.

The dispersed, territorially defined community (Type 2)

In discussing Type 1 societies, we saw that even where conditions are suitable for the flourishing growth of a segmentary lineage system, they are never perfect enough to prevent sporadic movement of individuals and groups of a kind that threatens to disrupt the congruence between genealogical, spatial and social relations. We also saw that genealogical reckoning is so much a force in its own right that it can cope with quite a heavy incidence of anomalous migrants simply by redefining their positions in a way that denies the anomalies.

But although the limits to this process have never been clearly defined, and maybe vary with the special circumstances of each society, there obviously are limits. Where there are gross inequalities in the peripheral land supply, some segments become almost totally blocked in the process of expansion, whilst others have more than enough space for their needs. In these circumstances, disjunctive migration becomes the order of the

12 See Bohannan and Bohannan, *The Tiv . . .*, pp. 31–2.

day.[13] Blocked groups pass through the territories of all their closer genealogical relations and end up begging land from groups to which they acknowledge distant or nil genealogical ties. Where an area is filled up in this way the result is a series of aggregates, each of which is composed of a number of lineages who define their solidarity, not in terms of a further genealogical link, but in terms of co-residence on a more or less clearly defined tract of land.

Many populations throughout West Africa exhibit this dispersed but territorially defined pattern of settlement and social organisation. In Nigeria, for example, some Idoma[14] and Ibo[15] groups provide good illustrations. But the *locus classicus* of populations that exhibit this pattern is undoubtedly the country extending from the headwaters of the Volta up toward the Niger bend—the country occupied by such stateless peoples as the Nankanse, the Birifor, the Konkomba, the Lowiili and the Lodagaa.[16] This whole region seems to have been a field for disjunctive migrations rather than even expansions.[17]

Disjunctive migration, with consequent exchange of a genealogical for a territorial definition of group identity, has momentous consequences for those involved. Earlier we noted how, in the 'pure type' segmentary lineage systems, the all-important principle of strict equivalence between segments got its strength (*a*) from the genealogical idiom, and (*b*) from the fact that coordinate segments and their members were in identical relations to the land. In the populations we are now considering, (*a*) has disappeared at the highest level or organisation. As for (*b*), disjunctive migration has meant a division of lineages into 'landowners' and 'latecomers'. A result of this is that the principle of equivalence and opposition between segments has been replaced by the principle of non-equivalence and complementarity.

Let me spell this out in a little more detail. In the first place, there is a natural tendency to look on the 'landowners' and their representatives as

13 For an interesting discussion of types of migration, see Paul Bohannan, 'The migration and expansion of the Tiv', *Africa*, xxiv, no. 1, 1954. Bohannan distinguishes 'expansion migration', which preserves the relative positions of expanding lineage segments, from 'disjunction migration', which alters these positions and disrupts the genealogical order. Though he stresses that both types of migration have been going on in Tiv country, he makes the point at the end of his article that an inordinate increase in disjunction migration, now a feature of some areas, will inevitably bring about basic changes in the social organisation.

14 For an outline of Idoma social organisation, see Daryll Forde, Paula Brown and Robert G. Armstrong, *Peoples of the Niger-Benue Confluence* (Ethnographic Survey of Africa), London, 1955.

15 See Forde and Jones, *op. cit.*

16 For a general survey of this area which is still of considerable relevance, see R. S. Rattray, *The Tribes of the Ashanti Hinterland* 2 vols, Oxford, 1932. For a more recent survey which throws light both on the history and on the present-day social organisation of the area, see J. Goody, *The Ethnography of the Northern Territories of the Gold Coast West of the White Volta*, Colonial Office, London, 1954.

17 See Goody, *op. cit.*, esp., pp. 31–2.

having a special status *vis-à-vis* the 'latecomers' and their representatives. This tendency is reinforced by prevailing ideas about the spiritual essence of the earth. Now the idea of an earth spirit is almost universal in West Africa. So too is the idea that it can prosper those living on the earth if they treat it with respect, and punish them if they anger it by breaking certain prohibitions. This complex of ideas seems to be present in some degree even in 'pure type' segmentary lineage systems such as that of the Tiv. But in such systems it tends to stay in the background. Where the territorial criterion of group identity takes precedence over the genealogical criterion, however, ideas about the spiritual force of the earth come to the forefront. Appropriately, the cult of this force is vested in the 'landowning' lineage, and the head of the lineage discharges the functions of cult priest on behalf of the community as a whole. Since the earth spirit sanctions a body of laws that apply to all men living on a particular tract of land, irrespective of lineage, the cult priest has the makings of an authority figure of a kind not much in evidence in the 'pure type' segmentary lineage systems. On the one hand, he has the licence, not just to represent his group against outsiders, but also to preside to some extent over its internal affairs. On the other hand, this licence is valid, not just within the 'landowning' lineage, but in all the lineages that make up the community.[18]

Secondly, the differentiation of status between 'landowners' and 'latecomers' implies complementarity. The 'latecomers' need land from the landowners', and the 'landowners' need the 'latecomers' to help them hold their land. Now where complementarity rather than equivalence is seen to be the governing principle of relations between lineages, the latter can serve as the basis for a considerable division of labour. Different lineages can perform different services for the community, or bring out different types of office-holders. Some of the Voltaic peoples such as the Lodagaa, it is true, have only one significant community office—that of the earth priest vested in the 'landowning' lineage.[19] More commonly, several different offices are distributed among the several different lineages. A typical pattern is that in which the office of 'Owner of the Land' (earth priest) is vested in the autochthonous lineage, whilst the office of 'Owner of the People' is vested in one of the immigrant lineages. This pattern may well have arisen in circumstances where the autochthones were greatly outnumbered by the immigrants, and where, in a very real sense, the former supplied the land and the latter the people. A good example of it is provided by the Konkomba of Northern Ghana. With them, as probably with

18 For ideas about the importance of replacement of a genealogical by a territorial definition of group identity, I am much indebted to discussions with John Boston and James O'Connell. Some of Boston's views on the subject are well set out in the closing paragraphs of his 'Igala political organisation', *African Notes*, iv, 2, 1967.

19 See J. Goody, 'Fields of social control among the LoDagaba', *Journal of the Royal Anthropological Institute*, lxxxvii, 1, 1957.

other populations exhibiting the same pattern, the balance of authority between the Owner of the Land and the Owner of the People varies from group to group. Like that of the Owner of the Land, however, the office of Owner of the People also carries the connotation of authority over the territorial group as a whole, and not just over the lineage in which it is vested.[20]

In the 'pure type' segmentary lineage system, it is very difficult to point to any level of grouping as 'the political community'. A given group becomes merged with others of its kind in opposition to distant enemies, or dissolves into its component segments as soon as it drops out of conflict with outsiders; for where the principle of equivalence remains supreme, it is mainly conflict with outsiders that unites. But in Type 2 societies, a group does not dissolve in quite the same way when it drops out of conflict; for where the principle of complementarity defines the relations between segments, they see each other as interdependent parts of an organic whole, and are therefore set for cooperation even in the absence of external pressures. This set-up makes for a fixed focus of political allegiance, and so potentially reinforces the other factors that encourage the emergence of at least a rudimentary form of authority. The Konkomba, with their little bundles of organically related lineages and their dual Elderships, provide a good illustration of this outcome.[21] So too do many of the Idoma 'Lands'.[22]

Sometimes there is a complication which leads to rather different results. For wherever 'latecoming' lineages settle down in their new homes, they do not at once lose memory of all ties with their areas of origin. Where migration is recent and of short range such ties continue to be particularly significant. Indeed, given a dispersed settlement pattern with no clearcut breaks in population, and given the tendency for social distance to vary with spatial distance, it is clear that when a lineage migrates in such a way that it ends up not much farther from its community of origin than it is from parts of its community of adoption, its ties with the former must compete in strength with its ties with the latter. The pattern of dual allegiance which arises in such circumstances results in large areas of population in which it is extremely difficult to single out discrete political units. Instead of isolable communities, we find what Goody[23] has described as 'a continuous intermeshing of social relations'. Here again, then, we have context-relative political allegiance. It is, however, of a different kind from that which we found typical of the 'pure type' segmentary lineage systems. In the latter, the individual gives his allegiance within a single series of progressively more inclusive groups. The level in the series on which he

20 See D. Tait, 'The territorial and lineage system of the Konkomba', in *Tribes Without Rulers,* ed. J. Middleton and D. Tait, London, 1959.
21 Tait, *op. cit.*
22 Forde, Brown and Armstrong, *op. cit.*
23 Goody, *The Ethnography of the Northern Territories* . . . , p. 27.

focuses at a particular moment in time varies with context. But his allegiance is always confined within the one series. In Type 2 situations, by contrast, the individual's allegiance does not shift from level to level within a single series, but oscillates between two or more groups which are in a relation of partial overlap. In distinguishing these two kinds of context-relative allegiance, it may be useful to talk of escalating versus oscillating allegiance.

Summing up our discussion of Type 2 populations, we can say that even where settlement pattern remains dispersed, the switch from expansion to disjunction results in a set of organisational principles markedly different from those that characterise the 'pure type' segmentary lineage system. At the highest level of organisation, territorial co-residence replaces common descent as the criterion of political identity; the principles of differential status and complementarity replace those of equivalence and opposition; authority and institutional differentiation begin to emerge; and fixed or oscillating political allegiance replaces escalating allegiance.

Below the top level of integration, however, the lineages remain the dominant units of social grouping. It is still *through* their lineages that people are integrated into the total community. The territorial organisation builds on the lineage organisation and caps it. It does not work against it. The continuing paramountcy of the lineages in Type 2 societies is not really surprising; for where spatial distance is an important determinant of social distance, the continuance of a dispersed settlement pattern means that the lineages must remain significantly more cohesive than the total community. A challenge to the paramountcy of the lineages can only occur where this basic demographic condition no longer obtains.

The large compact village (Type 3)

We cannot yet claim to be fully clear as to why some West African populations are addicted to a dispersed settlement pattern, whilst others have opted for life in large, compact villages. But as I mentioned in discussing the 'pure type' segmentary lineage system, one thing that does seem clear is that whilst dispersed settlement is a single-minded adjustment to subsistence farming, village settlement results from a partial neglect of the organisational demands of farming in the face of those of efficient defence. This is vividly brought out by the fact that, so far as the evidence of contemporary travellers' descriptions and the recollections of old men go, many West African village communities were once stockaded and fortified—often in a most elaborate and spectacular manner.[24] What seems probable is that in precolonial times, the dispersed settlement pattern was characteristic of peoples who were expanding or maintaining themselves territorially against negligible or relatively uncoordinated resistance, whilst the

24 For details of village fortifications in Liberia, see G. Schwab, *Tribes of the Liberian Hinterland* (Peabody Museum Papers, vol. xxxi), Cambridge, Mass., 1947; also H. Labouret, *Paysans de l'Afrique Occidentale*, Paris, 1941, pp. 109–12.

compact village pattern was characteristic of peoples who were defending their territory and their lives against formidable opponents intent on annexing the one and extinguishing the other.

Whatever the exact determinants of the 'clotting' of the settlement pattern, the result is a social aggregate markedly different from either of the two types we have considered so far. The reasons for this difference are fairly evident.

Let us remember that in the sort of ecological conditions we are dealing with here, spatial distance is an important determinant of social distance. Now all spatial distances within the village are small, and differ from each other relatively little in comparison with spatial distances between the village and its neighbours. Thus the spatial distance between houses of members of the same village segment, and the spatial distance between houses of members of different village segments, are of a similar order of magnitude when compared with the spatial distance from the village to its nearest neighbour. So far as spatial relations are concerned, then, they tend to produce a situation in which the social distance between members of the same segment and the social distance between members of different segments are both small and of comparable magnitude relative to the social distance between members of the village and members of other villages. Put simply, everyone within the village tends to feel close to everyone else within it, and distant from everyone outside it. This effect of the purely demographic pattern is reinforced by the effect of the defensive aims that underpin it. Where the village is essentially a unit constituted for the permanent defence of its members against lethal attack by outsiders, there is a tendency for each member to consider himself equally bound to all others within the village, and equally on guard against all those outside.

From this basic social situation flow a number of important consequences. First, there is the absence of an embracing genealogical scheme for conceptualising relations both within and without the village. Instead of a progressive increase in the social distance between sub-units with size of total aggregate, we have low social distance between sub-units for all aggregates within the village, and a high distance for all aggregates larger than the village. Since the use of an embracing genealogical calculus is compatible with the first situation but not with the second, genealogical reckoning can have only limited importance as a principle of village organisation (see again Fig. 3.2).

Given that most West African village communities seem to be the products of disjunctive migration, it is not surprising that they display a number of the features characteristic of Type 2 societies: for example, relations of status difference and complementarity between lineage segments; a fixed focus of political allegiance; and the emergence of a degree of authority. But there are other consequences of the basic village social situation which make communities of Type 3 very different from those of Type 2.

Most important of these consequences is the proliferation of institutions that ignore, cut across and even work against the lineages and the lines of division they create. Now although the village itself is seldom defined in genealogical terms, lineages usually remain at some level in its organisation, as landholding units. However, because social distance between village segments can never be much greater than social distance within such segments, lineages no longer enjoy the priority of allegiance which they have in societies of Type 2. Whereas members of a dispersed, territorially defined community relate to the total community *through* their lineages, the members of a compact village community have an allegiance to the total community which stands alongside and is independent of allegiance to the lineage. Hence in the organisation of life at village level, the possibility arises of using principles which ignore the lineages. That such principles *are* extensively used in the organisation of Type 3 communities is probably due to the fact that they are far more suited to the purpose than are the lineages.

Even where the eclipse of an embracing genealogical scheme has made it possible to define coordinate lineages as complementary parts of an organic whole, some element of equivalence and rivalry lingers on. This is because coordinate lineages still retain similar internal structures and similar landholding functions. The latter promote not only the idea of a residual equivalence underlying the superficial complementarity, but also a very real possibility of conflict. Cross-cutting institutions, on the other hand, set up a radical complementarity which is not marred by any taint of equivalence. This becomes obvious when we consider their main forms: age grades and associations. Thus age-grading divides the community into old men and younger adult men (or into a larger number of such units), whilst associations divide it into the qualified and initiated and the unqualified and uninitiated. These are units with no trace of equivalence. The only possibility of tension between them arises from envy of the prerogatives of the higher status unit on the part of members of the lower. But the sting is taken out of this by the fact that members of the lower status unit hope to succeed to the place occupied by those of higher status. There is little point in quarrelling about power and position when one is going to get it from others soon enough by peaceful means. Cross-cutting institutions, then, are much more efficient tools for organising a harmonious village life than are the lineages; and this is undoubtedly why they are so extensively developed in large, compact settlements.[25]

25 After reading an earlier draft of this chapter, Professor Daryll Forde pointed out to me that it is not strictly correct to say that cross-cutting institutions occur in Type 3 systems only. I agree that, within the basic three- or four- generation lineage, if not beyond, some form of solidarity between age-mates exists in all three types of social organisation. Such solidarity is an inevitable result (*a*) of children playing together within the neighbourhood occupied by the basic lineage; and (*b*) of the fact that certain agricultural operations carried

(*continued overleaf*)

Coming down to greater descriptive detail, let us start with those features of village organisation which most resemble features of Type 2 societies, and then go on to consider the more distinctive aspects of village life. Most West African villages contain a congeries of unrelated lineage groups which are the basic holders of settlement and farm land. Typically, the group that arrived in the area first is regarded as the senior, and the head of this group enjoys some degree of authority over the total community. Among the village-organised peoples of Guinea, hinterland Liberia and western Ivory Coast,[26] and among some Cross River peoples such as the Mbembe,[27] the head of the community is also priest of the earth cult which sanctions communal morality and law.

Where there are several complementary political and ritual offices in the community, these are often distributed among the various lineages in a more or less equitable manner. In the villages of the Kru Coast of Liberia, for example, communal government involves such diverse offices as Chief, Controller of Army and Public Works, Historian, Spokesman and Priest. And these are distributed evenly among the various lineage groups that make up the community.[28] Again, in the villages of the eastern Niger Delta, a dozen or more different priesthoods are carefully divided up among the different lineages.[29]

This use of lineages as vehicles of a village-wide division of labour is probably more widespread in West Africa than the current literature indicates. For the reasons I have given, however, much of the community-wide social organisation of the villages simply ignores the lineages. And it is to this cross-cutting organisation that we must now turn.

The simplest form of cross-cutting organisation found in West African village life is the age grade. Good examples of this institution are to be found in the Kalabari Ijo villages of the eastern Niger Delta, in the northern Edo villages, and in some eastern Ibo groups. Usually, age grading divides adult males into elders and young adults—or more rarely into elders, middle-aged, and young adults. The age-grade system is usually fed by a

(25 *continued*)
out within the framework of the basic lineage are most efficiently performed by people of a certain age—i.e. youths. Nonetheless, part of Tiv country seems to be devoid even of age sets; and where they occur they are not of great political importance (Bohannan and Bohannan, *op. cit.*, p. 46). Again, in the one monographic study we have of a more or less pure-type segmentary lineage system in Iboland, age organisation is dismissed as being of little sociopolitical importance (Green, *op. cit.*, p. 25). In the case of Type 2 social organisations, we find, once more, that our authors feel little need to mention age organisation in their sociopolitical outlines (Goody, 'Fields of social control . . .'; Tait, *op. cit.*). As for secret societies, these really do seem virtually confined to Type 3 village communities.

26 See Murdock, *op. cit.*, p. 263.

27 See Rosemary Harris, *The Political Organisation of the Mbembe, Nigeria*, London, 1965 (esp. chaps. 5 and 6).

28 See M. Fraenkel, 'Social change on the Kru coast of Liberia', *Africa*, xxxvi, 2, 1966.

29 See my 'From village to city-state', in *Man in Africa* (Essays presented to Daryll Forde), ed. M. Douglas and P. Kaberry, London, 1969.

system of age sets, whose members move from one grade to the next.

In age-graded villages, the way the system should work is often laid down by an ideology which describes the qualities of these grades and the way in which they should interact. In Kalabari villages, for example, the young adults are defined as 'hot-faced'—unreflective, bold, quarrelsome and bodily strong; whilst elders are defined as 'cool'—unhasty, reflective, cautious and bodily weak. Village ideology makes it clear that these two sets of qualities are complementary; and in this it points to the main lines of actual relations between the grades. Thus young adults are responsible for the actual labour in public works; for the brunt of active operations in war; for the expression of dissatisfaction about the state of village life; for the continual suggestion of solutions to village troubles; and for starting most quarrels. Elders, on the other hand, are advisers on the conduct of war; moderators having the last word in village affairs generally; and settlers of the quarrels provoked by the young. In the village assembly, the two groups sit opposite one another; and for the western observer familiar with parliamentary institutions, their behaviour is superficially reminiscent of that of 'government' and 'opposition' in debates. But although considerable tension often arises between the two grades, both are well aware of their mutual indispensability. And even where strong disagreement arises between them on the conduct of village affairs, the matter at issue tends to be tossed back and forth until a compromise is reached upon which both can agree.[30]

A tentative view of the West African scene suggests that this simple form of village organisation prevails where lineages are rather weak.[31] Stronger lineages with more acute rivalries pose a threat of disruption which can only be overcome by more subtle devices. I suggest that it is as an answer to the lineage threat that we can best understand the various devices associated with those typical West African institutions, the so-called 'secret societies'.

The majority of West African secret societies can be looked at as variants of a broad institutional pattern which is recognisable throughout the area. This pattern has four major elements:

a) Admission to the society is open to adult or adolescent males irrespective of lineage.
b) Admission is by payment of fees and/or an initiation ritual in which the candidate is both tested for certain skills and dramatically separated from his previous social partners. Often, separation involves not only a cutting-off of ties with family and lineage, but also a forging of new ties

30 For an outline of Kalabari village government, see Horton, *op. cit.*
31 In the Kalabari case, the *de facto* matrilineal constitution of the village lineages makes for a blurring of the sharp cleavages one might expect to find with agnatically constituted lineages. Again, the fact that lineages are holders of residential land but not of productive resources tends to weaken their hold as foci of allegiance.

with the guardian spirit of the society.
c) The society is typically a judicial body, deciding the more intractable intra-village disputes. But it may also have policy-making functions. Its deliberations in this sphere are kept strictly secret from the public.
d) Execution of the society's decisions is typically by junior members whose identity is concealed by masks.

Different peoples emphasise different aspects of this broad general pattern. Thus in the *okwa* of the Cross River Mbembe, initiation is a fairly simple matter, with little emphasis on learning and qualification, and with a one-stage entry.[32] Among the peoples of the Liberian hinterland initiation into the *poro* involves elaborate rituals and fierce tests of the candidate's knowledge of community lore. It takes place in a number of stages—each stage admitting the candidate to a higher grade within the society.[33] Again, whilst the Cross River *okwa* and *okengka* emphasise the executive rather than the decision-making aspects of the pattern—often carrying out orders that have originated from the village head or elsewhere—the Liberian *poro* and the Cross River *ekpe* emphasise both.[34]

As yet, no one has worked out the sociological correlates of these variations. But they seem, nevertheless, to be variations on a single theme. Now the best way to understand this theme, as I hinted earlier, is to treat it as a cluster of adaptations to the problem posed by the continuing presence in the community of strong and rivalrous lineages.

Let us take first the initiation rituals. These bring all the power of symbolism and drama to bear on the task of compelling the impressionable adolescent to 'die' to his old life and wake up 'reborn' in a new life. The old life, of course, is the life lived in the bosom of the family and the lineage; whilst the new life is the life in which the prime allegiance is to the community as a whole. By plunging the adolescent into an intense attachment to the guardian spirit of the society, the rituals again help to wean him away from deep emotional ties with parents and lineage members.

Secondly, let us consider the secrecy that invests the judicial and policy-making deliberations of the society—a secrecy which contrasts very strongly with the open free-for-all of the age-graded assembly. This secrecy counters the influence of lineage rivalries in two ways. On the one hand, it protects those engaged in the deliberations against pressure from their various lineages. This makes it easier for them to consider any situation on its merits, and to avoid taking up positions inspired by purely sectional interests.[35] On

32 Harris, *op. cit.*, chap. 4.
33 See Schwab, *op. cit.*; also G. W. Harley, *Masks as Agents of Social Control in North-East Liberia* (Peabody Museum Papers vol. xxxii, 2); Cambridge, Mass., 1950.
34 For *poro*, see Schwab, Harley, *op. cit.*; for *ekpe*, see Daryll Forde, ed., *Efik Traders of Old Calabar*, London, 1956.
35 On this, see G. I. Jones, *Report of the Position, Status and Influence of Chiefs and Natural Rulers in the Eastern Region of Nigeria*, Enugu, 1957, pp. 17–18.

the other hand, it enables the society to announce its decisions to the public at large as things collective and unanimous. So promulgated, they are likely to receive general acceptance. Had they been arrived at in open debate, with everyone aware of the sectional affiliations of those for and against, the chances are that some sections would have accepted them and others rejected them.

Finally, let us consider the masking of the society's executives. This makes immediate sense when considered as a device to ensure acceptance of the harsher sanctions applied by the society to offenders against community laws—sanctions which may include death, corporal punishment, or confiscation of properties. Where the executives are masked, it is possible for the public to accept their actions, however harsh, as impersonal manifestations of the collective will. If they were unmasked and identifiable, their actions might cause dangerous resentment through suspicion of sectional interest.[36]

We can now see why the West African secret society is an institution so particularly associated with village life; and why, in the context of village life, it has surrounded itself with the mysterious paraphernalia that have given it fame and notoriety far beyond the shores of Africa. First, it is only in the village that allegiance to the total community has a strength comparable to that of allegiance to the lineage. Hence it is only in the village that the secret society, as a tightly-knit, community-wide organisation, can wax strong. Secondly, even in the village, lineages and their rivalries are apt to survive. Hence to be an effective form of community-wide organisation, the secret society must evolve a whole battery of subtle devices to neutralise them.

In this presentation, I have put the village and its cross-cutting institutions last in a series of three types. In so far as the series shows a progressive institutional complexity, this order seems as good as any. Nevertheless, the causal factors I have invoked are all reversible; and I do not wish to imply a unidirectional scheme of evolution. Whilst it is quite probable that 'pure type' segmentary lineage systems, under the appropriate conditions, have on occasion given rise first to dispersed, territorially defined communities, and then to compact villages, other sequences are just as likely to have occurred. Thus, again under appropriate conditions, there may have been cases of a lineage breaking out of a Type 2 or Type 3 community, only to expand and give rise to a Type 1 segmentary lineage system. What I have presented here, then, is a set of three social types, together

36 Users of secret society masks often have a shrewd appreciation of the purely political value of such devices in village life. As elders of the Dan villages of the western Ivory Coast say: 'Our chiefs have never had any soldiers or policemen to enforce obedience. So the elders decided that the masks should be given final respect above men. Otherwise, how could law and order be maintained in our country?' Quoted from H. Himmelheber, Sculptors and sculptures of the Dan', in *Proceedings of the First International Congress of Africanists,* ed. L. Bown and M. Crowder, Ibadan, 1964.

with a tentative specification of the factors that make for transition from one to another. I am not insisting on some particular direction of transition.

THE PASTORALISTS

The Fulani, who are by far and away the most important pastoral people in West Africa, are also one of the few stateless peoples for whom it is possible to give considerable historical depth. This is not so much because of any great richness of the sorts of sources beloved by orthodox historians, as because of a combination of cultural and physical traits so odd as to permit of only one possible theory of origin.

Briefly, the Fulani are a group who speak a Niger-Congo (negro African) language, but who are markedly caucasoid in their physical make-up. In searching for the historical roots of this strange combination, we must take note of two facts. First, that the Fulani language is one of the West Atlantic sub-family whose base area is in and around the Senegal valley, where its variants are spoken to this day by such peoples as the Wolof, the Serer and the Toucouleur. Secondly, that this area witnessed an early infiltration by Berber herdsmen from North Africa, and a subsequent miscegenation whose results are still visible today. ('Toucouleur', incidentally, appears to be a corruption of the French 'all-colours'.) Putting two and two together, historians have concluded that the Berber infiltrators intermarried with their hosts and adopted their language, but largely ignored the already elaborate political ideas of the area, which were not suited to their way of life. Later, finding the pastures south of the Senegal Valley overcrowded, they started to spread out eastward. Once started they were able to spread very quickly; for existing landowners had no reason to treat them as competitors. Between the twelfth and nineteenth centuries, indeed, they succeeded in dispersing themselves throughout the length and breadth of the West African savannah.[37]

The pastoral Fulani depend for their livelihood almost entirely on their herds of cattle. They subsist largely on their own dairy products and on grain, which they acquire in exchange for milk in the markets of local farming communities. The basic productive unit is the compound family made up of a man, his wives and his children. This is the unit that owns and tends the herd. During the dry season, when Fulani have to move southward and scatter in search of viable grazing, it is at times isolated and virtually autonomous. Over much of the year, however, several agnatically-related families live and move together. Though cooperation within the resulting lineage is less intensive than that within the individual family, it is nonetheless very important. Thus a family with personnel inadequate to the tending

37 For reasoned reconstructions of pastoral Fulani history and summaries of the data upon which such reconstructions are based, see (*a*) Murdock, *op. cit.*, chap. 55; and (*b*) Robert G. Armstrong, *The Study of West African Languages*, Ibadan, 1964, pp. 4–9, 25–8.

of its herd expects to borrow help from other families in the lineage. Again, a family with a herd insufficient to support its personnel expects to borrow cattle from the same source.

For at least a few weeks of the year, usually at the height of the wet season, several putatively related lineages gather together into a clan camp. Though not so important as the family and the lineage, the clan too is a significant unit of pastoral cooperation.[38]

Granted the considerable differences between cattle-herding and sedentary agriculture as ways of gaining a livelihood, the pastoralists nonetheless face certain basic ecological conditions which are rather similar to those which we mentioned in connection with the farmers, and which give rise to similar social forms. Thus they have a subsistence economy with a poorly developed exchange and monetary sector—an economy based on long-term utilisation of particular productive resources which are relatively scarce goods. Again, though, their basic unit of production is the compound family, some aspects of the productive process require mutual aid and cooperation on a larger scale.

We have already rehearsed the social consequences of such conditions in dealing with the farmers. Let us recapitulate them briefly here. First, because of the necessities of economic cooperation, the group of neighbouring compound families acquires a high degree of cohesion. Second, because inheritance is the only channel for orderly acquisition of the basic productive resources, young men settle down with those they aspire to inherit from; so that after several generations of expanding population, the cohesive group of neighbours comes inevitably to be based on a core of males related through the line of cattle inheritance. Hence, for the pastoralists as for the farmers, the lineage of three or four generations in depth is an ever-present social grouping.

There are further parallels. Thus pastoral life seems to require very intensive cooperation within the small family group, fairly intensive cooperation within a somewhat larger group, occasional cooperation within a still larger group, and so on. Again, it seems to require that the larger the group the greater the period during the year for which its components must be physically scattered. Both these requirements make for a situation in which a progressive increase in group size is accompanied by a progressive increase in social distance between group components. This, as we saw in our discussion of the agriculturalists, is the situation optimally suitable for thoroughgoing use of the genealogical calculus; and in fact, pastoral Fulani tend toward segmentary lineage systems very much akin to the Type I systems of the farmers.

38 For descriptions of the ways of life of two of the more easterly pastoral Fulani groups, see C. E. Hopen, *The Pastoral Fulbe Family in Gwandu*, London, 1958; and D. Stenning, *Savannah Nomads*, London, 1959, esp. part i, chap. 2.

Some of the literature[39] suggests that, in pre-colonial days, the requirements of defence at times over-rode those of pastoral life, with the result that the pattern of cyclical scattering and regrouping gave way to one of large-scale, compact, semi-permanent village settlement. Unfortunately the literature in question gives little further detail, so we are unable to say how far this settlement pattern was accompanied (as one might expect) by a social organisation akin to the Type 3 agriculturalists. But it seems likely that the Fulani, because they were not competing with other peoples for the land itself, attracted aggressive intentions rather less often than did agricultural groups. And in any case, they appear to have sought out areas of the savannah where the requirements of pastoral life did not have to be balanced against those of defence.[40] Even in pre-colonial times, then, the Type 1 system was probably their most characteristic form of social organisation.

Despite the parallels between their own social organisation and that of the agriculturalists, Fulani have a strong feeling of the distinctiveness and superiority of their way of life. They are immensely conscious of being in but not of the societies that give them grazing rights. And inevitably, with their caucasoid physical features, they add racial overtones to their feelings. In so far as their conviction of cultural distinctiveness has any objective foundation, this perhaps derives from the absence of ties to any particular territory which is a consequence of the pastoral way of life. When a group of farmers divides a tract of land, the resultant pieces still remain physically together and hold their owners in spatial proximity. When pastoralists divide up a herd, there is nothing to stop cattle and owners from moving apart. One result of this is a very high rate of fission and permanent dispersion in Fulani segmentary lineage systems, a rate which prevents them from attaining anything like the size of their agricultural counterparts. Another result is the feeling that they have a kind of freedom and independence which the earthbound farmer can never have.

GODS AND OUTSIDERS IN THE STATELESS SOCIETIES

To conclude my survey of the stateless societies, I should like to say a little more about the relation of religion to their social organisations. I have made some scattered references to this question in previous paragraphs, but some more general comments are called for.

In West Africa religion is first and foremost a theoretical interpretation of the world, and an attempt to apply this interpretation to the prediction and control of worldly events. Now theory always involves the drawing of analogies between puzzling facts that demand an explanation, and areas of familiar, well-ordered experience. In traditional West African cultures, with their well-defined, slowly changing social organisations and their

39 Hopen, *op. cit.*, pp. 41–7.
40 Stenning, *op. cit.*, p. 5.

relatively undeveloped technologies, human social relations rather than inanimate phenomena are the experiential locus of order and regularity. Hence their theories are couched in a predominantly personal idiom. In these cultures, man sees himself as living in a world controlled by an invisible order of personal beings, of whom he has to take account at every turn.[41]

In such a world, the life of social groups, like other things, is thought of as underpinned by spiritual forces. Since these forces are conceived of as working for the strength and prosperity of their groups, it follows that human action making for the disruption of the groups will arouse their anger. The belief that they punish such action by sending sickness and misfortune is a logical consequence. Again, since these forces are conceived of as working for group strength, it follows that authority figures, such as lineages or village heads, must be in a relation of special intimacy with them. Indeed, such authority figures as exist in the stateless societies are thought to be backed by the spiritual forces of their groups, who 'walk with them' whenever they are in the legitimate exercise of their authority. Such figures are often regarded as living symbols of the group spirits.

All this, however, is but one side of the coin. For the world views of West African peoples are not idealisations, but attempts to come to terms with life as it is. As such, they feature not only the forces underpinning orderly group life, but also the forces behind the selfish and antisocial behaviour that threatens this life. Cults of group forces are shadowed by cults, often clandestine, of the antisocial and disruptive forces. In the villages of the eastern Niger Delta, for example, there are cults of communal gods and of lineage ancestors; but there are also cults of water-spirits that are associated with 'natural man' as well as with nature *sensu stricto*. Such cults are thought to be particularly attractive to those in pursuit of selfish, antisocial ends.[42] Again, spiritual beings that appear to be forces of order when viewed in one social context look more like forces of disorder when viewed in another. Thus the ancestors underpin orderly life *within* lineages, but they can also promote and approve conflict *between* lineages.

Since the West African religious world view typically alludes to and suggests means of utilising both social and antisocial, integrative and disruptive forces, we can hardly make any valid general statement about its net consequences for the social life of the stateless societies. We certainly cannot say that religious beliefs and practices have a net integrative effect. What we can say is that there is a constant dialectic between religious ideas and principles of social organisation. Not only do social forms exert a profound influence on religious ideas. They themselves are defined in terms of religious ideas and are even moulded by such ideas. Thus relations

41 For a longer exposition of all this, see my 'African traditional thought and Western science: Part I', *Africa*, xxxvii, 1, 1967.

42 See my 'The Kalabari world-view: an outline and interpretation', *Africa*, xxxii, 3, 1962.

between landowners and latecomers in Type 2 societies are what they are because they are defined in terms of ideas about the spiritual forces of the earth. And such positions of authority as exist in the stateless societies can only be understood if one takes into account the religious ideas that define them.

So much for the religious world view considered as a system of explanation, prediction and control. Being personal in idiom, this world view also presents a set of extensions to the purely human social field. In short, the gods are not only theoretical entities; they are people. Hence we need to ask ourselves not only about the consequences for West African societies of a predominantly religious world view, but also about the consequences for such societies of the presence in them of extra non-human people. The basic point here is that a man's social field includes not only relations with other men, but also relations with gods, and that the two kinds of relations have significant effects on one another.

Let me give some examples that are of particular significance for the social organisation of the stateless societies. First, it follows from what we have said about the typical West African world view that when a man enters a new group, or even when he takes up office within a group of which he has previously been an ordinary member, he enters into a new and intimate relation with the spiritual forces that underpin the group. And since this relation normally contains a strong element of dependence and subordination, its effect is to free the man involved from some of his dependence on his fellow men. One situation where this is very important has already been mentioned. That is the situation of the young villager who, on entering his community's secret society, is introduced to an intense personal relationship with a powerful guardian spirit, and is thereby liberated from his previous dependence on members of his family and lineage. Another such situation is that of the man whose installation as head of a lineage or village involves a new intimacy of relationship with the spiritual forces of the group—an intimacy which, again through freeing the man from some of his previous dependence on fellow group members, in a very real sense gives him a new source of power over them.[43]

A second very important feature of the gods' involvement in the human social field derives from the fact that although they are defined as personal beings, they are nonetheless 'outsiders' and figures of altogether higher status than men. This has one consequence of great significance for the maintenance of orderly social life. Where two factions within a group are in radical conflict, it is often impossible for any purely human member of

43 Though he does not analyse the situation in quite the same terms, Fortes gives a compelling picture of the religious backing of office in traditional African societies. See for instance his 'Pietas in ancestor worship', *J. Roy. Anthrop. Inst.*, xci, part ii, 1961. See also his 'Ritual and office', in *Essays in the Ritual of Social Relations*, ed. M. Gluckman, Manchester, 1962.

the group to reconcile them. For any such person is likely to be seen as partial to one side or the other. Hence one of the factions will see his settlement terms as victory, while the other will see them as defeat. But where the onus of reconciliation can somehow be placed on the spiritual forces of the group, the situation may be transformed. Before a high-status, impartial outsider, both factions can climb down to compromise without loss of face. Sometimes, the fact that the spiritual forces of the group are thought to be behind all the acts and decisions of its head is enough to give the latter's intervention the 'outsider effect'. Sometimes, where the dispute is too grave, this will not suffice. A more drastic device involves soliciting the spiritual forces to appear and give judgment in person, while possessing a human being. This is a widespread device in the stateless societies, and often works wonders where the intervention of the group head has failed.[44]

In some cases even this drastic device is not thought sufficient. Not only must the dispute be put before spiritual forces; it must be put before alien forces in a strange land. In this way, many communities in Eastern Nigeria used to take their disputes to the great oracle of Aro Chuku, often travelling a hundred miles through foreign territory in order to do so.[45]

It is at this point that the use of spiritual forces in the resolution of disputes fades into the use of human outsiders. One category of person widely coopted to act as mediating outsider is the blacksmith, who, while a member of the community involved, is nonetheless an outcaste.[46] Another kind of resident outsider who frequently gets called in the rôle of mediator is the visiting anthropologist! Often, however, the disputants go beyond their own community in search of the appropriate mediator. Where the dispute is within a single community the parties may go to a well-disposed neighbour. Where it is between two communities, they may go to a neutral third.

This brief mention of outsiders may seem an odd note on which to end a review of stateless social organisation. But, as we shall see in what follows, it gives us the basis for a fresh assessment of many received ideas about the origins of West African state institutions.

STATELESS SOCIETIES AND STATES

Of all the questions that have preoccupied historians of West Africa, perhaps the most vexing has been that of the origins of the states. Are the states indigenous developments, or the result of external influences? For

44 For examples of this, see my 'Types of spirit possession in Kalabari Religion', in *Spirit Mediumship and Society in Africa,* ed. J. Beattie and J. Middleton, London, 1969. The implications of intervention in a quarrel by secret society masks are of course similar. For examples of this, see Harley, *op. cit.*

45 S. Ottenberg, 'Ibo oracles and intergroup relations', *Southwestern J. Anthrop.*, xiv, 3, 1958.

46 For the blacksmith as mediating outsider, see J. Capron, 'Univers religieux et cohésion interne dans les communautés villageoises Bwa traditionelles', *Africa,* xxxii, 2, 1962, p. 146. See also D. Paulme, *Organisation sociale des Dogon,* Paris, 1940, p. 185 ff.

many years, this question was answered in terms of what is commonly known as the Hamitic Hypothesis. Put crudely, the Hamitic Hypothesis states that negro culture, left to itself, was never able to produce more than a very low level of political organisation. State ideology and organisation, like everything else considered valuable by Europeans, was brought into Africa by non-Negro invaders. In West Africa, proponents of the Hypothesis noted with delight the caucasoid features of the Fulani, and promptly cast them in the rôle of state-forming invaders. Some even went so far as to assert that it was Fulani experience with cattle that had prepared them for their rôle as rulers of men.

Now a great deal has been written over the last few years to show the flimsiness of the evidence for this theory. We have come to see how the ethnocentric prejudices of an earlier generation of European chroniclers led them to build massive edifices of fact out of small scraps of ambiguous legend. We have also come to see that a good deal of the legend itself was the product of similar prejudices on the part of the Arab chroniclers who wrote hundreds of years earlier still. But the Hamitic Hypothesis, though moribund, is not quite dead.[47] Let us therefore see what contribution the student of stateless societies can make to its evaluation, and, if necessary, to the suggestion of a plausible alternative.

In the first place, the little we know of the history of the pastoral Fulani enables us to give a clear verdict as to the validity of the theory that it was these caucasoid invaders who created higher forms of political organisation by imposing their rule on stateless negro agriculturalists. For we know that the Fulani herdsmen started their spectacular dispersal through the savannah long after the creative period of state formation in this zone. It is true that throughout the centuries of their dispersal existing savannah states were conquered, Islamised and reorganised by Fulani dynasts. But the leaders of this movement seem to have been sedentary Fulani hailing from the ancient Negro states of the Senegal valley, rather than the caucasoid pastoralists who had infiltrated into the latter's domains and adopted their language, but who had moved on without assimilating any of their elaborate political ideas.[48]

47 For critiques of the Hamitic Hypothesis, see J. Greenberg, 'The Negro Kingdoms of the Sudan', *Transactions of the New York Academy of Sciences*, Ser. ii, vol. xi, no. 4, 1949; Saint-Clair Drake, 'The responsibility of men of culture for destroying the "hamitic myth"', *Présence Africaine*, special issue (English language version), Paris, 1959; R. Armstrong, 'The development of kingdoms in Negro Africa', *Journal of the Historical Society of Nigeria*, ii, 1, 1960. Social anthropologists now seem to take these critiques as read. The same, however, cannot be said of historians. Thus Roland Oliver and J. D. Fage, in the latest edition of their *Short History of Africa* (London, 1968), still propound a modified form of the Hamitic Hypothesis. Though they no longer invoke hordes of conquering caucasoid pastoralists, they propose an Egyptian origin for African state ideologies, and suggest that such ideologies were superimposed on an indigenous infrastructure which had nothing in common with them. See Oliver and Fage, *op. cit.*, pp. 44–52.

48 See Murdock, *op. cit.*, chap. 55; and Armstrong, *op. cit.*, 1964, pp. 25–8.

The pastoralists certainly played a part in these conquests. As an element in the population of most of the existing savannah states, they were often disgruntled by the efforts of the rulers of these states to pin them down to fixed abodes and subject them to heavy tributes. And they responded eagerly to the blandishments of conquerors who not only promised to better their lot, but also called on them in the name of a common language and culture. However, their part in the conquests was that of followers rather than of leaders, of irregular cavalry rather than of rulers and administrators. They were certainly not the apostles of a state ideology. Nor, as their sedentary 'brothers' were to find out in due course, were they even very enamoured of the idea of being citizens of states.

If we want to discover more about the origins of the West African states, then, it is to the negro agriculturalists rather than to the caucasoid pastoralists that we must turn. Here again, the material presented earlier in this chapter is highly relevant to our discussion. For the factors suggested as the main determinants of social organisation among the stateless farming peoples are factors that have almost certainly been operative over the last thousand years.[49] In saying this I am not suggesting that these societies have been static for a thousand years. What I am suggesting is that, in so far as they have not turned into centralised states, their social organisation over this period has probably varied between the three types described above. Now if this contention is valid, it means that we can take the foregoing discussion of the varieties of stateless social organisation as a fair indication of the range of raw material from which many of the pre-colonial West African states must have developed. We are thus in a position to rephrase and answer at least tentatively the question posed a few paragraphs back. Is there such a gulf in ideology and organisation between stateless societies and states that to explain the transition from one to the other we have to invoke influences from outside West Africa? Or are there points of continuity which make it unnecessary to assume external influences?

If we start by looking at the overpublicised Type I organisations, it is discontinuity rather than continuity that strikes the eye. First, the individual in such systems thinks of the locus of his political allegiance as varying with context, whereas the state requires from him an allegiance which endures through all possible contexts. Again, the stress on equivalence and opposition as the dominant mode of relationship between coordinate segments militates against any one segment emerging as a 'royal lineage' charged with providing rulers recognised as such by all the others. Finally, the stress on equivalence and opposition of segments and their representatives acts as a block against the rôle specialisation and division of labour necessary in

49 My principal authority for this rather startling assertion is Murdock, *op. cit.*, esp. chaps. 7, 11, 28. If Murdock's analysis is correct, the crops, agricultural technology and rather dense population, which are crucial parameters in my model of the dynamics of West African stateless societies, have all been in evidence for well over a thousand years.

the development of a consequential state organisation. Between the 'pure type' segmentary lineage system and the state, then, there seems a great gulf fixed.

When we turn to Types 2 and 3, the gulf is not nearly so apparent. Here we quickly become aware of germs from which state organisation and ideology could sprout. In both these types, common residence on a defined tract of land and common submission to the laws sanctioned by the spirit of the land emerge as important principles of political integration. And these principles pave the way for ideas of sovereignty—that is, of a defined territory within which all comers are automatically subject to a definite body of laws.[50] Again, the fact that the first occupants of the defined tract of land have a relation to it which differs from and is more intimate than that of later comers provides the germ of a potential differentiation between royal and non-royal lineages. In many societies of Types 2 and 3, it is true, the landowning lineage does not have very much in the way of special privileges, and its head is little more than a mediator between the community and the earth spirit. In others, however, the differentiation is much more marked.[51] And it is interesting to note that in some of the states in our area, the royal lineage is the landowning lineage and the ruler the intermediary between his subjects and the land.[52] In this respect it is easy to see how small changes in the balance of power could have turned stateless communities of Types 2 and 3 into petty states.

Another point of continuity that links Types 2 and 3 to the states is provided by the relation of complementarity which holds between their lineages. This relation, as stressed earlier, makes for a set-up in which different lineages perform different services for the community, or bring out different kinds of office-holders. Here, it seems, we have the prefiguration of an arrangement common in the states: an arrangement in which the ruler is assisted by a council of chiefs who are appointed from the more important lineages of the community on a one-to-one basis, but who have specialised, mutually complementary functions. Some of the Yoruba and Akan states provide good illustrations of this pattern.[53]

Yet another point of continuity, this time between Type 3 and the

50 For a discussion of the earth cult as a source of concepts of sovereignty, see the closing paragraphs of Boston, *op. cit.*

51 For an example of a society where the 'landowning' lineage and the earth-priest are not highly differentiated in status, see Goody, 'Fields of social control . . .'. For examples of earth-priests who are more clearly authority figures, see Murdock, *op. cit.*, chap. 11, pp. 75–6; also Harris, *op. cit.*, pp. 50–72.

52 See Murdock, *op. cit.*, chap. 11; also C. A. Quinn, 'Niumi: a nineteenth-century Mandingo kingdom', *Africa*, xxxviii, 4, 1968, pp. 448–9. A transition from earth-priest to ruler is implied in V. Paques, *Les Bambara*, Paris, 1954, pp. 53–6.

53 For Oyo, see P. Morton-Williams, 'The Yoruba kingdom of Oyo', in *West African Kingdoms in the Nineteenth Century*, ed. D. Forde and P. Kaberry, London, 1967, pp. 52–7. For states in the Ashanti confederation, see R. S. Rattray, *Ashanti Law and Constitution*, Oxford 1929, pp. 77–8, 88–90.

states, is provided by the secret society. Earlier, I showed at some length how the paraphernalia of mystery surrounding this institution could be regarded as a series of devices designed to counteract the rivalry between still-powerful lineages. The same paraphernalia would seem to have an equal potential as supports of state organisation in the face of powerful sectional dissensions. Again, insulated as they are from sectionalism and from all those forms of organisation stressing equivalence and opposition, the secret societies would seem well fitted to act as enclaves for the development of that differentiation and specialisation of political rôles which is essential to the growth of a state apparatus.

It is not surprising, then, that we find secret societies as integral parts of state organisations over much of West Africa. In the east of the area, the best examples come from the kingdoms of the Cameroons and of Yorubaland. Further west, we find them playing key parts in the states of the Mende, the Temne, the Bambara, and other peoples of the far western forest and savannah. Their presence does much to account for the nice constitutional balance which scholars have found to be characteristic of many West African state organisations. For although they function as instruments of the ruler, they have their own independent sources of power which enable them to act as a very effective check on him.[54] Perhaps it is this latter aspect which accounts for the fact that although so widely distributed among West African states, secret societies are notably absent from some of the most powerful and highly centralised of them—including, for example, Dahomey and the Hausa states. For where events have conspired to allow the ruler to gather an overwhelming degree of power into his own hands, he is likely to crush any organisation which poses a serious threat to his absolutism.

The final point of continuity I shall deal with in this brief survey relates to the question of kingship. Now proponents of the Hamitic Hypothesis maintain that it is precisely in their kingships that West African states show most clearly their *lack* of continuity with the stateless societies. First, they hold that something called 'divine kingship' is characteristic of all West African states, and is recognisably the same institution wherever it occurs. Secondly, they hold that this institution has very strong affinities with the kingships of the ancient Near East. Thirdly, they hold that there is nothing corresponding to it in the stateless societies which are the products of

54 The dual rôle of the secret society, as a palliative for sectional cleavages and as a check on the power of the king, has been particularly well analysed for Yoruba and Mende states. For Yoruba, see P. Morton-Williams 'The Egungun society in south-western Yoruba kingdoms', *W.A.I.S.E.R., Proceedings of the Third Annual Conference*, Ibadan, 1956; 'The Yoruba Ogboni cult in Oyo', *Africa*, xxx, 4, 1960; 'The Yoruba kingdom of Oyo', *loc. cit.* See also P. Lloyd, 'Conflict theory and Yoruba kingdoms', in *History and Social Anthropology*, ed. I. Lewis, London, 1968, esp. pp. 41–5. For Mende, see K. Little, 'The political function of the Poro: Part II, *Africa*, xxxvi, 1, 1966; 'The Mende chiefdoms of Sierra Leone' in Forde and Kaberry, *op. cit.*

indigenous African political ideas. Fourthly, they hold that even where the origin myths of the West African kingships do not explicitly point to a non-negro origin, they *do* point to an external origin.[55]

Let us tackle these assertions in turn. First, let us look at the claim that there is some uniform thing called 'divine kingship' which turns up wherever there is state organisation, and that this institution has a strong flavour of the ancient Near East. Now analysts of West African political systems have been pretty free with the label 'divine king', and none too explicit about the actual relation of man to god involved. In fact, a wide range of such relations is found. At the one extreme, there are kings like those of the Akan states and of Dahomey, who appear to be in a close relation to the spirits of their dynastic ancestors, without actually being vehicles of those spirits.[56] At the other extreme, there are kings like the Alafin of Oyo and the Obi of Onitsha, whose bodies, on installation, are apparently imbued with at least some of the powers of the dynastic ancestors or the communal gods.[57] Curiously, though, there is little unambiguous evidence of cases where people believe that the king's body, on installation, is fully taken over by a spirit or god. In West Africa, then, the term 'divine kingship' is little more than an umbrella for a wide range of institutions; and West African kingships seldom approach the fully divinised pattern typical of Egypt and other states of the ancient Near East.

Let us turn next to the claim that there is nothing in the stateless social organisations which corresponds to the institution of 'divine kingship'. Now in the case of those rulers who are in a close association with the spirits but are not in any sense their vehicles, this claim is obviously wrong. For, as we have already seen, the predominantly religious emphasis of the world views of the stateless peoples makes it inevitable that such authority as exists among them should be defined in terms of the spiritual forces underpinning group life, and that holders of such authority should be thought of as backed by these forces. In the case of those rulers (if any) whose bodies are actually conceived of as receptacles of gods, the argument is at first sight a little less implausible. For the lineage, parish and village heads of the stateless societies are not conceived of as divine in this sense. Even here, however, there are significant continuities with stateless social organisations. The reader will recall that factions in the stateless communities often resolve their disputes by calling up spiritual forces onto the head of a medium, and accepting the decision handed down by these forces. Where the spiritual forces concerned are those of the group divided by conflict, they can

55 See reviews of the Hamitic Hypothesis cited above, p. 110, n. 47.
56 See descriptions of Ashanti and Dahomean kingships in K. A. Busia, 'The Ashanti'; and P. Mercier, 'The Fon of Dahomey', both in *African Worlds*, ed. Daryll Forde, London, 1954.
57 For Oyo, see P. Morton-Williams, 'An outline of the cosmology and cult organisation of the Oyo Yoruba', *Africa*, xxxiv, 3, 1964. Talking of the Alafin, Morton-Williams characterises him as 'the vessel for some of Sango's powers'. For Onitsha, see C. K. Meek, *Law and Authority in a Nigerian Tribe*, London, 1937.

almost be said to 'rule' the group for the brief duration of the settlement episode. Now it seems but a short step from such temporary rule by possession to the permanent condition involved in the more full-blooded kind of 'divine kingship'. For the essence of the latter is really no more than a sort of permanent possession, which begins at installation and ends at death.

An item from my own fieldwork experience in fact suggests that under certain conditions, the first kind of kingship could easily pass over into something approaching this second extreme. Thus oral traditions and contemporary traders' accounts relating to the present ruling dynasty in the Niger Delta state of New Calabar suggest that while its first three members were defined as kings of the first kind, its fourth member was well on the way to a 'divine kingship' of a much more full-blooded kind. Amakiri, the dynastic founder, and his sons Amakoro and Karibo, held an office whose definition was a simple extension of ideas about authority current in the village communities of the area. They were thought of as men powerfully backed by ancestral and communal spirits, but not as vehicles of such spirits. Abbi, the fourth member of the dynasty, was thought of in rather different terms. Oral tradition remembers him as 'having the spirits of the town always with him', and as being 'more like a spirit than a man'. Even contemporary traders and administrators sensed that he was different in this respect from his predecessors, and complained about his absorption in 'juju matters'. Unfortunately for our purposes, British administration was established in the area during the latter part of Abbi's reign, so these changes in the definition of the kingly office were cut short at a rather early stage. Clearly, however, Abbi was moving toward a definition of himself as the vehicle of group spiritual forces.

If we accept that these changes were in large measure due to Abbi himself, we are bound to ask about his motives. The answer, I think, lies in the fact that while the first three members of the dynasty had powerful personal followings which they could use to control factional divisions in the community at large, Abbi came to the throne with no such following. Tradition stresses the importance of Abbi's 'more spirit than man' aura in the context of his ability to settle factional disputes. And I think we can understand his development of this aura as a political device to compensate for the human backing which his predecessors relied upon to bolster their rule. This, alas, is an isolated example; but it does show quite vividly how the more full-blooded kind of 'divine kingship' *might* have arisen in the absence of any obvious external influence.[58]

Finally, let us deal with the claim that the mythology of West African

58 For a good picture of the political position of the New Calabar king, see G. I. Jones, *Trading States of the Oil Rivers*, London, 1963. Jones does not deal with the changing relationship between the king and the gods, but he shows very clearly how Abbi came to the throne without the personal following available to Karibo.

kingship always indicates an external origin. This would appear to be no truer than the other claims. As mentioned earlier (p. 112), the mythologies of at least some kingships indicate that the dynastic founders, far from being outsiders, were the earliest arrivals or autochthones of a particular area. Many West African royal dynasties *are* talked of as having come in from elsewhere to conquer the peoples they now rule, or, less frequently, as having been asked in from elsewhere. But there is something a little suspicious about a good many of these traditions of alien origin. In a lot of cases, admittedly, the traditions are corroborated by contemporary written documents, as with the Songhai, Ashanti or Dahomeyan dynastic conquests; or by cultural evidence, as with the Benin-claiming Obiships of the western Ibo. But in other cases, such as those of the Igala and Mossi kingdoms, claims to alien origin are unsupported by corroborative evidence.[59] One suspects that they are as mythical as the claims to a divine aura often made by the same rulers. It begins to look, indeed, as though claims to 'outsider' status, whether divine or human or both, are, above all, means whereby rulers attempt to consolidate their positions in divided societies. In using such means, the rulers are drawing on an ancient and thoroughly indigenous heritage.

It should now be clear that in West Africa, the transition from stateless to state organisation has not, by and large, involved any drastic discontinuities. Rather, it has involved changes of balance and emphasis at the several points of continuity that link the one type of organisation to the other. Let me end this chapter with a brief mention of some of the factors that may have led to such changes.

There can be little doubt about the importance of commerce in relation to West African state formation. A glance at a good historical atlas shows how closely, at any given period, the areas covered by the great states tally with the junctions, termini and tentacles of the major trade routes.[60] Again, the general pattern of development of state organisations, beginning on the sub-Saharan fringe, continuing steadily down into the forest areas, then ending up with a blossoming of small principalities on the Atlantic coast, follows fairly closely the broad pattern of development of the great trade routes.[61]

59 For doubt as to the historicity of traditions asserting the foreign origin of the Igala royal dynasty, see J. S. Boston, 'Oral tradition and the history of Igala', unpublished paper read at a seminar on Non-Written Sources in the Reconstruction of African History held at Ibadan University during the second term of the 1966–67 session. For doubt as to the historicity of similar traditions among the Mossi, see D. Zahan, 'The Mossi kingdoms', in Forde and Kaberry, *op. cit.*, pp. 156–7.
60 See for example J. D. Fage, *An Atlas of African History*, London, 1958.
61 For an early suggestion by a historian that trade rather than alien ideology may have been one of the root causes of state formation in West Africa, see Michael Crowder, *The Story of Nigeria*, rev. ed., London, 1966, pp. 35–6. For a more recent and more detailed discussion of this question, see the opening paragraphs of P. Morton-Williams, 'The influence of habitat and trade on the policies of Oyo and Ashanti', in *Man in Africa*.

More detailed evidence for the importance of trade comes from a number of cultural areas in which most of the communities stayed rooted in agriculture or fishing and remained stateless, whilst a few became involved in major commerce and developed states. One such area is that inhabited by the eastern Ijo peoples of the Niger Delta. A glance at the fishing communities of the area shows us compact agglomerations of unrelated lineages, with founding lineages responsible for bringing out largely symbolic village heads, and with strong age grades cross-cutting the segments. In those communities that switched from fishing to the Atlantic Trade, the founding lineages became royal lineages, and the village heads became more or less powerful kings. These kings had no monopoly of trade; but their position was powerfully boosted by the fact that the European traders held them responsible for the safety of their personnel and ships, and in consideration paid them a substantial protection money known as 'comey'.[62]

Another such area is that inhabited by the Mbembe-speaking peoples of the middle Cross River. Here there are three groups of villages, two of which remained attached to yam-farming, whilst the third entered deeply into the nineteenth-century trade between the Cross River and the Cameroons, becoming particularly involved in the arms traffic. In all three groups, there were village heads who were at once heads of senior lineages and priests of communal earth cults. In the two purely agricultural groups, these heads had largely symbolic and priestly rôles, and could hardly be described as 'rulers'. In the trading group, one of these heads came to exercise a measure of real authority, not only over his own village but also over all the other villages of the group. As a student of the Mbembe puts it, he became the chiefly head of a 'pocket state'. Here again, the ruler had no monopoly of the trade; but his position was nevertheless boosted by protection and its rewards.[63]

Before leaving this topic, we should note two prominent negative cases: those of Tiv and Ibo. Though many Tiv and Ibo groups remained almost exclusively rooted in subsistence agriculture through the nineteenth and early twentieth centuries, others became extensively involved in trade. But although in these latter groups wealth became an avenue to prestige and leadership,[64] there was no corresponding growth of state organisation. What is of special interest about these two negative cases is that both involve areas of Type I social organisation. Tiv country, at least, conforms wholly to Type I, whilst a good deal of Ibo country does so too. Far from casting doubt on the importance of trade in state-formation, then, they

62 For the development of the New Calabar state in response to the Atlantic trade, see Jones, *Trading States of the Oil Rivers*; also Horton, *op. cit.*, 1969.

63 For the development of an Mbembe state, see Harris, *op. cit.*, pp. 151–98.

64 For trade and wealth as an avenue to prestige among Tiv, see Bohannan and Bohannan, *op. cit.*, pp. 31–6, 53. For a number of references to Ibo trade in palm products and other commodities, and to titles based on the wealth accruing from such trade, see Forde and Jones, *op. cit.*

lend support to my earlier remarks about the differential suitability of Types 1, 2, and 3 as raw materials for state-building.

These few examples show the considerable potential of studies of particular cultural areas in which some communities have remained agricultural whilst others have become involved in commerce. A little ingenuity should unearth many more such areas.

Other factors involved in state formation emerge from the picture a good deal less clearly than commerce. Warfare, perhaps, was of some importance. Thus the need for prolonged periods of defensive vigilance seems to have stimulated the growth of little kingdoms among certain peoples living on the borders of large, predatory states. In such places, where it seemed feasible to stand and organise defence rather than cut and run, people willingly granted greater powers to their community heads.

Of late, it has even been suggested that chronically destructive internal divisions may, in certain circumstances, have acted as stimuli toward state formation in previously stateless communities. Harris believes this to have been a contributory factor in the rise of the Adun 'pocket state' among the Cross River Mbembe. She suggests that because the Adun people were under strong external pressures, they reacted to their chronic internal schisms not by agreeing to split up, but by according more power to the senior *ovat* or earth-priest, who was then able to take effective action on the internal situation. The suggestion, in other words, is that whereas in the ordinary way, chronic internal disputes tended to bring about fission in the stateless societies, internal disputes combined with a strong external threat tended rather to bring about state formation.[65] The hypothesis certainly merits testing against other West African data, if suitable situations can be found.

It seems that state organisation, once developed, spread rather readily from those who had it to those who did not. One way in which this happened was by conquest. Rulers conquered neighbouring peoples to extend their control over trade routes and entrepôts. They also conquered in order to acquire a large taxable population: for during the period we are concerned with, most parts of the area had an agricultural technology efficient enough to permit the extraction of sizeable crop surpluses which could be used to maintain a corps of specialist administrators.[66]

Another probable way in which state organisation spread from those who had it to those who did not was by more or less voluntary borrowing. Social anthropologists are apt to give the impression that members of stateless societies are tremendously happy with their lot, and that they never cast envious glances at the great states which are often their neighbours. That this is not so can easily be gathered from the folklore of such

65 Harris, *op. cit.*, pp. 151–98.

66 For a discussion of this and other types of exploitation in the pre-colonial African states, see R. Armstrong, 'State Formation in Negro Africa', unpublished Ph.D. thesis, University of Chicago.

peoples, which frequently betrays fascination with life in the great states. In West Africa, unfortunately, the historian and the anthropologist have not been able to see with their own eyes the spectacle of people deliberately submitting to or acquiring kingly rule in order to exchange the relatively insecure life of a stateless area for the peace and freedom to be enjoyed within a large state. But the work of Southall in East Africa has alerted us to the fact that such things can happen.[67] And in West Africa, many of the better-corroborated traditions of 'outside' origins of royal dynasties suggest voluntary acceptance rather than conquest. Examples are the Benin tradition of an Ife dynasty, the western Ibo traditions of Benin dynasties,[68] and the traditions of Mande expansion in the Western Sudan.[69] Other communities, such as those of the western Niger Delta, have circumstantial traditions of borrowing the apparatus of kingship, though not kings, from their stately neighbours.[70]

For stateless communities accustomed to making use of outsiders in the settlement of their disputes, there would have been nothing particularly odd about asking stately neighbours to send them kings, or even about welcoming such kings when they appeared unasked. Indeed, many so-called conquests were probably subtle blends of compulsion and acceptance.

By now, I hope, the reader will have come to see that in reconstructing the history of West Africa, we need to invoke no mysterious Hamitic *Führerprinzip* in order to understand the transition from statelessness to state organisation. In repudiating the Hamitic Hypothesis, of course, we must avoid the opposite extreme of denying any trans-Saharan influence on pre-colonial West African political development. We know that the scale and efficiency of administration in several of the great states owed much to the presence of literate Muslim chamberlains who hailed from over the desert. We also know that the ideology of Islam itself contributed immensely to the power of the great kings of the Western Sudan. Nonetheless, the balance of the evidence makes it seem likely that a good deal of the basic business of state formation took place through the development of indigenous principles of social organisation.

67 A. Southall, *Alur Society*, Cambridge, n.d. (1955?)

68 For these, see R. Bradbury, *The Benin Kingdom* (Ethnographic Survey of Africa), London, 1957; and D. Forde and G. I. Jones, *op. cit.*

69 Goody's (*The Ethnography of the Northern Territories* . . .) summary of oral tradition and linguistic evidence bearing on Mande expansion in the Western Sudan leaves it very much open as to whether such expansion depended upon force of arms or upon the prestige accruing from trade, literacy, governmental know-how, and other skills. Zahan (*loc. cit.*, p. 156) raises the question of whether the relatively small numbers that seem to have been involved in this expansion were in any way sufficient for forcible domination.

70 For a brief mention of kingship in the western Niger Delta, apparently borrowed from Benin, see my 'A note on recent finds of brasswork in the Niger Delta', *Odu*, ii, no. 1, 1965.

CHAPTER 4

The early states of the Western Sudan to 1500

NEHEMIA LEVTZION

The agricultural revolution and the introduction of iron ore were two of the most significant developments in the prehistory of West Africa. With them the stage was set for the subsequent developments, those of the historical period, when the growth of long distance trade and the process of state building were the dominant themes. In the Western Sudan these were followed by the spread of Islam.

Arabic sources provide the earliest contemporary evidence about the trade and states that flourished in the Western Sudan before 1500. Al-Fazārī, writing towards the end of the eighth century, describes the extensive kingdom of 'Ghana the land of gold'.[1] The fame of Ghana reached beyond the Sahara, even as far as Baghdad, where al-Fazārī lived at the court of the Abbasid Caliph. By then, Ghana must have been a kingdom of some antiquity, though the date of its foundation cannot be fixed with any certainty. There is, however, little doubt that the emergence of Ghana, located in the Sahil—'the shore' of the huge sea of sand—is to be associated with the growth of traffic across the Sahara.

The introduction of the camel into the Sahara, at the beginning of the Christian era, caused a significant revolution in the desert. Horses and bullocks used before that period afforded limited mobility to the Berbers of the northern fringes of the Sahara, both in their nomadism and in their commercial relations with the countries to the south. The chariots, depicted by rock paintings across the Sahara, clearly suggest trans-Saharan contacts, but according to the available evidence the volume of the trade carried over the desert had been insignificant before the introduction of the camel.[2]

1 Quoted in al-Mas'ūdī, *Murūj al-dhahab; les praieries d'or*, texte et trad. C. Barbier de Meynard et Pavet de Courteille, Paris, 1861–77, iv, pp. 37–8.
2 R. Mauny, *Tableau géographique de l'ouest africain au moyen âge*, Dakar, 1961, pp. 287–9, 299.

Scholars have yet to explain why the camel had not reached the Sahara earlier than the beginning of the Christian era. Once the North African nomads became acquainted with this highly useful animal, they lost no time in adopting it. Mounted on camels, the nomad tribes, roaming beyond the *limes* which protected the agricultural population of Roman Africa, began to move southwards into the Sahara. They settled the oases in the middle of the desert, and reached its southern fringes. From the earliest Arabic records we learn of Berber tribes inhabiting the western and central Sahara, from North Africa to *Bilād al-Sūdān*, 'the land of the Black Peoples'. Most of the Saharan nomad Berbers belonged to the great confederation of the Ṣanhāja, which also counted among its members sedentary tribes of North Africa. The close ties between the Ṣanhāja of the Sahara and the Maghrib, as recorded between the ninth and eleventh centuries, indicate not only a common origin to both parties, but also suggest that their separation and dispersion over the huge desert had taken place not very long before. Constant communication was maintained between the Berbers on both shores of the Sahara, who, with their camels, bridged the desert, and carried an ever-growing trade, in which south-bound salt was exchanged for northbound gold.

When the Ṣanhāja nomads reached the southern fringes of the Sahara, this region was by no means empty. Archaeological and traditional evidence confirm that the sedentary Sudanese Negro population had previously extended farther north from its present habitation, covering the Hodh, Tagant, and Adrar. The gradual desiccation of the Sahara, caused by climatic changes, initiated the retreat of the sedentary population, and this retreat was accelerated by the invading nomads, who pushed the Sudanese southwards. Only isolated communities of Sudanese, the *haratin*, were left behind as subjects of the nomads, Berbers and later Moors. So the southern fringes of the Sahara changed both its population—from Sudanese to white Berbers and Moors—and its landscape—from cultivated land to nomads' domain.[3]

Some time between the second and the fifth centuries, the northern among the Sudanese peoples—Wolof-Serer, Soninke, and Songhay—came into direct contact with the newcomers from across the Sahara. This contact, accompanied by the well-known pressure of nomads on sedentary peoples, stimulated development of political organisation among the Sudanese. Historical traditions of the latter often attribute the creation of the early states, associated with their own ancestors, to dynasties of white origin. There are two ways of examining these traditions. One is to regard them as reflecting actual historical events, which may be explained by the imposition of alien rule, that of aggressive warlike nomads over a peaceful sedentary population. On the other hand the same traditions may be taken

3 *Ibid.*, pp. 199–211.

as projecting values of later periods back to the past: an attempt to raise the prestige of noble clans by claiming white origin, which, under Islamic influence, takes the form of an Arab or *sharifian* descent. Significantly, none of the early Arabic sources until the mid-twelfth century implies white origin to ruling dynasties in Takrūr, Ghana, or Songhay. Yet, since that period—with al-Idrīsī—this theme becomes more and more frequent. This may be associated with the spread of Islam, because al-Idrīsī was the first Arabic author to describe events after the Almoravids' conquest. The two Sudanese *Ta'rīkhs* of the seventeenth century—presenting oral traditions—suggest white origin for the earlier rulers of Ghana and Songhay. Current traditions are even more affirmative, claiming white origin for many, too many, local dynasties, and drawing on the stock of Muslim historiography for adopting historical and legendary persons as their ancestors. It might have been easier to admit white origin for a few early dynasties than for the many which claim it, but one is tempted to apply the same critical view to the former as to the latter.

Even if white nomads did not intervene directly in the process of state building, by furnishing dynasties, it is likely that their presence and pressure contributed to that process. The Sudanese had to mobilise their own social and political resources and reorganise themselves on a larger scale in order to face the pressure from the north. Not less important for this political development was the growth of the trans-Saharan trade during the centuries preceding the Arab conquest of North Africa. Berbers carried the trade and controlled it across the Sahara, but the gold came from farther inland, from beyond a country inhospitable to the desert people and their camels. The gold was carried by Sudanese traders from its sources in the south to the Sahil, where it was exchanged for the salt brought there by the Berbers from mines in the Sahara. In the Sahil goods changed hands and were transported by asses, bullocks and porters instead of camels.

Ṣaḥil is the Arabic word for 'a shore', which is well understood if the desert is compared to a sea of sand, and the camel to a ship. Hence the towns which developed in the Sahil—Takrūr, Ghana, and Gao—may be regarded as ports. These towns became both commercial entrepôts and political centres. Their rulers endeavoured to extend their authority in order to achieve an effective control over the trade. Trade stimulated a higher level of political organisation, while the emergence of extensive states accorded more security to trade routes. Subsequent historical developments in the Western Sudan may be better understood by tracing changing patterns of intercontinental and trans-Saharan trade.

The Arab conquest of North Africa gave the trans-Saharan trade a new impetus by linking it with a vast empire, anxious to obtain as much as possible of its gold, on which the monetary system of the Muslim world depended. Traders from the eastern parts of the Muslim world, mainly from Iraq, were attracted to towns at the northern end of the trans-Saharan

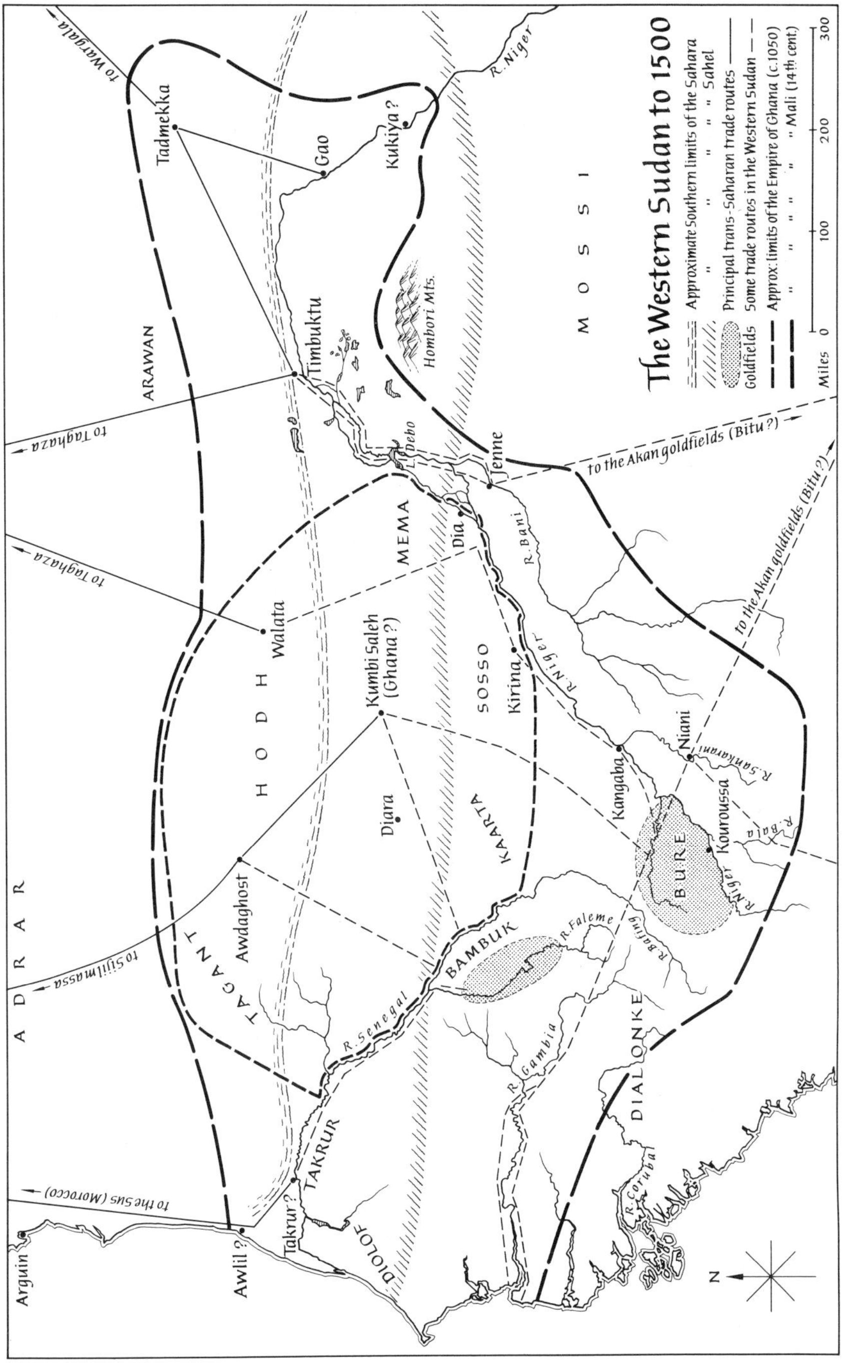
The Western Sudan to 1500
Approximate Southern limits of the Sahara
" " " " Sahel
Principal trans-Saharan trade routes
Some trade routes in the Western Sudan
Goldfields
Approx: limits of the Empire of Ghana (c.1050)
" " " " Mali (14th cent.)
Miles 0 100 200 300
to Wargala
Tadmekka
Gao
Kukiya ?
R. Niger
ARAWAN
Timbuktu
Hombori Mts.
M O S S I
to Taghaza
to Taghaza
L. Debo
Jenne
to the Akan goldfields (Bitu ?)
to the Akan goldfields (Bitu ?)
MEMA
Dia
R. Bani
Walata
H O D H
Kumbi Saleh (Ghana ?)
SOSSO
Kirina
R. Niger
Niani
R. Sankarani
Kangaba
Kouroussa
R. Baja
BURE
R. Niger
Diara
KAARTA
A D R A R
Awdaghost
to Sijilmassa
TAGANT
BAMBUK
R. Faleme
R. Bafing
R. Senegal
R. Gambia
DIALONKE
TAKRUR
Takrur ?
to the Sus (Morocco)
Arguin
Awlil ?
DJOLOF
R. Corubal
N

4:1

trails, such as Zuwaila in Fezzan and Sijilmasa in Morocco.[4] The spread of Islam among the North African Berbers was rather slow, but among the earliest converts were the urban population and enterprising traders. Hence, during the eighth and ninth centuries, most of the traders engaged in the trans-Saharan trade were Muslims. These Muslim traders brought Islam to the Saharan nomads and sowed its first seeds in the Sudan.

In the commercial centres of the Sahil the North African Muslim traders came in contact with two elements of the local population: with the Sudanese traders between the termini of the trans-Saharan trails and the gold sources, and with the rulers of the Sudanese states, who controlled the trade. Islam began to win converts among traders and rulers, and for a long time it was limited to these two influential elements. On the other hand, Islam left little impression among the stateless peoples or the commoners, whose way of life had hardly been changed by their incorporation into the political framework of the states. Patterns of trade and of political organisation conditioned the spread of Islam, while on the other hand Islam played an important rôle in the fortunes of the Sudanese states, both as an external force (Ghana facing the Almoravids), and as an internal factor of cohesion or disintegration. The history of the Western Sudan revolves, therefore, round these three themes: trade, states, and Islam.

THE SONINKE STATE OF GHANA

The Soninke are the northern among the peoples of the great Mande family, whose other branches extend as far south as the forest. In their northern position, the Soninke had the longest contact with the white nomads of the Sahara, and it is sometimes suggested that the name Sarakollé, a synonym for Soninke, means 'red (white) people'.[5] Yet, whatever contribution the white nomads may have made to the ethnic composition of the Soninke, more important historically is the fact that their pressure uprooted many Soninke communities, which spread southwards in various directions. On the Senegal, the Gambia and the Niger there are clans which claim to be Soninke, though some do not even speak their original language any more. They are united by their national consciousness, and by their pride in having once been part of the ancient Soninke kingdom of Wagadu. Everywhere in their dispersion the bards tell the legend of Wagadu, a tradition with many versions, but one theme.[6]

4 al-Yaʿqūbī, *Kitāb al-Buldān*, ed. M. J. de-Goeje, Lugduni Batavorum, 1892, p. 345; (*Les pays*, trad. G. Wiet, Cairo, 1937, p. 205). Ibn-Ḥawqal, *Kitāb Ṣurat al-Arḍ*, ed. J. H. Kramers, Lugduni Batavorum, 1938, p. 61 (*Configuration de la terre*, trad. J. H. Kramers et G. Wiet, Paris, 1964, p. 58).

5 M. Delafosse, 'Le Gāna et le Mali et l'emplacement de leurs capitales', *Bulletin du Comité d'Etudes Historiques et Scientifiques de l'Afrique Occidentale Français*, 1924, p. 494.

6 The many different versions of this tradition have been collated by Ch. Monteil, 'La Légende du Ouagadou et l'origine des Soninké' in *Melanges Ethnologiques*, Mem. de l'Institut Français de l'Afrique Noire, no. 23, Dakar, 1953, pp. 359–408.

Wagadu was a prosperous kingdom, with its capital at Kumbi, a town in the part of the Sahil still known to the Soninke by the name of Wagadu. Its kings bore the title of *Magha* or *Manga*, and were of the Sisse patronymic group. Wagadu was blessed with vast quantities of gold, replenished annually, thanks to the guardian of the kingdom, a snake. The snake was worshipped in an annual sacrifice of a virgin. Catastrophe came about when the lover of the virgin chosen to be sacrificed killed the snake. The dying snake pronounced a dreadful curse, causing the desiccation of the land and the cessation of the gold, which moved to Bure on the Upper Niger. As a result the people dispersed and their country turned into desert.

From current traditions let us turn back to traditions recorded three or four centuries ago. In reviewing the political history of the Western Sudan, the two *Ta'rīkhs* from Timbuktu mention traditions about the kingdom of Kaya-Magha as predecessor of Mali. The author of *Ta'rīkh al-Fattāsh* says: 'Mali rose to power only after the downfall of the kingdom of Kaya-Magha, ruler of the west. . . . Kaya-Magha in the Waʿkore [Soninke] language means "king of gold" . . . . The name of his capital was Qunbi, an important town.' In the middle of the seventeenth century, al-Saʿdī wrote: 'The first kingdom in that part of the world was that of Kaya-Magha. His capital was Ghana, an important town in the country of Baghana.'[7]

The current traditions about Wagadu and the older traditions about the kingdom of Kaya-Magha refer, in all probability, to the same ancient kingdom of the Soninke. 'Wagadu' in Soninke and 'Baghana' in Malinke are two names for the same region. Other parallels are the memory of gold, the recurrence of the title 'Magha', and the reference to Kumbi as the capital. It was this reference to Kumbi by *T. al-Fattāsh* and oral traditions that led to the hypothesis that Kumbi-Saleh, in the south-eastern corner of Mauritania, may have been the capital of that kingdom. Excavations carried out there have revealed the remains of a Muslim town, abandoned probably about the thirteenth century. This may have been the Muslim ward of the capital of Ghana, described by al-Bakrī in 1067–8.[8] Al-Bakrī placed the capital in Awkar, which is the Berber name for the region of Wagadu. Al-Saʿdī's identification of the kingdom of Kaya-Magha with that of Ghana seems plausible. The ancient Soninke kingdom which figures as legendary in oral traditions becomes concrete in documentary evidence. Indeed, the historical elements in the traditions fit rather well with what can be learned from contemporary Arabic sources.

7 *Ta'rīkh al-Fattāsh*, texte arabe et trad. fr., O. Houdas et M. Delafosse, Paris, 1913–14 (repr. 1964), p. 41 (trans. pp. 75–6). Al-Saʿdi, *Ta'rīkh al-Sūdān*, texte arabe éd. et trad., O. Houdas, Paris, 1900 (repr. 1964), p. 9 (trans. p. 18). On the author of *T. al-Fattāsh*, see N. Levtzion, 'A seventeenth century chronicle by Ibn al-Mukhtār: a critical review of *Ta'rīkh al-Fattāsh*', *Bull. S.O.A.S.*, 1971 (in press).

8 P. Thomassey, et R. Mauny, 'Campagne de fouilles à Koumbi Saleh (Ghana?)', *Bulletin de l'Institut Français de l'Afrique Noire*, ser. B., 1956, pp. 117–40. R. Mauny, 'The question of Ghana', *Africa*, 1954, pp. 200–13.

Since its first mention by al-Fazārī towards the end of the eighth century, Ghana, 'the land of gold', is referred to by all Arab geographers who had anything to say about the Sudan. Yet very little is said in these sources about the kingdom, beyond its rôle in the gold trade and some reference to its relations with the Berbers on its borders.[9] We have to wait until 1067–8, when al-Bakrī—relying on information collected from visitors to the Sudan—wrote an exceptionally detailed description of Ghana and its neighbours.

Though al-Bakrī used the name Ghana for both the kingdom and its capital, he says explicitly that 'Ghana is the title of their kings'. *Gāna* or *kāna* in Malinke still has the meaning of a war chief.[10] The reigning king in 1067–8 was *Tunka* Menin, who ascended the throne in 1063, succeeding his maternal uncle, King Basī. 'It is their custom that a king is succeeded only by his sister's son.' Matrilineal succession prevailed among the Berbers of the southern Sahara, and may suggest a Berber influence on the ruling dynasty.[11]

'The king's conduct is praiseworthy, being a lover of justice and favourable to Muslims. . . . Tunka Menin wields great power and inspires respect as the ruler of a great empire.' Sons of the vassal kings are present in the king's audience, the ceremonial pomp of which is vividly described. The king can mobilise a great army of bowmen and cavalry. He levies taxes on imported salt and exported gold, as well as on other merchandise. The best nuggets found in his country's mines are appropriated by the king, and only the gold dust is left for the people, 'otherwise gold would be so abundant that its value would depreciate'.

> The city of Ghana consists of two towns situated on a plain. One of these towns is inhabited by Muslims. It is large and possesses a dozen mosques, one being for the Friday prayer, and each having imams, muezzins and salaried reciters of the Koran. There are jurisconsults and scholars. Around the town are sweet wells, which they use for drinking and for cultivating vegetables. The royal city, called al-Ghāba [grove] is six miles away, and the area between the two towns is covered with habitations. Their houses are constructed of stone and acacia wood. The king has a palace with conical huts [around], surrounded by a fence like a wall. In the king's town, not far from the royal court, is a mosque for the use of Muslims who visit the king on missions. . . . The interpreters of the king are Muslims, as are his treasurer and the majority of his ministers.

9 Ghana is described among others by al-Yaʿqūbī (870), Ibn al-Faqīh al-Hamadhānī (d. probably 903), Ibn-Ḥawqal (977).

10 Delafosse, 'Le Gana et le Mali', p. 487.

11 On matrilineal succession among the Masufa of Walata, see Ibn-Baṭṭūṭa, *Tuḥfat al-Nuẓār fī Gharā'ib al-Amsār wa-'Ajāib al-Asfār (Voyages)*, texte arabe et trad. fr., C. Defremery et B. R. Sanguinetti, Paris, 1922, iv, p. 388.

> Their religion is paganism, and the worship of idols. . . . Around the royal town are domed dwellings, woods and copses where live their sorcerers, those in charge of their religious cults. There are also their idols and their kings' tombs. . . . When the king dies they construct a large dome of wood over the burial place. . . . They put [into the grave] the king's ornaments and arms, his eating and drinking vessels, food and drink, and bring in those people who used to serve his food and drink. Then the dome's entrance is locked. . . . They sacrifice for their dead and make offerings of intoxicating drink.[12]

A mighty king, the ruler of Ghana administered justice in his kingdom, controlled its trade, and extended its sphere of influence over neighbouring territories. The king himself kept to his ancestral religion, which accorded him some superhuman dimension, but was liberal towards Muslims, strangers and subjects. Muslims were important not only in trade, but also in administration, where they were distinguished by their literacy.

The extent of Ghana's dominions may only be guessed by following al-Bakrī's information about other towns and kingdoms in the Western Sudan. To the west, the Senegal river formed the border between Ghana and the independent kingdom of Takrur; in the south, Ghana's authority touched the gold-bearing region of Bambuk (at the confluence of the Senegal and the Faleme rivers), stopping short of the Mandingue mountains; to the east Ghana reached the Niger, while to the north it dominated, until 1054/5, the Berber town of Awdaghost.[13]

At this period, the middle of the eleventh century, Ghana reached its zenith. In 1076, only nine years after al-Bakrī's literary memorial to the greatness of Ghana had been written down, this kingdom, mistress of the Western Sudan, was overrun by the Almoravids.

THE ALMORAVID MOVEMENT AND ITS AFTERMATH

The conquest of Ghana by the Almoravids (Arabic: *al-Murābitūn*) came after a long period of tension between this Sudanese state and its northern neighbours, the Ṣanhāja nomads, also known as 'the people of the veil'. The three important tribes of the southern Sahara—Juddāla, Lamtūna, and Masūfa—came under a loose confederation, with a certain degree of central authority, to ensure control over the trans-Saharan trade. Awdaghost, an oasis in the desert fifteen or twenty days' march north-west of Ghana, was the commercial centre of the Berbers.

12 *Al-Bakrī, Al-Masālik wa-'l-Mamālik; Kitāb al-Mughrib fī dhikr Bilād Ifrīqīya wa'l-Maghrib* [1067/8], *Description de l'Afrique Septentrionale*, Paris, 1911–13 (repr. 1965), pp. 174–7 (trans. pp. 327–31). The passages were rearranged in the quotations. Here and elsewhere the translation of the Arabic text was compared with the passages quoted by J. S. Trimingham, *A History of Islam in West Africa*, Oxford, 1962.

13 See Mauny, *Tableau*, pp. 509–10.

Awdaghost is first mentioned by al-Yaʿqūbī in 891. Its king, a pagan, raided the peoples of the Sudan to the south.[14] From later sources of the fourteenth century—Ibn abī Zarʿ and Ibn Khaldūn—we learn of a dynasty which ruled over the Ṣanhāja from the beginning of the ninth century to 918–19, when internal troubles caused its collapse. In 951–2 Ibn Ḥawqal recorded the name of the king of Awdaghost who had been reigning for twenty years, while al-Bakrī mentioned a king of Awdaghost, who held authority in 961–71.[15] All these sources imply that the Ṣanhāja rulers of the ninth and tenth centuries extended their authority over both Berber and Sudanese peoples. During these centuries Ghana seems to have been on the defensive. The king of Awdaghost of 961–71 intervened in the affairs of the Sudan, by aiding the chief of Māsin against that of Awghām, the latter having been a tributary to Ghana.

The unity of the Ṣanhāja, however, went through periodical crises. One of these crises occurred in 918–19; another probably towards the end of the tenth century, because al-Bakrī tells us that before the Almoravid conquest of Awdaghost, in 1054–5, this town had been subject to Ghana. The Almoravids treated Awdaghost with much severity because its people had paid allegiance to the ruler of Ghana.

Prominent in the population of Awdaghost were North African traders, Arabs and Zenāta. The latter were members of a Berber confederation, and were rivals and enemies of the Ṣanhāja. In 976 Zenāta became masters of Sijilmasa at the northern end of the trans-Saharan route. Hence in the first half of the eleventh century the Ṣanhāja of the Sahara had enemies in control of the two important oases—Awdaghost and Sijilmasa—at both ends of the route of which they had previously been the sole masters. In this situation the Ṣanhāja tribes—Juddāla, Lamtūna, and Masūfa—reunited to regain authority over the whole of the Sahara and its trade.[16]

By that time Islam had spread among the Ṣanhāja nomads, and their political regeneration had a flavour of Islamic zeal. Their leader Tarsina,

14 Yaʿqūbī, *K. al-Buldān*, p. 360 (*Les pays*, p. 277).

15 Ibn Khaldūn, *Kitāb Taʾrikh al-Duwal al-Islāmīya bi'l-Maghrib*, pub. M. G. de Slane, Alger, 1847, i, pp. 236–7 (*Histoire des Berbères et des dynasties musulmanes de l'Afrique du Nord*, trad. par M. G. de Slane, nouv, trad. par P. Casanova, Paris, 1925–56, ii, pp. 65–7). Ibn Abī Zarʿ, *Rawḍ al-Qirtās*, ed. Tornberg, 1939, p. 43 (*Histoire des souverains du Maghreb et annales de la ville de Fes*, trad. par A. Beaumier, Paris, 1860, p. 167). Ibn-Ḥawqal, *Ṣūrat*, p. 100 (*Configuration*, p. 98). Al-Bakrī, *al-Masālik*, p. 159 (trans. pp. 351–2).

16 The sources for the Almoravid movement are: al-Bakrī, *al-Masālik*, pp. 164–70 (trans. pp. 311–20); Ibn Abī-Zarʿ, *Rawḍ*, pp. 43–9 (*Histoire*, pp. 169–89); Ibn Khaldūn, *K. Taʾrīkh*, i, pp. 237–9 (*Histoire*, ii, pp. 67–73). These sources do not agree in all details, and what follows is a result of the collation of these texts. See also P. Semonin, 'The Almoravid Movement in the Western Sudan, a review of the evidence', *Transactions of the Historical Society of Ghana*, vii, 1964, pp. 42–59. P. F. de Moares Farias, 'The Almoravids: some questions concerning the character of the movement during its periods of closest contact with the Western Sudan', *Bull. I.F.A.N.*, xxix, 1967, pp. 794–878. N. Levtzion, 'Abdallāh ibn Yāsīn and the Almoravids' in *Studies on the History of Islam in West Africa*, ed. J. R. Willis, London (in press).

of the Lamtūna, went on pilgrimage. Back in the Sahara he launched a war against the Sudanese (directed probably against Ghana), but was killed in 1023. His successor and son-in-law, Yaḥyā b. Ibrāhīm, was of the Juddāla, the most western of the Ṣanhāja tribes on the Ocean side. He also went to Mecca in 1035. On his way back he visited Qairawān, where he conferred with the famous *faqīh* (jurist) Abū ʿImrān b. ʿIsā (died 1038). Their conversation revealed how superficial Islam was among the Ṣanhāja of the desert. Yaḥyā asked for a disciple who would accompany him to teach his people the true doctrine. None of the scholars in Qairawān was ready to undertake the hardship of the Sahara, and Yaḥyā was directed to Wajjāj ibn Zalwī of Naffīs (or Malkūs) in southern Morocco. Wajjāj, a Ṣanhāja of the Lamṭa tribe, was the head of *Dār al-Murābiṭīn*, a centre devoted to worship, study, and the propagation of the faith. This was a centre of the orthodox Māliki school in southern Morocco, where heretical tendencies were widespread. It was also a stronghold of the Ṣanhāja facing the Zenāta advance. There Yaḥyā found a ready response. Indeed it seems that Wajjāj saw from the beginning great prospects for his own cause in alliance with the southern Ṣanhāja.

Yaḥyā was accompanied to the Sahara by ʿAbdallāh ibn Yāsīn, a disciple of Wajjāj. ʿAbdallāh started his preaching among the Juddāla, Yaḥyā's tribe, but had little success. After Yaḥyā's death the Juddāla even turned against ʿAbdallāh, who was ready, in his despair, to give up his mission. But, encouraged by his master Wajjāj and supported by two Lamtūna brothers, Yaḥyā and Abū-Bakr, sons of ʿUmar, ʿAbdallāh retreated to consolidate his power, before coercing the Berbers into accepting his authority. When he came back, the Lamtūna rallied to his cause, but the Juddāla had to be forced into acceptance. The latter remained reluctant and troublesome. Once his authority had been established over the Saharan tribes, ʿAbdallāh took his force northwards to attack Sijilmasa, responding to the call of his master Wajjāj. The conquest of Sijilmasa served the cause of both partners to the movement of the *Murabiṭūn*, and helped to cement the alliance between Wajjāj and the Ṣanhāja of the desert. The same year, 1054–5, ʿAbdallāh drove back southwards to capture Awdaghost, accomplishing the recovery of the Ṣanhāja power throughout the Sahara, and in the two termini of the route.

While the Almoravids were fighting at Awdaghost, their garrison at Sijilmasa was massacred. This could not have been left unavenged, and the main force was taken once again to the north. Yet Yaḥyā b. ʿUmar, the military commander of the Almoravids, had to stay behind to deal with a mutiny of the Juddāla. In the battle which followed Yaḥyā was defeated and killed (1056–7), while the Juddāla seceded definitely from the Almoravid movement.

Abū-Bakr b. ʿUmar succeeded his brother as the military commander. After the second conquest of Sijilmasa he was engaged, together with

ʿAbdallāh ibn Yāsīn, in conquering southern Morocco. In the fighting against the heretic Barghawāta ʿAbdallāh was killed (1059). While fighting in Morocco was going on Abū-Bakr heard of a new mutiny in the desert. The Sahara was the base of the Almoravids, the source of their power since their new recruits came from there. Abū-Bakr therefore hurried back to restore order at home, leaving behind his cousin Yūsup. Tashufīn as deputy in Morocco. Abū-Bakr pacified the Sahara, but his way back to leadership in Morocco was barred by Ibn Tashufīn, who forced him back to the desert. Thus, the Almoravid movement split into two. One part under Ibn Tashufīn established an empire over Morocco and Spain, carrying further its religious mission in securing the predominance of the Māliki *fuqahā'* ; the other remained in the Sahara, under Abū-Bakr b. ʿUmar.

It was at that stage only, after having been deprived of authority in the north, that Abū-Bakr turned against the kingdom of Ghana. The fighting probably spanned several years, and Ghana was conquered in 1076–7.[17] The Almoravids' conquest destroyed the power of Ghana, contributed to the Islamisation of the Soninke, and accelerated their dispersion. Yet the Almoravids' domination over the Sudan was short. In 1087 their leader Abū-Bakr was killed in fighting against the Sudanese in Tagant, and after his death the Almoravid movement in the Sahara disintegrated and passed away.

The Almoravid episode weakened not only the kingdom of Ghana, but also the Ṣanhāja of the south-western Sahara. Their best contingents were absorbed in Morocco and Spain. Those which remained in the desert lost much of their warlike nature. This made easier the invasion of the Banū Ḥassan, Arab nomads, during the fourteenth and fifteenth centuries. The Ṣanhāja were subjugated, and some were reduced to the status of clients, known as the Zenaga. Others carried on the Islamic legacy of the Almoravids, by retreating to *zawāyā*, centres of learning. These formed the clans of the Marabouts, who under the Arabs retained their prestige as holy men.[18]

Following the collapse of the Almoravid movement, Ghana regained its independence. According to al-Idrīsī, writing in 1153–4, Ghana was still the greatest kingdom in the Western Sudan. Its trade flourished, and vast quantities of gold enriched its king. The most remarkable change noted by al-Idrīsī was the spread of Islam; the king and many of his subjects were Muslims.[19] Al-Idrīsī's account, however, seems deficient, probably because his sources belonged to different periods, and he handled them

17 The date is given by al-Zuhrī (*floruit* 1137), quoted in Youssouf Kamal, *Monumenta Cartographica Africae et Aegypti*, Leide 1934, vol. iii, fasc. iii, p. 802.

18 See, F. de la Chapelle, 'Esquisse d'une histoire du Sahara occidental', *Hésperis*, xi, 1931, pp. 35–95.

19 Al-Idrīsī, *Kitāb Nuzhat al-Mushtāq fī Ikhtirāq al-Afāq (Description de l'Afrique et de l'Espagne)*, ed. et trad. R. Dozy et M. J. De Goeje, Leyde, 1866, pp. 6–7 (trans. pp. 7–8).

carelessly. His contemporary, Abū Ḥāmid al-Andalūsī (writing in 1162), adds hardly anything on the political situation, and like al-Idrīsī he was more interested in the gold trade.[20] These were the last authors who could furnish contemporary evidence on Ghana, because this kingdom was eliminated early in the thirteenth century.

THE EMPIRE OF MALI

Ibn-Khaldūn, the great Arab historian of the fourteenth century, relying on previous Arabic sources and on oral traditions he had collected from Sudanese visitors to North Africa, summarily relates the political history of the Western Sudan from the eleventh to the thirteenth centuries:

> The authority of Ghana waned and its prestige declined as that of the veiled people—neighbours on the north next to the land of the Berbers—grew. The latter triumphed over the Sudanese, destroyed their dwellings and country, levied tribute, forced many of them to join Islam, and subjugated them.
>
> Consequently the authority of the rulers of Ghana dwindled away, and they fell under the domination of the Sosso people—their Sudanese neighbours—who subdued and crushed them completely.
>
> Later, the people of Mali, increasing in population more than any of the Sudanese nations, overran the whole region. They vanquished the Sosso, and took all their possessions, both their ancient kingdom and that of Ghana, as far as the Ocean to the West.[21]

Sosso, the intermediate state between Ghana and Mali, is not mentioned in any other Arabic source, but it figures in oral traditions. According to these traditions, the Sosso—people related to the Soninke—inhabited Kaniaga, south of Wagadu (Ghana) and north of Beledugu (the region of Bamako). They had been subject to Ghana, probably until the Almoravid conquest when the Sosso, together with other tributary peoples, asserted their independence. During the twelfth century Sosso extended its authority, and reached the height of its power during the reign of Sumanguru Kante, early in the thirteenth century, when the territories of Ghana and the Malinke chieftaincies came under his rule. Sundjata, founder of the Mali empire, led a successful revolt of the Malinke against Sumanguru. The victory of Sundjata put an end to the Sosso kingdom, and opened the way for the extension of Mali's authority over the Sahil.[22]

20 Abū Ḥāmid, *Tuḥfat al-Albāb,* ed. et trad. G. Ferrand, *Journal Asiatique,* ccvii, 1925, pp. 41–2.

21 Ibn Khaldūn, *K. Ta'rīkh,* pp. 263–4 (*Histoire,* ii, pp. 109–10).

22 All versions of the traditions about Sosso and Mali are discussed by Ch. Monteil, 'Les Empires du Mali. Étude d'histoire et de sociologie soudanais', *Bull. Com. Etud. hist. scient. A.O.F.*, 1929, pp. 291–447. This is a most stimulating work, and much of what is said about Mali in this paper follows Monteil's analysis. A colourful account of the traditional history is given in D. T. Niane, *Soundjata ou l'epopée mandingue*, Paris, 1960.

The transfer of the hegemony from Ghana to Sosso, and then to Mali, marks a gradual shift of the political centre of gravity southwards, from the Sahil on the fringes of the Sahara deeper inland to full Sudanese savannah. Three factors go some way to explain this process. First, the weakening of the northern Soninke, masters of Ghana, through the long conflict with the Berber nomads, which reached its climax in the Almoravids' conquest of Ghana. Second, the replacement of Bambuk, at the confluence of the Senegal and the Faleme rivers, by Bure, on the Upper Niger, as the principal goldfield of the Sudan, which probably occurred in the eleventh and twelfth centuries. Third, with the extension of the trade routes southwards towards the new gold sources, mainly by Soninke traders, a wider section of the Sudan became part of the intracontinental trade complex, stimulating the development of political organisation.

Such a political development among the Malinke began at least as early as the eleventh century, as attested by al-Bakrī. He describes a line of commercial towns on the northern bank of the 'Nile', the Upper Senegal and its tributaries, where the Muslim Sudanese traders came from Ghana to collect the gold. Beyond that river he mentions two kingdoms, Do and Malel. The king of the latter was converted to Islam by a Muslim (trader?) resident in his kingdom. Al-Idrīsī, writing about a century later, regarded Do and Malel as the only two towns in the country of the Lamlam, as he called the loosely organised peoples south of Ghana's dominions.[23] Both authors, therefore, refer to the emergence of two of the earliest chiefdoms among the Malinke. Indeed, oral traditions tell of several small Malinke chiefdoms before the rise of Mali to hegemony. One of these was Do (or Dodugu), a name mentioned also by al-Bakrī and al-Idrīsī. The other, Malel, may refer to any Malinke chiefdom.

The traditionalists count several rulers, whose number and names may vary in different versions, of the Keyta dynasty, ancestors of Sundjata. Some traditions, coloured by Islamic influence, trace the origin of the dynasty back to Bilāl, the black companion of the Prophet. Some of the early rulers are said to have gone on pilgrimage. An echo of this tradition is found in Ibn-Khaldūn, who mentions Barmandana as the first Muslim king of Mali who performed the pilgrimage. The authenticity of the kings in the pre-Sundjata period cannot be ascertained, but from Sundjata on, until the end of the fourteenth century, we have a detailed chronicle of the kings of Mali recorded by Ibn-Khaldūn.[24]

This chronicle starts with Mārī-Djāṭa, the great king of Mali who overcame the Sosso, conquered their land and wrested power from their hands. Mārī-Djāṭa should, undoubtedly, be identified with the Sundjata of the

23 Al-Bakrī, *al-Masālik*, pp. 177–8 (trans. pp. 332–4); al-Idrīsī, *Nuzhat*, p. 6 (trans. pp. 6–7).
24 Ibn Khaldūn, *K. Ta'rīkh*, i, pp. 264–8 (*Histoire*, ii, pp. 110–16). For a detailed analysis of this chronicle, see N. Levtzion 'The thirteenth and fourteenth-century kings of Mali', *Journal of African History*, iv, 1963, pp. 341–53.

oral traditions. Sundjata, an exiled prince from a Malinke chiefdom on the Sankarani (a tributary of the Upper Niger, on the border between modern Guinea and Mali), was called back by his people to free the country from the yoke of Sumanguru Kante, the oppressive king of Sosso. A collation of various traditions suggests that Sundjata had first endeavoured to unite under his authority the different Malinke chiefdoms, both by contracting treaties of alliance and by coercion. At the head of the united force of the Malinke, Sundjata defeated the powerful Sumanguru. The combat between the two great warriors is presented by the oral traditions as a struggle between two powerful magicians.

The victory over the Sosso opened the way for expansion northwards, where Mali gained control over the termini of the trans-Saharan trails. At the same time the commanders of Sundjata's army and his allies extended the rule of Mali westwards over the upper valley of the Senegal and towards the Gambia. Mali thus held sway over all the internal trade routes over which gold was carried northwards to meet the trans-Saharan trade.

It is difficult to date stages in the territorial expansion of Mali. It is likely, however, that the conquests initiated by Sundjata (alias Mārī-Djāṭa) were followed by his son and successor Mansā (king) Ulī, whom Ibn-Khaldūn regarded as one of the most powerful kings of Mali. Mansā Ulī went on pilgrimage during the reign of the Mamluk Sultan of Egypt, Baybars (1260–77). Mansā Ulī was succeeded by his brother Wātī and then by another brother Khalīfa. The latter was weakminded, amusing himself by killing people for sport. He was deposed and killed, an event which marked the beginning of decadence in the dynasty and of troubles at the court. The throne was then given to Abū-Bakr, a grandson of Mārī-Djāṭa by one of his daughters. He was probably a nominee of the court officers, whose power grew with the weakness of the kings. This became even more apparent when Sākūra, a freed slave, usurped the throne.

Sākūra proved a great ruler, as he expanded (or recovered) the possessions of Mali and encouraged trading activities. He followed the example of other great rulers of the dynasty and went to Mecca. On his way he visited Cairo during the second reign of al-Mālik al-Nāṣir ibn Qalā'ūn, the Sultan of Egypt (1298–1308). Sākūra died on his way back from the pilgrimage, and the throne returned to the legitimate heirs. Mansā Qū son of Mansā Ulī reigned, and was succeeded by his son Mansā Muḥammad.

Then the kingship passed from the descendants of Mārī-Djāṭa to those of his brother Abū-Bakr. The latter, according to the traditions, was Sundjata's right hand both in exile and in the foundation of the empire. This change of branches within the dynasty infused new life to the kingship. Mansā Mūsā, grandson of Abū-Bakr, distinguished himself as the greatest king of Mali known to the Muslim writers, both oriental and Sudanese. In the oral traditions, however, Mūsā is belittled compared with their god-hero Sundjata.

During the reign of Mansā Mūsā, also known, after his mother, as Gongo Mūsā (1312–37), Mali reached its peak in prosperity, fame, and territory. Some Muslim authors attribute to him the conquest of the two important towns of Timbuktu and Gao, but a critical review of the evidence suggests that these towns had already been part of Mali before his reign. With Mansā Mūsā, Islam became well established at the royal court. Mūsā's fame outside the Sudan was due to his pilgrimage in 1324. His visit to Cairo left a strong impression, and his generous gifts and expenditure of gold caused it to be devalued in Egypt.[25] The appearance of this great Sudanese king was well remembered in Egypt. A later historian, Ibn-al-Iyās (died 1524), mentioned it as the most outstanding event of the year A.H. 724 (A.D. 1324).[26] From Egypt and North Africa the name of Mansā Mūsā reached Europe. 'Rex Melly' appears on the map of Angelino Dulcert in 1339, and 'Mussa Melli' on the Catalan map drawn for Charles V by Abraham Cresques of Majorca *c.* 1375.[27] Wishing to strengthen the links of his empire with the outside Muslim world, Mansā Mūsā initiated diplomatic relations with the Marinid sultans of Morocco. Embassies were exchanged during his reign and that of his brother Sulaymān (died 1360).[28]

Mansā Mūsā was succeeded by his son Maghā, who reigned for four years only. By appointing his son as deputy, during his absence in Mecca, and later by ensuring him the succession, Mansā Mūsā deprived his brother Sulaymān of his right to the throne, as the eldest male in the family. The short reign of Maghā raises the suspicion that he was deposed by his uncle, Sulaymān, who claimed the throne. This caused an internal conflict.

Mansā Sulaymān was a strong ruler, and during his reign the policy and prosperity of Mansā Mūsā's reign continued. But even during his reign there were troubles at the court, recorded by Ibn-Baṭṭūṭa who visited it in 1352–3. He describes a plot planned by an exiled prince Djāṭa and the king's senior wife.[29] The *coup d'état* was avoided, but soon after Sulaymān's death there was a civil war. The succession of Qāsā, Sulaymān's son, was challenged by Mārī-Djāṭa son of Mansā Maghā son of Mansā Mūsā, probably the same as the conspirator mentioned by Ibn Baṭṭūṭa. Mārī-Djāṭa killed Qāsā and seized power, so avenging the deposition of his own father by Qāsā's father and restoring the house of Mansā Mūsā.

Mārī-Djāṭa II reigned for fourteen years, 1360–73/4, and was an oppressive ruler. He depleted the treasury and nearly ruined the whole kingdom.

25 Al-ʿUmarī, *Masālik al-Abṣār fī Mamālik al-Amṣār. L'Afrique moin L'Egypte*, trad. et annoté Godfroy-Demombynes, Paris, 1927, p. 79. Ibn Kathīr, *al-Bidāya wa'l-Nihāya,* Cairo, 1932, xii, p. 122. Al-Maqrīzī, *Kitāb al-Sulūk fī Akhbār al-Mulūk,* Cairo, 1936, ii, p. 255.

26 Ibn al-Iyās, *Badā'iʿ l' al-Zuhūr fī Waqā'iʿ al-duhūr*, Cairo, 1893–4, i, p. 163.

27 Ch. de La Roncière, *La découverte de l'Afrique au moyen âge*, Cairo, 1924, plates VII and XI.

28 Ibn Khaldūn, *K. Ta'rīkh*, ii, pp. 394–5, 459–60 (*Histoire*, iv, pp. 243–4, 342–4).

29 Ibn-Baṭṭūṭa, *Voyages*, iv, pp. 417–19.

He died of sleeping sickness, and was succeeded by his son Mūsā. Mansā Mūsā II had good intentions, but he was a weak king, and took no part in the government. He was secluded by his chief minister, who held the authority during the fourteen years of Mūsā's reign. This chief minister, Mārī-Djāṭa (probably a member of the royal family), succeeded in restoring the empire which had deteriorated during the civil war and the irresponsible reign of Mansā Mārī-Djāṭa II. His military expeditions north-eastwards, to Gao and beyond, were probably carried out against rebellious provinces. Once again, as in the case of Sākūra, when weak kings undermined the foundations of the empire, a court official restored power.

Mansā Mūsā II died in 1387, and was succeeded by his brother Mansā Maghā II who was killed within a year, when the throne was seized by a usurper, Ṣandaki, probably a slave. This usurpation was avenged a few months later by a man from the house of Mārī-Djāṭa II. In this ferment the throne once again changed hands, when taken by Maḥmūd, a descendant of Mansā Qū son of Mansā Ulī son of Mārī-Djāṭa the Great, who had come from the lands of the pagans beyond Mali. He succeeded to the kingship, under the name of Mansā Maghā (the third) in 1390.

Thus towards the end of the fourteenth century the wheel came full circle. About four generations or eighty years earlier the laxity and impotence displayed by the descendants of Mārī-Djāṭa the Great caused the throne to pass to the descendants of Abū-Bakr, his brother. But here again, after a first generation of able rulers—Mansā Mūsā and his brother Sulaymān—succeeding generations proved a failure. The regeneration of the empire was ensured until the end of the fourteenth century by transferring authority from one branch of the Keyta dynasty to the other, and by the intervention of court officials, guardians of the state.

During the period of its greatness the authority of Mali reached to Takrur and the Gambia in the west, to the Upper Niger and the Malinke colonies beyond in the south, to the foothills of the Bandiagara scarp in the east, to Gao and Tadmekka in the north-east, and to the nomad Berbers of the Sahil, including Walata, in the north.[30] In such a vast and heterogeneous empire troubles at the centre led to revolts and secessions in the outlying provinces. Powerful rulers restored these provinces, but this cycle could not last long, and the end of the fourteenth century marked the beginning of a new phase: the disintegration of the empire, which lost, one by one, many of its important provinces. Some of these provinces had their own history before they became part of Mali, and some rose as new states. We now turn to the history of these states.

TAKRŪR AND DYARA

Arabic authors, after the fourteenth century, often refer to the Western Sudan by the name *Bilād al-Takrūr*, and to the Sudanese Muslims as

30 See Mauny, *Tableau*, p. 511, and map on p. 512.

Takārir, or the people of Takrūr. Al-ʿUmarī, knowing that the Egyptians called the king of Mali by the name of 'King of Takrūr', helped them out of the confusion by noting that 'Takrūr is only one of the regions in his empire'.[31] Two reasons may go some way to explain how it came about that the name of one region in the far west, on the Senegal, has been applied to the whole Western Sudan. First, Takrūr was one of the earliest Sudanese kingdoms to embrace Islam, and its people remained devoted to this faith. Second, these Muslim people of Takrūr—the Takārīr of the Arabs, or the Toucouleur of the French—spread during the centuries over large parts of the Sudan, along with their Fulani kinsmen.

Takrūr was first described by al-Bakrī:

> Takrūr, a town on the 'Nile' (the Senegal), is inhabited by black people. These, like the rest of the Sudanese, had been pagan and worshipped idols until the reign of Wār-Djābī (or, Wār-Ndyāy) son of Rabīs. He became Muslim, introduced Islamic law, and enforced the religion upon his subjects, opening their eyes to the truth. He died in 432 (A.D. 1040–1). Today (1067–8) the people of Takrūr are Muslims.[32]

Elsewhere al-Bakrī says that Labī son of Wār-Djābī, king of Takrūr, fought with Yaḥyā b. ʿUmar, the Almoravid leader, against the Juddāla in 1056–7.[33] Hence the Muslim state of Takrūr aided the Almoravids as brethren in faith, but also probably as allies against a common adversary, the pagan king of Ghana.

Al-Idrīsī, writing in 1153–4, describes the king of Takrūr as an independent sovereign, possessing slaves and troops, and renowned for his resolution, firmness and sense of justice. Traders from the Maghrib used to come to Takrūr, importing wool, copper, and beads, and exporting gold and slaves.[34] Silla, another commercial town on the Senegal, east of Takrūr, is described by both al-Bakrī and al-Idrīsī as a tributary of Takrūr. 'Its people are Muslims having been converted by Wār-Djābī. The king of Silla fights the pagans inhabiting the country between his own towns and Ghana.'

Ibn Saʿīd, a contemporary of al-Idrīsī, distinguished between two sections of the population of Takrūr; sedentaries and nomads. This is the distinction between the Toucouleur and the Fulani.[35] On the map of Angelino Dulcert, of 1339, one finds the names 'Felle' and 'Tochoror' in this region.

31 Al-'Umarī, *Masālik*, pp. 53–4.
32 Al-Bakrī, *al-Masālik*, p. 172 (trans. p. 324).
33 *Ibid.*, pp. 167–8 (trans. p. 316).
34 Al-Idrīsī, *Nuzhat*, p. 3 (trans. p. 3).
35 Abū'l-Fida', *K. Taqwīm al-Buldān*, pub. M. G. De Slane et M. Reinauld, Paris, 1840, p. 153 (*Geographie d'Aboulfeda* trad. M. Reinauld, Paris 1848, p. 208). Ibn Saʿīd al-Maghribī, *K. Basṭ al-Arḍ fi 'l Ṭūl Wa-' l-ʿArḍ*, ed. J. V. Gines, Tetuan 1958, p. 24.

This is all the documentary evidence available for the early history of Takrūr, and it is left for the oral traditions to fill in the wide gaps.[36] The task of writing this history becomes all the more complicated because it involves the elusive problem of the Fulani origin, for which too many solutions have been advanced. Two statements about the Fulani may be made without reservation: first, that their herdsmen are physically different from the Sudanese, including the Toucouleur, displaying non-negroid traits; second, that they speak the same language as the Toucouleur, which is closely related to the languages of the Wolof and the Serer. This leads to the suggestion that the Fulani ancestors were nomads of foreign origin, who had migrated to the Futa Toro in the Senegal valley, where they acquired their present language. Any further hypothesis about these ancestors—who they were, where they had come from, when, and in what circumstances—must be, at the present state of our knowledge, conjectural.

It is likely that the arrival of the Fulani's ancestors to the Futa is represented in the oral traditions by the first ruling dynasty of Takrūr, the Dyaʿogo, said to have been of white origin. The Futa had then been inhabited by the Serer, who became subjects of the Dyaʿogo. The Dyaʿogo ruled over the Futa in the later part of the first millennium A.D. In the tenth century the Dyaʿogo were overthrown by a new dynasty known to the traditionalists as Manna. These were Sudanese, said to have been a branch of the Nyakhate clan, rulers of Dyara, a Soninke state in the Sahil between Ghana and the Futa. Wār-Djābī (or Wār-Ndyāy), the first Muslim king of Takrūr, who died in 1040–1, was probably of this dynasty, because al-Bakrī regarded Takrūr as a Sudanese, black, kingdom.

It was at that period that the people of Takrūr, the Toucouleur, became fervent Muslims. The increasing pressure of the Saharan Berbers pushed the Sudanese southwards, across the Senegal and beyond. At that time the differentiation between the Toucouleur, Wolof, and Serer may have taken place. The last two remained pagan, and while the Wolof developed their Jolof state, probably in the fourteenth century, the Serer states developed later.

The claim that the Manna dynasty of Futa was dependent on Dyara in the eleventh and twelfth centuries is not supported by al-Bakrī and al-Idrīsī, who regarded Takrūr as an independent kingdom with its own tributaries. In the thirteenth century Dyara became part of Mali. It is possible that it was as vassals of Mali that the rulers of Dyara extended their influence over Takrūr. Indeed, following the migration of Soninke groups to the Senegal valley, after the collapse of Ghana and Sosso, Soninke and Malinke influence in the Futa became apparent.

Under pressure from all directions—Berbers and Moors from the north, Soninke and Malinke from the east, and Wolof, Serer, as well as Malinke

36 For a collection of traditions, annotated by the editors, see M. Delafosse et H. Gaden, *Chronique du Fouta Senegalais*, Paris, 1913.

(approaching from the Upper Gambia) in the south—conditions in the Futa became unstable. In the fourteenth and fifteenth centuries the traditions record a rapid succession of dynastic changes, all associated with invasions from outside the Futa. The Manna dynasty, of Soninke origin, was overthrown by that of the Tondyon, probably a combination of Serer (of the Dyūf clan) and Malinke (Tondyon in Malinke means 'the crown's slave', and governors of the Tondyon carried the Malinke title of *farba*). This dynasty, in its turn, was followed by those of Lam-Termes and Lam-Taga, both invading groups from the Hodh (just west of the site of the capital of Ghana), which were probably a mixture of Fulani and Berber nomads. One may imagine a fragmentation of the Futa, with several dynasties ruling petty chieftaincies. The growing Jolof state of the Wolof also took its share of the Futa in the later part of the fifteenth century. During all this period the kingdom of Dyara had access to the right bank of the Senegal.

The centre of the kingdom of Dyara was in Kingui—in the present *cercle* of Nioro. According to the traditions it was founded by the Soninke clan of the Nyakhate when anarchy reigned in the country after the collapse of Ghana. Dyara had probably been vassal to the Sosso of Kaniaga, and later came under the domination of Mali. As vassals of Mali, the Nyakhate were left to rule their kingdom, with a resident commissioner from Mali to ensure their loyalty. At that period the Nyakhate even extended their sphere of influence to include Kaniaga, Takrūr and other neighbouring provinces.[37]

Towards the end of the fourteenth century the Nyakhate were overthrown by a new dynasty, the Dyawara. Their ancestor, according to the traditions, stayed for some time in Mali. The Dyawara exploited internal troubles in Mali, killed the representative of Mali at Dyara, and became independent. The independent state grew stronger. Its capital was frequented by caravans and became a commercial centre, and the army, based on cavalry, manifested the power of the Dyawara. The kings were noted for their modesty and could hardly be distinguished when sitting in council. This is all the more significant when compared with the ceremonial pomp of other Sudanese rulers.[38] From the late sixteenth century the kingdom was weakened by continuous civil wars between two branches of the dynasty, until it fell under the Bambara rulers of Kaarta in 1754. As will be discussed later in this chapter, the expansion of the Songhay empire since the second half of the fifteenth century was mainly along the Niger river. Hence, the inland state of the Dyawara remained independent, paying due respect to the power of Songhay.

37 For the traditions of Dyara, and a reconstruction of their history, see G. Boyer, *Un peuple de l'Ouest africain: les Diawara*, Mém. de l'I.F.A.N., no. 29, Dakar, 1953.
38 *T. al-Fattāsh*, pp. 39–40 (trans. pp. 70–2).

TIMBUKTU, JENNE, AND MASSINA

The commercial centres of Ghana and Awdaghost were replaced by Walata, which served as the terminus for the trans-Saharan caravans as late as 1352, when it was visited by Ibn-Baṭṭūṭa. From the termini of the Sahil, trade was carried along overland routes to the goldfields of Bambuk and Bure. The Niger became important as a commercial waterway only with the development of Timbuktu and Jenne as the principal entrepôts of the Western Sudan trade.

Early in the sixteenth century Valentim Fernandes described the salt bars from the Sahara sent by canoes from Timbuktu to Jenne. Unloaded at Jenne, the salt was then carried by the Wangara traders on porters' heads to the gold mines.[39] Raymond Mauny rightly suggests that there was no reason why the salt for the goldfields of Bure on the Upper Niger should be unloaded at Jenne, as it could be carried by boats up the main course of the Niger, as far as the river was navigable. It is likely, therefore, that the salt brought to Jenne was destined for the new sources of gold in the Akan forest (in the modern republics of Ghana and the Ivory Coast).[40] Located at the south-eastern end of the inner delta of the Niger, Jenne proved an ideal entrepôt for trade with these goldfields. A busy trade on the Niger between Timbuktu and Jenne is described also by Leo Africanus in 1512–13.[41] In the seventeenth century, al-Saʿdi, who knew both Timbuktu and Jenne well, describes the basis of this trade system:

> Jenne is one of the greatest Muslim markets, where traders with salt from the mine of Taghāza meet traders with gold from Bīṭu [probably Beʿo, the old trading centre which preceded Bonduku in the same region]. . . . It is because of this blessed town [Jenne] that caravans come to Timbuktu from all points of the horizon.[42]

If this is accepted, Timbuktu and Jenne must have developed as trading centres about the same time. Timbuktu, in its turn, replaced Walata as the principal terminus for the desert caravans; as al-Saʿdī put it: 'The prosperity of Timbuktu was the ruin of Bīru (Walata).'[43] Contemporary evidence may help us to suggest a date for this change in the pattern of trade. In 1352 Ibn-Baṭṭūṭa joined a large caravan which took the old route: Sijilmasa–Taghaza–Walata. He describes Walata as the busy 'desert port' of Mali, while he had very little to say about Timbuktu, which he also visited, beyond the fact that it was inhabited by Berbers.[44] But, only

39 V. Fernandes, *Description de la Côte d'Afrique de Ceuta au Sénégal*, pub. et trad. P. de Cenival et Th. Monod, Paris 1938, pp. 85–7.
40 Mauny, *Tableau*, pp. 359–60.
41 Jean-Léon L'Africain, *Description de l'Afrique*, trad. A. Épaulard, Paris 1956, ii, p. 465.
42 Al-Saʿdī, *T. al-Sūdān*, pp. 11–12 (trans. pp. 22–3).
43 *Ibid.*, p. 21 (trans. p. 37).
44 Ibn-Baṭṭūṭa, *Voyages*, pp. 385–7 (Walata), 430–1 (Timbuktu).

twenty-three years later, in the map of Abraham Cresques dated 1375, the trans-Saharan route goes 'Sigilmasa-Tagaza-Tenbuch (Timbuktu)'. From then on this was the principal route described, and it is likely that Timbuktu superseded Walata as the main terminus of the caravan trade in the second half of the fourteenth century. It was about that period that the Niger waterway gained importance, and Jenne developed as the port for the gold trade with the Akan forest.[45]

We may now turn to the history of Timbuktu as related by al-Saʿdī, a native of that town. Timbuktu started as a summer camp of the Tuareg in their transhumance between Arawan and Lake Debo on the Niger, at the end of the fifth century A.H. (beginning of the twelfth century A.D.). Gradually people began to settle there, and it became a market, first for the region of Wagadu, and later for a wider section of the country. Then the cosmopolitan community of Walata—merchants and Muslim scholars, Sudanese, Berbers and North Africans—moved to Timbuktu, leaving Walata to decline. Temporary dwellings were replaced by huts and houses, but the building up of Timbuktu—as it was known to al-Saʿdī—had not been accomplished before the middle of the tenth century A.H. (middle of the sixteenth century A.D.). Timbuktu, therefore, reached its height only during the reign of the Askiya dynasty of Songhay.

The Tuareg, founders of Timbuktu and its immediate neighbours, lost control of the town when the empire of Mali reached the fringes of the desert, probably about the middle of the thirteenth century. Even the Tuareg in the neighbourhood of Timbuktu may have become vassals to Mali. But with the decline of Mali, at the beginning of the fifteenth century, the Tuareg began to raid Timbuktu and its environs. In 1433-4 they drove away the agents of Mali and became masters of Timbuktu. The chief of the Tuareg, however, did not change his way of life, and remained the nomad of the desert. He exercised authority at Timbuktu through the governor, Muḥammad Naḍḍi, a Ṣanhāja from Shinqit, who had held the same office under the suzerainty of Mali. The governor levied tribute for the Tuareg, retaining a third of the income for himself. At that time Walata also fell to the Tuareg, because the Tuareg chief took refuge there when Timbuktu was conquered by Sonni ʿAlī of Songhay in 1469.[46]

The growth of Timbuktu as an important centre of Islamic learning took place alongside its development as a commercial town. The reputation of its scholars had already become known during the reign of Mansā Mūsā (1312–37). Among the scholars of Timbuktu there were Sudanese but Berbers, Ṣanhāja of the desert, seem to have been in the majority. Significantly, al-Saʿdī says that the important office of the Imam of the great mosque had been held by Sudanese when Mali ruled Timbuktu,

45 On the Mande trade to the Akan forest, see I. Wilks, 'A medieval trade route from the Niger to the Gulf of Guinea', *J.A.H.*, iii, 1962, pp. 337–41.
46 Al-Saʿdī, *T. al-Sudān*, pp. 20–4 (trans. pp. 35–42).

but that office went to the 'white' Berbers under the Tuareg.[47] Timbuktu may be regarded as an outpost of Berber Islam in the Sudan, a link between the Maghrib, the Sahara and the Sudan.

Jenne, the other important centre of trade and Islamic learning—over two hundred miles up the Niger river—was in all respects a Sudanese town. The old inhabitants of Jenne were the Bozo fishermen. These have remained until the present day 'owners of the earth and the water', in the ritual sense of this expression, but they became politically subject to the Nono, a branch of the Soninke. The Nono had probably left the Sahil in the twelfth century, with the Soninke dispersion. They had stayed for some time at Dia before they moved to build the new town of Jenne.[48] Jenne was founded in the thirteenth century, and developed into a commercial centre in the following century. Its Islamisation was linked with its growing trading activities, as illustrated by the tradition, recorded by al-Saʿdī. The first Muslim king of Jenne gathered Muslim *ʿulamāʾ* and asked them to pray for the town and to bless it. The three blessings the king asked for were all concerned with the influx of strangers and the growth of trade.[49]

Jenne is surrounded by water, and during the flood the town is turned into an island. This made Jenne a safe place for traders, unlike the open country around Timbuktu which was vulnerable to raids. Compared with his easy conquest of Timbuktu, Sonni ʿAlī had to engage in a long siege of Jenne before it was captured. Al-Saʿdī says that Mali did not succeed in its attempts to conquer Jenne, but according to *T. al-Fattāsh* Jenne was vassal to Mali.[50] The latter seems more plausible, and it is likely that both Timbuktu and Jenne, as well as the Niger in between, were part of Mali during the thirteenth and fourteenth centuries. But with the weakening of Mali at the beginning of the fifteenth century, when it lost control over Timbuktu, Jenne also asserted its independence. It is to this period, which lasted about half a century until its conquest by Sonni ʿAlī (1473), that al-Saʿdī's description of Jenne as an independent kingdom with its own vassal chiefs should be applied. At that time the trade between Timbuktu and Jenne flourished in an independent country lying between the declining Mali and the rising Songhay. This region was then deprived of the security provided by the great empires, and attracted the raids of the Mossi in 1430, and again in 1470–83.[51]

South-west of Timbuktu, near the lakes formed on the river, was the old kingdom of Mema, mentioned by the oral traditions as a great kingdom which flourished before the rise of Mali.[52] Later Mema was a province of

47 *Ibid.*, p. 57 (trans. p. 92).
48 Ch. Monteil, *Une Cité soudanais: Djenné, metropole du delta central du Niger*, Paris, 1932, pp. 29–36.
49 Al-Saʿdī, *T. al-Sūdān*, pp. 12–13 (trans. pp. 23–4). The dates suggested by al-Saʿdī are not necessarily correct.
50 *Ibid.*, pp. 13–14 (trans. pp. 25–6). *T. al-Fattāsh*, pp. 37–8 (trans. p. 65).
51 Al-Saʿdī, *T. al-Sūdān*, pp. 27, 68–70 (trans. pp. 46, 112–15).
52 Niane, *Soundijata*, pp. 70–1.

Mali, but became independent at the beginning of the fifteenth century. Its independence, however, was short, because it was destroyed by Sonni Sulayman Dandi (died 1464), predecessor of Sonni ʿAlī the Great of Songhay.[53]

South of Mema is Massina, the pastureland of the Fulani nomads. The Fulani reached Massina about 1400, coming from Termes in the Hodh. They were allowed to stay there by the Governor of Mali, the *Baghana-fari,* and their leader was recognised as chief (*ardo*). They became subjects of the Songhay in 1498–9 when Askiya Muḥammad defeated the *Baghana-fari,* who was still governing in the name of Mali. It is probable, therefore, that the Fulani, unlike their neighbours in Mema and Jenne, remained loyal to Mali, and fought with its governor against the Songhay. Their resistance to the Songhay is shown by Sonni ʿAlī's hatred of the Fulani and the hostility they displayed towards the Songhay government during the sixteenth century. As late as 1599 the Fulani of Massina joined Mali in the attempt to conquer Jenne, then under the Moroccan Pasha of Timbuktu.[54]

THE BEGINNINGS OF THE SONGHAY EMPIRE

Songhay was the last of the great empires of the Western Sudan. The period of its greatness, which lasted just over a century, will be dealt with in another chapter. Here we are concerned with the Songhay state from its earliest days to the reign of Sonni ʿAlī who turned it into an empire, and with the effect of the rise of Songhay on the disintegration of Mali.

The Songhay are now spread in a large arc along the Niger from Dendi (on the Nigerian border) in the east to lake Debo (south of Timbuktu) in the west. There are also Songhay communities in Mopti and Jenne. In the Hombori mountains, inside the Niger bend, are to be found the only land-locked, non-riverain Songhay peoples. The Niger played a decisive role not only in the dispersion of the Songhay, but also in the expansion of their imperial dominions when the empire became dominant in the Sudan. Their dependence on a water course for expansion is best illustrated by the plan of Sonni ʿAlī to dig a canal from Ra' s al-Mā' to Walata in order to conquer this town of the Sahil.[55] The fleet was most important in the military exploits of Songhay.

This is explained by the fact that the dominant element among the Songhay were the Sorko fishermen of the Niger. The complementary elements—which together with the Sorko formed this heterogeneous people—were the Gow hunters and the Do farmers. The Sorko navigated up the river from Dendi and reached the region of Bentia, north of Tilla-bery, where they found hippopotami in abundance. Mobile and warlike

53 *T. al-Fattāsh*, pp. 42–3 (trans. p. 81).
54 Al-Saʿdī, *T. al-Sūdān*, pp. 185–7, 76, 181–2 (trans. 281–5, 124, 277–9).
55 *Ibid.*, p. 70 (trans. pp. 114–15).

people, the Sorko became not only 'masters of the water' but also rulers of the farmers, 'owners of the earth', who lived in the region of Bentia. There they were joined by the hunters, and a town by the name of Kukiya developed as the capital of the Songhay nation.[56]

In this region the Niger flows in arid country, an extension of the Sahara, inhabited by Berber nomads. The contact between the Berber and the Songhay introduced the latter to the trans-Saharan trade and stimulated among them a more cohesive political organisation. This may be inferred from the traditions about the Dya, the first Songhay dynasty. The founder of this dynasty, a stranger, was recognised as sovereign by the Songhay after he had killed a fish dragon, worshipped by the Songhay people, who were subject to its stringent laws.[57] The myth of the dragon-killer becoming a ruler is widespread in West Africa. It may represent a departure from a society dominated by oracle priests to that ruled by chiefs. Yet the new Songhay chiefs were by no means secular, as magic played an important rôle in their authority.

It was probably in the eighth century that a new town—Gao—developed north of Kukiya as a terminus for a trans-Saharan trail. Through this trade the kingdom of Songhay became known to the Arabs by the name of Kawkaw, which may refer to the Gao-Kukiya complex. It is likely that with the growing importance of Gao as a commercial entrepôt the Dya rulers moved there, but retained Kukiya as the ancestral traditional capital, where the ceremonial investiture of the kings took place.

Close commercial relations between Kawkaw and the Kharejite state of Tahert (in Western Algeria) developed soon after the establishment of the latter, in the late eighth century.[58] In 874, the famous Kharejite revolutionary, Abū-Yazīd, was born in Kawkaw, where his father was a trader.[59] Kawkaw is mentioned by al-Khwarizmī (died 846/7), and in 872 it was described by al-Yaʿqūbī as the most powerful kingdom in the Sudan with many vassal chiefs paying tribute.[60]

In 985 the Egyptian author al-Mahallabi described Kawkaw as divided into two towns on both sides of the Niger. On the right bank (facing the desert) was the traders' town and on the other bank was the royal town. The king of Kawkaw was then Muslim.[61] His Islamisation was a result of the influence of the Muslim traders resident in Kawkaw. He was probably the first important Sudanese ruler to adopt Islam, preceding even Takrūr.

56 J. Rouch, *Contribution à l'histoire des Songhay*, Mém. de l'I.F.A.N., no. 29, Paris, 1954, pp. 165–9.
57 Al-Saʿdī, *T. al-Sūdān*, pp. 4–5 (trans. pp. 6–9); see another version in the fragment, second appendix in *T. al-Fattāsh*, pp. 329–31.
58 T. Lewicki, 'L'état nord-africain de Tahert et ses relations avec le Soudan occidental à la fin du VIIIe et au IXe siècle', *Cahiers d'Études Africains*, 1962, pp. 513–35.
59 Ibn Khaldūn, *K. Taʾrīkh*, ii, 17 (Histoire, iii, 201).
60 Al-Yaʿqūbī, *Kitāb al-Taʾrīkh*, ed. M. Th. Houtsma, Lugduni Batavorum, 1883, p. 220.
61 Quoted by Yāqūt, *Kitāb Muʿjam al-Buldān*, ed. F. Wustenfeld, Leipzig, 1866, iv, p. 329.

Islam, however, was confined to the court, and even there it seems to have been superficial, because al-Bakrī (1067–8) described a Muslim king, hedged by traditional non-Muslim ceremonial customs, ruling over a pagan population.[62] Royal steles discovered near Gao in 1939 have epitaphs calling kings and other members of the royal family by their Arabic names, which they had beside the traditional ones. The steles are dated between 1100 and 1256, and some of these are carved on marble, the work of an Andalusian sculptor. This suggests some contact between the Muslim kings of Gao and Spain.[63]

At that period Gao had a position similar to that of Ghana, with its northern neighbour the Berber town of Tadmekka as parallel to Awdaghost. While Ghana and Awdaghost traded with Morocco, Gao and Tadmekka traded with Algeria, and probably also with Egypt. The Songhay kingdom did not intervene in the country west of the Niger bend, though the Sorko fishermen continued their advance along the Niger in this direction.

In its attempt to control all the termini of the Western Sudan, Mali extended its authority over Gao and Tadmekka, about the middle of the thirteenth century. Songhay, however, was a remote province, and periods of weakness in Mali were occasions for trying to secure independence. About 1275, during the troubles caused by Khalīfa's reign, Songhay revolted under the leadership of ʿAlī Kolon, who, according to one version, was a son of a Songhay king residing in Mali as a hostage, and according to another version, an official of Mali who made himself independent of his sovereign.[64] In his bid for independence ʿAlī Kolon founded the new dynasty of the Sonni, replacing that of the Dya. Songhay, however, came back under the rule of Mali in the reign of the usurper Sākūra, and was visited by Mansa Mūsā on his way back from the pilgrimage. It was within the dominions of Mali during Ibn-Baṭṭūṭa's visit (1353). Mārī-Djāṭa, the minister who ruled in the name of Mansa Mūsā II (1373–87) had to subdue territories in the direction of Gao, probably to restore the authority of Mali which had been weakened during the civil war following Mansa Sulaymān's death and the oppressive reign of the next king.

This was the last time Mali sent troops to the north-east. From the beginning of the fifteenth century Mali was unable to secure the northern provinces. With the increasing pressure of the Tuareg in the region of Timbuktu, Songhay could go its own way. Free from foreign domination, the Sonni rulers of Songhay built up military power. In about 1420 Sonni Muḥammad Daʾo raided a territory of Mali, and the booty carried back by this expedition, including slaves, strengthened the resources of the kingdom.

62 Al-Bakrī, *Masālik*, p. 183 (trans. pp. 342–3).
63 J. Sauvaget, 'Les épitaphes royales de Gao', *Bull. I.F.A.N.*, 1950, pp. 418–40. M. -M. Viré, 'Steles funéraires musulmanes soudanosahariennes', *Bull. I.F.A.N.*, sér. B., 1959, pp. 459–500.
64 Al-Saʿdī, *T. al-Sūdān*, pp. 5–6 (trans. pp. 9–12); Appendix II in *T. al-Fattāsh*, pp. 334–535.

The territorial expansion of Songhay began in the reign of Sonni Sulaymān Dandi (died 1464) who annexed the kingdom of Mema, then already independent of Mali.[65]

This had been a prelude to the military exploits of Sonni ʿAlī the Great (1464–92), who transformed the kingdom of Songhay into an expanding empire. He conquered Timbuktu in 1469 and Jenne in 1473. These two towns, like Mema, had already been independent of Mali; the disintegration of Mali preceded the Songhay conquest. In the next stage, during the reign of Askiya Muḥammad (1493–1528), founder of the last Songhay dynasty, Songhay expanded at the expense of Mali, and wars were waged against governors of Mali. During the period 1499–1509 the provinces of Baghana, Kaarta, and Galam were conquered.[66] Mali lost all power in the Sahel, and retreated south of the inner delta of the Niger and the Upper Senegal, to the territories of the Malinke and kindred peoples. In 1512 Leo Africanus described Mali as a declining kingdom, lying along the Niger south of Jenne.[67] Songhay, on the other hand, expanded until it became the largest of all the Sudanese empires, only to disintegrate in 1591 after its defeat by the Moroccan army (see Chapter 9).

Even at this time, when Mali was losing power in the north, there is evidence from Portuguese sources that its authority was recognised on the Gambia. The expansion of Mali in that direction had been accompanied by a migration of Malinke, who settled on the Gambia.[68] Mali's power lasted longer in territories inhabited by Malinke and kindred peoples, while it lost territories of alien groups—Tuareg, Songhay, Toucouleur and Soninke.

Ghana and Songhay passed away suddenly in periods of greatness. Mali, on the other hand, declined gradually, and it survived over two hundred years after the tide had turned against it. This may be explained by the geographical fact that the capitals of Ghana and Songhay as well as their power centres were in the Sahil, the region in which the Sudanese powers competed with each other, and which was also coveted by the people of the Sahara and the Maghrib. Mali was the only empire which had its capital and centre of power south of the Sahil. This is why Mali could build up its power when Sosso was still in its prime, and why it could survive its own successor, the Songhay empire. Ghana and Songhay were destroyed by powers from the north—the Almoravids and the Moroccans—while Mali was eliminated only with the rise of a new local power, the Bambara, with their roots in the Sudanese Savannah.

65 *T. al-Fattāsh*, pp. 55–6, 42–3 (trans. pp. 107, 80–1).

66 *Ibid.*, pp. 70, 75 (trans. pp. 135, 143). Al-Saʿdī, *T. al-Sūdān*, pp. 75–6 (trans. pp. 124–6).

67 Leo Africanus, *Description*, ii, p. 466.

68 Ca da Mosto, *Alvise de, Relation des voyages à la côte occidentale d'Afrique, 1455–57*, pub. Ch. Schefer, Paris 1895, p. 158. V. Fernandes, *Description de la côte occidentale d'Afrique (Sénégal, au Cap de Monte, Archipels)*, pub. et trad. Th. Monod, A. Teixera da Mota et R. Mauny, Bissau, 1951, pp. 35–7, 59.

GOVERNMENT IN THE WESTERN SUDAN

Lineages and clans, representing the kinship system, and villages and districts, representing the territorial setting, form the basis of the social-political structure of societies in the Western Sudan. Above this level one should take account of the ethnic groups, of which the principal ones—Soninke, Malinke, Bambara, Songhay, Toucouleur, etc.—may be described as 'nations'. Each of these nations had in common language, history, customs, religion, and a territory. Territory, however, should be redefined for each period in the history of a nation. A nation is formed by different clans, which fall into different categories of status: nobles, freemen, castemen, serfs and slaves. The political history is generally that of the noble clans, and the process of state building is that of one noble clan asserting its authority over other groups and over the territories they occupy. The dominant clan can then become the wealthiest by drawing from the resources of its subjects. There was no single pattern, and some examples of state building have already been given above in the account of the political history.

Petty states or chiefdoms may be limited to a few villages or to a district. Their numbers have always been legion, but though these formed the basis for more elaborate forms of political organisation, historical evidence about them is scanty. Geographers, travellers, and historians were concerned more with the few great kingdoms or empires. These may cautiously be called 'national states'. Ghana, for example, was a Soninke state; its rulers were Soninke and its dominions covered most of the country inhabited by the Soninke, and little, if any, of the territories of other groups. Mali, on the other hand, ruled also over alien groups other than the Malinke, but its national character is revealed both at the dawn of its history and towards its end. By mobilising the resources of the Malinke, Mali emerged as the dominant power, and when its government proved too weak to hold the empire together it contracted back to the Malinke national territory.

For that later period al-Saʿdī left a description of the organisation of Mali. It was divided into three provinces, and each of these was divided into smaller chieftaincies. The latter may have been local Malinke chieftaincies which had been united under the Keyta rulers to form the nucleus of the Mali empire.[69]

In the conquered territories Mali, like the other Sudanese empires, tended to retain the local rulers. Sons of vassal kings were held at the court—in Ghana or in Mali—undoubtedly as hostages. Governors or commissioners were appointed over the local rulers, and were responsible to the central government. They were recruited from members of the ruling family or from among the royal slaves.

Slaves and serfs were of prime importance in the structure of the states in the economic, military, administrative and political spheres. In the Western

69 Al-Saʿdī, *T. al-Sudan*, pp. 9–10 (trans. pp. 19–20).

Sudan there was no shortage of land, and production depended on the availability of manpower. Lands cultivated by serfs or slaves could supply agricultural products for the chiefs to maintain their courts, their administrations and their armies. The crown was the biggest owner of slave settlements, but other citizens also derived income from such settlements. This institution was inherited by Songhay from Mali, and it is likely that in Mali, as in Songhay, the king gave slave villages as gifts to his favourites. Slaves also rendered services, attending the ruler or looking after his horses.[70]

Slaves were the core of the army, as bowmen. A small kingdom had to mobilise its own citizens to form an army; but an empire with heavy military commitments needed a standing army.[71] As the empire grew stronger its ruler could obtain more slaves, and part of these were taken to the army. The cavalry—the striking force of a Sudanese army—was that of the freemen, whose commanders were given estates and generous gifts from the king to win their loyalty.[72] Horses were very expensive in the Sudan, and most were imported, first by the Berbers and later also by the Portuguese. The sources, Arabic and Portuguese, say that horses were bought in exchange for slaves.[73]

The personal loyalty of slaves or freed slaves to the ruler made them a good choice for responsible posts in the provincial administration and the court. At least some of the provincial governors in Mali were slaves, as was the comptroller of the commercial town of Walata, the Mansā-dyo (royal slave).[74]

Slaves were prominent at court: they intervened in conflicts within the royal family, and were among the 'king-makers'. When troubles weakened the legitimate dynasty, members of this group seized the throne, as did Sākūra the freed slave (*floruit c.* 1300), and Sandiki (1387–8), whose title may have been that of *Sandigi*, 'chef des achats'.[75]

The recorded history of Mali in the thirteenth and fourteenth centuries shows that during the reign of powerful kings the empire prospered, while it was shaken to its foundations when weak kings were on the throne. This indicates the importance of the king's personal rôle in the running of the government. This is supported by Ibn-Baṭṭūṭa, who recorded the personal intervention of Mansā Sulaymān in punishing the comptroller of Walata for abusing his office, and by al-Idrīsī, who describes the daily inspection of the capital by the king of Ghana.[76]

70 *T. al-Fattāsh*, pp. 55–8, 94–110 (trans. pp. 107–12, 178–202).
71 *Ibid.*, p. 116 (trans. p. 211); Al-Saʿdi, *T. al-Sudan*, p. 72 (trans. p. 118).
72 Al-ʿUmarī, *Masālik*, pp. 66–7.
73 *T. al-Fattāsh*, p. 56 (trans p. 109). Leo Africanus, *Description*, pp. 480–2 (on Bornu and Gaoga). Ca da Mosto, *Relation*, pp. 48, 116–17. Fernandes, *Description* (1951), pp. 20–1, 77.
74 Ibn-Baṭṭuṭa, *Voyages*, p. 34. Monteil, *Les Empires*, p. 417. M. Delafosse, *Haut-Senegal-Niger*, Paris, 1913, ii, p. 194.
75 Mauny, *Tableau*, p. 450.
76 Ibn-Baṭṭuṭa, *Voyages*, p. 416. Al-Idrīsī, *Nuzhat*, p. 7 (trans. p. 8).

The monarchies of the Sudanese kingdoms and empires had their origins in the office of head of a clan or chief of a small chieftaincy. In both of these, secular authority had been combined with religious priesthood. But it appears that as they developed into monarchies, the sacred element was emphasised. Indeed elements of divine kingship may be traced in these monarchies. The best descriptions are from Kanem, which is outside the scope of this chapter, but we have a similar note about the king of Kawkaw (Songhay) by al-Bakrī: 'No one is free to go about the royal town until he [the king] has finished his repast, the remnants of which are thrown into the Nile.' Al-Bakrī's description of the burial of the king of Ghana carries similar evidence. The audience of the king, both in Ghana and in Mali, is described in much detail, and it is full of ceremonial customs: people approached the monarch, prostrating, rolling on the ground and putting dust on their heads, and no one was allowed to sneeze in the presence of the king. The king did not speak directly with his people, but only through a linguist.[77]

The king was above the people, but this gave him no licence to act arbitrarily, as the case of the deposed Khalīfa proves. In other kingdoms even dynasties were overthrown, but in Mali, in spite of continuous troubles and conflicts at the court, and occasional interventions by outsiders, the sanctity and prestige of the Keyta dynasty ensured the ultimate return of the throne to one of its members. The same dynasty ruled Mali for at least the four centuries of its recorded history.

TRADE

Of all the subjects related to the early history of the Western Sudan, trade is the best documented. Information reached the Muslim world along trade routes, carried by the traders who frequented the Sudan. These traders communicated mainly with other traders, both foreign and local, and their main interest was to collect whatever information was available on the economic resources of the country, and on the prospects of trade. Here we will only be able to deal briefly with this subject; for more details on trade and other economic aspects the reader is advised to consult R. Mauny's monumental work, in which he has collected and analysed all the documentary evidence from Arabic and Portuguese sources.

Gold was the most important staple in this trade, and until the discovery of America, the Sudan was the principal source of gold both for the Muslim world and for Europe. It is significant that though much was known about the trade in general, little reliable information was available to the Arabs about the goldfields themselves. Common among Arab geographers

77 Al-Muhallabī on Kanem, quoted by Yāqūt, *Muʿ jam*, ii, pp. 932–3. Al-Bakrī, *Masālik*, pp. 176; 183 (trans. pp. 330, 342). Ibn-Baṭṭuṭa, *Voyages*, iv, pp. 407–9. Al-ʿUmari, *Masālik*, pp. 65–8.

is the description of the gold growing in the Sudan 'like carrots'.[78] The Sudanese—chiefs and traders—tried to keep the sources of the gold secret from the foreign North African traders. Indeed, these Sudanese themselves had uneasy relations with the peoples of the gold-producing countries. This is well illustrated by that peculiar method of barter known as 'the silent trade'. The traders laid down their merchandise, mainly salt, on the bank of a river, and retreated. Then the local people came with their gold, laid some of it against each pile of goods, and withdrew. The traders then came back, and if satisfied with the amount of gold they took it. As soon as they had disappeared the local people came back to collect the merchandise they bought with their gold.[79] Though this kind of trading relation may not have been general, it does indicate the reluctance of the local masters of the goldfields to come into direct contact with the more sophisticated Sudanese traders. That they came out at all was because of their great need for salt.

The Sudanese traders and chiefs had to respect the customs of these masters of the gold, for it was considered that only through the ritual association of the local people with the gold-bearing country did the land yield that precious metal. Mansā Mūsā related in Egypt that whenever he had tried to impose Islam on the people of the gold-bearing country, the gold diminished. He therefore left them on their own, and was satisfied with the income he gained from controlling the gold trade through his dominions.[80] These people resisted not only Islam, but probably also any central authority. It is likely that the great empires of the Sudan did not rule the gold-bearing regions, but held them as exclusive spheres of influence.

Following the scanty contemporary evidence and the recent information furnished by travellers and geologists, it is now possible to suggest three main goldfields, besides some of less importance, which supplied gold for the trans-Saharan trade. The earliest, and most northern, were the goldfields of Bambuk (at the confluence of the Senegal and Faleme rivers), which were exploited at the time of Ghana. In about the twelfth century the goldfields of Bure, on the Upper Niger, gained importance. These goldfields contributed to the emergence of Mali, which controlled the routes approaching Bure. About the fourteenth century rich new fields, far south in the Akan forest, began to feed the trans-Saharan trade, with Jenne as the starting point of the southward routes to this region.

Gold was extracted as dust and nuggets (the king of Ghana monopolised the latter), and in this form it reached the trading centres of the Sahil. It was prepared for transport across the Sahara in places like Awdaghost and

78 Ibn-al-Faqīh al-Hamadhānī, *Mukhtaṣar Kitāb al-Buldān*, ed. M. J. De Goeje, Lugduni Batavorum, 1885, p. 8. Yāqūt, *Muʿjam*, v, p. 822; al-ʿUmarī, pp. 71–2.
79 Al-Masʿūdī, *Akhbār al-Zamān*, quoted by Youssouf Kamal, *Monumenta*, iii, p. 628. Yāqūt, *Muʿjam*, i, pp. 821–2, Ca da Mosto, *Relation*, pp. 57–8.
80 Al-ʿUmarī, *Masālik*, pp. 58–9.

Tadmekka, but was turned into coins only at the other end of the desert, at places such as Sijilmasa and Wargala.[81]

Some peoples in the Western Sudan, those nearer to the goldfields, were ready to pay an equivalent measure of gold for salt.[82] This account of the Arabic sources illustrates the great need for salt. Maritime salt was unsuitable for distribution over vast and remote areas in the humid climate of the Sudan. On the other hand, the salt bars extracted from mines in the Sahara were dry and solid enough to be carried unspoilt over long distances. The salt of Awlīl, near the coast in southern Mauritania, was sent by boats up the Senegal, and distributed in the countries on both sides of the river. This mine was only of local importance compared with the mine of Taghāza, on the route from Sijilmasa to Ghana.[83]

The salt bars carried on camels across the Sahara to centres in the Sahil were then taken, whole or broken into pieces, by the Sudanese traders to be distributed along the routes leading ultimately to the goldfields. These traders were mainly Soninke, who through their contact with the North African traders became Muslims. They are called in the Arabic sources Wangara, a name still current in West Africa. Among the Malinke, the Sudanese traders are better known as Dyula, a name which became a synonym for 'Muslim trader'. The Wangara were itinerant traders, carrying their merchandise on asses, bullocks, porters or even their own heads. Wangara communities developed along the routes to form a widespread network of trading and family relations. Travellers of the nineteenth century left vivid descriptions of the Wangara, but it is likely that the scene had not changed much, because al-Bakrī's account of the routes and centres between Ghana and the goldfields tells a similar story.

In a town like Jenne, Sudanese traders were responsible for even more important transactions as agents of the trans-Saharan trade. They distributed the imported goods to the retailers, the itinerant traders, and collected from them the goods destined to be exported northwards. The same is true, but mainly at later periods, for other inland commercial centres. During the period we are considering the big traders in the centres of the Sahil were mostly North Africans, Berbers and Arabs.

The trade which bridged the two shores of the huge desert was very elaborate. This is well illustrated by the story of one firm, that of the Maqqarī brothers in the fourteenth century. These five brothers from Tlemcen were engaged in the prosperous trans-Saharan trade. They started by reorganising the route Sijilmasa—Taghāza—Walata, by digging wells, maintaining them, and by supplying guides to caravans. Two of the brothers stayed at Tlemcen where they obtained goods for the Sudan. One brother settled at Sijilmasa where he could obtain information about

81 For references, see Mauny, *Tableau*, pp. 375–7.
82 Al-ʿUmarī, *Masālik*, p. 83. Al-Bakrī, *al-Masālik*, p. 174 (trans. p. 327).
83 On the salt mines, see Mauny, *Tableau*, pp. 323–32.

markets and prices both in North Africa and the Sudan. He could therefore regulate the flow of goods to obtain maximum profits. The other two brothers lived at Walata, where they distributed the goods received from the north to local itinerant traders, and collected from them goods to be sent in the caravans to their brothers in the north. The brothers at Walata maintained good relations with the authorities of Mali, who encouraged their trading activities throughout the country.[84]

The kind hospitality accorded to North African traders by the Sudanese governments is recorded also in contemporary Arabic sources. We have already referred to the traders' wards at the capital of Ghana and at Gao. There the foreign traders lived a somewhat secluded life, but at the capital of Mali these foreigners became more closely involved in the life of the country, because Islam, which had formerly divided the foreigners from the local people, now united them as brethren in faith. Ibn-Baṭṭūṭa found Moroccan compatriots in all the important towns. His Moroccan host at the capital of Mali was married to the king's cousin, and maintained close relations with the court.[85]

Ibn-Baṭṭūṭa mentions among the virtues of the people of Mali that they did not touch the property left by a foreigner who died in their country. It was kept with one of his compatriots until recovered by the legitimate heir. Throughout his visit to Mali Ibn-Baṭṭūṭa was impressed by the love of justice displayed by the king.[86] The justice which reigned in the Sudan became known also to the Portuguese on the Gambia.[87] Justice and the internal security maintained by the rulers encouraged the development of trade under the Sudanese kingdoms.

Gold and salt were the two principal goods in the trade, but as the trade developed more goods were added to the list both for export and import. Among the imported goods were horses, cloths of all kinds, copper, silver, beads, glassware, dried dates and figs, and all kinds of manufactured goods. After gold, slaves were the next most important export of the Sudan to North Africa, and since the fifteenth century also to the Portuguese. Most of the slaves were probably captured in raiding expeditions on the loosely organised peoples beyond the borders of the Sudanese kingdoms, often referred to in the Arabic sources as Lemlem. Among other exported goods were spices, kola nuts, shea-butter, hides, civet, musk, ivory, etc.[88]

The organisation of the trans-Saharan trade began in the North African towns of Tlemcen, Fes, Sijilmasa, Wargala, and others. All these towns are inland at different distances from the coast. Although they traded with Europe they tried to avoid the participation of European traders in the

84 H. Pérès, 'Relations entre le Tafilelt et le Soudan à travers le Sahara du XIIIe au XIVe siècle', *Mélanges géographiques et orientalistes offerts à E. F. Gautier*, Tours, 1937, pp. 409–14.
85 Ibn-Baṭṭūṭa, *Voyages*, iv, pp. 397–8, 400, 420–1, 435–6.
86 *Ibid.*, pp. 390–1, 416, 421.
87 Fernandes, *Description* (1951), pp. 41, 47.
88 Mauny, *Tableau*, pp. 368–80.

trans-Saharan trade itself. Nevertheless at least two Europeans succeeded in getting beyond the Maghrib. In 1469 a Florentine, Bendetto Dei, is reported to have reached Timbuktu, while in 1447 the Genoan Malfante stayed for some time at Tuat. Tuat was then an important commercial centre where traders from Tunis and Egypt came to change goods for the Sudanese gold.[89] Important Jewish communities in North-Africa and the Saharan oases, such as Tuat, also took part in this trans-Saharan trade.[90]

The best description of the journey of a caravan across the Sahara is that of Ibn-Baṭṭūṭa, who recounted his own experience. He described the dangers a caravan faced in the desert, and the need for effective organisation and a qualified guide. For a long time, at least since the tenth century, the Masūfa Berbers were famous as guides to the caravans.[91] Other Berber tribes of the Sahara also had vested interests in the trade, not the least through levying tribute for protection, that is for refraining from attacking the caravans. In spite of occasional attacks by the Saharan Berbers, the necessary measure of security prevailed. Conditions along the western route leading to Walata changed in the second half of the fourteenth century, with the arrival of nomad Arabs in the western Sahara. Banū-Salaymān began to raid caravans, and this route had to be abandoned for a more eastern itinerary which brought the caravans to the region of Timbuktu.[92] This was another reason for the decline of Walata and the growth of Timbuktu at that period.

Most of the trade of the Western Sudan was with the Maghrib, but Egypt also had its share at certain periods. The Arabic sources mention an old route from Ghana via Gao to the oases in the desert west of Egypt. But this route is said to have been abandoned because it proved too dangerous.[93] New evidence about the commercial relations between Egypt and the Western Sudan appears in the second half of the fourteenth century. Ibn-Baṭṭūṭa, who saw Egyptian-made clothes at Walata, passed Air where one route turned north-east via Ghāt to Egypt. Ibn-Khaldūn heard of a huge caravan, twelve thousand camels it was said, which passed Tadmekka every year.[94] It is possible that the impressive visit of Mansā Mūsā to Cairo (1324) and the wealth he displayed stimulated the interest of Egyptian traders to re-open direct communication with the Western Sudan.

Indeed, the pilgrimage of Mansā Mūsā serves as a good example for the

89 Ch. de La Roncière, *La Découverte de l'Afrique au Moyen Age. Cartographie et explorateurs*, Cairo, 1925, i, pp. 143–58, 163. Cf. Mauny, *Tableau*, p. 463.

90 H. Z. Hirschberg, 'The problem of the Judaised Berbers', *J.A.H.*, iv, 3, 1963, pp. 319–25.

91 Ibn-Baṭṭūṭa, *Voyages*, iv, pp. 377–85; see also, Ibn-Ḥawqal, *Ṣurat*, p. 101 (*Configuration*, pp. 99–100).

92 Ibn-Khaldūn, *K. Ta'rīkh*, ii, p. 81; (*Histoire*, iii, p. 288).

93 Ibn-al-Faqīh, *Mukhataṣar*, p. 68. Ibn-Ḥawqal, *Ṣūrat*, p. 61 (*Configuration*, p. 58). al-Idrīsī, *Nuzhat*, p. 43 (trans. p. 50). Al-ʿUmarī, *Masālik*, p. 80.

94 Ibn-Baṭṭūṭa, *Voyages*, iv, pp. 387, 445. Ibn-Khaldūn, *K. Ta'rīkh*, ii, p. 73 (*Histoire*, iii, pp. 287–8).

correlation between trade, Islam, and the foreign policy of Mali. The greatness of Mali was due not least to the fact that it became part of the wider Muslim world.

ISLAM

The mid-eleventh century, when al-Bakrī wrote his book (1067–8), was a crucial period in the spread of Islam in the Western Sudan. It was after the rise of the Almoravid movement but before the fall of Ghana. It will be instructive, therefore, to follow al-Bakrī's account in order to survey the position of Islam about that time.

By the middle of the eleventh century the trans-Saharan trade had already been pursued by Muslims for about three centuries. Muslim traders from the Maghrib lived in their own wards in the capitals of the three principal kingdoms, Ghana, Gao and Takrūr. In the last two, Muslims had already succeeded in winning over the kings. But, whereas in Gao the Islamisation of the king and his entourage seems to have been only nominal, and pre-Muslim customs persisted, in Takrūr Islam was adopted with much zeal. Islamic law was introduced, subjects were forced to join Islam, and the ruler even extended Islam to the tributary town of Silla. In 1059 we find the king of Takrūr fighting on the side of the Almoravids. Thus the two earliest Muslim rulers in the Western Sudan served as examples for the two main trends in the spread of Islam: a compromise between Islam and the traditional religion on the one hand, and militant Islam, seeking to impose the new religion by force, on the other.

Ghana of the mid-eleventh century offered the example of resistance to Islam. Muslims lived in the traders' town with all the institutions of a Muslim community. Apart from dominating commercial activities, they also entered the political field as interpreters and ministers. Yet, in spite of close association with the Muslims, the king of Ghana adhered to his ancestral religion. This is surprising because Sudanese rulers in contact with Muslims usually adopted Islam, at least partially, as we learn not only from the examples of Ghana's neighbours—Gao, Takrūr and Malel—but also from other regions in later periods. One reason for the reluctance of the king of Ghana to accept Islam may have been his hostility towards the Berbers of the desert, who represented militant Islam. By fortifying the traditional religion, the king may have tried to protect his kingdom from the impact of the north. Ghana, however, was overcome by the Almoravids, and its resistance to Islam broke with the destruction of its political power. The Ghana of al-Idrīsī, in the twelfth century, was a Muslim kingdom.

Even before the Almoravid conquest, Islam had made some advance in Ghana, among the Soninke traders, who operated on the internal routes of the Western Sudan. As traders they were in close contact with the Muslims of North Africa, and through their trade they became detached from the agricultural and tribal way of life in which the traditional African religion is rooted. They adopted Islam more easily, and in their wanderings could find hospitality as well as a sense of community among fellow Muslim traders in the communities which developed along the trade routes.

Such communities are described by al-Bakrī on the routes leading to the goldfields. It was these traders who carried Islam further into the interior. The conversion of the chief of Malel beyond the Upper Senegal is a good example of the process of Islamisation. Malel was afflicted with drought for some years, but all prayers and sacrifices were of no avail. Then a Muslim resident promised the king that if he accepted Islam, he, the Muslim, would pray for his relief. He persisted until the king agreed. The Muslim taught the king the prayers, some passages from the Koran, and the basic obligations of the faith. Then, on Friday, the king had to undertake his ablutions, to put on a cotton robe, specially made for him by the Muslim, and the two went to a rise on the ground. The Muslim prayed all night, while the king repeated the 'amen'. At dawn abundant rain came down, and the king, firm in his new faith, ordered the expulsion of the magicians and the destruction of the idols. Together with his heir and courtiers he became sincerely attached to Islam, but the people of his kingdom remained 'idolators'. 'Since that time their kings have borne the title of *al-Musulmānī*.'[95]

Islam became a factor of division: the ruling group was Muslim while the commoners remained pagan. This crisis in relations between the two was of considerable concern to the king of Aluken, tributary to Ghana, of whom al-Bakrī says that having become a Muslim he concealed this from his subjects.[96] The way out of this dilemma was for rulers to maintain a middle position between Islam and the traditional religion, so that most of them were neither real Muslims nor complete pagans.[97] From the middle position some chiefs turned towards the true Islam, while others fell back on their traditional religion.

The Malel of al-Bakrī was a Malinke chieftaincy, though not necessarily the one that later emerged as the empire of Mali. Traditions are explicit that the kings of Mali had been Muslims before Sundjata, the founder of the empire. Mūsā Allakoi of the oral traditions and Barmandana of Ibn-Khaldūn are said to have gone to Mecca, probably in the twelfth century. Yet the traditional history of Sundjata contains hardly any elements of Islam; rather it emphasises the rôle of Sundjata as the great magician. Though Sundjata came from a dynasty which had already accepted Islam, at least nominally, in the critical hour of history when he had to mobilise the national resources of the Malinke he turned to the traditional religion

95 Al-Bakrī, *al-Masālik*, pp. 177–8 (trans. pp. 333–4).
96 *Ibid.*, p. 179 (trans. p. 335).
97 For a study of a comparable situation, see N. Levtzion, *Muslims and Chiefs in West Africa: a study of Islam in the Middle Volta Basin in the pre-colonial period*, Oxford, 1968.

for support, to the particularist spirit of the nation rather than to the universalistic appeal of Islam. The same is true of Sonni ʿAlī, who made the Songhay masters of a large empire. It is these rulers who remain the god-heroes of the national traditions rather than their successors, like Mansā Mūsā of Mali or Askiya Muḥammad of Songhay, who were to become famous as great Muslim rulers through the Arabic records.

From its centre on the Upper Niger, Mali spread into the Sahil. Old centres of Islam—Dia, Walata, and others—became part of the empire. The Muslim Wangara traders were active over the wide network of routes which covered the empire. These traders as well as North African merchants came to live at the capital of the kings of Mali. The military conquest of a vast and heterogeneous empire had to be followed by a policy which would give the empire more cohesion. Islam as a supra-tribal religion could provide the cement needed; the routes and the Muslim traders' traffic could serve as the veins that would make the empire a functioning organism. Islam demands the pilgrimage, and this adventurous voyage, undertaken by several rulers of Mali, brought them nearer to the Muslim world north of the Sahara. Fes in Morocco became not only another commercial centre in the great trade system, but also the centre where scholars from Mali went to further their studies in the Muslim sciences,[98] as well as the capital of a Sultan regarded as brother to the king of Mali. At the court of the king of Mali a memorial ceremony for the late Abū 'l-Ḥasan, king of Morocco, was held in 1352.[99]

This all added strength to Islam in Mali. It was during the period of its greatness that Mali looked like a real Muslim empire. Our information about the state of Islam in Mali comes from Arabs who knew Mali at the time of Mansā Mūsā and his brother Sulaymān. Of the latter al-ʿUmarī says that he continued the work of his brother Mūsā in spreading Islam throughout his dominions. He built mosques and instituted the Friday public prayers. He attracted Muslim scholars to his country, and was himself a student of the religious sciences.[100]

Ibn-Baṭṭūṭa was an eye-witness to what he describes. The Muslim leaders had official status at the court, and were present at royal audiences. The king and all members of the court took part in the public prayers held on the two great Islamic festivals. The preacher's sermon consisted of admonition and warning, eulogy of the king and exhortations to persist in obedience to him.[101] The presence of the king in this prayer made it an official occasion. Non-Muslims also attended it. This was the support accorded to Islam by the king, and in return the whole prestige of this religion was directed to exhorting loyalty to the ruler.

98 Al-Saʿdī, *T. al-Sūdān*, p. 57 (trans. p. 92).
99 Ibn-Baṭṭūṭa, *Voyages*, iv, p. 400.
100 Al-ʿUmarī, *Masālik*, p. 53.
101 Ibn-Baṭṭūṭa, *Voyages*, iv, pp. 409–410.

Ibn Baṭṭūta was impressed by the punctiliousness with which people in Mali observed the Muslim prayers. On Fridays a man had to go early to the mosque if he wanted a place, so great was the crowd. On Fridays and festival days all were dressed in white. The people were very concerned with learning the Koran by heart.[102] All this leaves us with the impression that we are in a real Muslim centre, like Fes or Qairawān. However, Ibn-Baṭṭūṭa spent most of his time in the Muslims' quarter and not among the Malinke commoners of whom he might have given a different description. Yet Ibn-Baṭṭūṭa himself was critical enough to record customs inconsistent with Islam. On the Festival day, in the afternoon, there was a traditional ceremony when dances were performed in the presence of the king and the dignitaries, and the *dyeli* (griots) dressed in garments of feathers with wooden masks representing birds performed their rites which included the recital of traditional history.[103] This shows the duality existing in the king's court. The Muslim festival became an official one, and on such an occasion a traditional ceremony, providing a bond between the people and their king, between the king and his ancestors, should also be performed. Ibn-Baṭṭūṭa also deplored the custom of putting dust on the head when greeting the king. It is likely that in Mali, as in Ghana, stranger Muslims were exempted from this custom, and greeted the king by clapping hands.[104]

A crucial problem in Islam is the application of Muslim law. There were Muslim Cadis in the principal towns, but their jurisdiction was probably limited to the foreign Muslim community, and to those Sudanese Muslims who became completely detached from the traditional way of life. The gap between orthodox Muslim law and customs was most apparent in marriage procedure and sexual behaviour, which more than once shocked Ibn-Baṭṭūṭa.[105]

Islam was observed in different degrees by different groups in the kingdom. Through its adaptability to, and compromise with, the African way of life, Islam appealed to a wide section of the population. The unity and purity of Islam was maintained by that group of real Muslims, prominent among whom were the scholars. They had a privileged status, and had much influence. The mosque and the preacher's house at the capital were sanctuaries for wrongdoers.[106] Dia, an old Muslim town in Massina, was autonomous under the rule of its Cadi, and the Sultan could not pursue into the town one who had sought its sanctuary.[107]

102 *Ibid.*, pp. 422–3.
103 *Ibid.*, pp. 410–14.
104 *Ibid.*, pp. 423–4; see also, Al-ʿUmarī (*Masālik*, pp. 64, 69), on sorcery and pagan burial customs in Mali.
105 Ibn-Baṭṭūṭa, *Voyages*, iv, pp. 388–90; see also, al-Saʿdī, *T. al-Sūdān*, p. 5 (trans. pp. 9–10). Sonni 'Alī's father was married to two sisters, and al-ʿUmarī, *Masālik*, pp. 72–3, tells that Mansa Mūsā took free women as concubines.
106 Ibn-Baṭṭūṭa, *Voyages*, iv, pp. 418–19.
107 *Ibid.*, p. 395. See also *T. al-Fattāsh*, pp. 60–1, 179 (trans. pp. 115–18, 314).

Of all the Muslim centres Timbuktu was the most famous. Though it reached its height under the Songhay it had already been important under Mali. It was in that period that the two important mosques, the Friday mosque and the Sankore mosque, were built. These served not only for prayers, but also for studies. Shaykh ʿAbd al-Raḥmān al-Tamīmī, who came from the Ḥijāz with Mansā Mūsā, found that scholars in Timbuktu were more learned than he was, and went to Fes to study before coming back to Timbuktu.[108] It was in the time of Mansā Mūsā that Abu-Isḥāq al-Sāḥilī, to whom the introductions of Muslim architecture is attributed, lived in Timbuktu.[109]

In the fifteenth century Mali lost Timbuktu, Jenne, and the other Muslim centres of the Sahil. With its decline, the foreign Muslim community probably left the capital. We have no information about the state of Islam at that period, but from what we know about the Malinke in the nineteenth century, it is likely that Islam declined with the disintegration of the empire into its component parts. Muslims remained around the courts of the chiefs, but chiefs returned to the middle position between Islam and the traditional religion, with a greater emphasis on the latter. Only the Wangara, the ubiquitous Muslim traders, remained attached to true Islam, and it was they who continued to spread it during the following centuries.

108 Al-Saʿdī, *T. al-Sūdān*, p. 51 (trans. pp. 83–4).
109 Ibn-Khaldūn, *K. Taʾrīkh*, i, pp. 265–6 (*Histoire*, ii, pp. 113–14). Ibn-Baṭṭūṭa, *Voyages*, iv, p. 431. Leo Africanus, *Description*, ii, p. 467.

CHAPTER 5

The early states of the Central Sudan

ABDULLAHI SMITH

THE PEOPLING OF THE REGION

The region with which we shall be concerned in this chapter is the area circumscribed by a line running from the mountains of Tibesti in the north-east, southwards (through the Jurab depression) to Lake Fitri in Kanem, and thence slightly south of west (across the middle course of the Shari-Logone river system and the great bend of the Gongoḷa) to the northern foothills of the central Nigerian highlands; from there north and north-east across the valley of the Gulbin Kebbi to the southern end of the Azben plateau; returning to Tibesti via the great *erg* of the Tenéré. This rough parallelogram has an area of something over 400,000 square miles, which is nowadays roughly equally divided between the Republics of Nigeria, Chad and Niger.[1]

During the last 20,000 years or so, the region, though free of tectonic movements, has been subject to sensational climatic changes, and these have in turn brought about radical modifications in the conditions of human life in the area. Some general account of these changes is essential for any understanding of the development of human society in this region which eventually became known to the Arab geographers of a thousand years ago as the central part of *bilād al-Sūdān*.

The study of palaeoclimate and its effects on human ecology in this area is still in its early stages, and such conclusions as have been reached up to the present can only be tentative and probably subject to substantial modifications as investigation proceeds. But even at this stage it is perhaps possible to speak with some confidence of certain developments the significance of which, so far as we are aware, has not yet received the discussion which it appears to merit.[2]

1 I wish to acknowledge my thanks to Malam Ado Jos for his help in the preparation of the map on p. 159 and to Mr Ibrahim Mamuru for typing the MS.

2 For useful summaries of work done on palaeoclimatic and associated studies in this
(*continued on p.* 160)

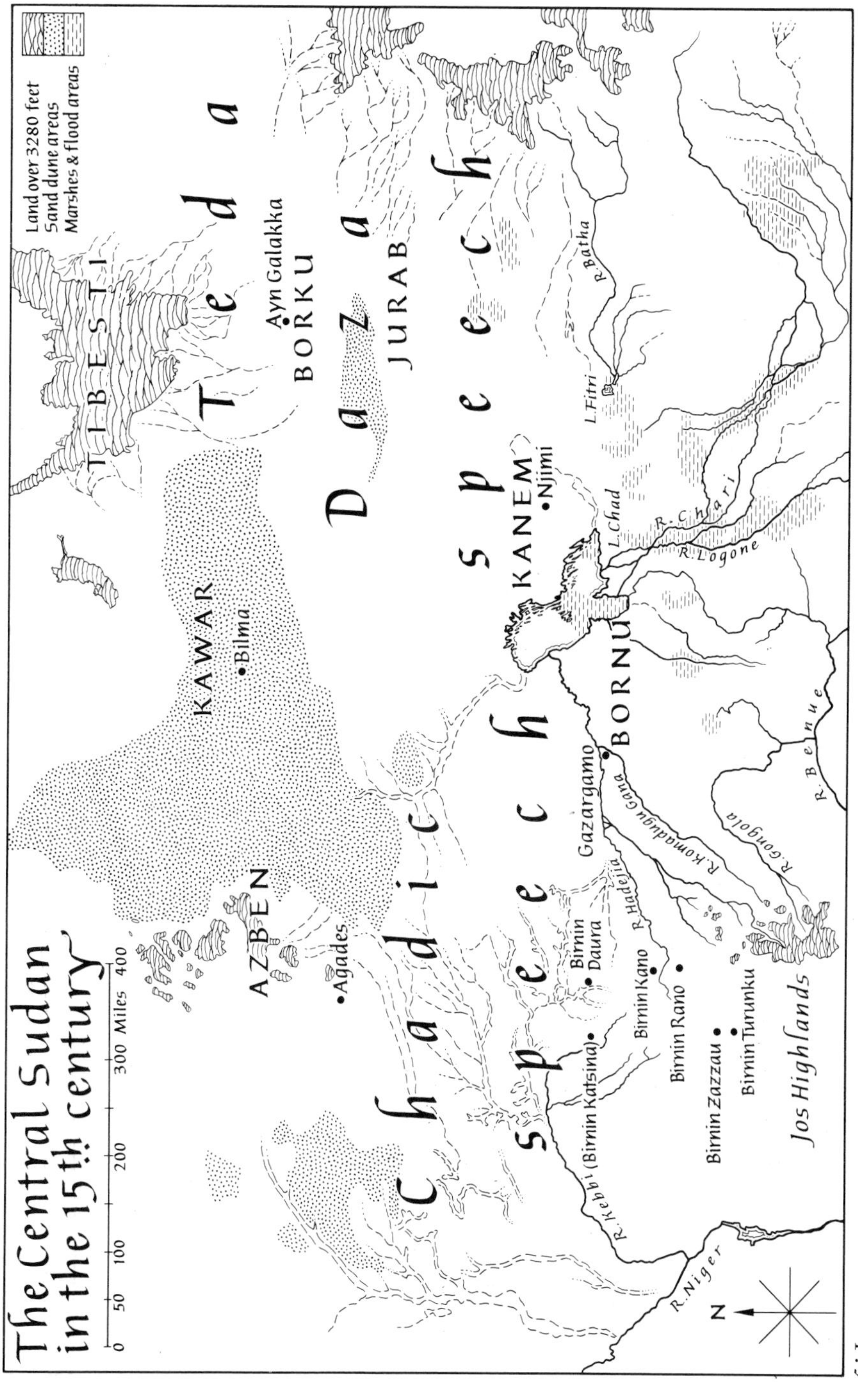
The Central Sudan in the 15th century
Land over 3280 feet
Sand dune areas
Marshes & flood areas
0 50 100 200 300 400 Miles
TIBESTI
Teda speech
Daza speech
Chadic speech
KAWAR
•Bilma
AZBEN
•Agades
Ayn Galakka
BORKU
JURAB
KANEM
•Njimi
BORNU
Gazargamo
L. Fitri
L. Chad
R. Batha
R. Chari
R. Logone
R. Benue
R. Gongola
R. Komadugu Gana
R. Hadejia
R. Kebbi
R. Niger
Birnin Daura
Birnin Kano
Birnin Rano
Birnin Katsina (Birnin Katsina)
Birnin Zazzau
Birnin Turunku
Jos Highlands
N

5:1

First, it would appear that anciently this region was divided into two roughly equal zones east and west of a line running in a south-westerly direction from Kawar on the northern edge of the region towards the north-eastern edge of the Jos Plateau. The zone east of this line 20,000 years ago was almost entirely occupied by a large lake, the Mega-Chad. This great sheet of water, the size of the present Caspian Sea, stretched as far south-west as modern Bama and Gashua in Nigeria, and in the north-east to the foothills of Tibesti. There is little doubt that the shorelands of at least the northern part of this lake provided a suitable habitat for the hunters and food gatherers of Old Stone Age times. But of these people, or their contemporaries, the Old Stone Age hillmen of central Nigeria, we know practically nothing.[3] It is said that the Mega-Chad may have remained full until about 5,000 years ago.[4]

The western zone of our region was very different in this era of the Mega-Chad. Here was a swell of land traversed by rivers flowing either south-eastwards from the massif of Azben in the north-west into the Chad, or south-westwards from the watershed stretching between Azben and the Jos Plateau, to the Niger beyond the western edge of our region. This upland is believed to have supported a parkland flora merging into denser vegetation in the south-west during this period. But again we know practically nothing about its Old Stone Age inhabitants.[5]

Then after about 7,000 B.P., dramatic changes in climate appear to have begun in this region: changes which brought about not only a substantial alteration in the distribution of surface water, but also a series of revolutionary modifications in the fauna and flora and consequently the conditions of human life. Speaking in very general terms we may describe these changes as the progressive substitution of a hot dry climate for a cooler, wetter one. This process has continued down to recent times and may still be going on.[6] The process of desiccation cannot be described in detail. We are dealing with a very long period of time (7,000 years or

(2 *continued*)
region see F. C. Howell and F. Bourliere, eds., *African Ecology and Human Evolution*, London, 1964, especially the chapters by T. Monod and A. T. Grove and R. A. Pullen. A brief but more recent summary is in R. E. Moreau, *The Bird Faunas of Africa and the Islands*, New York and London, 1966, ch. 3. See also H. J. Hugot, ed., *Missions Berliet: Tenéré-Chad*, Paris, 1962, *passim*; and A. T. Grove and A. Warren, 'Quaterny landforms and climate on the south side of the Sahara', *Geographical Journal*, cxxxiv, 2, 1968, pp. 194–209.

3 R. C. Soper, 'The Stone Age in Northern Nigeria', *Journal of the Historical Society of Nigeria*, iii, 2, 1965, pp. 176–94.

4 Grove and Warren, *op. cit.*, suggests that Borku immediately south of Tibesti continued to enjoy a Mediterranean flora until as late as 5000 B.P. This opinion is based on the carbon-dating of pollen recovered from the area. Carbon-dating of shell from other parts of the Mega-Chad zone confirms that the lake surface stood at 320 metres above sea-level as late as 5000 B.P. Its present height is 282 metres. The well-known Bama ridge of Bornu Province of Nigeria is a shore line of the Mega-Chad.

5 Soper, *op. cit.*

6 See Chapter 1, above.

more) during which many fluctuations of climate may have taken place.[7] But about the general trend there can be no doubt, and here we are merely concerned with certain undeniable effects of this trend. First, the great Chad began to dry up, leaving eventually only the shallow lake which we know today in its south-western corner. Secondly, the dense vegetation of the southern edge of our region retreated to leave in its place the Guinea savannah of today. Thirdly, the northern half of the region suffered extreme desiccation to produce a desert of sand dunes stretching from near Agades eastwards into the Jurab depression which had once been the deepest part of the Mega-Chad. This last change, producing what is called the great *erg* of the Tenéré and its eastward extension, may perhaps have been completed only in the second millennium B.C.

Of the hunters, farmers, and pastoralists who lived in the region during the era of desiccation we know much more than we do of their predecessors of the era of the Mega-Chad. Neolithic and early Iron Age men have left many traces of their material culture, not only in the implements they used, but also in the monuments they built and their *art rupestre*.[8] And though our knowledge is only slowly accumulating and remains entirely fragmentary for any time before the end of the first millennium A.D., there are certain extremely important general suggestions we can, with some confidence, make about the effect on human society in the region of the advancing desiccations of the last seven millennia: suggestions which may eventually form a sound basis for our understanding of how the pattern of ethnic grouping known to us in historical times in this region came to be established.

The desiccation produced an entirely new configuration for this region so far as conditions for human settlement are concerned. First, there developed a roughly triangular stretch of country, Azben-Borku-Chad, practically uninhabitable by human beings, except along the route Chad-Bilma-Jado. This has meant that for the last three or four millennia there have existed in our region two zones where men have been able to live, effectively separated from each other (so far as mass contact of people is concerned) by the great *erg*, and only contiguous in the area immediately surrounding Lake Chad. Even in the neighbourhood of Chad, east-west communication probably remained difficult for a long time, because of the swamps adjoining the lake on the south side. This has in turn meant that the historical development of the region south-west of the *erg* has been

7 Palaeo-climatologists are confusedly divided in their views on this.
8 See Hugot, *op. cit.*, *passim*; H. Lhote, 'Gravures, peintures et inscriptions rupestres du Kaouar, de l'Air et de l'Adrar des Iforas', *Bulletin de l'Institut Français de l'Afrique Noire*, xiv, 4, 1952; P. Huard and J. M. Massip, 'Monuments du Sahara Nigero-Tchadien', *Bull. I.F.A.N.*, xxix, 1-2, 1967, pp. 1-27. For recent discoveries in the area just south of the present Lake Chad see G. E. Connah, in *First* and *Second Interim Reports of the Northern History Research Scheme*, Ahmadu Bello University and University of Ibadan, Zaria, 1966 and 1967.

separate in many ways from that of the eastern inhabited zone.

This separateness is not only reflected in the persistence of two very different language systems: the so-called Chadic languages of the west[9] and the Teda-Daza languages of the east,[10] but has also been manifest in the different processes of state formation which have characterised the two zones in historical times and which we shall be considering in this chapter. In the west we have the formation of the Hausa states proceeding separately from the formation of the first Kanuri empire in the east. It is only right at the end of the period we are dealing with in this chapter, namely in the fifteenth century, that the barrier between east and west is effectively breached by the establishment of the second Kanuri empire west of the Chad in the plain of Bornu. Even then the Kanuri of Bornu can only with the greatest difficulty maintain contact with their homeland beyond the lake and the ancient barrier closes behind them again in the eighteenth century.

Another important effect of the desiccation was to cause a thinning out of the population in the northern part of the region on both sides of the *erg* barrier and a concentration of population in the south. As conditions of life in the north became more and more difficult as a result of the declining rainfall, northern peoples would have no alternative but to move southwards into the relatively more humid lands of the Mega-Chad basin and the country between the Chad and the great bend of the Niger (which remains well watered down to the present time). It is suggested that this hypothesis of a substantial north–south movement of peoples during the era of the desiccation may touch on the oft-disputed basis of the many legends of ancient migration which characterise the orally preserved traditions of the people of Hausaland and Bornu-Kanem at the present day.[11]

9 These are listed in J. H. Greenberg, *Languages of Africa*, rev. edn, Bloomington, 1966, pp. 45–8. Examples are Hausa, Ngizim, Mober, Bolewa, the Kotoko languages, Margi, Bachama, Angas.

10 These are listed in *ibid.*, pp. 130–3. Examples are Teda, Daza, Kanembu, Kanuri, Zaghawa. The position of Kanuri in this group is not entirely clear (see J. Lukas, *A Study of the Kanuri Language*, London, 1937, pp. ix–x). The hypothesis we suggest is that a mixture of elements mainly from various old Daza languages, occasioned by the political unification of a number of tribal groups in Kanem, eventually produced the language nowadays known as Kanembu and which is widely spoken in Kanem at the present time. Then much later (fourteenth century A.D.) when large sections of the politically unified people speaking this language moved west of the lake and cut their connection with the peoples remaining east of the Chad (see below, p. 179), their language began to become differentiated from the speech of Kanem (partly no doubt through the assimilation of elements from Chadic languages already spoken west of the lake) to produce what we now know as Kanuri. If there is any truth in this, then Kanembu is really 'classical' Kanuri. A fragment in support of this hypothesis is to be found in the tradition among the Kanuri *'ulamā'* that Kanembu is the classical language of *tafsīr* in Bornu. This is of course a very tentative suggestion, as linguists have as yet paid no attention to this problem.

11 These legends of migration are specifically stories of north-south movement in the case of some Hausa groups. Elsewhere they are stories of migration from the east, but these ideas of eastern origin may well have gained currency in recent times through the eventual cultural orientation of the peoples concerned (i.e. Islamic and Christian). For ancient

(*continued opposite*)

And in a very general sense it can no doubt be argued that this concentration of population in the south eventually provided one very important condition for the emergence of statelike forms of government in the southern part of the region. We shall return to this question of movements of people and state formation later when we consider the origin of the Hausa states and the first Kanuri empire.

Finally, in connection with the hypothesis of north-south movement there arises the question of the fate of peoples already living in the southern zone. In the area of the Mega-Chad the desiccation is likely to have attracted people into the bottom-lands from all directions, creating a fertile source of conflict between immigrant groups: conflict which may have produced the Kanuri people. It is likely that this conflict was eventually resolved by the Kanuri domination of Kanem involving the assimilation or driving away of the southern peoples, though we lack evidence on this.

West of the Chad the development was different as no great imperial northern power emerged to dominate the southern area. The real position is in fact still obscure. The area of Hausaland and Bornu is linguistically homogeneous, all ethnic groups here (if one excepts the recent intrusion of the Kanuri) speaking Chadic languages, which certainly appear to have been the languages of our northern immigrants. The southern frontier of the region here is a linguistic frontier (as it is east of Chad), marking the dividing line between Chadic speech and the quite different Niger-Congo speech to the south.[12] This frontier may have been established as a result of the southward displacement of Niger-Congo-speaking peoples in face of an invasion of Chadic language-speaking groups from the north. Certainly some Niger-Congo language-speaking groups immediately south of the frontier, such as the Gwari people, have traditions of ancient migration from the north. And again, the area of the central Nigerian highlands which stand astride the frontier appears with its remarkable linguistic variety to have been a place of refuge for Niger-Congo language groups previously spread over a much wider area.[13] But traditions of conflict which such displacement must have involved are hard to come by. This may be because it all happened too long ago or because what traditions of ancient conflict once existed have by now all been assimilated to the preserved traditions of much more recent conflict in historical times between

(11 *continued*)
north-south movements among the Teda-Daza-speaking peoples east of the Chad, a fragment of evidence of a different sort is provided by the fact that the place-name *Kanem* is certainly derived from the word for 'south' in those languages (*anem*).

12 See map in J. H. Greenberg, *Studies in African Linguistic Classification*, New Haven, 1955, p. 47.

13 Greenberg (*Languages*, p. 175) claims that some thirty different Niger-Congo languages are spoken in the highlands, mainly on the western side. There is also a concentration of Afro-Asiatic languages (some fifteen) on the eastern side of the pleateau. But this latter is likely to have been caused by the expansion of the Kanuri in historical times.

northerners such as the Hausa people and more southerly groups of Niger-Congo speech. Yet what actually happened is still a mystery because it is difficult to see how small groups of Chadic-speaking settlers never achieving any great central organisation until historical times could possibly have displaced the more southerly peoples in the systematic and comprehensive way indicated by the clearcut east–west linguistic frontier.

A possible alternative hypothesis here is that the area of Hausaland and Bornu was only very sparsely populated before the immigration from the north, and that therefore the coming of the northerners did not give rise to any substantial displacement of people at all. It may perhaps have been the case that before the desiccation this area was covered by a network of streams and swamps (of which the river systems of the Gulbin Kebbi and the Komadugu Yobe are the remains) inimical to dense settlement, and only became able to support a large peasant population after it had dried out.[14] We cannot decide this with any certainty and the question of possible displacement of peoples in the Niger-Chad zone must for the present remain obscure.

The upshot of this discussion is that there is plenty of evidence to indicate with regard to the peopling of our region that the desiccation of the central Sahara produced two separate patterns of settlement: a concentration of Teda-Daza-speaking people in the area north-east of Lake Chad, and a concentration of Chadic-language-speaking people in the area of Hausaland and Bornu to the west of the lake. The era of the emergence of this settlement pattern may be provisionally regarded as the last millennium B.C. and the first A.D. We must now consider the cultural developments to which it gave rise, namely the rise of the first Kanuri empire and the development of the Hausa states.

THE FORMATION OF THE KANURI PEOPLE

The use of the word Kanuri in referring to events in Kanem in the first millennium A.D. is no doubt open to many objections. The antiquity of this word as an ethnic title is unknown. It may be of quite recent origin.[15] But it is proposed to use it here as the name of a group of Teda-Daza-

14 Even if the Mega-Chad had never been surrounded by swamps on its western side, it is clear that in the pluvial age a number of lakes and rivers had existed on the western edge of our region. How far this system extended into the region itself is not clear, but it must have represented a great volume of permanent surface water because it was into these lakes that the 'Upper' Niger discharged in pluvial times.

15 The meaning of the word is obscure. Attempts to derive it from the Arabic *nūri* ('people of light') or to regard it as a corruption of *Kanemri* are unsatisfactory. The earliest known occurrence of the word in written sources is eighteenth-century (in the poetry of the Fallata Bornu scholar Muḥammad al-Ṭāḥir b. Ibrāhīm). We cannot follow H. R. Palmer in claiming that this word occurs in the writings of the Arab geographer al-Gharnāti (d. A. D. 1169). What Palmer read there as 'Kanuri (Ganuri)', we read as *Fāwaha* (or *Qitāwaha* in the variant text) (*Sudanese Memoirs*, vol. ii, p. 90; *Tuḥfat al-albāb*, ed. G. Ferrand, *Jour. Asiatique*, 1925, p. 42).

speaking tribes forming a unified group in Kanem from the end of the first millennium A.D. who now go by that name, as no earlier name for them appears to have been preserved.

The precise date of the formation of the Kanuri people by some sort of coalition of previously separate Teda-Daza-speaking groups is unknown. But there is reason to believe that it took place during the first millennium A.D. as it appears to be closely connected with the emergence of a central ruling dynasty among them which we can, with some degree of confidence, assign to the ninth or tenth century A.D. The richness of the oral traditions about the origin of this people would also suggest a rather late origin, in contrast with the lack of traditions properly referring to the origin of the Hausa people, indicating the possibility of a very early origin of which memory has been lost.

The traditions of the Kanuri, many of which have been committed to writing in very recent times, say generally (though there are a number of versions which differ in detail) that a great Arab hero named Sayf b. Dhi Yazan gained control of a group of nomads, the Magumi, living to the north-east of Lake Chad.[16] The legends go on to say that he and his descendants subsequently established ascendancy, as chiefs of the Magumi, over a number of other tribal groups or sections of such groups who together came to constitute the Kanuri people: the Ngalaga, the Kangu, the Kayi, the Kuburi, the Kaguwa, the Tomagra, the Tubu.[17] Sayf and

16 This legend of origin has been the subject of much publication in recent times, particularly by H. R. Palmer, (*Bornu, Sahara and Sudan*, London, 1936; *Sudanese Memoirs*, 3 vols, Lagos, 1928) and Y. Urvoy, (*Histoire de l'empire du Bornou*, Paris, 1949 (abbreviated *infra as Bornu, SM,* and *Hist. Bornou*). The works of Palmer and Urvoy cited here may be taken as the basic secondary works available on the Kanuri empire. In the light of more recent unpublished work, however, it should be noted that these writers represent a largely outmoded historiography and they should be used with great caution. Palmer's publications in particular are extremely difficult to use. They are very confused, having no doubt been hastily produced in the spare time of an exceptionally busy colonial administrator. Even where clear they tend to be misleading because of the author's predilection for basing historiographical interpretation on apparent similarities of vocabulary in the languages of the peoples studied extending even to the acceptance of far-fetched parallels with ancient Egyptian and Greek. But Palmer was not a trained linguist and much of his writing in that field is in fact nonsensical. Below, we quote the documents he recovered, never his interpretation of them.

17 This is the general thesis of G. Nachtigal, *Sahara und Sudan*, 3 vols, Berlin, 1879–89, i, pp. 415–8. This valuable but neglected treatment of the origin of the Kanuri is largely followed here. The list of 'original' groups we give is confirmed in an anonymous MS of unknown provence recovered by Palmer (Jos Museum Arabic MSS, Palmer's 'Army Book'). Kangu is missing from Nachtigal's list but this is confirmed again by J. Lukas, (*A Study of the Kanuri Language*, London, 1937, p. x) who also identified two further groups, Ngema and Kennena, on whom we lack other information. Some Kayi and Magumi are still to be found as separate groups in Kanem today (A. Le Rouvreur, *Saheliens et Sahariens du Tchad*, Paris, 1962, p. 93). The modern 'Konkou' of that area may perhaps be Kangu (*ibid.*). The Ngalaga may have an ancient connection with Ain Ngalaga in Borku. Tomagra exist separately in present-day Tibesti where they are the ruling group (J. Chapelle, *Nomades noires du Sahara*, Paris, 1957, esp. pp. 83–95). Tubu is a general name for the people of Tibesti (*ibid., passim*).

his descendants thus established the dynasty of the *mais* (lords) of the Sefawa. This dynasty, founded in the ninth or tenth century A.D., continued, though with many vicissitudes, to rule the Kanuri people and their dependents for the best part of a millennium.[18] Here we have a political achievement of some magnitude and it is important for us to examine the bonds which held the tribes of the Kanuri people together in loyalty to the Sefawa over this remarkably long period and in addition brought under its control over the centuries a considerable number of non-Kanuri peoples.

The legends attribute all to the charisma of Sayf b. Dhi Yazan as a great Arab hero whose name is known throughout the Arabic-speaking world. These tales however do not tell us whence the *héros civilisateur* derived his power.[19] We do not really know, of course, what exactly happened to enable the Sefawa to establish their ascendancy in the way they did. But the emergence of dynasties having political control over several tribal groups is not an unknown phenomenon in the world of the desert nomads. It occurred again in our region towards the end of the fifteenth century in the foundation of the sultanate of Azben. In this instance, as we shall see later,[20] centralised political authority appears to have arisen by agreement among several groups of the desert Tuareg as a means of reducing inter-tribal conflict. But the tribes involved there never abandoned their individuality nor professed unquestioning obedience to the sultan. Thus the authority of that central government was always strictly limited and the sultans never emerged as the leaders of a new people. The conditions of intergroup conflict which prevail in that world where men are continually involved in struggle for the control of inadequate natural resources can always produce the temporary ascendancy of one group over another. But to extend this ascendancy, make it permanent and forge a new people from the groups involved, as happened north-east of Lake Chad in the first millennium A.D., is more difficult.

Let us examine the conditions which appear to have made possible the emergence of the Sefawa. Certainly they were a product of the nomad world. They maintained a pride in their nomad origin and preserved customs of nomad life long after they had built their cities and became the rulers of settled peoples in Kanem.[21] And it is no doubt significant that the first Kanuri empire was mainly established by conquering the desert dwellers of the central Sahara rather than by the conquest of the settled

18 The last of the mais of the Sefawa was executed in 1846.

19 I have dealt with this story in detail in 'Considerations relating to the origin of the Sefawa', *J.H.S.N.*, forthcoming.

20 Chapter 9, below.

21 The Arab geographer Al-Maqrīzi (d. 1442), probably deriving his information from the thirteenth century writer Ibn Saʿid al-Maghribi, says that the king of Kanem was still a nomad in mode of life. Down to the nineteenth century the Koyam of Bornu, who claim an ancient association with the dynasty, continued to attach great importance to the rearing of camels long after they had settled south of the Yo River in Bornu (Nachtigal, *loc. cit.*).

peoples of the savannah. The importance of military superiority in the process by which the Magumi forged the other tribal groups into a people loyal to the Sefawa must also be emphasised. Much seems to have depended on the effective use of cavalry. We do not know exactly whence they obtained their horses, but the valley of the Bahr al-Ghazal in which these developments are most likely to have taken place retains its reputation for horse-breeding down to the present day.[22] Yet victory in the tribal wars of the nomad world tends to be a temporary thing, merely suppressing the blood feud without removing the source of it. The feud can only be ended, if at all, by fusion of the warring groups through intermarriage. And indeed this also seems to have been a policy systematically pursued by the early leaders of the Sefawa. The overriding importance of this is to be seen in the fact that the only information preserved for us of the early rulers (besides their names and the length of their reigns) is on this very subject of intertribal marriage.[23] Thus Ibrahim (the second ruler) married Afalu of Kayi; Katuru (the sixth ruler) married Tsumagu of Ngalaga; Adyoma (the seventh ruler) married Ganjaya of Kayi; Bulu (the eighth ruler) married Azisana of Tomagra; Arku (the ninth ruler) married Tagasu also of Tomagra; ʿAbd al-Jalīl (the eleventh) married Takama of Kayi; Humai (the twelfth) married Kintā of the Tubu; and so on down to the sixteenth ruler who may have married a Magumi.[24] Intertribal marriage by itself, of course, is only a step in the direction of cementing tribal alliances. But the full importance of this policy as practised by the early Sefawa is indicated by the fact that, according to the kinglists, it was through the offspring of these non-Magumi women that the kingship descended. This gave the other groups a real stake in the ascendancy of the Sefawa by providing the necessary basis of self-interest for a continuing common allegiance to the dynasty.[25]

22 Race-horses for use in Nigeria are at present imported from this region.

23 This information derives from the traditional histories of the mais known as *girgam*. These exist written in Arabic or orally preserved in Kanuri verse. Published versions are in Palmer, *S.M.*, ii–iii, and *Kitāb fī shaʾn al-Sulṭān Idrīs b. ʿAlī*, Kano, 1930, pp. 130–7, and Introduction, pp. 1–9 (abbreviated as *K.S.I.*); English trans. in Palmer, *History of the First Twelve Years of the Reign of Mai Idris Alooma* Lagos, 1926; H. Barth, *Travels . . .*, repr., London, 1965, vol. ii, appendix i. Unpublished versions are in Deutsche Morganlandische Gesellschaft, Halle, Arabic MS 53; Jos Museum Arabic MSS, Palmer collection (microfilm in Northern History Research Scheme collection, Zaria). Some attempt has been made to analyse and collate the published sources by Urvoy, 'Chronologie de Bornu', *J. Soc. Afr.*, xi, 1941, pp. 21–32, and R. Cohen, 'The Bornu Kinglists', *Boston Papers on Africa*, ii, 1966, pp. 41–83. But these attempts have not proceeded very far and involve errors of interpretation.

24 Even this is not certain. The tribe of the woman concerned is given as *M?g?r?m?h*. This *may* be a corruption of Magumi, but as it occurs in both texts available (*K.S.I.*, p. 132, Halle MS, f. 1 (b)), this may really be said to be unlikely. *Mageri* is, of course, the Kanuri name for the people of the lower Shari-Logone valley (Lukas, *op. cit.*, p. x), and therefore *Magerima* might equally be the ruling people of that area. The Mai in question is Selemma b. Bukar, father of Dunama Dibbalemi (see pp. 175–6).

25 We should note in passing that here we may also have the origin of the influential position occupied throughout the history of the Sefawa by the *Magira* or 'Queen mother'.

This allegiance seems further to have been strengthened in the course of time by a religious factor: the development of the 'divine kingship'. The way in which the Sefawa became divine kings is not clear. The conditions of nomad life would not appear to facilitate the emergence of this type of authority where the ruler lives in a ritual seclusion from his subjects surrounded by much mystery and taboo. It is possible that the Sefawa adopted this institution from settled peoples with whom they came in contact in the region of Kanem. It may even be that some of the groups which came together under the Sefawa from the beginning were sedentarised before their incorporation in the Kanuri and had previously developed such an institution. Whatever the origin, it is probable that divine kingship existed in Kanem as early as the tenth century A.D. The evidence for this is to be found in the writings of the early Arab geographers.[26]

The first mention of Kanem in such works is in al-Yaʿqūbī who says that it is a country inhabited by people called Zaghawa. Now these Zaghawa appear in many Arabic works on the Sahara and Sudan, and modern writers[27] have gone so far as to attribute the foundation of the Kanuri people and empire to them. This appears to be a quite unwarranted assumption as the Kanuri sources make no mention of this people. It is also the case that they no longer live in Kanem, but far to the east in the north-western corner of what is now the Sudanese Republic. A more plausible assumption would seem to be that they were a group driven out of Kanem by the emergent Kanuri and never incorporated in the latter. Confirma-

26 Much respect has in the past been paid to the writings of the Arab geographers as source material for the history of Sudan. Those who have found favour in the study of the Kanuri empire are mainly Al-Yaʿqūbi (fl. late ninth century A.D.), *Kitāb al-buldān*; al-Muḥallabi (fl. late tenth century A.D.), *Kitāb al-masalik wa-l-mamalik*; Al-Idrisi (d. 1166) *Ṣifat al-maghrib wa arḍ al-sudan*; Ibn Saʿīd al-Maghribi (d. 1274 or 1286) *Ṣurat al-arḍ fi-l-ṭūl wa-l-ʿarḍ*; Al-ʿUmari (d. 1348) *Taʿrīf fī musṭalat al-sharīf*; Al-Maqrīzi, (d. 1442) *Kitāb al-mawāʿiẓ w-al-iʿtibār fi dhikr al-khiṭaṭ wa-l-athār*, etc. These texts have mostly been translated into French in Youssouf Kamal, *Monumenta cartographica Africae et Aegypti*, 16 vols, Cairo and Leiden, 1926–51. But the literature is difficult to obtain, and non-Arabic-speaking students may have to be content with the summaries given in R. Mauny, *Tableau géographique de l'ouest africain au Moyen Age*, Dakar, 1961. At the same time it should be noted that these works, as a whole, provide unsatisfactory source material. They are defective for Kanem because none of them are eye-witness accounts and they generally lack any criticism of the indirect sources of information which they use. Some, like the works of Al-Maqrīzi, borrow estensively from much earlier writers and the surviving texts do not always indicate what is quotation and what is not. Some incorporate palpable errors of topographical description and betray a childish predilection for 'tall stories' of monsters and marvels. Finally it is important to realise that these writings show substantial racial prejudice against the Negroes on the part of the authors, prejudice which destroys their value as source material for African history. A readily available example of this is in the *Tuḥfat al-albāb* of Abū Ḥāmid al-Gharnāṭī (d. 1169) (quoted in Palmer, *SM*, ii, pp. 90–2). This source material therefore must be used with great care. As an example of such a text, both useful and misleading, we have appended at the end of this chapter a hitherto unpublished English translation of a passage from Ibn Saʿīd (ed. J. V. Gines, as *Libro de la Extension de la Tierra en Longitud y Latitud*, Tetuan, 1958).

27 Such as J. S. Trimingham, *A History of Islam in West Africa*, London, 1965, pp. 104–5.

tion of this is perhaps provided by the fact that certain sections of the Zaghawa today actually claim a Bornuan origin.[28] Whatever the truth of this, there is no reason to doubt that the Zaghawa did inhabit Kanem in the ninth century A.D.

The next piece of information about these people is provided in the tenth century by al-Muḥallabi (A.D. 985) who tells us that their religion is king-worship (*ʿibādat mulūkihim*) and gives the further detail that no one is allowed to see the king eat. Now whether the Sefawa took over this institution from the Zaghawa *in toto* we do not know. But there is good reason to believe that the dynasty did develop some at least of the characteristics of divine kingship and that these were well established among them before the end of the twelfth century A.D. This can be inferred from the fact that even though the dynasty was officially converted to Islam at that time the ritual seclusion of the monarch (which is of course very un-Islamic) continued to be practised long after.[29]

A final bond which cemented the unification of the Kanuri in common obedience to the Sefawa appears to have been provided by the increasing sedentarisation of the whole group. Some clans of the tribes which formed the Kanuri people have of course retained their nomadism down to the present, some of the Tomagra for example. But it seems clear that the full development of the Kanuri people could not take place until the whole group had become anchored firmly to a particular territory (Kanem) and developed sedentary habits. It is significant that those clans of the Tomagra which continue to nomadise in Tibesti at the present time do not regard themselves as Kanuri and were probably never at any time integrated into the people.

This sedentarisation of the tribes clearly took a long time to accomplish. The eventual success of the Sefawa in bringing it about is perhaps to be measured by their ability to establish urban centres in Kanem. The foundation of cities as a stage in the process of state formation and national development generally will be considered in greater detail when we discuss the Hausa states, where much material is available on this subject. Here we can only note the fragments which have come down to us about the early efforts of the Sefawa in this direction. For the ninth century al-Yaʿqūbī says that the Zaghawa of Kanem 'dwell in huts made of reeds,

28 A. J. Arkell, 'The medieval history of Darfur, II', *Sudan Notes and Records*, xxxii, 2, p. 218.

29 Even in the early nineteenth century the Mai granted audience from behind a screen. See below, p. 173, n. 41, for a discussion of other aspects of the 'divine kingship'. The power of the monarch appears for example to have been partially derived from the fact that he was the custodian of certain sacred objects, such as *mune*, in which the power of the supernatural resided. Much interesting material on divine kingship in the Central Sudan generally is given in Arkell, *op. cit.*, pp. 225–38. Concerning other details of the old Kanuri religion we know practically nothing. Pre-Islamic survivals such as belief in 'bush demons' (as Lukas calls them) which now forms part of the 'fairy-tale' side of rural Kanuri folklore may derive from the religions of the pre-Kanuri inhabitants of Bornu.

for they do not live in towns'. In the tenth century al-Muḥallabi mentions 'the towns of Bilma' (*Madā'in Bilmā'*), and Manan and Tarazaki of the Zaghawa. It is al-Idrīsī (d. 1166) who first gives us information about towns in Kanem: Mānān and Anjīmī. He suggests that Mānān was the seat of the ruler and Anjīmī was a small town farther south. Mānān (if it is the Mātān of Ibn Saʿīd) was situated 'in the direction of the corner of the lake' and Anjīmī (the Jīmī of Ibn Saʿīd) away to the south-east. Ibn Saʿīd al-Maghribi (d. 1274 or 1286) states that Mātān was the capital (*qāʿida*) of Kanem down to the time of the Islamisation of the Sefawa, and thereafter Jīmī became the seat of the kings. Mānān/Mātān does not often appear in the Kanuri sources, but Njimi is everywhere accepted as the ancient seat of the dynasty.[30] It is not clear when the Sefawa established themselves there (probably in the mid-thirteenth century A.D.[31]), but its emergence as the permanent capital city no doubt marks an important stage in the development of the Kanuri state.

These considerations relating to the emergence of the Kanuri people under the rule of the Sefawa have been presented here at some length as this is a subject strangely neglected in recent writings. Palmer and Urvoy,[31a] who devoted most attention to the early history of the Sefawa, accepted uncritically the simple hypothesis that this history is merely the story of the way in which a group of Hamitic (Berber) invaders from the Sahara imposed a statelike political structure on a number of politically segmented Negro peoples of the central Sudan. This treatment of the subject is defective on two counts. First the Magumi and their followers were not Berbers but negroid nomads of the south-central Sahara bordering on the Sudan, speaking a Nilo-Saharan language and belonging to the same stock as the present day Tubu of Tibesti, Bidayat and Qurʿān of Ennedi, and the Zaghawa of north-western Durfur. Secondly, this 'Hamitic hypothesis' offers no explanation of the way in which these nomads, whose traditional political system, dictated no doubt by the conditions of desert life, was (and still is to an extent) one of extreme segmentation, came to evolve the highly centralised political institutions which, in the form of the Sefawa monarchy, they are said to have imposed on the settled Negro inhabitants of Kanem. But it has been widely applied to the problem of state formation in West Africa, and the exposure of its weaknesses in the field we are now considering should perhaps alert students to an examination of its inadequacy elsewhere. We shall return to this question in our consideration of the origin of the Hausa states.

Meanwhile we should proceed with the consideration of the next stage in the development of the Kanuri people under the Sefawa, namely that of

30 But strangely enough no archaeological investigation of its site has yet been attempted.
31 The first mai to be buried in Njimi, according to the *girgam*, was Biri b. Dunama (second half thirteenth century).
31a See above, p. 165, n. 16.

the introduction of Islam. We have seen that the early religion of the Kanuri appears to have involved the concept of the divine king, a concept widespread among the old religious systems of West Africa. This concept is essentially un-Islamic in nature. Yet the Kanuri people were developing at a time when Islam was beginning to spread in Africa, and the geographical situation of Kanem was such that the people of that country were bound eventually to come into contact with carriers of the new faith. The earliest recorded appearance of Muslims in the vicinity of Kanem occurred in 46 A.H. (A.D. 666–7) when raiders under the command of the emir ʿUqba b. Nāfiʿ reached the region of Kawar.[32] This indeed pre-dated the rise of the Sefawa, and although these raiders withdrew and we hear no more of Arab military penetration into this area, the fact is that the old road which they followed connected Kanem directly with the Tripolitanian coast and provided a gateway through which Islamic influences could enter the territory of the Kanuri throughout the period of the rise of the Sefawa.

Much attention in recent times has been paid to the early development of trans-Saharan cultural and economic connections by the far-western routes, especially those linking Morocco with the Sudan between the Senegal and Niger valleys, and much has been said about the importance in this traffic of the Moroccan desert-port of Sijilmasa which flourished from the tenth century onwards if not earlier.[33] This has somewhat obscured the fact that an equally practicable and important trans-Saharan link lay from Kanem to Tripoli via Bilma in Kawar and the great Fezzani desert port of Zawīla. Most of the early Arab geographers pay some attention to this last town, describing it as an important market for trade between Ifriqiyya and the Sudan. The southbound trade from Zawīla appears to have been mainly in cloth, while slaves were imported from the south. It was well-known in al-Bakrī's time for a special type of leather called *zawīliyya* and it is not impossible that this (like the famous 'Morocco' leather of the far west) was imported from the Sudan. These geographers also say that Zạwīla was a frontier town of the Maghrib set against the country of the Negroes,[34] and it is clear that it maintained close contact with the Saharan nomads belonging to that group of peoples who in our opinion figure so largely in the early history of the Sefawa.

It would appear that it was by this road that Islamic influences penetrated into Kanem rather than from the west (beyond the barrier of the *erg* and the Chad) or from the east (where the Christian kingdoms of the Upper

32 Ibn ʿAbd al-Ḥakam, *Futūḥ Miṣr*, ed. C. C. Torrey, New Haven, 1922, p. 195.
33 For example, E. W. Bovill, *Caravans of the Old Sahara*, London, 1933, re-ed. as *Golden Trade of the Moors,* London, 1958; 2nd edn, 1968. See chapter 4 above.
34 On Zawīla see Al-Iṣtakhri (b. 951), *Kitāb al-Masālik wa-l-mamālik*, ed. M. J. de Goeje, Leiden, 1876, p. 44; Al-Bakri, *Kitāb al-mughrib fi dhikr bilād al-Ifriqiyya wa-l-Maghrib,* ed. de Slane, Paris, 1911, pp. 10–11; Al-Idrisi, *Ṣifat*, ed. Dozy and de Goeje, Leiden, 1866, p. 133; Al-Yaʿqūbi, *Al-buldān*, ed. de Goeje, Leiden, 1892, p. 345.

Nile continued to flourish). It would also appear that it entered by peaceful means, through the activities of traders and itinerant scholars. We can thus surmise that the early towns of the Sefawa contained colonies of Muslims (as did the ancient city of Ghana), and that these became important, especially to the rulers, because of their connection with foreign trade. In such circumstances, it is suggested, the conversion of the dynasty eventually took place. Kanuri sources suggest that the first ruler to adopt Islam was Humai, son of Selemma, the twelfth mai, whom we can with some confidence assign to the late eleventh century.[35] His teacher is said to have been one Muḥammad b. Māni, and the latter's descendants continued for a long time to hold a privileged position at the court, the Islamic advisers of the mais claiming descent from him as late as the sixteenth century.[36] This is roughly confirmed by Ibn Saʿīd al-Maghribi (d. 1274 or 1286) if we assume that he was writing about the reign of Mai Dunama Dibbalemi as he says that the great-great-grandfather (*al-jidd al-rābiʿ*) of the mai of his time was the one who converted to Islam.[37] Al-Maqrīzī's conflicting suggestion that it was Dunama Dibbalemi himself (mid-thirteenth century) who was first converted may no doubt be explained by the fact that this geographer was writing much later and lacked reliable sources of information. It is also no doubt the case that the international fame of Dunama Dibbalemi far exceeded that of his predecessors.

Now it is not easy to say just what impact on the Kanuri as a whole this conversion of the dynasty to Islam had. There used to be a tendency among writers on the history of the Western Sudan (such as the great Delafosse) to assume that the early conversion of dynasties to Islam was not followed by the conversion of their people. The rulers in question are said to have opposed widespread conversion for fear that this would detract from their veneration as divine kings. But we have no documentary evidence that this was their attitude in Kanem, and whatever may have been the views of the Sefawa in this matter it is quite clear at least that they took the new faith seriously. Dunama, the successor of Humai, performed the Hajj with great pomp twice and was drowned in the Red Sea on his way for the third time. The next mai, Biri, is remembered as a *faqīh*; his grandson Selemma was a mosque builder and honoured the learned Imam ʿAbdallah b. Bukar. There is in fact indication that during this early period the privileged position of the Kanuri *ʿulamāʾ* was established and this of course was a necessary prerequisite for large-scale conversion among the people.[38] The first period of the Islamic era in Kanem comes to a climax with the

35 By working backwards through the reign lengths of the Mais given in the *girgam*.
36 Thus the famous Masbarma family.
37 See appendix to this chapter.
38 The Kanuri *ʿulamāʾ* eventually came to occupy a position of great authority in the Kanuri empire, and their fame extended to Egypt and the Far Maghrib.

mid C13th

reign of Dunama Dibbalemi. Ibn Saʿīd says that in his time the ruler of Kanem was well known for '*jihād* and other good works of an Islamic nature'. This fame is echoed in the writings of al-Maqrīzī.[39] It was also probably he who established the *madrasa* of al-Rashīq in Cairo from the 1240s for the use of Kanuri students in that city.[40]

This climax of religious development[41] seems to have been shortly followed by political crisis. But before considering this in detail we must turn back to trace the political developments which had been going on since the end of the eleventh century. The welding together of the constituent parts of the Kanuri people appears to have proceeded far by the time of Mai Humai. But it was a process which still continued thereafter. The successor of Humai, Dunama, appears to have played an important rôle in this. The Kanuri sources emphasise his importance, especially his military strength. He is said to have disposed of 100,000 horses and a fabulous number of fighting men. Indeed the *girgam* states that 'there was no other king of his class among all the sons of Humai' (*walam yakun aḥad malik mithl darjatihi min bani Humai*).[42] There is indication also that during the twelfth century at least two further Teda-Daza language groups were incorporated in the nation. Thus the inhabitants of the oases of Kawar (called Dirku by the Kanuri) were brought under control of Mai Bukar b. Biri.[43] These are the Tura, who became a tribe of the Kanuri and are so recognised at the present time. This development no doubt had to do with the growing importance to the Sefawa of the trans-Saharan route which passed through Kawar and was thus controlled by the Tura. Similarly it

39 See translation of a passage in Palmer, *Bornu*, p. 192.
40 Al-Maqrīzi, *Khiṭaṭ*, ed. M. G. Wiet, Paris, 1922, iii, 2, p. 266.
41 Dunama Dibbalemi is also said to have made a clean break with the old religion by destroying the sacred *mune*. Palmer, *K.S.I.*, p. 132, *S.M.*, i, pp. 69–70. But it is possible that the significance of this action has been misjudged by recent non-Muslim writers such as Trimingham (*op. cit.*, pp. 117–18). A careful reading of Ahmad Fartuwami's account of this incident translated in *S.M.*, i, immediately indicates that, in the opinion of the Kanuri *ʿulamāʾ*, Dunama's destruction of the *mune* was *not* a defence of Islam against paganism but an act of irreligion. To them, it seems, the *mune* was *sakīna* (Qur'*ān*, ii, 248) which may perhaps be translated as 'an indication of the omnipotence of God preserved in some inanimate object' (like the tablet of the Ten Commandments preserved in the Jewish Ark of the Covenant, to which Qur'ān, ii, 248 refers); and Ahmad Fartuwami clearly states that 'but for the opening of this talisman, known as *mune*, in the time of Dunama Dibbalemi, no infidel would have opposed the Beni Sef till the end of time'. This is not to dispute that *mune* belonged to Kanuri religion before the rise of Islam in Kanem. But this would not prevent its incorporation in Kanuri Islam any more than the fact that the Old Testament was a sacred book of pre-Christian Palestine prevents its incorporation among the sacred texts of Christianity. Thus the destruction of the *mune* was not calculated merely to precipitate a conflict between Muslim and non-Muslim interests in the Kanuri sphere of influence (this conflict no doubt already existed). It was calculated to bring about a conflict between the Sefawa and *all* other interests, both Muslim and non-Muslim (see below, pp. 177 ff.).
42 *K.S.I.*, p. 131.
43 *S.M.*, iii, p. 5.

seems that Mai Bukar was the first ruler to marry a woman of Dibbiri.[44] Dibbiri seem to have been a group inhabiting Kanem and they too eventually became a constituent tribe of the Kanuri.[45]

At the same time it is not to be supposed that all people with whom the Sefawa came into contact were eventually assimilated to the Kanuri. Thus a tradition of Mai Duku, the third of the dynasty, suggests that in his time Magumi settlers in the south lost their connection with the Sefawa and became assimilated to the Mbum.[46] Other traditions suggest ancient conflict with the same people.[47] But we have as yet no real evidence to show that under the early Sefawa anything like an empire developed in which other peoples, while retaining their ethnic identity, became subject-peoples of the Kanuri.

THE FIRST KANURI EMPIRE

It is not until the thirteenth century that there are indications of a rising Kanuri imperialism. Ibn Saʿīd speaks of a Kanuri base on the eastern side of Lake Chad (Maghzā) whence the rulers of Kanem raided the peoples living around the lake. Again on the eastern side of Chad he speaks of the country of Jājā, separate from Kanem but subject to the Sefawa in his day. On the north side of the lake he mentions Badī, a people also subject to Kanem. Al-Maqrīzī, on unknown authority, states that the ruler of Kanem in 650 A.H. (1252–3) invaded a region 'covered with many great trees and with pools from the overflowing of the Nile' and 'killed many of the inhabitants or enslaved them'.[48] What all this really amounted to in terms of Kanuri domination of the lakeland peoples is not clear. But much more sensational extension of Kanuri power at this time seems to have taken place in the far north.

It is believed that in the mid-thirteenth century the Sefawa gained control of the Fezzan by establishing a post in the oasis of Traghan about twenty miles east of modern Murzuk and some seventy miles west-south-west of ancient Zawīla. This region since the eighth or ninth century had been under the rule of the Berber dynasty of Banu Khaṭṭāb, but their power had been destroyed by Turkish raiders from Egypt at the turn of the twelfth and thirteenth centuries. In the anarchy which followed, it is said, the local people appealed to the mai of Kanem, and Dunama Dibbalemi in person led an expedition into the Fezzan and established a governor at Traghan.[49] This Kanuri domination of the Fezzan is confirmed in the Arab

44 *K.S.I.*, p. 132, where the name of this Mai is given as ʿAbdalla. See also Urvoy, *Chronologie*, p. 28, n. 1.
45 Nachtigal, *op. cit.*, i, p. 120.
46 *S.M.*, ii, p. 107.
47 *S.M.*, ii, pp. 103–6.
48 Cited in Palmer, *Bornu*, p. 193.
49 Chapelle, *op. cit.*, p. 50.

geographers.[50] Traghan is over eight hundred miles from Njimi and these events represent imperial activity on a remarkable scale.

Here was the first Kanuri empire and it appears to have reached its peak of development under Mai Dunama Dibbalemi. The Kanuri sources may be referring to this northern expansion when they speak of the wars which this mai fought against the Tubu 'for seven years, seven months and seven days',[51] and it is possible that the great expedition was mounted by Mai Dunama to prevent the oases falling under the control of hostile Tubu tribes. The *girgam* also mentions his military strength (41,000 horses[52]) without which, of course, this imperial activity would have been impossible.

Concerning the political structure of this first empire our information is fragmentary, but several important aspects of organisation may perhaps be traced back to this period. One is the development, by the Sefawa, of a delegated military command necessitated by the raiding undertaken over the extremely wide area described. There is some reason to believe that powerful rulers like Dunama Dibbalemi employed their sons as military commanders,[53] and it may be that here we have the origin of the influence of the *maina* class (princes) which was to be substantial in later times. Again it is perhaps in these wars of the thirteenth century, in which the ascendancy of the Sefawa was extended beyond the tribal lands of the Kanuri, that the feudal system[54] of later times has its origin. Newly conquered territory could, as elsewhere, be most easily organised by granting it as a fief to military commanders. The Kanuri word for fiefholder, *cima*, does in fact mean 'master of the frontier'.[55]

We preserve a copy of a grant of privileges (*mahram*) made by Mai Selemma b. Bukar, datable, if it is genuine, to the early thirteenth century, which gives an important list of officials bearing the following titles: *arjinoma, mustrema, yerima, ciroma, tegoma*. Some of these at least appear originally to have been officers of the royal household (such as *mustrema*, chief eunuch; *ciroma*, heir apparent to the throne), but in the course of

50 Abū Al-Fidā' (d. 1331), quoting Ibn Saʿīd: 'The country of Fezzan is also one possessing water and palm groves. It has towns inhabited mostly by Waddān and all are now under the control of the king of Kanem' (*Taqwīn al-buldān*, ed. Reinaud and de Slane, Paris, 1860, p. 127). It is said that even at the present time Kanuri place-names are to be found in the oasis of Traghan.

51 *S.M.*, i, p. 50; Barth, ii, p. 583 (which, however, is misleading in this section).

52 *K.S.I.*, p. 132.

53 Barth's interpretation of the girgam (*Travels*, ii, p. 583).

54 A political system based on the recognition of contractual obligations between lord and vassal, where fief-holding office is the reward of military service.

55 For an account of feudalism in Bornu in the nineteenth century see R. Cohen, 'The Dynamics of Feudalism in Bornu', *Boston Papers on Africa*, ii, pp. 87–105.

time to have become fiefholders.[56] In this way a second class of feudatories, distinct from the *mainas* (and possibly created as a counterweight to their influence), was developed; though how far this had proceeded in the time we are speaking of is not clear. Such fiefholding courtiers eventually formed the group known as *Kogena*.[57] The *mahram* of Selemma b. Bukar also lists the following Islamic offices: *wazīr, khāzin, ṭālib, qāḍi*. The functions of the treasurer (*khāzin*) are not clear. The *ṭālib* in later years was a high ranking judicial officer. The importance of these Islamic officials probably became very great at a later time as they might be expected to be above factional interests. We do not know if they held fiefs.

A further political development in the ruling class which may be traceable back to this period is the emergence of groupings within the kinship structure of Magumi. This was a development to be expected as a result of the rapid expansion of the royal family in those early times (through unlimited polygamy, pursued over some nine generations, and probably little affected by Islam, in the beginning at least). The Sefawa were thus bound to form many collateral branches, and between these the possibility of political opposition (over the succession to the maiship for example, or the distribution of *ci*) was no doubt ever present. In such circumstances each group of the Sefawa would seek for followers, particularly among the Magumi, and the groups would thus tend to be continually growing. These groupings may indeed be of considerable antiquity, some of them going by the names of the early mais, e.g. Magumi Uméwa (the people of Humai), Magumi Selemwa (the people of Selemma), etc.[58] Similarly the policy of intermarriage, if it extended to the marrying of Magumi women to men of other tribes, must have produced a situation in which such tribes developed a blood relationship with the Magumi but were excluded from the patrilinear succession to the maiship. The group known as Bulala, claiming to be the people of a daughter of one of the early mais,[59] appears to have developed this uneasy position *vis-à-vis* the Sefawa. The earliest mai whose relationship with the Bulala is mentioned in the Kanuri sources is Dunama Dibbalemi.[60]

56 The *mahram* is in Palmer, *Bornu*, pp. 19–20 (*S.M.*, iii, pp. 13–14). The office of *Magira*, essentially a household office, certainly had fiefs attached to it in later times. The office of *Galadima* may also have originated as an old household office which did not have fiefs attached to it until the seventeenth century when it was held by the governor of the Western marches.

57 Urvoy, *Hist. Bornou*, pp. 39–40.

58 Nachtigal, *op. cit.*, i, pp. 418–19.

59 The Bulala song recorded in Palmer, *Bornu*, p. 181, speaks of their chief ʿAbd al-Karīm Lafiyami Dunamarammi, ‘Abd al-Karim son of Lafiya son of the daughter of Dunama’. The name Dunama appears to mean ‘master of the world’. This name was commonly given to the Mais of the Sefawa, but does not occur in the kinglists of associated, lesser dynasties. At the present time the Bulala are a Kanembu-speaking group living in the region of Lake Fitri. See A. M-D. Lebeuf, *Les Populations du Tchad*, Paris, 1959, pp. 61–5.

60 *S.M.*, ii, p. 42.

The extension of the feudal system outside the Kanuri tribal lands must also have raised the question of the relation between the Kanuri governors and the pre-existing local political authorities in each region. The indication here is that where the Kanuri did not drive off the earlier inhabitants they incorporated those local rulers who submitted, as subordinate chiefs. These chiefs, who formed the lowest grade of the officials in the imperial system, were no doubt known by the general title of *bulama* (master of the country), and this is the title of village heads in Bornu at the present-day, appointed in accordance with local tradition rather than as representatives of the central government.

THE TIME OF TROUBLES

The Kanuri empire of which we have this glimpse, the greatest Negro power in the opinion of al-Maqrīzī,[61] ruled by kings of international fame, did not in fact remain intact very long. It seems, like many political organisations, to have rested on an unstable balance between centralising and disintegrating forces.[62] Indeed the Kanuri sources emphasise the difficulties rather than the achievements of Dunama Dibbalemi. The *girgam* states that 'in his time the sons of the ruler became separated in different regions, though before this there had been no division among them'.[63] There is also mention of war with the Bulala.[64] These sources seem to attribute political disintegration to Dunama's crucial destruction of the sacred *mune*.[65] The point here perhaps is that with the destruction of the *mune* the mai ceased to be the custodian of the sacred symbols, and this would mean a reduction in his authority. That all was indeed not well with the Sefawa after his time is indicated by the fact that his successor, Kadai, was assassinated. Dunama's grandson, Ibrahīm Nikale, reigning at the end of the thirteenth century, is said to have been the first mai to kill one of his sons, and was himself assassinated. There was civil war in the next reign.[66]

The trouble into which the dynasty then plunged was reflected in the loss of the Fezzan, where the mai's representative declared himself independent and founded a dynasty known as the Banu Naṣūr which was destroyed by

61 Palmer, *Bornu*, p. 193.

62 A remarkable characteristic of the Sefawa is that, according to the *girgam*, the rulers very seldom appear to have been buried in their capital city. This is true of the whole period dealt with in this chapter and, if it is an indication that in order to maintain their authority the mais had continually to be touring their domains (like the sherifs of the Far Maghrib in later times), then here we have some measure of the disintegrating forces at work in the state.

63 *Wa fi zamānihi tafarraqat ibn* [sic] *al-Sulṭān nāḥiyya ilā nāḥiyya wa lam yakun tafarruq qabl hadha* (*K.S.I.*, p. 132, cf. Barth, ii, p. 583).

64 *S.M.*, ii, p. 42.

65 See p. 173, n. 41, above.

66 That of Mai ʿAbdullah b. Kadai; *K.S.I.*, p. 133.

5:2 SEFAWA GENEALOGY
(*c.* 1250–1500)

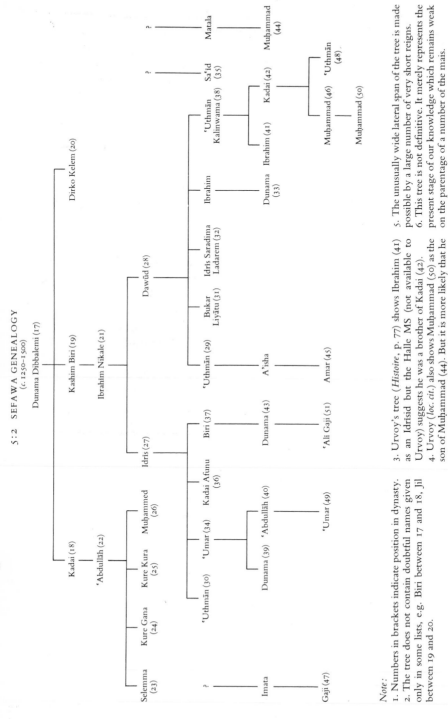

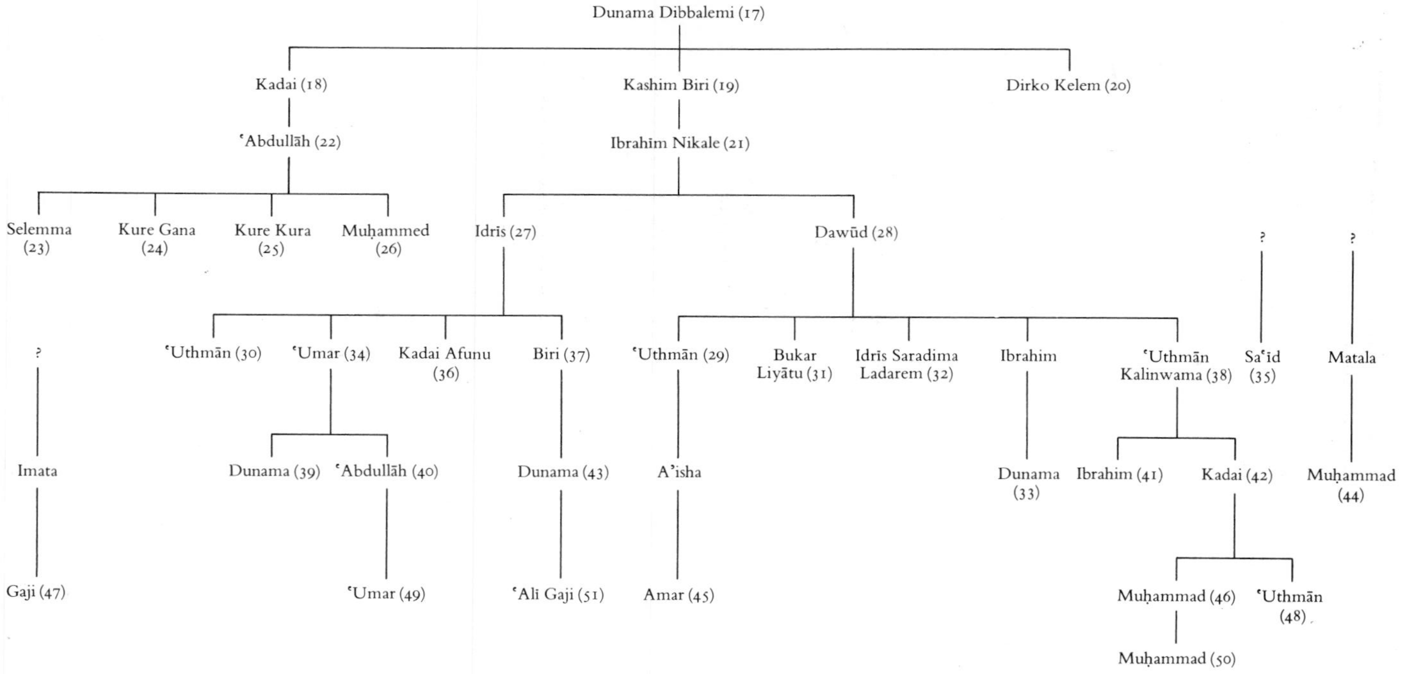

Note:
1. Numbers in brackets indicate position in dynasty.
2. The tree does not contain doubtful names given only in some lists, e.g. Biri between 17 and 18, Jil between 19 and 20.
3. Urvoy's tree (*Histoire*, p. 77) shows Ibrahim (41) as an Idrīsid but the Halle MS (not available to Urvoy) suggests he was a brother of Kadai (42).
4. Urvoy (*loc. cit.*) also shows Muḥammad (50) as the son of Muḥammad (44). But it is more likely that he belonged to the Sefawa proper as the *girgam* praises him. He is therefore shown as son of Muḥammad (46).
5. The unusually wide lateral span of the tree is made possible by a large number of very short reigns.
6. This tree is not definitive. It merely represents the present stage of our knowledge which remains weak on the parentage of a number of the mais.

Arabs from the Maghrib late in the fourteenth century.[67] The Sefawa had overreached themselves in this imperial venture. Their imperial activities in the region of Lake Chad fared even worse. There, particularly on the southern and western sides of the lake, they appear in the early years of the fourteenth century to have met fierce resistance from the non-Kanuri peoples generally referred to in the *girgam* as the So.[68] Four mais in succession, all great-grandsons of Dunama Dibbalemi, were killed fighting these people[69] and by the time of the accession of Idrīs b. Ibrahīm Nikale in about 1325 the fortunes of the dynasty had fallen to a very low ebb indeed.

Idrīs b. Ibrahīm Nikale reigned for about twenty-five years and seems to have died a natural death. But this was only an interlude in the troubles, which recommenced under his successor, Dawūd, whose reign saw the real onset of the wars between the Sefawa and the Bulala. In the sources we are not told the reason for these wars. Certainly, as we noted above, there are grounds for assuming an uneasy relationship between the Bulala and the Kanuri proper, but we can only surmise that perhaps it was an attempt by Mai Idrīs or Mai Dawūd to recoup the position that the dynasty was losing elsewhere by extending their control south-east of the Baḥr al-Ghazāl into the Bulala country which precipitated the hostilities. Whatever the immediate cause, there is no doubt that the Bulala wars filled most of the second half of the fourteenth century, and in them the Sefawa fared badly. Dawūd was killed fighting the Bulala king (*malik*) ʿAbd al-Jalīl.[70] The Bulala were then able to carry the war into the heart of Kanem where the two following mais, ʿUthmān b. Dawūd and ʿUthmān b. Idrīs, were also killed; and when the successor of ʿUthmān, Bukar Liyātu, had also died on the battle field, the crisis point was reached.[71] Thus it was that the Mai ʿUmar b. Idrīs who followed Bukar determined to leave Kanem and seek refuge in the country of Bornu, west of the lake. As the *girgam* puts it, he 'took out his armies and all his possessions and his people into Kaga; and down to this day none of our rulers have ever returned to Kanem to re-establish their residence there'.[72]

The first Kanuri empire was now in ruins, and the Sefawa had been driven from their homeland. But the Bulala wars were not ended and two

67 Chapelle, *loc. cit.*

68 The So culture of the lower Shari valley has been dealt with by J. P. Lebeuf (e.g. Lebeuf and Detourbet, *La civilisation du Chad*, Paris, 1950). For more recent archaeological work on pre-Kanuri culture farther to the west see G. E. Connah in *Second Interim Report of the Northern History Research Scheme*, Zaria, 1967. Places mentioned in the *girgam* in connection with the So are, Ndufu, Ngala and Ngalewa, all south and south-west of Lake Chad. It is to be suggested that the peoples classified as So were Afro-Asiatic language-speaking groups ancestral to the present-day Buduma, Kotoko, Margi, etc.

69 Mais Selemma, Kure Gana, Kure Kura and Muḥammad, all sons of ʿAbdullāh b. Kadai.

70 *K.S.I.*, p. 133.

71 Unfortunately the accounts of these wars given in the fragments published by Palmer (*S.M.*, ii, pp. 33–53) are so extraordinarily confused that it is extremely difficult, if not impossible, in the present state of knowledge, to reduce them to any kind of order.

72 *K.S.I.*, p. 134.

more mais (Saʿīd and Kadai Afunu[73]) were to die before a respite was obtained in the reign of ʿUthmān b. Idrīs at the end of the fourteenth century. This mai reigned for over thirty years, but where precisely we do not know. His headquarters appears to have been in Kaga, south-west of Lake Chad[74] but how far his authority extended we do not know. Certainly it did not extend to Kanem. And the Bulala wars merely gave place to other troubles. It is during his reign that we first hear of the penetration of nomad Arabs into the region of the Chad. These appear to have been descendants of the Banu Hilāl tribesmen deported from Egypt two centuries previously by the Fatimid caliph al-Mustanṣir and the ancestors of the Shuwa tribes of present-day Bornu and Kanem. In the time of ʿUthmān b. Idrīs they took advantage of the troubles, enslaving Kanuri refugees and even killing the mai's brother, ʿUmar.[75]

This was not all. ʿUthmān b. Idrīs was also at war with the *kaigama* Muḥammad b. Dalatu.[76] This is the first time that we hear of the title *kaigama* in the sources, and its origin is obscure. The country of Kaga was probably a territory which the Sefawa had succeeded at great cost in conquering from the So peoples, and it is possible that the office of kaigama had been created for the government of this region. It also may be that its early incumbents were members of the *maina* class enjoying a considerable degree of independence from Njimi, and that the establishment of the mais in their territory was therefore resented. Whatever the case they certainly made trouble for the refugee government which lasted for several reigns. Mai ʿUthmān Kalinwama b. Dawūd was actually deposed by the kaigama Nikale b. Ibrahīm, and exiled to Hausaland.[77] Similarly, after the short reign of Dunama b. ʿUmar,[78] the mai ʿAbdullāh b. ʿUmar was deposed by the kaigama ʿAbdullāh Digelma who replaced him by his own nominee, Ibrahīm b. ʿUthmān.[79]

Put to flight by the Bulala and harassed by their own feudatories, the Sefawa then entered the third phase of disaster. ʿAbdullāh b. ʿUmar was eventually reinstalled by the kaigama, but his successor, Ibrahīm b. ʿUthmān,

73 Saʿīd's parentage is not given in the *girgam* and he may not even have belonged to the Sefawa. Kadai Afunu means 'Kadai, the Hausa-man', but it is not known why he was so-called.

74 His contemporary, the Egyptian writer Al-Qalqashandi (d. 1418), says that the capital of Bornu was Kākā (*Subḥ al-ʿashā*', Cairo, 1918–22, v, pp. 279–81).

75 Letter quoted in *ibid.*, viii, p. 116; trans. Palmer in *Bornu*, p. 218. For Shuwa Arab origin see J. R. Patterson, *Stories of Abu Zeid*, London, 1930. For a brief description of them at the present time A. M-D, Lebeuf, *op. cit.*, pp. 89–99.

76 *K.S.I.*, p. 134.

77 The *Yerima* Kadai Kaʿgu also took part in this coup (*K.S.I.*, p. 134). ʿUthman Kalinwama is possibly the *dagaci* who is said to have come to Kano from 'south Bornu' in the reign of Sarkin Kano Dauda dan Kanajeji (1420s and 30s) and who subsequently acquired great influence in that city (*S.M.*, iii, p. 109).

78 Who was killed by his horse (*K.S.I.*, p. 134. Contrast Palmer's trans. in *Mai Idris*, p. 89).

79 *K.S.I.*, p. 135.

was assassinated by his brother Kadai[80] who seized the throne only to fall into conflict with a rival claimant Dunama b. Biri who, in turn, succeeded him after a reign of only one year. Dunama b. Biri ruled five years, but dynastic instability continued, for this reign was followed by three very short reigns: those of Muḥammad b. Matala who may not have been of Sefawa blood at all as his father's name is omitted from most of the kinglists available; his successor Amr whose mother was the daughter of ʿUthmān (b. Dawūd?) but whose father's family is unknown; and Mai Muḥammad b. Kadai who is particularly mentioned as a 'blood-thirsty and overbearing' ruler.[81] Mai Gaji, also of unknown parentage, who followed, stayed in office five years but was eventually killed by the Bulala chief of Kanem, Muḥammad b. ʿAbdullāh. Gaji's successor, ʿUthmān b. Kadai was at war with a rival claimant ʿAlī b. Dunama, and at his death ʿUmar b. ʿAbdullāh seized power but was never properly installed.[82]

Thus this rapid succession of rulers (nine in about twenty years), rivalry for the throne and disregard of proper succession procedures clearly indicate the development of disintegrating influences on the central government from opposing political groups. Through it runs the thread of opposition between the descendants of Mai Idrīs b. Ibrahīm Nikale and those of his brother Dawūd. Earlier the hostility between these two powerful groups was no doubt averted by an alternation of the maiship between them.[83] But Kadai b. ʿUthmān of the house of Dawūd fell into violent conflict with Dunama b. Biri of the house of Idrīs; ʿUthmān b. Kadai of the Dawūdids with the Idrīsid ʿAlī b. Dunama; and ʿUmar b. Abdullāh of Idrīs seized power from Muḥammad b. Muḥammad of Dawūd. This disunity within the Sefawa appears to have created opportunities for outsiders like Muḥammad b. Matala and Gaji b. Imata to seize power temporarily, and for the Bulala to strike again. It is possible also that Amr b. A'isha was placed on the throne by the sons of Dawūd, in violation of the tradition, withdrawing their support from the legitimate Dawūdid claimant, Muḥammad, in order to postpone the violent conflict they expected between this blood-thirsty prince and ʿAlī b. Dunama the Idrīsid whose father (Dunama b. Biri) had already been at war with Muḥammad's father (Kadai b. ʿUthmān Kalinwama).

Out of these conditions of instability however there eventually emerged a new power in the person of ʿAli Gaji b. Dunama b. Biri of the house of Idris, who flourished in the last quarter of the fifteenth century. He is traditionally regarded in Bornu as one of the three greatest rulers of the Sefawa.[84]

80 Son of a different mother. Halle MS, f. 2 (b).
81 *K.S.I.*, p. 135.
82 Halle MS, f. 2 (b).
83 See fig. 5:2.
84 The other two being Dunama Dibbalemi and Al-Ḥājj Idrīs Aloma. His name is Gaji, 'the little', not Ghazi as suggested by Trimingham, *op. cit.*, p. 121.

'In his time', says the *girgam*, 'the war of the Sefawa abated'.[85] This came about first through the destruction of the power of the sons of Dawūd and the permanent seizure of the sultanate by the sons of Idrīs. At the time of the accession of ʿAli Gaji the Idrīsids had been excluded from the succession for the preceding seven reigns (except for the one year when ʿUmar b. ʿAbdullāh was on the throne). But during this time the sons of Dawūd, in spite of their attempts to manipulate the succession, had proved unable to prevent outsiders from seizing power or to bring an end to the chronic political instability by producing an outstanding leader. In these conditions it is not surprising that a mature and determined man such as ʿAli b. Dunama was able to muster a powerful following for the house of Idrīs. On his accession he was in fact opposed by a Dawūdid claimant ʿUthmān b. Kadai. But the latter (who had already, it seems, been passed over for the maiship in favour of his nephew Muḥammad b. Muḥammad) was no match for Mai ʿAlī. ʿUthmān b. Kadai was killed in battle and the sons of Dawūd disappear from the history of the Sefawa.

Traditions also indicate that ʿAlī Gaji defeated the Bulala, possibly north of Lake Chad,[86] thus preparing the ground for his successor Idrīs Katagarmabe who was to be first mai since the flight from Njimi who mounted a successful invasion of the Bulala country beyond the Chad, and actually re-entered Njimi sometime in the early sixteenth century. This was ʿAlī Gaji's second great achievement, bringing to an end another group of troubles which had plagued the Sefawa for over a century.

Finally this mai is said to be the founder of a new capital city which the Sefawa were to occupy for the next three centuries and which was to be the base from which they founded the second Kanuri empire.[87] This was Gazargamo, in the fork of the Komadugu Yobe and the Komadugu Gana, not far from the modern town of Geidam. The exact circumstances under which the city was founded are not known. But it is clear that its foundation was an important achievement. Since the loss of Njimi they had not, it seems, had a permanent base. The troubles they had experienced in Kaga apparently forced them to move northwards towards the valley of the Komadugu Yobe and there is some indication that they were established for a time at the north-west corner of the lake.[88] But now at Gazargamo they were in a country far from their old enemies in the south and east and well

85 *Thumma sakana ḥarb Bani Sayf* (*K.S.I.*, p. 135, Halle MS, f. 3 (a)).
86 Palmer, *Bornu*, p. 222. The treatment of this question in *S.M.*, ii, p. 34 and Barth, ii, p. 589, is confused. The Kanuri version of the *girgam* (Palmer, *Mai Idris*, pp. 96–7) is also confused on this matter. It gives Mai Arri Gaji Zeinami (as no. 44 in the list), Arri Dunamami (as no. 48) and Ali Gaji Zeinami (as no. 51). It is to the first of these that the title *Kange bula Bulalabe* (smoke of the Bulala country) is given in this version.
87 Palmer, *Bornu*, pp. 222–4.
88 *Ibid.*, p. 222. There are a number of burnt-brick sites in this area (Nguigmi, Garoumélé, etc). See A. D. H. Bivar and P. L. Shinnie, 'Old Kanuri capitals', *J.A.H.*, iii, 1, 1962, though the speculations on the location of Njimi in this article are unfounded.

placed for the future extension of their power into the eastern marches of Hausaland. The story of the expansion of their influence from this new base will be dealt with in a later chapter.[89]

HAUSALAND BEFORE THE RISE OF THE GREAT STATES

When we turn our attention to developments in the western zone of our region following the great desiccation we find a different set of conditions from those prevailing east of the Chad. In the east, as we have seen[90] the most striking development was the emergence of the Kanuri people closely connected with the rise of the Sefawa who eventually came to dominate the whole area. West of the lake we can hardly speak of the 'emergence of peoples'. The peoples who lived in the western zone at the end of the fifteenth century appear to have existed there from time immemorial (though their distribution within the zone had undoubtedly changed from time to time as a result of the progressive desiccation and other factors) and there is no evidence of the formation of new peoples in historical times comparable with the formation of the Kanuri.

The most populous groups comprised here are the Hausa people, the Bolewa, the Ngizim, the Manga, the Margi, the Buduma, and the Kotoko. The Hausa people are of course by far the most numerous and occupy the greater part of the territory. But we have no evidence that this people were formed by any process of sociopolitical unification of previously separate groups as with the Kanuri. Recent writing on the origin of the Hausa people has attempted to show that they are a people formed at the beginning of the second millennium A.D. by a mixture of Berber immigrants from the Sahara with a Negro population of the savannah. But this writing[91] is purely speculative and merely constitutes a variation of the Hamitic hypothesis which we discussed above.[92] In this case there is no satisfactory evidence for Berber (Tuareg) penetration into this zone of our region before the latter part of the fifteenth century, and linguistic evidence certainly does not indicate that the Hausa language is a mixture of Tamesheg and 'Sudanic' elements developing less than a millennium ago.[93]

With regard to the other groups speaking Chadic languages there is equally little that can be said about ethnic origins in the present state of

89 Mr P. F. de M. Farias of Birmingham University read the chapter up to this point in manuscript and offered some useful suggestions on points of detail. But he is not responsible for any errors of interpretation.
90 See p. 164 ff., above.
91 e.g. M. G. Smith, 'The beginnings of Hausa society', in *The Historian in Tropical Africa*, ed. Vansina, Mauny and Thomas, London, 1964, pp. 338–45; Hogben and Kirk-Greene, *The Emirates of Northern Nigeria*, London, 1966, pp. 145–50; H. A. S. Johnston, *A Selection of Hausa Stories*, London, 1966, pp. xiv–xvii, and *The Fulani Empire of Sokoto*, London, 1967, pp. 4–6.
92 See p. 170, above.
93 I have dealt with this legend of ethnic origin in detail in 'Some considerations relating to the formation of states in Hausaland', *J.H.S.N.*, v, 3, 1971.

knowledge. These languages are not mutually intelligible and the peoples speaking them seem to have lived in a degree of social isolation one from the other for a very long time. If we are to hazard a sketch of the developing demography of this area after the desiccation of the Mega-Chad we can merely suggest that Chadic-language populations began then to move southwards and south-eastwards into the well watered country of the Gulbin-Kebbi and its affluents and into the newly exposed western bottom lands of the Chad. And we may perhaps assume that this movement, or series of movements, involving the dispersal of groups over a very wide tract of territory, gave rise during the last millennium B.C. to linguistic differentiation: those speaking what became the Hausa language occupying the western part of our zone; those speaking what became the other languages we have mentioned occupying the plains of Bornu.[94]

In this section we shall be concerned with the story of the Hausa-speaking people because we still know very little about the early history of the others.[95] The territory we are studying is the western part of our zone but it has no name derived from its natural features. It is *Kasar Hausa*: the land of the Hausa language. The derivation and antiquity of the word Hausa are unknown,[96] but no earlier term has come down to us. Again, the extent of this territory during the last millennium B.C. and the first A.D. is uncertain as we do not know precisely when the southward movements of Hausa-speaking groups occasioned by the desiccation of the central Sahara took place. By the beginning of the present millennium however, when statelike political organisations among this people begin to appear, it would probably be safe to say that communities of Hausa-speakers were established throughout the country roughly bounded by a line running from Azben southwards as far as the north-eastern corner of the Jos Highlands, thence westwards to the great bend of the Kaduna River, thence north-west to the valley of the Gulbin-Kebbi and thence north-eastwards to Azben. This has more or less,

94 It is possible that other Chadic-language peoples also moved into the Chad bottom-lands but were eventually driven thence by the Kanuri in much later times. Thus the Angas peoples now occupying the south-eastern part of the Jos Highlands have a tradition of Bornuan origin. See also p. 163, n. 13, above.

95 Some traditions relating to Buduma are recorded in *Documents Scientifiques de la Mission Tilho*, ii, Paris, 1911, pp. 310–17. C. K. Meek, *Tribal Studies in Northern Nigeria*, i, London, 1931, gives some information on the Margi (pp. 213–51) and vol. ii on the Ngizim (pp. 247–69) and the Bolewa (pp. 288–310). Generally speaking however, the traditions of the Chadic-language-speaking peoples of Bornu have not yet been recorded. O. Temple and C. L. Temple, ed., *Notes on the Tribes . . . of Northern Nigeria*, 1922, repr. London, 1965, provides very little authoritative material. A. M-D. Lebeuf, *Les Principautés Kotoko*, Paris, 1969, was not available to the present writer.

96 This word does not appear to have been known to the Arab geographers. But this may merely be because, with the exception of Muḥammad al-Wazzān (Leo Africanus), they had no direct connection with Hausaland and only heard of it from non-Hausa informants. Thus Al-Maqrīzi gives *Afnu*, the Kanuri word for Hausa. The traditional attempt to derive 'Hausa' from 'hau sa' ('ride a cow') is not convincing. But an indication of the antiquity of the word is perhaps given by the fact that it is used in Songhay to mean 'east'.

in fact, remained down to the present the country where the inhabitants speak Hausa as their mother tongue. Adjustments to its frontiers occasioned by the intrusion of other peoples (Tuareg and Kanuri in the north particularly and also the pastoral Fulbe), by the assimilation of peoples not originally Hausa-speaking (such as the Songhay of the Gulbin-Kebbi), or by the foundation of Hausa colonies in other countries (for example in the territory of the Kambari, Acipawa, Dakarkari, Kamuku, Gwari, etc. to the south-west and south), appear to have taken place much later (late fifteenth, sixteenth, and seventeenth centuries).

Within this ancient Hausaland we are concerned with the development of a changing pattern of sociopolitical grouping and with the various cultural factors (economic, religious, etc.) which gave rise to it. In general terms we have to deal, not as in Kanem, with the rise of one great centralised state, but with the emergence of a shifting pattern of centres of political power arising in different places over a long period, and each the potential nucleus of a separate state, some surviving in political independence from their neighbours, some becoming absorbed into the sphere of influence of others and losing their political separateness. These centres of political power, the capitals of the states of the future, were cities, *birane* (sing. *birni*); and it is theoretically at least possible to divide the political history of Hausaland into the pre-*birni* times and the era of the *birane*.

What then can be said about Hausa society before the emergence of statelike political organisations? We have very little direct knowledge of this era because even where it persisted down to recent times the necessary ethnographic investigations have not been carried out,[97] and elsewhere ancient institutions have long been superseded by those of the emergent states. But by cautious inference from what are apparently archaic survivals in present day Hausa-speaking society, and from what we know of natural conditions in ancient times, we can attempt a provisional indication of some at least of the main features of early Hausa society.[98]

There is some reason to believe that the period between the desiccation and the rise of the *birane* saw the development throughout Hausaland of small agricultural communities known as *ḳauyuka* or *unguwoyi* (sing. *ḳauye*, *unguwa*). These were nucleated hamlets organised for crop production and consisting of family groups whose farmland (*gona*, *gandu*) was contiguous and separated from that of other *ḳauyuka* by waste (*daji*). In these hamlets authority appears to have been of two kinds. Overall leadership (*sarauta*), vested in a ruler (*sarki*), seems to have been recognised only for specific

97 There is an incomplete study of the Arewa in M. H. Piault, 'Populations de l'Arewa, introduction à une étude regionale', *Etud. Niger.*, xiii, mimeo., Niamey, 1964. Pre-Islamic Hausa institutions are also dealt with in J. Greenberg, *The Influence of Islam on a Sudanese Religion*, New York, 1946. L. Reuke, *Die Maguzawa in Nord Nigeria*, Bielefeld, 1969, was not available to the present writer.

98 See M. G. Smith, in 'The Historian in Tropical Africa', *loc. cit.* But this gives little idea of the antiquity or duration of the pre-*birane* era in the different parts of Hausaland.

purposes where communal discipline transcending the family group was required: mainly in the economic field. Thus a very ancient office was that of *sarkin noma*,[99] the king of farming, whose business was to organise the agriculture of the hamlet, including the religious ritual relating to the seasons. In matters not connected with agriculture authority appears to have resided in individual family heads, for the *ḳauye* was basically a collection of patrilinear family groups, *gidaje* (sing. *gida*) recognising no superior to the family head (*maigida*).

Here was a society in which political authority was based on kinship relations: even where authority over several *gidaje* was wielded by *sarkin noma* this still held, because all families within the *ḳauye* group would in any case be related to each other. Kinship terminology was indeed sometimes used to describe offices like that of *sarkin noma*. Thus the chief hunter who organised the men of the hamlet for hunting in the wasteland was known as *uban farauta*, father of hunting. This importance of kinship relations is to be seen also in the ancient religious organisation. Traces for example of an ancient totemism may survive widely in current beliefs of misfortune resulting from the killing of certain animals, and it is noteworthy that such animals are known as *kangida*, the head of the *gida*.[100] More precisely, among the non-Muslim Hausa of the present day the same expression is used to describe the particular spirits (*iskoki*; sing. *iska*) whose cult is practised by a family group.[101] It is the *maigida* also who has important duties in connection with the propitiation of spirits. The Hausa word for God is *Ubangiji*, father of the home.[102]

Of course it is to be expected that even in very ancient times Hausa society did not consist entirely of hamlets of the type we have described, for conditions must continually have been arising which favoured the growth of larger settlements where distantly related family groups would congregate, and which might even contain stranger elements not owning land in the vicinity but plying non-agricultural trades to meet the needs of the farmers. Thus convenient places might become centres for the production of industrial goods and for general trade. Larger settlements of the form of a *gari* (town) would perhaps tend to grow up in such places. The introduction of the use of iron into Hausaland, presumably in the early part of the first millennium A.D., was probably a factor in the growth of such towns.[103]

99 See e.g. Greenberg, *Influence*, p. 25.

100 A. J. N. Tremearne, *The Ban of the Bori*, London, 1914, pp. 35, 44, 203.

101 Greenberg, *Influence*, p. 44.

102 This term continues to be used by Muslims and Christians, but its antiquity is indicated by the fact that Hausa-speaking Muslims say 'Ubangiji Allah'.

103 Iron-smelting is a widely distributed industry in Hausaland and is often done in the vicinity of the black hills where iron-stone is mined. No archaeological study has yet been made of iron-working sites, but the *maḳera* (blacksmiths) of Gaya figure in the legend of the foundation of the Hausa Bakwai as the suppliers of Bayejida's magic knife. The 'Nok' iron-working sites so far investigated lie to the south-east of Hausaland and nothing is yet known about the spread of 'Nok' techniques.

Again religious factors could work in the same direction as particular places became centres associated with the cult of certain *iskoki*. Such centres are the great inselbergs, the black hills, of Hausaland. Even the great Hausa cities of later times were often built around such hills (e.g. Dutsen-Turunku, Dutsen-Kufena, Dutsen-Dala).

It is probably in such *garuruwa* that general political authority exercised over many family groups in the interest of communal organisation became vested in an individual: the *sarkin gari*, supported by ward-heads (*masu unguwa*). Even in the *gari* however the main bonds of political connection continue to be kinship ties and the authority of the *sarki* does not extend beyond the farmland of the settlement itself.

This vague picture of a country dotted with agricultural settlements of varying size, some with markets and the workshops of artisans and some without, but all mutually independent of each other in the political sense, is all we can draw for Hausaland in ancient times. How long this era lasted we cannot say, but eventually, at different times in different places, a political revolution took place in this country.

THE EMERGENCE OF THE HAUSA STATES

The revolution may perhaps be described as the replacement throughout the greater part of Hausaland of a political system in which authority was based on kinship relations, by one in which authority was based on control of territory; accompanied by the replacement of a very large number of very small and mutually independent political units by a much smaller number of large units possessing institutions of a centralised character. In short the emergence of states in a previously stateless society. The general problem of political developments in stateless society has been discussed in chapter 3. We are now concerned with the case of Hausaland.

East of the Chad we have seen that the foundation of the Kanuri state was closely associated with the rise of the Sefawa. In Hausaland the emergence of states appears to have been closely associated with the foundation of the great *birane*,[104] as centres of political power: capital cities. The *birni* in Hausaland differs from earlier types of settlement mainly in two ways. First it is cosmopolitan; an urban settlement with a population comprising many groups of diverse origins lacking kinship relations one with the other. Such settlements seem to have developed not so much as a result of the natural increase of one community but rather by the immigration of groups and individuals from outside, resulting from the fact that the site in question had become a centre of attraction in some way.

We do not know precisely why individual *birane* came to be established in particular places, but we can surmise that economic factors played an

104 Trimingham, *op. cit.*, p. 127, has briefly drawn attention to the importance of these cities. See also my 'Some considerations relating to the formation of states in Hausaland', *loc. cit.*

important rôle. Large urban populations with their complicated needs could obviously only be established in locations capable, through their agricultural and industrial resources, of supporting such groups. Thus Birnin-Kano (probably the greatest of the *birane*) is situated in the midst of some of the most fertile land in Nigeria, producing, in addition to food, industrial crops such as cotton. It also possesses abundant and easily workable iron-stone (in Dutsen-Dala, for example). Places where long distance trade routes converged would also come to support a permanent trading population of diverse origins. Over the centuries again certain places may well have acquired unusual attraction as the dwellings of the great *iskoki*: thus Dutsen-Dala of Kano and Kurmin-Jakara of the same place, the abode of Tsumburburai.

It is evident in addition that strategic factors relating to the protection of communities from attack were important in the foundation of *birane*, for the second characteristic of such settlements is that they are invariably fortified. The *gari* may or may not be a walled town and it is likely that the fortifications of some *garuruwa* were associated with wars post-dating the foundation of the states. But the *birni* is always a walled city and its fortifications, of which many examples still stand in Hausaland today, appear to have been an essential element in the emergence of such cities as centres of unusual political power.[105] The walls were obviously built to protect the urban community from outside attack, and, because they encircled farmland as well as dwellings, could offer a means of protection even in protracted siege. But the walls also provided a place of refuge for people of the surrounding countryside, and this was no doubt one at least of the factors which made the *birni* a centre of political power extending far beyond its walls.

Here we have the third characteristic of the *birni* which differentiated it from the *gari*; it was the seat of a new type of political power. Of course the *birni* like the *gari* had its own government necessitated by the organisational requirements of urban life. This government eventually became very complicated with power invested in a whole hierarchy of specialised officials whose titles we still preserve in the local government terminology of Hausaland (e.g. *magajin gari*, 'heir of the town', perhaps a general administrator; *sarkin kasuwa*, 'king of the market'; *sarkin kofa*, 'gate-keeper'; *mai-unguwa*, 'ward-head'; presidents of immigrant communities such as *sarkin turawa*, chief of the Arab trading group in Kano; etc.). But over all was the authority of the *sarki* who also had his seat in the city. This *sarki* was not *sarkin birni* (an expression not apparently used in Hausa) but *sarkin ḳasa*, king of the country, which consisted not only of the *birni* and its farmlands but a large tract of surrounding territory containing many *garuruwa* and *ḳauyuka*, all of which recognised the superior political power of the king in the city. This was the form of the Hausa state.

105 No scientific study of the ancient fortifications of Hausaland has yet been attempted.

States of this type came into being as the result of the cooperation of many factors: anything indeed which tended to promote in different places the emergence of large urban communities possessed of resources far in excess of those enjoyed by the small settlements of ancient times and whose power could effectively upset the political equivalence of the old kinship groups on which the highly segmented political system of those times had rested.

The government of this type of state was centred in the person of the *sarki* and was essentially dynastic in nature (i.e. vested in a particular family). But it was no simple hereditary autocracy. First, it was essentially feudal in nature,[106] the power of the king depending on the degree to which he could command the service (*barance*) of supporters of his authority; this degree in turn being dependent on the wealth of the *sarki* which could be used for rewarding his supporters, and on the needs of potential supporters which they might expect that the *sarki* could meet for them. Wealth lay in land, its produce, and its inhabitants: the basic need of individuals and groups was perhaps for protection and for a means of increasing their own prosperity. Thus to be successful the *sarki* is required to surround himself with people serving him (with military support and with assistance in the control of wealth-producing territory) in return for rewards (territory held as fiefs). This government therefore was by a king and fiefholding officials. The latter might in some cases belong to the royal lineage (*ʼyan sarki*, sons of the king) but generally they did not, their relationship with him being a feudal one, not one of kinship.

Far therefore from being a hereditary autocracy, this type of government was one where the power of the king rested on the maintenance (often, it seems, difficult to achieve) of a delicate balance between the interests of the *sarki* on the one hand and the fiefholding *masu sarauta* on the other. Even the hereditary principle was qualified by the emergence of powerful officials as king-makers. The royal lineages of Hausaland, like that of the Sefawa, developed many collateral branches and choice of the *sarki*'s successor from among many claimants reflected the balance of feudal power in the state. At the same time, of course, because of the limitations on the independent power of the *sarki* as a distributor of fiefs, the fiefholding offices themselves tended to become hereditary.

Finally, the establishment of this new form of government entailed a substantial reorganisation of society. New territorial groupings—the states—emerged, and, in addition, new classes. In the old villages permanent class distinction can hardly have arisen, authority within the family group being mainly a matter of age. Now in the states, however, there developed a sharp distinction between rulers and subjects, between *masu sarauta* on the one hand and *talakawa* (people holding no 'official' position) on the other. The ways in which *talakawa* could enter the ruling class in view of the development of fiefholding lineages were very few. There is indication that this

106 See above, p. 175, n. 54.

was sometimes achieved as a reward for outstanding military service.[107] With the development of the *sarki*'s court also there grew up a class of palace officials (*fadawa*) who could be of *ba-talake* origin. Again, there is evidence of the eventual emergence of a class of slave officials obviously recruited from the *talakawa*.[108] But generally the society of the states appears to have lacked mobility between political classes.

In considering the rise of states in Hausaland a number of important points must be borne in mind. First, this movement did not take place everywhere at the same time. Because of the fact that no archaeological investigation of *birni*-type sites in Hausaland has yet been undertaken we cannot indeed speak with precision about their antiquity. What evidence we have is from the kinglists of the state-governing dynasties which have been preserved.[109] This material is extremely difficult to interpret largely because it does not appear to have been committed to writing until comparatively recent times, and, as now recorded, contains many obvious errors. One characteristic corruption of doubtful significance is the attribution of very long reigns to early rulers.[110] Thus for Daura we have 150 years for Bayejida (the tenth ruler), 90 for Bawo (the eleventh), 110 for Gazaura (the twelfth) etc. For Kano we have the first seven dynasts ruling over 30 years each and two for 60. For Katsina none of the first seven reigned for less than 60 years, and the first three are given reigns of 140 years each. For Katsina also we have been able to show that recorded kinglists involve an error of over 100 years even in the fifteenth century.[111] For Zazzau preserved kinglists do not give reign lengths for the first seventeen rulers. Again even within the territory of the great states mentioned here there appear to have been earlier dynasties whose duration is uncertain, centred either in the same place (as the Dala dynasty of Kano[112]) or in some neighbouring *birni* (as the Kufuru dynasty of Tsohon-Birni near Daura[113]). Yet again there exist the remains of *birane* for

107 Offices common in many Hausa governments are those of *Barde* (cavalry man) and *Jarumi* (brave man).

108 Sarkin Kano Muḥammad Rumfa created slave offices. See p. 199 below. It is likely that slavery only became common in Hausaland when the great states began to fall into conflict with each other and to raid non-Hausa country.

109 Published kinglists include Palmer, *S.M.*, iii (Daura, Kano, Katsina); *Documents Scientifiques de la Mission Tilho*, ii (Gobir, Katsina); Urvoy, *op. cit.* (Gobir); E. J. Arnett, *J.A.S.*, ix, 34, 1910, and *Gazetteer of Zaria Province* (Zazzau); E. J. Arnett, *Gazetteer of Sokoto Province*, London, 1920 (Gobir); P. G. Harris, *Gazetteer of Sokoto Province*, mimeo., Sokoto, 1936 (Gobir). Many were reprinted in Hogben and Kirk-Greene, *op. cit.* There is much unpublished kinglist material in the Nigerian National Archives, Kaduna, and the Jos Museum MS collection.

110 Cf. the kinglists of the Oba dynasty of Benin in R. E. Bradbury, 'Chronological problems in the study of Benin history', *J.H.S.N.*, i, 4, 1959, pp. 263–87.

111 H. F. C. Smith, 'A fragment on 18th-century Katsina' and 'Further adventure in the dynastic chronology of Katsina', *H.S.N., Bull. News*, v, 4, March 1961, pp. 4–6 and vi, 1, June 1961, pp. 5–7. Also unpublished papers of J. O. Hunwick.

112 Palmer, *S.M.*, iii, p. 97.

113 *Ibid.*, p. 142.

which we have no dating material at all (such as Birnin-Kudu south-east of Kano or Birnin-Turunku south of Zaria). Moreover the states for which detailed kinglists are preserved did not constitute the whole of ancient Hausaland but the southern half of it only; and even if the emergence of the *birane* in that part can be provisionally assigned to the first three centuries of this millennium (an admittedly speculative interpretation of the evidence available), the same cannot be suggested for the north. Here, in the territory of the Republic of Niger, the emergence of *birane* (such as Birnin-Lalle of Gobir, Birnin-Dare of Adar, the Sosebaki centres of Washa, Miriya, and Dungus; and Geza, the early centre of Damagaram) appears to have been much later, and in some areas (such as Damargu and Arewa) the Hausa-speaking populations have preserved highly segmented institutions without any great centres of political power right down to recent times.[114]

Secondly, the establishment of states must have been a lengthy process. According to tradition, it took over two hundred years of conflict to establish the state government of Kano, as we shall see below. Again, the movement does not appear to have been successful everywhere. At Turunku, for example, there stand the ruins of what appears to have been a flourishing *birni* abandoned probably several centuries ago. Some early states seem to have lost their independence to become absorbed as dependent units in other larger polities. Thus perhaps Rano, though its precise relations with Kano are obscure.

In this general consideration of the emergence of states in Hausaland, we must briefly examine the significance of the story of the *Hausa Bakwai* (the Hausa seven). This is a legend of unknown antiquity current in the southern half of Hausaland which assigns a particular importance to a group of seven state-governing dynasties which appear to have emerged during the first three centuries of this millennium. This legend gives a common family origin to these dynasts by making them descendants of the hero Bayejida. Thus Biram, a son of Bayejida, was the founder dynast of Garun-Gabas;[115] Bawo, another son, was father of the remaining founders: Gazaura in Daura, Kumaiyu in Ḳatsina, Bagauda in Kano, Zamagari in Rano, Gunguma in Zazzau, Duma in Gobir. But, though firmly embedded in the folklore of southern Hausaland, this legend is of doubtful historical significance.[116] The legend is also disputed by the folklore of Gobir which dissociates its dynasty from the sons of Bawo. It appears indeed that the centre of Gobir in the period we are considering (down to the late fifteenth century) lay considerably to the north of the territory of the other six (in Azben, in fact) and only came into close contact with them in the late fifteenth century.[117]

114 For this area see Y. Urvoy, *Histoire des populations du Soudan Central*, Paris, 1936, pp. 217–71, and F. Nicholas, *Temesna*, Paris, 1950, pp. 45–7.
115 Near modern Hadejia in Nigeria. The name means 'the eastern walls'.
116 See my 'Some considerations relating to the formation of states in Hausaland'.
117 *Ibid.*

Neither would it appear that these seven dynasties and the states they ruled were the most important in Hausaland. Garun-Gabas, Daura, and Rano never appear to have embraced any substantial territory or at the most must have lost land at an early date to Kano, Katsina, and Zazzau. Very little is known about their history at any time before the nineteenth century, and they do not appear to have played any important rôle in interstate relations.

It is clear also that the emergence of the dynasties of the Hausa Bakwai was not the beginning of state formation in Hausaland. In Daura the Bayejida tradition speaks of an earlier dynasty, as we have seen. In Kano a dynasty of chiefs with power over the surrounding country was already reigning from Dutsen-Dala before the coming of Bagauda. The real significance of the Bayejida legend must therefore for the present remain a mystery. Four members of this group however, Katsina, Kano, Zazzau and Gobir, can be said to have been the most powerful of the Hausa states.

GOBIR, KATSINA AND ZAZZAU, DOWN TO C. 1450

Unfortunately we know very little about these states before the late fifteenth century.[118] The early political history of Gobir is particularly obscure, as we do not know where the *birni* of the early kings was, or even, indeed, whether they had one. Traditions merely say that the Gobirawa lived in Azben down to the fifteenth century. But we entirely lack information about the organisation of this state in early times. The question of its political institutions is further confused by the legend that the Gobirawa were actually an alien aristocracy ruling over Hausa-speaking people.[119] But this again may only be a distorted description of much later conditions when the Gobirawa did come (in the eighteenth century) to dominate other Hausa-speaking groups such as the Zamfarawa and the Kebbawa.

Concerning the early history of Katsina a little more information is available. The Kamaiyu dynasty appears to have established itself at Durbi-ta-Kusheye, eighteen miles south-east of the present Birnin-Katsina, but with another centre at Bugaje ten miles to the west of it. These kings of the Durbawa (eight according to the kinglists) appear to have reigned down to the middle of the fifteenth century, and their graves are still to be seen at Durbi. During their time also another centre of political power appears to have emerged in the area of Katsina-Laka away to the south-west (region of modern Chafe). But the development of Birnin-Katsina (the modern city

118 Nothing has yet been written on the early history of Gobir, whose kinglists give no information beyond the names of the kings for any period before the seventeenth century. For early Katsina and Zazzau there is little available beyond what is published in Palmer, *S.M.*, iii, and E. J. Arnett, *Gazetteer of Zaria Province* (London, 1920). This is material recovered by early British administrators and is summarised in Hogben and Kirk-Greene, *op. cit.*, pp. 156–63 and 215–16. These works represent a generally low level of historiography and embody many demonstrable errors. For early Gobir see Urvoy, *loc. cit.*

119 Hogben and Kirk-Greene, *op. cit.*, p. 118.

of Katsina) does not seem to belong to this period.[120]

In Zazzau, according to the kinglists, seventeen kings reigned before the middle of the fifteenth century. Their seat of government appears to have been at Dutsen-Kufena (modern Zaria) but the extent of their territory is not clear, as other *birni*-like settlements also seem to have developed in the neighbourhood[121] at an early date and it is not known when these were brought under the control of the Sarkin Zazzau. There appears to have been a particularly important *birni* at Turunku some twenty miles north of modern Kaduna. But it has long been deserted and its significance in the history of Zazzau cannot yet be defined.

KANO DOWN TO C. 1450

It is only in respect of Kano that we possess detailed information about state development before the middle of the fifteenth century. Here our material derives from a remarkable document of unknown authorship recovered by Palmer from the *ʿulamāʾ* of the city.[122] This dynastic history of Kano is unique among the kinglists so far 'recovered' in the Hausa states because of the detail which it gives of the activities of each ruler. But the very detail which it gives, particularly on early reigns, must be the subject of caution in its use.

The picture of the early history of Kano which emerges from this document is as follows. Dutsen-Dala, around which Birnin-Kano was eventually built, was, as we have already mentioned, a centre of political power before the foundation of the Bagauda dynasty. Fifth in the earlier dynasty of the chiefs of Dala was Barbushe whose influence extended over the surrounding countryside. His power was basically religious as he was the priest of Tsumburburai, the spirit of Dala hill and the adjacent grove of Jakara. The authority of the spirit of Dala and Jakara extended over a large area including the countries of Gazarzawa, Zadawa, Fangon-Zaura, Dundunzawu, Shariya, Sheme, Gande, Gija, and Tokarawa. This area may have extended from Dan-Bakoshi (forty miles west of Dala) in the west to beyond Ringim (forty-eight miles east-north-east of Dala) in the east and from Kazaure forty-five miles north of Dala) in the north to beyond Barkun (twenty-five miles east-south-east of Dala) in the south.[123] It was into this area that the Bagaudawa came sometime after the death of Barbushe. It appears that they came from the north-east, probably from the Sosebaki region immediately

120 For early Katsina see *ibid.*, pp. 156–7.
121 M. G. Smith, *op. cit.*, p. 343 mentions Gadas, Karigi, Rikoci, and Wucicirri.
122 Published in English translation as the *Kano Chronicle* in *S.M.*, iii, pp. 97–132 (abbreviated below as *K.C.*). Arabic MSS exist in the Jos Museum and N.H.R.S. Collections, Zaria. Other sources for the history of Kano are Alhaji Abubakar, Wazirin Kano, *Kano ta Dabo Cigari* (Zaria, 1959), based on oral tradition and following the *K.C.*; 'The Song of Bagauda' (ed. and trans. Hiskett, *B.S.O.A.S.*, xxvii, 3, 1964, pp. 540–67; xxviii, 1, 1965, pp. 363–85), a Hausa poem of unknown authorship and antiquity.
123 *K.C.* (*S.M.*, ii, 98–9).

north of the present Nigerian frontier.[124] Some traditions suggest that the immigration into the fertile country of Kano was prompted by famine conditions prevailing elsewhere.[125] Bagauda, the leader of the immigrants, established his capital in the town of Sheme, some thirty miles north-west of Dala. He is traditionally believed to have founded the state of Kano in this territory and to have wielded general authority as sarki, supported by *masu sarauta* chosen from among his followers.[126] But the extent of his authority is not clear. It did not embrace all the countries listed above, neither did it replace the authority of the spirit of Dala and Jakara. This was the work of his successors: territorial conquest reinforced by the eventual destruction of the power of Tsumburburai.

The first step in this development of the state was the building of the new Birnin-Kano around Dala hill. It was from this base that further territorial conquest was made, and it is likely that the fortifications surrounding the dwelling place of the spirit were intended to prevent communication between Tsumburburai and the people of the countryside, thus restricting the authority of the former and replacing it by that of Sarkin Kano. The fortifications surrounding Dala hill are said to have been begun in the reign of the third sarki, Gijimasu, and these earliest walls of Kano city were completed by Tsaraki dan Gijimasu, the fifth ruler.[127] Outside the walls Gijimasu unsuccessfully attempted to exert authority over the people of Santolo, fifteen miles south-east of Dala, but Tsaraki was able to raid Karaye forty-five miles south-west of the *birni*.[128]

Naguje dan Tsaraki (the sixth sarki) was again unsuccessful against Santolo and was in conflict with the people of Dala, who retained confidence in the power of Tsumburburai. Naguje's successor, Guguwa dan Gijimasu, continued to live in fear of the spirit who is said to have struck him blind.[129] This conflict with the authority of Tsumburburai was not settled until the reign of Tsamiya dan Shekarau (the ninth sarki) who finally destroyed the shrine of the spirit. In order, no doubt, fully to incorporate this ancient authority within the new state structure he also appointed two priests of Tsumburburai as *masu sarauta*. Tsamiya is said to have been assassinated by his brother Zamnagawa who succeeded him. But it is clear that his reign marked an important stage in the development of the politico-religious power of Sarkin Kano.[130]

124 *Song of Bagauda*, trans., p. 115, says that the followers of Bagauda came from Washa and Tunbi, towns of Sosebaki (not 'pagan forebears' of the Hausawa as suggested by Hiskett).

125 *Ibid.*, trans., pp. 114–15.

126 *Ibid.*, text, p. 546, says 'sukai sarki Bagauda mai tsarewa' (they made Bagauda, the protector, *sarki*). See below for the names of his associates who were given *sarauta*.

127 *K.C.*, pp. 100–1. *Song of Bagauda*, trans., p. 116, says Nawatu, predecessor of Gijimasu, began the walls.

128 *K.C.*, pp. 100–1.

129 *Ibid.*, p. 102.

130 *Ibid.*, pp. 103–4; *Kano ta Dabo Cigari*, pp. 21–3.

These developments paved the way for further conquest in the reign of the eleventh sarki, Yaji dan Tsamiya, who is said to have driven Sarkin Rano from his *birni* (some thirty miles south of Dala), to have subdued Santolo,[131] and to have raided as far as Warji (one hundred miles south-east of Dala and beyond the borders of Hausaland). He is even said to have entered the country of the Kwararafa beyond the Gongola river.[132]

This period of territorial conquest culminated at the beginning of the fifteenth century in the reign of Kanajeji dan Yaji (the fifteenth sarki). It was he who is said to have introduced new military equipment in the form of padded horse-armour (*lifidi*), iron helmets (*kwalkwali*) and coats of chain-mail (*sulke*), and to have spent most of his reign in the battlefield. It is claimed that he invaded Zazzau, penetrating as far as Turunku, and although it is not clear that any of the territory of Zazzau was permanently occupied, Sarkin Zazzau was killed in the fighting.[133]

With regard to the development of the structure of government in Kano during this period it appears that the extension of the authority of the sarki necessitated the development of various classes of *sarauta*, the holders of which, while supporting the sarki, required him to share power with them. The earliest class of *masu sarauta* comprised the descendants of the leading followers of Bagauda (Buram, Isa, Baba, Kududdufi, Akasan) holding the offices of Dan Buram, Dan Isa, Dan Baba, Dan Kududdufi, and Dan Akasan.[134] But as time went on these lost importance, giving way partly to officials deriving power from religious sources such as Sarkin Gazarzawa, Sarkin Tsibiri, Sarkin Suri (priests of Tsumburburai); and partly to warrior chiefs (such as Galadima, Madawaki, Barde). The offices of Galadima and Madawaki appear to have become powerful from the time of the Sarki Yaji and in the first half of the fifteenth century the *galadima* came to overshadow the sarki himself. This seems to have started in the reign of the Sarki Umaru, successor to Kanajeji, who left public affairs in the hands of the Galadima Dana; and culminated in the reign of Abdullahi Burja dan Kanajeji whose *galadima*, Dauda, is remembered for his successful raids into the southern country. The Galadima Dauda acquired great wealth in slaves and other booty and is known in tradition as *Dauda Karfin Birni* ('Dauda, the city's strength').[135] Finally the chiefs of important *garuruwa* in the territory of Kano, such as Gaya, came to form a further class of *masu sarauta*.[136]

These political changes were also accompanied by economic developments. Most important among these appears to have been the emergence

131 Santolo was an inselberg and apparently an important religious centre. *K.C.*, pp. 105–6.
132 *K.C.*, p. 106.
133 *Ibid.*, p. 108.
134 *Ibid.*, p. 100.
135 *Ibid.*, pp. 109–10; *Kano ta Dabo Cigari*, pp. 27–8.
136 K.C., pp. 110–11.

of Birnin-Kano as a great centre of wealth and commerce with long distance international connections. The conquests undoubtedly aided this development and the *Chronicle* makes particular note of the commercial prosperity of the reign of Yakubu dan Abdullahi Burja, the last ruler in this period.[137]

THE ERA OF MUḤAMMAD KORAU, MUḤAMMAD RABBO AND MUḤAMMAD RUMFA

The Rise of Islam in Hausaland

The second half of the fifteenth century is a period of important change in the history of the great Hausa states; change associated with the reign of three sarkis all of whom ruled for at least twenty-five years and who appear to have been almost exactly contemporaries: Muḥammad Korau in Katsina, Muḥammad Rabbo in Zazzau, and Muḥammad Rumfa in Kano. The pre-eminence of these rulers is partly due to the rôle they are believed to have played in the spread of Islam in Hausaland. Muḥammad Korau and Muḥammad Rabbo are stated in the kinglists to have been the first Muslim kings of Katsina and Zazzau respectively,[138] while Muḥammad Rumfa is regarded as an Islamic reformer.

We know much more about the ancient religion of the Hausawa than we do about the old Kanuri religion. It has not been so completely obliterated by Islam and is still practised by substantial communities at the present day.[139] Here we can only give the briefest outline of its beliefs and practices. In general structure it appears to belong to a very widespread class of religions of tropical Africa involving belief in a high and distant god not actively connected with the everyday life of men and, in addition, in a great array of supernatural forces directly in touch with mankind and controlling its destiny.[140] The high god of the Hausawa was *Ubangiji*, the nearer spirits, *iskoki*; and the maintenance of correct relations with the latter was the object of ritual. Communion with the spirits was partly achieved by sacrificial procedures carried out by family heads and also by 'possession'. Spirits in possession of human beings are termed *bori*, and the '*bori* cult' continues to be widely practised in Hausaland at the present time. The system supported a priest class (the *bokaye*) especially skilled in the mysteries of the spirits and playing an important political rôle in the Hausa states. The sarki himself seems also to have been a leader of public ritual.

137 *Ibid.*, p. 111.
138 For Muḥammad Korau see Hogben and Kirk-Greene, *op. cit.*, pp. 159–61. The only information about Muḥammad Rabbo which has yet become available is the bare statement in the kinglists of Zazzau that he was 'the first to be a proper Muslim' (*awwal man badā li-Islam*).
139 The Nigerian census of 1953 gave a figure of 49,893 for the pagan Hausa community (the Maguzawa) of Kano alone.
140 The best general account of the religion is in Greenberg, *Influence*.

The spread of Islam in Hausaland appears to have taken the form of a gradual modification of the old beliefs and practices in which *Ubangiji* became progressively of greater and greater significance in the affairs of men while *iskoki* became progressively relegated to the essentially subordinate and harmless position of jinn.[141] Politically, the *bokaye* came to share power with the *malamai* (the *ʿulamāʾ*), and the sarki to occupy the uneasy position of leader of both groups.

The date of the first appearance of Muslims in Hausaland is unknown. Neither can we speak with any confidence of influences coming across the Sahara into this region in the early centuries of Islam as, unlike Kanem, Hausaland seems to have lacked direct contact with North Africa prior to the fifteenth century A.D. It is indeed most likely that the earliest Islamic influences in Hausaland were of western rather than northern origin. Thus in both Katsina and Kano the introduction of Islam is traditionally associated with the eastward migration into Hausaland of people called the Wangarawa. Wangara is well known in West African history as the gold-producing country of the Upper Niger from which the wealth of ancient Ghana and Mali was derived. But when exactly people from that country began to come into Hausaland is not clear. The Sarki Muḥammad Korau belonged to the Wangarawa and it is possible that their influence had been developing in Katsina-Laka for some time before the middle of the fifteenth century. The *Kano Chronicle* states that they came to Kano first in the reign of the Sarki Yaji dan Tsamiya who may be assigned to the second half of the fourteenth century and who is said to have been a Muslim. But although a Muslim community in Kano may date from this time it probably remained a largely foreign community, and the influence of Islam on the government of Kano was not permanent.[142] Thus the Sarki Kanajeji is said to have revived the cult of Tsumburburai and to have attributed his success against Zazzau to this. His successor Umaru seems only to have been able to pursue his career as a *muʿallam* by retiring from public life. Against this background the Sarki Muḥammad Rumfa is to be seen as a *mujaddid*, a renewer and developer of Islamic society in Kano.

Concerning the contribution of the three late fifteenth century rulers to the Islamisation of society in the Hausa states, it is of Muḥammad Rumfa's

141 *Ibid.*, pp. 60–8.

142 A seventeenth-century Arabic work of unknown authorship (ed. and trans., Muḥammad al-Ḥajj as a 'Chronicle on the origins and missionary activities of the Wangarawa', (*Kano Studies*, iv, 1968, pp. 7–16), states that Wangarawa brought Islam to Kano, not in the reign of Yaji, but in that of Muḥammad Rumfa, and the truth of the matter is as yet obscure. While it is possible that the 'History of the Wangarawa' is the work of a member of the community founded by Muḥammad ʿAbd al-Karīm al-Maghīlī in the time of Muḥammad Rumfa (see below) and therefore assigns the coming of Islam to that time, it is also true that important events appear to be misplaced in *K.C.* (e.g. Amina of Zazzau is placed in the fifteenth century by the author of *K.C.*, while the Zazzau kinglists clearly put her in the sixteenth century. *K.C.* also says that Kano paid tribute to Bornu in the early fifteenth century which is again very unlikely).

work that we know most. He was the first sarki who appears to have applied himself seriously to the problems of ruling a multireligious community in accordance with the Islamic law. For this purpose he went as far as consulting a jurist of international fame: Muḥammad b. ʿAbd al-Karīm al-Maghīli.[143] Al-Maghīli not only entered into correspondence with him and wrote a treatise on the art of government for his use, but actually settled in Kano and established a community of North African Muslims there which eventually became assimilated into the society of the *birni*. The leader of this community became a *mai sarauta* in the Kano government with the title of *Sidi Fari*. Muḥammad Rumfa also converted the Kurmin Jakara into a market (the Kasuwar Kurmi), built mosques, and even appears to have established his own seat of government in a Muslim quarter built in the form of a *qasba* outside the old walls on to which he built a substantial extension on the southern side.[144] In Katsina also al-Maghīli is traditionally regarded as having exerted much influence and his treatise on government was intended for use there as well.

This seems to indicate that government in Kano now entered an era of Islamisation as a result of which the office of sarki assumed the characteristics of a sultanate. This immediately meant great social changes in the society of the *birni*. One such change was the emergence of a class of *ʿulamāʾ* under the patronage of the king. This in turn is likely to have prepared the way for the spread of Islam into the surrounding countryside. But when this took place we do not know. Similar developments probably took place in Katsina under Muḥammad Korau and his immediate successors, Ibrāhīm Sura and ʿAlī Murabus (al-Murābiṭ). But we lack detailed information on this. They probably also took place in Zazzau under Muḥammad Rabbo. But on this we possess at present no information at all.

The Political Changes

Associated with the emergence of Islam as a political force in Hausaland were other changes in government in the great Hausa states. In Katsina this association is clear and simple. Besides being the first Muslim sarki, Muḥammad Korau was the founder of a new dynasty of Katsina-Laka origin which replaced the kings of the Durbawa, whose descendants holding the office of Durbi eventually sank to the level of subordinate *masu sarauta*.[145] The new rulers, the Wangarawa, founded Birnin-Katsina whose walls are said to have been built by ʿAlī Murabus.

143 For Al-Maghīli of Tilemsan see for example, Ibn ʿAskar, *Dawḥat al-nāshir* (Fez, 1309 A.H., pp. 95–7). His treatise on government is *Tāj al-din fi ma yajib ʿala al-mūluk* (ed. and trans., Baldwin as *The Obligations of Princes*, Beirut, 1932).

144 This extension increased the fortified area by about half. The final extension of the walls which brought the city to its present size was made in the eighteenth century.

145 Durbi continued to function as one of the king-makers.

In Zazzau the precise significance of the reign of Muḥammad Rabbo is not clear. But here also, within a decade of his death, dynastic changes appear to have taken place. The twenty-second sarki was Bakwan Turunku (reigning at the end of the fifteenth century). This name is usually believed to mean 'the stranger from Turunku', and if this is correct it may indicate that the main political power in Zazzau passed at this time from the ancient line to descendants of the dynasty of Turunku. This reign is traditionally regarded as opening a new era of political development in this state. A citadel appears to have been built at the eastern end of the old settlement at Dutsen-Kufena. This suburb was called Zaria after a daughter of Bakwan Turunku, and became the capital of Zazzau,[146] but the precise significance of these changes is not clear at present.

In Kano the reign of Muḥammad Rumfa is also regarded as the beginning of a new political era: the era of the kings of *Gidan Rumfa* (the house of Rumfa).[147] And although government did not pass into the hands of a new dynasty the palace of the kings was certainly moved at this time (as we have already noted) and a number of reforms were made in the structure of the central government. Thus Muḥammad Rumfa is said to have established a consultative council of nine members (Taran Kano) and to have created a number of slave offices to deal with the financial side of government. The fate of this reformed regime in the later times will be dealt with in chapters 6 and 12.

Finally towards the end of the fifteenth century important political changes appear to have taken place in the far north-east of Hausaland. These resulted from the establishment of the Tuareg sultanate of Agades, the detailed history of which is given below. Tradition suggests that the foundation of this sultanate was followed by a southward migration of the Gobirawa in the direction of the frontiers of Katsina. They eventually established a capital at Birnin-Lalle, but when exactly we do not yet know. This southward movement of the Gobirawa, as we shall see, was to have important repercussions in the rest of Hausaland.[148]

Appendix
Ibn Saʿīd's description of Kanem

In this region is the lake of Kūrā from which flow the Niles of Egypt, Mogadishu and Ghana. . . . Ibn Fāṭima said that he had not met anyone who had seen its southern shore. However, the people of Kanem, and their neighbours whom we have found on the northern shore, sail on it. Around

146 The history of Zazzau at this point is indeed very obscure. Local tradition as currently recorded (Hogben and Kirk-Greene, p. 216) suggests that the capital of Zazzau had previously been at Turunku and was then transferred to Zaria. But this is clearly inconsistent with the idea that the *sarki* was a stranger from the former place.
147 *K.C.*, pp. 111–12; *Kano ta Dabo Cigari*, pp. 29–31.
148 The section on Hausaland was read by Dr R. J. Gavin.

the lake on all sides are brutish, heathen peoples of Negro race who are cannibals, and we shall mention most of them here. On the northern side are Badī, and their town is known by the same name. From below this town which stands in the midst of its domains emerges the Nile of Ghana. Adjoining them on the west are Jābī who file their teeth. If anyone dies among them they hand over the corpse to their neighbours who eat it (and their neighbours do likewise to them). On the southern side of the lake are Ankazār and to the east of it Kūrā after whom the lake is named. To the east of the town of Badī, belonging to the Muslim people of Kanem, is the town of Jājā which is the capital of a separate kingdom with cities and towns but which also belongs at present to the ruler of Kanem. This country is characterised by fertility and abundance of natural resources. In the land of Jājā are peacocks, parrots, guinea fowl, piebald goats and sheep shorter than young donkeys and different in appearance from our rams, and many giraffes. To the east of the town of Jājā at the corner of the lake is *Al-Maghzā*[1] where there is the arsenal of the ruler of Kanem who, with his fleet, makes many raids from there on the heathen peoples surrounding this lake, capturing their vessels, killing them and taking them prisoner. . . . And in the direction of the corner of the lake . . . is Mātān . . . and to the south of it, the capital of Kanem, Jīmī. . . . There lives the ruler of Kanem, famous for jihad and other good works of an Islamic nature, a descendant of Sayf b. Dhi Yazan. The capital of his pagan ancestors[2] before they adopted Islam was the town of Mātān. Then his predecessor four generations back converted to Islam at the hands of the Islamic scholars in this country of Kanem. Thus the government there is like that of Tājūa and Kawar and Fezzan. May God support him and increase his progeny and multiply his armies. Clothing is exported there from Tunis. And there are learned men there. Also in the direction of Jīmī at the end of this section is Nay [?] where there are gardens belonging to the ruler, and a pleasure ground, bordering on the Nile of Egypt forty miles from Jīmī. Their fruit are different from ours. They have many pomegranates and peaches. They make use of sugar-cane and grow a little of good quality. But they do not devote themselves to it, except the ruler, and thus it is also with grapes and wheat. . . . At the point where the Nile of Egypt emerges from the lake is the town of Kūrā belonging to the cannibals. This is on the north side of the river where there is the highland of al-Muqassim [?][3] encircling the lake from where the south-east corner begins. From below this highland also issues the Nile of Mogadishu near the

1 This in fact seems unlikely to be a proper name; though it is regarded as such by Mauny, Trimingham, and others. It is perhaps a corruption in this particular text of *dār al-Maghzā(t)* meaning 'base of operations'.
2 The printed text reads *ḥudūdihi*. But we prefer *jidūdihi* as making better sense.
3 This is an obscurity: the printed text reads *jabal al-m?q?s?m*. It could perhaps be a technical expression: 'the highland of the divide' (between geographical regions?).

equator. Beyond the equator also they say that there is a mountain in the lake called Lūrātīs. . . . They also call it the hill of gold, and the Negroes claim that the gold which is found along the Nile at the time of the flood actually comes from the deposits of this mountain. But no one can approach the hill because of the multitude of snakes and dangerous animals that infest it, even the surrounding beaches being full of crocodiles and hippopotamuses. Indeed it is said that the hippopotamus is not hunted in this lake, but is hunted in the Nile of Ghana and the Nile of the Nuba. To the east of Mount Maqūris, which is the divide between the highlands of Kanem and Kawkau, are the domains of the people of Kanem and their Barābar followers who adopted Islam at the hands of Īdi b. Jabal, ruler of Kanem. They are his slaves,[4] and he raids them, and makes use of their camels which are numerous in those parts. In the domains of Mātān are those of the Zaghawiyyin. Most of these are also Muslim and obey the Kanemi. To the north of Mātān and the domains of Kanem are the domains of Kawar whose towns are well known. . . . They are also Muslims who obey the Kanemi.[5]

4 The printed text reads ʿ*amīduhu*. But we suggest ʿ*abīduhu* as making better sense.
5 Mr M. A. Al-Hajj of Abdullahi Bagero College, Kano, offered advice on obscurities in this text. He is not responsible for any error of translation.

CHAPTER 6

Songhay, Bornu and Hausaland in the sixteenth century

J. O. HUNWICK

Historical periods rarely conform to the arbitrary framework of centuries. Although, with hindsight, one may be able to point to a particular event as a turning-point, in general the processes leading up to that event and the consequences resulting from it form part of the never-ending chain of the historical process. We are unusually lucky in the case of Songhay and the Central Sudan states in finding that the sixteenth Christian century, and even more aptly the tenth Islamic century (1494–1591), forms a meaningful unit for study as it marked both the beginning and end periods of certain phases in the history of these areas.

The year 1493 saw the overthrow of the Sunni (or Shi) dynasty by al-ḥājj Muḥammad b. Abī Bakr who took the title Askia and whose brothers and descendants formed the ruling oligarchy of the Songhay empire until its collapse under the impact of a Moroccan invasion in 1591. In Bornu the period was ushered in by the powerful rule of Mai ʿAlī Gaji, founder of Ngazargamu (1470–1503), from whom all other mais of the sixteenth century were descended. His rule brought to an end the fratricidal succession struggles which had sapped Bornu's strength for over a century. It closed with another powerful rule, that of mai Idrīs Aloma (1569/70–*c.* 1619) whose campaigns and reforms have been so fulsomely celebrated by his chronicler Ibn Fartuwa.

Between these two great empires lay the seven Hausa states (*Hausa bakwai*), of which two, Kano and Katsina, were entering upon a period of major economic and military growth (and increasing conflict) during the late fifteenth century, a time at which they also received their most lasting Islamic influences. By the early seventeenth century they, like Bornu, were already seriously threatened by the marauding cavalry of the Kwararafa from the Benue valley and were soon to make peace in the face of this common enemy. Of the seven 'upstart' states (*banza bakwai*) we shall be concerned only with Kebbi, which early in the sixteenth century broke free of Songhay tutelage to became a powerful buffer between it and the Hausa states, even becoming a contender with Bornu for control over them and the Air region. We shall also consider separately the sultanate of Agades, not as a state—which it was not—but rather as an area of vital importance for the trans-continental trade to North Africa and Egypt and hence a key area to control.

Above all, the importance of the sixteenth century for Bornu and the lands of the Niger bend was that it opened up a new era in international relations. Although economic and cultural links had existed between Bornu on the one hand and North Africa and Egypt on the other for some three centuries, it was not until the latter part of the sixteenth century that Bornu, face to face with the expanding Ottoman empire, had a common border with a world power whose boundaries encompassed both areas and extended to the Balkans and Persia. Songhay itself came into increasingly bitter conflict with the Ottomans' chief rival in Africa, the Saʿdian dynasty of Morocco. This conflict culminated in the overthrow of the Askia dynasty in 1591 as part of an attempt by the sultan al-Manṣūr to gain control of the Sudan belt from the Atlantic to Lake Chad in his bid to challenge Ottoman supremacy. Complementary to this ambition was his hope of controlling the sources of West African gold so as to obtain the necessary capital to enable him to buy gunpowder, firearms and the services of mercenaries and artisans—all from Europe—to pursue his first and major objective. The consequences of these encounters will be studied in chapters 12 and 13.

The sixteenth century is, for our area, the period richest in written sources prior to the nineteenth century and there exists a wide range of material both in regard to type and value. In order not to overburden the present study I have discussed them in a separate paper intended as a bibliographical background to this chapter.[1] I have also discussed in another recent paper the much vexed question of dynastic chronologies for the Central Sudan states in the sixteenth century.[2] Although the chronologies I suggest there are admittedly tentative, they have been used, *faute de mieux*, as the basic chronological framework for the first part of this chapter. The chronology of the Songhay empire under the Askias is sufficiently well established not to need specialised treatment.

Although the dominant power in the Sudan belt in the sixteenth century was undoubtedly Songhay, I have chosen to deal first with the states of the Central Sudan as an understanding of their history will provide an essential background to the wider picture of power during the period.

1 'Source materials for the study of Songhay and the Central Sudan states in the sixteenth century', *Research Bulletin of the Centre of Arabic Documentation,* University of Ibadan, vi, 1971.

2 'The dynastic chronologies of the Central Sudan states in the sixteenth century: some reinterpretations', *Kano Studies,* new series, i, 1, 1971.

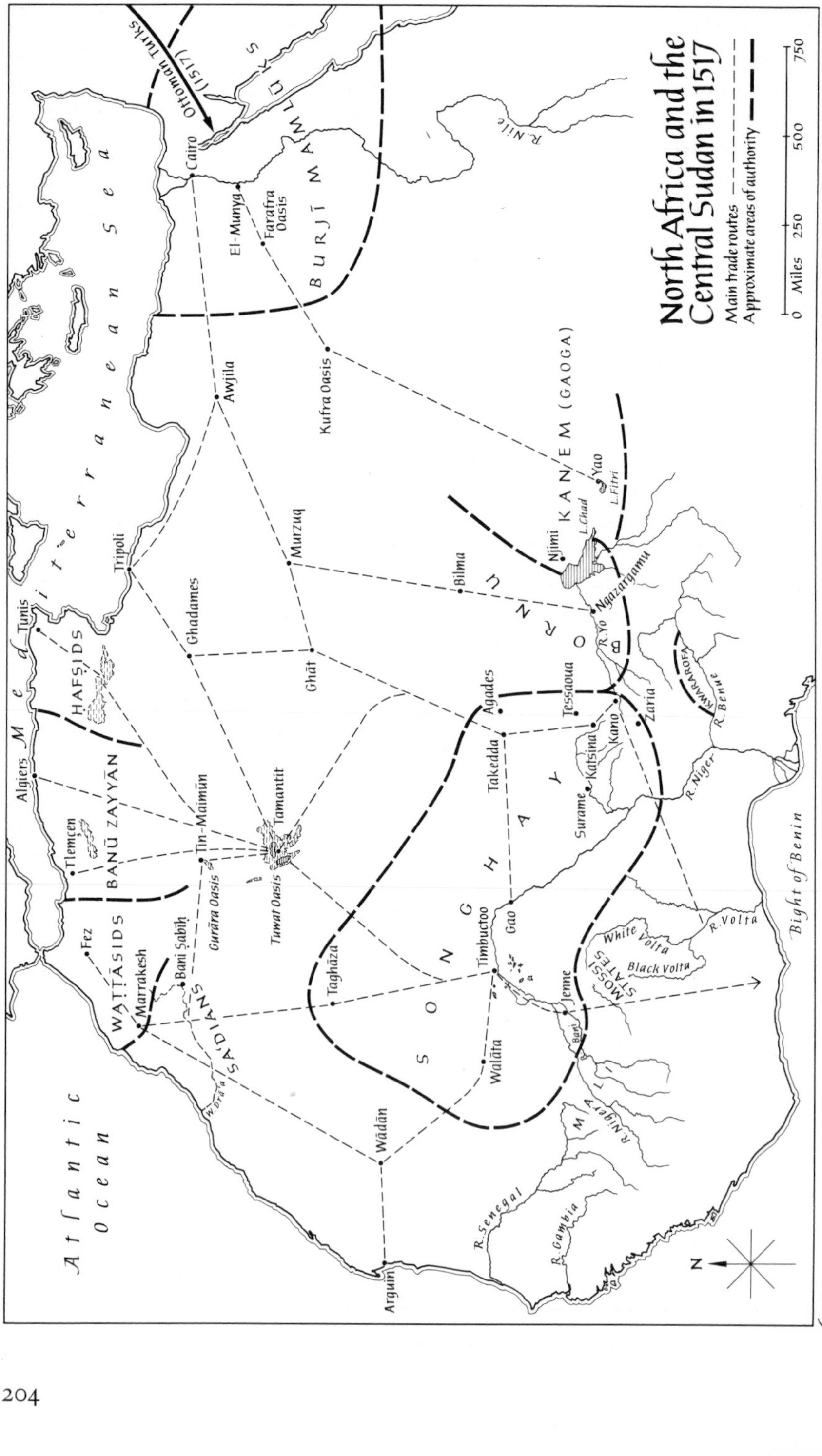
North Africa and the Central Sudan in 1517
Main trade routes
Approximate areas of authority
0 Miles 250 500 750
Mediterranean Sea
Atlantic Ocean
Ottoman Turks (1517)
Cairo
El-Munya
Farafra Oasis
BURJĪ MAMLUKS
R. Nile
Awjila
Kufra Oasis
KANEM (GAOGA)
Yao
L. Fitri
L. Chad
Njimi
Murzuq
Bilma
BORNU
Ngazargamu
R. Yo
Tripoli
Tunis
HAFṢIDS
Ghadames
Ghāt
Agades
Tessaoua
Zaria
KWARAROFA
R. Benue
Algiers
BANŪ ZAYYĀN
Tlemcen
Tin-Maimūn
Tamantit
Gurāra Oasis
Tuwat Oasis
Takedda
Katsina
Kano
Surame
R. Niger
SONGHAY
Gao
Timbuctoo
Taghāza
R. Volta
White Volta
Black Volta
MOSSI STATES
Bight of Benin
Fez
WAṬṬĀSIDS
Marrakesh
Bani Ṣabīḥ
SA'DIANS
W. Dra'a
Jenne
Bani
Walāta
Wādān
MALI
R. Niger
R. Senegal
R. Gambia
Arguin
N

6:1

BORNU

A new era in Bornu history opened with the reign of Mai ʿAlī Gaji (Kanuri = the younger), son of Dunama Aḥmad (1470–1503). The previous hundred years had been marked by bitter civil strife between the descendants of Mai Idrīs and Mai Dāwūd, both sons of Ibrāhīm Nikale, and it was the chronic instability of this period which led to the loss of Kanem to the Bulala in the late fourteenth century. ʿAlī Gaji was a descendant of the Idrīsid line and it was his direct descendants who held power throughout the sixteenth century, providing Bornu with a new period of internal strength which enabled it to withstand the many external threats which faced it. The stabilisation of Bornu was marked by the construction of a permanent walled capital at Ngazargamu (also called Birnin Bornu) on the banks of the river Yo.[3] As a result of the dynastic feud and through fear of Bulala attacks the mais had had no fixed capital since their expulsion from Njimi a century earlier.

When ʿAlī Gaji died in 1503 he was succeeded by his son Idrīs who took advantage of a period of internal peace to march against the Bulala sultan Dunama (ʿAbd al-Jalīl) b. Salama, whom he drove out of Njimi, afterwards occupying the town for a while before returning to Bornu. Dunama was later killed by his brother Ādam who seized power and began a reoccupation of Kanem. Mai Idrīs launched a second campaign, again expelled the Bulala from Njimi and again occupied the city for a period.

When Leo Africanus visited the Bulala state, which he calls Gaoga, in *c.* 1513 he ranked it second in power to Songhay while he considered Bornu the least powerful of the Sudanese kingdoms;[4] all the other states he visited were at the time subordinate to one of these big three. He also tells us of Gaoga's flourishing trade with Egypt[5]; the terminal point of the route in that country was El-Munya[6], a little downstream from Asyūṭ, and the caravan route would probably have passed through the Farafra and Kufra oases.[7] It is in Leo's account too, that we first learn of the appearance of firearms in the area, though the hand-gun he saw presented to the sultan by an Egyptian merchant may have been indeed more for prestige purposes than for combat. Nevertheless one may legitimately speculate on whether further supplies were obtained for military purposes and whether such a technological advance on the part of the Bulala may not have spurred Bornu to obtain similar arms half a century later when Mai Idrīs Aloma campaigned

3 This site, near modern Geidam, has been described in A. D. H. Bivar and P. Shinnie, 'Old Kanuri capitals', *J.A.H.*, iii, 1962, pp. 1–10.

4 Jean-Léon l'Africain (Leo Africanus), *Description de l'Afrique*, trad. A. Epaulard, Paris, 1956, i, p. 10.

5 Leo Africanus, *Description*, ii, pp. 482–3.

6 *Ibid.*, p. 531.

7 For the rôle of the Kufra oasis and the route from Egypt to the Niger bend in the Middle Ages see T. Lewicki, 'A propos du nom de l'oasis de Koufra chez les géographes arabes du XIe et XIIe siècles', *J.A.H.*, vi, 1965, pp. 295–306.

against them. The Bornu army at the time is described by Leo as consisting of 3,000 horsemen and 'as much infantry as the ruler requires as all the people are in his service'.[8] The mai's revenue was obtained solely from the booty of his campaigns, the most important commodity being captives whom he could barter for horses with the North African merchants in the ratio of fifteen or twenty to one.[9]

Early in the reign of Mai Muḥammad (1525–43/4), the son and successor of Idrīs, there was an actual attack on Bornu by the new Bulala sultan Kadai b. ʿAbd al-Jalīl, but it was warded off. Kadai was killed in the encounter and for the next twenty years there were no major engagements with the Bulala, though there were constant petty raids and forays. According to one source[10] it would be during the reign of this mai, in 1532, that Air, first subjugated about a century earlier and subject to Songhay in the early sixteenth century, was again made tributary to Bornu.[11] Bornu domination of Air during the middle years of the century seems confirmed by the fact that when Kebbi was harassing it, it was to Bornu that the ruler turned for aid, leading to the celebrated war (of 1561?[12]) in which Bornu was so disastrously defeated.

Muḥammad was succeeded by his brother ʿAlī who only ruled for one year and was noted by the *Dīwān*[13] for his love of justice. An anonymous French surgeon who wrote an historical account of Tripoli while a captive there in the late seventeenth century, attributes to a Mai ʿAlī the establishment of commercial relations with the Knights of St John of Malta when they were occupying Tripoli, but dates this 1534; however his chronology is notoriously inaccurate. On his death ʿAlī left an infant son, Idrīs, and there being no adult male heirs the succession passed to Dunama Muḥammad, son of his brother Muḥammad. Between these two rulers the Kanuri *girgams* place ʿAlī Fannami, a full brother of Dunama; Palmer suggests, following on local tradition, that ʿAlī acted as regent for Dunama who was also too young to rule, but the matter remains far from clear.[15]

Under Dunama (1545–62/3) there was apparently diplomatic contact with the Ottoman Turks who had established themselves at Tripoli in 1551. The French surgeon speaks of an 'alliance' between Mai Muḥammad (to whom he also, and perhaps rightly, attributes the Kebbi war) and Dragud

8 Leo Africanus, *Description*, ii, p. 480.
9 *Ibid.*
10 See H. R. Palmer, *Sudanese Memoirs*, iii, p. 160 (translation of the Masbarma family history).
11 *The Kano Chronicle* (*apud* H. R. Palmer, *S.M.*, iii, p. 109).
12 See p. 222, for further details of this war. I have discussed its date in my 'Dynastic chronologies' (see p. 203, n. 2, above).
13 *Dīwān salāṭīn Bornu*, apud Aḥmad b. Fartuwa, *Ta'rīkh Mai Idrīs wa ghazawātihi*, Kano, 1932, p. 136.
14 See 'Chronologie des rois de Bornou de 1512 à 1677', appendix to M. Fresnel, 'Mémoire sur le Waday', *Bulletin de la société de géographie de Paris*, 3e série, xi–xii, 1849, pp. 252–9.
15 See H. R. Palmer, *The Bornu Sahara and Sudan*, London, 1936, p. 231.

(i.e. Turgut Re'is), pasha of Tripoli in 1555.[16] Under both Dunama and his son ʿAbdullāh (1562/3–1569/70) there was continued trouble with the Bulala, though Dunama was able to pursue the forces of ʿAbd al-Jalīl b. Kadai into Kanem and inflict a defeat on them in their own territory. It is evident that the occupation of Njimi by Idrīs b. ʿAlī was ephemeral and that the Bulala, strengthened through their contacts with Egypt, continued to present a formidable problem to Bornu whose rulers, for the most part, had to be content with merely maintaining the balance of power.

The years immediately preceding the reign of Mai Idrīs Aloma (1569/70–*c.* 1619) present a special problem. Sources written in Arabic (and hence reflecting the Arab-Islamic ideal of patrilineal succession) name the preceding ruler as ʿAbdullāh son of Dunama. Kanuri tradition, which gives at least equal weight to matrilineal considerations, ignores ʿAbdullāh and in his place puts Aisa (ʿĀ'isha) Kili Ngirmaramma, daughter of Dunama, and *magira*.[17] The probable answer to this contradiction is that while in fact Aisa was the effective power in Bornu after the death of her father, formal Islamic tradition could not record a woman as ruler as this is in direct conflict with its principles of sovereignty.[18] How far she was protecting the throne for Idrīs as Palmer, basing his statement on 'present-day tradition', claims, it is not possible to say.[19] By 1562/3 Idrīs was at least nineteen years old, but even so he may perhaps have been considered too young to take on the responsibilities of rule.

The sixteenth century closed with the rule of the best known of all the mais of Bornu, 'the learned, just, courageous and pious Commander of the Faithful'[20] Idrīs Aloma, whose mother was Amsa, a Bulala princess. The first twelve years of his reign and his campaigns against the Bulala have been described and panegyrised by the imām Aḥmad b. Fartuwa, a contemporary of his, and it is not unnatural that the wealth of detail we possess about his reign should have made him appear to tower above all the other mais of Bornu. This is not to belittle the very remarkable achievements of Idrīs both on the battlefield and in home administration. He came to power at a difficult period. There had been long famines in the reigns of his two predecessors; the western frontiers with the Hausa states were not yet secure, nor yet were those to his north and north-west with the Teda and Tuareg, while to the east the Bulala still presented a very real threat. Within Bornu the So, Ngizim and many other lesser groups who remained unislamised had not yet been fully pacified or integrated into the dominant Kanuri structure, while in the hills to the south of the Bornu plains lay the territory

16 See n. 4, above.

17 Usually translated as 'queen-mother', but it is not in fact exactly equivalent, i.e. the *magira* was not necessarily the wife of the deceased ruler. The term seems rather to mean senior female of the royal household.

18 According to all the Muslim theorists it is a *sine qua non* of a Muslim *amīr* to be a man.

19 Palmer, *The Bornu Sahara and Sudan*, p. 232.

20 Ibn Fartuwa, *Ta'rīkh*, p. 2.

of many a non-Muslim tribe upon whose territory the Kwararafa from the Benue valley were already beginning to encroach, with all that implied for the security of Bornu.

Ibn Fartuwa presents us with the picture of a vigorous ruler who embarked on a planned policy of securing his borders and pacifying his own domains. His victories he paints as victories for Islam and his virtues as those of a pious caliph. He also tells us of how Idrīs campaigned relentlessly against lax morals, how he first built mosques of mud-brick to replace the old style made of reeds and established an Islamic juridical system under *qāḍīs* to replace the indigenous system of customary law. All this recalls the reforming zeal of askia al-ḥājj Muḥammad of Gao, though like him also Idrīs seems to have stopped short of islamising the actual administration of the state; the Kanuri titles, Galadima, Kaigama, Hirima, Yerima etc., and their duties remained unchanged, though we do find mention of the Islamic office of *wazīr*,[21] or chief adviser, which did not apparently exist in Songhay.

Ibn Fartuwa's account of Mai Idrīs's external expeditions against the stockades of Kano, the lowland Tuareg of Damergu and the Teda of Jawana and Bilma, and his internal campaigns against the Kotoko, Buduma, Ngizim and So, are replete with fine detail but totally lacking in any chronology other than indications of the day of the week. Many of the expeditions were led by the mai in person while others were led by his wazīr; in some cases he sent off his military governors to conduct their own campaigns in their own areas of jurisdiction. The core of his army, in particular the corps bearing firearms, was certainly regular; the cavalry was also in a sense regular, being made up of members of the mai's household and title-bearers and other chiefs within the system of royal patronage, whereas the infantry was probably recruited or pressed into service separately for each campaign. Mai Idrīs also introduced a specialised arm, the camel cavalry who could be drafted into service for long-range expeditions into the scrub and desert lands to the north and north-west of Bornu.

His strategy would obviously have varied according to the terrain in which he was fighting and the tactics of his enemy. In his internal campaigns against the So and Ngizim he pursued a scorched earth policy to break their fierce resistance.[22] The psychological effect alone of his newly acquired firearms was very great; in the attack on the So town of Amsaka he needed no other force than his musketeers.[23] Large numbers of captives were taken which was important to Bornu as slaves were a major source of foreign exchange, enabling Bornu to obtain the horses, arms and other goods it needed from the Arab world.

Relations with the Bulala began on a good footing. Idrīs's mother was

21 *Ibid.*, p. 10, p. 32 *et passim.*
22 See, for example, *ibid.*, p. 5 (against the Ngizim) and pp. 8–12 (siege of Damasak).
23 *Ibid.*, p. 4.

a Bulala princess and he himself married from the ruling family; indeed while ʿAbdullāh b. Abd al-Jalīl was sultan there was a formal state of peace and friendship.[24] Under the brief rule of his successor Muḥammad, relations remained friendly but under the next ruler, ʿAbd al-Jalīl, the brother of ʿAbdullāh, trouble again flared up over three border towns which were claimed by the Bulala by right of seizure during the reign of Mai Dunama b. Muḥammad. Unable to negotiate a settlement, Idrīs conducted a series of successful campaigns against Kanem, at the end of which he was able to conclude a pact of non-aggression with the Bulala based on the sworn homage of their sultan and leaders. He made no attempt to reintegrate Kanem into the empire, preferring to leave it as a semi-autonomous dependency. This illustrates the relative weakness of Bornu which evidently could not effectively control such a large area; it would appear also to reflect the wise statesmanship of Mai Idrīs in maintaining a more compact state dominated by the Kanuri to whom most of the other groups became in time acculturated.

Bornu's relations with the Ottoman Empire

In 1517 the victorious Ottoman sultan Salīm had marched into Cairo to wrest Egypt from the last of the Burji mamlūks and to establish it as an Ottoman province. In the following year two Ottoman corsairs of Greek extraction, the brothers Barbarossa, drove the Spaniards out of Algiers, took possession of it in the name of the Ottoman sultan, and during the following quarter of a century expanded their domains along the coastal lands and down to Tunis. On land the eastward thrust came from Egypt under the command of Sinān Pasha who, in 1551, was able to drive the Knights of St John of Malta out of Tripoli. It was shortly after this, in 1555, that we hear of the first diplomatic contacts between Bornu and the Ottoman empire referred to above. The next contact reported by the French surgeon is an exchange of embassies under Mai ʿAbdullāh, though the date ascribed to this, 1579, would seem to be at least a decade too late.

One result of these Ottoman contacts with Bornu via Tripoli was to begin to open up the area to the attention of Europe which had already been stirred by the publication of Leo Africanus's *Description* in 1550. In 1573 there was published in Venice, the same city from which Leo's work had first appeared, the *Universale Fabrico del Monde* of Giovanni Lorenzo d'Anania in which a small section is devoted to Bornu. Of particular interest is the mention at this early date of the 'many Turks who go there to seek their fortune'. The third edition of the work in 1582 contains considerably more detailed information which the author apparently obtained through a friend of his who had fallen into the hands of the Pasha of Tripoli and been enslaved. He describes how the mai received both

24 *Ibid.*, p. 57.

vassals and foreign visitors in a manner similar to the 'King of Timbuctoo' (i.e. the Askia of Gao) which recalls very precisely the etiquette which Ibn Baṭṭūṭa had described at the court of Mali two and a half centuries earlier. For the first time the names of some of the So village-states of the Shari-Logone delta appear in European writing with occasional important details, such as the mention of a considerable iron trade from Mandara to a town which he calls Quamaco, or the ritual putting to death of the courtiers of the ruler of Logone when he died.

He also mentions a piece of Arabic correspondence from the mai to the Pasha of Tripoli which his friend actually saw. This was most probably part of a diplomatic exchange which took place in the late 1570s between Mai Idrīs and the Ottomans and of which a fragment has recently come to light in the archives of Istanbul.[25] It comprises two drafts of a reply from Sultan Murād III to Mai Idrīs both dated 5 Rabīʿ I, 985 (23 May 1577). The main subject of the letter, which is in Arabic, is a refusal to give up to Bornu 'the fortress of Gurān' or to give military aid.[26] It was in this same year that the Ottomans had annexed the Fezzan, formerly a part of Bornu territory. At the time of annexation it was under the control of the Awlād Muḥammad, a sharifian family originating from Fez, who were probably vassals of Bornu and had been aided to power by the mais. This southward thrust of the Ottomans brought them to the borders of Bornu territory and the 'fortress of Gurān' may well have been a Bornu outpost in Teda country south of the Fezzan, annexed by Maḥmūd Bey.[27]

As a result of these incursions Idrīs sent an embassy to Istanbul headed by a certain al-ḥājj Yūsuf who would have brought back the final version of the letter referred to above.[28] It is clear from the tone of the letter and the Turkish language instructions accompanying it that Maḥmūd Bey had been over-zealous on behalf of the Sublime Porte for he was instructed to give safe passage to Bornu travellers and to respect their frontiers.

Although direct military aid to Bornu was refused, it is well known that Turkish musketeers were employed by Mai Idrīs. D'Anania noted the many Turks who went to Bornu to seek their fortune, implying that they were freelance mercenaries, and Ibn Fartuwa stresses the value of the Turks—'the people of the *bunduq*'—and the many mulatto slaves expert

25 I am most grateful to my friend and colleague Mr M. A. al-Ḥājj, who came across these items during the course of his own researches, for drawing my attention to them and kindly providing me with photocopies of the letters. They are preserved in the Bash-bakanlik Arşivi, Istanbul, *Mühimme Deftere, jild* 30 (*ṣaḥīfa* 213, no. 494 and *ṣaḥīfa* 215, no. 496).
26 For a translation and discussion of these letters see B. G. Martin, 'Mai Idrīs of Bornu and the Ottoman Turks, 1575–8', in *Documents from Islamic Chanceries*, ii, ed. S. M. Stern, Oxford, 1969. For a general study of relations between Bornu and Fezzan-Tripoli, see B. G. Martin, 'Kanem, Bornu, and the Fazzān: notes on the political history of a trade route', *J.A.H.*, x, 1969, pp. 15–27.
27 Gurʾan is the Arabic name for the Teda-Daza, who are also called Tubu (people of Tu = Tibesti) by the Kanuri (see A. Lebeuf, *Les populations du Tchad*, Paris, 1959, p. 5).
28 Ibn Fartuwa, *Taʾrīkh*, p. 127.

in using the *bunduq*.[29] Another possible explanation of the origin of the Bornu musketry corps is that put forward by the anonymous Spaniard of Morocco (1591) that the core was established from captives taken by Bornu during an Ottoman expedition against them and later expanded as other weapons were captured.[30] If this is true then the expedition may well have been part of an offensive launched by Maḥmūd Bey which penetrated far beyond the Fezzan and into Bornu as seems to be hinted at in the Turkish instructions accompanying Murād's letter.[31]

In spite of Ottoman protestations of peace and friendship Mai Idrīs evidently did not feel secure against the threat from the north and so, in the tradition of great power diplomacy, having failed to obtain what he wanted from one power he turned to its rival, in this case the Saʿdians of Morocco. In 1582 he sent an embassy to the court of Sultan al-Manṣūr, accompanied by a gift of male and female slaves, cloth and 'other luxuries of the Sudan', asking for military aid in the form of troops, muskets and cannon, ostensibly to pursue the *jihād* against his non-Muslim neighbours.[32] It is reported that there was a marked discrepancy between the contents of the letter and the representations of the ambassador and it is not unreasonable to suppose that the actual purpose of mai Idrīs was to use the military aid he hoped to obtain against the Ottomans on his borders. Al-Manṣūr took advantage of the situation to endeavour to establish his influence in the area by making aid conditional upon the mai, swearing allegiance to him as *amīr al-mu'minīn*. This diplomatic coup would have been of immense value to him in his overall strategy. Firstly, it would provide him with important support in his challenge to the Ottoman sultan for recognition as supreme head of the Muslim community, in Africa at least. Secondly, it would secure the submission of one of the great empires of the Sudan, leaving him with only Songhay to subdue—a plan which was no doubt already in his mind. With the areas of Tuwat and Gurara, which he was to annex in the following year, the loyalty of Bornu and finally the wealth and might of Songhay, he would have had the Ottoman possessions in

29 *Ibid*., p. 4. The term *bunduq* is a general word for hand-guns. We do not know the precise kind which had reached Bornu by this time, though they were most probably some type of matchlock. The miquelet, a variant of the snaplock, which later became very popular in North Africa, had probably not yet come over from Spain where it was invented in the late sixteenth century.

30 *Relation d'un espagnol anonyme*, apud H. De Castries, 'La conquête du Soudan par el-Mansour (1591)', *Hespéris*, iii, 1923, pp. 433–88. See p. 475 where the author claims that the expedition came from Egypt, but Egypt may simply mean 'Ottoman territory'.

31 Against this we must also consider the testimony of the 'Anonymous Surgeon' to the effect that Giaffer (Jaʿfar) Agha, Pasha of Tripoli made a gift of firearms to mai ʿAbdullāh (sic) in 1578.

32 ʿAbd al-ʿAzīz al-Fishtālī, *Manāhil al-ṣafā*, abridgement of part II only by an unknown hand, ed. A. Ganūn, Rabat, 1964, pp. 61–3. See also Aḥmad b. Khālid al-Nāṣirī, *Kitāb al-Istiqṣā*, Casablanca, 1954, *v*, pp. 104–11, where the full account of Al-Fishtālī is quoted including the text of the *baiʿa* agreed to by Mai Idrīs. In the text he is simply called *al-ra'īs* Abū 'l-ʿAlā Idrīs.

North Africa surrounded from the south, whence he might well have been able to launch campaigns to drive them out of all the lands west of Egypt.

Bornu, for its part, was apparently willing to pay the price al-Manṣūr demanded, assuming no doubt that Morocco was too distant for allegiance to its ruler to be anything more than a formality. However, on his way back to Morocco for the third time with the copy of the *baiʿa* agreed upon by Idrīs, the ambassador died at Gurara; the gifts he brought were sent on to Marrakesh and presumably also the *baiʿa*, but we are not informed whether the promised military aid was ever sent to Bornu. Perhaps, considering al-Manṣūr's other commitments in Africa at the time, both in Tuwat-Gurara and by 1584 in southern Mauritania, they were not. In this connection it is significant to note that no appeal for support was made to Bornu by al-Manṣūr when his forces were engaged in subduing Songhay during the last decade of the century. On the other hand, Bornu seems to have continued to maintain close contacts with the Ottomans in Tripoli; the French surgeon mentions two more 'renewals of alliance' during the reign of Mai Idrīs and gives interesting details of some of the Bornu embassies which visited Tripoli down to the time at which he was writing in *c.* 1680.

KATSINA AND KANO

By the end of the fifteenth century Katsina was beginning to emerge as a small but increasingly powerful state with an Islamic core. In the reign of Sarkin Kano Muḥammad Runfa (1463–99) the first war between Kano and Katsina is recorded and throughout the sixteenth century there were to be numerous other wars between these two neighbouring states.

It was probably early in the second half of the fifteenth century that a new dynasty came to power in Katsina, founded by Muḥammad Korau, the first ruler whom tradition claims as a Muslim. His adoption of Islam as the royal cult was probably due to the influence of Wangara (Dyula) trading groups who were, at this time, moving away from 'metropolitan' Mali in search of new areas of commercial activity. New centres for the trade in gold and kola, in which the Wangara specialised, were being opened up to the east of Mali in Jenne, Timbuctu and Gao while from the beginning of the fifteenth century Dyula traders had pushed south to develop such towns as Bobo-Dioulasso, Kong and Begho in their quest for the gold which Europe was demanding. By the time the Portuguese reached Elmina in 1471 they were already on the coast.[33] According to the *Kano Chronicle* a trade-route between Kano and Gonja (at the confluence of the Black and White Volta) had been opened up in the reign of

33 I. Wilks, 'A medieval trade route from the Niger to the Gulf of Guinea', *J.A.H.*, iii, 1962, pp. 337–41.

Muḥammad Runfa's predecessor Yaʿqūb (1452–63)[34] and it is at about this time that kola is said to have been introduced into Hausaland. Although the Gonja state established by Mande warrior groups did not arise until the late sixteenth century, it is not unlikely that Mande traders (Dyula) were operative in the area long before this.[35] Songhay incursions into the middle Niger in the mid fifteenth century may also have encouraged the Dyula to look for outlets for their trade through the northern Hausa states.

As the economic importance of the Dyula increased so also would their cultural influence. Wilks' important study of the rôle of Muslim traders in early nineteenth century Ashanti has clearly demonstrated how this process can work,[36] and we may suppose that the influence of the Muslim Dyula merchants and their symbiotic 'clerical' lineages made itself felt in similar ways in fifteenth century Kano and Katsina. The second Muslim ruler of Katsina, Ibrāhīm Sūra (Mandinka = white, Arab) who ruled c. 1493–8, was singled out along with Muḥammad Settefen of Agades by Al-Suyūṭī for mention in his tract addressed to the kings and sultans of Takrūr (Central Sudan),[37] the general tone of which seems to indicate that Islam was still a comparatively new element in the social and political structure.

The third ruler of the new dynasty, ʿAlī (1498–1524), under whom the city's fortifications were built, bears the Islamic sobriquet *murābiṭ*—religious warrior. The clearly Islamic character of the new Katsina is again demonstrated by the visit of the celebrated North African scholar al-Maghīlī in the mid-1490s, by the settlement of the *qāḍī* Aida Aḥmad of Tāzakht (d. 1529–30) in the city after a long study tour of Mecca and Cairo, and the visit of Makhlūf al-Bilbālī (d. 1533–4), a well known peripatetic scholar from the Ḥawḍ. It may therefore be that the original character of the new Katsina was akin to that of the *ribāṭ*, the fortified place of devotion and study whose members were also warriors, and that the name *murābiṭ* given to ʿAlī was more than a mere honorific.

This may at first sight appear contradictory in view of the disparaging picture of Katsina given by Leo Africanus: 'All the inhabited areas are hamlets made up of straw huts of wretched appearance. None is larger than three hundred hearths [which might give an estimated population of 2–3,000]. Poverty is here accompanied by baseness.'[38] Several factors must

34. Palmer, *S.M.*, iii, p. 111.
35 J. Goody and M. Mustafa, 'The caravan trade from Kano to Salaga', *J.H.S.N.*, iii, pp. 611–16. See also N. Levtzion, *Muslims and Chiefs in West Africa,* Oxford, 1968, pp. 17–18.
36. I. Wilks, 'The position of Muslims in metropolitan Ashanti in the early 19th century', *Islam in tropical Africa,* ed. I. M. Lewis, London, 1966, pp. 318–39.
37 The text of this letter appears in ʿUthmān b. Fūdī, *Tanbīh al-Ikhwān,* of which several MSS exist, and in Adam ʿAbdullāh al-Ilūrī, *Al-Islām fī Nījiriyā wa ʿUthmān b. Fūdī,* Cairo, n.d., pp. 25–6. The *Tanbīh* was translated by H. R. Palmer under the title 'An early Fulani conception of Islam', *J.A.S.*, xiii, 1913–14, pp. 407–14 and xiv, 1914–15, pp. 53–9 and 185–92.
38 Leo Africanus, *Description,* ii, p. 477.

be borne in mind however. First, Leo evidently did not actually visit Katsina town, and secondly, his interest was in politically or economically powerful states rather than religious learning. Further Katsina had recently become tributary to Songhay and probably greatly impoverished thereby.[39] It is also possible that the establishment of the fortified town took place after he gathered his information and represents a response to Songhay attacks and the belligerency of Kano.

On the other hand Leo devotes considerably more attention to the commercially flourishing and militarily powerful city-state of Guangara, though its exact location still remains doubtful. He describes it as bordering Zamfara on the south-east and later as lying between the empire of the Askia and Bornu. Lhote suggests that it was a Wangara-inspired state in the region of Tessaoua (north-east of Zamfara) and points to the existence of a place called Gangara in that area.[40] Leo's description of the rich merchants who trade to distant gold-bearing lands in the south seems to lend support to the hypothesis of a Gonja-Hausaland trade link operated by the Wangara, as suggested above. In all probability Leo actually passed through this area, having come from Gao via Agades (at that time a Songhay colony) on his way to Bornu, skirting the northern edge of the Hausa states without actually visiting them.

Palmer, however, is of the view that Leo's Guangara existed at Katsina-Laka (about 100 miles north-west of Zaria) being the same city that was famed for learning, the present Katsina being until the Fulbe conquest of 1807 merely a caravan terminus.[41] No immediate solution to the problem seems possible, but it may be suggested that while Katsina-Laka was the seat of the former dynasty, the Durbawa, the present Katsina grew up as an Islamic city under Wangara influence. This may be the origin of Leo's name Guangara, or his city of that name may have had a separate existence at his time and been later abandoned or absorbed by Katsina, its merchants finding a safer refuge in the new walled town which was also the seat of political power. Neither Songhay, Kano or Katsina sources make any separate mention of a place of this name.

The new city-state of Katsina probably became tributary to Songhay early in the sixteenth century, having earlier been tributary to Kano. If Leo is correct, it would appear that Kano was soon after attacked by the Askia,

Ibid. Another Songhay expedition against Katsina took place in 1514, shortly after Leo was in the area; the cursory mention this receives in the sources tends to reinforce the view that Katsina had already been subdued and that this was a punitive expedition against a rebellious tributary. See ʿAbd al-Raḥmān al-Saʿdī, *Ta'rīkh al-Sūdān,* ed. and trans. O. Houdas, Paris, 1898–1900, p. 78 (text) and Maḥmūd Kaʿti *et al.*, *Ta'rīkh al Fattāsh*, ed. and trans. O. Houdas and M. Delafosse, Paris, 1913, p. 77 (text).

Leo Africanus, *Description*, ii, p. 478, n. 97. This assumes the name to be connected with the term Wangara, which it may well be. On the other hand, we should note that *gangara* means 'declivity' in Hausa and hence could be applied to many localities.

41 H. R. Palmer, 'History of Katsina', *J.A.S.*, xxvi, 1926–7, pp. 216–34.

probably as a result of its having tried to establish its authority over Katsina. A marriage alliance was contracted by the Askia with Sarkin Kano and a tribute of one-third of the annual revenue imposed. But this, like the subduing of Katsina, was precarious and ephemeral; Songhay sources do not even mention it. As for Katsina, by 1514 another Songhay expedition was already necessary, suggesting that tribute was not being paid regularly and had to be exacted by forceful seizure. The loss of Kebbi three years later effectively sealed off the Songhay empire from the Hausa states and it was forty years before another raid was attempted, early in the reign of Askia Dāwūd, a raid moreover which ended in disastrous defeat for the small Songhay force at the hands of the Katsina cavalry.

At this latter date the ruler of Katsina was Ibrāhīm Maje (1549–66/7) whom tradition portrays as an Islamic reformer, indicating that the initial zeal of Ibrāhīm Sura and ʿAlī Murābiṭ had cooled in the intervening years. The un-Islamic sobriquets of some of the rulers of this period (Toya Rero, Karya Giwa, Tsaga Rana) may be a further indication of the trend, though some lists also give them Islamic names as well and some later rulers also bore such names.

Little is known about the history of the second half of the sixteenth century in Katsina. The *Kano Chronicle* records another expedition against Katsina in the reign of Sarkin Kano Muḥammad Shashere (1573–82) in which Kano forces were routed, though under his successor, Muḥammad Zāki (1582–1618), they were successful in a major expedition, inflicting heavy losses on the Katsina forces. This marked a change in the fortunes of Kano. They had been subjected to Kwararafa attacks and a decade of famine during which time Katsina had also been pressing them very hard. Another major war took place under Muḥammad Nazāki which, though Katsina was defeated, compelled Kano to undertake major improvements to its defences. It was not until the mid-seventeenth century after further exhausting conflicts that peace between the two states was concluded, no doubt owing to the need to face the Kwararafa, a common enemy from the south whose cavalry were raiding both Kano and Katsina at the time.

We have already looked at Kano in its relations with Katsina and it now only remains to examine the internal situation of the city and its relations with its other neighbours, particularly Bornu.

Our period properly opens with the last ruler of the fifteenth century, Muḥammad Runfa (1463–99) under whom the effective islamisation of Kano took place. The *Kano Chronicle* describes him as 'a good man, just and learned; he can have no equal in might from the time of the founding of Kano until it shall end'.[42] The same source attributes the first Islamic impulses in Kano to the reign of Yaji (1349–85), due to Wangara influence, with the tale familiar in the annals of islamisation in West Africa of the

42 Palmer, *S.M.*, iii, p. 111.

first *mallams* helping the ruler to succeed in an important expedition by their prayers and advice. While early Muslim infiltration may have occurred as early as this, the major Wangara immigrations occurred about a century later. Kano Wangara traditions, which compress a long process into a single immigration under the charismatic leader ʿAbd al-Raḥmān Zaghaite (Diakhite?), place the movement into Kano in the reign of Muḥammad Runfa and also link it with the coming of Al-Maghīlī,[43] though they indicate that the exodus from Mali began some sixty years earlier.

By the latter years of the fifteenth century Kano was a centre of attraction for Muslim scholars from more distant regions. Aḥmad b. ʿUmar b. Muḥammad Aqīt of Timbuctu, the great-great-grandfather of the famous Aḥmad Bābā, visited Kano and taught there *c.* 1487.[44] In 1491–2 al-Maghīlī was in correspondence with Muḥammad Runfa and shortly afterwards visited Kano and wrote a small treatise on government for him.[45] At some time between 1504 and 1518–19 ʿAbd al-Raḥmān Suqain, a scholar of Moroccan origin and a pupil of the historian Ibn Ghāzī, arrived in Kano from Egypt and taught there for a while. Another pupil of Ibn Ghāzī, Makhlūf al-Balbālī (d. post 1534) also taught in Kano and Katsina. The teaching activities of these scholars seem to mark the emergence of Kano as a Muslim city; its 'conversion' is symbolised by the cutting down of the sacred tree, an event which both the *Kano Chronicle* and Wangara sources attribute to the reign of Muḥammad Runfa.

Kano at this time was in a stage of economic growth and military ascendancy. Under Runfa's grandfather, ʿAbdullāh Burja, enormous numbers of slaves had been obtained from the southlands. These slaves formed the nucleus of a labour force upon which Kano built its prosperity, using them for agricultural and other labour, as porters and guards on the trade routes soon to be opened up with Bornu, Gonja and Agades, as soldiers for military campaigns and as barter items for Mediterranean imports, in particular the all-important horses. The power and prosperity of Kano at this time is reflected in the building of markets and major extensions to the walls as well as in the vast proportions of the royal *ḥarīm* (with accompanying purdah) and the elaboration of court ceremonial with the intro-

43 An anonymous document written in 1651 and entitled *Aṣl al-Wanghariyyīn alladhīna bi Kano* (The Origin of the Wangara who are at Kano), has recently come to light in northern Nigeria and has been published and translated into English by M. A. al-Hajj in *Kano Studies,* v, 1969. It relates the emigration of shaikh ʿAbd al-Raḥmān Zaghaite and his people from Mali (*c.* A.D. 1431) to the Hausa states and their settlement in Kano. I have discussed Wangara immigration in my 'Dynastic Chronologies' under 'Katsina'.

44 Al-Saʿdi, *T/Sūdān,* p. 37. See also J. O. Hunwick, 'Religion and state in the Songhay empire, 1464–1591', *Islam in Tropical Africa,* p. 305.

45 The letter is to be found in ʿUthmān b. Fūdī, *Tanbīh,* and al-Ilūrī, *Al-Islām,* pp. 21–4. Many MS copies of the treatise are extant. It was published as *Risālat al-mulūk*, Beirut, 1932 and translated by T. H. Baldwin, *The Obligations of Princes*, Kano, 1932.

duction of long copper horns (*kakakai,* from Agades) and ostrich-feather fans.[46] It was in the time of Runfa and his son ʿAbdullāh (1499–1509) that Katsina and Zaria became tributaries and although Katsina at least was soon lost to the Askia and even Kano itself became temporarily subject to him, Leo Africanus testifies to the agricultural prosperity of the area and the rich commerce and skilled artisanry of the city in the early years of the sixteenth century.[47]

Under both ʿAbdullāh and his son Muḥammad Kisoki (1509–65) there were threats from Bornu. Under ʿAbdullāh a Bornu army made to attack Kano but the Sarki was able to come to terms with the mai. In the reign of Kisoki the war was begun by Kisoki who took possession of Nguru, a town on the margins of Bornu and Kano territory. This resulted in a reprisal in which Bornu forces came right up to the walls of Kano, but finding its defences too strong had to retire. As in more recent times, the walls must have encompassed a large area of cultivated land whose produce enabled a long siege to be withstood.

One interesting detail in the *Kano Chronicle's* account of Kisoki's reign is the arrival of a certain Shaikh Tūnis and other scholars who brought with them Islamic books previously unknown in Kano; shaikh Tūnis is said to have ordered the building of a special mosque for the *Rumawa.* Whether these persons were actually Turks (*Rumawa*) is open to question, but it may be suggested that they were scholars who came from Tunis after the Ottoman occupation of that city (1534)—another testimony to the Islamic reputation of Kano, to which students were now also coming from Bornu and Zaria.

Following the death of Kisoki attempts were made to give power to his son Yakufu (Yaʿqūb) and the latter's son Dāwūd, but both were quickly deposed and exiled, though the Galadima offered to restore the unwilling Yakufu. The way was then clear for the aged Abū Bakr Kado, son of Muḥammad Runfa, to take office. He was over sixty-six at the time and had no interest in the offices of state; he devoted himself to religion and through his weakness in matters temporal the Katsinawa were able to ravage the surrounding countryside.

Inevitably he was deposed (1573) and another son of Yakufu, Muḥammad Shashere, came to power, though he too could not prevent another defeat at the hands of Katsina. Mai Idrīs of Bornu also launched an expedition which laid waste the stockaded towns of the Kano–Bornu marches though he was unable to conquer Kano itself.[48] Following the defeat by Katsina a plot was laid by the brothers of Muḥammad Shashere to assassinate him; the attempt was foiled but his rule came to an end in 1582, either as a result

46 Palmer, *S.M.,* iii. p. 112.
47 Leo Africanus, *Description,* ii, p. 476.
48 Ibn Fartuwa, *Taʾrīkh,* pp. 24–5. The *Kano Chronicle* does not mention these attacks.

of his deposition or death during the epidemic of 'plague' which struck Kano in that year.[49]

He was succeeded by his uncle Muḥammad Zāki (1582–1618), from whose descendants were appointed all the rulers of Kano down to the Fulbe conquest of 1807. Prior to Muḥammad Runfa succession in Kano had generally been collateral. From his time onwards there appears a tendency towards a rule of primogeniture (perhaps another sign of Islamic influence), though the older principle periodically re-established itself as in the case of Abū Bakr Kado. In Songhay, on the other hand, the collateral principle was unaffected by Islamic notions of filial succession.

The main events of Muḥammad Zāki's reign, the Katsina wars and the Kwararafa attacks have already been discussed, but if it marked a resurgence of Kano's might, it also marked a stagnation of the Islamic zeal which had characterised the early part of our period and the corresponding revival at state level of some elements of the indigenous cults. We see the reappearance at court of the venal mallams against whom al-Maghīlī had inveighed, hiring their occult powers to the ruler. In the same period was begun the *dirki*, a non-Islamic taboo similiar to the ancient *mune* in Kanem, now thinly islamised. It consisted of a copy of the Qur'ān wrapped in a goat's hide, symbolising the sealing up and preserving of *baraka* for the state and never to be opened on pain of doom to the community. More wrappings were added periodically so that by the end of the eighteenth century it required men with axes to open it up, though by that time no one was any longer aware of what the talisman consisted. In the late seventeenth century under Sarkī Dadi (1670–1703) the *maguzawa* rites of *bundu* and *tsibiri* were revived and under his successor a variety of un-Islamic taxes became common, so that it was not perhaps without just cause that ʿUthmān b. Fūdī fulminated against their pagan practices when he sent against Kano his victorious *mujāhidūn* to extinguish finally the ancient dynasty in 1807.

AIR

The mountainous region of Air, or Abzin[50] as it is called in Hausa, did not constitute a state as such. Rather its loose political organisation reflected the needs of the largely nomadic society which inhabited this important commercial crossroads and consequently needed to carry out some of the functions of a state. The most striking of these was the office of sultan which was instituted in the early fifteenth century. He was a sedentary figurehead who represented the interests of the various nomadic Tuareg groups of the

49 The *Kano Chronicle* says he was deposed. The *Song of Bagauda* records that he died of the plague (see M. Hiskett, 'The "Song of Bagauda"; a Hausa kinglist and homily in verse'. *Bull. S.O.A.S.*, xxvii, 1964, p. 547). I have discussed this in my 'Dynastic chronologies'.
50 And not, as Abadie points out, Azben or Asben, despite the currency of this deformation. (See M. Abadie, *La Colonie du Niger*, Paris, 1927, p. 40).

area to the outside world and in particular to their southern neighbours and the rising Songhay power to their west.

Rennel considers that the earliest Tuareg groups arrived from the area of Bornu in the late eleventh century,[51] though Nicholaisen thinks that some Tuareg were in Air before A.D. 1000 and that the exodus of the Banū Hilāl and the Banū Sulaim from Upper Egypt in the eleventh century drove others from the Awjila area into the Sahara and towards Air.[52] Among those who arrived at this time was a group of seven tribes who formed a confederation named after its senior member, the Itesan. At the time of their arrival the Air region was inhabited by the Hausa-speaking Gobirawa whose chief settlement was at Asode. Their presence was at first tolerated by the Tuareg, but by the sixteenth century they had been completely driven out to their new homeland north of Kebbi and Zamfara.

It was at the beginning of the fifteenth century that the Aṛumbulu, or supreme chief, of the Itesan confederation, took the initiative of seeking out a neutral figure who could be ruler, or rather arbiter, of the Tuareg of Air. The need for such a person arose from both economic and political circumstances; firstly in order to render more secure the trade route from the Niger bend to Egypt which had first been revived in the heyday of the Mali empire in the early fourteenth century. An acknowledged leader could ensure that the tolls which different Tuareg tribes randomly levied on the caravans did not become so excessive as to kill the trade and would allow for the establishment of a more regular system of duties in which each group obtained its due. Secondly, the hostility between the different Tuareg tribes, arising from their being intruders in the area who had not yet agreed upon a division of pastures, had reached a point where an uncommitted arbiter was necessary. This heightened hostility probably arose at a period when the Gobirawa had been largely driven out, leaving the Tuareg with no common enemy to give their warring factions a semblance of unity.

According to an Air manuscript they went to look for a sultan at Aṛrem Settefen (Tamacheq: town of the Blacks) which led Palmer to suggest that the first sultan came from an area south of Air.[53] Lhote, however, suggests that it was Asode, the old Gobirawa centre in Air,[54] which has to this day maintained strong connections with Hausaland.[55] Nicholaisen points out the similarities between some of the sultan's qualities and those of the Sudanic divine kings.[56] At all events the sultan was an outsider to Tuareg squabbles and probably of servile origin; to this day the sultan can only be

51 Lord Rennell of Rodd (formerly Francis Rodd), *People of the Veil,* London, 1926, pp. 373–5.
52 J. Nicholaisen, *The Ecology and Culture of the pastoral Tuareg,* Copenhagen, 1964, p. 412.
53 Palmer, *S.M.*, iii, pp. 46–8; *The Bornu Sahara and Sudan*, pp. 55–6.
54 Leo Africanus, *Description*, ii, pp. 474–5, n. 85.
55 J. Nicholaisen, *Pastoral Tuareg*, p. 416.
56 *Ibid.*

chosen from the offspring of mothers of servile (Buzu) origin.[57]

The first sultan, Yūnus b. Tahanazete (*c.* 1405–25), had his seat at Tadeliza, but soon the centre of the sultanate was moved to Tin-Shaman.[58] But neither of these places proved satisfactory and finally the town of Agades was selected, probably on the grounds of its being in a neutral area. As Rennel remarks, 'with the advent of a figurehead king there sprang up a figurehead capital'.[59] Agades, on the southern edge of Air, just off the main caravan routes and away from the best grazing areas seemed to fulfil the necessary conditions for such a seat. The date of its foundation is uncertain. Leo Africanus, the first writer to describe it, simply remarks that it was built by 'the modern kings', probably meaning by one of the sultans whose descendants then ruled.[60] Marmol, whose *Descripcion* was first published in 1573 says it was built one hundred and sixty years before his time, that is in *c.* 1413.[61] The *Asben Record* states that before the seat of the sultanate moved to Agades the area had been inhabited by the Gobirawa, but as a result of a subsequent war with the Itesan the Gobirawa were driven out.[62] Independent confirmation of this comes from the *Kano Chronicle* which tells of the coming of the 'Asbenawa' to Gobir in the reign of Yaʿqūb (1452–63).[63] Although we may allow both of these statements a measure of historical truth, it seems likely that the Gobirawa had been emigrating southwards for some considerable time prior to this owing to Tuareg pressures and that this exodus marks their final expulsion from the Air region.

The problem of the security of the caravan routes was one which plagued the sultans of Agades. While the third sultan, Alsu (1429–49) sought a *fatwā* from 'the lands of Islam' which confirmed the right of the tribes to levy tolls of horses and cloth, later *fatwās* from al-Suyūṭī (1493) and al-Maghīlī (*c.* 1494) condemned the practice.[64] It was almost certainly the

57 According to one tradition the first sultan of Air was the son of a concubine of the sultan of Istanbul. This is no doubt a fabrication designed to give added prestige to the office, though it serves to confirm the servile origin of the sultans since Tuareg descent is matrilineal. Istanbul at the time (early fifteenth century) was still the seat of the Christian Byzantines. See 'An Asben Record', in Palmer, *The Bornu Sahara and Sudan*, p. 63.

58 Rennell, *People of the Veil,* pp. 364–5 discusses the location of this town which was probably not very far north of Agades. See also G. Brouin, 'Du nouveau au sujet de la question de Takedda', *Notes Africaines*, xlvii, 1950, pp. 90–1.

59 Rennell, *People of the Veil*, p. 116.

60 Leo Africanus, *Description*, ii, p. 473.

61 Luis de Marmol y Caravajal, *Descripcion general de Affrica,* Granada, 1573. Edition consulted, Paris, 1667 (trans. Nicholas Perrot), see iii, p. 66. On the basis of Marmol's remark Cooley estimates the date of the foundation of Agades to be 1438 (W. D. Cooley, *The Negroland of the Arabs,* London, 1841, p. 25, n. 43). Barth, again based on Marmol, gives 1460 (H. Barth, *Travels and Discoveries in North and Central Africa*, London, 1890, Minerva edn, i, p. 203).

62 Palmer, *The Bornu Sahara and Sudan*, p. 64.

63 Palmer, *Sudanese Memoirs*, iii, p. 111.

64 The *fatwā* obtained by Alsu appears in Palmer, *The Bornu Sahara and Sudan*, p. 56. Al-

(*continued on next page*)

inability of the sultans to control the predatory inclinations of the Tuareg which led to the expedition launched by askia al-ḥājj Muḥammad in 1501 against Agades in order to secure this vital commercial highway to Egypt. The result of the expedition was the deposition of the ruler, Muḥammad Talzi Tanet and the imposition of a tribute which Leo Africanus estimated at 150,000 ducats. Agades was probably left semi-autonomous; Leo reports (*c.* 1513) that the town was largely inhabited by Berber or Arab merchants and that 'the few blacks are almost all artisans or soldiers of the king'.[65]

This arrangement proved unsatisfactory to Songhay and in 1516 a punitive expedition was sent to Agades and spent a year in the area enforcing Songhay authority and exacting tribute.[66] It was probably after this expedition that the askia, having learnt his lesson, left a Songhay garrison in the town and, one may presume, his own administrator. No further Songhay expedition to Air is recorded, though the Songhay language, called there Emghedesi, remained the *lingua franca* until the mid-nineteenth century,[67] presupposing substantial settlement and continuous contact. It is not clear how far Air remained tributary to Songhay throughout the sixteenth century. Bornu is said to have subjugated it in 1532 and some years later it was troubled by Kebbi. Later in the century mai Idrīs made three expeditions against the Tuareg, but these appear to have been lowland tribes inhabiting Damergu, though owing at least nominal allegiance to Agades.[68]

At the turn of the century (*c.* 1601) Air was still a plaything in the hands of Kebbi and Bornu, with Kano and Katsina aiding the latter. According to the *Asben Record*, the sultan Yūsuf was deposed by his cousin Muḥammad b. al-Mubārak but restored with the help of Kebbi and Asben (Gobir ?). Ibn al-Mubārak then sought aid from Kano, Katsina and Bornu and returned at the head of an army. Yūsuf was defeated and fled to Kebbi, raised an army and returned to expel his cousin who fled to Bornu from whence he was later recaptured and imprisoned.[69]

Such was the precarious existence of the sultanate of Air in the sixteenth century, its own rulers virtually powerless in the hands of the Itesan kingmakers, not ruled as a state but as a nomadic confederation and apparently with no standing army to enable it to withstand the buffetings of Songhay, Kebbi and Bornu. It probably suffered little from the ravages of the Moroccan conquest of Songhay in 1591. The pasha's troops did not reach

(64 *continued*)
Maghīlī expressed his views in his *Replies* to the questions of askia al-ḥājj Muḥammad. For al-suyūṭī's *fatwā* see J. O. Hunwick, 'Notes on a 15th century document concerning *Al-Takrūr*' in R. W. Johnson and C. H. Allen (eds.) *African Perspectives: papers in the History, Politics and Economics of Africa, presented to Thomas Hodgkin*, Cambridge, 1970.

65 Leo Africanus, *Description*, ii, p. 473.

66 Al-Saʿdī, *T/ Sūdān*, p. 78.

67 H. Barth, *Travels*, i, pp. 176, 179 and 205.

68 Ibn Fartuwa, *Taʾrīkh*, pp. 25–6, 29.

69 Palmer, *The Bornu Sahara and Sudan*, p. 65.

Agades, so far as we know, and any loss of trade due to insecure conditions to its west was probably made good by increased commerce with the south, in particular with the expanding commercial entrepôt of Katsina.

KEBBI

The heartlands of Kebbi which lie to the west of Sokoto fall between the lands bordering the Niger, inhabited by the Songhay-speaking Dendawa and the Hausa-speaking territories of Zamfara and Katsina. Muḥammad Bello represents the Kebbawa as a mixed Hausa-Songhay people[70] and to this day the *taubashi* or tribal 'cousinship' between them and the Katsinawa is maintained.[71]

Nothing definite is known of the history of the area before the rise of the first Kanta, Kuta, who rose from being an insignificant local chief to become a vassal and military support of the Songhay empire. He was probably a client of the Dendi-fari, governor of the extreme south-easterly province of Songhay, with responsibility for the left (*ausa*) bank. In 1516–17 he and his army took part in a Songhay expedition against Agades but afterwards quarrelled with the Dendi-fari over the division of booty and, breaking his ties with Songhay, established himself as an independent ruler. From this time on he remained independent and was able to build up a powerful state on the eastern edges of the Songhay empire which, during its two hundred years life-span is said to have held sway at one time or another over Katsina, Kano, Gobir, Air and a part of Songhay.[72]

The capital of the early Kebbi state was at Leka,[73] but by the time of the celebrated Bornu attack (1561 ?) the walled city of Surame had been built.[74] The *casus belli* of this war was Kebbi's raids on Air, whose ruler then called on Bornu for help.[75] Air had been a dependency of Songhay since 1501, but in 1532 had been wrested from the askias by Bornu,[76] which would explain the request for Bornu aid. This Bornu attack, though perhaps only one among many, was evidently a major attempt to crush the power of Kebbi. Its fame even reached Europe where in 1573 d'Anania could claim that the ruler of Bornu had 'several times put into the field 100,000 men against the king of Cabi'.[77] The kanta was at first defeated but thanks to the

70 Muḥammad Bello, *Infāq al-maisūr fi ta' rīkh bilād al-Takrūr,* Cairo, 1964, p. 46. See also P. G. Harris, 'Kebbi Fishermen', *J. Royal Anthrop. Soc.,* 1942, pp. 23–33 and J. Rouch, 'Les Sorkâwa, pêcheurs itinérants du Moyen Niger', *Africa*, xx, 1950, pp. 5–21.

71 S. J. Hogben and A. H. M. Kirk-Greene, *The Emirates of Northern Nigeria,* London, 1966, p. 239.

72 Muḥammad Bello, *Infāq al-maisūr,* p. 64. ʿAbd al-Qādir b. al-Muṣṭafā, *Rawḍāt al-afkār,* Centre of Arabic Documentation, Ibadan, no. 289.

73 Muḥammad Bello, *Infāq al-maisūr*, p. 64.

74 The ruins of Surame have been described by E. J. Arnett. See Palmer, *The Bornu Sahara and Sudan*, p. 229, n. 3.

75 Muḥammad Bello, *Infāq al-maisūr*, pp. 64–6. ʿAbd al-Qādir b. al-Muṣṭafā, *Rawḍāt.*

76 Palmer, *Sudanese Memoirs*, iii, p. 160.

77 G. L. d'Anania, *L'Universale fabrico del monde*, 2nd edn, Venice, 1576, p. 296.

stout resistance of Surame itself, was able to rally his forces to pursue the withdrawing Bornu army to Nguru (?) where he was able to inflict a series of defeats on them. It was on his return from this expedition that the kanta (Muḥammad ?) died as a result of a wound received in another combat at Dugul in Katsina territory.

Able to withstand the military might of its powerful eastern rival, Kebbi was no less able to stand up to threats from its erstwhile overlord to the west. In the 1530s a Songhay expedition was launched against Kebbi under the personal command of Askia Muḥammad Bunkan Kirya (*reg.* 1531–37), probably fairly early in his reign. With surprising candour, the *Ta'rīkh al-Sūdān* admits that the askia's forces were completely routed and that he was fortunate to get away with his life.[78] This was the last attempt of Songhay to subdue Kebbi, though in 1552 a 'dispute' is recorded between the new Askia Dāwūd and Kanta Muḥammad which was peacefully settled in the following year.[79]

At present no further information is available for Kebbi in the sixteenth century apart from what may be deduced from a letter from the Moroccan Sultan al-Manṣūr to Kanta Dāwūd in the mid-1590s.[80] In it he accuses the kanta of giving asylum to the fleeing Songhay leaders and aiding them with cavalry reinforcements. From al-Manṣūr's demand that the kanta should hand over to him the annual gift of boats and their equipment which he was accustomed to give to the askia, it would appear that Kebbi was again in some sort of tributary relationship with Songhay, though it may be that the annual gift resulted from the peace negotiations of 1553 and formed part of a mutual defence agreement.

The sultan further accused the kanta of preventing the people of Kano and Katsina from passing through his territory to make their submission to him—presumably through his pasha in Timbuctu. In the light of the *baiʿa* concluded with mai Idrīs in 1583 it seems clear that al-Manṣūr intended to make the whole of the Central Sudan, indeed all the lands to the south of Ottoman territory in Africa, tributary to him. Although he threatened to attack Kebbi if Dāwūd did not accede to his demands and himself pay homage to him, he was unable to carry out his threat, due in the main to his meagre forces being over-extended and too preoccupied with pacifying the Songhay domains, but perhaps also because Kebbi itself was still powerful enough to present a formidable obstacle to carrying out these plans. In the event, the Moroccan forces were only able effectively to hold down the area of the Niger bend from Jenne to Gao and had virtually to abandon the provinces of the south-east. Kebbi, on the other hand, was to continue as an independent state for another century or more until internal weakness led to its being divided up among the rulers of Air, Gobir and Zamfara.

78 Al-Saʿdī, *T/Sūdān*, p. 88.
79 Al-Saʿdī, *T/Sūdān*, p. 103.
80 *Rasā'il Saʿdiyya*, ed. A. Ganūn, Tetuan, 1954, pp. 127–32.

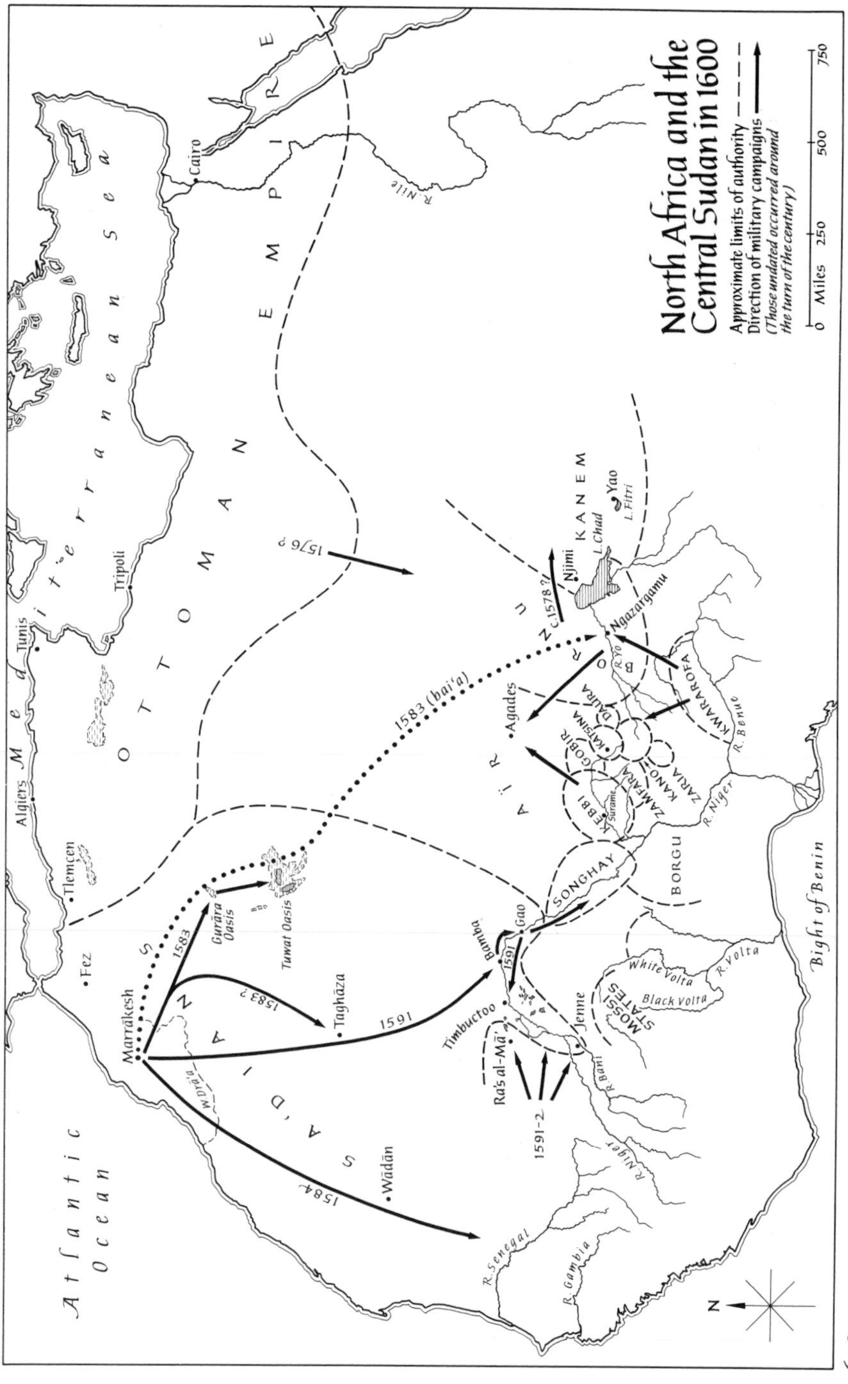
North Africa and the Central Sudan in 1600
Approximate limits of authority
Direction of military campaigns
(Those undated occurred around the turn of the century)
0 Miles 250 500 750
Atlantic Ocean
Mediterranean Sea
OTTOMAN EMPIRE
SA'DIAN S
BORNU
KANEM
AIR
SONGHAY
BORGU
MOSSI STATES
KEBBI
GOBIR
KATSINA
DAURA
ZAMFARA
KANO
ZARIA
KWARAROFA
Surame
Tlemcen
Algiers
Tunis
Tripoli
Cairo
Fez
Marrākesh
Gurāra Oasis
Tuwat Oasis
Taghāza
Wādān
Timbuctoo
Ra's al-Mā'
Bamba
Gao
Jenne
Agades
Njimi
Ngazargamu
L.Chad
Yao
L.Fitri
R.Nile
R.Senegal
R.Gambia
R.Niger
R.Bani
R.Benue
R.Yo
R.Volta
White Volta
Black Volta
W.Drā'a
Bight of Benin
1583
1583 ?
1583 (bai'a)
1584
1591
1591-2
1576 ?
c.1578 ?
N
6:2

SONGHAY

If the chief difficulty in writing the history of the Hausa states and Bornu in the sixteenth century has been the scarcity of source materials, the major obstacle to synthesising Songhay history over the same period is due to the relative abundance of material, which, however, still awaits critical analysis and evaluation.[81] The following pages will therefore merely attempt to sketch in the main lines of the period as a preliminary to a more detailed study which the author of this chapter is currently engaged in.

Inevitably we must begin with the reign of Sunni ʿAlī (1464–92), for it was under his energetic and imperial spirit that Songhay was transformed from a relatively small homogeneous state into a large multi-ethnic empire. ʿAlī Bēr, as he was also known, was the last effective ruler who bore the title Sunni or Shi (probably more correctly *Sõṅyị*), inherited from the days of ʿAlī Golom, the Mali commander and son of a Songhay ruler, who wrested his homelands from the suzerainty of Mali in the late thirteenth century.[82] Although his predecessor, Salmān Dāma (or Dandi) had devastated Mema, a province of northern Mali, it was not integrated into Songhay proper. The *Taʾrikh al-Sūdān* is explicit: 'The sovereignty of none of them (the Sunnis) extended beyond "Songhay" except for Sunni ʿAlī.'[83]

In less than thirty years Sunni ʿAlī's restless military energy built up an empire stretching from the borders of Kebbi in the south-east around the Niger buckle to beyond Jenne in the south-west and including much of the *gurma* (right bank) as well as the *aussa* (left bank) territories. Whereas his predecessors all had a single royal residence at Kukiya, his continual campaigns necessitated a series of other 'capitals' at Gao, Kabara and Wara in Tindirma. It would be tedious to enumerate all his many expeditions, but the following main lines of conquest may be noted. Early in his reign he made a series of expeditions into the southern Saharan fringes aimed at pacifying the Tuareg whose incursions into the settled riverain areas were a constant menace. A campaign of 1467–8 into the 'desert of the Moors'

81 Our chief sources are the two voluminous local chronicles, the *Taʾrīkh al-Sūdān* and the *Taʾrīkh al-Fattāsh* (see p. 214, n. 39 above). Their accounts of sixteenth-century Songhay overlap a great deal, but also supplement each other. Many problems arise from their conflicting accounts, while other serious difficulties arise from textual obscurities, particularly in the orthography of personal and place names.

82 The date is uncertain. I have discussed the matter briefly in my 'Religion and state in the Songhay empire 1464–1591', in I. M. Lewis, ed., *Islam in Tropical Africa*, London, 1966, pp. 296–315. See also chapter 4 of this present volume, p. 144. The origin of the title Sunni (thus spelt in *T/Sūdān*, p. 64) or Shī (*T/Fattāsh*, p. 43, but in the Fragment, p. 334 (trans.) Suʾi or Suʿi) appears to be from the Mandinka Sõ-ṅyị = subordinate (or confident) of the ruler. See M. Delafosse, *La langue mandingue et ses dialectes*, vol. ii, Dictionnaire Mandingue-Français, Paris, 1955. This accords exactly with the meaning given the title by the *T/Fattāsh* (p. 43) which is *koi-banandi* (Song.) or *khalīfat al-sulṭān* (Ar.), i.e. deputy of the ruler.

83 *T/Sūdān*, p. 6, 'Songhay' here would mean the heartlands of the Songhay people, i.e. the banks of the Niger and adjoining bush lying between Dendi and Gao.

(*sūra bantamba*) to the north and north-west of Timbuctu was followed a year later by the occupation of Timbuctu city which for the preceding forty years had been in the hands of the Ṭuareg. This was the occasion of his first and most ruthless persecution of the Muslim scholars (many of whom were 'men of the desert'), which led to large scale emigration of the *literati* to Walata. In 1469–70 he campaigned in Azawād (north-east of Timbuctu)[84] after which date he appears to have established sufficient control over his northern territories for there to be no need for further expeditions.

To the south of the Niger buckle there was another constant threat, the Mossi state of Yatenga. Just before 1336 the Mossi had sacked Timbuctu,[85] in 1410 they had raided the Lake Débo region and may also have besieged Walāta in *c.* 1446.[86] In 1477 Naba Nasere led his army into Bāghana and on to Walāta and it was only in 1483 that Sunni ʿAlī was able to drive him out of the area.[87] This was an enemy he had every cause to fear and for this reason he had directed three expeditions against the Mossi in the early years of his reign, though evidently none was devastating enough to reduce them to submission; in fact the Mossi remained a constant source of danger to the Songhay and none of the askias was able to establish direct rule over the Naba's territory.

In the south-west Sunni ʿAlī was able to add to his empire the province of Jenne which was still firmly a part of the empire at the time of the Moroccan invasion in 1591. Again the chronology is not very clear, but it would appear to be in 1472 that he began his siege of the city which was almost defeated by the annual flooding of the river Bani. However, a hastily assembled fleet of small boats enabled him to impose an effective blockade and within six months the city capitulated.[88] It was from Jenne that Sunni ʿAlī then launched two expeditions into Mali, probably in the province of Kala which then became a tribute-paying satellite of Songhay. Others of his campaigns were directed against the Fulbe, who were migrating into Masina and the lacustrine area south-west of Timbuctu during the fifteenth century, and against the Dogon (or Tombo) of Bandiagara-Hombori or al-Ḥajar as the area is generally known in the Arabic sources. It was in this area that he lost his life in November 1492

84 The desert area south of Air, and another about eighty miles east of Niamey, are also called Azawa(t), and it may well be in this latter area that Sunni ʿAli campaigned: the names of all three localities derive from the Tamacheq word *azwagh* (see Rennell, *People of the Veil*, p. 61).
85 *T/Sūdān*, p. 8.
86 See Y. Person, 'Le moyen Niger au 15e siècle d'après des documents européens', *Notes Africaines*, lxxviii, 1958, pp. 45–7.
87 The accounts of this episode in the *T/Fattāsh* (pp. 47–8) and *T/Sūdān* (p. 70) are difficult to piece together into a coherent narrative. Delafosse in his note to p. 93 of the translation gives a plausible reconstruction of the sequence of events.
88 *T/Fattāsh*, p. 50. *T/Sūdān* estimates the duration of the siege as variously seven years and seven months (p. 14), four years (p. 15) or perhaps thirteen months (pp. 15–16).

while returning from an expedition against the Fulbe and their client *dyawamBe* (Ar. *zaghrāna*). The circumstances are mysterious. The *Taʾrīkh al-Fattāsh* merely records that he died suddenly at Qunna; the *Taʾrīkh al-Sūdān* claims that he was drowned in a flooded river at Kuni, though as Rouch points out, the Niger tributaries would be long since dry at that time of year.[89] Oral tradition, on the other hand, asserts that he was killed by Mamar, a son of his sister Kassey (and later to be askia al-ḥajj Muḥammad I),[90] who was at the time, according to Arabic sources, Tondi-farima, or 'governor of the rock' (the Hombori/Bandiagara region).

No less mysterious is the origin of Muḥammad himself. The Arabic chronicles, perhaps wishing to emphasise a clean break with the 'pagan' past of the Sunni dynasty indicate that his male ancestors came from Sila or Futa Toro,[91] and from this one would assume his paternal origins to be Soninke or Tokolor. According to the chronicles his mother, Kassey, was a daughter of Kura-koi Bukar,[92] but oral tradition makes her a sister of Sunni ʿAlī. It is not altogether unlikely that Muḥammad was in some way related to Sunni ʿAlī, a fact which the *Taʾrīkh al-Fattāsh* also appears to confirm,[93] and that he made a bid for power through an attempted *coup d'état*—a method which was certainly characteristic of many of his successors. His bid, however, was not immediately successful as the army confirmed ʿAlī's son Abū Bakr Dāʿū (known as Sunni Bāru) as their new ruler while they were still on route back to Gao. Meanwhile Muḥammad had assembled an army with which to pursue his challenge to the throne, although he was only supported by one of the major commanders, the Bara-koi.[94] The two armies assembled at Anfao (or Angao) near Gao on 19 February 1493, but negotiations between the two sides continued for fifty-two days.

According to the *Taʾrīkh al-Fattāsh* Muḥammad challenged Sunni Bāru to declare himself a Muslim and Sunni Bāru 'refused absolutely; he had fears for his sovereignty as is natural on the part of a ruler'.[95] This statement highlights the struggle between Islam and indigenous cults as the *élan vital* of Songhay sovereignty. Sunni ʿAlī's charisma had rested largely on his position as supreme master of the indigenous cult structure; at the same time, however, he had found it profitable to add elements of Islam to the

89 *T/Fattāsh*, p. 51; *T/Sūdān*, p. 71. J. Rouch, *Contribution à l'histoire des Songhay* (Mémoires de l'I.F.A.N., no. 29), Dakar, 1953, pp. 185–6. Qunna or Koni is perhaps to be identified with Konna, S. E., of Lake Débo between the river Bani and Bandiagara.
90 J. Rouch, *Contribution*, pp. 187–8. Mamar is a Songhay corruption of Muḥammed.
91 *T/Fattāsh*, pp. 59 and 71. *T/Sūdān*, pp. 71 and 134.
92 *T/Fattāsh*, p. 59, though it is remarked that some genealogists trace his mother's descent from a grandson of Jābir b. 'Abdullāh, a Companion of the Prophet!
93 *T/Fattāsh*, p. 48.
94 *T/Fattāsh*, p. 54. The Bara-koi was the governor of the area of the river Bara (Bara-issa), north of Lake Débo.
95 *T/Fattāsh*, p. 53.

Songhay pantheon and to mould them into the total system. It is for this reason that, for Muslim scholars, there arose the question of whether or not he was in fact a Muslim and why the question was discussed in some detail by al-Maghīlī. Sunni Bāru felt it impossible to reject his inherited Songhay spiritual authority, which an outright 'acceptance of Islam' would have entailed. On the other hand Askia Muḥammad felt able to make Islam the basis of royal authority (though doubtless he too had to pay deference to the power of Songhay cults) and early in his reign sought to supplant the purely Songhay charisma of the Sunnis with the more international authority of Islamic *baraka* acquired after his pilgrimage and appointment as 'caliph of Takrūr'. The process may be seen as a reflection of the changing political nature of the expanding Songhay state. On the battlefield on 12 April 1493 Askia Muḥammad's apparently smaller force was able to defeat the armies of Sunni Bāru who fled into exile.

Askia Muḥammad inherited an empire that was still fairly closely knit, stretching around the Niger from Dendi (north of Borgu) to beyond Jenne. Gao was the fixed capital throughout the sixteenth century and the centre of an elaborate system of government whose machinery had, in general, existed in the days of Sunni ʿAlī and perhaps before. In spite of his reputed zeal for Islamic reform Askia Muḥammad, the 'pilgrim-king', appears to have made no attempt to shape his administration on Islamic models.[96] Territorially the empire was divided into provinces—Dendi, Aribanda (= beyond the river), Hombori, Timbuctu, Benga (or Bangu = lake), Dirma, Bara, Bani, Jenne, Kala and later Bāghana (or Bakhunu)—each governed by an official with the title *koi* or *fāri*/*farima*, more often than not a relative of the askia.[97] There were also town governors (probably revenue collectors) in Timbuctu, Jenne, Masina and Taghāza with the title *mundyo* and officials at the ports of Gao and Kabara who performed the functions of harbour-master and customs officer.

Muḥammad also created a new post, that of *gurman-fāri* (or *kan-fāri*), the jurisdiction of which is not wholly clear in the early period, though later its holder had overall responsibility for all the western provinces. The first title-holder was the askia's brother ʿUmar Komdiagha ('captor of Diagha'[98]), appointed in 1494, who built the town of Tindirma as his seat of government. There were also a number of officials charged with specific administrative tasks at the centre. While the exact nature of these

96 The titles *amīr* and *wazīr*, for example, were not used; our Arabic sources use the Songhay terms and it is clear that court ceremonial and protocol remained non-Islamic. See *T/Fattāsh*, pp. 98 and 114.

97 *Koi* is a Songhay word meaning possessor or master. *Fāri*, or more correctly *fāriñ* is a Mandinka word meaning brave, powerful, and by extension war-lord. *Farima* (= *fariñ-ma*) and *fariba* (= *fariñ-ba*) which are also used with the general meaning of chief or governor may be considered comparative or superlative forms of the root *fāriñ*.

98 ʿUmar had been responsible for the conquest of Diagha (or Dia) in southern Masina in 1494.

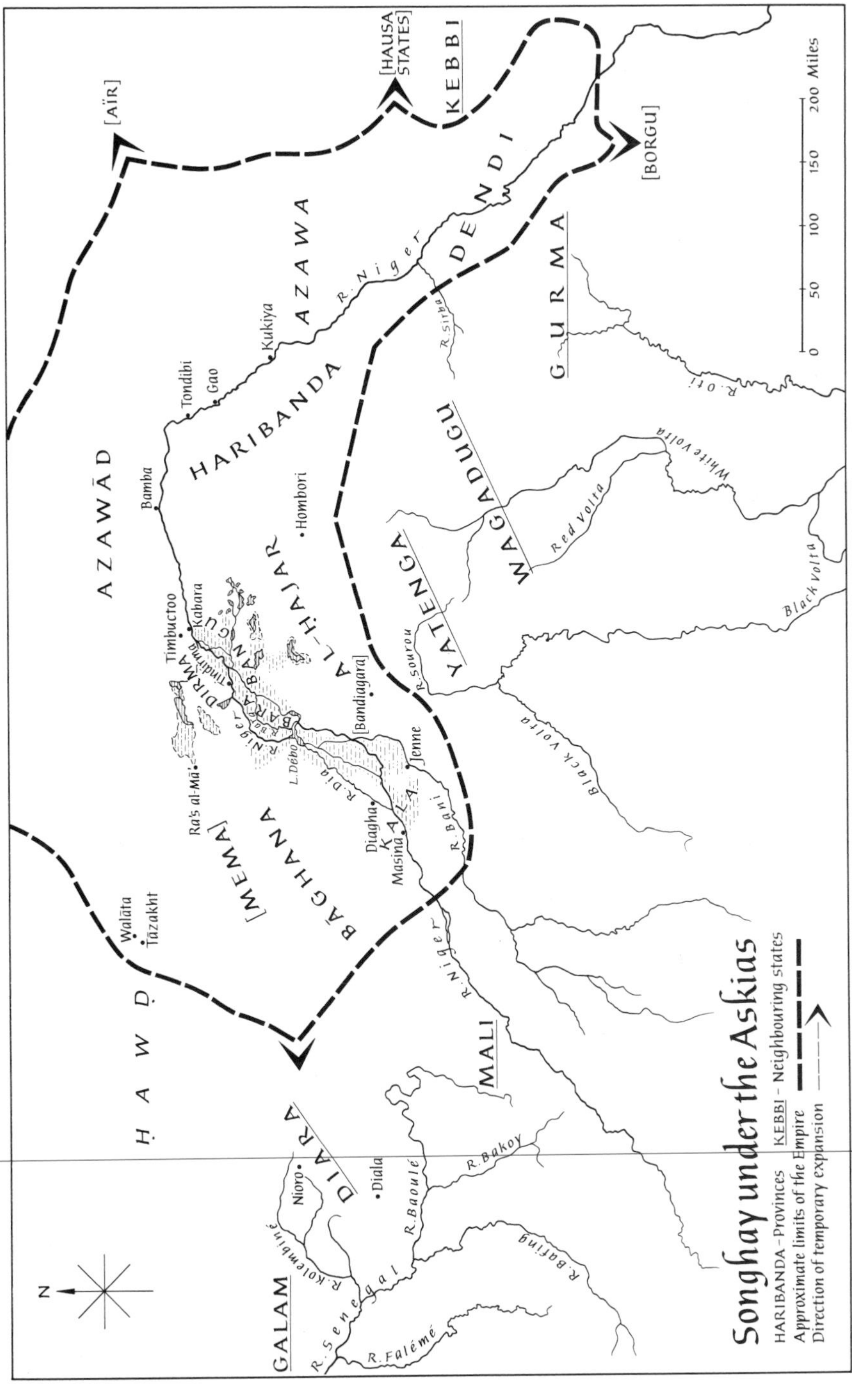
Songhay under the Askias
HARIBANDA - Provinces
KEBBI - Neighbouring states
Approximate limits of the Empire
Direction of temporary expansion
0 50 100 150 200 Miles
N
[AÏR]
[HAUSA STATES]
KEBBI
[BORGU]
AZAWĀD
AZAWA
DENDI
HARIBANDA
GURMA
WAGADUGU
YATENGA
AL-HAJAR
BARA
DIRMA
BANGU
BAGHANA
[MEMA]
KALA
ḤAWḌ
DIARA
GALAM
MALI
Timbuctoo
Kabara
Tindirma
Bamba
Tondibi
Gao
Kukiya
Hombori
[Bandiagara]
Jenne
Diagha
Masina
Ra's al-Mā'
Walāta
Tāzakht
Nioro
Diala
L. Débo
R. Niger
R. Sirba
R. Oti
White Volta
Red Volta
Black Volta
R. Sourou
R. Bani
R. Dia
R. Baoulé
R. Bakoy
R. Bafing
R. Falémé
R. Senegal
R. Kolombiné

6:3

offices is by no means clear, the more important officials seem to have been the following: the *Fāri-mundyo* (royal estates),[99] the *Hou-kokorai-koi* (master of the royal household), the *Korei-farima* (responsible for 'white' Arab and Berber traders and settlers), the *Sā-farima* (?)[100] and the *Wanei-farima* (responsible for 'property'—perhaps the booty obtained from military expeditions). The chief state military offices were the *hi-koi* (master of the fleet) and the *Balama* (garrison commander of Kabara)[101]; like the medieval kings of Europe, the askia himself generally took command in the field while regional governors had their own forces which were also at the disposal of the central government. Justice, in the large centres, was in the hands of Muslim *qāḍīs* who were appointed, at least in some instances, by the askia. The askia himself also heard complaints and disputes[102] and so, presumably, did his provincial governors.

Early in his reign, in October-November 1496, Askia Muḥammad left Gao to perform the pilgrimage to Mecca and during the nearly two years of his absence left the empire in the hands of his brother ʿUmar the Gurman-fāri. While in Cairo he was invested by the ʿAbbāsid caliph as his deputy (*khalīfa*) over the 'lands of Takrūr' and presented with a ceremonial turban and sword. Almost immediately on his return (July-August 1498) he set out on a *jihād* with the object of compelling Nassere, the Naba of Yatenga, and his people to accept Islam. In this objective he failed, but so great was the number of captives taken that a special quarter had to be built for them in Gao.

It was probably at this time that he received a visit from al-Maghīlī, who had been preaching and teaching in Kano and Katsina since 1493. In his written replies to the questions of Askia Muḥammad, al-Maghīlī encouraged him to undertake *jihād*, but pronounced that *jihād* against crypto-Muslims and backsliders was more important than waging war against self-confessed unbelievers. Although none of Askia Muḥammad's subsequent campaigns was a formal *jihād*, they all seem to have been directed at populations which were either in general declared Muslims or

99 *Fāri* means 'field' in Songhay. There were large and lucrative royal estates cultivated by slave or serf labour along the course of the Niger. See *T/Fattāsh*, pp. 94–5.
100 The nature of this office is not clear. Delafosse and Rouch, who call it *Sao-farma*, both think it means 'Minister of forests' (Song: *sao* or *sago/sadyo* = forest), but where the 'forests' were or what such a minister did with them remains obscure, unless there were royal plantations where wood for the construction of royal barges and buildings was grown. It is possible that the word *sāʿ* is derived from the Arabic *al-sāʿī*, a title used in classical Islamic terminology as equivalent of *ṣāḥib al-barīd* (master of the [royal] mail). Another possibility is that he was in charge of collection of *zakāt*; there was an official in the early nineteenth-century Sokoto state of ʿUthmān b. Fūdī who bore the title *al-sāʿī* and was responsible for the collection of tax on cattle, and the term has classical legal authority (see D. M. Last, *The Sokoto Caliphate*, London, 1967, p. 51).
101 The existence of a Djina-koi (commander-in-chief of the army) as claimed by Delafosse and Rouch seems doubtful and the word should probably be read Jenne-koi. At all events the office was not synonymous with Balama as Rouch suggests (*Contribution*, p. 192, n. 2).
102 Leo Africanus, *Description*, ii, p. 471.

ruled by a Muslim sovereign. They all went beyond the riverain cradle of the Songhay empire and were for the most part only successful in establishing tribute-paying satellites which proved difficult to rule. This pattern of expansion also seems to reflect Muḥammad's desire to establish his authority as 'caliph' of Takrūr.

To the east an attempt was made to gain control of the Air region which lay astride the important caravan route to Egypt. From Askia Muḥammad's questions to al-Maghīlī it is apparent that caravans were being interfered with and the North African scholar gave religious sanction to punitive action taken against such brigands (*muḥāribūn*). His incursions into Air have been discussed above. The breakaway state of Kebbi has also been discussed and though attempts were made under Askia Muḥammad Bunkan (at an unknown date during his reign, 1531–37) and under Dāwūd in 1554, Songhay was unable to re-establish its dominion. Katsina and perhaps also Kano and Gobir were for a brief period tributaries of Songhay. These city-states would have been important sources of revenue for the askia, particularly if they were entrepôts for Dyula gold, as has been suggested.[103]

To the west the main impetus seems to have been against the now autonomous northern states of the old Mali empire. Bāghana, to the west of Lake Débo was subdued in 1499–1500, though another expedition was necessary twelve years later. In 1501–2 a successful expedition was launched against Dialā, possibly a seat of the ruler of the Diawara state. Ten years later ʿUmar Komdiagha was called upon by the ruler of Diara (the Kaniaga-faren) to suppress an attempt by Teniella (or Tenguella), a Pulo chief established in Futa Kingui, to overthrow him.[104] In 1518–19 however, ʿUmar made another raid on Dialā and put its ruler to death. Both Askia Dāwūd (in 1550) and Askia al-ḥājj Muḥammad II (in 1583) found further expeditions in this area necessary. One even more distant expedition to the west was undertaken by the first askia; in 1507–9 an attack was made on the Galam region near the Senegal–Falémé confluence, but we have no indication of the outcome or whether the area became tributary to Songhay for any period.

During the last ten years of Askia Muḥammad's reign there were no expeditions. The askia was now an old man and steadily going blind. In this state of weakness he became increasingly dependent on his Hou-kokorai-koi, ʿAlī Fulan, to the vexation of his numerous sons. The appointment of his youngest son, Bala-farma, to the important post of Bangu-farima on ʿAlī's advice in 1525–6 was particularly slighting to the others and Fāri-mundyo Mūsā, the eldest and most immediately ambitious, began a cam-

103 See p. 213 above.
104 The *T/Fattāsh* describes Teniella as a pseudo-prophet (*mutanabbī*) which perhaps indicates that his real danger was as a challenge to the sole authority of Askia Muḥammad as 'caliph of Takrūr'.

paign of intimidation which led to ʿAlī fleeing for refuge to the new Gurman-fāri Yaḥyā in Tindirma.[105] In the following year Mūsā and his brothers began to plot a revolt from near Kukiya. The askia, blind and too infirm to deal with it himself, called his brother Yaḥyā from Tindirma and asked him to settle the matter, but with the minimum bloodshed. The unfortunate Yaḥyā was met by an army prepared for battle and in the encounter which ensued Yaḥyā died under circumstances of extreme humiliation. Askia Muḥammad himself did not last out the year in power. On Sunday, 15 August 1529, the festival of ʿ*Īd al-aḍḥā*, Mūsā entered Gao with his forces as the communal prayer was about to start. His octogenarian father submitted to the inevitable and as a token of his new authority Mūsā led the community in the ʿ*Īd* prayers.

The detailed history of the reigns of the other askias cannot be entered into here; details of their expeditions and their genealogical relationships can be found in accompanying tables. Territorially the empire remained unchanged. Before the end of Muḥammad's reign the south-eastern satellites in Hausaland were lost and effective control over Air probably did not last much longer. The askias who followed Muḥammad, Mūsā (1528–31), Muḥammad Bunkan (1531–37), Ismāʿīl (1537–39), and Isḥāq I (1539–49) appear to have spent the early parts of their reigns eliminating their rivals (for the most part brothers) and a good part of their other years forestalling *coups* from the successors to these rivals. It was undoubtedly the quarrels arising from this nepotic system which proved the greatest source of instability within the empire; all the askias were lineal descendants of al-ḥajj Muḥammad with the exception of Muḥammad Bunkan, who was his nephew. The key offices were redistributed by each askia among those of his brothers (or more generally half-brothers) whom he considered most loyal to him. Only the long reign of Dāwūd (1549–82) stands out as worthy of separate mention.

He came to power peacefully when Isḥāq I died on 24 March 1549; although he immediately had his own appointees installed in the key offices of *Gurman-Fāri*, *Hi-koi*, *Fāri-mundyo* and *Dendi-fāri*, he does not appear to have had any of his brothers put to death.[106] From the large number of campaigns undertaken by him in all areas we may infer that most of the satellite states had ceased paying tribute after his father's death. Like his father, too, he was not content to leave the powerful Mossi states outside the Islamic orbit, though none of his four campaigns achieved the desired subjugation. Other motives cannot be ruled out. Although the area was

105 In 1519 his trusted brother ʿUmar had died and was replaced in office by another brother, Yaḥyā (see *T/Sūdān*, p. 781, *T/Fattāsh* p. 77).
106 The *T/Sūdān*, however, records that his chief rival to the throne, the Aribinda-farima Bukar (a nephew) died at a time when Dāwūd was having homeopathic magic performed against him (p. 98). He was also responsible for the liquidation of the Hi-koi Mūsa (*T/Sūdān*, p. 101).

6:4 GENEALOGICAL TABLE OF THE ASKIAS IN THE SIXTEENTH CENTURY

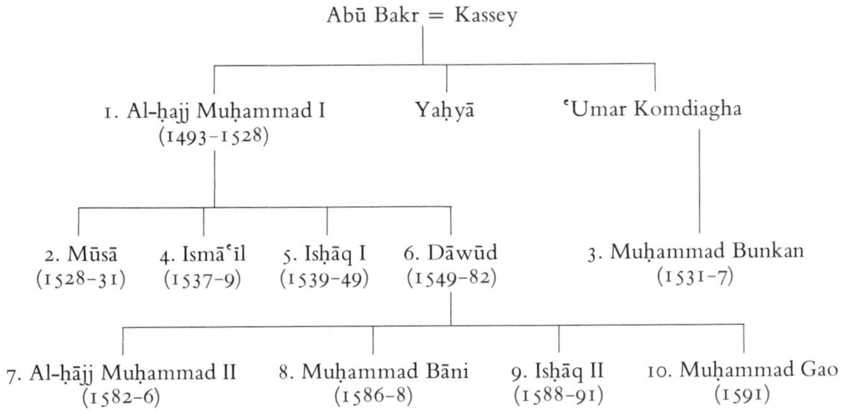

not important either strategically or economically in its own right, it was a rich source of booty and slaves while it could also be argued that it was in the askia's interests to make periodic pre-emptive strikes against a neighbour whose armies had traditionally posed a threat to the security of the Niger buckle.

The *Ta'rīkh al-Fattāsh* makes much of the Islamic virtues of Dāwūd: his memorisation of the Qur'ān, his studies of the *Risāla* (of Ibn Abī Zaid al-Qairawānī), the establishment of libraries and treasuries, annual alms and the endowment of gardens for the poor in Timbuctu and his contribution towards the rebuilding of the Great Mosque of Timbuctu. He did not, however, perform the pilgrimage, nor yet did any other askia after the founder of the dynasty apart from al-ḥājj Muḥammad II b. Dāwūd. As the eldest surviving son of Muḥammad I, he inherited the authority which his father had been given in Cairo: with the growth of Islamic authority within his own territory he had only to go to the scholars and saints of Timbuctu, and in particular its *qāḍī* Al-ʿĀqib, for the moral authority and spiritual guidance he needed.

When Askia Dāwūd died—a peaceful death on a royal estate near Gao—there was little to suggest that within ten years the Songhay empire would lie in ruins, askias would be made and unmade at the whim of eunuchs and renegades, scholars would be exiled in chains and the security of the Niger buckle again be shattered by marauding Tuareg, Fulbe and Bambara. But certain distant signs of danger were already clear. In 1578 Dāwūd had appointed his son Muḥammad Bunkan to the post of Gurman-fāri and then virtually divided the empire with him, giving him overlordship of all the western provinces. The effect that this was to have on the ambitions of Muḥammad Bunkan and his successors was almost sufficient to tear the empire apart even without trouble from outside. But it was in the

6:5 EXPEDITIONS OF THE ASKIAS

	al-ḥājj Muḥammad I (1493–1528)	Muḥammad Bunkan (1531–1537)	Ismāʿīl (1537–1539)	Isḥāq I (1539–1549)	Dāwūd (1549–1582)	al-ḥājj Muḥammad II (1582–1586)	Isḥāq II (1588–1591)
Eastwards							
Aïr	1500–1; 1515–17						
Katsina	1513–14				1554		
Kebbi	(1516–17 independence)	between 1531 and 1537			1552–3		
Dendi				1544–5	post 1570*		
Borgu	1505–6				1555–6		
Inner Buckle							
Gurma		between 1531 and 1537	1537–8				Twice between 1588 and 1591
Mossi	1498–9				1549; 1555; 1561–2 post 1570*		
Westwards							
Ḥawḍ					1570 (to Sūra bantamba)		
Bāghana	1499–1500; 1511–12				1550	1583 (Wagadu)	
Diawara/Diala	1501–2; 1512–13; 1518–19						
Central Mali				1539–40 or 1542–3 1545–6	1558–9 Post 1570*		
Galam	1507–9						

Notes
Askias Mūsā (1528–31) and Muḥammad Bāni undertook no recorded expeditions.
*In these expeditions no fighting occurred.

same year, 1578, that Sultan Aḥmad al-Manṣūr came to power in Morocco and immediately demanded that the tax levied on loads of salt from the central Saharan salt-mines of Taghāza should be paid to him. This was not a new demand. During the reign of Askia Isḥāq I the sultan Aḥmad al-Aʿraj had claimed that the tax levied by the askia on the Tuareg caravans (*aẓalai*) which carried the salt to the cities of the Niger buckle should be paid to him. Isḥāq's response had been swift and devastating; two thousand Tuareg cameleers were sent to plunder the flourishing southern Moroccan market town of Banī Ṣabīḥ. A Moroccan attempt to launch a major expedition against the Songhay as a reprisal for this provocation got no farther than Wādān.[107] In 1556–7 the sultan Muḥammad al-Shaikh instigated trouble at Taghāza which led to the death of the Taghāza-mundyo and some of the Tuareg caravaneers. For a time exploitation of the mine was abandoned while the Tuareg opened up another source at Taghāza ʿl-Ghizlān.[108]

Dāwūd's response to the latest Moroccan request was the opposite of his predecessor's. Al-Manṣūr asked for the tax of one year to help finance the 'armies of Islam' which were fighting against the Christians. Whether for reasons of piety or diplomacy, Dāwūd sent a 'gift' of 10,000 *mithqāls* of gold which avoided recognising that the sultan had any actual rights over the tax. Al-Manṣūr's designs, however, were much grander than mere fiscal control over Taghāza. As soon as he had finished pacifying the Sūs region in the early years of his reign he went farther into the Sahara and in early 1583 an expedition departed for the oases of Tuwāt and Gurāra. By 1586 the area was under Moroccan control and a governor and tax-collector had been installed.[109]

The seizure of Tuwāt by the Moroccans may have been a serious blow for Songhay foreign trade as it was the focal point of all the major routes from North Africa to the Niger buckle. Even if no attempt was made at this time to block trade through Tuwāt, the presence of an occupying military force would certainly have had an adverse effect on trade. In addition it was an excellent advance post for intelligence about the Songhay empire which al-Manṣūr was anxious to gather. Some attempt was also made at direct spying at the askia's court. In 1584 an embassy was sent to the court of al-ḥajj Muḥammad II (1582–6) with rich presents which the askia reciprocated. Moroccan sources also admit the sending of a spy who managed to survive initial suspicion and spent three years at Gao 'winning

107 See Luis de Marmol y Caravajal, *Descripcion*, iii, p. 67. See also R. Mauny, 'L'expédition marocaine d'Ouadane (Mauritanie) vers 1543–4', *Bull. I.F.A.N.*, xi, 1949, pp. 129–40.
108 Al-Fishtālī, *Manāhil*, p. 55, claims that Muḥammad al-Shaikh, after seizing the mines of Taghāza, agreed to share the tax with the askia.
109 Al-Fishtālī, *Manāhil*, pp. 36–45. It was no doubt a column from this expedition which was sent to take control of the mines of Taghāza (see *Manāhil*, p. 55, *T/Sūdān*, p. 120). The workers fled and again the askia forbade commerce with Taghāza; new mines were opened up at Tin-Wadar (Tin-Warad?) and the old ones at Taghāza finally abandoned.

favour and giving advice', eventually returning in 1589 with a man who claimed to be a brother of Askia Isḥāq II.[110]

At the same time al-Manṣūr had been active on other fronts in an attempt to encircle Songhay with territory he controlled directly or which was in alliance with him. In 1584 an expedition was sent to pacify the desert Arabs of Mauretania which then pushed on to the borders of the river Senegal where the submission and formal oath of allegiance of some Pulo chiefs was obtained. It is doubtless to this expedition that the *Ta'rīkh al-Sūdān* refers and perhaps also the *Anonymous Chronicle* of the Saʿdian dynasty, though both claim that it ended in complete disaster.[111] On the eastern side al-Manṣūr managed to obtain an agreed written act of homage from mai Idrīs of Bornu in 1583.[112]

By the time al-Manṣūr's spy returned from Gao in April 1589, with the supposed brother of Askia Isḥāq II, the sultan had completed his plans for the encirclement of Songhay. The spy's report included convincing evidence of the internal weakness of the Songhay empire. He was able to give a full account of the civil war which had begun in early 1588 as a petty quarrel between the Kabara-farima and the Balama Muḥammad al-Ṣādiq and which had ended in April of the same year as a full-scale revolt of all the western governors against the centre which Isḥāq, on assuming power, was fortunate to be able to put down. As a result, all the governors of the western provinces had to be dismissed and their armies which had fought against the askia had either been decimated or dipersed. Even the Gurman-fāri's army had taken part, though the Gurman-fāri himself (Ṣāliḥ, a son of askia Dāwūd) had been killed in a quarrel with the Balama at an early stage. The *Ta'rīkh al-Fattāsh* sadly comments: 'This revolt was the ruin of Tindirma. Of all those who came out in revolt with Kanfāri Ṣāliḥ none returned except a few of low rank.'[113]

Encouraged by these reports of internal strife, al-Manṣūr began to plan a military expedition which would bring the Niger buckle under his control, thus, as he hoped, completing his ambition to rule the Sahara with its lucrative salt mines and the 'lands of the Sūdān'[114] with their much greater wealth of gold dust. While planning the military campaign he also began formal diplomatic negotiations with the askia, based on his claim

110 The 'brother' was actually the son of a slave born in the royal household and exiled in disgrace to Taghāza from where he 'escaped' to Morocco (see H. De Castries, *La Conquête du Soudan*, p. 458; *T/Sūdān*, p. 137). When the askia's tax-collector at Taghāza, Ḥamma b. ʿAbd al-Ḥaqq al-Darʿī came to Gao in early 1591 he was arrested and imprisoned for spying, but more probably for complicity in this plot (*T/Sūdān*, p. 139). This seems borne out by the fact that he was later released by the Moroccan army and made an *amīn* in the service of sultan al-Manṣūr at Timbuctu (*T/Sūdān*, p. 142).

111 *T/Sūdān*, p. 120; also G. S. Colin, ed., *Chronique anonyme de la dynastie saʿdienne*, Rabat, 1934 (publ. de l'Institut des Hautes-Etudes Marocaines), p. 68.

112 See above p. 211.

113 *T/Fattāsh*, p. 143.

114 *T/Sūdān*, p. 143.

as *amīr al-mu'minīn*, to collect the total revenue of the Saharan salt mines. In Ṣafar 998 (Dec. 1589–Jan. 1590) he wrote to Askia Isḥāq II informing him that he proposed to place a tax of one *mithqāl* of gold on every load of salt leaving Taghāza. He also informed the askia of the arrival of his 'brother', enclosing a forged letter from him to al-Manṣūr asking for his aid against the askia.[115] Isḥāq's reply was brusque and challenging: an intemperately worded letter accompanied by some spears and two iron (horse) shoes.[116] Armed with this gross insult to his Islamic dignity al-Manṣūr summoned his council to lay before it his plans for conquering Songhay. At first he met total opposition to his plans, but eventually convinced its members that the advantage which firearms would give to a small mobile force would be decisive, even against a numerically much superior force. In this judgment he was proved correct and he had already had bitter experience of the logistic problems involved in sending a large force across the Saharan wastes.[117] What he did not clearly foresee was the difficulty, or, as it proved, the impossibility of governing such a distant area as a province of his empire.

On 16 October 1590 al-Manṣūr handed over command of a force numbering some 4,000 fighting men and 600 engineers to a young Spanish renegade from Las Cuevas and favourite of his called Jodar Pasha. Two weeks later they left for the Draʿa valley to obtain provisions, taking with them ample supplies of powder and shot, ten mortars firing stone balls, tents and all other necessary equipment carried on the backs of 10,000 camels and 1,000 pack-horses. Finally, having completed their preparations in the Draʿa, they entered the Sahara on 22 December 1590.[118] Travelling during the coolest season of the year the expedition, in spite of its slow-moving beasts of burden, was able to reach the banks of the Niger after only two months journey at a place called Karabara, near the present-day town of Bamba.[119] After a brief rest, during which they suffered some harassment from small Songhay columns, the army moved towards Gao

115 *T/Sūdān*, p. 137; *Manāhil*, p. 57; where it is claimed that the 'brother's' letter was written under pressure and as a result of a trick by al-Manṣūr. The text of the letter of sultan al-Manṣūr is to be found in A. Ganūn, *Rasā'il Saʿdiyya*, pp. 132–6 and G. Pianel, 'Les préliminaires de la conquête du Soudan par Maulāy Aḥmad al-Manṣūr', *Hespéris*, xl, 1953, pp. 185–97. In both these sources is to be found an extract of another letter to the askia (Isḥāq) inviting him to obedience (*ṭāʿa*) and threatening military action, which may be the second letter referred to in *Manāhil*. A third extract, also calling for obedience, but in more gentle terms, seems to belong to neither letter and is further complicated by a reference to the recipient's ancestor as Saif b. Dhī Yazan, which would suggest that it was addressed to the ruler of Bornu.

116 Pianel, *Préliminaires*, p. 191, n. 1, reads *naṣlain* (two spear or arrow heads) for *naʿlain*, which does not really seem a necessary emendation.

117 See p. 236, n. 111 above.

118 The dating is from *Manāhil*, pp. 67–9. The information on stores and personnel is to be found in the account of the anonymous Spaniard, for which see p. 211, n. 30 above.

119 *T/Sūdān*, p. 139. See also H. De Castries, 'Kabara et Karabara', *Hespéris*, v. 1925, pp. 125–8.

and on 12 March 1591 met a mixed Songhay force, numbering perhaps 40,000 at Tankondibo near Tondibi, some thirty-five miles north of the Songhay capital.[120]

The small Moroccan force formed ranks with their backs to the river, but neither the Songhay stratagem of advancing behind a herd of cattle nor their vastly superior numbers could shake the well-disciplined ranks of the Andalusian and renegade musketeers. As al-Manṣūr had predicted, the firearms proved absolutely decisive and the Songhay army, hastily assembled and with no tried tactics against gunpowder and shot, was soon routed, though casualties on both sides were light. The askia fell back on Gao whose inhabitants hastily fled to the right bank with the exception of the *khaṭīb* (preacher) and the scholars who were there to welcome Jodar and his men when they entered the town some days later. Jodar was greatly disappointed with the poverty and drabness of Gao and when Isḥāq sent word of a peace offer which would provide for recognition of Moroccan suzerainty and payment of a heavy annual tribute in exchange for a military withdrawal, Jodar immediately communicated the terms to his master in Marrākush.[121] He and his troops spent only seventeen days in Gao, where the unhealthy climate claimed many lives,[122] and then made for the more salubrious air of Timbuctu.

Initially it appears that he was also made welcome in that city, but the ruthless fashion in which he seized upon the quarter of the prosperous Ghadames merchants and knocked it into a fortress for his troops, and the monthly grain levy he imposed on the city's merchants, inevitably aroused the resentment of the élite; the boorish behaviour of the troops also served to incense the general populace. This, no doubt, is what lay behind the serious rioting which broke out in the city later in the year and which accounted for seventy-six Moroccan lives in less than two months. Similarly, it must have been this insurrection which caused the new pasha, Maḥmūd Zarqūn[123] to take such serious measures of reprisal after he returned from his campaigns against the askias in Dendi—reprisals which led to the exile of the celebrated scholar Aḥmad Bābā and a number of members of his family.[124]

120 *T/Sūdan*, p. 140, estimates the strength of the Songhay force at 30,000 infantry and 12,500 cavalry and is probably the most accurate. *T/Fattāsh*, p. 146 gives 18,000 cavalry and only 9,700 infantry. The Anonymous Spaniard estimates a total strength of 80,000 while *Manāhil* (p. 71), not surprisingly, vastly exaggerates the enemy strength at 104,000.
121 See *T/Sūdān*, p. 141; *T/Fattāsh*, p. 155; *Manāhil*, p. 79; H. de Castries, *Relation*, p. 473.
122 Over 400 men died of various diseases and also many horses while Jodar's force was in Gao (see H. de Castries, *Relation*, p. 473).
123 Al-Manṣūr had been so angry when he received Jodar's letter containing the askia's peace offer that he immediately revoked his appointment and appointed the eunuch Maḥmūd (b. ʿAlī) b. Zarqūn to his post. Maḥmūd arrived at Timbuctu with an additional force of 80 men on 17 August, 1591. See H. de Castries, *Relation*, p. 474; *Manāhil*, pp. 81–2; *T/Sūdān*, p. 144.
124 The matter is discussed in J. O. Hunwick, 'Aḥmad Bābā and the Moroccan invasion of the Sudan (1591)', *J.H.S.N.*, ii, 1962, pp. 311–28.

The immediate effect of the Moroccan invasion was to produce a state of physical insecurity due to the breakdown of the normal Songhay administration and, it may be supposed, a corresponding economic slump. Soon after the Moroccan invasion Fulbe groups and their client Diawambe were ravaging Ra's al-Mā', Bara and Dirma, while other Fulbe together with Bambara were raiding Jenne and the Kala region; the Tuareg, too, seized the opportunity to plunder Timbuctu in December 1591. All effective control of the western provinces of the empire was lost under the Pashas except for Jenne; in the east the heart of the old Songhay empire was split in two. The pashas controlled the area from Gao around to Jenne and appointed their own puppet askias; to the south-east of Gao lay the more ancient home of the Songhay to which the remnants of the askia dynasty and its army retired. Far to the south in Dendi they continued to lead an independent existence under their own askias, hardly touched by Moroccan rule—no longer the fulcrum of a mighty empire, but now just another minor Sudanic state hardly to be distinguished from their neighbours, Gurma, Kebbi and Borgu.

CHAPTER 7

The Atlantic slave trade 1600–1800

PHILIP D. CURTIN

The Atlantic slave trade was the largest intercontinental migration in world history before the nineteenth century. As part of the great Atlantic migration which repopulated the New World from the Old, its demographic importance is sometimes obscured by the even more massive movement of Europeans in the nineteenth and twentieth centuries. Nevertheless, for 300 years more Africans than Europeans crossed the Atlantic each year. This migration was not merely important for its demographic results; it also lay at the heart of a wide net of commerce and production that touched every shore of the Atlantic basin. This economic complex, sometimes called the South Atlantic System, centred on the production of tropical staples in Brazil, the Caribbean, the southern North America. Even though it was divided into competing national spheres, each under the separate rule of a European power, the patterns of society and economy had much in common. The system's influence reached far beyond the tropical plantations themselves—to Africa for labour, to Europe for managerial staff and commercial direction, to northern North America for timber, food, and shipping, and to mainland South America for monetary silver.

The history of West Africa would be incomplete without a view of the forces that drew so many Africans overseas, alongside the more intimate and local view of the slave trade that appears in other chapters. Since the South Atlantic System touched so many aspects of Atlantic history, it is important to see it in Atlantic perspective. The history of the slave trade, however, presents certain barriers to objective understanding. The controversy over the trade and over Negro slavery was the crucial point at which western society confronted the moral issues flowing from its rise to world dominance in the nineteenth century.[1] The emotional overtones of that controversy are far from dead. In the United States the heritage of

1 See D. B. Davis, *The Problem of Slavery in Western Culture*, Ithaca, New York, 1966 for a recent survey of the controversy.

Negro slavery has been the principal bar to achieving the kind of society Americans have held as a goal since the eighteenth century. In Europe racial prejudice persists, alongside the reaction against colonialism. In Africa the intellectual history of the past century has been dominated by the search for an identity in the colonial and postcolonial world. On all three continents, and in South America as well, the foundation was laid in the era of the slave trade, when European thought about Africa and Africans rested on the fact that the Africans most widely known to Europeans were the uprooted migrants, inserted on the bottom rung of a plantation society created by Europeans.

For the Europeans of the eighteenth century, Negro was synonymous with slave. One long-term result was the low status given to Africans in the pseudoscientific racism of the nineteenth century, and racial prejudice from this source only began to diminish towards the middle of the twentieth century.[2] Still another result for western thought was a sense of guilt, heightened by the great anti-slavery campaigns of the nineteenth century. Both western guilt and western prejudice are reflected in African thought. Yet it is possible to seek objectivity. We can admit that the slave trade was evil—that Africans captured slaves and sold them to the Europeans, that Europeans bought slaves and forced them to work on the American plantations. Beyond the long-debated moral problem, however, remains another problem of understanding how the South Atlantic System came into existence and why it achieved its enormous scale and influence for all of Atlantic history.

FORMS OF SLAVERY

The problem begins with the institution of slavery itself. This is an extremely common institution in world history, but the word 'slave' remains one of the most ambiguous in the lexicon of the social sciences. The ordinary dictionary definition will emphasise the slave's status as a chattel, a 'thing' that can be bought and sold like any other movable property. But legal saleability is only one factor in the extremely complex links of law and custom which tie the individual to his society. Whatever the legal status, no human being can become simply a piece of property, lacking any other social dimension. As a member of society, his status is made up of a much more intricate bundle of rights and disabilities, both present and potential. All of these inevitably help to set the limits of what he can and cannot do, of what he can and cannot become. The nature of slavery will therefore vary enormously from one society to another, depending on what other rights and disabilities, beyond mere saleability, the individual may actually possess.

Although Africa, Europe, and the Middle East all had traditions of

2 For a study of racist thought applied to Africa see P. D. Curtin, *The Image of Africa*, Madison, Wis., 1964.

slavery going back for millennia, the form of slavery differed so much from one society to another that it can be misleading to talk of slavery as a single institution. Under the Roman Empire, to be a slave of an important person might open channels of upward mobility that were closed to poor freemen, and many slaves served as important officials of the Empire.[3] In the Islamic world as well, chattel status was only one factor in determining a man's rank or power. In eighteenth-century Morocco, for example, the *ʿabid*, a royal bodyguard of slave-soldiers recruited by purchase from Negro Africa, very nearly dominated the state, making and unmaking sultans at will.

Slavery in the West African tradition was highly variable from one country to another. In the Islamic belt of the northern savannah, it was influenced to a greater or lesser extent by the prescriptions of the *shariʿa* law, which allowed the enslavement of unbelievers as a means to their conversion. The law, in short, imposed an obligation on the owner to watch over the religious well-being of the slave, and slave status took on overtones of the trusteeship that might be exercised over a ward or a minor child.[4] Even where Islam was unknown, slavery was a social rather than an economic institution. It was at once a mark of social status and a means of recruiting new members into a social group. The rights of a slave could be various, even within a single society. A war captive was at first normally at the mercy of his captor. He could be killed or sold, but, after a series of sales from one trader to another, he ordinarily came into the hands of a 'consumer'. From that point, his assimilation to his master's culture began, and he gradually acquired rights. These differed from one African society to another, but a second-generation slave often ceased to be a chattel in the legal sense. He could be sold, but only after judicial condemnation. His rights would still be less than those of a free man, but he was a full member of the community into which he had been born.[5]

Even where he remained a legal chattel, the slave in West Africa often enjoyed a variety of opportunities for advancement. Like the Roman slave, he could sometimes partake of the status of his master and rise as his master's agent to positions of authority over low-status freemen. (Where kinship ties were of crucial importance in the political structure, it was often unsafe for a ruler or other important person to depend on those who were not kin; and an assimilated slave was an artificial member of the family of his master.) Most slaves, however, were kept as domestic servants or

3 For recent comparative studies of slavery in the ancient and modern worlds see M. I. Findley, 'Between slavery and freedom', *Comparative Studies*, vi, 1964, pp. 233–49, and A. A. Sio, 'Interpretations of slavery: the slave status in the Americas', *Comparative Studies*, vii, 1965, pp. 289–308.

4 M. G. Smith, 'Slavery and emancipation in two societies', *Social and Economic Studies*, iii, 1954, pp. 240–90.

5 Deherme, 'L'esclavage en A.O.F.', Archives du Sénégal, Dakar, p. 25.

settled on the land. But even agricultural slaves established households that worked the land in the way a free household did. In some places, the owner set aside a piece of land as his own, and the slaves were obliged to work it in addition to their private plots. In others, the slave was merely responsible for giving up a portion of the total yield. In any case, most West African societies made no distinction between the kind of work appropriate to the status of slavery and the kind of work that might be done by freemen. Furthermore, slaves rarely differed recognisably from the physical type of their masters. They might begin as aliens unwillingly assimilated into a new social setting, but nothing in their racial appearance branded them and their descendants as the offspring of slaves. This in itself was a crucial difference from the plantation slavery that arose with the South Atlantic System.

Few of the forms of slavery practised in the Ancient Mediterranean or in Africa were very close to the type of slavery that developed with the South Atlantic System. The closest approximation was in Italy under the Roman Empire, where latifundia, or large-scale landed estates, were worked by slaves, up to a thousand serving on a single estate with a single owner—but this situation was exceptional. With the fall of the Empire, the western tradition of servitude changed. Instead of a clear line between a latifundia slave and a free man, distinctions in the kind and degree of servitude became blurred. Chattel slaves, serfs bound to the land, and sometimes even the subordinate followers of a military leader fell heir to a variable set of disabilities that set them apart from the nobility. In most of northern Europe, the status of chattel slavery disappeared, though it continued on both the Christian and Muslim shores of the Mediterranean. Even there it was no longer the dominant institution for the control of labour. Slaves were widely used in domestic service, to row galleys, in some urban crafts, but only occasionally in agricultural work. The crucial fact for the future American slavery, however, was the survival of the Roman legal status in the Mediterranean, ready to play a rôle in the development of colonial slavery as a special kind of forced labour.

MEDITERRANEAN ROOTS OF THE SOUTH ATLANTIC SYSTEM

The evolution of western-controlled plantation slavery began long before the discovery of the New World. When, in the wake of the Crusades, the Italian city-states like Genoa and Venice set up trading-post empires in the eastern Mediterranean, they discovered certain exotic crops and the possibility of growing them for the European market. Sugar, for example, was all but unknown in Europe, though it had grown throughout the Middle East and in Muslim North Africa. Christian merchants could buy it from the Muslim growers whenever trade was open, but in the prevalent conditions of religious warfare it was more secure to create a source of supply under Christian control. Venetians began directing some sugar production in the conquered Levant as early as the second quarter of the twelfth century. After the Muslim reconquest of the Levant, Cyprus became the principal source of sugar for the European market, a position it held from the early thirteenth century to the middle of the fourteenth.

Here the pattern of the later South Atlantic slave plantation began to emerge, as the European rulers and European merchants on Cyprus began to use old institutions in new ways. In Europe the peasant, whether free or unfree, worked the land according to the customs of the village. The *seigneur* held a bundle of rights over the land and the people alike, and he received a share of the total production, but he was rarely a manager who could introduce drastic changes, even if he wanted to do so. On Cyprus, however, the mixed group of Venetians, Catalans, French, and Genoese who had seized control of the land found themselves in a different position. If they were to produce an exotic crop for export to Europe, they had to innovate. Cane fields had to expand far beyond the island's domestic needs, and the cane juice itself had to be processed for shipment. In this way a sugar plantation was both agricultural and industrial. Whether the planters' European origins were feudal or mercantile, they found themselves in the position of early capitalists, investing in land, industrial plant and slaves, and managing the intimate details of production through their agents.[6]

The labour force was initially a mixture of free men from Europe, a few local serfs, and some slaves captured in the Levantine wars. But the planters soon ran into problems of labour scarcity. Sugar production was extremely labour-intensive compared to the ordinary wheat, wine and olives of the Mediterranean countries. This meant that the existing population had either to be concentrated on a small part of the available land, or else labour had to be imported from somewhere else. It might have been possible to attract voluntary migrants, as voluntary migrants were attracted from western to eastern Germany to open up new lands at this same period. But that solution was not tried—perhaps because the institution of slavery had survived in the Mediterranean and provided a cheaper source of labour supply. In the eastern Mediterranean, in any event, the need to concentrate people for new economic enterprises, whether planting or mining, was met through the existing links of a Mediterranean slave trade.

Slaves were regularly bought and sold and transported from one part of the Mediterranean basin to another—in both the Christian and Muslim sectors. Both religions held that it was licit to enslave war prisoners of the other faith, which was one source of slaves. Licit or not, there were also many Christian slaves in Christian lands and Muslim slaves in Muslim countries, and it was not uncommon to sell slaves from one religious zone to the other. In addition to the sources of slaves within the Mediter-

6 C. Verlinden, 'Les origines coloniales de la civilisation atlantique', *Journal of World History*, i, 1953, and *Précédents médievaux de la colonie en Amérique*, Mexico, D.F., 1954.

ranean basin itself, two external sources came to be important. The earliest of these was the series of slave markets in the ports along the northern and eastern coasts of the Black Sea. This trade was opened to Latin Christians with the fall of Byzantine Constantinople in 1204, and it continued as the leading source of slaves for the whole Mediterranean, Christian and Muslim alike, until the middle of the fourteenth century.[7]

The second external source was sub-Saharan Africa. Long before the Atlantic slave trade began, a trade in slaves had existed in West Africa. Part was an export trade to North Africa, but much of the West African slave trade (probably most of it) was internal. As Mungo Park noted toward the end of the eighteenth century, a long-distance trade in slaves within West Africa had a definite economic base. The price of a war prisoner close to his home was low; he might well try to escape. The further from home, the more difficult escape would be, and slave prices varied directly with distance from the scene of capture. Slaves were often passed from one dealer to another for a considerable period before they were finally settled into a new community—or exported by way of the Sahara or the Atlantic.[8] By the early fourteenth century Negro slaves began to appear in Europe—first as captives in cross-Mediterranean warfare and later by purchase from North Africa. When, in 1453, Constantinople fell to the Turks, the Black Sea slave trade was cut off, and Africa became the only external source of forced labour for the Mediterranean slave plantations.

Meanwhile the sugar plantation as an economic institution had spread far to the west of its original home. Plantations appeared in Crete, Sicily, and later in southern Spain and Portugal—Valencia, Málaga, and the Algarve—and the management of the enterprise was equally international. Capital came mainly from the complex of early capitalist trading cities in northern Italy and southern Germany. Managers and technicians were attracted from old plantations to direct the creation of new ones. As they moved they transmitted the institutions to which they were accustomed. These included not merely slavery, but a particular form of slavery. The labour force were chattels, but this was not the crucial aspect of their position. What counted far more was the fact that they worked as gangs minutely supervised on a day to day, hour to hour basis by the owner's representative. They were thus a rural proletariat, with minimal control over their lives or actions, kept separate from the rest of society, and with no possibility of upward mobility.

By the late fifteenth century this form of slavery was already linked to

7 C. Verlinden, 'La colonie vénitienne de Tana, centre de la traite des esclaves au xive et au début du xve siècles', *Studi in onore di Gino Luzzatto,* Milano, 1950, ii, pp. 1–25, and *L'esclavage dans l'Europe médiévale. Péninsule Ibérique-France,* Bruges, 1955.

8 M. Park, *Travels in the Interior Districts of Africa*, London, 1816, ii, p. 443. For representative itineraries of slave in transit see P. D. Curtin, ed., *Africa Remembered*, Madison, Wis., 1967; S. W. Koelle, *Polyglotta Africana*, 2nd edn [Freetown], 1963, pp. 1–24.

West African sources, and the plantations of that period already suggested the American plantations of the South Atlantic System. But there were also marked differences. The scale of plantation production was still small, and plantation slaves were still derived from a variety of sources—not yet from a single region of the world, whose physical type could serve as a badge of slave origin. Another century would pass before an example of the full-blown South Atlantic System came into existence in Brazil—and three centuries before the system reached its greatest growth and importance.

THE MOVE TO THE ATLANTIC

The key to further development was a revolution in maritime technology. Over the two centuries from 1400 to 1600 or so, Europeans developed the art of navigation in a way that changed the whole geo-political order of human societies. Shortly after 1500 European ships were able to reach any seacoast in the world. Even more, European society, which up to this time had been relatively insignificant in comparison with the Islamic world or with China, began to achieve the combination of sails and guns that was to give it naval dominance over any possible challenger.[9] The economic and commercial revolution that ensued may have been still more important than the relocation of military power. All the coasts of Africa were now open to European seaborne trade. The isolation of the Americas was also ended, and one long-term consequence was to make American crops like maize, manioc, pineapple, and cocoa available to African farmers. For the future South Atlantic System, however, the crucial change was the accumulation of maritime experience which made the sailing ship the most effective machine for using natural sources of energy that man had known up to this time. The real costs of ocean transport dropped steeply through the sixteenth and seventeenth centuries, as more efficient ships made possible lower crew-to-tonnage ratios. It became gradually more feasible to carry bulky cargoes (such as sugar and slaves, among others) over long distances. This change made it economic to produce sugar for European consumption at a distance of 4,000 miles from the market, and to supply the centres of production with labour brought 6,000 miles by sea. In short, the maritime revolution made it possible to reproduce on a gigantic scale the earlier innovation which had allowed Europeans to import cane sugar grown on Cyprus by slave labour brought from southern Russia.

This maritime revolution affected West Africa by stages. Like most technological advances, this one proceeded through the accumulation of small, discrete improvements followed by a dramatic breakthrough to a new level of efficiency. The first and most dramatic breakthrough, for West Africa and for the whole world, was achieved in the early fifteenth century by Portuguese mariners whose names are not even recorded. Their problem

9 See C. M. Cipolla, *Guns and Sails in the Early Phase of European Expansion 1400–1700*, London, 1965.

was navigation along the Sahara coast of Mauritania. These waters were extremely difficult for early sailing ships—not because of storms and rough seas, but because the north-east trade winds blow all year long in the same direction, accompanied by a strong southward-flowing ocean current. Mariners had long been able to sail against the wind by tacking back and forth, but it was much more difficult to make headway against both wind and current. Medieval Mediterranean ships, both Christian and Muslim, were perfectly capable of sailing south along the Sahara coast. The problem was to get back to the north of the desert.

One part of the solution was the gradual improvement of sailing ships, until a type had emerged that could sail sufficiently close to the wind. By the beginning of the fifteenth century such ships were available, based on modifications of hull and rigging drawn from the experience of the Mediterranean, the Indian Ocean, and the Atlantic coasts of Europe. This made possible a series of experimental Portuguese voyages down the coast toward Senegal. The Portuguese mariners apparently learned sometime in the early fifteenth century that they could return northward if they used the small diurnal alternation of wind direction, by which the wind shifted slightly onshore during daylight and offshore at night.[10] But, even with this discovery, the coastal route northward from Senegal was too time-consuming and difficult for use as a regular trade route. It was, however, a necessary step to the real breakthrough—the discovery that if a ship sailed north-west from the vicinity of Dakar, keeping as close as possible into the north-east trades on a long tack, she would finally come to a part of the ocean near the Azores, where winds blow from all points of the compass but mainly from the west. From there it was an easy sail back to Portugal, Spain, Morocco, or the Straits of Gibraltar. It would be hard to overestimate the importance of this discovery, which lay behind the better publicised achievements of Columbus, Da Gama, and their successors.

It also lay behind the next steps toward the formation of the South Atlantic System, first, the movement of Mediterranean plantation agriculture out into the Atlantic basin, and then its direct link to West Africa by way of the maritime slave trade. The westward migration of sugar planting began even before the discovery of America. In 1449 an improved sugar press was invented in Sicily, and its use soon spread to the Iberian peninsula. In the next few decades sugar production increased and spread to the Atlantic islands. With the new Sicilian techniques (and often with Sicilian technicians), with Genoese capital and Portuguese maritime expertise, Madeira and then the Canary Islands began shipping sugar to Europe.[11] At exactly the same period, Portuguese ships were developing their trade with

10 R. Mauny, *Les Navigations médiévals sur les côtes sahariennes anterieures à la découverte portugaise*, Lisbon, 1960. For naval architecture see J. H. Parry, *The Age of Reconnaissance*, London, 1963, pp. 53–68.
11 Verlinden, *Précédents médiévaux*, pp. 49–55.

West Africa. By the 1450s, they had made direct contact with the West African slave trade, buying slaves along the coast from Arguin Island southward to the Senegal and Gambia rivers and shipping them back to Europe by sea. The numbers purchased in this way were still small, only a few hundred each year, and African labour was not yet the dominant group on the plantations; but the maritime slave trade had begun.

Further steps followed in short order. In the decades immediately after 1500 Portuguese capitalists began sugar planting on the island of São Thomé in the Gulf of Guinea, taking advantage of the cheap slave labour available on the nearby African coast to counterbalance the long sea route to the European markets. Here for the first time the plantation system depended solely on imported African labour, though most of the slaves came from the region near the Congo mouth, rather than from West Africa.

After the discovery of America, sugar planting was tried there as well. The Spanish on Hispaniola brought cane and technicians from the Canaries, and a little sugar was exported as early as 1522. Planting then spread in the second quarter of the sixteenth century to Puerto Rico, Jamaica, and coastal Mexico, but none of these Caribbean experiments was an outstanding success. The crucial problem was labour. Local Indians could be enslaved, but they died on contact with unfamiliar European and African diseases. The Atlantic islands still dominated the European plantation system, in spite of a trickle of slaves imported from Africa to the Caribbean islands. Sugar exports from Hispaniola as late as 1560 were less than half those of São Thomé.[12]

The first outstanding boom for slave plantations in the New World came in Brazil. After a half-century of experiments with other forms of enterprise, the Portuguese found that sugar grew well on the coastal plains of the north-east. They solved the labour problem by a combination of raiding far and wide for native Indians and importing African slaves—a possibility more open to them than it was to the Spanish, since Portugal dominated the trade of coastal Africa to the end of the sixteenth century. By 1580 Brazil had become the most important source of sugar for Europe, displacing the Atlantic islands just as the Atlantic islands had earlier displaced Mediterranean sources. By 1590 the Portuguese settlements in Brazil had already reached an estimated population of 57,000—about 44 per cent European, 32 per cent Indian, and 29 per cent African—and the African proportion continued to increase.

The pattern of the South Atlantic System was now established. Large sugar plantations, much larger than the Mediterranean forerunners, surrounded the principal port towns. Their owners formed the dominant class

12 M. Ratekin, 'The early sugar industry in Española', *Hispanic American Historical Review* xxxiv, 1954, pp. 1–19. For the general history of sugar planting see N. Deerr, *The History of Sugar*, London, 1949–50.

in colonial society. The plantation owners were not only *de facto* rulers of their own domains; they also controlled the agencies of local government through their control over the municipalities, which theoretically ruled the countryside as well as urban areas. The plantation as an economic unit was very different from the nearly self-sufficient manor of medieval Europe, or from the African village. Its reason for existence was a market for sugar (and later for indigo, tobacco, cotton, or coffee) many thousands of miles away. The American plantation was, in fact, an intensely specialised off-shoot of the metropolitan economy. Never before in world history had agricultural enterprises on such a large scale depended so heavily on an export market. The planters also needed metropolitan power for protection of the trading posts in Africa, for protection of the sea lanes, and for the whole range of skills and services that could only be found in the much more diversified setting of the European cities. Plantation society in tropical America has sometimes been characterised as patriarchal, a kind of neo-feudalism grown up in a new country. This may be so, to a degree, and in the social setting of the plantation alone, but specialised production and dependence on other distant specialised suppliers through a broad commercial system was distinctively 'modern' and market-oriented.

This fact explains in part why plantation slavery was so different from African slavery, or from the slavery of the ancient Mediterranean. The individual slave was purchased as a labour-unit, and treated as a labour-unit. There was little or no room for individual decision, individual initiative, or even the play of individual personality. As long as he remained a field slave on a plantation, he remained part of a dehumanised economic enterprise. This is not to say that there was no escape from field work. Even within the slave caste, differentiation of status and rewards existed on every plantation. Some slaves served the household of the master or his subordinate officials. Others held positions of trust and leadership over the other slaves. Still others did skilled work or were allowed to take up occupations off the plantation in return for periodic remission of part of their earnings. In spite of these exceptions, however, field work on the plantation was the norm.

Once the slave plantation was established in Brazil, and its economic advantages were recognised, it spread to other suitable regions in tropical America. As it spread, the details were changed, but its essential nature was preserved, and many features were, in fact, copied directly from Brazil. The first agents of this further diffusion were the Dutch, who had become the most efficient Europeans at seaborne trade early in the seventeenth century. They began to move into the African trade. Between 1630 and 1654, the Dutch West India Company seized control of a part of north-east Brazil, where they learned how the existing plantation order worked. With their superiority at sea and their understanding of the South Atlantic System, they were able to sail to the Caribbean islands that were already occupied by France and England, offering, in effect, a package that included technical assistance in setting up sugar estates, a supply of slaves from Africa, and carrying services to take off the sugar that might be produced.

Dutch assistance of this kind was contrary to the spirit of mercantilist commercial policy (and often contrary to the letter of French and English commercial law), but it was profitable. Up to this point, the Lesser Antilles —Barbados, Martinique, Guadeloupe, St Kitts, and Antigua in particular —had been settled by Europeans on small farms that produced tobacco and a few other crops suited to small scale enterprise. Over a few decades from the 1640s through the 1660s, they were transformed into sugar colonies. White settlers gave way to African slaves; small farms gave way to large plantations; tobacco gave way to sugar. Once the 'sugar revolution' was accomplished in the Lesser Antilles, it spread westward. Jamaica and the French part of Hispaniola (the colony of Saint Domingue) were acquired by England and France respectively before 1700. Within a half century they were the most prosperous of all the sugar islands. Thus, while Brazilian sugar production stabilised at a level near that achieved in the early seventeenth century, the growing demand in Europe was met by the expansion of the system into new territory.

In the eighteenth century the system continued to expand, and it became more and more diverse. Slave plantations were set up beyond the fringes of the Caribbean, which had now become the heartland of the system, and these often followed West Indian models. Virginia for tobacco, South Carolina for rice and indigo, and from the end of the eighteenth century the whole of southern North America east of the Mississippi entered the system as a centre of cotton production. In North America the slave plantations were intermixed with white settlement, and most of these settlers were not slave owners: they were small farmers who worked their own lands. Thus even the southern United States were only a partial member of the South Atlantic System, and the northern states never entered it. Even on the islands of Cuba and Puerto Rico, numerous small farmers of European extraction worked the land alongside the enormous sugar estates that were established in the late eighteenth and nineteenth centuries.

At the risk of oversimplification, the pattern of American development in the seventeenth century through the nineteenth can be thought of as containing three different sectors with three distinct patterns of demography and society. One type of development was typical of highland Peru and Mexico, where the Indians survived better than they had done in the lowlands, and where relatively small cadres of Spanish officials, miners, ranchers, and planters ran a society that was dominantly Indian. A second type was typical of northern North America, where the Indians were few to begin with, and where the European settlers created a new society on the model of the Old World they had left behind. Finally, there was the South

Atlantic System, most fully typified by Jamaica, Barbados, and Saint Domingue in the eighteenth century, where virtually all manual work was done by slaves from Africa, and white settlers and Indians were equally few in number.

THE CHOICE OF A LABOUR FORCE

From 1650 Negros outnumbered Europeans in the Americas as a whole.[13] Even though Negro slavery was most closely associated with the South Atlantic type of development, both slaves and free men of African descent were to be found throughout the Americas. The very existence of large concentrations of slaves in the American tropics made them available for further sale into the settler sector or into the true empire of Spanish America. They were used as domestic servants in northern North America. They were bought even more extensively as mine labour—for silver in Bolivia and Mexico, or for gold and diamonds in eighteenth-century Brazil.

Just as Negroes filtered into the other two sectors of American development, both European and Indian labour was used in the South Atlantic System, at least in the early centuries. On the first Brazilian plantations, Indian slavery was important. Both England and France also tried in the seventeenth century to colonise the Lesser Antilles with white settlers. But the tropical lands had a bad reputation, and settlers without capital preferred North America. It was possible, however, to attract some settlers by allowing the shipowner to advance the passage money, in return for which the would-be emigrant signed an indenture or labour contract for a period of a year. Once in America the indenture could be sold to an employer of labour in much the same way a slave from Africa was sold to a planter. Condemned criminals were also sentenced to transportation overseas, and their labour could be purchased by planters as still another alternative to Negro slavery. For France the official policy was to depend on white bondsmen—in the Antilles from 1626 until at least the 1680s, and the last shipment took place in 1763.[14] The English began their settlement of Barbados in much the same way. As late as 1643 the working population was estimated at 18,600 Europeans as against only 6,400 Africans. Yet in each of these cases, the non-African workers were finally replaced by Africans, and in later decades the planters throughout tropical America expressed a preference for African labour—a preference that finally led to the dominance of Negro slavery for all economic development of the South Atlantic type.[15]

The planters at the time explained the superiority of African to European

13 A. Rosenblat, *La población indígena y el mestizaje en América*, Buenos Aires, 1954, i, p. 59.
14 L. Vignols, L'institution des engagés, 1624–1774', *Revue d'Histoire Economique et Sociale*, i, 1928, pp. 12–45, and 'Une question male posée. Le travail manuel des blancs et des esclaves aux Antilles', *Revue historique*, 1935, pp. 308–16; Gaston-Martin, *Histoire de l'esclavage dans les colonies françaises*, Paris, 1948, pp. 11–24.
15 See Eric Williams, *Capitalism and Slavery*, Chapel Hill, N. C., 1944, pp. 9–23.

labour by saying that Africans could work in hot climates, while Europeans could not. This belief became, in time, one of the cornerstones of pseudo-scientific racism, though scientists now recognise that physical type has little or nothing to do with tolerance to hot weather. (For that matter, the climate of West Indian islands is not as hot as Ohio or Illinois in the summer.) But the planters were empirically correct, however wrong their explanation. The answer lies, rather, in epidemiological factors. Students of the spread and incidence of disease now recognise that a host population will acquire immunity during childhood to severe attacks of the diseases endemic in its own part of the world. They also point out that disease environments differ from one region to another, since germs and viruses characteristically evolve new diseases and new strains of disease with great rapidity. In the modern world of intense communication, these new forms will spread rapidly, unless their range is limited to special climatic conditions.

The pre-Columbian Atlantic world was far different: disease environments were more isolated, hence far more distinct than they are today. West Africa and Europe shared many of the diseases common to the whole Afro-Eurasian land mass, but some West African diseases like yellow fever were limited to the tropics. Thus Africa had a wider range of disease than Europe. The Americas had been cut off for millennia from effective contact with the Old World; the range of disease known there was still narrower. Men who had grown up in any of these environments were somewhat protected against local disease, but they were extremely vulnerable to patterns of disease away from home; and the whole of the Americas was vulnerable to a great range of African and European disease.[16]

With the maritime revolution, both people and diseases crossed the Atlantic. The combination of African and European diseases wiped out most of the lowland population of the American tropics within a century. This development was fundamental to the future slave trade, since it created an immediate need for new population as the basis for any development at all.[17] But that was not all. West Africa was deadly to outsiders. Nineteenth-century statistics (from a period before the development of modern medicine) suggests that newcomers from Europe regularly died at a rate of 400 to 600 per thousand during their first year of residence in the 'white man's grave'.[18] Europeans also died in the West Indies from malaria and yellow fever of African origin, often at a rate ten times the ordinary death rate for people of the same age group in Europe. Africans newly arrived in tropical America died as well at something like twice their normal African death rate, but they had the enormous advantage of coming from

16 See P. D. Curtin, 'Epidemiology and the slave trade', *Political Science Quarterly* lxxxiii, 1968, pp. 190–216.
17 P. M. Ashburn, *The Ranks of Death*, New York, 1947.
18 Curtin, *Image of Africa*, pp. 483–7.

a disease environment where both the tropical diseases and a wide range of common Afro-Eurasian diseases were present. The statistics now available suggest that their death rate was about a third as high as that of European newcomers.[19]

In these circumstances it is hardly surprising that planters preferred workers from Africa. Whether they purchased the indenture of a European bondsman, bought the labour of a European criminal condemned to transportation, or bought a slave from Africa, they were laying out capital in return for a claim to later labour. If the European workers died out three times as rapidly as their African counterparts, the choice was clear. An American-born worker would, of course, be accustomed to the disease environment from childhood, and the price of creole (or American-born) slaves was always markedly higher than that of new migrants from Africa. Creole slaves, however, were always in short supply, and prices on the American slave markets appear to have been determined mainly by the cost of supplying new recruits from Africa.

If the prices of African-born slaves had not been competitive with those of labour from other sources—native born or European—the slave trade could never have come into existence, no matter what the epidemiological consequences of movement across the Atlantic. The cost conditions of the slave trade itself were therefore equally basic to the South Atlantic System.

The operations of the slave trade can be divided into three functionally and institutionally distinct segments. As a first step the slave had to be captured in Africa—a process equivalent to the production of some other commodity that later becomes an article of commerce. In the earliest phases of the trade Europeans occasionally captured people in Africa, but they soon learned that Africa was far too dangerous to their own health. Enslavement came to be a function performed by Africans alone; and, since second-generation slaves in Africa were rarely sold, the stream of people fed into the slave trade at its point of origin were mainly captives.[20] Some were certainly captured in warfare begun for other reasons—not simply in order to acquire slaves for sale. In this case they were a byproduct of a par-

19 British army medical records compiled by A. M. Tulloch in *Parliamentary Papers*, 1837–38, xl, [C. 138]; 1839, xli [166]; and 1840, xxx [C. 228] show a mortality rate of British troops serving in the Jamaica command at 130 per thousand per annum over the period 1817–36, compared to a civilian death rate among men of the same age group in Britain at 11.5 per thousand. Troops recruited in West Africa and serving in the West Indies during the same period had a death rate of 40 per thousand. A survey of wartime mortality rates over the period of 1796–1807 in the West Indies finds an annual average mortality for European troops at 244 per thousand per annum, compared with 59.2 per thousand per annum for African troops. See F. Guerra, 'The influence of disease on race, logistics and colonization in the Antilles', *Journal of Tropical Medicine and Hygiene*, lxix, 1966, p. 34; Curtin, 'Epidemiology', for tables summarising Tulloch's findings.

20 One statistical sample of causes of enslavement was based on the interviews conducted by S. W. Koelle among Sierra Leone recaptives in 1850. Of 179 individuals interrogated, 34 per cent were taken in war; 30 per cent were 'kidnapped' (which could mean capture by

(*continued overleaf*)

ticular military action, which would have taken place in any case. From an economic point of view, such byproduct prisoners of war had a negligible cost of production to their captor. He could sell them at a low price and still consider he had made a profit on the transaction. A raid mounted for the sole purpose of capturing slaves, on the other hand, was an 'economic' operation requiring the allocation of scarce resources. Leaders and other voluntary participants could measure the probable yield against the danger and expense to themselves. In this case, the supply of slaves could be expected to depend on a slave's value to the captor or on his anticipated sale price. Little is known about the prices of slaves within Africa, but available evidence indicates that the captors received only a small part of the price that would ultimately be paid for a slave once he had arrived in the New World.

A larger part of the final selling price went to those who performed a second function—the shipment of slaves to a coastal point and accumulation of enough slaves to create an attractive market for European slave ships. The institutions used for transportation and bulking of slaves for shipment were extremely variable throughout West Africa. Slaves were only rarely purchased directly from the captor and sold to the European slaver by a single African merchant. More often they passed through several hands, as individuals or in small lots, until they were finally gathered in large groups for sale on the coast. Where a long-distance slave trade existed, as it did in the eighteenth century between the upper Niger and the coast of present-day Guinea-Conakry or the navigable Senegal and Gambia, the merchants who conducted the slaves were also involved with other commodities, such as kola nuts, salt, and textiles of both European and African manufacture. Almost everywhere the state was likely to be involved, but the type and degree of involvement varied greatly. In Dahomey the external slave trade became a state monopoly. Other states merely milked the trade by collecting tolls and fees from passing caravans and from the European ships on the coast. Still others carried out some state trading but left the rest up to private enterprise under appropriate controls. At times economic and political activity became so intertwined it is hard to distinguish one from the other, as in the intricate canoe-house system of the Niger Delta.[21]

The third and final segment of the slave trade was shipment by sea to the Americas. European shipowners who managed this part of the trade normally received at least half the sale price, which meant that theirs was

(*20 continued*)
slave raiders, capture while travelling abroad, or surreptitious capture and sale by members of one's own society); 7 per cent were sold to pay debts; and 11 per cent were sold as a result of judicial processes (P. E. H. Hair, 'The enslavement of Koelle's informants', *J.A.H.*, vi, 1965, pp. 193–203). Koelle's sample, however, was skewed by the fact that he chose his informants to represent as many different languages as possible, which would over-represent individual cases of enslavement and underrepresent mass enslavement in warfare.

21 G. I. Jones, *The Trading States of the Oil Rivers*, London, 1963, pp. 88–101.

the largest of the three shares. From this sum they had to cover the cost of trade goods in Europe, transportation of these goods to Africa, and the transportation of the slaves to America. This could be an extremely profitable trade to the individual merchant, but the risks were also great, and the trade was intensely competitive.

Whatever the profits to individual merchants, the trade exacted heavy costs from European society. At least half of all personnel sent to the African coast must have died of disease. The crews of the slave ships also died. From a sample of 598 ships sailing from Nantes to Africa between 1748 and 1792, the average crew losses were 169 per thousand per voyage. This compares unfavourably with the mortality of the slaves themselves in the notoriously bad conditions aboard the slavers. A similar sample of 465 slaves from Nantes in the same period shows a slave mortality per voyage of only 152 per thousand. Furthermore, the mortality rate for the slaves dropped by more than half during the period of the survey, whilst that of the crews remained relatively constant.[22]

In spite of the number of people involved in the slave trade, in economic terms the real cost of a slave delivered in the New World was extremely low. To take 1695 as a date at which the South Atlantic System was fully established in the Caribbean, a slave could be bought in Jamaica for £20 currency—roughly the same value as 600 pounds of muscavado sugar sold on the London market, or the European cost of sixteen trade guns for exchange in Africa.[23] This was a low price in the islands, because a prime slave would be expected to add more than 600 pounds to the production of an estate in the first year. It was also low compared with alternate prices of labour. In the 1680s, a criminal condemned for labour in the colonies sold for £10 to £15, and the buyer still had to pay his transportation to America and assume the risk of his escape or death from disease before he had even arrived on the plantation.[24]

These prices as of 1695 are representative of a single year and of the British segment of the South Atlantic system. Prices elsewhere could be very different, and the price of slaves fluctuated greatly from one part of Africa to another, depending on conditions of supply and demand. But the secular trend was one of rising prices. The prime cost of goods to purchase one able-bodied slave in Africa rose from about £3 to £4 at the beginning of the seventeenth century to more than £20 at the end of the eighteenth.[25] This price rise represents more than a mere decrease in the

22 These rates have been calculated from the lists of ships in the Nantes slave trade published in D. Rinchon, *Le Trafic négrier d'apres les livres de commerce du capitaine gantois Pierre-Ignace-Liévin Van Alstein, Tome Premier*, Paris, 1938, i, pp. 243–302.

23 K. G. Davies, *The Royal African Company*, London, 1957, pp. 356 and 364.

24 R. Pares, *A West-India Fortune*, London, 1950, p. 9.

25 *Report of the Lords of the Committee of Council for . . . Trade and Plantations . . . Concerning the Present State of Trade to Africa, and Particularly the Trade in Slaves* . . . London, 1789, Part II (cited hereafter as *Board of Trade Report*).

value of the pound sterling. In barter terms-of-trade, the Europeans were forced over time to put down more and more goods for each slave they exported from the African coast.

Nevertheless, in the conditions of 1695, eight trade guns or six cwt. of iron bars represented the coastal African price of a slave. From present-day perspective, it may seem curious that an African society could capture a man and deliver him on the coast so cheaply. Too little is known about the African economies of this period to explain this phenomenon fully, but part of the answer seems clear. Europe was already on its way to the enormous technological achievements of the later industrial revolution, while African technology was relatively backward. Many West African societies could produce high-quality blades, but they could not produce them (or any other kind of iron) in large quantities without a very high cost in labour to gather wood, manufacture charcoal, mine iron ore, and build the high clay furnaces that were common at the time. Yet the value of imported iron within Africa depended on these costs—not on the much lower cost in time and materials to manufacture the same iron in Europe. Measured against African metal technology, 300 pounds of iron in bars delivered to the interior and ready for the manufacture of hoe blades or spear points, may well have been a profitable exchange for a newly captured unskilled slave. Similar technological differences in firearms, textiles, and distilling would tend in the same way to create a comparative advantage for the African as well as the European partners in the slave trade.

Firearms were something of a special case. Unlike textiles, or iron, which were produced in Africa as well as in Europe, firearms were an innovation —and an innovation that could bestow power on any African society that managed to acquire them before its neighbours did the same. A change in power relations among African states could have far wider consequences than cheaper iron or a new supply of luxury goods. It is possible that firearms did not merely make possible a gun-slave cycle, where an African state used the arms to capture more slaves, to buy more arms, and so on. The availability of firearms may also have forced African states to take up slave raiding in self-protection, since guns could only be bought with slaves. But the importance of the gun-slave cycle is still a matter of controversy among historians. It may not have counted for much before the nineteenth century. The long reloading time of earlier trade muskets made them less than universally dominant, either against the cavalry of the savannah or skilled bowmen with poisoned arrows in the forest.

THE DEMOGRAPHIC ROOTS OF THE SLAVE TRADE

In any event, the very cheapness of slaves set up economic and demographic patterns that turned the slave trade into a permanent feature of the South Atlantic System, rather than a brief migration for a century or so until the American tropics had been repopulated. The crux of the matter was a negative rate of natural population growth in tropical America. This came about for a variety of reasons. Initially, epidemiological factors dictated that migration was costly in human life, but this should have been a short-run influence, since creoles of African descent would have developed immunities to the American disease environment. The more persistent cause was a very low birth rate in the American tropics, and this was tied directly to the low real cost of slaves in Africa. Planters wanted more men than women on their estates, calculating that it was cheaper to buy a young African of working age that it was to import African women who would sit idle raising families.

The slave traders responded to demand conditions, normally importing two men from Africa for each woman. Since birth rate depends on the number of women of child-bearing age, this meant an automatic reduction of 30 per cent in the potential birth rate for each group of migrants from Africa. In addition, the planters regarded female slaves as labour units, and they did little to encourage either a high birth rate or a low rate of infant mortality. When slave women found themselves in a situation without stable family life, where the demands of field work were constant, and where the rearing of children was difficult, if not actually discouraged, they simply had few children (and they knew about both abortive and contraceptive techniques). The result was a low birth rate, not merely in terms of total population, but in terms of female population. Slave populations in tropical America thus normally experienced a net natural decrease caused by very low fertility rates.[26] This rate of natural decrease sometimes ran as high as 40 per thousand per annum, and 20 per thousand appears to have been common in the Caribbean.[27]

The failure to create a society with a self-sustaining population made the slave trade necessary not merely for the gradual expansion of the plantation regime, but simply to maintain the population level of existing plantations. Thus, the cheapness of African manpower led the South Atlantic System into a pattern of consuming manpower as other industries might consume raw materials. Estimates for the French colony of Saint Domingue indicate a total of about 860,000 slaves imported between 1680 and 1791, but its Negro population in 1791 was only about 480,000. For Jamaica, the net immigration from Africa was about 750,000 during the whole period of the slave trade, yet the Negro population on emancipation in 1834 was only about 350,000.[28]

26 G. W. Roberts, *The Population of Jamaica*, Cambridge, 1957, pp. 219–34.

27 Roberts, *Population*, p. 37; Gaston-Martin *L'esclavage* p. 125; E. V. Goveia, *Slave Society in the British Leeward Isalnds at the End of the Eighteenth Century*, New Haven, Conn., 1965, p. 234.

28 P. D. Curtin, *The Atlantic Slave Trade*, Madison, 1969, pp. 71, 78, 79. But this pattern was not universal, as Kuczynski indicates (*Population Movements*, London, 1936, pp. 15–17), British North America was a striking exception. The thirteen colonies that were to become

(*continued overleaf*)

The planters recognised that their enterprise consumed manpower, and they also understood the link between this pattern and the low prices of slaves on the African coast. As slave prices rose towards the end of the eighteenth century, some planters responded by seeking a better balance of the sexes as a way of producing a self-sustaining slave gang. One study of the island of Nevis shows this new policy successfully put into practice as early as 1775.[29] The point at which this policy was to the planters' economic advantage must have differed considerably from one colony to another. It appears to have been reached about 1788 in Jamaica, for example, where an able-bodied slave straight from Africa sold for £62 to £65, and a creole slave sold for £80 to £100—roughly the cost of rearing a slave up to the age of fourteen, when he could first be used for field labour.[30] But the change to a self-sustaining population took time. Even in Jamaica, where slave imports were cut off by imperial legislation in 1807, the population did not begin to achieve a natural increase until the 1840s. On other islands, like Cuba, where the plantation system was still expanding, the demand for slaves from Africa continued at a high rate; and the proportion of men to women continued to be very high far into the nineteenth century.[31]

FLOW AND TIMING

These demographic peculiarities of tropical slave societies had important consequences for the timing and flow of the slave trade. Rather than rising to a peak and then declining, as the American territories filled their own need for population growth, the trend in numbers transported was steadily upward from the fifteenth century until about the 1780s, after which the Atlantic slave trade decreased, gradually at first, then sharply after the 1850s. But the trade did not draw continuously from the same parts of West Africa, nor did it send the slaves continuously to the same destinations in the New World. Though the stream of migrants grew in size from decade to decade, it was supplied by a series of variable tributary streams flowing from the coast of Africa, and it branched out into a number of changing outlets on the American side of the ocean.

In all, about ten million Africans were landed in the Americas by the Atlantic slave trade.[32] Since they were brought for sale to the European

(*28 continued*)
the United States imported about 350,000 to 500,000 slaves over the whole period of the slave trade, but their demographic pattern was one of net natural increase at rates nearly as high as those of the white population. As a result, there were more than 4.5 million Negro North Americans at the time of emancipation.

29 Pares, *West India Fortune*, pp. 123–5.

30 *Board of Trade Report*, Part II; Roberts, *Population*, p. 241.

31 R. Guerra y Sanchez, ed., *Historia de la nación cubana*, Habana, 1952, iv, pp. 167–81.

32 This figure represents a scaling down of the older estimates that sometimes went as high as 20 million or more, and it may still be on the high side. Recent monographic (*continued opposite*)

TABLE 7:1

ESTIMATED SLAVE IMPORTS INTO THE AMERICAS, BY IMPORTING REGION, 1451–1870 (000 OMITTED)

Region and country	1451–1600	1601–1700	1701–1810	1811–1870	Total
British North America	—	—	348.0	51.0	399.0
Spanish America	75.0	292.5	578.6	606.0	1,552.1
British Caribbean	—	263.7	1,401.3	—	1,665.0
Jamaica	—	85.1	662.4	—	747.5
Barbados	—	134.5	252.5	—	387.0
Leeward Is.	—	44.1	301.9	—	346.0
St Vincent, St Lucia, Tobago, and Dominica	—	—	70.1	—	70.1
Trinidad	—	—	22.4	—	22.4
Grenada	—	—	67.0	—	67.0
Other BWI	—	—	25.0	—	25.0
French Caribbean	—	155.8	1,348.4	96.0	1,600.2
Saint Domingue	—	74.6	789.7	—	864.3
Martinique	—	66.5	258.3	41.0	365.8
Guadeloupe	—	12.7	237.1	41.0	290.8
Louisiana	—	—	28.3	—	28.3
French Guiana	—	2.0	35.0	14.0	51.0
Dutch Caribbean	—	40.0	460.0	—	500.0
Danish Caribbean	—	4.0	24.0	—	28.0
Brazil	50.0	560.0	1,891.4	1,145.4	3,646.8
Old World	149.9	25.1	—	—	175.0
Europe	48.8	1.2	—	—	50.0
São Thomé	76.1	23.9	—	—	100.0
Atlantic Is.	25.0	—	—	—	25.0
Total	274.9	1,341.1	6,051.7	1,898.4	9,566.1
Annual average	1.8	13.4	55.0	31.6	22.8
Mean annual rate of increase*	—	1.7%	1.8%	−0.1%	

*These figures represent the mean annual rates of increase from 1451–75 to 1601–25, from 1601–25 to 1701–20, and from 1701–20 to 1811–20.
Source: P. D. Curtin, *Atlantic Slave Trade*, p. 268.

(*32 continued*)
research has tended to reduce almost all of the older guesses at the number of slaves landed. A common estimate for imports into the United States was 1 million, but recent studies have reduced this to the range of 330,000 to 350,000 (J. Potter, 'The growth of population in America, 1700–1860', in D. V. Glass and D. E. Eversley, eds, *Population History: Essays in Historical Demography*, Chicago, 1965, p. 641). Brazilian estimates for the slave trade to that country often ran to 9, 12, or even 15 million; 3½ million is now the accepted guess, and this may well be too high (F. Mauro, *L'Expansion européene (1600–1870)*, Paris, 1964, pp. 335–6; J. H. Rodrigues, *Brazil and Africa*, Berkeley, 1965, pp. 40–1).

colonists, their destinations in the Americas varied according to the patterns of European activity and economic development. In the first half of the sixteenth century, even before the South Atlantic System had begun to emerge, Africans accompanied the Spanish in the conquest of the great Indian civilisations. As a result, in the 1570s, when Europeans still outnumbered Africans in Brazil, Africans outnumbered Europeans in both Mexico and coastal Peru.[33] With the seventeenth-century expansion of tropical agriculture, the main flow of slaves went to Brazil in the first half of the century—and to the islands of the Caribbean in the second. During the eighteenth century, North America, central and southern Brazil, and the Spanish mainland colonies entered more strongly, but the mainstream of the trade continued toward Jamaica, Saint Domingue, and north-east Brazil. Finally, in the nineteenth century, with the slave trade to English- and French-speaking territories cut off, Brazil and Cuba remained as the only rapidly growing segments of the plantation economy. Hence they were the principal destination of the trade.

Origins on the African side of the Atlantic are harder to trace, partly because European records most often give only the coastal shipping point, not the country or ethnic origin of the men and women who were embarked. Where large supplies of slaves at low prices can be traced to African conditions, however, political instability was often the cause—warfare, the rise of new states, the fall of old ones. All of these produced prisoners for sale. But the correspondence between political disturbance and slaves exported from a particular part of West Africa is far from perfect. The European demand, for instance, fluctuated according to war and peace in Europe, dropping steeply when war made the sea lanes dangerous and then rising to new peaks with the return of peace. In addition, Europeans were not the only buyers. The internal slave trade absorbed many captives who were never exported, and the trans-Sahara slave trade ran during the whole period of the Atlantic trade. The influence of political instability, however, is striking in cases like that of the Yoruba, who were rarely victims of the slave trade before the 1820s. From then onwards the Yoruba Wars produced so many captives that the Yoruba became the most important single ethnic group in the populations of Cuba, Brazil, and Sierra Leone.

Geography also counted for something in the distribution of African peoples in the New World. From the Senegambia or the coast southward to Sierra Leone, ships could pick up the north-east trade winds for a direct trip to America north of the equator. Further east in the Gulf of Guinea it was necessary to drop south of the equator in order to sail for America on the south-east trades. Ships bound to the Caribbean from, say, Lagos,

33 J. Lockhart, *A Colonial Society*, Madison, Wis., 1968, pp. 171–98; G. Aguirre Beltrán, *La población negra de México, 1519–1810*, Mexico, D. F., 1946; D. M. Davidson, 'Negro slave control and resistance in colonial Mexico, 1519–1650', *Hispanic American Historical Review* xlvi, 1966, pp. 235–53.

thus had to cross the equator twice, and each time they stood the chance of being caught for long periods in the equatorial calms. Brazil could be reached on the south-east trades, making it necessary to cross the equator only once with a full cargo of slaves. The voyage from Angola to Brazil was even easier, carried on the south-east trades the whole way.

As long as maritime advantage was not cancelled by political factors, it was common for slavers from Senegambia to make for the Caribbean, while slave populations in southern South America came mainly from the hinterland of Angola and Mozambique. As early as 1615, when slaves in the Caribbean came mainly from Senegambia, those in Chile were mainly from Angola—brought overland from the Rio de la Plata.[34] Later, too, a large sample of arrivals in the Plata basin between 1742 and 1806 shows 40 per cent from East Africa, 23 per cent from Angola, and only 37 per cent from West Africa.[35] In the nineteenth-century trade to Brazil, Rio de Janeiro and the south were mainly served by Angola, while Bahia and the north were still served from West Africa.[36]

The West African slave trade at all times appears to have supplied more people to the Caribbean than to Brazil. Although almost all parts of the coast supplied some slaves at all periods, the main source shifted through time from the far west of West Africa toward the east and south. In the sixteenth century, for example, not only Mexico but also Peru had a high proportion of Africans from Senegal, the Gambia, and Guinea-Bissao. Of eighty-three African-born slaves on a Mexican plantation in the late sixteenth century, for example, 88 per cent were from this West Atlantic region.[37] Another sample of 207 slaves listed in the notarial registers of Lima and Arequipa in Peru between 1532 and 1560 showed 74 per cent from the Senegambia, with Wolof predominating, 16 per cent from the Guinea coast between Sierra Leone and the Bight of Biafra, and only 10 per cent from the Bantu-speaking areas of Central and East Africa.[38] In the eighteenth century, by contrast, the Senegambia contributed relatively little to the slave trade, only about 6 per cent to the combined Anglo-French exports (see Table 1). Furthermore, the small Senegambian contribution of the eighteenth century was no longer derived from the coastal region; it was mostly Bambara and others brought overland from the upper Niger.

The shift to the east and south was highly irregular. The British slave trade drew on Angola for about a tenth of its supply at the end of the seventeenth century, then dropped to much less in the early 1770s, only to shift very decisively to this source at the end of the eighteenth century. The French slave trade, which reached its peak in the period between 1783

34 R. Mellafe, *La Introducción de la esclavitud negra en Chile*, Santiago de Chile, 1959, p. 200.
35 E. F. S. de Studer, *La Trata de negros en el Rio de la Plata durante el siglo xviii*, Buenos Aires, 1958, p. 325.
36 P. Verger, *Bahia and the West Coast Trade, 1549–1851*, Ibadan, 1964, pp. 32–3.
37 Aguirre Beltrán, *Población de México*, pp. 244–5.
38 Lockhart, *op. cit.*, pp. 357–8.

and 1789, also shifted to Angola at this time, with less than half of its supply drawn from West Africa (see Table 1).

Along the eighteenth-century Guinea coast, a regional shift to the east is also perceptible. The English slave trade in the first half of the century drew mainly from the Gold Coast and subsidiary regions to the west. In the second half of the century it depended much more heavily on the areas between the Volta and the Cameroons. The Portuguese slave trade to Brazil moved in a similar pattern. After drawing mainly from Angola during the seventeenth century, the Portuguese returned to West Africa in the eighteenth. Up to about 1770 they worked the Bight of Benin between the Volta and Ouidah. Then, in the last quarter of the century, the traders from southern and central Brazil joined the general rush to the markets of Angola, while the Bahians shifted eastward along the Guinea coast to Porto Novo, Badagry and (later on) Lagos.[39]

As slaves from these shifting sources of supply arrived in the Americas, the timing of the strongest flow of immigration tended to influence the ethnic make-up of the population. Jamaica, for example, received its largest imports of the eighteenth century in the decade of the 1790s, with net imports at more than 10,000 a year.[40] The distribution of slaves sold there included the same high proportion from the Bight of Biafra and from Central Africa as the English slave trade as a whole. But this correspondence between the ethnic make-up of slaves shipped from Africa and those arriving in a particular American port was not always the case.

Buyers often had marked preferences for particular ethnic groups, and these preferences were taken into account by the slave traders, along with other market conditions. These market factors produced striking differences in the content of slave cargoes arriving in the territory of the present-day United States. The Middle Atlantic colonies like New York and New Jersey bought relatively small numbers of slaves, destined mainly for non-agricultural work. The buyers therefore preferred slaves born in the Americas, English-speaking, and already accustomed to the western way of life. As a result, of a total of 4,551 slaves imported into these two colonies between 1714 and 1765, only 20 per cent were from Africa. The remainder were creole Negroes from the West Indies. In Virginia, on the other hand, 86 per cent of a sample of 52,500 slaves imported by sea between 1710 and 1769 were born in Africa. South Carolina represented still another step in this direction; since the indigo and rice plantations were closer to the West-Indian plantation pattern, a higher proportion of the slaves there came directly from Africa.[41]

Similar preferences played a rôle in the West Indies as well as in North

39 Verger, *Bahia and the West Coast Trade*, p. 3.
40 Robert B. Le Page, *Jamaican Creole*, London, 1960, p. 83.
41 This and the following paragraphs are largely based on the detailed calculations found in Curtin, *The Atlantic Slave Trade, passim.*

America. French slavers, for example, delivered an approximate ethnic cross-section of their whole trade to Saint Domingue in 1748–92, but their sales in Martinique during the same period included a disproportionate number from the Senegambia and the Guinea coast (see Table 3). In the same way, the North American markets in Virginia and South Carolina took many more Senegambians than Jamaica did, while Jamaican buyers of the 1780s showed a marked preference for people from the Gold Coast.

AFRO-AMERICANS IN NEW WORLD SOCIETIES

The patterns of Negro folk culture that survived in the New World depended on many other factors than the simple arithmetic of slave imports by ethnic origin. One of these was priority of arrival. In Jamaica, Akan culture tended to dominate in creole speech, even though the immigrants from the Bights of Benin and Biafra over the whole period of the trade may have been twice as numerous as those from the Gold Coast. In Saint Domingue, where the number of slaves imported from the Guinea Coast and Angola was roughly equal between 1748 and 1792, Dahomean culture nevertheless became dominant, since the Dahomeans formed a high proportion of the slaves in the early settlement of the colony. They dominated the patterns of creole culture which others, later to arrive, assimilated. In the United States, on the other hand, the survival of African culture is much weaker than it is in the West Indies, mainly because the large population of Negro Americans owes its size to natural increase—not to a continuous stream of new recruits from Africa.

In some parts of the Americas African culture survived the slave trade still more fully than was possible on the plantations. The history of the African states of the New World during the era of the slave trade is one of the least-known aspects of Afro-American history, mainly because settlements formed by escaped slaves took pains not to call attention to their affairs. Nevertheless, one byproduct of slavery was the desire to rebel or escape, and both were occasionally successful. As a result, one or more regions of *de facto* African domination existed somewhere in the Americas from at least 1570 onward. When Haiti emerged as an independent republic in 1804, and obtained the recognition of the European powers after the Napoleonic Wars, it became the first ex-colony to achieve this status in western eyes. But, from another point of view, it merely continued a political situation that had existed for centuries elsewhere in the New World.

Some of the settlements of escaped slaves were relatively isolated from Western culture, such as those inland from the Guiana plantations on the South American coast.[42] Other escaped Africans set up small states, which remained in military contact with the European colonists. At least ten of these refuges or *quilombos* (as they were known in Portuguese) were

42 See M. J. Herskovits and F. S. Herskovits, *Rebel Destiny. Among the Bush Negroes of Dutch Guiana*, New York, 1934.

established in Brazil during the seventeenth and eighteenth centuries. Many were short lived, but Palmares, the most famous of all, lasted through most of the seventeenth century until its capture and destruction in 1694.[43] Others lasted even longer in 'Spanish' America. On the faraway Pacific coast, a cargo of African slaves was wrecked in 1570 in the present-day Republic of Ecuador. The ex-slaves conquered the local Indians, married some of the Indian women, and set up an independent Afro-Indian community, which maintained its freedom from the European-dominated highlands until the twentieth century.[44]

Some independent African settlements recognised the formal hegemony of a European colony in return for the right to run their own affairs. One of the most successful of these was in seventeenth-century New Spain. It began with small bands of runaway slaves, who terrorised the hinterland of Vera Cruz from the 1560s onward. As these bands became more stable, one of them, in 1609, successfully challenged the forces sent to hunt it out. The result was a formal peace treaty, still preserved in the Mexican archives. The rebels won the right to their freedom from slavery and to an independent municipal government. In return, they promised the Spanish help in time of war and in capturing other escaped slaves. The new town, San Lorenzo de los Negros, lasted and was apparently properous at the end of the seventeenth century. In the longer run, however, the Negroes of San Lorenzo merged with the rest of the Mexican population.[45]

Similar colonies of maroons, as they were called in the Caribbean, existed from time to time on all of the islands. On Jamaica several groups are resonably well known, and some maintained treaty relations with the Jamaican government from 1739 until 1795–6, when they lost a war against the Europeans and were expelled, first to Nova Scotia, and finally to Sierra Leone in 1800.[46] Still another area of maroon activity was the height of land separating the French and Spanish parts of Hispaniola. Several groups there survived until the 1790s, where they merged with the general slave rebellion against the French. Other settlements elsewhere also lasted until the general emancipation of the slaves, when they settled down as another group of free peasants, indistinguishable from the rest of the population.

In the century since the end of the slave trade, the descendants of the slaves have everywhere met a similar problem of finding an adequate place for themselves in a society where they are recognisably descended from the former servile caste. By 1940, a little more than 10 per cent of

43 R. K. Kent 'Palmares: An African state in Brazil', *J.A.H.*, vi, 1965, pp. 161–75.

44 J. L. Phelan, 'The Road to Esmeraldas', in *Essays in History and Literature: Presented by the Fellows of the Newberry Library to Stanley Pargellis*, Chicago, 1965, pp. 91–108. See also R. C. West, *The Pacific Lowlands of Colombia*, Baton Rouge, 1957.

45 Davidson, 'Negro slave control', pp. 246–50.

46 R. C. Dallas, *The History of the Maroons from their Origin to the Establishment of their Chief Tribe in Sierra Leone*, London, 1803.

the population of both Americas was partly of African descent, though their distribution over the two continents was (and remains) extremely uneven.[47] They are a majority, and a very large majority, in many Caribbean countries, such as Haiti, Jamaica, and Barbados. In the larger American countries, Negroes and mulattoes together make up about 37 per cent of the population of Brazil, while the largest Negro population in a single country is found in the United States, though it is only about 10 per cent of the total.

With such demographic diversity it is hardly surprising that the social position of Afro-Americans is also extremely diverse. Nevertheless, the heritage of slavery was not easily removed, either from the former masters or the former slaves. Where Euro-Americans built barriers of caste and privilege to defend their own interests, the Afro-Americans suffered from lack of education, medical care, and home training that might have brought a more rapid advance to higher wealth or status. No American state—not even Cuba, Brazil, or Jamaica—has succeeded in creating a completely integrated society free of racial prejudice, though the remnants of the old caste lines are sometimes weaker there than they are, say, in the southern United States. Class distinctions, even in these countries, tend to parallel racial appearance, the upper classes being more often white or light coloured, while the lower class are more often black or dark mulattoes.

But colour was not the only variable, and integration could take many forms. In countries like Mexico and Peru, for example, which were outside the old South Atlantic System and where the majority of the people were dark coloured Indians in any case, racial integration has gone much farther than it has in the Caribbean. In both countries intermarriage has been so extensive that the recognisable Negro racial type is in decline. In Mexico, where the Negro population was perhaps 10 per cent of the whole in 1650, recognisable Negroes today form less than 1 per cent of the Mexican nation. In Peru, the census enumeration of Negroes and mulattoes declined from 18 per cent in 1895 to 1.6 per cent in 1940.[48] The African strain has simply melted into a generally mixed European-African-Indian population.

But integration can take many forms, and race prejudice in the Americas has often been mixed with cultural and class prejudice in surprising ways. Haiti, for example, may have the strongest class lines still remaining in the hemisphere, even though all Haitians are at least partly of African descent. The line, in this case, is drawn between those who are lighter in colour and more European in culture, as opposed to those who are both darker and more African in their way of life. In Jamaica, survivals of a three-caste society are still evident, with distinctions drawn between white, coloured,

47 See table of American populations in Rosenblat, *Población indígena*, facing p. 20.
48 F. Romero, 'The slave trade and the Negro in South America', *Hisp. Amer. Hist. Rev.*, xxiv, 1944, p. 386.

and black in which the line between black and coloured was harder to cross than that between coloured and white. In the United States the old caste line was drawn in a way that considered everyone of any recognisable African descent as Negro, even if his appearance might indicate that seven-eighths of his ancestors were probably European. This two-caste system persisted in law in the southern United States until the 1960s; the social prejudice continues as a severe problem in American society, even though some Negroes can be found at every level of wealth and status.

The influence of the slave trade on West Africa was more limited in time. The ending of the South Atlantic System brought a painful commercial readjustment in the nineteenth century, but that was all. The crucial question is whether the slave trade warped the course of African development and prevented economic and political progress that might otherwise have taken place. Historians will continue to debate this issue, even though a secure answer may never be possible. Among the other imponderables is the possibility that, if there had been no slave trade, there would have been very little trade of any kind. On this assumption, it has been argued that the slave trade, evil as it was in many respects, was better for West Africa than no trade at all—that it gave Africa a more developed commercial system, a more intense contact with the outer world, and hence a better preparation for meeting the European impact and the challenge of modernisation.

But the contrary assumption can also be made, that the slave trade presented Africans with an opportunity for short-term profit at the cost of long-term economic stagnation—that it was all too easy to sell captives to the Europeans, and this easy entry into world trade foreclosed the healthier alternative of producing goods that foreigners would come to buy. If this challenge had existed, it might have been met by productive innovation. As it was, innovation took place, but its direction was that of forcing one society after another to become more efficient hunters of slaves rather than more efficient producers of goods.

In spite of might-have-beens and remaining problems, some of the older beliefs about the slave trade can be dismissed. Among these is the myth that some racial characteristics of Negroes made them desirable as slaves and led to their predominance as the working force of the South Atlantic System. Nor was the slave trade forced on Africa by the Europeans. Europeans bought, but Africans sold; and the numbers of Africans engaged in the slave trade at any moment was certainly larger than the number of Europeans. It is equally clear that some African societies profited from the slave trade, at least in the short run, while other societies were destroyed or hopelessly crippled by continuous slave raids. An assessment of the trade, based on what did happen rather than what might have happened, can only come after weighing the evidence of detailed regional studies which historians of Africa are only now beginning to provide.

TABLE 7:2

PROJECTED EXPORTS OF THAT PORTION OF THE FRENCH AND ENGLISH SLAVE TRADE HAVING IDENTIFIABLE REGION OF COASTAL ORIGIN IN AFRICA, 1711–1810

Region	1711–20	1721–30	1731–40	1741–50	1751–60	1761–70
Senegambia		22,500	26,200	25,000	22,500	21,400
%	16.5	10.0	8.2	7.4	7.6	5.5
Sierra Leone	5,900	15,000	14,900	18,400	9,900	5,300
%	3.2	6.7	4.7	5.4	3.4	1.4
Windward Coast	30,600	47,600	55,200	65,300	29,800	67,600
%	16.4	21.2	17.3	19.3	10.1	17.4
Gold Coast	44,000	54,200	65,200	67,000	41,800	52,400
%	23.5	24.2	20.5	19.8	14.2	13.5
Bight of Benin	72,500	48,400	59,400	30,900	35,600	48,400
%	38.8	21.6	18.6	9.1	12.1	12.5
Bight of Biafra	—	4,500	45,100	71,300	100,700	139,300
%	—	2.0	14.2	21.1	34.1	35.9
Central and southeast Africa	3,200	32,000	52,500	60,200	54,600	53,200
%	1.7	14.3	16.5	17.8	18.5	13.7
Total	187,000	224,200	318,500	388,100	295,000	387,700
%	100.0	100.0	100.0	100.0	100.0	100.0

Region	1771–80	1781–90	1791–1800	1801–10	Total
Senegambia	17,700	20,300	4,400	800	191,700
%	6.0	3.4	1.1	0.3	5.8
Sierra Leone	3,700	17,700	12,200	9,600	112,600
%	1.3	3.0	3.2	3.6	3.4
Windward Coast	49,700	24,400	14,700	11,200	396,100
%	16.9	4.1	3.8	4.2	12.1
Gold Coast	38,700	59,900	29,400	22,100	474,700
%	13.2	10.1	7.7	8.3	14.4
Bight of Benin	41,400	120,400	15,100	5,300	477,400
%	14.1	20.3	3.9	2.0	14.5
Bight of Biafra	100,000	114,800	137,600	110,400	823,700
%	34.0	19.4	35.9	41.5	25.1
Central and southeast Africa	42,900	234,400	170,400	106,700	810,100
%	14.6	39.6	44.4	40.1	24.7
Total	294,000	591,800	383,800	266,000	3,286,100
%	100.0	100.0	100.0	100.0	100.0

*Figures and totals have been rounded. Source: P. D. Curtin, *Atlantic Slave Trade*, p. 221.

This table is made up from the unsatisfactory statistics made available from a variety of different sources, but it nevertheless gives some indication of the coastal shipping points that were most prominent in particular years. For purposes of the table, the Senegambia is taken to be the coast and hinterland of the Senegal and Gambia Rivers. Sierra Leone includes the whole coast of present-day Guinea-Bissao, Guinea-Conakry, and Sierra Leone. The Windward Coast was a shifting designation, but it is used here for the coast windward of the Gold Coast, roughly the present-day territory of Ivory Coast and Liberia. The Bight of Benin is the 'slave coast', from the Volta eastward to Benin. The Bight of Biafra is the Niger Delta and the Cameroons. Central Africa is the entire north–sorth coast from Gabon through Angola.

TABLE 7:3
ORIGINS OF SLAVES SOLD BY SLAVERS FROM NANTES IN VARIOUS AMERICAN TERRITORIES, 1748–92
(IN PERCENTAGES OF SLAVES SOLD)*

Coastal region of origin	(1) Saint-Domingue	(2) Martinique	(3) Cuba and Puerto Rico	(4) Total Nantes slave purchases
Senegambia	3.7	8.4	—	5.0
Guinea	48.9	65.5	50.5	48.3
Angola	45.8	26.2	49.5	43.8
Mozambique	0.8	—	—	1.3
Not known	0.8	—	—	1.7
Total	100.0	100.0	100.0	100.0
Size of sample in numbers of slaves sold	181,025	11,321	3,263	314,289

*Calculated from the list of ships sailing to Africa from Nantes published by D. Rinchon. *Le Trafic négrier d'après les livres de commerce du capitaine gantois Pierre-Ignace-Liévin Van Alstein*, Paris, 1938, i, pp. 243–302. The samples are based on the number of slaves purchased, when reported—otherwise on the average number of slaves actually landed by ships in each range of tonnage, and these estimates adjusted for average reported loss in transit. The total sample consists of 861 ships, which purchased 314,289 slaves.

CHAPTER 8

The Niger Delta states and their neighbours, 1600–1800

E. J. ALAGOA

The term Niger Delta states is applied here only to the eastern delta kingdoms of Bonny, Elem Kalabari, Okrika and Nembe.[1] This classification is apt not only as a geographical description, but also because of the ethnic identity and the similarity of political, economic and social institutions of these states. They are bordered on the east and north by such related peoples of the delta periphery as the Andoni (Obolo), Ogoni, Ndoki, Abua, Odual, Ogbia, Engenni (Egene); and the Ibo. The Ibibio and the Efik state of Calabar (Old Calabar) on the Cross River estuary are farther to the east. To the west of the delta states are the bulk of ethnically identical Ijo subgroups of the Niger Delta. The history of these central and western delta Ijo groups is important for understanding the early development of the states. Other groups in the western delta, the Urhobo, and especially the Itsekiri kingdom of Warri also exercised influence, although ethnically different from the Ijo kingdoms of the eastern delta.

The geographical basis of the classification is that all the states named lie within the delta of the River Niger. A recent survey[2] has determined that only a limited number of the rivers flowing into the Atlantic on the Nigerian coast discharge waters of the Niger and Benue, that is, form part of the Niger Delta. These include the rivers between the Forcados on the west and Brass on the east. Soil analysis, however, indicates that the delta extended beyond the rivers Benin and Bonny in former times. It thus included the kingdoms of Bonny, Okrika, Kalabari, and Nembe, but not the Efik state of Calabar.

There are varieties of three major land and soil forms in the Niger Delta. First, the sandy beach ridges two to five feet above mean high water level. These are islands immediately bordering on the Atlantic with a width

1 The names applied to Bonny in European records were derived from Ibani, Okoloama and Okoloba. Elem Kalabari (New Calabar in the records) is known locally also as Owome and Kengema Kalabari. Nembe is the Brass of European records.

2 NEDECO (Netherlands Engineering Consultants), *The Waters of the Niger Delta, Report of an Investigation*, The Hague, March 1961, p. 11.

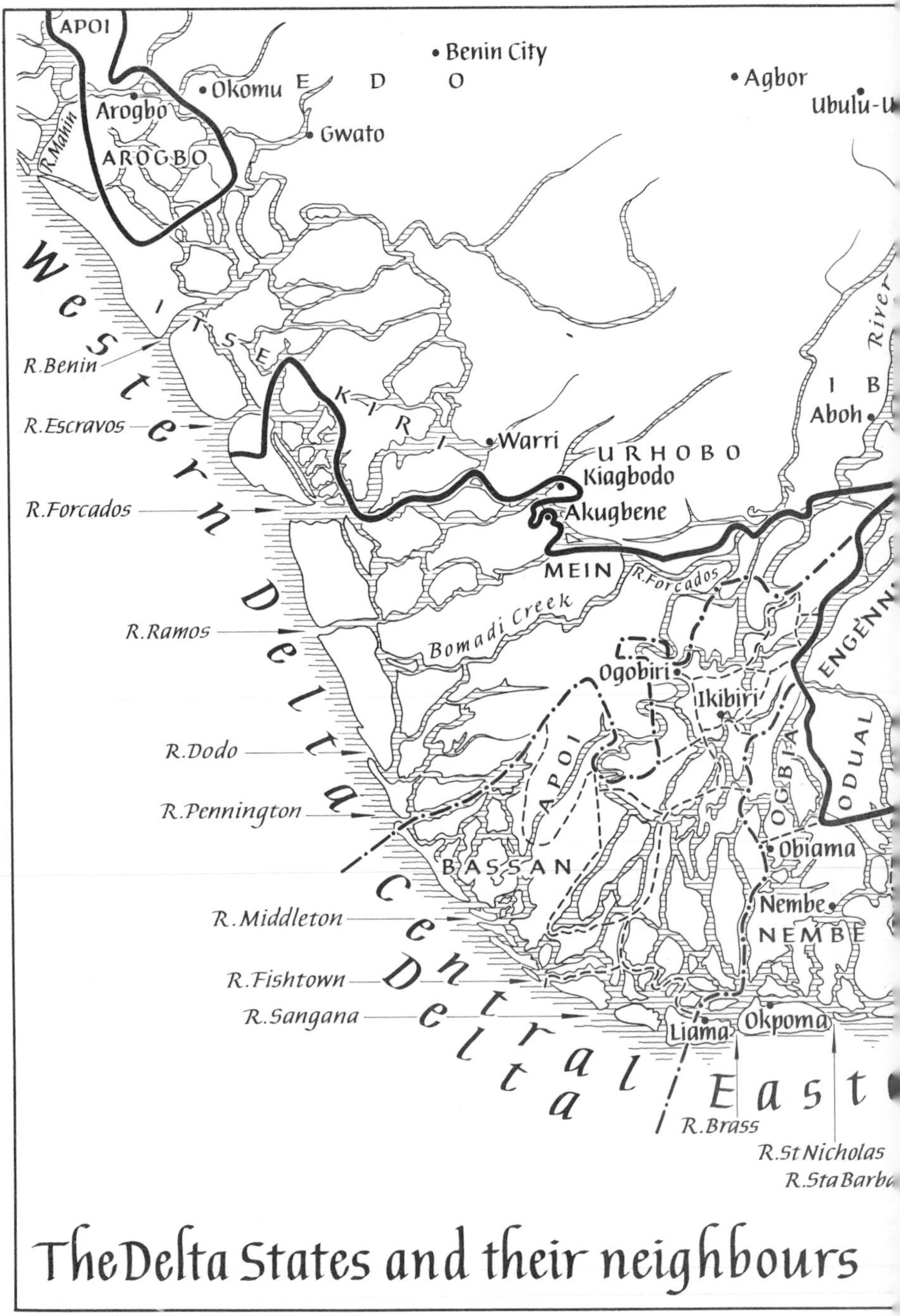

The Delta States and their neighbours

8:1

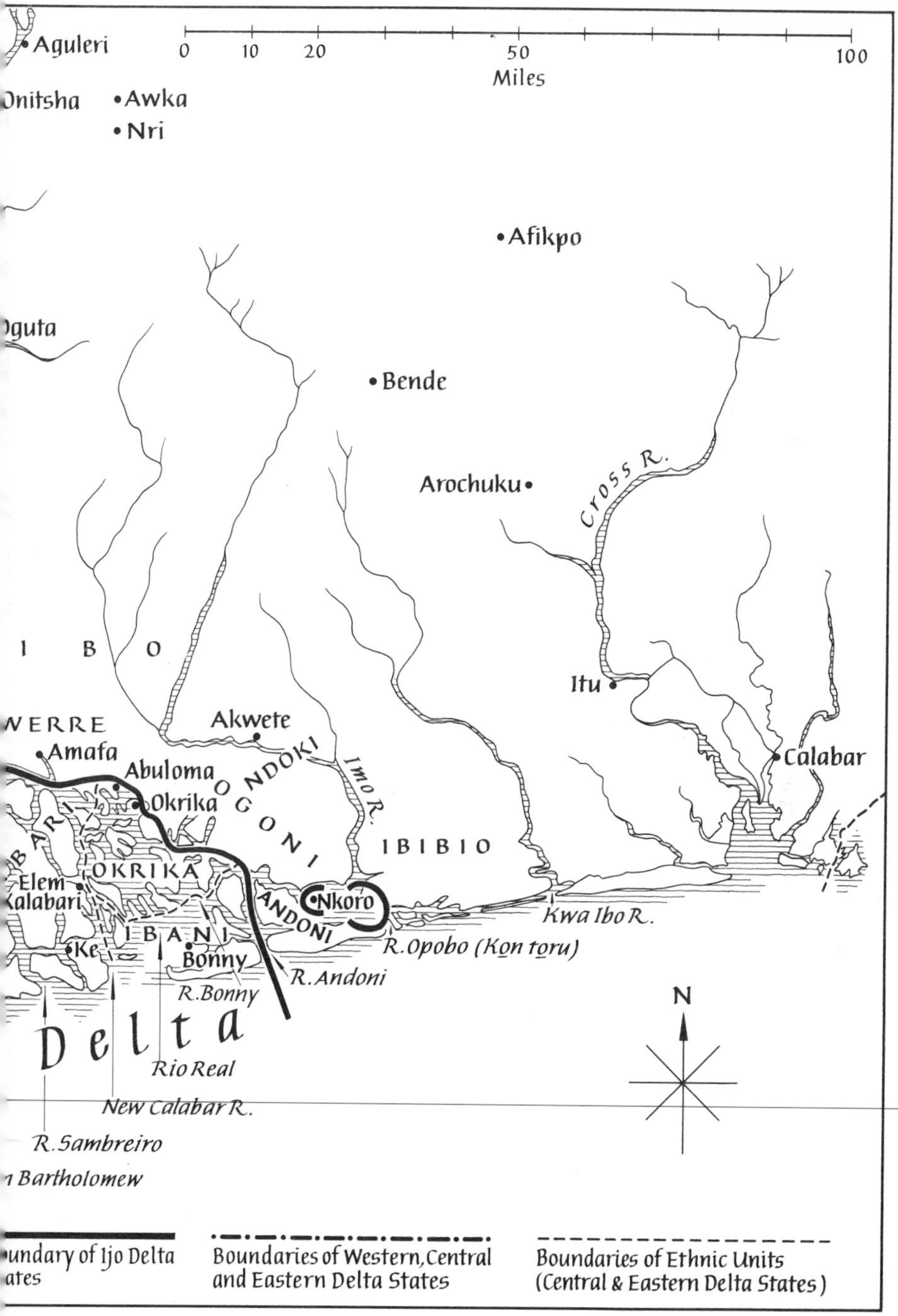

Aguleri
0
10
20
50
Miles
100
Onitsha
Awka
Nri
Afikpo
Oguta
Bende
Arochuku
Cross R.
I B O
Itu
WERRE
Akwete
Amafa
Abuloma
NDOKI
OGONI
Imo R.
Calabar
Okrika
KALABARI
IBIBIO
OKRIKA
Elem Kalabari
Nkoro
ANDONI
Kwa Ibo R.
IBANI
Ke
Bonny
R. Opobo (Kon toru)
R. Andoni
R. Bonny
N
Delta
Rio Real
New Calabar R.
R. Sambreiro
Bartholomew
Boundary of Ijo Delta States
Boundaries of Western, Central and Eastern Delta States
Boundaries of Ethnic Units (Central & Eastern Delta States)

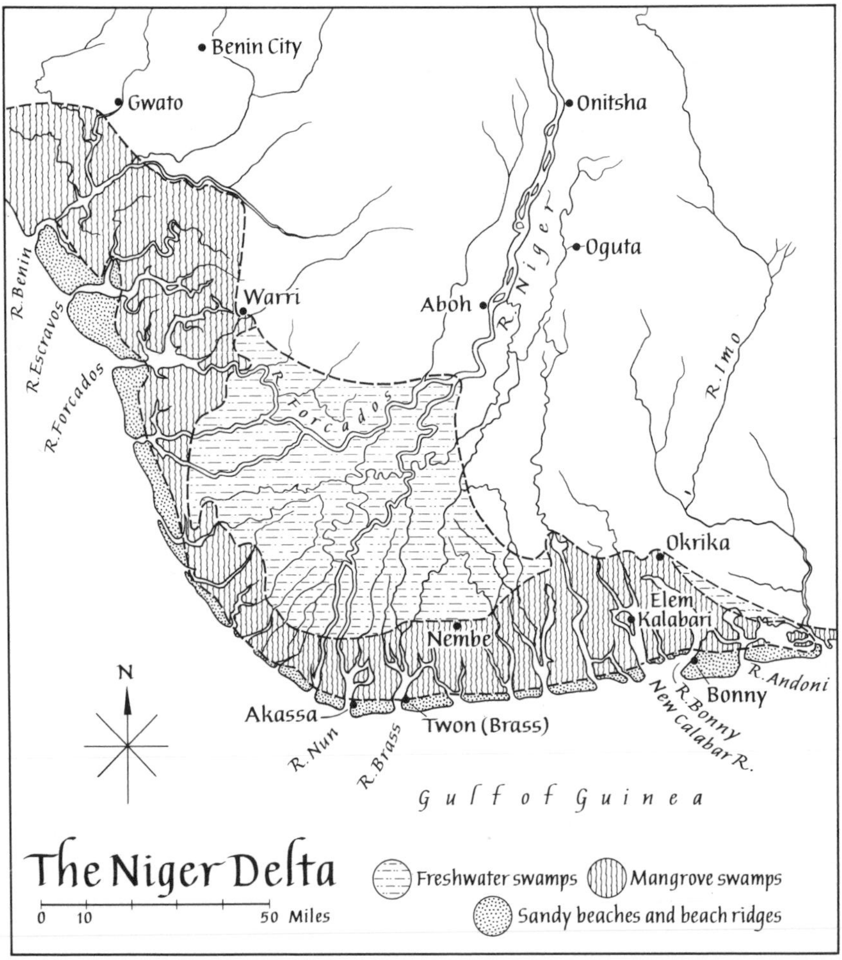

8:2

ranging from less than a hundred feet to ten miles. Second, the salt water swamp, covering a vaster area from twenty to twenty-five miles from the sandy ridge. Most of this territory is about two feet below normal high water level and is flooded daily at high tide. It also provides the popular image of the characteristic mangrove swamp environment of the Niger Delta. Third, the fresh water swamp at the northern extremity of the delta which is only flooded seasonally.

The sandy ridges are the youngest portion of the delta, being recent deposits raised above water level by the subsidence of the adjacent sea bed. But even this portion of the coast may have been formed between two and four thousand years ago,[3] and some of the oldest delta settlements are

3 J. R. L. Allen and J. W. Wells, 'Holocene coral banks and subsidence in the Niger Delta', *Journal of Geology*, lxx, 4, 1902, p. 391.

sited on these coastal ridges. The city of Bonny is sited on the inner edge of one of these sandy ridge islands as are some of the most ancient towns in the Kalabari region (such as Ke) and in Nembe (Okpoma, Odioma and Twon).

All of Okrika territory lies in the region of the tidal salt water mangrove swamp, as does most of Nembe and Kalabari.

The greater portion of the delta is freshwater swamp. Most of the central and western Ijo live in this region. The Ibo live in the hinterland beyond the delta. Since the soil of the freshwater delta is similar to that of the hinterland and is only flooded seasonally, the inhabitants of this part of the delta practise small-scale agriculture together with fishing. The seasonal floods deposit silt on the farms which are used year after year. These neighbouring delta planters were, accordingly, the earliest suppliers of food to the states and other inhabitants of the mangrove swamps and coastal ridges, rather than the larger farmers of the hinterland.

From a linguistic view, too, the Ijo of the delta states differs from neighbouring languages.[4] Ijo belongs to the wide Niger Congo family of African languages along with all the neighbouring languages; and more particularly to the Kwa sub-family along with Yoruba (Yoruba, Itsekiri), Ibo, and Edo (Bini, Urhobo-Isoko, Egene, Epie-Atissa, Udekama), within which it forms a distinct group—the Ijo group. Most of the eastern neighbours of the delta states speak languages of the Benue-Congo sub-family of Niger-Congo. Abua, Odual, Mini (Abureni), Ogbia and Abuloma belong to the Abua Group; Andoni, Efik, Ibibio to the Efik-Ibibio cluster; and Kana, Gokana, Eleme to the Ogoni Group of the sub-family.

The clear ethnic and environmental distinctions between the delta states and their neighbours did not prevent them from forming many links with each other.

EARLY HISTORY

Several traditions of Benin origin occur in the delta states as they do among other Ijo groups. These traditions and a number of bronze objects discovered at widely spaced spots in the lower delta suggest some early contact with Benin.[5]

The Mein traditions concerning their bronzes indicate the nature of Benin relationship with the delta. There had developed among the leaders of three Mein groups (Akugbene, Ngbelebiri, and Ogbolubiri) a dispute over who was to be chosen Mein Okosowei, that is, paramount elder of

4 The classification follows Dr Kay Williamson, 'Languages of the Niger Delta', *Nigeria Magazine*, xcvii, 1968, pp. 124–30; Hans Wolff, 'Niger Delta Languages I: Classification', *Anthropological Linguistics*, i. 8, 1959, pp. 32–53; J. H. Greenberg, *The Languages of Africa*, Bloomington, 1963.

5 R. Horton, 'A note on recent finds of brasswork in the Niger Delta', *Odu: University of Ife Journal of African Studies*, iii, 1, 1965, pp. 76–91.

all the Mein. Kalanama, head of Akugbene, decided to make a trip to Benin. He obtained various objects as emblems of office, and took the title of *pẹrẹ*. The leaders of the other groups similarly obtained Benin bronzes and took the title of *pẹrẹ*. These traditions indicate that Benin was considered distant even from the western delta, and the journey to the capital long and hazardous. Moreover, even these westerly parts of the delta were not an integral part of the Benin polity. The Oba was a distant, impartial potentate able to settle disputes. He had to be paid a number of slaves as a fee for his services and the bronze insignia of office.

The Mein evidence, therefore, suggests that even the western delta was merely on the edge of the Benin kingdom and not part of it. This is confirmed by evidence from among the Urhobo and Isoko who are located much closer to Benin.[6] The Ughelle also decided a succession crisis by the test of a trip to Benin, the successful candidate returning with a brass sword of office. The *ovie* or priest kings of the Agbor, Ozoro and Iyede were also installed only after presents had been sent to the Oba of Benin. That these acts did not mean direct subjection of the Isoko to Benin is shown by the fact that other groups such as the Abraka sent their kings to the Ibo ruler of Aboh to seek the external recognition thought necessary to their internal prestige. In fact, this type of informal relationship was practised in other parts of Nigeria. Even in quite recent times, the Tiv are reported to have sent their chiefs (*Tor*) to serve a period of apprenticeship to learn the ceremonial and obtain insignia at the Jukun courts at Wukari and Katsina Ala. For this the Tiv paid fees to their Jukun hosts, and did not consider themselves subject.[7]

There is thus little evidence that the main body of I̱jọ east of the Forcados River ever came under the direct sway of the Oba of Benin. But scattered groups of I̱jọ west of the Forcados, especially on and west of the Benin River, may have come into direct contact with Benin. One Benin historian states that the Oba Olua (*c.* 1473) gave 'orders' to 'Ijaw men' to carry his son Iginua (Ginuwa) and his retinue to found the Itsekiri kingdom of Warri.[8] The most westerly I̱jọ group, the Apoi of Okitipupa Division also claim that at one of their earlier settlements at Okomu or Akpaka, they served as paddlers for the messengers of the Oba of Benin. The non-Edo delta town of Arbo at which the Dutch established a trading post about 1644, and noted by them to have been under the suzerainty of Benin, may also be identified as Arogbo, home of the Arogbo I̱jọ group in Western Nigeria.[9]

6 O. Ikime, 'Itsekiri-Urhobo Relations and the Establishment of British rule, 1884–1936', unpublished Ph.D. thesis, University of Ibadan, 1965, p. 19.
7 Akiga, *Akiga's Story: The Tiv tribe as seen by one of its members*, trans. and annotated by Rupert East, reprinted London, 1965, pp. 364–7.
8 Jacob Egharevba, *A Short History of Benin*, 3rd edn, Ibadan, 1960, pp. 22–3.
9 A. F. C. Ryder, 'Dutch trade on the Nigerian coast during the seventeenth century', *Journal of the Historical Society of Nigeria*, iii, 2, 1965, p. 199.

There are, however, traditions of settlement by small groups of Itsekiri (Iselema in the Ịjọ accounts) at Ukubie in the Bassan area of the central delta, Liama, Nembe, and at Orusangama in the Kalaḅari area. The Itsekiri are associated with religious innovations at several of these places. At Liama in the Nembe kingdom, certain words are supposed to be spoken in a language believed to be Itsekiri during certain rituals. Similarly at Soku in Kalaḅari the words of particular religious songs are believed to represent those used by Itsekiri captives. These small migrant groups of Itsekiri have probably left their most enduring mark in the Nembe metropolis. They brought with them their national war god, as well as a magic sword, *ada*. They did not found the Nembe state, but are said to have taken over control of it within a generation or two. Their war god Ogidiga became the state god of Nembe.

All the four delta states have traditions deriving their founding ancestors from the central delta.[10] Nembe and Okrika have traditions of migration through the delta. The leaders of Elem Kalaḅari and Bonny are said to have taken routes through the Ibo hinterland before turning back into the delta, finally settling much closer to the sea than either Nembe or Okrika. The traditions concerning the metropolis of Nembe mention six or seven early settlements in a radius of about ten miles around the present town. Three of these settlements are best remembered: Olodiama, Oboloma and Onyoma. Nembe town itself grew out of the earlier settlements, all of which disappeared. The Iselema or Itsekiri migrants are stated to have arrived during the reign of Kala Ekule, the first or second on kinglists of the present metropolis. The founders of Okrika came from the dispersion of Ikibiri in the central delta. Okrika traditions mention Obiama and other stopping places in Nembe and Kalaḅari.

Elem Kalaḅari, like Nembe, may have comprised a number of early settlements with varying traditions of origin. The Endeme group claims to have left an unidentified original home in the central delta, probably in the region of Ogobiri. The ancestors travelled through the hinterland and settled at Amafa on the eastern delta fringe. They finally moved back into the delta in search of better fishing grounds.

The Ibani (Bonny) say their ancestors came from the central delta through the Ibo hinterland. After a period of sojourn in Ndoki territory, they came down the Imo River and through Andoni country to their coastal location. After the Bonny state was established, its traders used this same route to obtain the produce of the hinterland for the Atlantic trade.

CHRONOLOGY
When did these kingdoms come into being? We can only attempt to

10 E. J. Alagoa, 'Oral tradition among the Ijo of the Niger Delta', *Journal of African History*, viii, 3, 1966, pp. 405–19; 'Ijo origins and migrations', *Niger. Mag.*, xci, 1966, and xcii, 1967, pp. 47–55.

translate the relative chronology of the kinglists and royal genealogies into what must be but tentative dates. The available genealogies would thus indicate that Nembe was founded before about 1200 and that its first kings reigned around 1400.[11]

Thus the institution of monarchy is quite ancient in these states. The House (wari̱) lineage institution was, however, more recent. In Nembe the earliest known House is that of King Pe̱re̱suo, to be dated about 1660. Most surviving Nembe Houses are to be dated in the eighteenth and early nineteenth centuries. Accordingly, the period 1600 to 1800 was a significant one during which the delta states developed their socio-political institutions. This conclusion is largely confirmed by documentary evidence.

The Portuguese captain, Pereira, summarising his countrymen's knowledge of the West African coast at the beginning of the sixteenth century, saw all the coast from the Forcados River to the Bonny River (Rio Real) occupied by I̱jo̱—'Jos'.[12] This stretch of coast does, in fact, correspond to that currently inhabited by the I̱jo̱.

Pereira's record suggests that those I̱jo̱ groups now living west of the Forcados and east of the Bonny had not yet arrived at their present territory by 1500. Arogbo was first mentioned around 1644; and an estimate based on its kinglist dates the foundation of Nkoro (lying east of Bonny) at around 1700. It is, accordingly, fair to suppose that by 1500 the I̱jo̱ had already expanded to cover all of the delta between the Forcados and Bonny Rivers, but probably not beyond.

The evidence of this expansion is itself some indication that the date of between 1200 and 1400 for the migrations to found such eastern states as Nembe, Elem Kalaḇari̱, Okrika and Bonny is not too early. Pereira also recorded a 'large village of some 2,000 inhabitants' engaging in trade. This has been credibly identified as Bonny and some of its customers as Kalaḇari̱ from their hinterland settlement at Amafa, Okrika, or Andoni.[13] The settlement described by Pereira was definitely not a new one, and could have been over a hundred years old.

The direct accounts of Bonny and Elem Kalaḇari̱ in the seventeenth century leave no doubt about the advanced nature of their institutional development. Dapper in the first half of the century described Bonny, Elem Kalaḇari̱ and Okrika as established kingdoms. Barbot even gave names of kings and trading chiefs (who must have been House Heads) at Bonny and Elem Kalaḇari̱ in 1699.[14]

The consideration of West African states south of the savannah region

11 We use an average distance of 21.2 years between reigns, see E. J. Alagoa, 'Dating oral tradition', *African Notes*, iv, 1, October 1966, p. 8.

12 G. H. T. Kimble, *Esmeraldo de Situ Orbis by Duarte Pacheco Pereira*, London, 1937, pp. 128–32. Kimble dates the book *c.* 1505–8.

13 G. I. Jones, *The Trading States of the Oil Rivers: A study of political development in Eastern Nigeria*, London, 1963, p. 34.

14 John Barbot, *A Description of North and South Guinea*, Paris, 1732, p. 459.

has hitherto centred on the larger forest kingdoms. It may be useful to pay some attention to smaller scale states, such as the delta states wrestling with the problems of their peculiar environment.

POLITICAL HISTORY

Some speculation has surrounded the origin and development of the delta states. Dike, impressed by their territorial organisation on the basis of a central city with authority radiating to hinterland trading stations, called them 'city-states'.[15] Dike rightly noted the shift from an organisation based on kinship and descent to a more open society, but underestimated the Ịjọ cultural base of the state structure. That is, that although 'citizenship came increasingly to depend not on descent but on residence', the most important factor determining full citizenship was culture—the acquisition of the variety of Ịjọ culture developed in these states. Accordingly, although large numbers of slaves from the Ibo hinterland were admitted into these states in this period, they were deliberately acculturated.

Jones called attention to another important aspect of the delta kingdoms when he called them 'trading states'.[16] It does seem, indeed, that many of the peculiar features of these states were developed in response to the Atlantic trade in slaves, but it is possible to emphasise the Atlantic trade to the neglect of internal trade and other local factors.

Ịjọ political structure

The basic Ịjọ ethnic unit is the *ibe* (clan). There are not only basic differences between the structure of the *ibe* in the western, central, and eastern delta, but also a number of significant general characteristics. In the central and western delta, the members of the *ibe* recognise themselves as belonging together by reason of common descent from a single founding ancestor. The sense of kinship is reinforced by common language which is the outward symbol and seal of common culture. The common founding ancestor is usually presumed to have borne the name by which the group is known, and to have founded one town from which his 'sons' spread out to found each of the member towns and villages.

The only instrument of central control embracing all member settlements of central and western delta *ibe* was the cult of a national god. The high priest, *pẹrẹ*, was, accordingly, the only person wielding authority over the whole *ibe*. He determined the date of the yearly festival of the god, and presided at its performance. This religious office of *pẹrẹ* has been changed into a political leadership of the *ibe* in recent years.

There was, then, no traditional central authority over western and central delta *ibe*, with the exception of a few like the Mein who recognised

15 K. O. Dike, *Trade and Politics in the Niger Delta*, London, 1956, pp. 30–1.
16 G. I. Jones, *op. cit.*

the eldest son of their founding ancestor as Mein Okosowei (Mein elder); and the Apoi and Arogbo whose political titles of *kalashuwe* and *agadagba* may have been comparatively ancient. However, the general I̱jo̱ pattern was one where the member villages or towns of an *ibe* were held together by no central political institutions but only recognised a presumed blood relationship and religious and cultural affiliation. Above all they used a common dialect. However, the absence of central control gave individual villages complete political autonomy.

Village autonomy meant the elaboration of village political organisation. Here the main political authority was the *amagula*, village assembly. The oldest member of the village, the *ama-okosowei* (town elder), presided, but the executive leadership resided in a younger man, the *ogulasowei* or spokesman. There were specialised offices among some *ibe* such as a messenger, town crier, deputy president, hangman, and others. In every village, the priest of the *ama-oru* (town deity), known as *orukarowei,* carried out community religious duties, corresponding to those of the *pe̱re̱*, for the entire *ibe*.

Units of social and political division also existed within the village; the biggest subdivision of the village being the *polo* (ward), itself subdivided into *wa̱ri* (subward, household or 'family'). A further division across kinship lines into as many as six age sets has been reported for western Tarakiri villages.

Political structure of delta states

The areas over which the eastern delta states exercised influence coincided with the territory occupied by speakers of a common I̱jo̱ dialect and recognised by their neighbours as *ibe*. There was also the feeling of belonging together based on their common tongue and cultural institutions. The tradition of common descent and a common founding ancestor was, however, absent or very tenuous among these eastern *ibe*. As the state institutions developed and their territorial influence increased, even this cultural and linguistic unity tended to disappear, for these states came to include peoples speaking dissimilar languages and practising differing cultures. Thus Nembe was associated with Mini and Ogbia groups as well as with groups speaking the Akassa dialect rather than Nembe. The Kalabari have within their territory the Udekama, and Okrika the Abuloma, both of whom speak a different language. These groups remain small minorities within the eastern delta states, but their presence adds an element that differentiates these states from the I̱jo̱ *ibe* of the central and western delta.

The cult of a national god features in the development of the delta states. Their traditions usually tie up the growth of the political authority with developments in the worship of the national god or changes in the status of the high priest. But since in the eastern states the member communities do not necessarily accept traditions of common descent, their unity is often founded on the spiritual kinship of the village gods (*ama-oru*) to the national god (whose shrine would be sited at the metropolitan city).

The basic village organisation of the eastern delta before the development of the state institutions was also similar to the central and western delta system. There were the same descent groups or *wari* making up a *polo*, and the political authority of the village assembly. One obvious difference between the eastern delta village system of government and that of the west was the rejection of age as a qualification for office. The assembly president was not the oldest man (*amaokosowei*), but the *amanyanabo*, who was appointed because of his descent from a particular *wari* or *polo* ancestor claiming discovery of the village site. The only concession made to age was the separation of elders from the youths in the sitting arrangements at the assembly meetings and the greater respect paid to the aged.

The village political structure of the eastern delta, then, already showed departures from the basic forms of the west. Age was less important a qualification for office. The president of the assembly came from a particular lineage qualified by a priority of settlement. His title of *amanyanabo*, owner of the town, was also already a rudimentary form of monarchy. The eastern delta fishing village, accordingly, possessed forms of the traditional Ijo polity that could be fashioned into the city or trading state form of system characteristic of the four delta states.

How did one city gain in status and power above its neighbours in such a way as to be recognised as a city-state and to be accepted as leader of each of these eastern delta *ibe*? This development may be viewed in the perspective first of the increase in the power of the *amanyanabo* (the monarchical idea); second in the change in the idea of the *wari* as a lineage into the 'open' institution of the War Canoe House. All these changes were related to the trans-Atlantic trade in slaves.

The monarchy. The cities that gained leadership in their *ibe* either were already centres of population or became such by reason of their engaging in trade in addition to traditional fishing. The position of the *amanyanabo* changed along with the size and economic orientation of the population. It is evident that the earlier *amanyanabo* were much more like the ritual heads exemplified by the *pere* of the western delta. They presided at assembly meetings, decided on matters of ritual concerning village or national gods, and directed external wars. But occasions for external action were probably infrequent.

The beginning of the Atlantic trade increased the power of the *amanyanabo*. He was the representative of the people in their relations with the European traders who paid him comey and other duties for protection. His authority was also enhanced in relation to the other leaders of the community—the trading heads of the new type of House (*wari*)—since they could be introduced to the European traders and obtain credit (trusts) through him.

The history of all four delta states shows struggles over succession, and changes of dynasty resulting from the enhanced prestige and wealth of the monarchy. Earlier changes of dynasty were usually attributed to the arrival of new migrants.

The House system. The most revolutionary change occasioned by the Atlantic trade was probably the adaptation of the old Ịjọ *warị* or House to serve new ends. Enterprising trading leaders began to build up their personal households by various means. An aspirant, where he had sufficient funds, paid large dowries to the heads of the Houses of the women he married so that the children of such unions would belong to his House rather than theirs. He became protector or patron of persons in trouble, and most important, purchased slaves. By these means such a man increased his labour force and, accordingly, his wealth. When he considered himself wealthy and powerful enough, he equipped a war canoe and showed himself to the *amanyanabọ* and community as a political leader. He became a House head.

The position of House head meant that such a man had a following within the city large enough to provide a fighting contingent or war canoe (about thirty men) in defence of the state. He also had money to provide guns and ammunition. In political terms he became a member of the King's Council—the successor of the village assembly—which decided on internal and external relations.

The members of the House referred to each other by the kinship terminology of the original *warị* lineage, in spite of the different ways by which its members were recruited. All members belonged directly to the head's trading organisation or depended on him for recommendation to European merchants. Because of competition for political power within the city-states, succession was determined not by heredity, but by capacity in trade and for leadership, and on the vote of all adult members of the House.

The 'open' criterion for upward social mobility ingrained in the House organisation was a significant step in the development of the delta states. But the importation of large numbers of slaves to build the new Houses also posed problems of integrating these men and women into the society.

The House system itself was designed to turn a foreign slave into a member of his community and kin to all other members of the House. A slave had his hair ceremonially shaved and was given a new name to symbolise his rebirth. He was then handed to a senior woman in the House who became his 'mother'. Thenceforward, other members were expected to treat him as one of themselves. Other social and economic forces also induced slaves to acculturate quickly and completely.

First there were the rewards of enterprise and complete acculturation. A slave who learnt the culture of his new home and either conducted the trade of his House head or acquired wealth of his own, could be elected House head. Second there were the societies whose activities encouraged acculturation. The first of these was the prestigious masquerade playing society called *ekine* or *sekiapu*.[17] The members of *sekiapu* considered themselves particularly well-endowed citizens by reason of their ability to dance, their knowledge of the drum language embodying the historical lore of the state and their ancestors. Since the drum names called during *sekiapu* dances involved the rendering of archaic speech forms into drum rhythm, knowledge of it meant a thorough understanding of the local language.

Ekine or *sekiapu*, then, was one institution that enshrined the open society traditions of the delta states where careers were determined by talent. Rise within the society was based solely on artistic ability—to sing, dance, drum, or understand the drum language. Success within *sekiapu*, moreover, was publicly displayed and became the seal of full citizenship, acceptance within the community, and passport to political office. In other ways too, membership of *sekiapu* introduced a man to a measure of political action since the society came to assist the rulers of the states in the administration of justice. *Sekiapu* enforced a code of conduct on all its members, and also collected debts and punished pilferers and offenders against public morality.

The associations of successful warriors, *peri ogbo*, present in all the delta states, also offered opportunities for the exhibition of ability as well as punishment for slaves who would not assimilate thoroughly and quickly. Members of *peri* were men who had slain an enemy in war, taken a captive, or even killed an elephant, leopard or performed other feats of valour. They were distinguished by their use of eagle feathers, drinking with the left hand, and by their performance of a special war dance (*peri*) at the close of a war, the death of a king or of a member. Here again the emphasis was on individual achievement—the exhibition of enterprise and spectacular physical courage in the defence of the state or the execution of a dangerous mission. The enterprising slave could, therefore, become as renowned a *peri* member as a free citizen.

There were, however, aspects of *peri* which served the function of punishing poorly acculturated persons. There was among the Kalabari, an inner group of *peri* called *koronogbo* (the club of the strong) which terrorised such people. Members of *koronogbo* went into the streets on certain nights and challenged anybody they met. If the individual replied in a foreign accent, he was immediately seized and dispatched. There were similar vigilance committees in the other delta states designed mainly for the protection of the cities against enemy infiltrators, but which came also to serve as a further inducement for slaves to acculturate.

The new Houses served their purpose of turning foreigners into full and loyal citizens. They also served as defence units in the external wars of the states. However, the competitive nature of the society created by the House

17 R. Horton, 'Igbo: an ordeal for aristocrats', *Niger. Mag.*, xci, 1966, discusses the acculturative functions of *Ekine* among the Kalabari. See also his paper 'From fishing village to city state', presented at a seminar, University of Ibadan, 1967, now published in M. Douglas and P. M. Kaberry, eds, *Man in Africa*, London, 1969, pp. 37–58.

system and the Atlantic trade did not make for internal harmony within the states. It was difficult to contain the conflicts between Houses. The *amanyanabo* had to cope with these inter-House conflicts as well as to protect his position against the ambition of House heads who might expand their groups and wealth faster than he could.

These developments did not occur in a uniform manner in all the states. In the important consideration of turning foreign slaves into citizens of the state for example, some states achieved more success than others. Whereas in most of the states the slaves had no chance of affecting the culture of the state, in Bonny, Ibo, the language of the majority of the slaves, largely superseded Ibani.

Nembe

Some traditions say Nembe was settled from the central delta dispersion centre of Obiama as part of the same migration which started the other major towns of the Nembe *ibe* on the Atlantic coast, namely, Odioma, Okpoma, and Twon. Nembe was accorded primacy because the ancestor who settled there from Obiama was 'senior' in age to the ancestors who founded the other towns of the *ibe*. But the more probable argument for their acceptance of Nembe leadership at this time was the fact of prior settlement—that is, that the Obiama migrants to Nembe went to a settlement with an earlier population. Nembe accordingly had a larger population than the other towns, and naturally assumed leadership in their relations with neighbouring peoples.

The heads of the early settlements (Oboloma, Olodiama, and Onyoma) bore the western Ijo title of *pere* and probably performed similar ritual functions. The first changes in the system were precipitated by a combination of internal wars (between Olodiama and Oboloma) and external attack (by the Kalabari towns of Kula and Bile on Onyoma). The various settlements came together to form a union. Finally a number of royal refugees from the Itsekiri kingdom of Warri (Iselema) arrived about 1460. These incidents may have begun the process of change from a religious leader to one with political authority; although a religious base for the leadership of Nembe over the other towns of the *ibe* may have been laid about this time. Thus Ogidiga, brought by the Itsekiri, became the national god of the entire area, the gods of the other towns being conceived of as 'sons', 'daughters' or 'wives' of Ogidiga.

The changes in the nature of leadership set in motion by external pressure and by the arrival of the Itsekiri immigrants may have gone on for a century or more. A new element is said, by some traditions, to have been added with the arrival at Nembe of the tenth king, Ogio, from the ancient Mini town of Ebala. Ogio's reign is dated about 1639. He superseded the dynasty controlled by the Itsekiri, and all existing royal genealogies begin from Ogio.

The beginnings of the House system may have appeared in Nembe during the reign of Ogio's son, Peresuo, since the House of that name is the oldest remembered today. Peresuo's date of *c.* 1660 thus indicates a mid-seventeenth century origin for the city-state House institution in Nembe.

The building up of a personal following by individual aspirants to political and economic power may also explain the division of the Nembe metropolis into two parts in the first half of the eighteenth century. Mingi (*c.* 1745) fought a protracted feud with his cousin Ogbodo before seizing the throne. Ogbodo moved across the river to found his own parallel monarchy at Bassambiri, leaving Mingi in control at Ogbolomabiri.

The manner of Mingi's rise to power does not indicate that the Atlantic trade was yet an overriding factor in Nembe history even in the early eighteenth century. He prevailed on the people to accept him by forming an alliance with the Olodiama Ịjọ village of Ondewari to block food supplies to Nembe. This internal trade line was obviously the most important economic consideration at this time. Later, Mingi acquired his wealth by smithing and farming, and also by trading in slaves.[18] In the particular instance of Nembe, therefore, the new political leaders owed their rise as much to the traditional internal trade as to the Atlantic trade.

The ascendancy of Nembe over the outlying towns was also firmly established during the reigns of Mingi and of the three sons that succeeded him, namely, Ikata (*c.* 1766), Gboro (*c.* 1788), and Kulo (*c.* 1800–30). Mingi gained the support of Okpoma during his dispute with Ogbodo, and he drove the people of Odioma to seek the protection of Ogbodo. Twon also sought the protection of Kulo against slave raids. These later political affiliations merely formalised the existing feelings of kinship, ties in the religious sphere and the need for solidarity against neighbouring rival groups. Thus during his war against the Kalaḇarị community of Ḇile, King Ikata was assisted by Gọlị, the ruler of Okpoma.

Elem Kalaḇarị

The traditions which relate a migration from the central delta Ịjọ also present a simple explanation for the basis of the culture of Elem Kalaḇarị.[19] The suggested migration route across Ibo territory, and the short sojourn on the mainland close to Amafa at the head of the New Calabar River also indicate early contact with the main source for the goods Elem Kalaḇarị came to use for the Atlantic trade.

The other Kalaḇarị settlements, such as Tombia, Ḇile, Ifoko, Kula, and Ke, in the salt water swamp and beach ridges between Elem Kalaḇarị and Nembe claim to be as old as or older than Elem Kalaḇarị.

18 E. J. Alagoa, *The Small Brave City-State*, Madison and Ibadan, 1964, pp. 52–3.
19 H. Wenike Brown-West (Tienabeso), *A Short Genealogical History of Amachree I of Kalabari*, Yaba, 1956.

How did Elem Kalabari develop in the way it did in advance of the other Kalabari settlements to a position of leadership? It has to do with the power conferred by a large population and wealth. It is not clear why the earlier settlers from different places converged in the location of Elem Kalabari; but it became the greatest centre of population in this part of the delta. The traditions concerning the earlier kings of Elem Kalabari also show that there was probably more competition for political leadership among the different groups than in the other settlements. The names of the early kings suggest power shifts from one group to the other.[20] The hinterland connections or contacts of some of the Elem Kalabari sections together with the competitive nature of its society clearly cut that city out to take a greater advantage of the Atlantic trade than the other Kalabari settlements. Once this trade was in full swing, Elem Kalabari rapidly increased its advantage over the surrounding Kalabari towns in population, wealth, and power.

Many of the factors in the development of Elem Kalabari are evident in the story of the rise of Amakiri in the eighteenth century. When a fire destroyed Elem Kalabari, even the competing groups had to come together under a leader able to carry the burden of restoration. A wealthy man was indicated. Seleye Fubara of the Krome declined the offer of leadership and Amakiri of Endeme accepted. Amakiri was then engaged in the internal trade—mostly in mudskippers but, later, also in slaves—to restore the losses in population from the fire as well as from a war with Okrika.

The traditions also stress the importance of religious sanctions in the formation of the state and in its expansion. The unification of the Elem Kalabari sections was forced on the people by Owomekaso (Akaso) the goddess of Krome. Akaso thenceforth became the goddess of the Kalabari and the spiritual mother of the nation. Amakiri naturally used the spiritual kinship of Akaso to the gods of the surrounding towns to bind their people to him.

The majority of Kalabari towns acceded to the predominance of Elem Kalabari because of external pressure. Tombia and Ifoko sought aid and protection against Bonny. Pressure from Bonny and Okrika may, indeed, explain the phenomenon of east-west rebound in migrations among Kalabari groups in this area. Many of these settlements claim original migrations from the central delta eastwards to the Andoni country, followed by a return westwards into Kalabari territory. Amakiri's Elem Kalabari provided a protective umbrella.

Although Amakiri's peaceful methods in extending his and Elem Kalabari influence are contrasted in the traditions with the rapine and destruction of another Kalabari leader, Agbaniye Ejike of Bile, Amakiri also made wars of conquest. Kula and Soku are said to have been taken by force, and reconciled by superior diplomacy.

20 G. I. Jones, *op. cit.*, p. 26, gives the list collected by P. A. Talbot.

Representation of Amakiri of Elem Kalabari (mid eighteenth century) in ancestral shrine at Buguma. (In wood; 3 ft 6 in × 3 ft 6 in.)

Elem Kalaḇari̱ tradition, then, sees its history as passing through a period of inter-sectional or group conflict to one of unification and expansion in the reign of Amakiri in the eighteenth century. But the Atlantic trade had been in full swing before his time and the House system was operating before the end of the seventeenth century. Thus in 1699 Barbot recorded John Grazilhier as meeting a 'King Robert' together with four principal leaders.[21] These leaders were obviously trading House heads and the trade was already conducted on the basis of well established rules. The European visitors of 1699 clearly recognised Elem Kalaḇari̱ as predominant in the Kalaḇari̱ region and treated its rulers with respect comparable to that which they accorded those of the Bonny state.

Bonny

Bonny traditions of origin suggest a movement into the Ibo hinterland up the Engenni-Orashi river system and south-eastwards down the river system of the Imo.[22]

The beginning of the Atlantic trade is assigned by tradition to the reign of Asimini, one of the early kings. King Asimini's reign was a turning point in Bonny political history, since his recognition by the European traders seemed to confer authority on him greater than that exercised by earlier kings. This superior authority was sanctified by Asimini's reported act of sacrificing his daughter to the river gods in order to make the estuary navigable by ships.

The institution of the national god, Ikuba, symbolised by the monitor lizard or iguana, *varanus niloticus*, has been ascribed to contact with Andoni.[23] Introduction from Andoni seems confirmed by the fact that the characteristics of this war god, namely, a 'house of skulls' for war trophies, and the sacred monitor lizard, are reported for Andoni (Dony) in Barbot but not for Bonny. Against this may be set the tradition that Ikuba had come with the founders of Orupiri who left Opu Ikuba (Ikuba-senior) there and took with them only Kala-Ikuba (Ikuba-junior) to Bonny. If Barbot did not see evidence of the Ikuba cult at Bonny in 1699, it may only mean that its worship had not then gained strength there. The building of a 'house of skulls', for example, is said to have begun only in the reign of Queen Kanbasa (third ruler after Asimini) after a war against the Ogoni. It may be noted too that the use of special constructions for war trophies was common to all the delta states (called *ebeka* at Elem Kalaḇari̱ and *egbesu* at Nembe).

Wherever Ikuba may have come from, the indication is that after Asimini had established the monarchy on a firmer basis with the help of the new Atlantic contacts, new dimensions were added to an old cult. The war god flourished with the increase of the military and commercial power of

21 Barbot, *op. cit.*, pp. 461–2.
22 See traditions given by A. Fo̱mḇo̱ in E. J. Alagoa, 'The Settlement of the Niger Delta: Ijo oral traditions', unpublished Ph.D. thesis, Madison, 1965, pp. 72–88.
23 G. I. Jones, *op. cit.*, p. 71.

Bonny, and the skulls increased with the wars against the Ogoni and Andoni to open new markets, and against the Kalabari for predominance on the Rio Real.

The House system, too, started in Bonny before the end of the seventeenth century. The majority of the Bonny Houses trace their origin to King Perekule or Pepple, who must be identified with Barbot's 'Captain Pepprell', brother of the 'King William' of 1699.[24] Barbot's 1699 account mentions trading chiefs who were obviously heads of Houses, and although it has not been possible to identify 'King William', one Bonny House (Halliday) is named after King Awusa who preceded Perekule as ruler.

The period of Perekule's reign in the eighteenth century is referred to in Bonny traditions as a golden age. Opubo, who succeeded Perekule's son Fubara in 1792, features in the European accounts as an absolute monarch. The marked effectiveness of his reign made the nineteenth-century kings that succeeded Opubo appear only pale shadows, especially as the succeeding period was also one in which the House heads became close rivals of the king in wealth and power.[25]

Okrika

Recorded Okrika traditions derive the founding ancestors of all its sections (Opu-Ogulaya of Ogoloma, Oputibeya of Okrika, Oko who founded Okochiri on the mainland from where Fenibeso and others came to join Oputibeya) from the central delta in the region between Ikibiri and Amassoma.[26] As in the other states, the other towns of Okrika *ibe* do not have traditions of migration from Okrika.

Oputibeya, as first arrival on the Okrika side of the island, was the political leader as Opu-ogulaya was on the Ogoloma end. Leadership was handed down within the lineages of these founders but in less than ten generations at Okrika (*c.* mid-eighteenth century)[27] and a little later at Ogoloma, a change of dynasty occurred. The accounts suggest that the changes were due, in part, to shifts in the power structure of the state due to the overseas trade.

In Okrika leadership passed to Ado when he was the only person able to produce certain objects: *ovo* described variously as 'a currency' and as 'a big

24 G. I. Jones, *op. cit.*, p. 107, objects on the grounds that Fubara and Opubo (1792) who succeeded Perekule were both his sons. But W. B. Baikie, *Narrative of an Exploring Voyage 1854*, London, 1856, pp. 444–5 makes Opubo a grandson of Perekule. The succession could well have passed from Perekule to his son and grandson in the period 1699–1792.

25 It was in such an atmosphere that Jaja founded his own state at Opobo (named after Opubo) in 1869.

26 Alagoa, 'Niger Delta', pp. 96–109. K. Williamson, 'Okrika History: Notes taken in 1957', unpublished manuscript. My interpretation of Okrika traditions here is more impressionistic than authoritative, and may not be cited for litigation.

27 Using the Nembe mean of 21.2 years from Ibanichuka (1896), Ado would be dated 1769. Another founding ancestor, Krike, is sometimes opposed to Oputibeya as first arrival on Okrika island.

manilla'; and *ikaki-ikpo* (*ikaki-bite*), a type of cloth used as a unit of value. In some accounts these materials were required to be shown in a contest of affluence with Bonny. In other accounts they were needed for ritual purposes consequent on the death of the previous king, Igo, in a war against Elem Kalabari. Ado is also represented as having won the royal regalia from a lover after Igo died. In short, after the reign of Igo, Ado was the only man able to fulfil conditions demanded by the people and the times. And these conditions concerned rare objects used in the trade of the delta. They were present in Bonny, and Ado could produce them because his ancestors had brought them from Ke (Kalabari). The conclusion that the change of dynasty did follow a shift in economic power is supported also by the fact that the Ado kin group belongs today to the Tuboniju (the trading community), and the Oputibeya to the Koniju (the fisher folk) in Okrika.

The Ogoloma account of their change of dynasty makes it even plainer that a trader took over from a fishing lineage. Yechuku of the Opu-Ogulaya lineage took in a refugee from Bonny, Ikwo. Since King Yechuku and his closest advisers were all fishermen and out of town for long periods, the trader, Ikwo, became judge and prime minister. At Yechuku's death Ikwo took over as the first of a new dynasty.

In Okrika, the offices of king and high priest were separated at an early stage. Fenibeso who arrived on the island in the life time of the founder, Oputibeya, or soon after him, took over the priestly functions. At his death, Fenibeso himself was deified, and became the war god of the Okrika, serving thenceforth as one of the main symbols of unity in internal religious observances and in external wars.

The House system may have come into operation prior to the time of Igo and Ado (who were probably contemporaries of Amakiri of Elem Kalabari). In spite of the fact that Okrika took part in the overseas trade indirectly through Bonny, its control of hinterland markets probably ensured growth at a rate comparable to Bonny and Elem Kalabari which had direct contact with the Europeans.

Whether institutions like the House, *peri ogbo* and *sekiapu* came early or late to Okrika, she also had other institutions for regulating conduct. *Sekeni*, a masquerade society and warriors' club, also served as a court of appeal and carried out death sentences on murderers and other undesirables. Another masquerade society, *kiriowu*, checked misdemeanour among women; while the society of old women, *egbele irieme*, powerfully protected women's rights.[28]

The history of Okrika has been affected by its being cut off from the sea by Bonny and Elem Kalabari. She has had, therefore, to fight these states while maintaining friendship with Nembe. Elem Kalabari had even more enemies, since she had common borders with all three of the other states and shared

28 P. A. Talbot, *Tribes of the Niger Delta*, London, 1932, pp. 158, 304.

the same estuary with Bonny for the European trade. Nembe had only Elem Kalabari among the states as a traditional foe, being friends with both Bonny and Okrika with whom she had no common frontiers or markets.

Inter-state relations: wars

Wars feature prominently in oral tradition, and although they could give the erroneous impression of an Hobbesian state of nature, the accounts of these wars also reveal the existence of peaceful relations.

Three main activities of some delta communities provoked war: piracy, head-hunting, and slave raids. Piracy was practised by the Ijo *ibe* of the central and western delta. The victims of these activities were mainly the Itsekiri kingdom of Warri and Nembe, which had to take police action. But there were also particular communities in the eastern delta which combined head-hunting with piracy. Such communities as Idema, Soku, Abalama and Ogoloma were celebrated for their exploits and even took drum praise names proclaiming their addiction to these practices. These activities conferred honour on individuals within their communities because they were considered to signify manly prowess, to serve as a deterrent against an enemy attack, and sometimes because they were undertaken on the orders of tutelary deities. The organised kingdoms were officially opposed to piracy and head-hunting, but some of their members also engaged in them, and especially in slave raids on weaker neighbouring peoples.

These conditions of turbulence encouraged weaker communities to seek the protection of the city-states, and individuals or families to affiliate with House heads within them. Some communities, especially in the western delta, moved their settlements off the main river courses or into the centre of islands. Similar precautions were taken by minority elements in the eastern delta. Thus the coastal villages in Nembe (Egwema, Beletiema and Liama) built their settlements in the centre of their islands to avoid Nembe slave raiders. Elem Bakana in the Kalabari area similarly settled far enough away from the river bank to screen the smoke of their fires.

The city-states were best equipped to keep the peace, but even the smaller groups sometimes combined to destroy particularly troublesome communities in their midst. The states encouraged such societies as *peri* and *koronogbo* for combat. The House was not only a labour force, but also a fighting unit. It may be noted too that Nembe, Bonny and Okrika each had a war god as tutelary deity. Even Elem Kalabari, with a pacifist national god, had the subsidiary war cult of *okpolodo*.

The states and even the smaller communities, then, aimed above all to prevent attacks on them by preparing for war. But they also had conventions for the arbitration of disputes by a neutral neighbouring community; and the Ke (Kalabari) served as peacemakers, invoking religious sanctions to bind warring parties to observe conditions of peace mutually accepted. These conventions predisposed the states to accept the British consul in the nineteenth century as arbitrator and treaty maker.

Particular wars between the states are revealing with regard to inter-state relations. A few examples alone are selected as illustration of the extent, causes, and repercussions of these wars.

Nembe-Kalabari wars The earliest wars between towns in Nembe and Kalabari were those of Onyoma and Kula.[29] Kula was aided by Bile on the Kalabari side, but Onyoma fought alone and was defeated. The inhabitants moved to join the settlers at Nembe. The state of Nembe was clearly not yet strong enough to extend protection to Onyoma. It merely served to receive the refugees from the sack of Onyoma. Similarly Kula and Bile acted on their own without the assistance of Elem Kalabari.

The much later war between Nembe and Bile in the eighteenth century also reveals the trends of relationships and peaceful contact across the delta.[30] King Ikata of Nembe (dated *c.* 1766) had sent a trading mission to King Amakiri of Elem Kalabari and to Bonny, since European ships were not doing business on the Brass River. King Amakiri sent presents to Ikata. But the messengers were ambushed by Bile pirates, the two survivors of the attack being rescued by men from Ke. In the ensuing war, Elem Kalabari did not come to the aid of Bile; but Nembe towns, such as Okpoma, assisted her.

Nembe traditions of the Bile war also corroborate Kalabari traditions which refer to the independent and piratical activities of Bile during the reign of Amakiri. Agbaniye Ejike of Bile was a menace even to other Kalabari communities.

Nembe and Elem Kalabari did not, apparently, come into direct confrontation before the nineteenth century. Elem Kalabari was engaged in a struggle with Bonny and Okrika in the eighteenth century and courted the friendship of Nembe. And Nembe needed to trade with Elem Kalabari.

Okrika-Kalabari wars Elem Kalabari and Okrika traditions refer to many early wars but give prominence to wars in which Amakiri's city was decimated by a sneak attack and Okrika's King Igo died. These traditions probably refer to the same war in the mid-eighteenth century.

The unpreparedness of Elem Kalabari is explained by its leaders being absent on *orufe*: an expedition to the hinterland markets to buy things for sacrifice to the gods (*oru*). Only Chief Iju, who had returned with his men because of an ill-omen, offered stiff resistance to the attackers and provided a place of refuge in his quarter. The Okrika forces also succeeded in ambushing the chiefs and menfolk on their way back from *orufe*.

The results of this attack were that Elem Kalabari needed more urgently to use the slave trade to replenish her manpower and population in the

29 Alagoa, *The Small Brave City-State*, pp. 35–6. This war may be dated in the fifteenth century.
30 *Ibid.*, pp. 53–5.

eighteenth century than any other delta state. This urgency may also explain the drastic methods, such as the use of Ko̱ro̱nogbo, to achieve quick assimilation of slaves.

In Okrika the death of Igo led eventually to a change of dynasty. The rapid expansion in the power of Amakiri at Elem Kalab̲ari̲ could have convinced Okrika that they too needed a leader interested in the overseas trade to match the development of their rival.

ECONOMIC HISTORY

The delta states passed through some three stages of development in their effort to derive a living from their environment. There was an early stage of subsistence fishing, hunting, and gathering of the natural products of the delta. This was supplemented by exchange with the other delta communities pursuing various levels of agriculture in the freshwater area. This limited stage of exchange of produce was followed by what may be termed long distance trade with the peoples of the delta hinterland, and also with the western delta. The beginning of dealings with Europeans in the Atlantic slave trade transformed the delta states into centres of redistribution: collecting European merchandise for sale in the hinterland, and receiving hinterland produce for export.

However, the internal changes of institutions consequent on this last stage of economic development took time to unfold. Similarly the business of opening new markets and expanding the influence of the states by a show of the newly acquired economic power was carried out over a period covering a century or more. Accordingly, the period of the seventeenth and eighteenth centuries was the critical period of changes whose seeds had been sown many years before.

Early economic activities

The early delta populations relied on fishing for their livelihood, using rather inefficient methods. They used harpoons, basket traps, and poisons (such as the mashed endocarp of the fruit of *Raphia vinifera* or *oxytenanthera abyssinica*). Accordingly, there was probably little surplus from this occupation for exchange. The wide distribution of traditions using the stereotype of a quarrel over the division of the soup of a *wan* (Togo hare, duiker?) caught in communal hunting, also suggests hunting as a subsidiary source of protein.

Vegetable sources of nourishment were not plentiful in the beach ridge and saltwater swamp delta. There are, however, traditions of collecting and gathering palm nuts, certain species of banana, *amakoromo̱ idu* (city-founding banana), and other plants that grew wild. But the picture was brighter for the freshwater swamp areas where bananas and plantains (*musa paradisiaca*), cocoyam (*taro*), and the water yam (*dioscorea alata*) have been cultivated for a long time.

The earliest forms of exchange, therefore, occurred between the fishing

1

2

3

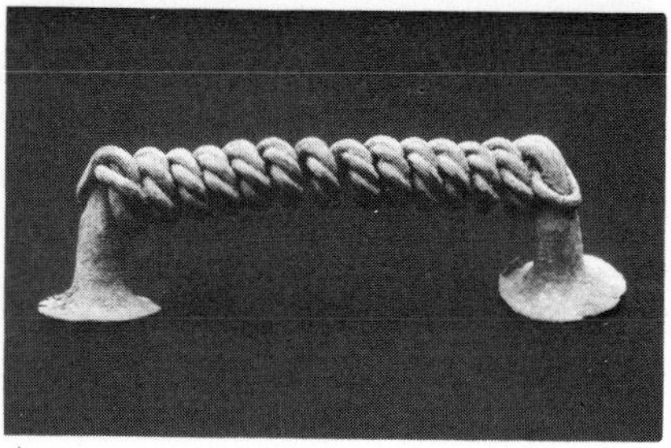

4

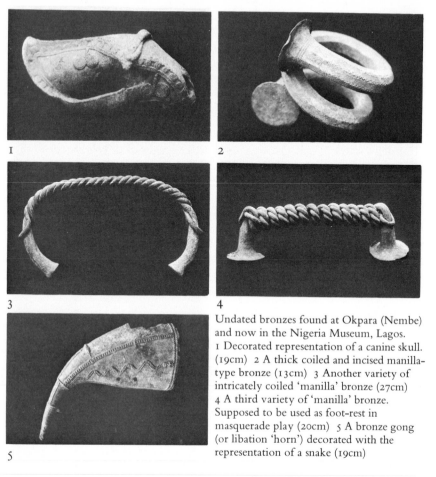

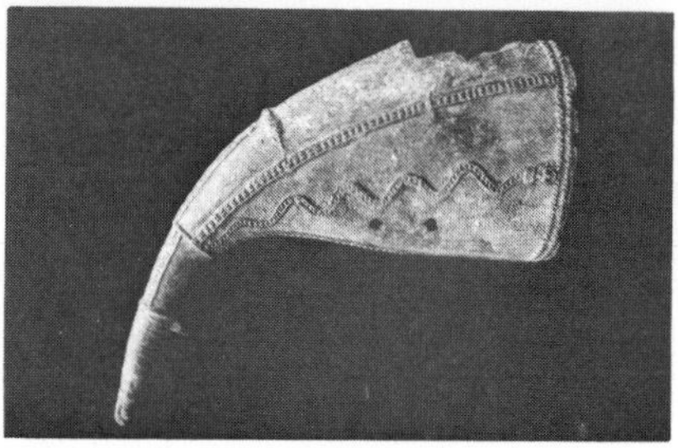

5

Undated bronzes found at Okpara (Nembe) and now in the Nigeria Museum, Lagos. 1 Decorated representation of a canine skull. (19cm) 2 A thick coiled and incised manilla-type bronze (13cm) 3 Another variety of intricately coiled 'manilla' bronze (27cm) 4 A third variety of 'manilla' bronze. Supposed to be used as foot-rest in masquerade play (20cm) 5 A bronze gong (or libation 'horn') decorated with the representation of a snake (19cm)

settlements of the saltwater swamp and beach ridges with the fishing and farming communities of the adjacent freshwater swamp.

It would be false to accept too rigid a picture of isolation of the early delta communities. The bronzes discovered in so many places in the delta, although as yet undated, presuppose early contact with places outside the delta. Mein traditions already indicate importation from Benin, while some pieces show affinities with bronzes excavated at Igbo-Ukwu in the Awka area.[31] And even if further research reveals centres of bronze-casting in the delta, the raw material at least had to be imported. These bronzes, therefore, indicate early contact with the outside. They also suggest the existence of groups pursuing leisure activities, for the bronzes were used in the courts of political leaders, the cult houses of religious leaders, or in the masquerade plays of cultural elites.

31 Horton, 'Brasswork in the Niger Delta', pp. 76–91.

Long distance trade

Long distance trading across the delta and into the hinterland was well established before the Portuguese arrived in the delta at the beginning of the sixteenth century. Pereira (*c.* 1508) reported such activity at a delta port on the Rio Real where large trading canoes made out of a single trunk brought yams, slaves, cows, goats and sheep from as far in the hinterland as 'a hundred leagues or more'.[32]

Barbot described trading canoes used at Elem Kalaḇari in the seventeenth century in terms similar to Pereira.[33] They carried javelins and shields for defence, with twenty paddlers, and were capable of carrying seventy to eighty warriors. These descriptions are fully consistent with traditions in the delta states and other Ịjọ groups concerning their trading canoes and canoe-making. The western delta group of Arogbo has traditions which explain their name with reference to their early canoe-building industry. That is, that the name Arogbo is derived from *aru̲ ogbo* (canoe forest) referring to the earlier use of the site for making canoes out of the single tree trunks noted by both Pereira and Barbot.

To the yams, slaves, cows, goats and sheep Pereira listed as the produce of the hinterland, Barbot added bananas, chickens, hogs, palm wine and palm oil. But it was Pereira who recorded what the delta people gave in exchange: salt.

Many European visitors to West Africa reported the manufacture of salt from sea water on the coast for sale in the hinterland. On the Gold Coast, Barbot reported that sea water was evaporated in pots or in pits in the ground. And in some places in the Accra hinterland, salt was in such great demand that 'a slave, and sometimes two, are given for a handful of salt'.[34] Pereira did not report how the salt was made on the Rio Real, but John Adams reported in the early nineteenth century that it was made by boiling sea water in 'earthenware of native manufacture' on the Benin River, and in 'neptunes, or large brass pans, taken from Europe to Bonny' in the eastern delta.[35] There are, indeed, traditions of salt manufacture among many Ịjọ groups (especially the Bassan) and the Itsekiri of the western delta, but no remembrance of salt boiled from sea water. Delta traditions know only of manufacture from the salt concentrated in the aerial roots of mangrove trees, *Rhizophora racemosa*.[36]

In the delta the concentrated solution filtered from the ashes of the mangrove parts was boiled in pots which determined the shape and size of the salt cakes that formed the unit of exchange. Since this salt was in

32 Kimble, *Pereira*, p. 132.
33 Barbot, *op. cit.*, p. 382.
34 *Ibid.*, pp. 205–6.
35 John Adams, *Remarks on the Country Extending from Cape Palmas to the River Congo*, London, 1823, pp. 118, 122.
36 Cf. G. O. Oweh, 'Salt- and soap-making in Warri Province', *Niger. Mag.* xiii, 1938, pp. 70–1.

great demand in the hinterland and food was short in the delta, a north-south trade link is easy to visualise. But there was also a west to east trade route across the delta linking the eastern delta states with the Itsekiri kingdom of Warri and with regions much farther west.

The fact of early Itsekiri religious and cultural influence in the central and eastern delta has already been suggested by the traditions of migrations. But Bassan traditions concerning their salt industry state that they bought the clay pots from Itsekiri traders. The most important produce distributed by the Itsekiri in the eastern delta was, however, a cassava meal known throughout the delta by variations of its original Portuguese (Brazilian) name of *farinha (de mandioca)*. The cassava (manioc) apparently spread to other parts of the delta from Warri. Barbot, who was in the delta in 1678 and 1682, did not list it among the produce of any other place in the delta except Warri. According to Barbot, the Itsekiri had a large number of 'magnoc bushes, which they call *mandi-hoka* in their language; of which they make the *cassaba* or *farinha de pao*, that is in Portuguese, wood meal, which is the bread they commonly feed on'.[37]

These Portuguese names confirm the view that the meal had come to Warri from Brazil, probably via Angola and the Atlantic islands.[38] Barbot's observation of its importance as a staple food also confirms the traditions and its present position in the diet of some delta groups. In Nembe where it was introduced by the Itsekiri and became a staple, it became a significant factor in military operations, since it is easy to carry and preserve.

It is doubtful if the pots and farina were traded across the delta by Itsekiri traders alone. In the Kalabari area to the east of Nembe, traditions attest to Itsekiri traders carrying farina or *ifenia*. But at Nembe the regular suppliers were Bassan traders from the central delta, apparently as middlemen. Bassan traditions also suggest that they went west into Itsekiri country to buy pots for their salt industry.

Any Ijo traders from the east and central delta who went west to Warri may have carried slaves for exchange, since salt was also made by the Itsekiri. After Warri, the other trading centres—established by the Europeans—were first, Ughoton (Gwato) serving as the port of Benin, and later Arogbo. There is yet little direct evidence from the Nigerian end for the suggestion of a bead trade from the Benin region to the Gold Coast (Ghana), but since the Bini themselves were not a maritime people, the carriers would have had to be one or all of the other peoples trading in this region (Ijo, Itsekiri, Ijebu).[39]

37 Barbot, *op. cit.*, p. 377.

38 W. O. Jones, 'Manioc: an example of innovation in African economies', *Economic Development and Cultural Change*, v, 2, January 1957.

39 J. D. Fage, 'Some remarks on beads and trade in Lower Guinea in the sixteenth and seventeenth centuries', *J.A.H.*, iii, 2, pp. 343–7. See Ryder, 'Dutch trade', for Nigerian traders in the Benin region.

The Atlantic trade

The first impact of the Portuguese on West African coastal commerce was probably to fragment local long distance trade routes running along the coast. By establishing contact with distribution centres at various points on the coast, they were able to take over the movement of goods from one point to the other along the coast.

Thus after the Portuguese had established posts at Warri and Ughoton (Gwato) in the western delta, they handled the trade between the Benin region and the Gold Coast. They exchanged Benin blue cloth and beads at Elmina for gold and in the Congo for copper made into manillas and redistributed in the Niger Delta as currency.[40]

Each delta state thenceforward concentrated on developing markets in its direct hinterland. Thus Elem Kalaḇari̱ opened the Obia markets, while Bonny had to go farther east and north to trade at Ohombele and other markets in Ndoki country, since the Okrika controlled the Ikwerre and Ogoni areas immediately east of the Elem Kalaḇari̱ markets. However, both Okrika and Andoni traders did business at Bonny. Nembe traders developed contacts up the Niger at markets in Aboh and Osomari, meeting Kalaḇari̱ expansion westwards in the nineteenth century in the Oguta Lake and in the Orashi River.

The Europeans also competed with local producers of goods used in local trade. The English, for example, began to import salt in competition with the local industry. By the end of the eighteenth century each English vessel trading to Bonny carried up to fifty tons of salt.[41] The abandonment of salt-making in the city-states may be viewed as part of the process by which these communities gave up traditional pursuits in favour of the European trade.

The slave trade

The overseas trade in slaves as in other articles could only be conducted by men with capital, who were able to equip the type of large canoes described by Pereira in the sixteenth century and by Barbot and others in the seventeenth. The canoes had to be large to carry a sufficient stock of merchandise to the hinterland markets, and to bring back enough slaves to make a profit. In turn these canoes required a large number of paddlers. Further, fighting men and armaments had to be provided against attack by pirates and trade rivals. Barbot described the armament of the first half of the seventeenth century as consisting of shields and javelins, but very soon cannon were to be mounted on trade canoes and the warriors supplied with firearms.

Although the trading canoes were armed, the main supply of slaves from

40 Kimble, *Pereira*, pp. 128–9. J. Vansina, 'Long distance trade-routes in Central Africa', *J.A.H.*, iii, 3, 1962, p. 380.
41 Adams, *op. cit.*, pp. 262–3.

the hinterland markets was obtained by peaceful trade. The peoples of Aboh, Ohombele and other markets obtained the slaves from other groups farther inland. The majority of slaves sold to the Europeans at the eastern delta ports came from Iboland, but some obtained by Nembe middlemen at Aboh may have come down the Niger from Idah and other parts of northern Nigeria. The delta states strove to maintain good relations with the peoples of the supply centres.

Oral traditions in the delta states do not mention raids as an important source of slave supply. The few raids reported were conducted within the delta. The main supplies came from trading expeditions to the northern borders of the delta.

Results of the Atlantic trade

Some of the internal results already discussed may be illustrated from the account of James Barbot and John Grazilhier of their visit to Bonny and Elem Kalaḇari̱ in July and August 1699.[42]

First it is clear that the kings had been enriched by the trade. King William of Bonny confessed it. The surest sources were the comey duties or customs paid by all Europeans' ships. Barbot paid goods worth 1,000 copper rings (manillas?) for his ship estimated capable of carrying 500 slaves. He also had to give presents both to kings and to House heads. But the kings also made direct profit by trade for which the Europeans gave 'trusts'—a loan or credit in goods to serve as capital to be exchanged in the hinterland for slaves and provisions. In the distribution of trusts, Barbot advanced most to King William, and to the chiefs 'each in proportion of his quality and ability'. The chiefs clearly depended on the king for recommendation to the visitors.

The giving of trusts added another dangerous element: a growing dependence of the rulers of the delta states on the European traders and on the Atlantic trade. That they did not fall completely under European control at this time was due to their firm control of the hinterland supply centres of the articles required by the Europeans. The Barbot account shows, in fact, that the rulers were very much in control of the situation, bargaining for the prices of everything before giving word for the start of business.

It may be noted too that in proportion as the overseas trade enhanced the power of the king over his chiefs, it also increased the chiefs' control over the House members. The member depended on the head for capital to engage in trade and for a wife, and for his welfare in society generally. This was greater economic control than any one person had over another in the earlier traditional village economy. However, in the competitive society of these city-states, the House members could become a House head.

42 Barbot, *op. cit.*, pp. 455–65.

Money objects: uses and distribution

The geographical distribution of the many money objects passing through the delta is a useful index of the areas penetrated by influences from the coast. The use of particular types of money was, of course, dictated by the scale and type of commercial operation. At the coast where the rulers of the delta states traded in slaves and goods in large quantities, money objects of large denomination could be used. In local market transactions in small units and in exchange in the hinterland, money objects of very small denomination were preferred.

The use of salt cakes as a means of exchange has already been mentioned. In the nineteenth century slaves too began to be so used. Both slaves and salt were in great demand and highly valued. They were used more often as accounting units or standards against which goods were valued.

Metal objects were accepted in the delta ports as money. In the early sixteenth century the Portuguese bought produce at the Rio Real with 'brass and copper bracelets'. In 1699 James Barbot noted iron bars as 'the standard coin' on the Rio Real. He had to sit in conference with the rulers of Bonny to convert all his merchandise into their equivalent in iron bars. The prices of articles to be supplied to the ships were also calculated in iron bars. In this case iron bars were used, in the main, as an accounting unit, and used only rarely in actual payment. Copper bars were also given out in payment at Bonny and Elem Kalabari, but valued in iron bars (four copper bars to one iron bar). At Calabar Barbot had to make most payments in copper bars.

Although accepted and used as means of payment, copper, iron and brass bars were often converted into other less bulky forms of money in the hinterland, and used as the raw material for the manufacture of ornaments. By the mid-seventeenth century Dapper had reported the use of an iron currency in the hinterland of the Rio Real that could have been made from the larger bars imported by the Europeans. Barbot also reported at the end of the century that at Elem Kalabari the copper bars were made into 'arm-rings'. Brass bars or rods were converted into leg-rings for girls at Awka and lead bars into slugs and balls on the coast. Iron currencies have been reported too for Arochuku, Awka, Idoma, and on the Benue.[43]

Manillas (made of copper or brass), and cowry shells were the most widely used money objects in the delta states and their hinterland. The 'brass and copper bracelets' used in Pereira's time may have been manillas, and the cowry was also seen in Benin during the sixteenth century.[44] These objects were in such small denominations that they penetrated the

43 G. T. Basden, *Among the Ibos of Nigeria*, London, 1921, pp. 198, 201, for Awka; Baikie, *Exploring Voyage 1854*, pp. 114, 220 for Idoma and Benue.

44 A. H. M. Kirk-Greene, 'The major currencies in Nigerian history', *J.H.S.N.*, ii, 1, 1960, p. 137. See also G. I. Jones, 'Native and trade currencies in Southern Nigeria in the 18th and 19th centuries', *Africa*, xxviii, 1, 1958, pp. 43–54.

subsistence sphere of the economy and largely eliminated barter. Thus the British were hard put to it to displace the cowry at the beginning of this century, since their smallest money unit, the tenth of a penny (*anini*), was still equivalent to between nine and eighteen cowries.[45]

Manillas and cowries, the only general purpose money of the delta states, spread inland along the rivers into the trading areas of Bonny, Elem Kalabari, and of the Efik. The extent of Bonny distribution of the manilla may be seen in the fact that when manillas were withdrawn from circulation, 1,722,870 were recovered from the Ndoki district alone.[46] In the hinterland of the Cross River, the Efik coastal middlemen treated with the Aro, operators of a wide network of trade routes in the Ibo hinterland. The extent of Aro operations may be seen in the list of money objects and trade goods recovered from a mound at Arochuku: cowry shells, beads, manillas, wire coils, ring money, and types of iron currency.[47]

NEIGHBOURS

The Ibo hinterland

The Ibo hinterland was crossed by a number of trade routes connecting important markets. The Aro, who exerted influence over most of these routes, lay close to one of these central Ibo markets at Bende.[48] Routes passed from Bende to other centres at Ihube, Nike, the Ezza region, and Uburu. Connection with the delta and coastal distribution centres was achieved mainly through Aro agents at Itu (to Ibibio, Umon, and Efik middlemen), in Ndoki at Akwete or Ohombele (to Andoni, Bonny, Okrika, and Kalabari traders). Some of the slaves and other produce of the Ibo area passed northwards from such markets as Nike (through Idah), and Uburu.

Aro predominance in the hinterland trade was achieved partly through their settlement pattern. They planted small settlements along the trade routes. In other cases bigger settlements were built to dominate a market centre, but leaving the local Ibo population its political autonomy. Finally there were the large-scale settlements in which the Aro took control of land and all religious ritual of a locality. Thus on the Bende-Ozuakoli-Ihube trade route there were the large Aro settlements of Ndizuogu and Ndienyi. In the Ezza region there were Aro quarters in the main markets, with their influence spreading north-east to Obubra and Yako. On the Uburu route, the Afikpo cooperated with the Aro on the basis of ancient kinship and mutual benefit.

45 Basden, *op. cit.*, p. 198.
46 O. O. Amogu, 'The introduction into and withdrawal of manillas from the Oil Rivers as seen in Ndoki District' *Niger. Mag.* xxxviii, 1952, pp. 135–9.
47 J. D. W. Jeffreys, 'Some Negro currencies in Nigeria', *South African Museums Association Bulletin* i, no. 16, Dec. 1954, p. 406.
48 The account of Ibo trade routes and Aro oracle and influence largely follows Simon Ottenberg, 'Ibo oracles and inter-group relations', S-W Journal of Anthropology, xiv, no. 3, 1958, pp. 295–317.

Two factors accounted for the extent of Aro influence and the success of Aro traders. First, they were protected by the reputation of the oracle at Arochuku, Ibini Okpabe. Second, Aro commercial operations as well as the reputation of their oracle were supported by the activities of Abam, Edda, Ohaffia, Abiriba, and other mercenaries.

In spite of their widespread influence the Aro neither attempted nor achieved political integration of Iboland. The hinterland communities remained essentially segmentary in structure. The Aro homeland was itself segmentary in structure, since, out of nineteen autonomous villages, six claimed Akpa origin, five Ibo, and two Ibibio.[49] The remarkable success of the Aro stemmed from the coincidence of the interests of all its members abroad and at home. The traders and settlers outside were unmolested wherever they went because they were considered the children of Ibini Okpabe. The operators of the oracle at home needed those outside to act as agents, guides and informants. Even the mercenaries worked with the Aro completely on a symbiotic basis. The Aro served as spies, provided camps and supplies on long forays for heads and booty. The Aro, of course, directed the mercenaries against trade rivals or groups which defied the decisions of their oracle, and took over the war captives as slaves.

Other oracles competed with the Aro for influence in the Ibo hinterland. The difference was that the rivals of the Aro oracle did not have the support of mercenaries and of agents with the wide-ranging activities of the Aro traders. Their closest rival was probably the Agbala (or Agbara) oracle at Awka. The Awka were famous blacksmiths and travelled widely. But the Awka operated in an area west of the main Aro routes.

Important as the Aro and other Ibo oracles were in promoting inter-group relations and in procuring slaves for the Atlantic trade, their influence can be exaggerated. Equiano's account of his childhood in, and six to seven months travel through, the Ibo hinterland to the coast in the second half of the eighteenth century contained no word about oracles. He knew of 'stout mahogany-coloured men from the south-west' who traded firearms, gunpowder, hats, beads and dried fish, mainly for slaves and salt.[50] The number of times he changed hands from these '*Oye-Eboe*' slave captors suggests too that no single Ibo group was in control of this trade route to the market from which the delta middlemen took him over. Equiano also indicates the sources of the overseas slave trade, namely, violent seizure by itinerant traders and in local wars, as well as persons cast out by society.[51]

Clearly there were parts of Iboland which lay outside the direct influence of the Aro oracle and its agents. The stimulus to developments in some of

49 G. I. Jones, 'Who are the Aro?' *Nigerian Field*, viii, 3, 1939, p. 102.
50 Paul Edwards, ed., *Equiano's Travels: The Interesting Narrative of the Life of Olaudah Equiano or Gustavus Vassa the African*, London and Ibadan, 1967, p. 7 ff.
51 Cf. J. S. Harris, 'Some aspects of slavery in Southeastern Nigeria', *Journal of Negro History*, xxviii, 1, 1942, pp. 47–54.

these areas, such as those west of the Niger, Aboh, Osomari, Oguta, Onitsha, the Anambara and Nsukka regions probably came from the Benin empire and the Igala kingdom of Idah. The Aboh and Onitsha claim to have received royal refugees from the Benin area. It has been suggested that the Benin immigrants to Onitsha arrived between 1650 and 1680.[52] The Umueri at the three centres of Aguleri, Nri, and Oreri also developed chiefly institutions uncharacteristic of the Ibo country. Their traditions claim Igala origin for the innovators, although in the Umueri, as in the other cases, the Benin and Igala institutions and ideas have been fully integrated into an Ibo cultural framework of age grades and titles.[53] It seems too that the date of arrival for these intrusive elements may be earlier than the seventeenth century suggested for Onitsha, for the ancient bronzes discovered at Igbo-Ukwu near Awka have been associated with 'a former Eze Nri—the priest-king of the Umueri clan'.[54]

The delta communities were indirectly concerned in many of the developments in the Ibo hinterland. Adams estimated that, at the close of the eighteenth century, three-quarters of the slaves exported annually at Bonny came from this area.[55] This trade contact presumably stimulated many of the developments in the hinterland. The Aro sold slaves to the delta traders at markets on the delta periphery. There are several nineteenth-century accounts of trips to the oracle at Arochuku from several delta states, and such ritual consultations may have begun at an earlier date. But there is little evidence of Aro settlements or mercenary operations within the delta, such as the Aro used to establish their influence in the Ibo hinterland. Traditions of Awka blacksmiths are more common, especially in the central delta, and direct contact was established by Nembe with the Ibo states on the Niger (Osomari, Aboh, Onitsha).

The Efik State of Calabar

In the seventeenth century the Efik in their four major settlements of Ikoritungko or Obio Oko (Creek Town), Obutong (Old Town), Atakpa (Duke Town) and Nsidung (Henshaw Town), became the main distributors for the Atlantic slave trade on the Cross River. These settlements, collectively known as Calabar (or Old Calabar), served as the distribution centre to the immediate east of the delta states, and although dissimilar in many respects, developed on comparable lines with those states.

Arochuku lies in the immediate hinterland of Calabar, and the majority

52 R. W. Harding, *The Dispute over the Obiship of Onitsha*, Enugu, 1963, p. 18.
53 Cf. J. S. Boston, 'Notes on contact between the Igala and the Ibo', *J.H.S.N.*, ii, 1, 1960, pp. 52–8. J. D. W. Jeffreys, 'The divine Umundri king', *Africa,* viii, 3, 1935, pp. 346–54.
54 Thurstan Shaw, 'Bronzes from Eastern Nigeria', *J.H.S.N.*, ii, 1, 1960, p. 164.
55 Capt. John Adams, *Sketches taken during Ten Voyages to Africa between the Years 1786 and 1800*, London, p. 38. Cited by G. I. Jones, 'European and African tradition on the Rio Real', *J.A.H.*, iv, 3, 1963, p. 391. The total annual export for Bonny of 20,000 slaves was probably closer to 10,000 according to the figures supplied by James Barbot for 1699.

of slaves resulting from the operation of the Aro oracle must have eventually come into Efik hands at the Itu market. Traditions have even been recorded to the effect that the Efik originally came from a home (Ibom) in the Aro region.[56] It does not necessarily follow that the Efik were Ibo, but it does reinforce other traditions of early contact with the Aro Ibo. The Efik are stated to have moved from Ibom to Uruan in Ibibio country, to Ikpa Ene, and finally to Creek Town on the Cross River. The development of a distinctive Efik state is supposed to have occurred at Creek Town from where they spread to the other settlements to take control of the Atlantic trade in this section of the Nigerian coast.

Efik movement to the Cross River is assumed to have occurred in response to the Atlantic trade and probably no earlier than the seventeenth century. This conclusion is based on the fact that the earliest mention of the Efik state on the Cross River occurs in seventeenth-century European accounts. Nor do Efik traditional sources suggest an earlier dating. Eyo Nsa (Eyo Honesty I) of Creek Town who died in 1820, is, for example, only three generations from Efiom Ekpo, a founding ancestor, in the genealogies.[57] Whatever the reasons for Efik settlement on the Cross River, the Calabar state came to depend on the Atlantic trade as much as the delta states from the seventeenth century onwards.

The Efik settlements were on firm land, and not within delta swampland. Calabar, accordingly, was more secure in its food supplies from the neighbouring Ibibio. The Efik also got food from their own agricultural efforts, for which they came to employ slave labour in farm settlements. The treatment of slaves was, in fact, one of the areas in which the Calabar state differed from the delta states. Slaves were not integrated into the lineage and political system. Mostly kept separate in the farms, they had no hope whatever of attaining positions of political or social leadership in the lineages or state. The *Ekpe* society of Calabar, more important politically than the *s̱eḵiapu̱* or *ekine* of the delta states, barred slaves from ever rising to the top.

The *Ekpe* society of Calabar played the rôle of the *amanyana̱bo̱* and House heads in the delta states. The heads of Efik lineages and those who came to assume the title of king (*obong*) apparently exercised their authority through their membership of the highest grades of *Ekpe*. The rulers of Duke Town, for example, had to strengthen their position by buying the highest *Ekpe* grade of Eyamba. Similarly, the Eyo dynasty of Creek Town had to occupy the next highest *Ekpe* grade, as well as to make a marriage

56 A. E. Afigbo, 'Efik origin and migrations reconsidered', *Niger. Mag.*, lxxxvii, 1965, pp. 267–80; J. D. W. Jeffreys, 'Efik origin', *Niger. Mag.*, xci, 1966, pp. 297–9.

57 A. K. Hart, *Report of the Enquiry into the Dispute over the Obongship of Calabar*, Enugu, 1964, pp. 125–7. The genealogies are clearly telescoped. They would date the founding of Creek Town in the eighteenth century or very late in the seventeenth. Cf. Daryll Forde, ed., *Efik Traders of Old Calabar,* containing the *Diary of Antera Duke, an Efik Slave-Trading Chief of the eighteenth century* . . . London, 1956.

alliance with the Ambo lineage from which the Eyamba title had passed to Duke Town. It is clear from Antera Duke's diary (1783–8) that it was *Ekpe* which made the trade regulations at Calabar. And it is probable too that the numerous 'kings' to whom Barbot paid trade duties in 1698, although they may also have been lineage heads and big traders, obtained their titles from *Ekpe* membership.[58]

The effects of the Atlantic trade on Calabar and delta political development, then, differed on the score of the preponderant influence of the secret society in Calabar. Whereas in the delta states the king and the House heads gained in stature because of the trade, in Calabar the political leaders appear to have exercised power only indirectly through *Ekpe*. Where in the delta states the wealth and power resulting from the trade went to build up the political leaders, in Calabar these were shared among an aristocracy of birth and wealth gathered in the *Ekpe* secret society. And where *ekine* integrated the new slave members into the community, *Ekpe* condemned them to subordinate status.

Benin

The Benin empire was a colossus in the southern areas of Nigeria east of Ọyọ. Its influence and prestige extended even to the regions over which its power could not be enforced.

According to Benin tradition the areas under effective control were wide down to the end of the eighteenth century.[59] In the west, the boundary with Ọyọ was established at Otun in Ekiti country. The rulers of Akure, Ilesha, and Owo looked up to Benin to settle succession disputes, or were required to pay homage. And Lagos, eight days by canoe through the creeks, was apparently a principality of Benin. Badagry to the west of Lagos and other places even farther west were reported to be subject to Benin at the close of the eighteenth century and early in the nineteenth.

To the east, Benin tradition records Ibo rulers from west of the Niger (Agbor, Aboh, Ubulu-Uku) seeking Benin assistance in resolving succession disputes. In each case the unsuccessful candidate was detained in Benin to serve as sword-bearer (*emada*). The rulers of these places were also invested at Benin.

The degree of control exercised over these territories seems to exceed the type of Benin influence ascertainable in the Niger Delta during the same period. In some of the Urhobo groups on the delta periphery and in Mein, only the first incumbent in political office went to Benin. Later rulers merely sent presents to Benin.

The kingdom of Warri founded by Benin migrants also ran its own affairs within the delta and dealt with the European visitors as a sovereign state. It is, however, clear from I̱jọ oral tradition that the prestige of

58 Barbot, *op. cit.*, p. 465. That is, they were holders of *Ekpe obong* grades.

59 Egharevba, *A Short History of Benin*, pp. 32–43 for the Oba between 1600 and 1800.

Benin was high throughout the delta.

Admitting European visitors and influence only through the port of Ughoton (Gwato), Benin does not seem to have been affected by the Atlantic contact as much as the coastal communities. The fluctuations in the power of the kingdom are ascribed by Benin traditions to weakness of individual Obas, rebellion, or succession disputes. The Benin monarchy was, however, fairly stable during the seventeenth and eighteenth centuries. Only one Oba was removed by the elders, and at the beginning of the eighteenth century, the rule of primogeniture was established by Oba Ewuakpe.

While European contact failed to become the decisive force for change in Benin, the European effort was much greater and sustained over a longer period than in the delta states. In Benin as in Warri, the Portuguese established Christian missions from the sixteenth century.[60] In each place these initiatives failed to take root.

CONCLUSION

The delta states developed from an I̱jo̱ baseline and were, accordingly, culturally distinct from the majority of their neighbours. During the seventeenth and eighteenth centuries the four cities of Bonny, Elem Kalabari̱, Okrika and Nembe changed from a fishing to a trading economy and eventually developed institutions appropriate to their new way of life. Under the stimulus of an older internal long distance trade and the Atlantic slave traffic, the states engaged in wide-ranging contacts with peoples in the Ibo hinterland and across the delta.

These states served as the clearing house of the Atlantic trade, supplying a large proportion of the slaves received by European slavers from the West African coast. Together with Calabar and Warri, they helped to give this part of the West African coast the name of The Slave Coast.

The coastal trading states stimulated developments in their hinterland, such as the network of trade routes that came under the control of the religious and commercial centre at Arochuku. There were, however, other areas which looked to Benin for their inspiration. The presence of this large forest kingdom actually drew the early European visitors inland past the western delta through the inland port of Ughoton to Benin.

In the period 1600 to 1800, then, the delta states developed their internal institutions and fortunes in free and voluntary relationships with the European traders and with their Nigerian neighbours. In the following century they were to reorganise their economic system from a base in the slave to palm oil trade; and also to combat growing European interference and threat to their sovereignty.

60 A. F. C. Ryder, 'The Benin missions', *J.H.S.N.*, ii, 2, 1961, pp. 231–57. A. F. C. Ryder, 'Missionary activities in the kingdom of Warri to the early nineteenth century', *J.H.S.N.*, ii, 1, 1960, pp. 1–24.

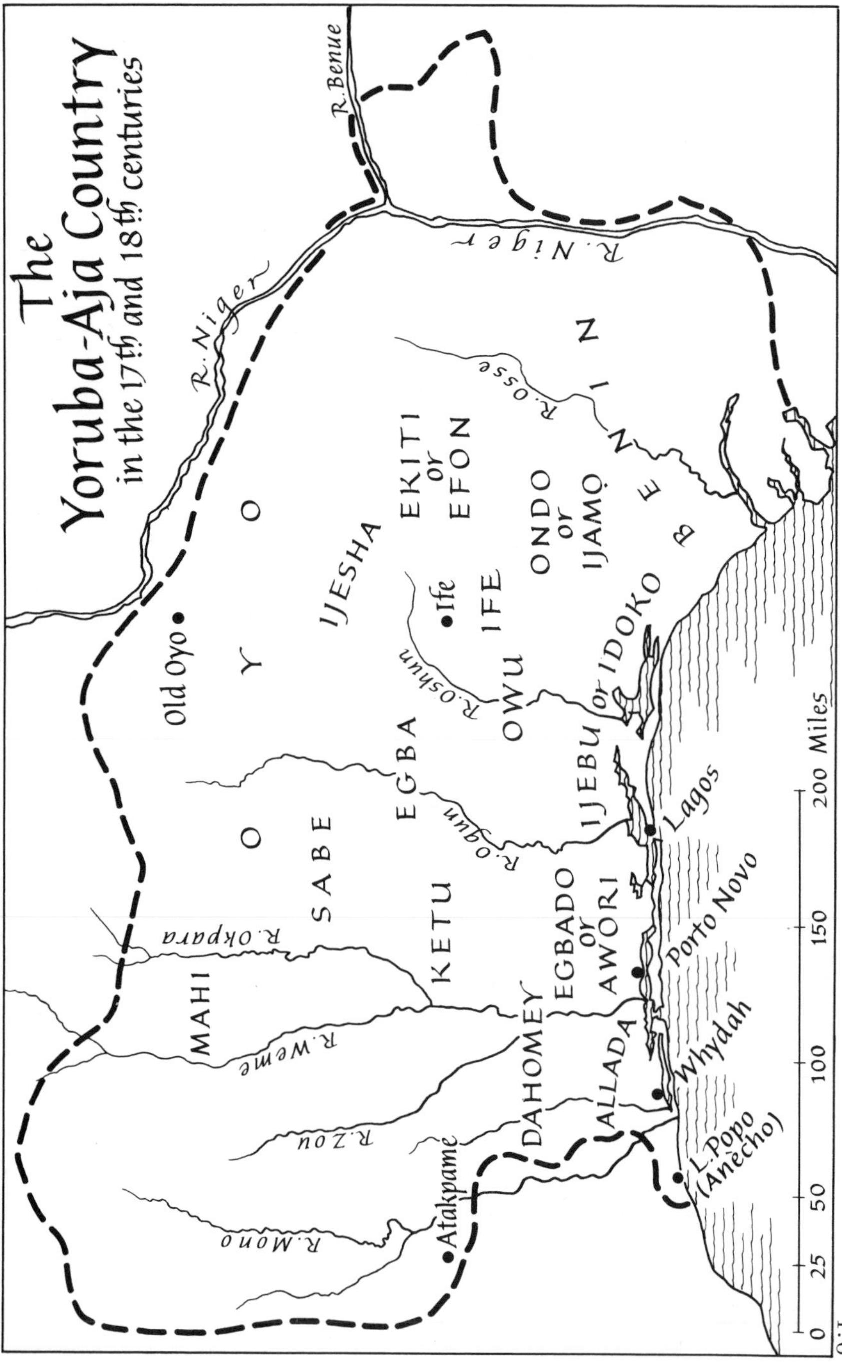
The Yoruba-Aja Country
in the 17th and 18th centuries
R. Benue
R. Niger
R. Niger
R. Osse
R. Oshun
R. Ogun
R. Okpara
R. Weme
R. Zou
R. Mono
Old Oyo
O Y O
IJESHA
EKITI or EFON
Ife
IFE
OWU
ONDO or IJAMO
B E N I N
EGBA
SABE
KETU
MAHI
DAHOMEY
EGBADO or AWORI
ALLADA
IJEBU or IDOKO
Lagos
Porto Novo
Whydah
L. Popo (Anécho)
Atakpame
0 25 50 100 150 200 Miles

CHAPTER 9

The expansion of Ọyọ and the rise of Dahomey, 1600–1800

I. A. AKINJOGBIN

YORUBA–AJA CULTURAL UNITY

The present boundaries of Africa, imposed by the European powers at the end of the nineteenth century, and preserved today by the need of independent African states for political stability, have created barriers between peoples who in precolonial times had very close contact with each other. Two such peoples are the Yoruba and the Aja of Dahomey and Nigeria.

It is easy to see that there are Yoruba on both sides of the border. Two things, however, are not often realised, at least as clearly as they ought to be. The first is that the Yoruba are spread both to the east and the west of the Aja, who seem to have been a later intrusion and to have cut the Yoruba settlers in two.[1] The second is that even the people here called Aja, which include the Egun (Gun), the Fon, the Arada, and a number of other small groups in modern Southern Dahomey, are very closely related to the Yoruba by language, beliefs, economy, political systems and social usages. And, as we shall see, large slices of both the Yoruba and the Aja areas were, at various periods, under the same political authority. In a real sense therefore, the Yoruba and the Aja can be regarded as belonging to a single cultural area.

Let us take language first. A recent linguistic study of West Africa classifies the Yoruba, the Aja and the Ewe languages as well as Edo and Igbo as belonging to the same 'Kwa' subfamily within the great Niger-Congo (Nigritic) family.[2] But Yoruba and Aja are more closely related languages one with another than they are with Edo or Igbo. It appears clear from contemporary travellers' reports that at the opening of the period under discussion, the *lingua franca* of the Aja country was 'Lucumi', which is undoubtedly the Yoruba language.[3]

1 Most linguistic maps of West Africa do not show this clearly, but anyone travelling from Abeokuta to Atakpame in Togo will easily discover the phenomenon.

2 J. Greenberg, *The Languages of Africa*, Indiana University, Bloomington, 1963, p. 3. G. Murdock, *Africa, Its Peoples and Their Culture History*, New York, 1959, pp. 14–15.

3 J. Ogilby, *Africa: Being an Accurate Description of Aegypt, Barbary, Libya, etc.*, London, 1670, p. 647.

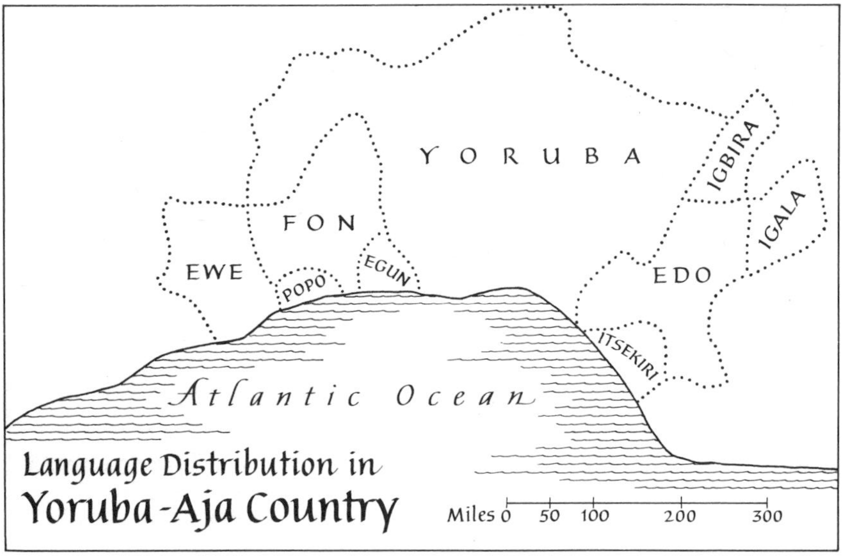

9:2

The close affinity between Yoruba and Aja is most obvious in their religious beliefs. The Dahomeans, for example, accept that most of their gods originated from Ife, a belief shared by all the Yoruba kingdoms.[4] In the eighteenth century, the highest Dahomean god was the Lisa, the male counterpart of Mawu.[5] This word Lisa is the same as Orișa, which is the shortened form of Orișa Nla, sometimes called Ọbatala, the god of creation in Yorubaland. There was also in Dahomey the cult of Șango (or Xevioso) and that of Legbara (Ẹlẹgbara or Eșu). In addition to these prominent ones, there are a number of less important religious cults which the Aja and Yoruba share in common.

In social organisation they shared many common characteristics. As with most Africans, the respect for age was a basic consideration in personal relationships among both the Yoruba and the Aja. The 'father' or 'elder brother' was given instant obeisance irrespective of acquired wealth or military reputation. With both, the system of inheritance was patrilineal. Furthermore, town-dwelling appears to be a strong characteristic of both the Yoruba and the Aja, and this distinguishes them from other African groups, with the notable exception of the Hausa. The town and its surrounding villages was a basic unit of social and political organisation.

4 Hazoumé, *Le Pacte du sang au Dahomey*, Paris, 1937, p. 139; Le Herissé, *L'Ancien royaume du Dahomey*, Paris, 1911, pp. 92–155; Jacques Bertho, 'La Parenté des Yoruba aux peuplades de Dahomey et Togo', *Africa*, 1949, pp. 121–32.

5 H. Labouret and P. Rivet, *Le Royaume d'Arda et son évangélisation au XVIIe siècle*, Paris, 1929, pp. 31–3.

The economic organisation of both peoples was similar. There was a system of periodic markets,[6] which were located in various places in Yorubaland and Dahomey. There were five-day markets, nine-day markets, and seventeen-day markets.[7] In addition, every town and every village had morning and evening markets. A most important factor was that cowry shells formed the common currency among the Yoruba and the Aja peoples. This not only emphasised their unity but also distinguished them from their eastern and western neighbours. For, to the west, among the Fanti and Ashanti, gold was the common currency, whereas east of the Niger, in the period under consideration, the manilla was the commonly accepted currency.

Therefore by language, religion, social and economic organisation, the Yoruba and the Aja formed one distinct cultural area. The existence of a *lingua franca* in the Yoruba language tended to knit them still more closely together. There is therefore every justification for treating their history in the seventeenth and eighteenth centuries together in this chapter.

The degree of cultural identity referred to above had its roots in the distant past. This is borne out by the 'histories' of the different Aja and Yoruba kingdoms as related in their various oral traditions and myths of origin. The migration stories of the Yoruba are well known. One version states that the Yoruba migrated into present-day Nigeria from the north-eastern part of Africa.[8] Another version, common in Ifẹ, states that Ile-Ifẹ was the dispersal point of the Yoruba. The two versions are not necessarily irreconcilable. There may well have been some immigration from areas outside the present Yoruba country. But it would appear that it was probably at Ile-Ifẹ that the Yoruba became conscious of their identity as a people with common bonds and interests different from others around them. And that from Ifẹ, various leaders went with their followers to found other kingdoms. One version of the traditions says that when Oduduwa was on his deathbed he called his sons together and asked them to migrate and found their own kingdoms, giving each of them certain symbols.[9] A likely reason for this dispersal, preserved in an Ifa verse, relates that at a stage in the development of Ifẹ there was a problem of overpopulation worsened by a prolonged drought which lasted for a number of years, thus causing great famine. According to this tradition various consultations were made with the

6 Karl Polanyi, *Dahomey and the Slave Trade*, University of Washington Press, 1966, pp. xx and xxii, insists that Dahomey had markets but no market system because 'these markets, being isolated, did not link up into a system'. This assertion is difficult to reconcile with the practice of organised market systems in Dahomey which has continued till modern times.

7 The counting of these days is 'inclusive' one day being counted twice; thus there are two five-day markets in a nine-day market and there are two nine-day markets in a 'seventeen-day' market.

8 S. Johnson, *The History of the Yorubas*, Lagos, 1956, pp. 15–18.

9 This tradition is current in Ifẹ and Ila. In 1958, when I collected oral traditions in Ila, the Ọrangun said his ancestors brought 'Ogbo' (a kind of cutlas) as their regalia from Ifẹ.

Babalawo (Ifa divination priests), to find out the causes of their afflictions and suggest cures. None seemed able to help until one of them, Agirilọgbọn, who came from Ita Asẹ, a quarter of Ile-Ifẹ, suggested migration as a cure. This was accepted and various groups went to settle in different areas of the country.[10]

Those who left during this 'primary' migration are variously said to be seven or sixteen groups. It will probably never be possible to know exactly how many, judging from the number of kingdoms whose rulers now claim direct descent from Oduduwa in order to validate their status. It would appear however that it was during this period that Oranyan became the ruler of Benin and later founded Ọyọ. The kingdoms of Owu, Ketu, Ilesha, Ilá and Òkò (later Ijebu) as well as some of the Ekiti kingdoms may also have been founded at this time. Other kingdoms were later founded by migrants from these kingdoms. These are the kingdoms of 'secondary' migration. Again, how many they were cannot now be traced. Among them might be Akurẹ, Ọṣogbo and Old Ikoyi. Because these are of fairly ancient foundations, some of them also claim direct descent from Ifẹ. Such claims make any attempt to distinguish between the kingdoms of the primary and secondary migrations still more difficult.

What is fairly certain is that the Aja kingdoms belonged to the secondary migrations. According to oral traditions current in Allada, Whydah and Abomey, and in Eweland in modern Togo, the founders of the Aja kingdoms migrated from areas around Ketu (a kingdom of primary migration) and went first to a place called Nuatja or Watchi in the modern Republic of Togo.[11] The exact name of their point of departure has not been preserved. This omission is at first surprising because *orírun* (place of origin) is of absolute importance in the psychological make up of the Yoruba-Aja peoples. But it becomes easier to understand when it is realised that they probably did not leave as a single united group, but as separate family groups.

Indeed the traditions are clear that in Watchi the people lived in separate autochthonous groups for a considerable length of time until someone decided to impose himself as a ruler over all the groups. That was the cause of the first major rupture among the Watchi inhabitants and a group of them who were unwilling to acquiesce in such a move broke away and migrated eastwards.[12] At Tado they founded their own kingdom and apparently became a more cohesive group. After an unspecified period of time, the traditions relate that a succession dispute forced another group of Tado inhabitants to migrate still further eastwards to Allada where they founded

10 The dispersal would appear to have been orderly, for the leaders of each group, all Ifẹ princes, met in a place in Ile-Ifẹ, still called Ita Ijero (the place of convenant) where they all agreed which way to go in order to avoid friction. They probably also agreed on how to maintain future contact.

11 Jacques Bertho, 'La Parenté des Yoruba . . .', *loc. cit.*, pp. 121–32.

12 *Ibid.*

a kingdom of that name.[13] This last migration to Allada brought the Aja people back into further contact with the Yoruba and will be looked at in some detail.

There is tradition that at Tado a princess encountered a male panther (Agasu) in the forest and eventually had a son by the panther. The descendants of this son came to be called Agasuvi (children of Agasu). During a vacancy on the Tado throne an Agasuvi contested but eventually lost because succession was patrilineal and he was related to the throne only through his mother. All the remaining Agasuvi and their sympathisers therefore migrated eastwards and eventually settled at Allada.[14]

Another version of this story is that the man who married the Tado princess was a Yoruba man from Ijebu called 'Adimola' (Ademola or Adumila). He had wandered into Tado and had impressed the ruler with his magical powers displayed in repelling Tado's enemies, and it was as a result of this that he was given the princess to wed. It was one of his descendants who unsuccessfully vied for the throne of Tado and who migrated with all his supporters to Allada.[15]

Succession disputes were a common feature in most West African societies where the monarchical system prevailed, and in this instance it was the immediate cause of migration towards Allada. However, other strands in the oral traditions suggest that there were associated causes. For example, one tradition relates that before the Alladanu (the people of Allada) migrated from Tado, Tado was subjected to constant raids by a group of people who used *Akatampo* (short guns).[16] It is therefore probable that another important cause of migration was the need for security. This they may have sought for in the Allada region, which is nearer the point from which their ancestors emigrated, perhaps many centuries before. There may have been geographical reasons as well. The Tado region was not as fertile as the area lying eastwards. With increase in the population there may have been a real need to seek more fertile lands. Once Allada was founded, other kingdoms followed, founded by people led by Allada princes. Such kingdoms included Whydah, Jakin, Za and Tori.

Jacques Bertho has suggested that all the migration stories of both Yoruba and Aja should be regarded as a continuous movement of a related group of people looking for suitable abodes,[17] and judging from the evidence available so far, his suggestion appears sound. A number of problems however remain with these stories of migration. Although we know from present-day evidence the approximate land area which these related peoples came to occupy, it is yet impossible to say exactly how many king-

13 Le Herissé, *op. cit.*
14 *Ibid.*
15 A. Akindélé and C. Aguessy, *Contribution à l'étude de l'histoire de l'Ancien Royaume de Porto Novo*, I.F.A.N., Dakar, 1953, pp. 2–22.
16 *Ibid.*, p. 21.
17 Bertho, *op. cit.*, pp. 121–32.

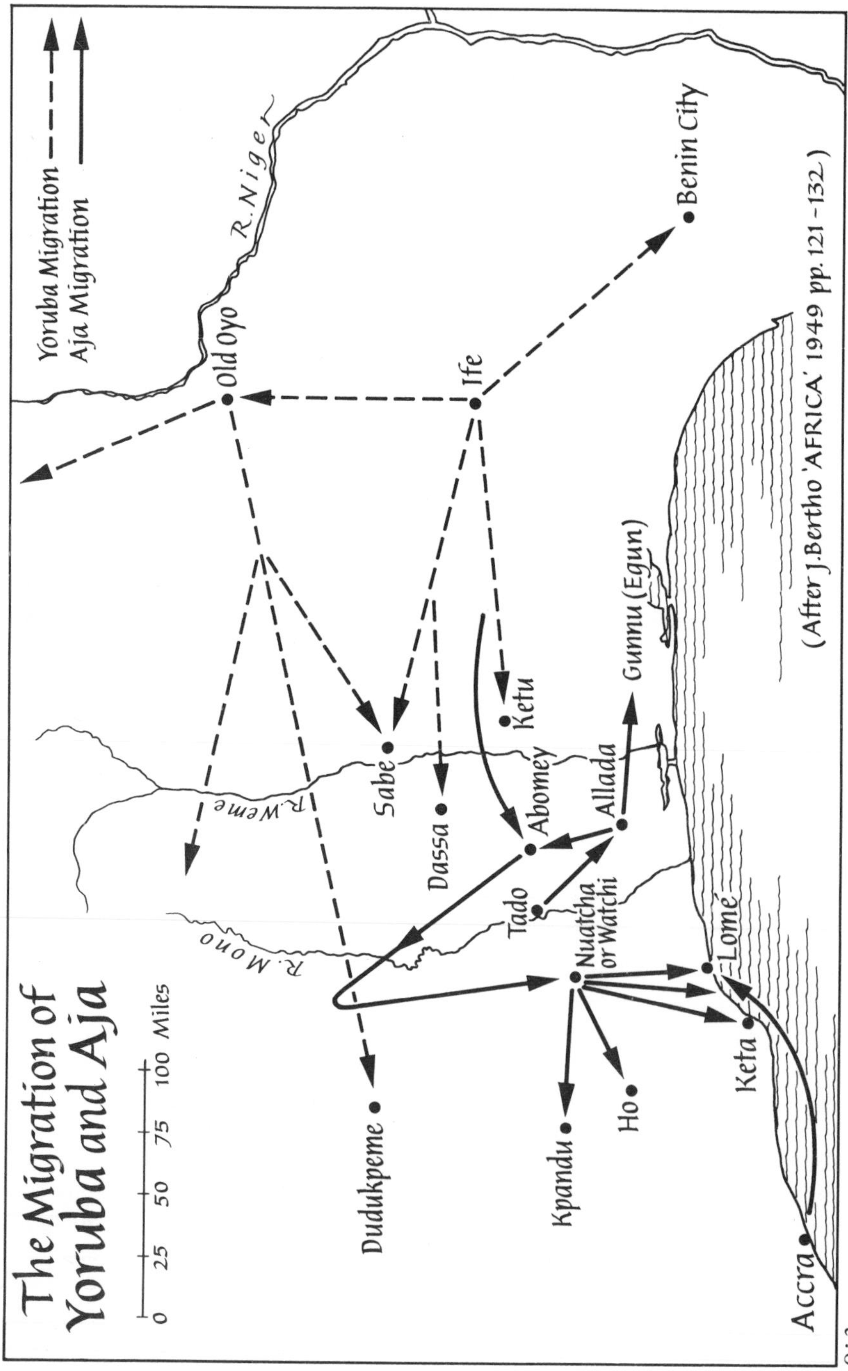
The Migration of Yoruba and Aja
0 25 50 75 100 Miles
Yoruba Migration
Aja Migration
R. Niger
Old Oyo
Ife
Benin City
Sabe
Ketu
Dassa
Abomey
Allada
Gunnu (Egun)
R. Weme
R. Mono
Tado
Nuatcha or Watchi
Lomé
Keta
Ho
Kpandu
Dudukpeme
Accra
(After J. Bertho 'AFRICA' 1949 pp. 121-132)

9:3

doms were founded by these migrants, not only in Yorubaland but also in Ajaland. Secondly we do not yet know when these migrations occurred. What is apparent is that this period of migrations and the founding of the different kingdoms extended over a considerable length of time. Certain kingdoms would appear to have reached a high degree of political sophistication while others were still migrating.

THE RISE OF ỌYỌ

One Yoruba kingdom which maintained the longest, though not entirely peaceful, connection with the Aja was Ọyọ. As we have noticed, it belonged to the primary migration and would seem to have been growing while the Aja were still migrating westwards and back again. Its reputed founder was Ọranyan (Ọranmiyan), an Ifẹ prince, who is also accepted as the progenitor of the present Benin dynasty. Exactly when Ọyọ was founded is not known, but various dates, from the tenth to the fourteenth century, have been suggested.[18]

Ọyọ appears to have had certain initial advantages, and also to have been exposed early to certain adversities. Both these conditions eventually aided its growth. First it was situated in the savannah region just south of the River Niger. It therefore seems to have benefited from the trans-Saharan trade, perhaps as early as the fourteenth century. It has been suggested that the Yoruba word for Muslims, *Imale*, embodies a reference to Mali, whence Muslim missionaries and traders could have come to Ọyọ. Almost certainly, Ọyọ benefited from the trans-Saharan trade during the period of the Songhai ascendancy. Precisely what Ọyọ sent north is not known, but could have included kolanut, (*obi abata* or *obi gidi*, *kola acuminata*, not the later *gbanja* or *goro*, *kola nitida*), *ori amọ* (shea butter), and oil palm products. In return, Ọyọ traders probably accepted horses and saddles, *kanun* (potash), *obuotoyọ* (rock salt) and perhaps goods manufactured in North Africa and the middle eastern countries. It was no doubt with the horses thus procured that Ọyọ eventually formed its cavalry force.

Exposure to outside influence also had its disadvantages, for Ọyọ did not escape external attacks from foreigners to the north. Sometime in the fifteenth century, the Nupe (Tapa) attacked Ọyọ and drove them out of their capital, Ọyọ Ile. The Alafin first took refuge in Kusu in the Bariba country and later came to Igboho, from where the reconquest of the old capital was organised. This early experience taught the Ọyọ a hard lesson. While the other Yoruba kingdoms within the forest could still regard themselves as 'relations' and deal gently with one another or report their quarrels to their 'father', the Ọọni at Ifẹ, or any of the 'brother' ọbas not directly involved in the quarrel, Ọyọ learnt that it had to rely on its strength

18 S. O. Biobaku, *Origin of the Yorubas* (Lugard Lectures), Lagos, 1956, p. 19; P. Morton-Williams, 'The Ọyọ Yoruba and the Atlantic slave trade, 1670–1830', *Journal of the Historical Society of Nigeria*, iii, 1, 1964.

to live with strangers who were, more often than not, implacably hostile. Before the final reconquest of Ọyọ Ile, therefore, the Ọyọ army was reorganised.[19] One Ọyọ tradition says that it was during this period of military reorganisation that Ikoyi, the town later renowned for producing the bravest of the Yoruba soldiers (Ẹṣọ), was founded,[20] though another tradition recorded in Johnson would seem to imply that the Ẹṣọ were in existence before the Nupe invasion. It may well have been that while the institution of Ẹṣọ was already in existence, the Nupe attack served as an impetus to create a whole settlement, which later grew into a sub-kingdom, where training in warfare became the main business of the inhabitants.

What happened between the time the Ọyọ reconquered their capital, flushing out the Nupe at the beginning of the sixteenth century, and the very end of that century is still obscure. There is little doubt however that Ọyọ was consolidating and expanding throughout the period. It may have been that during this period Ọyọ reconquered parts of the Nupe and Bariba countries. Certainly by 1591, when the Moroccans from across the Sahara conquered Songhai and brought that empire to an end, Ọyọ was in a position strong enough to benefit from the ruins. This increasing strength of Ọyọ also carried its power southwards towards the coast.

While Ọyọ was passing through its tribulations to greatness, the Europeans were beginning to appear on the West African scene. They reached Cape Verde in 1444. Between 1461 and 1471 the coastal regions of the Yoruba-Aja country had become known to them and Benin had been reached by 1483. For a long time the Portuguese remained unchallenged in exploiting the wealth of their new discoveries. From the early years of the sixteenth century, however, other European nationals joined them in the lucrative competition. First came the French in 1530, then the English in 1553, and finally the Dutch in 1595.

What gave impetus to these voyages of discovery was the desire to tap the riches of the orient and perhaps to earn greater economic strength than the Muslim rulers without passing through the Muslim world. Later each country in Europe also tried to ensure that its European rivals did not gain advantage over it. The initial activities of the Europeans consisted in looking for the natural products of the coasts of Africa—gum, ivory, gold and pepper. But from the very beginning of these voyages, seamen had, quite illegally, carried away peaceful and unsuspecting Africans into slavery. These were sometimes captured violently, occasionally resulting in the burning of villages. Gradually it was discovered that trade in Africans themselves was more lucrative than in African products. The pious appeal of the Catholic Church to save the souls of the Africans for Christianity, the

19 S. Johnson, *op. cit.*, pp. 161–7; R. S. Smith, 'The Alafin in exile', *Journal of African History*, vi, 1, 1965, pp. 57–77.

20 Personal communication with S. O. Babayẹmi, Research Fellow in the Institute of African Studies, University of Ibadan, who is working on Ọyọ.

discovery of the Americas and the consequent need for a labour force all combined with the economic motive to make slaves the principal African export by the end of the sixteenth century.

Exactly how European exploration and trade affected the Yoruba kingdom of Ọyọ during this early period is not yet known, but from the available evidence, European influence would appear to have been minimal.

The capital of Ọyọ, Ọyọ Ile, (known to northern neighbours as Katunga) was very far from the coast, being more than 200 miles by the shortest route. That need not have prevented contact, since Ọyọ's influence, if not its actual control, was undoubtedly being felt on the coast by the opening years of the seventeenth century. What probably repelled Ọyọ rulers was the experience of their first contact with the Europeans. An Ọyọ tradition, recorded in Johnson, relates how a European king got in touch with Ọbalokun, the reigning Alafin, and professed friendship with him. According to Yoruba custom, Ọbalokun then sent messengers (said to have numbered 800) to greet this friend. Unfortunately these messengers never came back,[21] and their memory continued to serve as a warning to subsequent Ọyọ rulers to beware of the professed friendship of strange peoples.

It would appear, therefore, that the rulers of Ọyọ did not encourage any official dealings with the Europeans on the coast. For, until the nineteenth century, guns and ammunition, which were the most useful European import for empire building, were conspicuously absent in Ọyọ military equipment. A few individual Ọyọ traders who went to the coast may have had commercial dealings with Europeans and may have brought back exotic European manufactures, but their activities did not seem to have counted much in the economy of the Ọyọ people. Nor did Ọyọ appear to be trading in slaves in any appreciable quantity with the Europeans during this period.[22] No doubt war captives were being made to work for their masters, a system that was later called domestic slavery, but such captives were only technically 'slaves' for they continued to possess the same rights as most citizens of the kingdom. They could marry their masters' daughters or become heirs to their masters' wealth.

EUROPEANS AND THE RISE OF DAHOMEY

The Aja, situated very near the coast, felt the impact of European intrusion much more than the Ọyọ. Allada, their 'father' kingdom, was founded around 1575. Their political institutions were therefore still unsettled when the Dutch arrived twenty years later, and could be easily influenced by any

21 Johnson, *op. cit.*, p. 168.
22 Morton-Williams, *op. cit.*, concludes that the foundation of Ẹgbado towns in the seventeenth century meant that the Ọyọ were trading in slaves from the seventeenth century. Nothing in his evidence supports this conclusion and circumstantial evidence would suggest the opposite conclusion. In any case, towns could be founded for defence and protection.

determined group of people, an opportunity which the Europeans did not miss.

During the first decade of the seventeenth century, the Dutch placed their agents in Assim, the capital of the Allada kingdom.[23] In 1640 the French Capuchin missionaries came in a bid to Christianise the Aja, but their mission, apart from giving us the earliest recorded form of the Aja language (Egun), was a failure.[24] Then in 1664 the French turned their attention to the Aja country. A French mission sent to the king of Allada in 1669 led to one sent by the king of Allada to France in 1670.[25] Both missions failed. The French mission wanted such favourable terms of trade as the Allada authorities could not grant. The leader of the Allada delegation to Paris refused to sign the treaty presented to him, in spite of a very flattering reception, on the grounds that it was against the interests of his country.

The failure of these French missions to establish an accord between France and Allada led to the establishment of a French trading station in Whydah in 1671. This greatly affected Aja politics, for hitherto Allada had been the only centre of European trade in Aja. With the French establishment at Whydah, economic rivalry between Allada and Whydah, hitherto suppressed, came into the open. More than that, the way was now open for any European trader to establish posts anywhere, thus causing further political complications. Between 1670 and 1700 other European nations, big and small, established trading posts, some for a very short time, in various places in the Aja country.[26] With these establishments the traditional sentiment of family relationship, which had existed among the Aja kingdoms and which had made for stability, started to be questioned. Economic rivalry took the place of traditional consultations between kingdoms. And within each kingdom, the chiefs, anxious to amass wealth, gradually weakened the traditional organisation which bound the state together.[27]

The earliest manifestation of this gradual persistent weakening of the traditional ties led to the foundation of Dahomey in about 1625. The oral traditions in connection with the foundation of Dahomey are well known. Two brothers were vying for the vacant stool of Allada. The younger won and was installed; the elder was apparently exiled. Later, the elder returned, seized the throne and forced the younger to migrate northwards.[28] The

23 Personal communication with Dr K. Daku, University of Ghana.
24 Labouret and Rivet, *op. cit*. This book reproduces in the appendix the Catechism of the Roman Catholic faith called *Doctrina Christiana*, written in both Portuguese and Egun.
25 T. Astley, *A New and General Collection of Voyages and Travels* (London, 1745–7), iii, pp. 65–79; J. Barbot, *A Description of Coasts of North and South Guinea*, London, 1732, pp. 325–50.
26 For example the Dutch established a factory in Whydah in 1682, the English in 1683 and the Brandenburgers in 1684 (see I. A. Akinjogbin, *Dahomey and Its Neighbours, 1708–1818*, Cambridge, 1967, p. 32).
27 Akinjogbin, *op. cit.*, pp. 33–7.
28 Le Herissé, *op. cit.*, p. 279; Akindélé and Aguessy, *op. cit.*, p. 23.

coming back of the elder brother, which in oral tradition is wrapped in mysterious circumstances, may indeed have happened with Dutch intervention and support.

The group that migrated with the expelled king went to the Abomey plateau and formed the nucleus of the new kingdom later to be called Dahomey. Dahomey was more than yet another African kingdom. Among the Yoruba–Aja peoples, its leaders were the first to realise that the traditional organisation based on real or formalised family ties was unlikely to meet the new economic challenge being posed by the Europeans. They therefore decided on a strong central monarchy. Instead of looking at their kingdom as a larger version of the family, they likened the state to a perforated pot, and the king to water which must be made to remain in the pot. Such a difficult job was possible if every citizen would ensure, by stopping each hole with a finger, that the water did not flow out. This meant that a direct relationship was established between the king and the individual subject instead of merely between him and the lineage. Citizenship was based on the individual's willingness to belong to the state and serve the king; advancement in the king's service depended on merit and not on lineage connections.

Although the early leaders of Dahomey settled on a piece of land given to them by the local owners, they did not remain willing for long to base their title on a gift. They appear to have believed that only such things as they could claim by force and guard successfully were theirs. The story is told that they started to pick quarrels with one local leader after another. Da, the chief who had given them land, complained that they were always asking for more land and asked whether they intended to build on his belly. The followers of Dogbagrigenu took offence at this, declared war on Da, killed him and laid the foundation of their big house on his carcass. From this episode is derived the name Dahomey (in Da's belly).[29] Furthermore, they had established that might was right, a doctrine hitherto foreign to accepted political concepts in the Yoruba–Aja area.

Altogether, therefore, the foundation of Dahomey was a quiet revolution, the result of which was bound to produce great changes in the Aja country. Dahomey expanded gradually. Dogbagrigenu, the leader of the migrants, was not made king, for his followers were, by and large, tenants on other people's land and there was no territory over which he could rule. By 1650, when Aho, Dogbagrigenu's son, succeeded his father, there was a sizeable territory which the Dahomeans could call their own. He was therefore crowned king under the cognomen Wegbaja. He reigned until about 1680 by which time he had added eighteen more towns and villages to the territory left by his father. By that date Dahomey had become the most powerful kingdom north of Allada and Whydah, and it was giving early warnings of its future actions. In 1670–71 and again in 1687–8, the

29 Le Herissé, *op. cit.*, p. 279.

Dahomeans barred the way to the Allada raiders who were going into the interior to procure slaves. On both occasions, the Allada raiders had to return home without slaves until they negotiated with Dahomey.[30]

ỌYỌ INVADES AJALAND

Until about the 1680s the existence of the Dahomean revolutionary experiment behind Ọyọ's backyard had not drawn any particular attention from Ọyọ. This was not only because Dahomey was still small and relatively weak, but because Ọyọ itself was too preoccupied, sometimes with consolidation and expansion and sometimes also with its own internal squabbles, to take much notice of faraway events. Alafin Abipa moved from Ọyọ Igboho to Ọyọ Ile in the last years of the sixteenth century and probably died in the early years of the seventeenth. The reorganised Ọyọ army and the newly introduced cavalry, with the renewed confidence which resulted from the reoccupation of old Ọyọ, started a period of expansion. The Nupe, who had driven the Ọyọ away from their homes, must have been convincingly conquered during the reign of Ajiboyede just as the Baribas had been convincingly defeated in the previous reign. Abipa who brought the Ọyọ back home was therefore able to consolidate and plan expansion.[31]

Ọbalokun, who succeeded Abipa, would seem to have initiated an imperial policy whereby a large part of the Yoruba country came under Ọyọ. From the scanty oral traditions recorded by Johnson,[32] it would seem that Ọyọ cavalry quickly swept southwards and became masters of the country down to the Ẹgbado town of Ijanna. They would also have swept south-eastwards to the boundaries of the Igbomina and Ijẹṣa kingdoms. An unsuccessful attempt was made on the Ijẹṣa kingdom and the utter defeat of the Ọyọ horsemen must have indicated the limit of the effectiveness of cavalry warfare in that direction.

When therefore Ajagbo[33] succeeded to the throne, he learnt from the military experiences of the previous reign. According to extant oral traditions, he concentrated on conquest towards the coastal regions where the savannah forest made cavalry warfare possible. He created a new military title, the *arẹ-ọna-kakanfo* (usually shortened to *arẹ* or *kakanfo*) as a foretaste of the seriousness with which expansionist wars would be undertaken. He is said to have been in the habit of sending out four expeditions at once under four commanders: the Baṣọrun, the Agbakin, the Kakanfo and the Aṣipa. This was calculated to promote healthy rivalry between them. In that way he extended his predecessor's conquest in the Egbado region by capturing Wẹmẹ and some Ẹgba towns including Ikereku-Iwere. The conquest of Wẹmẹ meant in practice that Ọyọ controlled the coastal regions of what

30 Delisle, 'Extrait du Registre', 26 August 1728 (A.N. C.6/25).
31 Johnson, *op. cit.*, pp. 162–7.
32 *Ibid.*, p. 168; Morton-Williams, *op. cit.*
33 Johnson, *op. cit.*, pp. 168–9.

later became Porto Novo and was therefore a next-door neighbour of the kingdom of Allada. North of Wẹmẹ the power of Ọyọ by this time probably extended to the River Ọpara, in which case Ọyọ shared a common boundary with the territories which were increasingly coming under the sway of Dahomey.

The Rev. Samuel Johnson, the only man on whom we rely for the oral traditions of this period, treats the next five reigns, which probably spans the rest of the seventeenth century, more from the point of view of morals than from their total political contribution to the growth of the empire.[34] There is therefore need to do more research into the Oriki (praise names) of the kings—Ọdarawu, Kanran, Jayin, Ayibi and Ọsinyago. Johnson says Ọdarawu had a short reign because he was bad tempered, that Kanran was an 'unmitigated tyrant', that Jayin was 'effeminate and dissolute', that Ayibi was 'unworthy of the honour and respect done him', and that Ọsinyago 'was equally worthless'. All these condemnations were based on little moral stories, usually minor episodes in the last years of the kings, and the preceding years are dismissed with hardly any comment.

Yet it is clear, from the few remarks tucked in amidst these stories of decadence, that the expansion of the Ọyọ empire continued during the greater part of the seventeenth century covered by these five reigns. Ọdarawu certainly fought some wars, for it was after one such war against a town called Ojo Segi that his soldiers revolted. Their reason for revolting is said to have been that they thought the king's excuse for ordering the expedition was a petty vendetta. Ọyọ's influence was asserted in the coastal regions during the reign of Jayin, when a boundary dispute between the Asẹyin Odo, who may then have been under Ọyọ, and the Olowu was settled. Whether the man sent to settle it later became *Awujalẹ* as the Ọyọ tradition relates or whether the title *Awujalẹ* has a more ancient origin is a question still awaiting research. The interregnum and the regency that preceded the reign of Ayibi probably saw the Ọyọ invasion of Allada in 1698.[35] This invasion is well authenticated in the contemporary documents but has not been mentioned in any Ọyọ court tradition. The explanation may therefore be that at the time of the successful invasion, Ọyọ indeed had no king.

Why was Ọyọ expanding southwards and westwards during the seventeenth century? A simple answer is that the presence of the Europeans on the coast was a powerful factor; that the Ọyọ were anxious to enter into commercial contact with the Europeans, and particularly to trade in slaves.[36] Such an answer does not take into consideration all the evidence at our disposal, scanty though it is. While Ọyọ would have derived certain

34 *Ibid.*, pp. 169–70.
35 W. Bosman, *A New and Accurate Description of the Coast of Guinea*, London, 1705, p. 397.
36 This is the view of P. Morton-Williams, *op. cit.*

economic advantages from its conquests, it does not appear to have benefited much from the slave trade with the Europeans in the seventeenth century. Ọbalokun's experience referred to above made all the other succeeding Alafins wary. The fact that Allada and Whydah were finally chosen as seats of their trade by the Europeans rather than any of the coastal towns controlled by Ọyọ is an indication that Ọyọ was not making much of the European presence. For Ọyọ at that date the coast was really a backwater.

Indeed, Ọyọ's expansion towards the coast can be placed firmly in context when it is remembered that attempts at expansion were made south-eastwards as well, if one may judge from the scanty surviving traditions. Conquest towards the coast achieved spectacular results and has therefore been remembered much more easily. But Johnson records that Ọbalokun sent an ill-fated expedition to Ijẹṣa. He also records that Ojigi sent an expedition which traced what was probably regarded as the boundary of Ọyọ authority.[37] An *oriki* of Yau Yamba, the Basorun in Ojigi's reign, relates that he died in a ditch while he was leading an expedition towards Ọffa. Ọyọ expansion during the seventeenth and eighteenth centuries was therefore both south-eastwards and south-westwards. The expansion to the west and south achieved notable results because the chances of using cavalry in those areas were most favourable. The savannah which stretched down to the coast in Egbado and Egun countries made it easy for horses to be used for warfare. The areas lying south and south-eastwards, being thickly forested, did not suit cavalry warfare and therefore remained impenetrable to Ọyọ soldiers.

Whatever may have been the reasons for the expansion of the Ọyọ empire, the area which they occupied brought them into physical contact with the Aja of Allada and Dahomey. And the political implications were soon plain to the Aja. At first, it would appear that the rulers of Aja did not see the Ọyọ as constituting any threat to themselves. Indeed, because of the close cultural affinities between the Aja and the Yoruba, the Aja people, particularly those of the Allada kingdom, saw the Ọyọ authorities as a party with whom they could lodge complaints against their own rulers.

Soon, however, these sentimental connections gave way to the realities of power, and clashes occurred. Details of these are not clear. But from Dahomean oral traditions, it would appear that between 1680 and 1682, both Allada and Dahomey felt the weight of Ọyọ.[38] Ọyọ's interests in the Aja area had increased as Ọyọ traders and citizens engaged in various occupations came into greater contact with the Aja. The interests of these Ọyọ citizens were probably adversely affected by the frequent wars waged between Dahomey and Allada. This probably aroused the Ọyọ authorities to protect their citizens. In any case, Ọyọ attacked both Dahomey and Allada between 1680 and 1682. It is not clear whether the two kingdoms

37 Johnson, *op. cit.*, pp. 168 and 174.
38 Barbot, *op. cit.*, pp. 351–2.

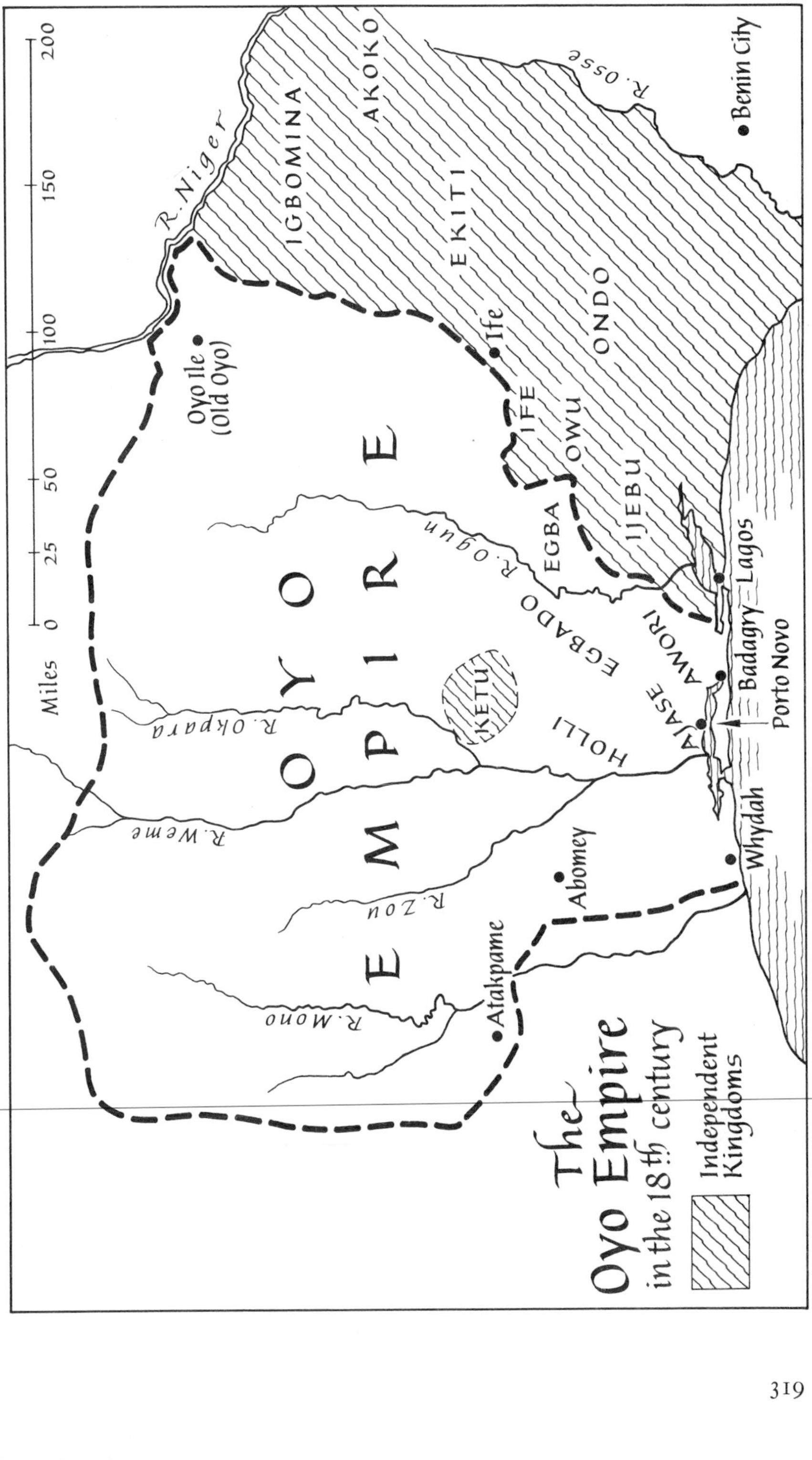
The Oyo Empire in the 18th century
Independent Kingdoms
Miles
0
25
50
100
150
200
R. Niger
IGBOMINA
AKOKO
EKITI
R. Osse
Benin City
Ife
ONDO
IFE
OWU
IJEBU
EGBA
Lagos
Badagry
Porto Novo
AWORI
AJASE
EGBADO
R. Ogun
OYO EMPIRE
Oyo Ile
(Old Oyo)
KETU
HOLLI
R. Okpara
R. Weme
Whydah
Abomey
R. Zou
Atakpame
R. Mono

9:4

were attacked more than once. What seems clear from Dahomean oral traditions, and from the written evidence that we have, is that as a result of the invasion from Ọyọ, the nascent Dahomey kingdom was almost destroyed, and over half of the old kingdom of Allada was overrun. Dahomey was rebuilt,[39] thanks to the thorough foundations laid by Wegbaja and to the exceptional abilities of Akaba, the reigning king of Dahomey. Allada would also appear to have sued for peaceful relations even if in bad grace. For over forty years after this, Dahomey took care not to offend Ọyọ. In Allada the mere mention of the name of Ọyọ created panic.

Having convincingly shown the Aja kingdom their power the Ọyọ rulers appear to have withdrawn their forces without participating in the internal affairs of Allada and Dahomey. Unlike its practice elsewhere, Ọyọ did not seem to have sent *ajẹlẹ* (intendants) to watch its interests in Allada or Dahomey. This exceptional treatment might suggest either that Ọyọ really had no expansionist ambition in that direction but was forced to fight in order to warn the kingdoms not to offend it, or that the victories were yet too insecure for Ọyọ to contemplate annexation. Whatever the reasons, Allada was soon to give grounds for another Ọyọ invasion. In order to understand the causes of this invasion of Allada, it will be necessary to survey briefly the internal political developments of the Aja since the foundation of Dahomey.

THE SLAVE TRADE WEAKENS THE COASTAL STATES

After 1625 the king of Allada had wanted, for security reasons, to concentrate European activities in Allada kingdom alone. Such a concentration would undoubtedly have been economically advantageous for Allada. But precisely also for economic reasons other Aja kingdoms, entirely discounting the security risks, wanted a share of the European trade.[40]

This share they started to get from 1671 onwards, when the French established a trading post at Whydah, as has already been noted. For the rest of the seventeenth century this rivalry for a share of the European trade led to disagreements between Allada and the other Aja kingdoms such as Whydah, Great Popo and others, and greatly weakened the common bond between them. By the 1680s civil wars had broken out among them, with each inviting mercenaries, including Europeans, to help put the other down,[41] thus introducing European participation into internal Aja politics.[42] The principal European traders took active part in installing kings who they judged would favour their activities, irrespective of whether such kings were acceptable to their subjects, or were the right candidates according to Aja traditions. The result was constant unrest within each Aja kingdom and

39 E. Dunglas, 'Contribution à l'histoire du Moyan Dahomey', *Études Dahoméennes*, xix, 1957, p. 96.
40 Akinjogbin, *op. cit.*, pp. 26–7.
41 *Ibid.*, p. 33.
42 Bosman, *op. cit.*, pp. 355–6; Barbot, *op. cit.*, p. 323.

constant antagonism between one Aja kingdom and another.

It was during this period of constant unrest and insecurity that the citizens of the Allada kingdom in 1698 sent messages to Ọyọ complaining about the bad government then obtaining in their kingdom. As has been noted, this message would appear to have reached Ọyọ during the interregnum that preceded the reign of Ayibi, an interregnum that may have been caused by Ayibi's minority. The baṣọrun, (probably Oluaja or Yabi) in whose hands the affairs of the government were entrusted, sent messengers to the reigning king of Allada advising that he should put his kingdom in order. The king of Allada, instead of heeding the advice, killed the Ọyọ messengers. This behaviour was against the accepted code of behaviour in the Yoruba-Aja kingdoms, as state messengers (called *ikọ* in Yoruba) were immune from attack or any form of molestation even during wars. The Allada authorities may have been led to this defiant breach of the traditions by the knowledge that Ọyọ lacked a king and was therefore not likely to retaliate. If that was so, they miscalculated. The baṣọrun and the regency council promptly mounted a punitive expedition against Allada with orders to conquer the country and bring the king alive or dead to Ọyọ. Allada was therefore again invaded and overrun, the second time within twenty years. However the king could not be captured as he had escaped, and for this the Ọyọ commander was said to have been disgraced.[43]

It is not clear how the issue was finally settled. Ọyọ traditions as recorded by Johnson do not deal with the episode and Allada traditions have disappeared with the destruction of the kingdom in 1724. It would appear from subsequent events that Ọyọ virtually incorporated Allada into the Ọyọ empire and that Allada never fully recovered from the effects of these two invasions.

This weakness of Allada altered the balance of power among the Aja kingdoms. Whydah, which appears never to have been affected at all by these Ọyọ invasions, gained advantages from the weak position of its principal economic rival. By 1701, when the French company, after a break, re-established there,[44] Whydah had become the most important slaving port in the whole of West Africa. European slave traders from Britain, Portugal, Holland and Brazil as well as France resorted there. In 1703 Whydah became an international port when all the European traders signed a treaty with the king that the port should be immune from attack by European ships and that its neutrality should be respected whenever there was war in Europe.[45]

In order not to lose everything, economically and politically, the rulers of Allada decided to come to an agreement with Whydah. Accordingly in 1705 Allada and Whydah agreed to settle their economic differences and to

43 Bosman, *op. cit.*, p. 397.
44 Capt. Paul Sorrell to R.A.C., Antega, 17 January 1702 (P.R.O. T. 70/13).
45 P. Labat, *Voyage du Chevalier des Marchais*, Paris, 1735, ii, p. 109.

accept the right of each to trade with Europeans. Neither was to impede the trade of the other. Moreover the weakening political links were repaired. Whydah, which had continuously disregarded these links in the last thirty years because of its European supporters, agreed to repair some of the damage done. Its new king, Aisan, who had avoided doing so, performed the traditional installation ceremonies, and paid to, as well as received from, Allada certain traditional dues.[46] The stage therefore seemed set for political regeneration in Aja.

Unfortunately this was not to be. In 1708, three years after this agreement, Aisan died, leaving behind him a twelve-year-old son. The succession struggle that followed brought to the surface again all the old internal antagonisms within Whydah and also resuscitated the strained relationships with Allada. The Europeans, who knew that they stood to gain from divisions among the Aja, backed one faction or the other and succeeded in prolonging chaos and the resultant power vacuum in Whydah.

The war of 1712 between Whydah and Allada, precipitated by Dutch traders, shows how inflammable was the situation in Aja country. A Dutch ship left Whydah port and attacked a Portuguese ship trading in Allada port. The latter immediately declared war on Whydah and closed all the trade routes used by Whydah traders to procure slaves from the interior. It is not necessary to go into the details of this internecine war. It is sufficient to say that it lasted actively until 1717 and did not finally end until 1722.[47] The bitterness it aroused made any cooperation between the two kingdoms impossible and it was finally responsible for their inability jointly to meet the common foe which eventually destroyed them both.

While Allada and Whydah were destroying each other militarily and economically, each was also destroying itself from within. In 1713 Huffon, the minority king of Whydah installed in 1708, fed up with squabbles of his principal men, ousted them from their positions of influence and nominated young men to advise him. These inexperienced young men became easily inflated with their own importance. They were corrupt and tyrannical and they soon had everybody complaining against them. In the meantime the elderly chiefs who had been jettisoned remained unhappy and some of them were planning rebellion. Every move that Huffon made to reassert the position of the monarchy or raise his own economic fortune offended one faction or the other and the danger of civil war was never far away.[48]

Inside Allada during the period the position is far less clear. But from scraps of information available it seems not too different from that of Whydah. The war against Whydah and the consequent closure of roads had caused great economic hardship to the chiefs and principal men at Allada. The inconclusiveness of the war made it impossible for any of them to

46 Astley, *op. cit.*, iii, pp. 41–3.
47 For a detailed discussion of these events, see Akinjogbin, *op. cit.*, pp. 46–50.
48 Akinjogbin, *op. cit.*, pp. 50–3.

regain whatever they may have invested in it, since each chief equipped his own army for the service of the king.

To add to the confusion, the European traders continued to vie among themselves for the greatest share of the slave trade, and to play one chief against another. They continually threatened to move their trade from one port to another in order to secure more favourable terms of trade than their rivals. If that failed they would threaten to prevent ships from calling. And it was not uncommon for them to resort to open fighting among themselves, into which they brought their African supporters, thus intensifying civil strife.[49]

This was the picture of the politics of the two leading coastal Aja kingdoms during the first two decades of the eighteenth century—wars and internal disorders constantly fanned by European economic interests.

THE ASCENDANCY OF DAHOMEY

During the same period Dahomey, which was slightly farther inland, presented a very different picture. It was growing in strength, size and internal cohesion. Akaba recovered from the almost total destruction of the kingdom in the 1680s and by the time of his death in 1708 he had managed to extend it.[50] Indeed by 1687 Dahomey had sufficiently recovered to be able again to bar the way to Allada raiders who were going inland to raid for slaves.[51] When Akaba died in 1708 Dahomey had become a sizeable kingdom containing about forty towns and villages.[52]

Two significant developments are discernible in Dahomey at the beginning of the eighteenth century. The first is the absolute central control, efficiently exercised by its kings. A kind of nationalism (with the king personifying the state) uncommon in other Yoruba or Aja kingdoms had emerged. By 1708 it had been accepted by every Dahomean citizen that his life must be devoted to the service of his king, and that to die in that service was his greatest reward.[53] Chieftaincy titles were controlled completely by the king, who could bestow them on any person who, in his opinion, deserved the honour. Any efficient chief could be promoted and an inefficient one demoted. Chiefs suspected of the least act of disloyalty were sentenced to death. The only man in the state whom the king was forbidden to execute was the *migan*, but even he could be exiled.[54] This strong central direction was lacking in the traditional system of government still being operated by the coastal Aja kingdoms.

The second development was that Dahomey's most significant expansion was mainly towards the south and south-east. Regions to the north and west

49 *Ibid.*, pp. 54–7.
50 Delisle, 'Extrait du Registre', 26 August 1728 (AN. C. 6/25).
51 P. Roussier, *L'Établissement d'Issigny, 1687–1702,* Paris, 1953, pp. 14–15.
52 Delisle, *op. cit.*
53 A. Dalzel, *History of Dahomey*, London, 1793, p. 69.
54 Akinjogbin, *op. cit.*, p. 25.

probably did not completely escape this expansion, but oral traditions in Dahomey do not record it. Expanding towards the coast meant eventually sharing a common boundary with the coastal kingdoms, thus raising possibilities of eventual clash between Dahomey and the rest.

This eventuality was probably foreseen by Agaja, the man who ascended the throne of Dahomey in 1708. Agaja was a younger brother of Akaba and therefore, strictly speaking, not eligible to become king if any of the sons of Akaba had been found suitable. But none of Akaba's sons was suitable. Neither Ahangbe, who was Akaba's twin sister, nor any of her sons could constitutionally ascend the throne in a patrilineal society. Agaja's accession turned out to be a blessing for the growth of Dahomey.

As soon as he ascended the throne, he established two new institutions to increase the effectiveness of the kingdom. He started a military training scheme for young boys under which each adult soldier was allowed at state expense to take with him to war a certain number of boys of about twelve years of age.[55] This system, though new in Dahomey, was probably not new in the Yoruba-Aja area for the Ọyọ may already have been using similar methods. In the nineteenth century, when the system was documented among the Ibadans, the cadets were called *baba ni ng joko* (*lit.* father says I should sit down, i.e. on the battle front). They were to sit and watch their appointed master fighting and they were not to leave the field until told to do so. In this way these boys grew up to become intrepid soldiers.

The second institution which Agaja established and which was probably unique was the *agbadjigbeto*.[56] These were a body of spies who were sent to the kingdoms around to find out details of their military strength and defences. If the king decided to attack such a place, the *agbadjigbeto* must produce and disseminate reasons why it must be attacked. In this way Agaja was kept constantly informed of the strength and weakness of the kingdoms around him and he was able to plan his campaigns accordingly.

Between 1708 and 1727 these two institutions were used to the utmost advantage by Agaja. The *agbadjigbeto* kept him informed of all the chaos in the coastal Aja kingdoms of Allada and Whydah, while his scheme for military training was producing seasoned soldiers. Around 1717 Agaja was ready to show his hand on the coast.[57] The situation was tailored to his designs. Allada and Whydah had been fighting for five years. Inside Whydah the chiefs were dissatisfied with the king's action and everybody was disgusted at the young counsellors around the king. The European traders were also looking for 'an extraordinary means' to bring Huffon to reason.[58] In that situation Agaja consulted the king of Allada as to the

55 W. Snelgrave, *A New Account of Some Parts of Guinea and the Slave Trade*, London, 1734, p. 78.
56 Le Herissé, *op. cit.*, pp. 64–5; Hazoumé, *op. cit.*, pp. 19–20.
57 'Conseil de Marine', 22 November 1717 (AN. C. 6/25).
58 W. Baillie to Governor, Cape Coast Castle, 10 May 1720 (P.R.O. T. 70/54).

possibility of joint action against Whydah. Allada agreed, but as that was at the time of its annual festival it could not go to war. Dahomey, lacking any accusations against Whydah, could not attack by itself and the whole project was dropped.

Agaja did not forget. Seven years after, in 1724, Allada played into his hands. Soso, the new king of Allada, died and a dispute ensued as to which of two brothers would succeed him. One of them won the contest and was put on the throne. The loser, unwilling to abide by the verdict, invited Agaja to aid him wrest the throne from his opponent. Agaja came down with his army and, instead of restoring his ally on the throne, occupied Allada and drove both the contenders out.[59] By this unexpected action, Agaja occupied the ancient capital of the Aja by force and destroyed the basis of the traditional ties that had bound the people together. The extraordinary nature of Agaja's behaviour was clearly recognised by his contemporaries in all the countries around,[60] though it was lost on subsequent generations.

The conquest of Allada by the king of Dahomey in 1724 raised a number of grave questions. On what basis would the Aja be organised henceforth? And would the surrounding peoples, the Popo, the Accra, and notably the Ọyọ, acquiesce in the new arrangements? The answers to these questions came all at once, but it will be convenient to treat them separately.

First, the basis of Aja reorganisation. Allada having been destroyed and occupied by force, it would seem obvious that all the other Aja kingdoms had to maintain their independence by force. But Huffon, the reigning king of Whydah, does not seem to have realised this. Strangely enough his faith in the traditional relationships appears to have been unshaken and he was confident that Agaja would not invade his own kingdom. In any case, he was confident of his military power to repel Agaja's army if he should attempt to invade.[61] Even when Gome, the northern province of Whydah adjacent to the new territory of Agaja, declared allegiance to Agaja,[62] Huffon still thought that very soon these erring 'sons' and 'brothers' would come back to beg for pardon.

His illusions were shattered in 1727. On a pretext that Huffon had not agreed that Agaja's agents should pass through Whydah to buy European goods, and that Huffon had threatened to seize Agaja and make him undertake the most menial jobs, Agaja invaded Whydah early in 1727. He met with very little resistance and within five days he was master of the whole kingdom. Huffon, grown fat with laziness, nevertheless managed to escape to the swamps of the Popo islands and there set up a government in exile[63] with the remnants of the Whydah people. Between 1727 and 1734, when

59 Akinjogbin, *op. cit.*, pp. 64–6.

60 The Little Popo and the Akwamu refused to recognise Agaja's right to the conquered lands. 'Conseil de Marine', 13 August 1728 (AN. C. 6/25). See below p. 326.

61 Snelgrave, *op. cit.*, pp. 6–9; Dalzel, *op. cit.*, p. 17.

62 Snelgrave, *op. cit.*, p. 9; Dunglas, *op. cit.*, p. 152.

63 Akinjogbin, *op. cit.*, pp. 70–1.

Huffon died, the people of Whydah made a number of attempts by force and by negotiation to regain their old kingdom. They were even ready to become Agaja's subjects if he would allow them to settle in their old homes.[64] But all attempts failed and Agaja became the effective ruler of the depopulated Whydah kingdom as he had been of the Allada kingdom since 1724. In the Aja section of the Yoruba-Aja country, might triumphed as the basis of right.

The incorporation of Allada and Whydah into the enlarged kingdom of Dahomey marked the end of the chaos in the old Aja kingdoms. The sagging faith in the traditional order, the civil wars, the inter-kingdom rivalries, all were ended by Dahomey's strong arm.

The problem that remained was how the other surrounding kingdoms would take Dahomey's victory. From the first conquest of Allada in 1724 it was clear that none of the countries around liked it. Little Popo and Akwamu refused to recognise the claim of Agaja to rule his conquered territory.[65] But, fret as they might, they were not strong enough, either singly or combined, to force him out.

ỌYỌ CONQUERS DAHOMEY

The only power which was in a position to do something about these developments in the Aja area was Ọyọ. It will be remembered that Allada, which Dahomey destroyed in 1724, had come under Ọyọ by the beginning of the eighteenth century. Therefore Ọyọ was unlikely to remain quiet at the loss. It would appear that soon after the 1724 conquest the Ọyọ authorities sent messengers to Agaja to find out what was happening,[66] and he was unable to reassure them. In 1726, therefore, the first Ọyọ invasion of Dahomey for forty years occurred. The traditional account, entirely from the Dahomean side, relates that Dahomey easily defeated the invading Ọyọ army. In the war, it was alleged, Dahomey was aided by the arms newly acquired from the sack of Allada and by a large supply of French wine with which the Ọyọ were baited and made drunk. Recent researches however have revealed that this story was originally formulated to boost the morale of the Dahomean army after what must have been the most crushing defeat they had suffered in forty years.[67]

According to documentary evidence, Agaja hoped to have an even chance against the invading Ọyọ army, and therefore made a stand. He reckoned that the Ọyọ had no firearms and hoped to match his guns with the Ọyọ cavalry. He forgot that horses were much swifter than the infantry which had been the usual opponents of the Dahomean army, and that once the initial discharges were fired reloading would take time, during which

64 For these attempts see *ibid.*, pp. 95–7.
65 'Conseil de Marine', 13 August 1728 (AN. C. 6/25).
66 Snelgrave, *op. cit.*, p. 56.
67 Director of Portuguese Fort, Whydah, to Viceroy of Brazil, 22 May 1726 (APB. OR. 21 doc. 61).

the cavalry could move much more swiftly than foot soldiers.

The result of the Dahomean miscalculation was that the battle with Ọyọ was short and sharp. A great number of Dahomean soldiers fell and the rest quickly dispersed. The king of Dahomey escaped to the forest areas of the river Mono where he was beyond the reach of Ọyọ horses. Having tasted the military might of Ọyọ, Agaja quickly submitted. The general opinion among the Europeans then resident at Whydah was that Agaja was militarily finished and would no longer be able to cause upheaval and annex other people's territories.[68] The Ọyọ also must have felt that with that experience Agaja would behave himself in future. Agaja's subsequent action showed that he regarded his defeat as only a minor setback and that, with proper planning, he could still carry through his programme of annexation of the Aja kingdoms. As soon as he had invaded Whydah in 1727 he immediately opened negotiations with Ọyọ[69] in the hope that by prolonging the negotiations into the rainy season, the Ọyọ cavalry would be unable to attack immediately and he would thus have a breathing space of one whole year in which to plan. On the Ọyọ side, the successful invasion of Whydah by Agaja must have come as a surprise. They too needed the façade of a prolonged negotiation to organise a war. In May 1727, when both sides were satisfied that the rains had started, they broke off the talks.

Agaja immediately started to plan how to outwit the Ọyọ when next they invaded. First he thought he would take refuge in the European forts on the coast[70] and from there organise resistance. Then, when he found that the Europeans were not sufficiently friendly, he decided to evacuate and burn Abomey, his capital, flee to a forest hideout and distribute his subjects in small batches to various parts of his territory which he thought the Ọyọ horses could not reach. The Ọyọ at the same time seem to have been getting ready for stiff Dahomean resistance.

When the Ọyọ army came in February 1728 they met no opposition whatsoever. Indeed, everything was so effectively destroyed by the Dahomeans that the Ọyọ soldiers were deprived of shelter and food. In the circumstances they could not stay for long and as soon as the rains started they returned home. The Dahomeans immediately came back to their towns and started rebuilding.[71] There was no indication that they submitted or sued for peace.

If the Dahomeans thought they would thus wear out Ọyọ aggression, they were mistaken. For Ọyọ at this time had at the head of its affairs a set of capable men who would brook no disobedience. Ojigi, the Alafin,

68 *Ibid.*

69 J. Bazilio to Viceroy of Brazil, 17 July 1730 (APB. OR. 28., f. 129); Snelgrave, *op. cit.*, p. 59.

70 'Conseil de Marine', 11, 18 and 24 August 1728 (AN. C. 6/25); Delisle, *op. cit.*, 26 August 1728 (AN. C. 6/25).

71 Viceroy of Brazil to King of Portugal, 5 April 1728 (APB. OR. 24, f. 40); Dupetitval à la Compagnie des Indes, 4 October 1728 (AN. C. 6/25); Dalzel, *op. cit.*, pp. 52–3.

was a warrior; Yau Yamba, the Baṣọrun, was one of the most capable warriors ever produced in Ọyọ; Gbọnka Latoyọ was an intrepid fighter.[72] Dahomey's obstinacy only served to make them determined to occupy the small impudent kingdom. Between 1728 and 1730, therefore, the Ọyọ organised their line of supply more securely by forming an alliance with the Mahi so that in case Dahomey burned all its harvest fields, food could be supplied from the north.[73] Moreover, it would seem that Ọyọ was prepared to import whole Ọyọ families to colonise Dahomey after it had been conquered.

Rumours of an Ọyọ invasion of Dahomey were strong by January 1729,[74] but the Ọyọ did not actually reach Dahomey until about March. Agaja, as before, had buried his treasures, burned his capital and the crops and sent his subjects into areas where he thought the Ọyọs would not come. The Ọyọ had expected this. They therefore pursued the fleeing Dahomeans much further south than the Dahomeans had anticipated, causing many more deaths. Next, the Ọyọ stayed much longer than the Dahomeans had expected. That again told heavily on the food provisions which the Dahomeans had stored. And when the rains came and the Ọyọ had not yet returned to their country as was expected, more Dahomeans died in their inconvenient hideouts.[75]

Finally the Ọyọ left. But early in 1730 they came again.[76] The Ọyọ tactics were now apparently to wear down the Dahomean resistance. Agaja, a tested military leader, got the message and started to sue for peace with the help of Bazilio, the Director of the Portuguese fort at Whydah.[77] After a brief negotiation an agreement was finally signed between Ọyọ and Dahomey. The text of this important treaty has not yet been found, but its principal provisions can be clearly seen from subsequent events.

Dahomey accepted the suzerainty of Ọyọ and agreed to pay annual tribute. The capital was removed from Abomey to Allada, the ancient Aja capital. In return Agaja was allowed to keep the whole of Whydah and a substantial part of Allada. However, a part of Allada kingdom was carved out as the new kingdom of Ajase which later came to be called Porto Novo. To this kingdom all former Allada citizens who so wished were brought. The old Allada dynasty was presumably restored here. The boundary between Dahomey and Ajase (Porto Novo) kingdoms was marked by Lake Nokoue and the So and the Weme rivers. East of that

72 Johnson, *op. cit.*, p. 174.
73 Mallis de la Mine to Premenil, 8 January 1732 (ADN. C. 739).
74 Accounts and Journals, Cape Coast Castle, 30 June 1729 (PRO. T. 70/393); Viceroy of Brazil to King of Portugal, 28 July 1729 (APB. OR. 25 f. 158); Dalzel, *op. cit.*, pp. 52–3.
75 Viceroy of Brazil to King of Portugal, 28 July 1729 (APB. OR. 25 f. 158); Accounts and Journal, Cape Coast Castle, 30 June 1729 (T. 70/393).
76 'Copybook and Diaries from Whydah', 30 December 1729, 3, 9–17 January, 9 and 25 February 1730 (T. 70/1466).
77 Viceroy of Brazil to King of Portugal, 10 July 1730 (APB. OR. 27 f. 140); Dalzel, *op. cit.*, p. 59.

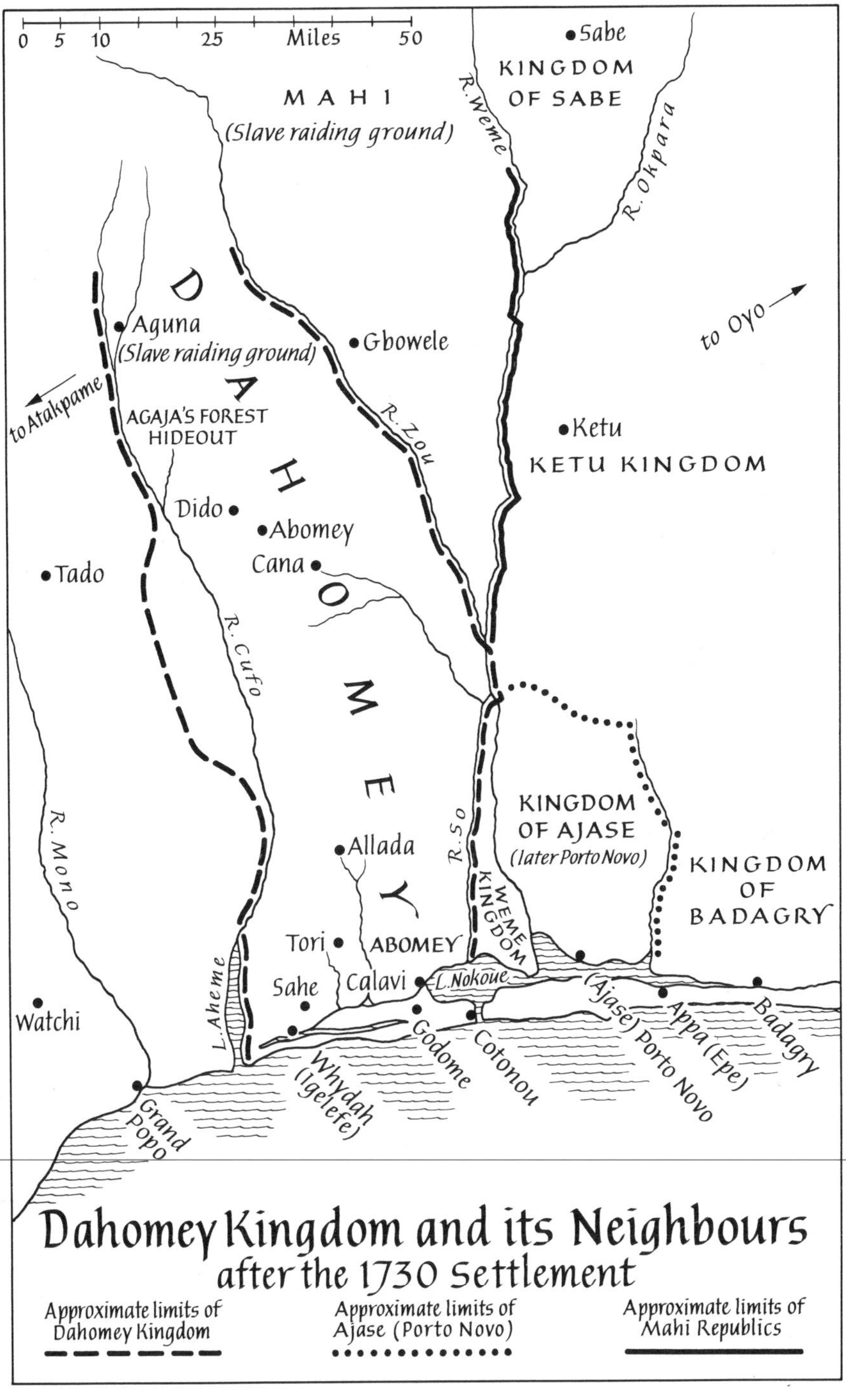

0 5 10 25 Miles 50
Sabe
KINGDOM OF SABE
MAHI
(Slave raiding ground)
R. Weme
R. Okpara
D A H O M E Y
Aguna
(Slave raiding ground)
Gbowele
to Oyo
to Atakpame
AGAJA'S FOREST HIDEOUT
R. Zou
Ketu
KETU KINGDOM
Dido
Abomey
Cana
Tado
R. Cufo
R. Mono
KINGDOM OF AJASE
(later Porto Novo)
R. So
Allada
WEME KINGDOM
KINGDOM OF BADAGRY
Tori
ABOMEY
L. Aheme
Sahe
Calavi
L. Nokoue
Watchi
Whydah (Igelefe)
Godome
Cotonou
(Ajase) Porto Novo
Appa (Epe)
Badagry
Grand Popo
Dahomey Kingdom and its Neighbours
after the 1730 Settlement
Approximate limits of Dahomey Kingdom
Approximate limits of Ajase (Porto Novo)
Approximate limits of Mahi Republics

9:5

line Ajase, Weme, and Badagri came directly under Ọyọ administration. West of it, Dahomey was a tributary kingdom but with a measure of initiative in its own internal government. A very significant aspect of this initiative was the fact that Dahomey was allowed to keep its army, which it was free to use northwards and westwards of its territory. Eastwards, in the direction of Ọyọ, Dahomey was forbidden to wage any wars, aggressive or defensive. As a proof that Dahomey intended to keep the terms of the treaty, a prince, who later reigned in Dahomey as Tegbesu, was sent to Ọyọ as hostage. The treaty was sealed by an exchange of princesses, with the king of Ọyọ sending his daughter to the king of Dahomey as a wife, and the latter reciprocating.[78]

AGREEMENT WITH EUROPEAN TRADERS

The treaty with Ọyọ in 1730 pacified what appeared to have been the most dangerous opponent of Dahomey's invasion of the coastal kingdoms. But there remained yet another one, the fraternity of European traders on the coast, equally dangerous in the long run, but quite within Dahomey's control in the short run. There is evidence to show that some of the European traders had encouraged Agaja's invasion of the coastal kingdoms in the hope that his occupation would provide a strong stable government in which trade could be advantageously carried on. Agaja played on their expectations and promised to be their friend if they did not oppose his invasion.[79] Once he had conquered the coastal kingdoms, however, the Europeans discovered that he did not quite play the rôle they had expected. Instead of slaves becoming plentiful for export, Agaja turned the slave trade into a royal monopoly and forbade his subjects, on pain of death, from trading in slaves.[80] Agaja's own sales were guided purely by his need for ammunition. As a result, he decided that the port of Whydah alone would be sufficient for his purposes and he therefore closed the two ports used at Allada before the invasion. In any case, the constant Ọyọ invasions between 1726 and 1730 prevented any peaceful trade.

The result was that the slave trade decreased tremendously, causing great disappointments—and losses—to European traders.[81] They therefore decided that the Dahomeans were great warriors but very bad traders. Between 1728 and 1730 these European traders tried to bring back the

78 For a discussion of the events which confirm these conclusions, see Akinjogbin, *op. cit.*, p. 91.

79 European traders had openly said they wanted an 'extra-ordinary means' to reduce the king of Whydah to reason and had entered into negotiations with Agaja before his invasion of Whydah in 1727. J. Blaney to Royal African Company, 4 August 1714 (PRO. T. 70/5); Snelgrave, *op. cit.*, pp. 12–13, 59–61.

80 W. Smith, *A New Voyage to Guinea*, London, 1744, pp. 171–89; Snelgrave, *op. cit.*, p. 94.

81 'Conseil de Marine', 13 August 1728 (AN. C. 6/25); Viceroy of Brazil to King of Portugal, 13 May 1729 (AHU. Codice 254 f. 61r 62r); Court of Assistants to J. Brathwaite, R. Cruikshank and B. Peak, 14 August 1729 (T. 70/54).

Whydah whom they regarded as expert traders.[82] First they attempted to persuade Agaja to accept them as his subjects, and when Agaja refused they plotted with the Whydah to drive the Dahomeans away from the coast. At times these plots were successful enough for the Whydah to occupy their ancient kingdom for weeks before the Dahomeans came down again to drive them away.

It was fortunate for Dahomey that the Europeans did not synchronise their plots with the Ọyọ invasions. Nevertheless Dahomey was forced to come to terms with the Europeans soon after making peace with the Ọyọ authorities. The Europeans were also convinced that their interests lay in reaching an agreement with Agaja. Even before the negotiations with Ọyọ started in 1730 the Royal African Company's West African headquarters at Cape Coast had sent out John Brathwaite, one of its three directors, to negotiate with Agaja.[83] He arrived while the negotiations with Ọyọ were in progress and he had to wait until July before he could begin his own negotiation.

Around 22 July 1730 Agaja gave indications that he was ready, and Brathwaite sent Edward Deane, the director of Whydah fort, to Allada, then the capital of Dahomey, to negotiate. Between then and 22 August all the points of disagreement between Agaja and the Europeans were discussed.[84] As in the case of the negotiation with Ọyọ, an account of this negotiation has not been found, but certain actions that were taken immediately after the talks are indicative of the broad lines of agreement.

First, Edward Deane, the English negotiator, recognised Agaja as the new political head of all Dahomey's conquered lands. In return Agaja accepted the responsibility for ensuring the safety of all Europeans within his kingdom. This was dramatised by Dahomean soldiers accompanying the Europeans from Allada to Whydah after the conclusion of the talks.[85] Secondly, Agaja apparently agreed to cooperate fully with the European slave traders. In return the Europeans would seem to have agreed also to remove all their trading posts in the other ports within the new kingdom of Dahomey and to concentrate all their efforts at Whydah. Agaja no longer harassed the slave traders as he had done before the talks, though he continued to maintain close control of the trade. The Europeans on the other hand moved from the old Allada ports of Jakin and Koko and came to Whydah.[86] One remarkable aspect of this agreement was that although

82 'Conseil de Marine', 11 August 1728 (AN. C. 6/25); Charlot Testefolle to R.A.C., Whydah, 30 October 1729 (T. 70/7); Memoire de la Compagnie des Indes', 8 November 1730 (AN. C. 6/25); Dalzel, *op. cit.*, p. 54.

83 J. Brathwaite to R.A.C., 1 June 1730 (PRO. T. 70/7).

84 'Copybook and diaries for Whydah', 29 July, 22 August 1730 (PRO. T. 70/1466); 'Accounts and Journals, Cape Coast Castle', May-December 1730 (PRO. T. 70/396).

85 'Copybook and diaries for Whydah', 22 August 1730.

86 'Copybook and diaries for Whydah', 25 August and 17 September 1730 (T. 70/1466); J. Brathwaite to R.A.C., 16 August 1730 (PRO. T. 70/7).

it was negotiated by an Englishman, it was accepted both by the Dahomeans and by the other resident Europeans as covering all the European traders in the kingdom of Dahomey. The success of Deane was hailed by all the other European directors of companies and large parties were held to celebrate it.[87]

The year 1730 therefore was an important date in the growth of Dahomey. In that year it definitely became a tributary of Ọyọ and was to remain so for almost a century. Also in that year Dahomey definitely accepted the slave trade and turned it into a royal monopoly. From then on the slave trade increasingly grew to be the basis of the economy of Dahomey, with consequences that became apparent by the end of the century.

INTERNAL ORGANISATION OF DAHOMEY

With peace agreed between Dahomey and Ọyọ, and between Dahomey and the Europeans, Agaja set out to introduce a new system of administration into the conquered areas. He had been uncertain whether it was the Europeans who dictated to which Dahomean chiefs they were to be responsible or whether it was his prerogative to appoint such overlords. When the Europeans themselves went to him and asked, he gave them three men, one in charge of the English trade, another in charge of the French and another in charge of the Portuguese.[88] By 1733 the European directors had found the courtesies of these local chiefs, who came to greet them in turns and had to be offered drinks, too expensive. They therefore asked that only one person be made responsible for the Europeans. In January 1733 the post of *Yovogan* was created and Tanga became the first incumbent.[89]

There was to be more fighting before the Whydahs would agree that their kingdom had been lost for ever. Their first reaction to the agreement between Ọyọ and Dahomey was to adopt a scorched-earth policy against the port of Whydah.[90] This was because they thought that once the port was unsafe and the trade dwindled, the Dahomeans would withdraw. But instead of making the Dahomeans withdraw, the constant harassment by the Whydah of the traders at the port only succeeded in uniting the European traders with the Dahomeans against the old Whydah. When Huffon died in July 1733[91] the succession dispute which ensued weakened Whydah resistance and Agaja was able to play one faction against the other. If internal discontent had not forced fresh Dahomean malcontents to join forces with the old Whydahs the latter would have given up after 1734.

But there was internal discontent in Dahomey. When in 1730 Agaja

87 'Accounts and Journals, Cape Coast Castle', May–December 1730 (PRO. T. 70/396).
88 'Extract du Registre', 13 September and 23 September 1728 (AN. C. 6/25).
89 Dubelay to la Compagnie des Indes, 26 August 1733 (AN. C. 6/25).
90 J. Bazilio to Viceroy of Brazil, Ajuda, 17 July 1731 (APB. OR. 28 f. 129).
91 Levet to la Compagnie des Indes, 26 August 1733 (AN. C. 6/25); Dalzel, *op. cit.*, pp. 81–2, report the death but with the wrong date.

agreed not to molest the European slave traders in his territory, he did not intend that the slave trade should return to the pre-invasion days when everybody participated in it freely. Rather he meant to take strict control. This attitude did not please the chief men in the state. They had probably fought in the hope that they would share in the profits of the slave trade. When Agaja prevented anyone but the king from taking part,[92] there was great resentment. There were strong rumours of important chiefs planning revolts or wanting to desert the Dahomean army. Agaja decided on firm action. Between 1733 and 1735 he ordered the execution of some of the most important men including the *Possu*, third in the rank in the Dahomean army, and the *Mehu*, the traditional treasurer of the kingdom and ranking only after the king and the *Migan*. Others like the Aplogan, chief of the province of Gome, and Ashampo, an important military leader with a large following, fled before they could be arrested. Ashampo later joined the old Whydahs at their Popo island settlement,[93] and was to give a great deal of trouble to Dahomey later.

For the time being these repressive actions left Agaja the undisputed leader of his kingdom. But they were not without their adverse effects. Dahomey was greatly weakened all round—politically, militarily and economically. In the decade following the settlement with Ọyọ and particularly between 1734 and 1743, only the reputation of Dahomey remained. The creation of the famous Dahomean 'Amazon' female army during this period shows how desperate the military situation was. The story is told that on one occasion when the old Whydahs invaded the Whydah port from their Popo island hideout, Agaja, finding that he had no adequate soldiers, armed such as he had, and gathered women, dressed up as soldiers to come up in the rear.[94]

The constant invasion of the old Whydahs and the acute internal dissensions succeeded in bringing internal and external trade virtually to a halt. While civil dissension continued, the European slave traders found it more profitable to go to other ports outside the jurisdiction of Dahomey to procure their slaves.[95]

The poverty and the chaos were to cause further sufferings for Dahomey. Because Dahomey was poor it was unable to pay regularly to Ọyọ the annual tributes imposed upon it by the 1730 treaty. Moreover, Agaja, in stubborn determination to keep the enemies of Dahomey at arms' length, invaded Badagry in 1737.[96] Badagry, it will be remembered, had been removed from Dahomean influence in 1730. Dahomey's failure to pay tribute and its impudent invasion of Badagry caused the Ọyọ army to

92 Levet to la Compagnie des Indes, Juda, 26 August 1733 (AN. C. 6/25).
93 Levet to la Compagnie des Indes, Juda, 26 August 1733 (AN. C. 6/25); J. Dubelay to la Compagnie des Indes, 7 January 1734 (AN. C. 6/25); Dalzel, *op. cit.*, pp. 68–71, 97–8.
94 Dalzel, *op. cit.*, p. 55.
95 Akinjogbin, *op. cit.*, p. 115.
96 'Enregistrement des rapports . . .', 3 February 1738 (ADN. B. 4587).

invade Dahomey early in 1739, with dire consequences.[97] Agaja fled and his kingdom was wasted. When he re-emerged in 1740 he had become a tired old man and died soon afterwards in May of the same year.

Agaja died under a cloud, with the very existence of Dahomey undermined. He must have been a disappointed man himself, for the greatness which he had spent his thirty-two years of reign seeking appeared to have eluded him. Dahomey was a tributary kingdom, poor economically, weak politically and chaotic in its internal administration. Yet certain fundamental achievements of Agaja proved durable. In all its vicissitudes, the authority of the king within Dahomey remained supreme. Within the terms of the 1730 treaty Dahomey remained a sovereign nation with its own army and a large measure of initiative in its deployment.

After a fairly fierce succession contest, Tegbesu, who in the last ten years had been in Ọyọ as a hostage, was chosen to succeed to the throne.[98] He found the treasury empty and the European trade gone but he faced his task with energy and grim determination. First he eliminated all those who had contested the throne with him and sold most of their supporters into slavery.[99] Then he invited the highest chiefs to nominate people to become the king's traders.[100] Finally, in 1743, he obtained the permission of the Ọyọ authorities to return to the ancient capital, Abomey.[101]

Conditions were not yet normal, for between 1743 and 1748 the threat of Ọyọ invasion hung over Dahomey. It is certain that Ọyọ again invaded the kingdom either late in 1742 or early in 1743 and threatened constantly to invade between 1744 and 1748.[102] The causes of these invasions may have been connected largely with Dahomey's inability to pay the regular annual tributes. However in 1748 Tegbesu again concluded another treaty with the Ọyọ authorities to confirm the 1730 treaty. After that, and until the third decade of the nineteenth century, Dahomey did not again provoke any invasion by the Ọyọ armies.[103] From 1748 until the end of the eighteenth century, therefore, it is proper to treat Dahomey and Ọyọ as two parts of the same empire.

During these years two parallel developments are discernible in Dahomey. One was the growing absolutism of the king and the increasing efficiency of the internal administration. The other was the growing weakness, after a brief period of prosperity, of the economic system based on the export of slaves.

As has been noted above, Tegbesu was determined, after his accession

97 Akinjogbin, *op. cit.*, p. 107.
98 Dunglas, *loc. cit.*, pp. 165–7, Le Herissé, *op. cit.*, pp. 161, 299–300; A. Dalzel, *op. cit.*, p. 67; Akinjogbin, *op. cit.*, p. 110.
99 E. Dunglas, *loc. cit.*, pp. 165–7; Le Herissé, *op. cit.*, pp. 299–300.
100 Levet to la Compagnie des Indes, 1 February 1746 (AN. C.6/25).
101 Levet to la Compagnie des Indes, 25 February 1744 (AN. C.6/25).
102 Levet to la Compagnie des Indes, 20 August 1743 (AN. C.6/25); Accounts and Journals, Cape Coast Castle, 1 January–30 June 1748 (T.70/424).
103 Le Herissé, *op. cit.*, p. 319; Dunglas, *loc. cit.*, pp. 146, 171.

in 1740, to brook no rivals. Having executed or sold most of his rivals and their supporters, he pounced on the rich ones who might become overmighty subjects. On one pretext or another, he caused many of them to be executed. The same treatment was meted out to various army captains who had either lived too long or were too popular for Tegbesu's liking.[104] He then promulgated new laws of succession by which only the direct sons of a reigning king could succeed him. This law excluded all the king's brothers, cousins or uncles from contesting a vacant stool. Of the sons of a particular king, only those born by one of the six wives designated as capable of producing heirs could succeed, and the king reserved the right to nominate his successor.[105]

By 1751 these measures had greatly increased the power of the king. In that year he designated his eldest son as his successor, and asked Guestard, the French director, to take him to France for education. Guestard, however, declined to do so, for he had been instructed not to send African princes to France for education. When the plan did not materialise, the king in 1754 decided to test the efficacy of his actions. He caused himself to be declared dead, and withdrew from all public engagements.[106] His intention was to see whether any of his subjects would seize the opportunity to challenge any of his laws. That none did, and that everyone was ready to abide by the constitutional procedure which he laid down, was a sign of his success.

The same measure of success attended the administrative reorganisation which he undertook with the same ruthlessness. Full details of this are not known, but the main outline is clear. Tegbesu had lived ten years in Ọyọ and must have been familiar with Ọyọ institutions. It is certain that he introduced one of them, the Ilari system, into Dahomey.[107] The Ilari were a group of royal messengers who were identified by the way they shaved alternate halves of their heads, so that when one half was clean, the other was hairy. That was why the English traders referred to them as 'half heads'. Tegbesu used them not only to carry messages to the Europeans on the coast, but also to move round the kingdom checking the activities of the various chiefs.

The administration of the coastal regions (old Whydah and Allada kingdoms) was of course very important. Not only was the export trade of the kingdom based there, it was also a region which continued to be disputed by the old Whydahs for many more years. Tegbesu therefore appointed two other chiefs to aid the yovogan.[108] In practice these two

104 Akinjogbin, *op. cit.*, pp. 115–16.
105 De Chenevert and Abbé Bullet, 'Reflexions sur Juda', 1776 (AN. C.6/27 bis).
106 Conseil de direction to la Compagnie des Indes, 10 July 1754; Guestard to la Compagnie des Indes, 10 July 1754 (AN. C.6/25).
107 Akinjogbin, *op. cit.*, p. 118.
108 Journals and ledgers, Cape Coast Castle, November and December 1746 (T. 70/704); Accounts and Journals, Cape Coast Castle, September–December 1747 (T. 70/423).

chiefs were spies on the activities of the yovogan. The result was that the yovogan of this period were very shortlived, for the least offence they committed was reported to the king and execution was often the result. Nor were the two subordinate officers, the *coki* and the *bunio*, any longer lived. Consequently all the officers appointed to govern Whydah felt very much the pressure of the king's strong hand.[109]

The European directors were not left out of the administrative organisation. Tegbesu recognised that they were very important to the national economy. He made plain early in his reign, when he drove the directors of the French and Portuguese forts out,[110] that he would not allow any director to stay in the kingdom who was not loyal to him. Between 1740 when Tegbesu ascended the throne, and 1774 when he died, he expelled four French and four Portuguese directors from Dahomey[111] for being unfriendly to the country and ruining its economy.

It was not only by coercive measures that he got the support of the European directors. He treated each of the directors as a chief, though he recognised their foreign nationality. He therefore became personally acquainted with each one on arrival and actually befriended some. He consulted them on national policy whenever he thought that such a policy would affect their interest. He invited them to Abomey annually during the Anubomey ceremonies, received their annual presents as he did from all the other chiefs in the kingdom, and gave them presents as he gave the others. And he encouraged them to bring whatever complaints they had to him.[112]

At first the European directors complained that going to meet the king frequently was irksome. But soon they got used to it and liked the opportunity of discussing their problems with him. They certainly came to know their rights, privileges and limitations and they preferred that to the chaotic situation which had characterised the last years of Agaja.

By 1751 Tegbesu had established himself as the absolute ruler of Dahomey and had established a very efficient administrative system. True it was a bureaucracy without paper or pen, but a very efficient bureaucracy nonetheless. Until the end of the century no one challenged the authority of the king. When disagreement arose towards the end of the century, it was the policy of the king rather than his authority that was in question. When, in the early nineteenth century, the other parts of the Ọyọ empire were disintegrating, the administration of Dahomey withstood all corrosive influences.

The economic picture of Dahomey was not as happy. As mentioned

109 Akinjogbin, *op. cit.*, pp. 119–20.
110 Levet to la Compagnie des Indes, 20 August 1743 (AN. C. 6/25); Extrait d'une lettre particulière écrite de Juda, 16 August 1743 (AN. C.6/25).
111 Akinjogbin, *op. cit.*, pp. 216–17.
112 *Ibid.*, p. 122.

above, when Tegbesu ascended the throne he found hardly any money left in the royal treasury. Having just come from Ọyọ where splendour was the order in court, the contrast must have struck him very forcefully. He therefore decided on a national policy that was the very opposite of his father's. He decided that it was 'better to trade than to make war'.[113] His administrative measures were meant partly to promote economic progress. He took steps to see that those European trading houses (then called factories) which had become dilapidated in the previous decade were repaired, and their European personnel, who had been badly impoverished, were loaned money and given other comforts in order to be able to carry on the slave trade.[114]

These steps, together with the administrative and constitutional steps being concurrently taken, increased the export of slaves through Whydah port and enriched the king. By about 1750 there was an air of prosperity in Dahomey. The slave trade was efficiently organised and it looked as if it was the answer to all the economic ills of Dahomey.[115]

By 1767, however, the picture began to change. European ships which used to crowd Whydah port because there were plenty of slaves to be had there, began to avoid the port and to go elsewhere. Tegbesu noticed and complained to the European directors resident in his kingdom. They replied at various times with different kinds of excuses. They said that his people were stealing their property and that was why the captains were unwilling to stay. At other times they said that so many people owed them debts which were not being repaid.[116] Whatever they complained of, the king made stringent laws to prevent a recurrence. Still trade did not improve. The king and his officers noticed that slaves were not being offered for sale in large quantities and he passed a law to force slave owners to sell a portion of their slaves. Finally when all peaceful methods failed to produce more slaves for export, Kpengla, one of his successors, decided that he would have to raid for the slaves himself and he set about organising war parties. But the Dahomean army had already been weakened by a long period of peace and consequent lack of practice and the raids were not spectacularly successful, though the Dahomean authorities made fantastic claims about their successes after every expedition.[117]

Despite all these measures, the economy continued to decline. What the Dahomean authorities failed to realise (and even today scholars are still arguing about it) was that the slave trade was destructive of itself and of every other economic activity. Human beings were not bred as cattle for sale. In eighteenth-century Dahomey only a small proportion of the

113 Thomas Melville to African Committee, 30 November 1754 (PRO. T. 70/1523).
114 Akinjogbin, *op. cit.*, pp. 127–9.
115 Guestard, 'Mémoire pour Servir à l'intelligence du Commerce de Juda. . . .', 1750 (AN. C. 6/25); Akinjogbin, *op. cit.*, pp. 134–7.
116 Akinjogbin, *op. cit.*, pp. 143–4.
117 *Ibid.*, chap. 5.

slaves were derived from condemned criminals, witches and debtors. By far the largest number were procured through wars and surprise raids conducted against unsuspecting neighbours engaged in some peaceful economic pursuit. The European slave exporters insisted on purchasing the healthiest of human beings in the prime of their life. The least physical defect or the slightest indication of age or infirmity disqualified any slave from being exported, though it did not set him free. And a slave who could not fetch a profit for his master was unlikely to be well cared for. The result was that people engaged in peaceful economic pursuit were either carried away, frightened away or, if they were strong enough, converted to slave raiders. Secondly, a large percentage of the virile section of the community were annually either carried away into slavery or killed while resisting capture. The result of this in time was economic depression. By 1774 when Tegbesu died and Agonglo ascended the throne the economic depression in Dahomey had not shown signs of any improvement. If anything it was getting progressively worse.

THE DECLINE OF ỌYỌ

The other part of the Ọyọ empire was going through a different ordeal and was affected by the slave trade in a different kind of way. It will be recalled that Ọyọ had never really shown much interest in the European slave trade export since the beginning of the seventeenth century, though undoubtedly a few Ọyọ slaves must have been transported across the seas. However, as a result of the Ọyọ expeditions into Dahomey, during which part of their booty must have consisted of rare European manufacture, there emerged an exaggerated opinion of the wealth conferred on the coastal kingdoms by the slave trade. The two treaties which Dahomey signed with Ọyọ in 1730 and 1748, and which compelled Dahomey to bring to Ọyọ certain European manufactured goods, must also have contributed to this notion.

From about 1754 there were two clearly defined factions in Ọyọ, one led by the Baṣọrun Gaha and the other by the successive Alafins. The traditions of this period have been transmitted to us by the supporters of the Alafin who overthrew Gaha. They therefore dwell at length on the excesses and wickedness of Gaha. No doubt Gaha was a strong-arm ruler but his excesses were probably the result and not the cause of the disagreement between himself and the supporters of the Alafins. There is evidence to show that a most important factor in the struggle between Gaha and the Alafins centred on a particular policy decision. One verse in Gaha's *oriki* (praise name) reveals that Gaha was incensed over one specific matter (*ọ̀rọ̀ kan, ọ̀rọ̀ kàn ni mbi baba ninú*) but does not say what the issue was. However from the surviving pro-Alafin traditions, the few extant traditions on Gaha and the events of the period, it is easy to see that the point of disagreement was whether the Ọyọ empire was to go on expanding or whether it was to concentrate on exploiting the already conquered areas. It is easy also to see that Gaha favoured the expansionist view while the Alafins favoured exploitation. Gaha was a descendant of Yau Yamba, one of the most successful generals of the early eighteenth century. He is known to have remained comparatively poor all his life. For a man in his position, this could only mean that he did not seek wealth. On the other hand all the Alafins who ascended the throne from 1754 to 1774 were either wealthy traders themselves before becoming kings or they had very powerful backers among the wealthy trading classes.[118] It is significant also that it was only after Gaha had been overthrown in 1774 that the export of slaves became greatly encouraged within the Ọyọ empire. Porto Novo, the Ọyọ port, became the leading slaving port in 1776 two years after Gaha's overthrow, and remained so until Abiọdun's death.

Each faction, no doubt, had a valid point of view. Ọyọ was by then a very large and powerful empire. For that reason, if it was to survive, it must continue to have a strong army both to discourage secessions and ward off external aggression. On the other hand, the size of Ọyọ was already placing a strain on the administration, as the means of communication were slow. Moreover, the apparent wealth of Dahomey might point out the advantages that could be derived from a peaceful policy. Neither side however saw the sense of the other's point of view. And from about 1754 to 1774 there was a great deal of instability in Ọyọ arising out of this conflict between the Alafin and the Baṣọrun. Until about 1770 the Baṣọrun faction was the stronger. He therefore encompassed the death of any Alafin who did not toe the military line.[119] As he grew older, however, his hold gradually weakened. When Abiọdun, an astute trader and a clever and ruthless politician, ascended the throne about 1770, Gaha's days were numbered.

Like his four immediate predecessors, Abiọdun was also a trader. He therefore supported the anti-expansionist policy. But for about four years he took care to cause no rupture with the Baṣọrun to whom he showed such an exaggerated respect as nearly disgusted the old Baṣọrun himself. But the Baṣọrun was deceived. Abiọdun was finding his feet and laying his plans. When the inevitable clash came in 1774, the Baṣọrun was defeated.[120] Abiọdun wreaked such vengeance on the fallen Baṣọrun as probably was later to have an ill effect on Ọyọ itself, for in suppressing all the families and known supporters of Baṣọrun Gaha, a large number of military families must have been involved.

Throughout this struggle two aspects appear strange. If Gaha started with superior advantage and power, it is difficult to explain why he was

118 Akinjogbin, 'The Oyo Empire in the eighteenth century: A reassessment', *J.H.S.N.*, iii, 3, 1966, pp. 449–60.
119 Johnson, *op. cit.*, pp. 178–82.
120 *Ibid.*, pp. 182–6; Dalzel, *op. cit.*, p. 157.

unable to influence the choice of a prince who would toe his own line. Secondly it would now appear reasonable for the two sides to have agreed on the pursuance of the two policies concurrently. Successful imperial enterprises must bring certain economic advantages to the metropolitan power. But for such advantages to continue, the imperial power must continue to maintain a competent army.

It must be remarked however that during this period of struggle, the Ọyọ empire remained strong. The studies which tend to see the seeds of the fall of the empire in this struggle do not take into consideration all the evidence at our disposal, scanty though this may be. For during these twenty years, the boundaries of the Ọyọ empire at its widest extent were maintained intact. Each part was kept obedient to the Alafin by the consciousness of the might of Ọyọ soldiers. The very mention of the name of Gaha anywhere in the empire sent shivers down the stoutest spine. It would appear also that strong military detachments were stationed at strategic points on the borders of the empire. For when in 1764 an Ashanti army of about 2,000 men strayed into Ọyọ territory near present-day Atakpame in modern Togo, the Ọyọ detachments there went into action and wiped out the Ashanti intruders.[121] Such a blow at a power which was very strong in the middle of the eighteenth century at once showed the strength of Ọyọ and warned any intending intruders to keep off.

From 1774, when Abiọdun was victorious over Gaha, until 1789 when he died,[122] Gaha's policy was completely reversed. Imperial expansion was stopped and it would appear that the army was kept weak. The exploitation of the resources of the empire developed. From about 1776, two years after Abiọdun's victory, the effects were already plain. Porto Novo, the main Ọyọ port, became the most important port for the export of slaves, and more European ships, particularly French ones, went there in large numbers to collect slaves. Between 1776 and 1786 there was talk of the French building forts in Porto Novo both to protect the trade and to prevent any military invasion by Dahomey,[123] which was beginning to grow jealous of the ascendancy of Porto Novo over Whydah.

Exactly where the slaves came from is uncertain. It seems that the bulk of them did not come from Yorubaland. It is more probable that they came largely from the Bariba, the Nupe and the Hausa. The fact that many Hausa slaves were still living in Ọyọ in the early years of the nineteenth century suggests that they may have been the remnants of those exported earlier. Parts of Tapa (Nupe) and Bariba (Borgu) being tributary to Ọyọ, Abiọdun may have increased their annual contributions in slaves. It is not impossible also that units of Ọyọ soldiers passed through these dependent territories to raid beyond their borders.

121 William Mutter to African Committee, 27 May 1764 (T. 70/31).
122 Akinjogbin, *Dahomey* . . ., p. 175, n. 1.
123 Akinjogbin, 'The Oyo Empire . . .', p. 457.

Apart from trade, Abiọdun also derived great advantages from the annual and periodical payment made to Ọyọ from dependent territories. As the head of the empire, Abiọdun was heir to all the most important chiefs within it. There is evidence that he extorted this right to the full in Egbaland and in Dahomey.[124] He may have done so in all the other parts of the empire but we have no clear evidence yet. In Dahomey there were instances when the king did not pay the right items of the annual tribute under the excuse that he could not obtain them. Whenever Abiọdun discovered that the king of Dahomey was not being honest, he reprimanded him so sternly that the king of Dahomey had to apologise and send still more presents. On an occasion when a Mehu of Dahomey died, the Alafin Abiọdun was not satisfied with the movable property of the dead Mehu which was sent to Ọyọ. He demanded the rest in such vehement terms that Agonglo was forced to procure more and send them.[125]

Abiọdun's exertion was momentarily beneficial to the Ọyọ people. The king's authority was such that there were no civil wars at home, nor were there any foreign wars. Trade boomed, money flowed and the populace was contented. For a long time the Ọyọ tradition remembered Abiọdun's reign as a glorious period in Ọyọ history.[126] Coming between the iron rule of Gaha and the chaotic period of Awolẹ, the reign of Abiọdun became romanticised, but there was no doubt that it was far more satisfactory to the Ọyọ than either the preceding or the succeeding reign.

In the long term, however, the reign of Abiọdun was not so glorious, and the long term was not far postponed. Before the death of Abiọdun, the slave trade was already producing the same sort of weakness as it had produced in Dahomey. The only difference is that whereas in the case of Dahomey it was the economic weakness that was the more prominent, in Ọyọ it was the military. In 1783 the Bariba subjects of the Alafin revolted and successfully defeated the attempt to resubjugate them.[127] Soon afterwards, the Egba also successfully declared their independence.[128] When, between 1782 and 1786, there were signs of unrest and disobedience in the coastal dependencies of Ọyọ, Abiọdun asked Kpengla to suppress the revolt for him because the places were too far for his army to reach.[129] As long as Abiọdun with his domineering personality was alive, the dangers inherent in this military weakness did not show. However, after his death in 1789, when he was succeeded by Awolẹ, a much weaker person, the cracks produced during his reign started to affect the edifice of the Ọyọ

124 S. O. Biobaku, *The Egba and Their Neighbours,* Oxford, 1957, pp. 8–9; Dalzel, *op. cit.*, pp. 173–4; p. 209.
125 Accounts and Daybooks for Whydah, 2, 24 and 27 January 1779 (T. 70/1162).
126 Johnson, *op. cit.*, pp. 186–8.
127 L. Abson to R. Miles, 26 September 1783 (PRO. T. 70/1545).
128 The date of Egba independence is still not settled. Biobaku puts it between 1775 and 1780; but a period of weakness in Ọyọ would appear more likely.
129 Akinjogbin, *Dahomey . . .*, pp. 164–8.

empire. In 1791, two years after his death, the Tapa (Nupe) again successfully revolted against Ọyọ rule. The unsuccessful war to crush them would appear to have been bitter and quite a number of Ọyọ generals lost their lives in the encounter.[130] The defeat of Ọyọ showed vividly its complete military helplessness and sealed the only remaining slave raiding route.

Awolẹ, in trying to revive both the military glory and the slave economy of Ọyọ succeeded only in committing greater blunders that brought the whole empire down. In 1793 he sent an expedition against Apomu, a market town in Ifẹ kingdom. The army was reluctant to set out because a war against Ifẹ was regarded as contrary to the traditional conventions of the Yoruba country. A face-saving device was arrived at when the then Balẹ of Apomu was asked to commit suicide and his head was sent to Ọyọ. But this did not stem the tide of decay. It appears that by such disregard of tradition Awolẹ drove his most important subjects to the verge of revolt. In 1795, when he ordered an expedition against Iwere, a town that had sentimental association with Ọyọ because Abiọdun's mother came from there, it was the last straw. The soldiers, instead of attacking Iwere, turned on all the known supporters of the Alafin and massacred them. They then demanded that Awolẹ himself must commit suicide. But his suicide created other problems. Two attempts to install new Alafins did not succeed and from about 1797 there was a long interregnum in Ọyọ.[131]

In the meantime Dahomey continued to wrestle with its own economic decline. Kpengla, who ascended the throne in 1774, tried to revive the military power and the economy of Dahomey by consciously sending military expeditions out to raid for slaves. Thus he hoped to kill two birds with a stone. But the attempt failed. The more the economy declined, the more dissatisfied the Dahomeans became. In 1787 Gourg, the French director in Whydah, said he noticed so much discontent that he was certain there would soon be a revolution in the country.[132] Kpengla died in 1789 without being able to solve his kingdom's economic problems. His son Agonglo tried other means. He invited the Portuguese to come in strength, but they demanded that he become a Christian first. When Agonglo showed signs that he was willing to be baptised his subjects objected and murdered him in 1797.[133] A short civil war that followed within the palace ended with Adandozan, Agonglo's son, on the throne. But there was no peace or progress again until Gezo deposed Adandozan in about 1818.

For the Ọyọ empire the eighteenth century ended around 1797 when both the Alafin and the king of Dahomey were violently despatched from their thrones. The century ended on a note of economic decline and political

130 Hogg to T. Miles, 19 March 1791 (PRO. T. 70/1560); Johnson, *op. cit.*, p. 187; Dalzel, *op. cit.*, p. 229.
131 Johnson, *op. cit.*, pp. 188–92.
132 Gourg to Ministre de Marine, 1 August 1787 (AN. C.6/26).
133 Akinjogbin, *Dahomey* . . ., pp. 185–6.

chaos which the nineteenth century would either aggravate or improve. Yet, the history of both Dahomey and Ọyọ during the two centuries 1600 to 1797 was not without its own valuable historical conclusions. The first of such deductions that may be noted is that conditions within the Yoruba–Aja country were not static, whether one thinks in political terms, in military terms or in economic terms. The second and no less important deduction is that such a large empire as that of Ọyọ could endure for a remarkably long time without Islamic concepts, without the bureaucracy of pen and paper, without telephones or telegraphs. Still another deduction that can be drawn is that European economic contact, necessary and sometimes useful, is not always bound to be beneficial. Unless the African kingdoms were able to consult their own interests and be active dictators of those interests, such economic contacts could result more in decline than in progress.

CHAPTER 10

The Mossi and Akan states 1500–1800

IVOR WILKS

The period of the sixteenth to the eighteenth century was one of far-reaching economic, political and social change in the hinterland of that part of the Guinea coast lying between the Komoé and Volta rivers. It was marked in particular by the emergence and consolidation of such southern Akan forest states as those of the Denkyira, Akwamu, Fante and, most powerful of all, Asante. These changes are significantly correlated with the growth of the European interest on the coast itself. In 1500 there was only one permanent European trading establishment there—the Casa da Mina of the Portuguese, built in 1482. By 1600 four such posts had been created, by 1700 about thirty-five, and by 1800 about forty-five: Portuguese, Dutch, English, Brandenburg, Swedish, Danish and French merchants all having become embroiled in the struggle for position on the beaches.[1]

The military power of the Akan forest states, where the horse could not readily be bred and was in any case of little utility, rested on the possession of foot soldiers. Revolutionary changes occurred, however, in the mode of warfare as in-fighting with swords and spears increasingly gave way to the use of missile weapons: the bow and, as supplies became available through the European merchants, the gun. Resources of organisation and management, brought into being as a result of the new scale of warfare, were utilised in the non-military sphere: army chiefs like the *kontihene* or commander-in-chief, and the *adontenhene* or commander of the main body, became at the same time the principal agents of civil government, so giving rise to the characteristic traditional Akan political formation.[2] North of the forest, in the savannahs that stretch away to the Middle Niger, lay another group of states, some by 1600 with a century and a

1 J. D. Fage, ed. 'A new check list of the forts and castles of Ghana', *Transactions of the Historical Society of Ghana*, iv, I, 1959. Intermittent occupation of some forts makes an accurate count difficult.

2 See e.g. R. S. Rattray, *Ashanti Law and Constitution*, Oxford, 1929, ch. 10.

half or more of development already behind them. These were the kingdoms of the Mossi complex: a southern group consisting of Mamprussi, Dagomba, and Nanumba, and a northern group, Tenkodogo, Wagadugu, Yatenga, and Fada N'Gurma. In contrast to the forest states, the power of these was based firmly on the possession of horses and a knowledge of the techniques of cavalry warfare. Using their heavy armoured cavalry principally for defensive purposes, the real strength of the savannah kingdoms lay in their employment of light cavalry for long-range raiding. Penetrating country where organised opposition was seldom encountered, battles were correspondingly rare; planners were concerned more with strategic than with tactical matters. Such conditions of warfare, however, did result in the extensive development of defensive works over a large area. Not only were larger towns frequently walled, but even village architecture was adapted to withstand sieges: many Sissala and Awuna villages, for example, have the appearance of miniature fortresses.

Comparatively little is known of the early history of the stateless societies ('tribes without rulers') of the northern savannahs. Certainly, during the formative years of the Mossi states, subjugated autochthonous peoples were sometimes dispossessed, but, more usually, they were integrated into the new societies as commoner lineages and allowed to continue in occupation of their lands. But the Mossi kingdoms remained surrounded by the territory of unassimilated and indeed never subjugated Bassari, Tallensi, Kassena, Awuna, Dogon, Konkomba and the like. As early as the seventeenth century some sort of equilibrium may have been established: that is, that although the stateless tribes remained subject to constant raids by Mossi cavalry parties, and were sometimes brought under a nominal overlordship like that of the Mamprussi over the Tallensi, no concerted attempts were made to integrate them more fully into the centralised systems. Unincorporated, they constituted pools of manpower from which the demands of raiding parties in search of slaves could be met; incorporated they acquired status and with it protection. It was perhaps in consequence of this situation that in the seventeenth century leaders of Mamprussi, Dagomba, and even Wagadugu cavalry groups created for themselves small chieftaincies, not in the vicinity of their homelands, but far to the west on the middle Black Volta. Best known of these are Wa in the country of the Dagaba, and Buna in that of the Kulango. Paradoxically, it was groups from as far west as the Komoé river, engaged as mercenaries by the Gonja and Mamprussi kings in the mid-eighteenth century, that were allowed to settle near the Mamprussi frontiers and to develop there a small state centred upon Sansanne Mango.

Between the southern Akan and the Mossi kingdoms, in the zone of ecological transition between forest and savannah, lay the northern Akan, or Bron, states. The largest and (through the works of Meyerowitz, some of which are cited below) best known of these was Bono. Founded earlier than any of the major southern Akan states, Bono had features that linked it with the savannah rather than the forest kingdoms: for example, the importance to it of the horse.[3] An intimate connection existed, nevertheless, between northern and southern Akan states, and some chiefly lines in the latter appear to have originated from the former. The Bono area passed under southern Akan (Asante) domination, however, in 1722–3: thereafter distinctively Bron cultural traits seem often to have become superseded by new fashions from the south.

In the mid-sixteenth century horsemen of Western Sudanese background, and probably Malinke and Bambara in culture, moved through the Bono area, and settled in the sparsely populated country along the valley of the southern Black Volta to create there the nucleus of what was to become the Gonja kingdom. The wars of the Gonja in the seventeenth century extended their territory as far east as the Oti River, and effectively isolated Akan from Mossi; only with the Asante invasion of Dagomba in the mid-eighteenth century was confrontation between the two blocs to occur.

The region under consideration here is one of great ethnographic complexity, reflected in the numerous languages of several major language families spoken within it; there has never been any *lingua franca*.[4] While the Akan are in general matrilineal, most other peoples are patrilineal (little resemblance though there may be between the loose cognatic social groups of the coastal Adangme and the highly structured agnatic clans of, for example, the Tallensi of the north). Some degree of cultural homogeneity has evolved through the progessive adoption of southern Akan forms by adjacent societies. Over the region as a whole, however, major differences of religion and ritual, and of social and political organisation, remain. Furthermore, the extremely uneven economic development which is still characteristic of the present-day republics of Ghana and Upper Volta, is a reflection of the fact that exploitation of the resources of the region has always tended to be concentrated in or near the forest zone; that is, of the gold that first attracted the European merchants to the coast, and of the kola that brought northern traders to the forest fringes. Nevertheless, if any one theme may be pursued to give some sort of unity to the history of the region, it is that of the successive emergence of ever larger state systems, transcending local 'tribal' particularism, establishing a structure of authority and maintaining a rule of law over increasingly wide areas, and, by the encouragement of production and trade, seeking to maximise economic benefits.

3 J. R. Anquandah, 'An Archaeological Survey of the Techiman-Wenchi Area', Supplement 1 to *Research Review, Bulletin of the Institute of African Studies, Legon*, December, 1965, *passim*.

4 Hausa gained very limited currency as a *lingua franca* in the region only at a late date and mainly in the newer urban areas. Portuguese was in use as a *lingua franca* until at least the later eighteenth century, but only in the coastal towns.

THE KINGDOMS OF THE MOSSI COMPLEX

João de Barros, writing of the reign of João II of Portugal (1481–95), told how the Portuguese had attempted to establish contact with the king of Mossi, a country which, according to reports received in Senegambia, 'began beyond Timbuktu and extended towards the Orient'.[5] At the time the Mossi were said to be at war with 'the king of Timbuktu Uli Mansa', that is, with Sunni ʿAli, ruler of Songhai from 1464 to 1492, who had taken Timbuktu in 1468. The struggles between the Mossi and the Songhai for control of the Middle Niger are documented in the Timbuktu chronicles, the *Taʾrīkh al-Sūdān* of al-Saʿdi and the *Taʾrīkh al-fattash* of Maḥmūd Kati. The particular campaigns mentioned by de Barros must be those of 1477–83, in the course of which the Mossi sacked the desert town of Walata but were later repulsed—Sunni ʿAli in person entering the capital of the Mossi ruler Na Siri.[6] This event constituted a turning point in Mossi relations with its northerly neighbours. In the earlier period the Mossi appear to have aspired to control of the region of the Niger Bend: their campaign against Walata had forerunners in that against Benga in the lacustrine area south of Timbuktu in the decade 1430–40, and in a still earlier attack upon Timbuktu itself, both reported in the *Taʾrīkh al-Sūdān*.[7] By the end of the fifteenth century the situation had changed, and the Songhai took the initiative in confining Mossi power to a more southerly locale. In 1498–9 Sunni ʿAli's successor, Askia al-Ḥājj Muḥammad (1493–1528), launched a *jihād* against the Mossi in the course of which Na Siri's capital was again occupied,[8] while half a century later Askia Daʾūd (1549–82) began the first of his three campaigns against the Mossi: those of 1549, 1561–2, and *c.* 1574.[9]

It may be assumed that it was primarily northern Mossi groups which were involved in the struggle with the Songhai in the late fifteenth century. Indeed, the Na Siri reported by the Timbuktu chroniclers to have been at war with both Sunni ʿAli and Askia Muḥammad is probably to be identified with the Na Siri or Na Sibiri or Na Seghe of northern Mossi tradition, whose son Na Yedega is generally accounted first ruler of the Yatenga kingdom.[10] The extent to which more southerly Mossi groups may have

5 J. de Barros, *Asia*: English translation of sections relating to West Africa in G. R. Crone, *The Voyages of Cadamosto*, London, 1937, iii, pp. 135, 144.

6 Al-Saʿdi, *Taʾrīkh al-Sūdān*, French edition by O. Houdas, Paris, 1900, pp. 112 and 115. Mahmūd Kati, *Taʾrīkh al-fattash*, French edition by O. Houdas and M. Delafosse, Paris, 1913, pp. 85, 89, 92.

7 Al-Saʿdi, *op. cit.*, pp. 16, 46. The sack of Timbuktu by the Mossi is often dated 1333, but this is not clear from the text of Al-Saʿdi, see pp. 16, 37. It may have taken place later, though certainly before 1433–4.

8 Al-Saʿdi, *ibid.*, pp. 121–2. Mahmūd Kati, *op. cit.*, pp. 134–5.

9 Al-Saʿdi, *op. cit.*, pp. 168, 173, 179.

10 M. Izard, *Traditions Historiques des Villages du Yatenga: Cercle de Gourcy*. Recherches Voltaiques 1. C.N.R.S., Paris, 1965, pp. 79, 125, but see also pp. 67, 84, 105 for a Na Seghe, son of Yedega. In Wagadugu tradition, Yedega's father is known as Na Siri alias Na Sibiri, son of Wubri. L. Frobenius, *The Voice of Africa*, two vols, London, 1913, ii, pp. 500 *et seq.* reports a Wagadugu story that Na Siri had campaigned north of the Niger.

been drawn into this conflict is not clear: early sources refer only to the Mossi as such. What does seem clear is that the various Mossi dynasties which emerged in the course of the fifteenth century were all closely connected ones, and this is reflected in the extant traditions of the ruling houses of these kingdoms. Their traditions, of which numerous versions have been recorded,[11] diverge at many points, but may be broadly compounded. The key figure in all is that of Na Gbewa (alias Kulu Gbagha, alias Nedega), whose domicile was at Pusiga in the extreme north-east of the present Ghana. The three southern Mossi kingdoms, Mamprussi, Dagomba, and Nanumba, have dynasties which claim descent from Na Gbewa through three of his sons, Tusugu, Sitobu and Nmantambu respectively. The northern Mossi dynasties, by contrast, claim descent from Yenenga, daughter of Na Gbewa, through her son Widraogo who became first ruler of the kingdom of Tenkodogo. Widraogo's son Rawa founded in turn the Zandoma kingdom, later to be incorporated into Yatenga, while Rawa's brother's son Wubri became the first ruler of Wagadugu, and Wubri's grandson Yedega the first ruler of Yatenga. Only in the case of Fada N'Gurma does any fundamental conflict in tradition arise: the founder of the dynasty, Jaba Lompo, is associated in some versions with the northern kingdoms, being regarded as another descendant of Na Gbewa's daughter, while in other versions he is treated rather as an agnatic kinsman of Gbewa. Paradoxically, it is in the traditions of the southern kingdoms that the Western Sudanese background of the Mossi is the more explicitly acknowledged. Thus the drum histories of the Dagomba start with a cycle of stories concerned with Toha Zie, the Red Hunter, who led his people from Tunga, east of Lake Chad, into Zamfara and thence into Mali. Serving in the wars of the Malian king, Toha Zie received in marriage one of his daughters, Paga Wabaga. Their son, Kpogonumbo, remained in Malian service for some time, but later migrated eastwards into Gurma country where one of his wives, Suhuyini, daughter apparently of a Gurma chief, gave birth to the Na Gbewa from whom the Mossi dynasties reckon descent. In the light of such stories one should not discount the possibility, which was earlier noted by Fage,[12] that the forebears of the early Mossi

11 For Dagomba see e.g. Khalīd b. Yaʿqūb, 'Ta'rīkh Daghabāwī', *Arabic Manuscript Collection, Library of the Institute of African Studies, Legon (I.A.S.A.R.)*/241, 250; H. A. Blair and A. Duncan-Johnstone, *Enquiry into the Constitution and Organisation of the Dagbon Kingdom*, Accra, 1932; E. F. Tamakloe, *A Brief History of the Dagomba People*, Accra, 1931; R. S. Rattray, *Tribes of the Ashanti Hinterland*, two vols, Oxford, 1932; D. Tait, F. N., 'Transcriptions and translations of the Dagomba drum histories', in I.A.S. For Mamprussi: D. V. Mackay, 'The Mamprussi', MS in the Balme Library, University of Ghana, n.d.; Rattray, *op. cit.* For Wagadugu: L. Marc, *Le Pays Mossi*, Paris, 1909; A. A. Dim Delobsom, *L'Empire du Mogho-Naba*, Paris, 1932. For Yatenga: L. Tauxier, *Le Noir du Yatenga*, Paris, 1917; Izard, *op. cit.* For Fada N'Gurma: P. Davy, 'Histoire du Pays Gourmantché', MS in Centre des Hautes Etudes sur l'Afrique et l'Asie modernes, University of Paris.

12 J. D. Fage, 'Reflections on the early history of the Mossi—Dagomba group of states', in *The Historian in Tropical Africa*, ed. Vansina, Mauny and Thomas, Oxford, 1964, p. 178.

rulers had mercenary cavalrymen in the service of the Malian kings.

New light may be thrown on the origins of the Mossi kingdoms if an Arabic account of the region reputedly written in 1410 by a Berber, Awdar, turns out to contain even some deposit of reliable early tradition. This work is said to report, for example, the migration of the Mossi from Bornu into the Dallol Boboye area east of Niamey.[13] In the absence of any full acount of the Awdar manuscript, one may suggest tentatively that in the course of the fifteenth century, while some Mossi groups retained a Western Sudanese involvement and became embroiled with the rising power of the Songhai, other groups were pressing far into the southern savannahs and laying the foundations of Mossi hegemony there. It was probably only after the middle of that century that the kingdoms of Mamprussi, Dagomba, Nanumba, Tenkodogo, Fada N'Gurma, Wagadugu and, latest of all, Yatenga, began to emerge as distinct political entities each with its own dynasty. By 1600, certainly, all these kingdoms had many years of growth and consolidation behind them.

The Mossi kingdoms were created in territory the indigenous inhabitants of which had little affinity in culture and tradition with the newcomers. The earlier peoples, Fulse, Ninisi, Kipirsi, Kassena, Nunuma, Konkomba and the rest, appear to have lacked centralised political institutions, but to have been organised on the basis of areas of ritual jurisdiction ('parishes'), each with its *tengasoba* (northern Mossi) or *tengdana* (southern)—a land priest having custody of the earth shrines. The policy of the immigrant horsemen towards the indigenous land priests seems to have varied. In western Dagomba, for example, where Na Nyagse established the early centres of the kingdom, the *tengdana* are reported to have been slaughtered, and replaced by immigrants.[14] In other areas, by contrast, the land priests were confirmed in office and vested with the symbols of political authority.[15] Some displacement of autochthonous people occurred; there is evidence, for example, for the flight eastwards of Konkomba groups before the Dagomba horsemen, and of Dogon northwards before the Zandoma.[16] In general, however, the indigenous populations, the *tengabisi* or *tengdamba*, were incorporated into the new systems as parts of the commoner class. In western Dagomba, it has been argued, the assimilation

13 M. Boubou Hama, President of the Assembly of Niger, kindly gave me some account of this work in May 1966. I was able to see only the last page of the MS, which shows it to have been a copy made in A.H. 1337, A.D. 1918, by Muḥammad Aḥmad Shāj (?) of Timbuktu. See also V. Monteil, *Bulletin de l'Institut Français de l'Afrique Noire*, B, xxviii, 1966, p. 675.

14 Tamakloe, *op. cit.*, chs 1 and 2.

15 E. P. Skinner, *The Mossi of Upper Volta*, Oxford, 1964, pp. 17, 26. D. Zahan, 'The Mossi Kingdoms', in *West African Kingdoms in the Nineteenth Century*, ed. D. Forde and P. Kaberry, Oxford, 1967, p. 157.

16 D. Tait, 'History and social organisation', *T.H.S.G.*, i, 5, 1955, p. 201. Skinner, *op. cit.*, p. 8.

of Konkomba was facilitated by assigning to them a military rôle as bowmen of the army.[17] Whatever the techniques employed, integration seems to have been the prevalent norm, and although Mossi society in general is still characterised by a basic polarity between those who possess *nam*, political authority, and those who possess *tengasobundo*, ritual relationship with the land, this distinction has in practice become progressively obscured through the attainment of political authority by some *tengdamba* groups, and through the loss of it (and assumption of commoner status) by some groups descended from the early invading horsemen. The indigenous people of the region spoke mainly Gur languages, particularly of the Lobi-Dogon, Grusi, Gurma and Mole-Dagbane subfamilies.[18] It was languages of the latter group that the invaders came to speak, doubtless as a result of intermarriage, but reflecting perhaps the fact of Na Gbewa's association specifically with the Pusiga district.[19]

In the course of half a millennium the Mossi kingdoms have shown a remarkable stability and adaptation to change. While their political systems have become progressively differentiated from each other as a result of successive modifications in some but not all, they remain alike in many respects.[20] Succession to highest office—the 'skin'—in the early kingdoms was perhaps by rotation between two or more segments of the royal lineage, each in possession of its own towns and villages. Such a system survives in Nanumba, where the paramountcy passes between two such segments. Wagadugu, Dagomba, and Mamprussi, however, have all abandoned polydynastic systems, presumably in the interest of developing a strong centralising monarchy. In this transformation Wagadugu went furthest in the evolution of a unilineal succession system: the strong preference there for the eldest son of the predecessor brought about the continued elimination of collateral lines from the class of eligible royals.[21] In Dagomba it is only sons of a previous ruler who succeed, though son need not follow father immediately; furthermore, since the eighteenth century, sons occupying one of the three 'gate' chiefdoms, namely, Karaga, Mion or Savalugu, have been preferred.[22] In Mamprussi grandsons of

17 Tait, 'History and social organisation', pp. 206–7.

18 For the Gur languages see D. Westermann and M. A. Bryan, *Languages of West Africa*, Oxford, 1952; J. H. Greenberg, 'The Languages of Africa', *International Journal of American Linguistics*, xxix, 1, 1963.

19 Kusal, the language spoken in the district of which Pusiga is part, appears virtually identical with Dagbane and Mamprule; all three are closely related to the Mole of the northern kingdoms.

20 To these generalisations Fada N'Gurma, on which few data are available, may be an exception.

21 Skinner, *op. cit.*, p. 36. For West African systems of succession in general, see J. Goody, Introduction in *Succession to High Office*, ed. Goody, Cambridge, 1966.

22 H. A. Blair and A. Duncan-Johnstone, *Enquiry into the Constitution and Organisation of the Dagbon Kingdom*, Accra, 1932. See further Ferguson and Wilks, 'Chiefs, constitutions and the British in northern Ghana', in *West African Chiefs, Their Changing Status under Colonial Rule and Independence*, ed. M. Crowder and O. Ikime, Ife, 1970.

former rulers, as well as sons, are eligible.[23] In Yatenga brothers are preferred to sons in the succession, and in theory all segments of the royal dynasty retain claims on the paramountcy. In practice, however, segments were constantly eliminated from the succession often as a result of civil wars.[24] That the middle Black Volta chiefdoms of Wa, Buna, Dorimon and Wechiau, created by Mamprussi and Dagomba cavalrymen in the seventeenth century, all have polydynastic systems, suggests that the constitutional changes in Mamprussi and Dagomba, and probably in Wagadugu also, did not take place earlier than that century. In the case of Dagomba this was certainly so: the drum histories report that adjustments in the succession system and the creation of the three 'gates' occurred after the long struggle for the skin following the death of Na Gungobile, in the settlement of which it became necessary to invite arbitration by the Mamprussi king Atabia. This took place around 1700, significantly at a time when the external threat from Gonja was becoming serious.[25]

The elimination of 'princes'—descendants of Na Gbewa—from highest office produced in the chiefly class (possessors of *nam*) a division between 'royals' and 'nobles', that is, between those eligible and those ineligible for such office. This led to the emergence of two distinct hierarchies of chiefdoms, namely those through which one might pass to the paramountcy and those through which one could not. Rulers of these latter often became extremely powerful in their own right, and sometimes created virtually autonomous principalities within the kingdom. Such were the *dindamba* of the kingdom of Wagadugu—the rulers of Bussuma, Yako and Riziam for example—whose power the king was often obliged to curb through military action.[26] While the (in some ways) comparable *na-yanse* chiefdoms of Dagomba enjoyed rather less autonomy, their rulers nonetheless wielded considerable power.[27]

To counteract the growing power of the principalities, the *dindamba*, *na-yanse*, and the like, the Mossi rulers acted to strengthen their own positions by assigning new rôles to palace officials, investing them with agencies of central government including finance and provincial administration. The reliability of these officials, and their dependence on royal patronage, was ensured by recruiting them from non-princely circles; the descendants of Na Gbewa, in other words, were in general barred from such offices. In Wagadugu groups arose which specialised in the performance of administrative tasks, and from these the king appointed not only the five senior ministers in the capital but also many lesser functionaries. One of the senior ministerial posts, that of the Kamsaogha Na, was

23 Mackay, *op. cit.* Rattray, *Tribes of the Ashanti Hinterland*, Oxford, 1932.
24 Tauxier, *Le Noir du Yatenga*, Paris, 1917, p. 348. Zahan, *op. cit.*, p. 173.
25 Tait, Field Notes, 'Transcriptions and translations of the Dagomba drum histories', in *I.A.S.*
26 Skinner, *op. cit.*, ch. iv.
27 Blair and Duncan-Johnstone, *op. cit.*, *passim.*

customarily held by a eunuch.[28] In Yatenga, similarly, senior officials were appointed by the king, who could and sometimes did select non-Mossi for important posts.[29] In Dagomba the independent status of the administrative class was defined even more clearly, for there most of the senior offices in the capital were held by eunuchs, who came to exercise both decision-making and executive functions.[30]

The putative ties of kinship between the founders of both northern and southern Mossi dynasties were expressed in a series of ritual pacts linking each ruler with his contemporaries in the other kingdoms. These pacts received overt acknowledgement in the institutionalised exchange of gifts between rulers: the Mogho Naba of Wagadugu, for example, sent goods from his predecessor's estate—wives, slaves, horses and the like—to Fada N'Gurmu and to Dagomba, and annual gifts of a horse, slaves and cloth to Mamprussi.[31] The existence of these pacts was reflected in the infrequency of war between one Mossi kingdom and another. Mutual assistance, on the other hand, might be offered not only in the form of military aid but, as instanced above (p. 351), in the resolution of internal conflict.

The mass of people in the Mossi states was engaged in agriculture: in yam, cereal and legume cultivation. Surpluses passed, by various forms of taxation, to the local chiefs, who were able to maintain courts, often small-scale replicas of that of the king, and to equip and train a number of their kin as cavalrymen who could be mobilized rapidly in times of war. The larger courts attracted the settlement of strangers, and in their vicinity towns of some size were arising in the course of the seventeenth and eighteenth centuries. Based on markets involved in the local exchange of goods and frequently in long-range trade with other towns, such urban centres also attracted communities of craftsmen engaged for example in weaving, leather-working, and smithery. The early capital of the Dagomba, reputedly founded by Na Nyagse, a grandson of Na Gbewa, was abandoned for a new site in the late seventeenth century. Its ruins lie near the White Volta some thirty miles north of modern Tamale. The seventeenth-century township covered an area of a square mile or more, was possibly walled, and excavations in one section have revealed the presence of elaborate complexes of buildings with storied houses adjacent to large but open enclosures: it was perhaps a merchants' quarter with corrals for the beasts of burden.[32] The Mamprussi capital of Nalerigu certainly lay within

28 Skinner, *op. cit.*, p. 67.
29 Zahan, *op. cit.*, p. 164.
30 Tamakloe, *op. cit.*, ch. 7. The recent fieldwork of Phyllis Ferguson has revealed the extremely powerful position of the eunuchs in the precolonial Dagomba capital.
31 Skinner, *op. cit.*, pp. 96–8.
32 P. Shinnie and P. Ozanne, 'Excavations at Yendi Dabari', *T.H.S.G.*, vi, 1962. For the dating see I. Wilks, 'A note on the early spread of Islam in Dagomba', *T.H.S.G.*, viii, 1966. Recent inquiries by Mathewson and Ferguson indicate that the quarter excavated is firmly believed by the local Dagomba chiefs to have been Zongbila's—a Ya Na. If so, the Dagomba royals were then building in western Sudanese style.

a large walled area; construction of the walls probably took place in the late seventeenth or early eighteenth century. The smaller and early site of Ketare, further south on the Oti river, is remarkable for its elaborate series of banks and ditches protecting the township; it was perhaps a trading community, and possibly within Nanumba jurisdiction.[33]

A most important component in the population of the early northern Mossi towns was that of the Muslim traders of Malinke and Soninke origins, and of Upper and Middle Niger background. The earliest movement of such trading groups into Yatenga appears to have taken place in the late fifteenth century when, during the reign of Na Yedega, communities grew up in such centres as Gourcy.[34] Other groups moved into Wagadugu at much the same time; their first settlement there is traditionally associated with the reign of the sixth Mogho Naba, Kundumie, regarded as a contemporary of Na Yedega.[35] The descendants of these early settlers are known as the Yarse. They have become largely Mossi in culture, but still retain their ancient connection with commerce. Although some groups apostatised, others have remained Muslim. There is no evidence of any substantial migration of Muslims into the southern Mossi kingdoms at this early date. In the seventeenth century, however, another major movement appears to have taken place into the Kaya and Mànė district of Wagadugu, and thence into Dagomba. Prominent among these settlers were members of the Baghayughu lineage; they are undoubtedly to be linked with the Baghayughu of Timbuktu, where many famous jurisconsults bore this name. At the beginning of the eighteenth century the office of Chief of the Muslims (Yeri-Na) in Dagomba was vested in the Baghayughu of Sabari, a town near the new Dagomba capital of Yendi; and later in the same century the Baghayughu of Wagadugu were appointed *imāms* to the Mogho Naba.[36]

Early accounts of the commercial structure of the Mossi kingdoms are lacking, but nineteenth-century references to the import trade in salt, and the export trade in cotton cloth and livestock, cattle, horses, donkeys and sheep, are probably equally applicable to an earlier period.[37] Nevertheless, none of the northerly Mossi kingdoms ever attained commercial importance of the first rank in West Africa. The great gold and kola producing countries

33 R. D. Mathewson, 'Kitare: A preliminary report', *The West African Archaeological Newsletter*, iii, 1965.

34 Izard, *op. cit.*, pp. 72–5. Touba, north-west of Gourcy, may have been founded by the ~~Dyula prior to the arrival in the area of the Mossi chiefs, see Izard, p. 129.~~

35 L. Tauxier, *Le Noir du Soudan*, Paris, 1912, pp. 464–6.

36 Wilks, 'A note on the early spread of Islam in Dagomba', in *T.H.S.G.*, viii, 1967. For the Baghayughu of Timbuktu see e.g. Mahmud Kati, *op. cit.*, pp. 227–9, 308–10. For a general account of Islam in the Voltaic region, see Levtzion, *Muslims and Chiefs in West Africa*, Oxford, 1968. Phyllis Ferguson is at present engaged on a more intensive study of the early phases of Islamisation in Dagomba.

37 See e.g. T. E. Bowdich, *Mission from Cape Coast Castle to Ashantee*, London, 1819, pp. 331–5; H. Barth, *Travels and Discoveries in North and Central Africa*, 3 vols, New York edition of 1857, iii, p. 202; L. G. Binger, *Du Niger au Golfe de Guinée*, 2 vols, Paris, 1892, i, pp. 478–501.

lay farther south, and the major trade routes from them to the Middle Niger and to Hausaland bypassed the Mossi states to west and east respectively. For this reason they remained comparatively little known to the outside world until late, and our knowledge of their development still remains in consequence inadequate. Only Dagomba, by virtue of its southerly position, came to benefit appreciably from the economic prosperity of the forest region.

BIGHU AND THE NORTHERN AKAN KINGDOMS

The settlement of Muslims in the early northern Mossi kingdoms appears part of a much wider movement that began perhaps in the late fourteenth century and gathered momentum in the fifteenth. One major impulse in the movement appears to have been the concern of the Malian governments to develop and rationalise the structure of their trade with the gold-producing regions of West Africa, and thereby gain advantage from the favourable conditions of exchange brought about by the growth in world demand for gold at the time. Malian trading groups appear to have been granted concessions in the new venture—rather as the Portuguese Crown offered concessions to its merchants for the same purpose—and as a result colonies of Malian Muslims, or Dyula, came to be established both near the sources of gold and at staging-posts for the caravans passing along the routes between these frontier settlements and the greater markets of the Western Sudan. Much of this activity was focused on the rich auriferous areas along the middle Black Volta (the so-called 'Lobi' goldfields), and on the forest country further south (the 'Akan' fields).[38] The nature of the evidence makes it impossible accurately to date the beginnings of Dyula enterprise in these two areas, and communities might often break up and be re-formed as different centres of the extractive industry competed in importance, and as different trade paths were opened. Nevertheless, certain primary centres of early Dyula activity are now becoming recognisable.

Near the edge of the Black Volta goldfields, on a north-south trade road that ran east of the river, the Dyula established the adjacent settlements of Nasa and Visi. The corporate identity of the former was expressed in the use by its members of the group name Tarawiri (Traoré), and of the latter, by Kunatay (Konaté): both refer to well known high-status groups in metropolitan Mali. To the west of the Black Volta, in an otherwise similar setting, other Dyula established themselves in the vicinity of Buna. The evidence suggests that these settlements arose in the sixteenth or seventeenth century. It was their prosperity that presumably attracted into the area the Mamprussi and Dagomba cavalry commandos in the seventeenth century, whose activities, already referred to, led to the foundation of such small 'neo-Mossi' chiefdoms as Wa, near Nasa-Visi, and Buna.[39]

38 I. Wilks, *The Northern Factor in Ashanti History*, Legon, 1961, ch. 1; also 'A medieval trade-route from the Niger to the Gulf of Guinea', *Journal of African History*, iii, 2, 1962.

39 For Buna see Tauxier, *Le Noir du Bondoukou*, Paris, 1921, pp. 96, 547. For Wa, see below p. 382.

Further west, probably at much the same time, Kong was developed as a caravan town by Tarawiri, Baro and other Dyula groups, as was Bobo-Dioulasso to its north, midway to the great market town of Jenne on the Middle Niger. Both Kong and Bobo-Dioulasso subsequently passed under control of the Watara (p. 382 below).

Central to the development of the Dyula interest in trade with the Akan goldfields was the growth of the most important commercial town of Bighu,[40] lying south of the southern loop of the Black Volta and a little north of the forest. The early presence there of Bamba, Kamaghatay, Jabaghatay, Timitay, Kurubari, Gbani and other Dyula trading groups is indicated, together with Numu blacksmiths, all of Malian origins. For at least part of its history, political leadership among the Dyula of Bighu appears to have rested with the Kamaghatay, while the imāmate was held by the Bamba.[41] Around the Dyula nucleus other communities grew up. Settlements of the (Akan-speaking) Bron, the (Guan-speaking) Dompo and the (Senufo-speaking) Nafana are still identified; presumably in these lived the 'landlords' who acted as intermediaries between their countrymen and the Dyula merchants.[42] The various ruined sites extend over several square miles, with those of the Dyula, the Bron and the blacksmiths (Numu) lying central.[43]

The final collapse of Bighu, as indicated by the archaeological evidence, occurred in the early eighteenth century, about the time of the first Asante incursions into the area (p. 375 below). The two events may be related. There is, however, evidence of tension, erupting into urban warfare, between the component communities of Bighu, involving not only Muslim Dyula and non-Muslim Bron, but also one Dyula group and another. It may be, then, that some sections of the town had been abandoned prior to the Asante campaigns.[44] The dispersion of the Dyula of Bighu, some of whom resettled as far away as Kong but others nearby, as

40 The name is variously rendered, in Twi as Bew: in locally written Arabic works, Bighu, Biʿu, and Bayku; in Western and Central Sudanese sources, Bitu; and in French, Begho.

41 Wilks, F. N., and especially interviews with Shehu Khalid Bamba of Bofie, 31 December 1965, 24 February and 22 June 1966, who drew on his memory of an Arabic history of Bighu no longer in his possession.

42 The earliest settlement in the area, to which the first Dyula were attracted before founding Bighu proper, was the Dumpo (Guan) town of Jorga. Trial excavations on the site by Duncan Mathewson of the University of Ghana have yielded material radio carbon dated to around A.D. 1000–1200.

43 I have visited these sites on several occasions between 1959 and 1966, accompanied either by Bron of Hani or Dyula Kamaghatay of Namasa. Both Hani and Namasa lie within the broad area of the former township.

44 See e.g. Tauxier, *Le Noir du Bondoukou*, Paris, 1921, p. 80, n.4. For the conflicts see e.g. M. Delafosse, *Vocabulaires comparatifs de plus de 60 langues au dialectes parlés a la Côte d'Ivoire . . .*, Paris, 1904, pp. 165–7; *Les Frontières de la Côte d'Ivoire, de la Côte d'Or, et du Soudan*, Paris, 1908, pp. 226 *et seq.*; I. Wilks, F.N., copies in I.A.S., Karamoko Yusuf b. Ibrahim of Bonduku, 17 June, 1966 and I. Wilks, F.N., Shehu Khalid Bamba of Bofie, 31 December, 1965, 24 February and 22 June, 1966.

at Bonduku and Banda, was of consequence not only for the spread of Islam in the region, but also for its effect in destroying the monopolistic position previously held by Bighu in the distributive trade.

The date of the first Dyula settlement at Bighu has been a matter of some controversy.[45] It is the opinion of the writer that the town was already established as a commercial centre by the middle of the fifteenth century. Certainly its crucial position in the West African gold trade was known to Portuguese merchants in the Senegambia by the latter part of that century. Bighu served as a collecting point for gold both from the southern tip of the Black Volta goldfields in its immediate vicinity, and from the Akan fields further south. The Dyula caravans brought salt, textiles and brassware along the trade paths from the entrepôts of the Western Sudan, and returned northwards with gold consignments. Bighu was particularly closely linked with Jenne. An early account of what must be the trade between the two was given by Valentim Fernandes, who seems to have derived his information from late fifteenth century Senegambia sources. To Jenne, Fernandes reported:

> the merchants come who go to the gold mines. These traders belong to a certain race called the Ungaros: these are red or brownish. In fact, no one is allowed to approach these mines but those of this race, to the exclusion of others, because they are regarded with a great deal of trust. . . . When these Ungaro arrive at Jenne each merchant brings with him a hundred negro slaves, or more, to carry the salt on their heads from Jenne as far as the gold mines, and from there to bring back the gold. . . . The merchants who make trade with the gold mines do considerable business. Certain among them have trade that can rise to 60,000 mithqals [1 mtq = $\frac{1}{8}$ oz gold]; even those who are content to bring the salt to Jenne make 10,000 mithqals' business.[46]

The 'Ungaro' of this account are the *Wangara*, a name by which the Dyula commonly refer to themselves. While the Dyula exercised a monopolistic control over trade between Bighu and the north, on the southern routes other groups were active, such as the 'Akanists' to whom reference will be made later (p. 366 below). The Dyula extended operations into the forest region, and their presence (as 'Mandingos') among others coming to do business with the Portuguese at Elmina around 1500 is documented.[47]

45 Y. Person, 'Enquête d'une chronologie Ivoirienne', in *The Historian in Tropical Africa*, ed. Vansina, Mauny and Thomas, Oxford, 1964, *passim*.
46 V. Fernandes, *Description de la Côte d'Afrique de Ceuta au Sénégal*, ed. P. de Cernival and Th. Monod, Paris, 1938, pp. 84–7.
47 P. Pereira, *Esmeraldo de Situ Orbis*, English edition by G. H. T. Kimble, London, 1937, p. 120; French edition by R. Mauny, Bissau, 1956, p. 125; Fernandes, *Description de la Côte Occidentale d'Afrique (Senegal au Cap de Monte, Archipels)*, ed. Th. Monod, A. Teixeira da Mota and R. Mauny, Bissau, 1951, pp. 46–7; Wilks, 'A medieval trade-route from the Niger to the Gulf of Guinea', *J.A.H.*, iii, 2, 1962.

Another writer of the early sixteenth century, Pacheco Pereira, again apparently using Senegambian information, was first to mention specifically the Akan goldfields. He wrote of 'a country where there is much gold, which is called Toom'—that is, Dyula *Ton* (compare the Hausa *Tonawa*), 'the Akan'. It lay, he noted, '200 leagues beyond this kingdom of Mandingua' (that is, Mali), and he named one of the great gold markets there as 'Beetu'.[48] Bighu appears to have been known as Bitu in the Western Sudan, and a number of references in the Timbuktu *ta'rīkhs* to a 'Biṭu' are probably to be taken as to it.[49]

A connection undoubtedly existed between the development of the gold trade of Bighu, and the rise of the northern Akan, or Bron, kingdom of Bono (which survives as the present Takyiman state in Ghana). The early Bono centres lay some thirty to forty miles south-east of Bighu, on the edges of the forest. Traditions that the ruling house of Bono was of Western Sudanese (and ultimately Saharan) origins, reported by Meyerowitz,[50] must be set side by side with others that claim for it autochthonous status, representing the ancestress of its kings as having emerged from a cave in the vicinity of Takyiman. Meyerowitz has recorded a king-list that has thirty-six occupants in office from Asaman, the putative founder of Bono, to the Takyimanhene Nana Akumfi Ameyaw III, whose reign began in 1944. Using local records of the years of each king's reign—gold pieces deposited in caskets kept in the 'Chapel of the Stools' at Takyiman—Meyerowitz dated the foundation of the Bono kingdom to the end of the thirteenth century.[51] But since the Asante conquest of Bono in 1722–3 took place in the reign of the twentieth king, a war with Jakpa of Gonja (reigned 1622–3 to 1666–7) in that of the twelfth king, while the Nabaga expedition of the later sixteenth century occurred in that of the eighth king, it is apparent that Meyerowitz's date for the foundation of the kingdom cannot be accepted. In fact, if the average length of reign over the known period is extrapolated to the earlier, then the reign of the first Bono ruler would seem to fall in the third and fourth decades, and certainly in the first half, of the fifteenth century.[52]

That the rise of both Bighu and Bono might thus seem to belong to the same period suggests that the two developments were not unrelated. Meyerowitz reported Takyiman traditions of the rôle of Malian Muslim traders in the development of the Bono kingdom. Muslim settlement there

48 Pereira, *op. cit.*, edn of 1937, pp. 88–9; edn of 1956, pp. 65–7.
49 Person, *op. cit.*, pp. 329–31, rejects the identification of the Bitu of the *ta'rīkhs* with Bighu. For a discussion of this point see Tauxier, *Le Noir de Bondoukou*, Paris, 1921, ch. 3.
50 E. L. R. Meyerowitz, *Akan Traditions of Origin*, London, 1952, pp. 33–4; *The Akan of Ghana*, London, 1958, pp. 103–4.
51 Meyerowitz, *Akan Traditions of Origin*, ch. 1.
52 These suggested revisions of Bono chronology agree closely with those put forward by Colin Flight, *J.A.H.*, xi, 2, 1970. Flight offers a convincing explanation of the distortions in the local records.

is said to date from the time of its second king. The third ruler Obunumankoma is reported to have travelled extensively in the Western Sudan, under Muslim auspices, before coming to the throne. By the time of the eight and ninth rulers, probably in the second half of the sixteenth century, sections of the Bono royal family are said to have adopted Islam, and with the support of the trading element to have constituted a faction within the state the interests of which were not always compatible with those of the rulers.[53] The early growth of Bono, like Bighu, seems then to have been stimulated by the Muslim Dyula connection. But whilst Bighu was a focus of the distributive trade, Bono was probably important primarily as a centre of the extractive industry.

Although washing of the rivers for gold was doubtless of high antiquity in the region, Takyiman tradition associates the beginning of gold mining as such specifically with the third king Obunumankoma,[54] whose *floruit* may tentatively be placed in the third quarter of the fifteenth century, and whose reputed travels in the Western Sudan look significant in view of the fact that mining techniques must surely have been introduced into the Akan and Black Volta goldfields from the Bambuk and Bure ones in western Mali. Indeed, the tenth king of Bono, Ali Kwame (probably late sixteenth century), is said also to have travelled in the Western Sudan, to the 'Mande Wangara' country, particularly in order to study mining,[55] while a major reorganisation of the Bono industry is reported to have been carried out by the thirteenth king Owusu Aduam (mid-seventeenth century), whose queen-mother Akua Gyamfiwa had likewise visited the Sudan and had a slave husband who was a miner and goldsmith.[56]

There is very little information in early written sources on the extractive industry. Indeed several writers commented on the secrecy by which mining enterprise was surrounded, this being fostered by those with a vested interest in production.[57] Such evidence as there is, from both traditional accounts as reported by Meyerowitz[58] and early literary sources, indicates first, the chiefly control of and involvement in mining; second, the extensive use of slave labour; and third, the application of not inconsiderable resources of management and technology. All three features are implicit in one of the earliest of these descriptions, that of Valentim Fernandes of *c.* 1500: 'The mines are very deeply driven into the ground. The kings have slaves who they put into the mines and they give them

53 Meyerowitz, *The Akan of Ghana*, pp. 106–7, 114–17; *At the Court of an African King*, London, 1962, pp. 79–80.
54 Meyerowitz, *The Akan of Ghana*, p. 107.
55 *Ibid.*, p. 117.
56 *Ibid.*, pp. 119–20.
57 See e.g. V. Fernandes, *Description de la Côte d'Afrique de Ceuta au Sénégal*, ed. P. de Cernival and Th. Monod, Paris, 1938, p. 89; J. Barbot, *A Description of the Coasts of North and South Guinea*, vol. v of Churchill's *Collection of Voyages and Travels*, London, 1732, p. 229.
58 E. L. R. Meyerowitz, *The Sacred State of the Akan*, London, 1951, ch. 12.

wives who they take with them, and they bring forth and raise children in these mines. . . .'[59]

The Numu blacksmiths, who unlike the Dyula were not Islamised, may have constituted a technological element in the mining communities, responsible for making and repairing tools while possibly participating in actual underground operations. Their enterprise was protected by ritual prohibitions, and areas of ritual jurisdiction arose, comparable with the 'parishes' of the land priests but based on a field of technical proficiency: in the case of the Numu, the use of high temperature forced-draught fires. The smiths retain to this day their ritual independence *vis-à-vis* the local political and religious authorities, as illustrated in the annual Apo ceremony at Takyiman, a basically Akan-type festival first described by Rattray.[60] On this occasion a ritual struggle between the smiths and both the Takyimanhene and the priest of the Tano cult is enacted, the former 'fighting' with their tongs. The smiths are finally pacified with drinks.[61] The smiths of Takyiman are today Akan in language and culture. Other groups, some to the west of Banda, retain a non-Akan culture and speak a Malinke dialect. Those of the small Bron chiefdom of Hani, which is near the former blacksmith quarter of Bighu, are culturally transitional: partly but not fully assimilated to Akan custom. They speak Akan but use Malinke in ritual, are organised as the Konti division of Hani under a Kontihene who is also Tonfohene, head of the smiths; and at the annual *odwira* ceremony purify not ancestral stools, but hammers and anvils.[62] Masked dancing cults found in the region, such as that of Sakrabundu, are Malinke in origin, and may have been introduced there by the Numu smiths, subsequently acquiring a wider clientèle among the Bron and others.[63]

The increase in economic activity in both Akan and Black Volta goldfields, beginning in the fifteenth century, stimulated the growth of towns as centres of trade and production. Pacheco Pereira mentions two other markets, Baha and Banbarana, both presumably in the same region as Bighu and possibly part of the one complex.[64] The small Bron chiefdom of Wenchi, between Bighu and Bono (and then at its old site of Ahwene), was described in 1629 as involved in trade with the 'Akanists' and as producing gold and fine cloths; the growth of secondary industries such as weaving was probably a feature of the period.[65] One result of the

59 V. Fernandes, *Description . . .*, pp. 86–7. The account is, of course, suggestive rather than accurate.
60 Rattray, *Ashanti*, Oxford, 1923, ch. 14.
61 Meyerowitz, *The Sacred State of the Akan*, pp. 35–6.
62 K. Ameyaw, F.N. in I.A.S., Traditions from Brong-Ahafo, I.A.S., BA/1–4; Wilks, F.N., copies in I.A.S., various visits to Hani, 1959–66.
63 It is possible that the masked dancing cults gave rise to such stories as that of Pereira: *op. cit.*, edn of 1937, p. 89, about the 'dog-faced' people of the mining areas.
64 'Baha' is probably Buya, the name of an old Dumpo and Dyula township near Bofie, which R. D. Mathewson has shown to be contemporary with Bighu.
65 Chart 743 dd. 25 December 1629, General State Archives, The Hague. See *Ghana N.Q.*, ix, pp. 14–15.

economic take-off in the region was the rise in demand for slaves, as carriers for the merchants and as labour in the mines. Thus, when the Portuguese began trading at Elmina at the end of the fifteenth century, they found there a demand for slaves, which they met by transporting men by caravel from Benin and the Congo. These slaves were sold to the interior merchants, until the whole enterprise was finally declared illegal by the Portuguese king João III (1521–57) on the grounds that many of the slaves became Muslim in their servitude.[66] The slave porters of Jenne, referred to by Valentim Fernandes (above, p. 356), may well then have originated from the Bight of Benin and beyond.

Although regarded as the earliest of all the major Akan kingdoms, Bono belonged to the distinctively northern, or Bron, subgroup of these. The very close resemblance between the northern and southern Akan today, in language and in social, cultural and political institutions, is probably largely a result of the spread of southern influences in the northern area from the early eighteenth century onwards. As already suggested, however, a northern Akan kingdom such as Bono was originally closely linked economically with the Western Sudan, had a strong Sudanese Muslim component in its make-up, and exhibited some markedly northern cultural traits in, for example, the importance of the horse in both ritual and everyday life,[67] and in other matters to which Goody has drawn attention.[68] Rattray's reference to the absence of the typically southern Akan matriclans (*abusua*) among the 'pure' Bron, and to their organisation by wards, may also indicate that northern Akan society was based on cognatic rather than matrilineal groups.[69]

The miners, and those who panned the rivers, were producing ultimately for world markets: much of the gold passed through the entrepôts of the Western Sudan and along the Saharan caravan trails to the ports of North Africa, whence it found its way into Europe and the East. Major structural changes in the pattern of trade resulted from the development of new markets on the Guinea Coast following the first arrival of Portuguese traders there. By 1500 the Portuguese were exporting through Elmina, on the most conservative estimate, some 20,000 ounces of gold annually, or somewhat over half a ton.[70] The expansion of this southern trade necessarily involved some contraction of the northern, at least until the production of gold might catch up with the growing demand in both quarters. Competition between Portuguese and (later) other European merchants, and their Western Sudanese counterparts, continued throughout the sixteenth and

66 Pereira, *op. cit.*, edn of 1937, p. 121; de Barros, *op. cit.*, edn of 1937, p. 124–5.
67 Anquandah, *op. cit.*; Meyerowitz, *At the Court of an African King*, p. 81.
68 Goody, 'The Akan and the North', *G.N.Q.*, ix, 1966, pp. 19–22.
69 Rattray, *Ashanti Law and Constitution*, Oxford, 1929, pp. 64–5.
70 A. F. C. Ryder, 'The Portuguese in West Africa'. Paper presented to the Third Conference on African History and Archaeology, SOAS, University of London, 1961. See also de Barros, *op. cit.*, edn of 1937, pp. 120–2; Pereira, *op. cit.*, edn of 1937, pp. 119–21.

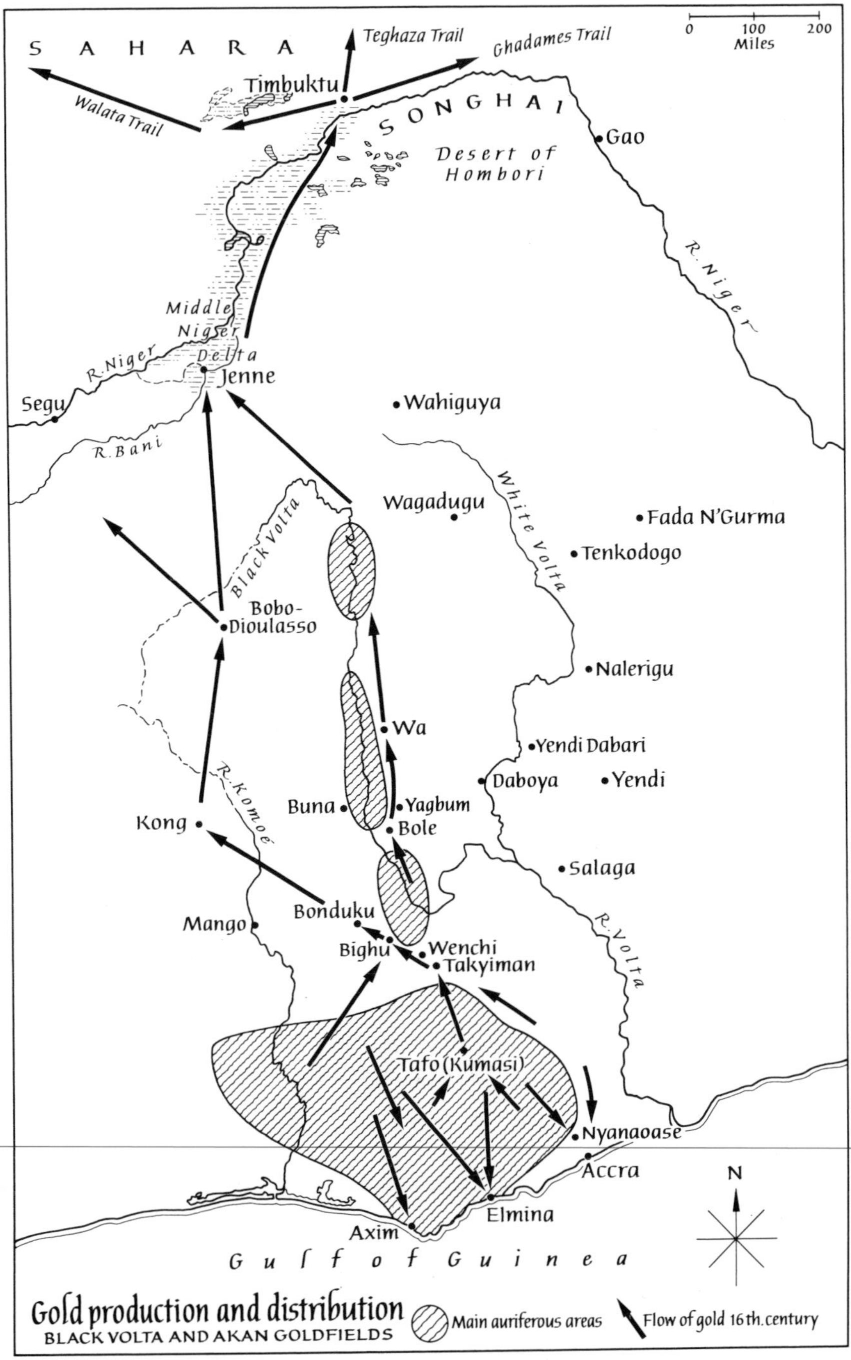
S A H A R A
Teghaza Trail
Ghadames Trail
0 100 200
Miles
Timbuktu
Walata Trail
SONGHAI
Gao
Desert of Hombori
R. Niger
Middle Niger Delta
R. Niger
Jenne
Segu
Wahiguya
R. Bani
Wagadugu
White Volta
Fada N'Gurma
Tenkodogo
Black Volta
Bobo-Dioulasso
Nalerigu
Wa
Yendi Dabari
Daboya
Yendi
R. Komoé
Buna
Yagbum
Bole
Kong
Salaga
Bonduku
Mango
Bighu
Wenchi
Takyiman
R. Volta
Tafo (Kumasi)
Nyanaoase
Accra
N
Elmina
Axim
Gulf of Guinea
Gold production and distribution
BLACK VOLTA AND AKAN GOLDFIELDS
Main auriferous areas
Flow of gold 16th.century

10:1

seventeenth centuries, until in the later part of the seventeenth century the trade in slaves largely superseded that in gold at the maritime markets. Portuguese missions to Western Sudanese rulers in the late fifteenth and early sixteenth centuries, sent from Elmina and elsewhere,[71] appear to have achieved nothing towards averting a trade war—if indeed such was their purpose—and no regularised diplomatic intercourse was maintained.

The creation of the Gonja kingdom in the sixteenth century may have been contingently an outcome of this struggle for gold supplies. Versions of Gonja tradition, committed to writing in Arabic possibly as early as the beginning of the eighteenth century,[72] suggest that the founder of that kingdom, Nabaga, was a member of a punitive expedition despatched by the king of Mali against Bighu as a result of the drastic fall in the consignments of gold reaching the Malian markets. It seems not unreasonable to suppose that the southern Dyula had found more favourable outlets for their trade, through Akan intermediaries, to the Guinea Coast. However that may be, Bighu—according to one Arabic text—was occupied by Malian forces, but Nabaga, choosing to remain in the prosperous Voltaic region, led his cavalry north to attack and sack Buna, before crossing the Black Volta to establish an encampment at Yagbum a little east of that river. Subsequently Yagbum became the base for Nabaga's wars of conquest against the autochthonous peoples of the area, to which reference is made in the mid-eighteenth-century Arabic work, the *Kitāb Ghunjā*. In these wars he was assisted by the *faqih* Isma'īl, of the Kamaghatay Dyula of Bighu.[73]

Yagbum became the capital of the Gonja rulers, the descendants of Nabaga. The main period of Gonja expansion, from its original nucleus around Yagbum, fell within the reign of the king Jakpa Lanta (1622–3 to 1666–7), who extended his conquests as far east as the Oti River, establishing a number of administrative divisions which he distributed among his (real or classificatory) sons.[74] It was this expansion that brought the Gonja into conflict with Dagomba, and started a series of wars between the two powers that culminated in the invasion of western Dagomba in 1713 (below, p. 381). In Gonja the Nbanya, as the descendants of the Malian settlers at Yagbum are known, came to form a princely estate dispersed

71 De Barros, *op. cit.*, edn of 1937, pp. 143–5.

72 Wilks, 'A note on the chronology and origins of the Gonja Kings', *G.N.Q.*, 1966. A copy of this work, *'Umūr Ajdādinā al-Ghunjawiyyīn*, was found in Yendi in 1968, see Wilks, F.N., 14 August 1968 (in *Muslim Office in Dagomba*, I.A.S., 1968).

73 *Kitāb Ghunjā,* opening section. (This section appears to follow an original of *c.* 1710, possibly by the same author as the work mentioned in the preceding note. An edition of this mid-eighteenth-century work from Gonja is in course of preparation by N. Levtzion and I. Wilks).

74 As a result of Jakpa's role in establishing the structure of the Gonja state, extant oral traditions refer to him as founder of the kingdom and as having himself come from Mali; see e.g. D. H. Jones, 'Jakpa and the Foundation of Gonja', *T.H.S.G.*, vi, 1962.

Larabanga: a traditional Dyula mosque in northern Ghana

throughout the territorial divisions created by Jakpa Lanta. Under Nbanya chiefs, the subject peoples constituted a commoner estate, the *nyamasi*. Within it, however, they retained their distinct identities, as Vagella, Anga, Tampolensi and the rest, and continued to maintain ritual control over the land, exercised through land-priests who, unlike the *tengdanas* of western Dagomba, were not dispossessed.[75]

Of intermediate status between the princely and commoner estates were the Muslims, the *Kramo*. In view of the proximity of Bighu, there had probably been some Dyula settlement in the Gonja region before the foundation of the kingdom: the Bamba of Bole in western Gonja, on a route between Bighu and Nasa-Visi, seem for example to be very early settlers. The dominant element in the Muslim estate, however, consisted of those Dyula from Bighu, especially Kamaghatay and Jabaghatay, who settled in Gonja under Nbanya patronage at the beginning of the seventeenth century, and who were granted the imāmates of Yagbum and of the divisional capitals.[76] In consequence of its contacts with other Dyula communities outside Gonja, the Muslim estate became prominent in the commercial life of the kingdom, and the early development of the kola trade between the forest country to the south and the Western Sudan must have been due partly to their initiative. Early in the nineteenth century a shift in trade occurred away from the older centres like Gbuipe in western

75 J. Goody, 'Circulating succession among the Gonja', in *Succession to High Office*, ed. Goody, Cambridge, 1966; 'The Over-Kingdom of Gonja', in *West African Kingdoms in the Nineteenth Century*, ed. Forde and Kaberry.
76 *Kitāb Ghunjā*, opening section.

Gonja, and to the new centre of Salaga in the easterly Kpembe division. In the course of time Salaga became the major entrepôt in the kola trade in West Africa, and attracted settlers from Hausaland and Bornu who came to dominate the older Dyula trading element.[77]

THE EARLY SOUTHERN AKAN KINGDOMS

The forest country between the Black Volta and the Guinea Coast is inhabited by Akan-speaking people belonging to a number of highly extended exogamous matriclans or *abusua*: Oyoko, Bretuo, Agona, Asene, and the like. The indications are that these matriclans became dispersed at an early date, and certainly long before 1600. A high degree of ideological conformity enforced by clan elders is designed to achieve subscription to a common tradition throughout the clan, and so obscures the fact that parts of the same *abusua* are frequently of quite different origins. The matriclan system has, in other words, been used as a device for integrating diverse elements into southern Akan society. Many groups regard themselves as autochthonous, and assert this claim through myths which link their founding ancestresses with particular localities in the central forest region. Thus the Oyoko royals of Kumasi derive themselves from Ankyaw Nyame, who descended from the sky by a golden chain at Asiakwa, while the Bretuo royals of Mampon look back to Asiama Nyankopon Guahyia, whose descent at Ahinsan was made by a silver chain.[78]

The fusion, in the forest zone, of different traditions into a distinct and fairly homogeneous southern Akan culture is in marked contrast to the situation in the savannahs to the north, where different traditions tended to accumulate layer by layer, so that there is not for example any distinct Gonja culture as such, but only the several cultures of the component estates. It may be suggested that Western Sudanese groups moving into more southerly savannahs, such as the founders of the Mossi kingdoms, found themselves in a familiar environment and, with little adjustment necessary, were able to retain their cultural identity. Savannah peoples moving into the forest region, by contrast, found themselves in a highly alien environment, and thus tended to become absorbed into the cultural tradition of the older societies. The fusion of many different elements into a distinctive southern Akan tradition made it a particularly vigorous one, and many of its features were borrowed by the predominately patrilineal Ewe, Ga, Adangme and Guan-speaking people who live to the east and south-east of the Akan, where the forest country gives way to the open grasslands of the Dahomey gap and Accra Plains.

77 The full history of the kola trade remains to be written, but see K. Krieger, 'Kola-Karawanen', in *Mitteilungen des Instituts für Orientforschung*, ii, 2, 1954.

78 A. A. Y. Kyerematen, 'Ashanti Royal Regalia: Their History and Functions', D. Phil. thesis, University of Oxford, 1966, pp. 103–8. J. Agyeman-Duah, 'Mampong, Ashanti: a traditional history to the reign of Nana Safo Kantanka', *T.H.S.G.*, iv, 2, 1960. Ahinsan and Asiakwa are some seventy miles apart.

By 1600 the Mossi kingdoms, and at least the northern Akan kingdom of Bono, were already well established. In the forest region, on the other hand, the situation appears to have been extremely fluid, and correspondingly difficult to appraise: only in the light of further research will it become possible to offer any definitive account of the early history of the southern Akan people.[79] Nevertheless, five basic and connected propositions about their progress may plausibly be argued. First, that a well developed agricultural complex must have existed in the forest from prehistoric times, but one that was greatly enriched by the introduction of New World crops through the maritime trade in the sixteenth century. Secondly, that the growth of the maritime trade after 1471 led to a period of rapid social and political change in the coastal hinterland,[80] and stimulated the emergence of comparatively large-scale kingdoms, of which Asante was latest and most powerful. Thirdly, that small-scale kingdoms, with all the accoutrements of centralised political authority, existed before the beginnings of the maritime trade with Europe: thus at Elmina in 1482 the Portuguese treated with the local 'king' who was attended by 'captains' and a following of stool-carriers, shield-bearers, drummers and musicians,[81] while shortly afterwards they made contact with various Akan 'kings' and 'princes' from inland.[82] Fourthly, that the emergence of the southern Akan kingdoms involved the intricate interplay of northern and southern Akan interests. Fifthly, that the progress of urbanisation, already advanced by the seventeenth century, extends back into the sixteenth and in some cases into the fifteenth. Ozanne has drawn attention to the existence of small towns in the Accra grasslands in the pre-1600 period, and has suggested that these may be associated with an early gold trade to the north.[83] Over one hundred miles from the coast, in the heart of the forest, the town of Tafo was already of some importance by the early sixteenth century, and probably played an important rôle in the rerouting of the gold trade from northern markets to southern ones in that century.[84]

The rise of the southern Akan kingdom of Akwamu illustrates some of these propositions. Its origins go back to about 1500, when a group of migrants, apparently traders accompanied by fighting men, moved from the northern Akan region and settled in the forest country behind Portuguese Elmina. There they founded the town of Kumkunso, some thirty

79 But see e.g. A. Boahen, 'The Origins of the Akan', and K. Y. Daaku, 'Pre-Ashanti States', both in *G.N.Q.*, ix, 1966.
80 See K. Y. Daaku, 'The European traders and the coastal states 1630–1720', *T.H.S.G.*, viii, 1965.
81 De Barros, *op. cit.*, edn of 1937, pp. 117–23.
82 A. F. C. Ryder, *Materials for West African History in Portuguese Archives*, London, 1965, various items, 112–51.
83 P. Ozanne, 'Notes on the early historic archaeology of Accra', *T.H.S.G.*, vi, 1962; Notes on the later prehistory of Accra', *J.H.S.N.*, iii, 1, 1964.
84 K. Y. Daaku, 'Pre-Ashanti states', *G.N.Q.*, ix, 1966; Wilks, *The Northern Factor in Ashanti History*, and 'A medieval trade-route from the Niger to the Gulf of Guinea', *loc. cit.*

miles inland: it is represented by the present Twifo-Heman. The leader of the migration of the Abrade, as the group was known, is remembered as Agyen Kokobo, to whom the ruler of the present Akwamu state, in the Lower Volta gorge, claims to be twenty-eighth in succession. As already noted, by 1500 over half a ton of gold was exported annually through Elmina, and the major changes brought about in the pattern of commodity flow in the late fifteenth century must have been in part the work of Abrade quick to seize opportunities offered by the opening of the new coastal trade outlets.

In the course of the sixteenth century Abrade participation in the gold trade, and their tendency to live off trade rather than by it, brought them into conflict with the surrounding southern Akan people, the 'Akanist' (Accani, Accanisten, Akanisterne, etc.) of the European reports of the period. Under Adow, fourth ruler in succession to Agyen Kokobo, a section of the Abrade with their followers moved slowly across the hinterland of the Gold Coast—as this part of the Guinea Coast inevitably came to be known—and finally, not long before 1600 and under their seventh leader Akotia, resettled some twenty miles behind Accra. This eastwards movement appears to have involved no diminution in Abrade involvement in the gold trade to the coast. The Portuguese had built a fort at Accra in 1577 or shortly after, and although forced by local hostility to abandon it in 1578, continued to trade from the beaches where they were joined by the Dutch in the early seventeenth century—the prelude to the fierce struggle for position at Accra by Dutch, Danes, English and Swedes in the middle part of the century. Many early seventeenth-century writers commented on the brisk gold trade at Accra, and, since gold was not produced locally, one must assume that inland traders often found it safer to travel to Accra by the open country to the north and south of the Volta gorge than to use the tortuous forest paths leading to Elmina.[85]

By 1600 already southern Akan in culture, and presumably with many southern Akan adherents, the Abrade under Akotia became clients of the Accra rulers, who sanctioned their settlement on the northern Accra frontier at Nyanaoase. Accra policy at this time was directed to creating for themselves a middleman rôle in trade between the European merchants on the coast and the 'Akanist' traders from the interior, by confining the former to the beaches while preventing the latter crossing the northern border. It was in pursuance of this policy that the Accra rulers encouraged the Abrade settlement, so strengthening the northern frontier against 'Akanist' attempts to pass through to the beaches. By the third decade of the seventeenth century this policy had proved successful, and in or near Nyanaoase the large gold mart of Abonse grew up, where

85 This section is based on the writer's fuller study of Akwamu, in preparation, and draws upon European archival sources, Akwamu traditions and the archaeological work of Ozanne.

traders from the interior were obliged to transact business with Accra middlemen. The power of the Abrade clients grew steadily throughout the first half of the seventeenth century, and by the middle of that century they were not only in control of the passage of trade through Abonse but also moving into positions of command to east and west of that market, cutting other trade paths that led from the interior to the coast windward or leeward of Accra and so channelling the flow of commodities into Abonse. By this period it becomes possible to speak of the Akwamu kingdom of Nyanaoase, which, although still technically under Accra, was rapidly becoming more powerful than its patron.

As a result of the pattern of its growth, the Akwamu kingdom of Nyanaoase acquired a dual character, a matter first noted by Rømer in the mid-eighteenth century.[86] On the one hand there was Akwamu proper, a trade state centred on Nyanaoase and its environs—'where the king could summon his nobles with a cannon-shot', as Rømer had it. There, surrounding the king, lived numerous officials concerned with the regulation of the Abonse market: with the control of commodity flow, with the taxation of trade, and with the price-fixing machinery.[87] On the other hand there was the tribute state, a political system for the control and exploitation of those peoples who had been brought under the authority of the Abrade rulers as Akwamu had extended its territorial jurisdiction in the attempt to engross trade over an ever larger area. The subject peoples included Guan, Ewe, Ga and Adangme as well as southern Akan of Akyem and Kwahu. They appear in some cases to have been placed under Akwamu and often Abrade overlords,[88] but in other cases to have been left under their own chiefs as tribute-paying vassals of Nyanaoase.[89]

Akwamu expansion fell into two distinct phases, the transition from the one to the other being in 1677. In the earlier phase it appears to have been slow and uncoordinated, a matter perhaps of infiltration rather than conquest. Groups spread along the Akwapim scarp, and into the densely forested region to its north, establishing settlements among the Guan and southern Akan people of the area over whom, by their greater organisational resources, they gradually gained an ascendancy. By contrast, the later post-1677 phase was one of concerted military campaigns which made the Akwamu presence felt westwards as far as the Fante country, northwards on the Afram Plains, and eastwards across the Volta to the frontiers of Dahomey. The major campaigns are recorded in the archives of the European trading companies on the coast: *c.* 1680, the western Adangme;

86 L. F. Rømer, *Tilforladelig Efterretning om Kysten Guinea*, Copenhagen, 1760, p. 122.
87 O. Dapper, *Naukerige beschrijvinge der Afrikaensche gewesten* . . ., Amsterdam, 1668, p. 455.
88 See e.g. I. Wilks, 'Akwamu and Otublohum: an eighteenth-century Akan marriage arrangement', *Africa*, xxix, 4, 1959.
89 For taxation and tribute see e.g. E. Tilleman, *En Liden enfoldig Beretning om det landskab Guinea*, Copenhagen, 1967, pp. 107–12.

1688–9, the Agona; 1702, Little Popo and Whydah east of the Volta; 1707, the inland Ewe, also east of the Volta; and 1710, Kwahu.[90]

The dividing line between these two phases of Akwamu expansion, so very different in character, occurred when the Abrade of Nyanaoase, under Ansa Sasraku (died 1689), seized power from their patron, the Accra king, by what may perhaps be regarded as a *coup d'état*. In this action the Abrade had the support of an influential section of the Accra people, probably the mercantile community which saw its interests best promoted under the dynamic Abrade rather than under its own traditional rulers: there were, for example, ritual prohibitions against the Accra kings even visiting the beaches in person.[91] In 1677 the Akwamu seized Great Accra, the capital town which lay midway between Nyanaoase and the shore,[92] and overcame loyalist opposition with the use of its cannons. In the course of the fighting the Accra king Okai Koi lost his life. The Accra royals took refuge in Small Accra on the coast, but, unable to organise a countercoup, went into exile first in Fetu to the west and finally in Little Popo beyond the Volta.[93] Atrocity stories about Okai Koi's mother, Dode Akabi, probably received currency at this time, as attempts to discredit the old regime.[94]

To a French mission that visited Nyanaoase in 1688 its ruler, by then styled king of Accra, appeared 'one of the greatest lords of Guinea'.[95] A decade later the Dutch factor Willem Bosman wrote of 'the great kingdom of Aquamboe', whose 'King and his nobles, or rather favourites, are so very rich in gold and slaves, that I am of the opinion that this country singly possesses greater treasures than all those we have hitherto described taken together'.[96] Estimates of the number of men that Akwamu could put into the field in the early eighteenth century ranged from 10,000 to 25,000 or over.[97] It is clear that its fighting forces were armed mainly with missile weapons, the bow, the musket, and the newest of all, the cannon.[98]

The kingdom of Nyanaoase disintegrated in 1730. Of the many factors underlying its collapse, three may be isolated as being of basic importance. First, by reason of the rapidity of its expansion, the organisational resources

90 For the expansion of Akwamu see I. Wilks, 'The rise of the Akwamu Empire, 1650–1710', *T.H.S.G.*, iii, 2, 1957, *passim*.

91 Tilleman, *op. cit.*, pp. 93–4.

92 Great Accra has been partially excavated, see Ozanne, Notes on the early Historic Archaeology of Accra, *T.H.S.G.*, vi, 1962.

93 Wilks, 'The Rise of the Akwamu Empire, 1650–1710', *loc. cit., T.H.S.G.,* pp. 106–11; M. J. Field, *Social Organisation of the Ga People*, London, 1940, pp. 144–6.

94 See e.g. C. C. Reindorf, *History of the Gold Coast and Asante*, Basle, 1895, pp. 18–19.

95 Sr Du Casse, 'Mémoire ou relation du Sr Du Casse', in P. Roussier, *L'Etablissement d'Issiny 1687–1701*, Paris, 1935, p. 13.

96 W. Bosman, *A New and Accurate Description of the Coast of Guinea*, first Dutch edition of 1704; London English edition of 1705, p. 70: the other countries being those of the Gold Coast.

97 *Ibid.*, p. 181. J. Rask, *En Kort og sandferdig Reisebeskrivelse til og fra Guinea*, Copenhagen, 1754, p. 150.

98 PRO. T. 70/175: letter from Sir Dalby Thomas dd. 13 May 1705.

of Akwamu ceased to be commensurate with the size of the territory it had to control, and undue strain was thrown on the agencies of central government. Secondly, as emphasis changed—with the growth of the sugar industry in the West Indies—from the trade in gold to that in slaves, the Akwamu authorities were not only unable to prevent the spread of illicit slave raiding, that is the seizure of freemen by marauding bands, but even came to participate in it: this gave rise to unrest among both Akwamu and the subject people who faced these depredations. Thirdly, the apparent failure to evolve clear rules of succession to highest office resulted in the formation of rival foci of authority within the state, and led to debilitating internecine strife.[99] In 1730 conflict arose between the Akwamu king and his mother's brother, and numerous rebellions broke out among the subject people of the Akwapim scarplands. Southern Akan chiefs in Akyem, long hostile towards the Abrade, seized the opportunity and sacked Nyanaoase, killing the king. A section of the Abrade royals retired into the eastern Akwamu territories, and in the Volta Gorge founded a new capital, the present Akwamufie. Other Abrade chiefs, such as those of Aburi and Asamankese, transferred allegiance to one or other of the three states among which the conquered Akwamu lands were apportioned: Akyem Abuakwa, Akyem Kotoku, and Akwapim,[100] all under rulers of the Agona *abusua*.

Akwamu has been treated at some length both because the records are particularly full and because, although small-scale states existed in the forest region and on its southern fringes earlier, the kingdom of Nyanaoase was the first large system to emerge there. It organised its resources on a hitherto unprecedented scale apparently to one basic end: the promotion of trade. Although the Abrade were of northern origins, Akwamu cannot be regarded other than as a southern Akan state. Indeed, the two other major southern Akan powers of the seventeenth century, the Denkyira and the Fante, appear also to have included a northern Akan element. The ancient capital of the Denkyira kingdom, Abankeseso, lay in the thickly forested country between Lake Bosumtwe and the River Offin. The kingdom probably came into being in the early seventeenth century, for Boa Amponsem, its sixth king according to the traditional regnal lists, is known from documentary sources to have been in office at the end of that century. Many prominent Denkyira lineages, including that of the royal house, maintain firm traditions of having migrated from the Bron area. Folk memories of the importance of gold in the early Denkyira economy receive support from contemporary writers. Bosman, for example, noted that the Denkyira 'are possessed of vast treasures of gold, besides what their own mines supply them with: either by plunder from others, or their own commerce'.[101] One very important centre of the extractive industry

99 See e.g. Bosman, *op. cit.*, p. 65. Tilleman, *op. cit.*, p. 105.
100 Wilks, 'Akwamu and Otublohum . . .', *loc. cit.*
101 Bosman, *op. cit.*, letter vi.

was at Manso Nkwanta, to the north of Abankeseso; its 'abundance of deep pits underground' was reported as early as 1707.[102] The sixth ruler of Denkyira, Boa Amponsem, is still commemorated in the saying, *Amponsem a odi sika atomprade*, 'Amponsem, who uses only newly dug gold'.

The main period of Denkyira expansion corresponded closely with the second phase of that of Akwamu. It is associated in tradition specifically with the reign of Boadu Akafu Brempon, predecessor of Boa Amponsem. By the end of the seventeenth century the Denkyira had established some sort of domination over the Twifo and the 'Akanists' of Assin, both to the south, and over the Wassaw and Aowin to the west, both rich gold-producing districts. Barbot referred to trade from Axim on the coast through Wassaw and as far north as the Niger.[103] While Denkyira expansion was thus, like that of Akwamu, a result of the attempt to engross trade, it also secured for the kingdom control of major centres of the extractive industry. It was probably on account of this that Denkyira came into early conflict with the rising power of Asante. It suffered a total defeat after a series of wars between 1699 and 1701. Numerous Denkyira chiefs transferred allegiance to the Asante king Osei Tutu, and were incorporated mainly into the Kumasi division. Other groups re-established themselves south of Abankeseso and, while retaining their Denkyira identity, came later to accept for a time the political overlordship of Asante.[104]

The Fante are distributed over a score of very small states: Bosman described them as 'republics'. About half of these were the creation of the Borbor Fante, who universally claim to have originated from Bono (Takyiman). It would appear that they arrived on the Guinea Coast after 1600, and probably after 1630.[105] They fought the local Etsi, about whom little is known, and took over as capital one of their towns and markets, Eduegyir, which they renamed Mankessim, 'the big town'. From it they established other centres, such as Ekumfi and Anomabu on the coast and Abora some little way inland. In 1707–13 the Borbor Fante overcame first the Asebu,[106] then later in the century the Oguanfo of Kommenda, Cape Coast and elsewhere. Four major elements thus comprise the Fante people of today: Borbor, Etsi, Asebu and Oguanfo. Although each small Fante state was a politically autonomous unit, with its own chiefs and elders, some sort of community of interest and unity of action existed between

102 Elimina Journal, Nuyt's Diary, entry for 16 April, 1707 (State Archives, The Hague).
103 Barbot, *op. cit.*, edition of 1746, p. 158. For the expansion of Denkyira see Bosman, *op. cit.*, p. 73.
104 For Denkyira in general see J. K. Kumah, 'Denkyira: 1600–1730', M.A. thesis, I.A.S., 1965; C. E. Aidoo, 'History of the Denkyiras', MS in I.A.S.; Ameyaw, *op. cit.* F.N., I.A.S., KAG/8, 9.
105 E. F. Collins, 'Borbor Fanti', paper presented to the Seminar on the Akan, University of Ghana, 1965.
106 R. B. Nunoo, 'Excavations at Asebu in the Gold Coast', *Journal of the West African Science Association*, February 1957. Asebu tradition tells of their ancestors' arrival from the sea.

them, based upon the ritual authority of the priests of Mankessim;[107] hence Barbot was led to describe the Fante as forming 'a sort of commonwealth'. The complex structure of Fante society,[108] with matriclans typical of the southern Akan existing side by side with patrilineal *asafo* companies—groups organised for war and other communal activities—may reflect its mixed origins. The Fante merchants formed a particularly close association with the English who made Cape Coast the headquarters of the Royal Adventurers and of its successor, The Royal African Company: the Fante acted as middlemen between them and the inland Akan. The growth in Fante power was rather later than that of Akwamu and Denkyira, and is more firmly associated with the slave trade of the eighteenth century than with the gold trade of the seventeenth.

The history of the southern Akan region in the seventeenth century is extremely complex, and only limited aspects of it have been treated here. Any appreciation of the period, however, must involve an understanding of the social implications of, first, the evolution of the gold-producing industry; second, the expansion and organisation of commerce in gold and, increasingly, in slaves; and third, the changing techniques of warfare. It seems possible to distinguish two phases in the development of the gold industry, both in its productive and distributive aspects. The first phase began in the fifteenth century when Malian Dyula traders systematically built up an organisation for maximising the flow of gold between the southern fields and the northern markets and in doing so greatly stimulated production. The second phase occurred with the development of coastal markets for gold after 1471. This new impetus to production resulted in waves of immigration into the southern goldfields, particularly from the northern Akan area. The struggle for control of the centres of production and of the trade routes brought into existence new concentrations of political power. Some of the new polities collapsed as rapidly as they had risen, but others, like Akwamu and Denkyira, succeeded in establishing for the time a rule of law (however imperfect) over wide areas and so prepared the way for the emergence of a yet larger power: Asante. Violent political change led in turn to advances in the techniques of warfare. Kyerematen reports Asante traditions that the introduction of the bow there took place in the time of Obiri Yeboa, that is, probably in the third quarter of the seventeenth century.[109] Over a century later the Akwamu bowmen were renowned for their skill.[110] The transition from personal combat with thrusting or cutting weapons to the use of missile weapons involved quite new tactical considerations, and made necessary the development of more elaborate forms of military organisation. With these, the

107 See e.g. PRO. T. 70/29: letter from Melvil dd. 23 July 1751.
108 J. B. Christensen, *Double Descent among the Fanti*, New Haven, 1954, *passim*.
109 Kyerematen, *op. cit.*, p. 124.
110 Bosman, *op. cit.*, letter xi.

replacement of the bow by the gun, as supplies became available, was smoothly accomplished.[111]

THE RISE OF ASANTE

The creation of the Asante kingdom in the late seventeenth century was the work of lineages belonging to various of the southern Akan matriclans, but especially to the Oyoko. Of six principal towns of metropolitan Asante founded or enlarged at this time, namely, Kumasi, Bekwai, Juaben, Kokofu, Nsuta, and Mampon, all but the latter had Oyoko chiefs. As is so often the case with such lineages, there is an ambivalence in their traditions of origin. Thus while the Oyoko royals of Asante maintain a claim to autochthonous status through the descent of their ancestress from the sky at Asiakwa (above, p. 364), yet there are also seldom publicised traditions that suggest links with the Kulango and Dyula town of Buna.[112] There is no doubt that the groups which founded Kumasi and the other early Asante towns had migrated immediately from the south, from the forest country of Adanse around and beyond Lake Bosumtwe. Their movement northwards was directed toward Tafo, now a suburb of Kumasi but then an old and prosperous trading town (above, p. 365) whose wealth had already attracted other settlers like the Domaa of Suntreso, a group of Akwamu emigrés who had established themselves there after their leader's unsuccessful bid for the chiefship of the Abrade, perhaps around 1600.

The struggles for power in the Tafo district, between the older settlers and the new immigrants from Adanse, are still recounted in detail in Asante tradition.[113] The earliest and fiercest was with the Domaa who, in one clash of arms, mortally wounded the leader of the new immigrants, Obiri Yeboa: this was probably in the 1670s. The newcomers elected as their next leader Osei Tutu of the Oyoko, who, significantly, had spent part of his youth in the court of Denkyira and who was, at the time of Obiri Yeboa's death, in that of Akwamu in Nyanaoase. The Akwamu, not averse to encouraging the growth of a new and allied power inland, and perhaps still wary of the Domaa, assisted Osei Tutu with men and arms, including a body of troops under one Anum Asamoa whose descendants are the present Adum of Kumasi. Osei Tutu returned to the Tafo area, marshalled his forces, and engaged the Domaa in war. They were defeated and moved westwards into the Ahafo area where, apparently with Asante approval, they founded a number of new towns such as Ahenkro and Sumaa. To the

111 *Ibid.* This letter contains a useful account of modes of warfare among the Southern Akan *c.* 1700.

112 See e.g. Meyerowitz, *Akan Traditions of Origin*, pp. 104–5. The writer has heard similar reports from reputable 'traditionalists'.

113 Kyerematen gives a useful account of these wars from traditional sources. The measure of agreement between these and contemporary written reports is high. For early Ashanti in general see Daaku, 'Pre-Ashanti states', and J. K. Fynn, 'The rise of Ashanti', both in *G.N.Q.*, ix, 1966.

north of these towns lay the kingdom of Gyaman, which had been created apparently by other Domaa groups from Suntreso, which had migrated there earlier in the seventeenth century and had slowly gained political ascendancy over Agni, Gbin, Nafana, Kulango and other indigenous peoples of the area.[114] The inclination of the newer Domaa settlers in Ahafo to look to Gyaman rather than Asante for leadership was to become one of the sources of recurrent tension between those two powers.[115]

After the defeat of the Domaa of Suntreso, Osei Tutu soon received the submission of the Tafo, of the neighbouring Amakom and Kaase and, some way to the east, of the Akyem ('Asante-Akyem') of such towns as Hwereso and Banka. By the 1680s it becomes permissible to speak of the kingdom of Asante. Osei Tutu made his capital at the new town of Kumasi near Tafo, while other of the Oyoko leaders and their associates established nearby their own centres, the *amanto*: Mampon of the Bretuo and Bekwai, Kokofu, Juaben and Nsuta all of the Oyoko. The institutions of government of the new kingdom appear to have been modelled closely on those of Akwamu; as in Akwamu, no clear distinction was made (at this time) between military and civil authority.

The overthrow of the Denkyira at the battle of Feyiase in 1701, after several years of warfare, resulted in numerous Denkyira chiefs transferring allegiance to Osei Tutu. For the most part they were assigned positions within the Kumasi political hierarchy, and their lands incorporated into Kumasi division. This perhaps did much to establish *de facto* Kumasi supremacy over the other Asante towns, a matter afforded *de jure* recognition in the institution of the Golden Stool of Asante, which symbolised the highest office in the land and was vested in that segment of the Oyoko to which Osei Tutu belonged. The defeat of Denkyira having opened for the Asante a path to the western Gold Coast (and thus access to guns, gunpowder and lead),[116] the Dutch made a rapid assessment of its growing power and from their headquarters in Elmina in 1701 hastened to despatch Van Nyendaal to Kumasi as ambassador to the court of 'the great Asjante Caboceer Zaay', that is, Osei Tutu.[117]

The remaining years of Osei Tutu's reign were occupied mainly with

114 For Gyaman see Tauxier, *Le Noir de Bondoukou*, Paris, 1921; E. A. Agyeman, 'Gyaman—its relations with Ashanti', M.A. thesis, I.A.S., 1965; K. Arhin, 'Brong Traditions', *Res. Rev.*, ii, 2, 1966.

115 The Akwamu Abrade, the Domaa, the Gyaman etc. all use the *abusua* name Aduana. In the southern Akan matriclan system this appears to have been some sort of residual category in which immigrants, particularly of northern Akan origin, were often placed. Similarly, the Portuguese, because of their southern connections, were apparently regarded as Agona, see Bowdich, *op. cit.*, pp. 230–1, to which *inter alia* the rulers of Denkyira belonged.

116 S. Tenkorang, 'The importance of firearms in the struggle between Ashanti and the coastal states', *T.H.S.G.*, ix, 1968.

117 For the *amanto* see Rattray, *Ashanti Law and Constitution*, Oxford, 1929, chs 17–23; Wilks, 'Ashanti Government', *West African Kingdoms in the Nineteenth Century*, ed. Forde and Kaberry, pp. 207–11 and 232–3.

the consolidation of Asante's position in the newly acquired lands, and with the task of their pacification. After the tumultuous events of the later seventeenth century, there was a general desire for peace—a sentiment reflected in an interview that the Dutch had with 'Akanist captains' from the interior in 1703:

> They declared that nearly all the trading people of Denkyira, Twifo, Asante and others were unanimously tired of war, and that after the end of the bad season, unusually heavy rains having flooded and made impassable the ways, the Denkyira would appear on the coast, but that trade might not at first be as great as in the old days, since all the old people had died off and the young men did not understand the business of trade.[118]

The main threat to peace came from parties of refugees who had retired into forest hideouts and taken to banditry. Denkyira groups for example were particularly active in preying on traders around 1706, and received support from small but ambitious local chieftains such as Ntow Koroko of Boaman near Bosumtwe. A massacre of Asante gold prospectors at Manso Nkwanta led Osei Tutu to take determined measures, and the bandits were hunted out and killed, while Ntow's petty chiefdom was destroyed. Ntow Koroko himself fled deeper into the forests to the south, where he succeeded in creating another small chiefdom, that of Akyem Bosome.[119] Despite such tribulations the Asante in this period systematically developed their trade with the western coast, especially with the Dutch in Elmina and Axim and with the English in Cape Coast, and also organised the exploitation of the major gold workings. In 1715, for example, there seem to have been about 4,000 Asante in the former Denkyira province of Aowin, for a head-tax of $2\frac{1}{2}$ *angels* imposed on them by the Asante king was estimated to yield 300 *bendas* of gold.[120] One of the first of the northern campaigns was clearly planned by Osei Tutu: that of 1711–12, against Old Wenchi and Domaa Abesim.[121]

In 1717 Asante armies came into conflict with the Akyem Kotoku to the south, then under Ofosu Apenten. Smallpox broke out in the Asante ranks, and a major reverse was suffered in an encounter with the Kotoku on the Pra River. In the course of these campaigns the Asante king died. This is usually considered to have been Osei Tutu, though there is a possibility that he had in fact died a few years earlier.[122] Whatever the case, the Golden Stool passed to Opoku Ware, Osei Tutu's sister's daughter's son.

118 W.I.C. 484, letter from de la Palma dd. 10 October 1703 (State Archives, The Hague).
119 Elmina Journal, letter from Landman dd. 11 April 1707; Kyerematen, *op. cit.*, pp. 219–21.
120 Elmina Journal, letter from Butler dd. 24 January 1715.
121 K. Y. Daaku, 'A note on the fall of Ahwene Koko', *G.N.Q.*, x, 1968.
122 M. Priestley and I. Wilks, 'The Ashanti kings in the eighteenth century: a revised chronology', *J.A.H.*, i, 1, 1960.

In a reign of some thirty years Opoku Ware extended the Asante power in all directions—from the Guinea Coast far into the northern savannahs—and laid the foundations of Greater Asante: the largest state system yet to have emerged in that part of West Africa. The major campaigns of Opoku Ware—which alone can be treated here—are known from both contemporary European and local written sources, and their chronology is reasonably clear.

In 1717 a counter-offensive against the Akyem Kotoku resulted in victory for the Asante forces and in the death of Ofosu Apenten.[123] A Sefwi raiding party having entered Kumasi whilst the Asante armies were engaged with the Kotoku, a campaign was launched against that country and (with the assistance of Wassaw levies) the Asante overran it and executed its ruler, Abirimuru.[124] A quarrel with the Wassaw over the division of spoils led to an invasion of that territory and to the death of its king, Animine Kwaw. This was in 1721.[125] All immediate danger from south and west thus averted, Opoku Ware turned his attention north-west to the rich towns of the Bono and Bighu region. Obtaining, through political negotiation, the active support of Nkoranza (a small state under Baffo Pim founded by Amakom groups in the late seventeenth century), and at least guarantees of neutrality from such other chiefs in the area as those of Nsawkaw, Wenchi and Banda,[126] Opoku Ware despatched his armies against Bono. This campaign, which is reported in both Dutch and Arabic sources, took place in 1722–3.[127] Bono was defeated, and its rulers left as subjects of the Asante kings, in possession of a greatly reduced territory, Takyiman. About this time Bighu appears finally to have been abandoned by the Dyula; of those that remained in the region some came to accept the protection of the rulers of Gyaman and developed Bonduku as an important centre of trade, while others settled in Banda, a small state ruled by Nafana immigrants from the west who were later to become staunch supporters of the Asante cause.

In 1726 Opoku Ware was threatening an invasion of Fante country with the use of Aowin and Takyiman troops,[128] but this seems not to have materialised. In 1732, however, Asante armies entered Gonja, perhaps occupying only the western divisions since conquest of the eastern ones was effected by Safo Katanka of Mampon in 1751.[129] A major Asante

123 Elmina Journal, letter from van Alsen dd. 30 October 1717; Kyerematen, *op. cit.*, pp. 242–6.
124 *Ibid.*, pp. 256–62.
125 *Ibid.*, pp. 263–4. Elmina Journal, entries for 1721.
126 Goody, Introduction to 'Ashanti and the North-West', Supplement 1 to *Res. Rev.*, 1965, pp. 9–18.
127 *Kitāb Ghunjā*, entry for A.H. 1135. Elmina Journal, letter from Beuns dd. 8 January 1724.
128 Elmina Journal, letter from Valckenier dd. 15 May 1726. For the use of such provincial troops, see Bowdich, *op. cit.*, p. 301.
129 *Kitāb Ghunjā*, entries for A.H. 1145 and 1165.

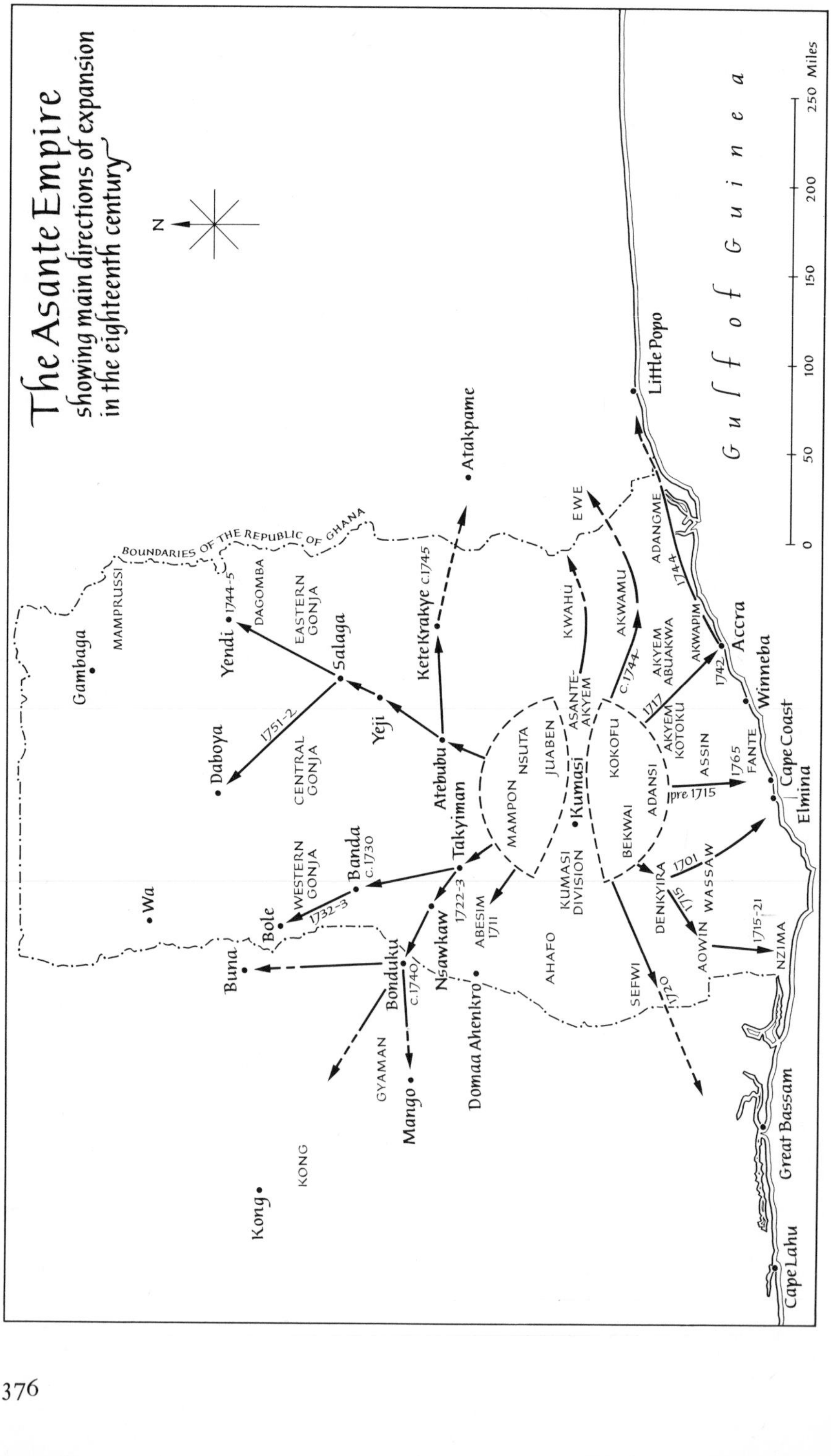
The Asante Empire
showing main directions of expansion
in the eighteenth century
N
BOUNDARIES OF THE REPUBLIC OF GHANA
Gambaga
MAMPRUSSI
Wa
Yendi
1744-5
DAGOMBA
EASTERN
GONJA
Salaga
1751-2
Daboya
CENTRAL
GONJA
Yeji
Kete Krakye c.1745
Atakpame
Atebubu
WESTERN
GONJA
Banda
c.1730
Bole
1732-3
Buna
Takyiman
1722-3
Nsawkaw
Bonduku
c.1740
GYAMAN
Mango
KONG
Kong
Domaa Ahenkro
ABESIM
1711
AHAFO
MAMPON
NSUTA
JUABEN
ASANTE-
AKYEM
Kumasi
KUMASI
DIVISION
KOKOFU
BEKWAI
ADANSI
KWAHU
AKWAMU
c.1744
EWE
ADANGME
1744
Little Popo
1717
AKYEM
ABUAKWA
AKWAPIM
1742
Accra
Winneba
AKYEM
KOTOKU
ASSIN
1765
FANTE
pre 1715
Cape Coast
Elmina
1701
DENKYIRA
1715
WASSAW
AOWIN
1715-21
NZIMA
SEFWI
1720
Great Bassam
Cape Lahu
Gulf of Guinea
0
50
100
150
200
250 Miles

10:2

advance in the north-west occurred with the thrust into Gyaman, when its ruler, Abo Kwabena, was slain.[130] There is some doubt about the exact date of this campaign, but it was probably *c.* 1740, for Abo's successor, Kofi Sono, who is said to have spent seven years in Kong before reaching an agreement with the Asante, was reigning over Gyaman by 1749.[131] In the course of the Gyaman invasion Asante troops are reputed to have advanced as far west as Mango (Groumania) on the Komoé River,[132] and as far north as Kong, a matter suggesting that the Asante army chiefs had by this time gained an impressive command of logistics as well as tactics.

Opoku Ware extended his power to both south-east and north-east, in two other major expeditions closely following the Gyaman campaign. In 1742 his armies overran Akyem Abuakwa, and went on to receive the submission of the Accra and Adangme towns on the plains to the east,[133] and, in or about 1744, of the Akwamu east of the Volta.[134] Next, in 1744, the king launched an invasion of Dagomba, of which an eye-witness account survives.[135] On this occasion the confrontation between the Asante infantry and the Dagomba cavalry produced deadlock; while the infantrymen were unable to outmanoeuvre their more mobile opponents, each cavalry charge was checked by the horses' terror of the gunfire. An Asante attempt to mount some of its troops on captured horses proved disastrous. In some disorder, the Asante retired southwards, but shortly afterwards the Dagomba sued for peace and accepted Asante protection.[136] Probably at much this time Asante seized control of the Afram Plains and crossed the Volta at Krakye.[137] In this latter action the forces of Juaben played a leading rôle, so establishing its interest in the Krakye area (a matter that became of crucial importance in British attempts to penetrate into the interior in the following century).[138]

Although the reign of Opoku Ware was above all a period of rapid territorial aggrandisement, commerce was not neglected: the government in Kumasi was in constant contact with the agents of the European merchant companies on the coast, with whom it maintained relations that were on the whole cordial. The production of gold probably rose steadily in the period, but since much of it continued to be despatched northwards, for which no statistics of any sort are available, the overall position cannot easily be assessed. The export of one other commodity certainly rose: on the coast keen competition for slaves between rival European trading

130 *Kitāb Ghunjā,* entry for A.H. 1162. Tauxier, *Le Noir de Bondoukou,* Paris, 1921, pp. 90–1. Delafosse, *Les Frontiers de la Côte d'Ivoire, de la Côte d'Or, et Soudan*, Paris, 1908, p. 231.
131 *Kitāb Ghunjā,* entry for A.H. 1162.
132 Kyerematen, *op. cit.*, p. 269.
133 Rømer, *op. cit.*, p. 185; Kyerematen, *op. cit.*, pp. 277–80.
134 J. Dupuis, *Journal of a Residence in Ashantee*, London, 1824, p. 234.
135 Rømer, *op. cit.*, pp. 218–21.
136 Bowdich, *op. cit.*, p. 235.
137 Kyerematen, *op. cit.*, pp. 274–7.
138 M. Johnson, 'Ashanti east of the Volta', *T.H.S.G.*, viii, 1966.

concerns created favourable market conditions for Asante. In exchange for war materials, the Asante despatched principally surpluses of prisoners-of-war who could not readily be absorbed into Asante society, but also criminals and other social outcasts.[139] There are indications of Opoku Ware's desire to diversify the economy by encouraging the local production of certain consumer goods: his employment of four Dutchmen to start distilleries was obviously intended to break the dependence on imported spirits, while innovation in the weaving industry based on the increased importation of silk was also made on his initiative.[140]

Towards the end of his reign Opoku Ware, aware that the evolution of an effective structure of government had not kept pace with the tremendous increase in the number of people to be governed, attempted to force through constitutional changes apparently designed to create a class of civil officials distinct from the military authorities—'new codes of laws, adapted for the government of the various departments of state', as Dupuis described it.[141] These changes were resisted by the army chiefs, who in 1748 carried their opposition as far as rebellion, so forcing Opoku Ware to abandon his proposals. He died in 1750.[142] A contemporary obituary notice, by an unsympathetic Muslim writer, testifies to the power exercised by this charismatic ruler:

> In this year Opoku king of the Asante died, may Allah curse him and place his soul in hell. It was he who harmed the people of Gonja, oppressing them and robbing them of their property at his will. He reigned violently as a tyrant, enjoying his authority. The people of all the horizons feared him greatly.[143]

There are difficulties in making any clear distinction between territories which became in a real sense part of Greater Asante, and those which were only loosely within the Asante sphere of influence,[144] dominated through the permanent threat of military intervention. But in the later eighteenth century and early nineteenth, when Asante was at the height of its power, the problem confronting its kings was that of evolving a system of political control over an area of perhaps approximately 100,000 square miles, with a population of possibly between two to three million people, highly

139 The export of slaves, as might be anticipated, began to fall immediately the main phase of Asante expansion ended in the mid-eighteenth century, see P. Curtin, *The Atlantic Slave Trade*, Madison, 1969, p. 225. For the trade from the Gold Coast, see also W. Rodney, 'Gold and slaves on the Gold Coast', *T.H.S.G.*, x, 1969.

140 Rømer, *op. cit.*, ch. 4.

141 Dupuis, *op. cit.*, pp. 235–6.

142 *Kitāb Ghunjā*, entry for A.H. 1163. Rømer, *op. cit.*, pp. 110, 226. The description of Opoku Ware given in Rømer shows him to have suffered from the condition of the pituitary giving rise to acromegaly.

143 *Kitāb Ghunjā*, entry for A.H. 1163.

144 See e.g. G. A. Robertson, *Notes on Africa*, London, 1819, p. 177; also K. Arhin, 'The Structure of Greater Ashanti', *J.A.H.*, viii, 1, 1967.

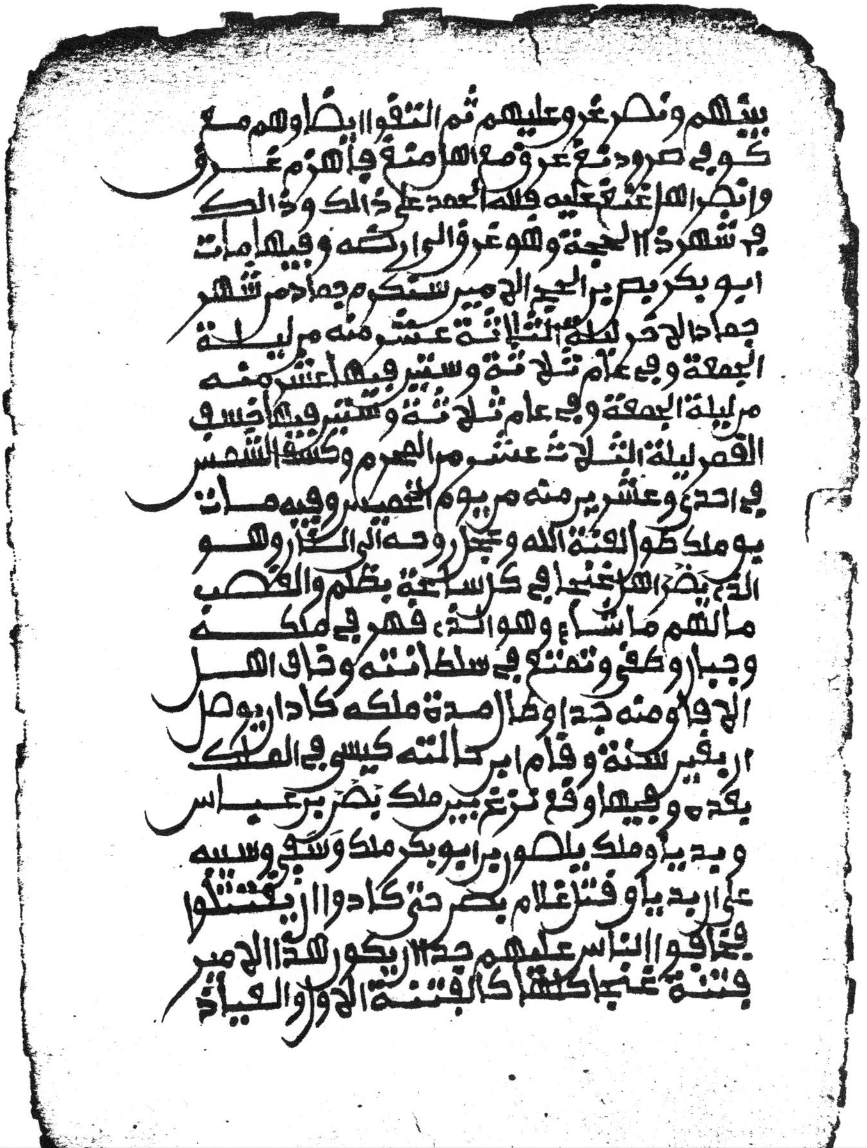

A page of the *Kitāb Ghunjā* with the obituary of the Asante king Opoku Ware.

diverse moreover in language, culture and economic development, and in forms of social and political organisation.

Comparatively little appears to have been accomplished in the reign of Kusi Obodom (1750–64)—though after the conquests of his predecessor even to maintain the *status quo* was something of an achievement.[145] Osei Kwadwo, however, who reigned from 1764 until 1777, was able to inspire major structural changes in government—probably continuous with those unsuccessfully pioneered by Opoku Ware—and these were in turn carried forward by his successors Osei Kwame (1777–*c.* 1798) and Osei Bonsu (*c.* 1801–24). These changes brought into being an appointive bureaucracy directly responsible to the king, and charged with the running of all agencies of central government: taxation and general finance, the management of state enterprises, the administration of the provinces, the conduct of foreign affairs, and the maintenance of internal security. At the same time new military formations were created, commanded by appointees of the king, and designed to strengthen his position *vis-à-vis* the older and traditionalist army chiefs. Senior posts in both bureaucracy and army became open to men of merit, and non-Asante from the provinces, and even from outside Greater Asante, not infrequently achieved high office within them.[146] While the cumulative effect of these measures was greatly to increase the power of the king in relationship to the old oligarchy, nevertheless the rulers of the *amanto*—the early Asante towns built up around Kumasi—clung tenaciously to their ancient privileges and resisted, to the point of civil war, any attempt to extend the power of the new bureaucracy into their domains. Thus by the beginning of the nineteenth century, while an administrative apparatus had been evolved that looked capable of sustaining programmes both of national integration and of general modernisation, nevertheless the 'pure' Asante towns at the heart of the empire retained this large measure of autonomy, and so constituted a barrier to the emergence of Asante as a unified nation-state.[147] Nevertheless, in the range of its managerial and proprietary control over land, manpower, trade and production, and in the high degree of its ideological organisation, by 1800 the Asante state exhibited a combination of institutional features far removed in character from those of the feudal systems with which Rattray and others have inclined to compare it.[148]

But the failure of Asante in the late eighteenth century effectively to consolidate its control over such southern regions as Wassaw, Assin, and

145 But see J. K. Fynn, 'The Reign and times of Kusi Obodom', *T.H.S.G.*, viii, 1965.
146 I. Wilks, 'Aspects of bureaucratisation in Ashanti in the nineteenth century', *J.A.H.*, vii, 2, 1966; 'Ashanti government', *West African Kingdoms in the Nineteenth Century*, ed. Forde and Kaberry.
147 *Ibid.*, pp. 232–4.
148 But see e.g. Rattray, *Ashanti Law and Constitution*, Oxford, 1929, pp. 75–6; but see e.g. K. A. Busia, *The Position of the Chief in the Modern Political System of Ashanti*, Oxford, 1951, pp. 57–60, for a contrary view.

Akyem[149]—which thus in the nineteenth century gradually became absorbed into a British protectorate—calls attention to one other aspect of its development which has consistently been overlooked: that for the greater part of its history Asante was essentially a northward-looking power. The fact that the greater part of the body of data available to the historian relates to the southern territories, and to relations between Asante and European mercantile interests, has led writers unduly to emphasise the problems which successive Asante governments faced in that quarter while largely ignoring the solid achievements—before 1874—of its administration in the northern provinces.

THE NORTHERN SAVANNAHS IN THE EIGHTEENTH CENTURY

The last phases in the struggles between Gonja and Dagomba occurred early in the eighteenth century. The military power of each lay in its possession of cavalry. The policy of the ruler Jakpa Lanta (abdicated 1666–7; died 1672–3) had brought Gonja into conflict with the southern Mossi kingdom of Nanumba, and indeed the eastern Gonja division of Kpembe came to incorporate a large area previously belonging to the Nanumba. Gonja pressure was also felt on the western frontier of Dagomba, and especially in the Daboya area where, along the White Volta, there were important salt deposits. Sometime in the later seventeenth century the Dagomba appear to have relinquished to the Gonja some of their westernmost territory, including Daboya. The court of the king, until then at Yendi Dabari near the White Volta, was transferred into eastern Dagomba, ultimately to the new (and present) Yendi some seventy miles away. Some cavalry commanders, however, remained in the west, so that today Tolon, whose chief is head of the cavalry and custodian of the Sacred Spears of Dagomba, is only some few miles from the Gonja divisional capital of Daboya. Intermittent border warfare appears to have continued until, in or shortly before 1713, Gonja cavalry under command of Kumpatia were thrown into a full-scale invasion of western Dagomba. The divisions of Kumbungu, Nanton and Savelugu were overrun, and Yendi Dabari, earlier seat of the court, was abandoned (above, p. 352). Despite its initial successes, Gonja had clearly overreached itself. The Dagomba forces were rallied by Andani Sigili, engaged the invaders in battle, and inflicted on them a crushing defeat that is still celebrated in the Dagomba drum chants.[150] The event is regarded as marking the end of hostilities between the two powers; whatever the precise content of the peace terms, however, Gonja retained control of former Dagomba territory west of the White Volta, including Daboya.

149 See e.g. M. Priestley, 'The Ashanti question and the British: Eighteenth-century origins', *J.A.H.*, ii, 1, 1961.

150 Tait, F.N., Transcriptions . . . of the Dagomba drum histories. Tamakloe, *op. cit.*, ch. 4; *Kitāb Ghunjā*, entry for A.H. 1125.

To the west, on the middle Black Volta, one of the petty chiefdoms founded by Mamprussi and Dagomba cavalrymen in the seventeenth century was, by the early eighteenth, in process of transformation into a small state that would in time achieve more than local importance as a centre of trade and of Islam. The state was Wa, and the reforms were the work of Na Pelpuo, aided by the Dyula from Nasa (above, p. 354). Wa is an interesting example of a pluralistic society built on a symbiotic relationship between three groups: immigrant cavalrymen, ancient Dyula settlers, and autochthonous people of the land, respectively the fighting, trading and farming components of the community. Office was distributed between the three interests, with the Wa Na, as head of the princely estate, being responsible for the security and protection of the society at large; the Shehu Wangara (or Yeri Na), as head of the Dyula, for the affairs of the Muslim community as such; and the Wida Na, as head of the commoners, for the land shrines. To these three groups Na Pelpuo added a fourth, by obtaining the services of a party of Muslims, Tarawiri like those of Nasa, from Dia in northern Massina: members of a society long famous for its cultivation of the Islamic sciences. In Yaʿmūsa, leader of this group, and his descendants, Na Pelpuo vested the imāmate of Wa.[151]

Further west, but at much the same time, the old Dyula communities of Kong and Bobo-Dioulasso were being incorporated into pluralistic societies of a kind similar to that of Wa. There the stimulus came from the Watara, Islamised horsemen from the Middle Niger valley probably in the Segu region, who moved into the Dyula caravan towns along the trail between Jenne and the Bighu area, and from these bases accomplished what the traders could not: the partial pacification of the hostile rural populations by which these towns were surrounded.

The creation of the states of Kong and Bobo-Dioulasso is particularly associated with Shehu ʿUmar Watara (died 1745/6) and his brother Fa Maghan Watara (died 1750–1) respectively, though friction between these two obliged them to employ Saghanughu Muslim scholars in a peace-keeping rôle. The Watara recruited autochthonous groups from around the towns as troops in their bid to obtain control over the whole region between the headwaters of the Komoé and those of the Black Volta. These local levies—precursors in some ways of the later *sofas* of Samori—to a large extent lost their distinct 'tribal' identities as Falafala, Gbin and the rest, and assumed a status within society of *sonangui*, warriors, as contrasted with the Dyula, traders.[152]

One of the lesser, and southernmost, of the Watara foundations was that

151 This section on Wa is drawn from the writer's study of the Dyula community there, in preparation. See also Wilks: A Note on the Arabic MS I.A.S.A.R./298, and others from Wa, *Res. Rev.*, xi, 2, 1966.

152 For Kong in general see E. Bernus, 'Kong et sa Region', *Études Eburnéennes*, viii, 1960 and particularly pp. 254–5 for the *Sonangui*. See I.A.S.A.R./454 for a history of the Watara of Kong.

of Mango, west of Bonduku, where northern Agni-speaking groups, the Anufo, were recruited into Watara service. In the middle of the eighteenth century, shortly after Asante armies had first penetrated the area (above p. 377), a section of the Mango Watara, with Anufo troops and probably Dyula clerics ('imāms of war'), were engaged by the Gonja king to assist him in an internal dispute with the northern division of Kandia. Subsequently the group transferred its services to the Mamprussi king, and was used in war against Kantindi, a Gurma chiefdom in (what is now) northern Togo. The campaigns concluded, the mercenaries settled in the region, where they founded the town of Sansanne Mango, 'the camp of the Mango'. Around it grew up the small but typically pluralistic Chakosi state—transplanted some 350 miles from its 'natural' setting—with Watara chiefs, Dyula traders and *imāms*, and Anufo commoners.[153]

In the eighteenth century the growth of Muslim influence in the kingdoms of the savannah was marked. It has already been noted that, at the beginning of the preceding century, Muslim immigration into Gonja had led to the emergence of a specifically Muslim estate from which the Gonja king and his divisional chiefs recruited *imāms* and other Muslim functionaries (responsible, for example, for regulating the Islamic festivals which had replaced earlier ones). In Dagomba a comparable development, by which Muslim officials became a recognised part of the political establishment, had occurred in the early eighteenth century, during the reign of Muḥammad Zangina, first Muslim to become Ya-Na. Muslim groups, such as the Baghayughu Dyula of Sabari (above, p. 353) and the Hausa Katsina settlers at Kamshagu, were awarded office, and their ranks enlarged by the encouragement of Muslim immigration. Not only Muslim *malams* or men of learning, but also weavers, butchers, smiths and well-diggers, moved into the Dagomba towns, so that, as the drummers say, 'Na Zangina brought a complete civilisation to Dagomba'. While Zangina's successors would show varying degrees of personal attachment to Islam, none sought to restore the pre-Zangina situation, and the *imāms* and other functionaries created by Muḥammad Zangina came to form a permanent Muslim hierarchy which later rulers enlarged.[154] Similar changes, about which much less is as yet known, appear to have taken place in Mamprussi in the same period, at the time of Na Atabia who died in 1741/2 after a long reign of half a century,[155] while in Wagadugu in the later part of the century the Baghayughu were officially recognised as *imāms* by the Mogho Naba Dulgu.[156]

153 N. Levtzion, *Muslims and Chiefs in West Africa*, 1968, pp. 174–85. Goody, Introduction to *Ashanti and the North-west*, Supplement 1 to *Res. Rev.*, 1965, pp. 20–4. Blair and Duncan-Johnstone, *op. cit.*, pp. 14–16.

154 I. Wilks, 'A note on the early spread of Islam in Dagomba', *T.H.S.G.*, viii, 1967.

155 *Kitāb Ghunjā*, entry for A.H. 1154. Levtzion, *op. cit.*, ch. 8.

156 Skinner, 'Islam in Mossi society', *Islam in Tropical Africa*, ed. I. M. Lewis, Oxford, 1966.

In the southern Mossi kingdoms political and social institutions were fully formed and already fairly rigid, before the main period of Islamic impact, and the Muslims had therefore to be accommodated within an essentially non-Islamic system. In the pluralistic societies of Wa and the Watara towns, by contrast, the Muslim presence was crucial in the very process of state building, and they came to play a correspondingly more central rôle in government and politics. In the northern Akan kingdom of Bono, near to the Dyula centre of Bighu, Muslim settlement occurred, as we have seen, shortly after its creation, and the conversion of royals produced divisions within the ruling house. Even among the southern Akan the Muslim impact made itself felt, and by the end of the eighteenth century the Asante king Osei Kwame was turning increasingly to Muslim advisers, and was thought to have had a personal attachment to the faith: a consideration apparently central to his removal from the throne in or about 1798 by his subordinate chiefs who saw in these developments a threat to their authority.[157]

The growth of Muslim influence in the region brought in its wake a development of literacy.[158] Not only were standard manuals of North African and Middle Eastern authorship brought into circulation, and Muslim law increasingly studied and taught, but a tradition of local scholarship arose which is well exemplified in the mid-eighteenth century *Kitāb Ghunjā* of al-Ḥājj Muḥammad b. Mustafā, a member of the Gonja Kamaghatay. This work, to which many references have been made, includes a compilation of Gonja traditions having relevance to the formative years of the kingdom, together with a year by year chronicle of events of the first half of the eighteenth century. Centres of learning grew up, representing an extension to the south of the older Western Sudanese tradition of Jenne and Timbuktu. Kong and Bobo-Dioulasso both developed as important teaching centres in the eighteenth century under the influence of Saghanughu scholars from Mali,[159] while by the end of that century Buna, by then broadly within the ambit of Asante, could attract *ʿulama* from as far afield as Futa Toto, Futa Jallon and northern Mali.[160] In Kumasi a rudimentary chancery was created, staffed with Muslim scribes who conducted the king's correspondence with the Muslim parts of Greater Asante, and who apparently maintained records of the judicial and administrative

157 I. Wilks, 'The position of Muslims in metropolitan Ashanti in the early nineteenth century', *Islam in Tropical Africa*, ed. I. M. Lewis, Oxford, 1966.

158 T. Hodgkin, 'The Islamic literary tradition in Ghana', *Islam in Tropical Africa*, ed. Lewis. I. Wilks, 'The Growth of Islamic Learning in Ghana', *J.H.S.N.*, xi, 4, 1963, and 'The transmission of Islamic learning in the Western Sudan', *Literacy in Traditional Societies*, ed. J. Goody, Cambridge, 1968.

159 Wilks, 'The Transmission of Islamic Learning in the Western Sudan', *Literacy in Traditional Societies*.

160 I. Wilks, 'Abu Bakr al-Siddiq of Timbuktu', *Africa Remembered*, ed. P. Curtin, Madison, 1967, p. 157.

departments of state.[161]

At the beginning of the eighteenth century Asante power had been confined to the forest, far south of the Black Volta. By the close of that century, in the north-east, Gonja was firmly and directly under Asante control,[162] Dagomba had accepted subordinate status, and even Mamprussi could be considered, perhaps improbably, as within 'the boundary of Asantee authority'.[163] In the nineteenth century, but probably earlier also, regular exchange of gifts between Kumasi and Wagadugu took place.[164] Under the influence of Asante the north-east became, as Dupuis observed, remarkably settled. No serious rebellion against Asante, as far as is known, occurred in the many years of Dagomba's association with it. The Dagomba towns rendered an annual tribute to Kumasi of slaves, cloth and livestock, and accepted a measure of political direction from it;[165] Dagomba traders, in return, gained free access to the Asante markets, while Asante army chiefs undertook the reorganisation and modernisation of the Dagomba army, creating within it a force of musketeers, the Kambonse.[166]

In marked contrast to the situation in the north-east, that in the north-west was highly unsettled. While the Komoé River was regarded as the limits of Asante authority in that quarter,[167] its position east of that river was far from secure, and a series of uprisings culminated at the close of the eighteenth century in a widespread rebellion, in which Gyaman and western Gonja received support from the Watara rulers of Kong. From this action the Asante emerged victorious but not unscathed.[168]

The ferment in the area is perhaps not fully to be understood without some reference to the growing power of the Bambara kingdom of Segu, on the Niger. The usurper N'Golo (died ?1790) had brought Massina under Segu control, and had extended his authority through the interior delta of the Niger as far as Timbuktu. Only the power of Yatenga, under Kango, halted the Bambara progress.[169] Under N'Golo's successors, his son Manson and his grandson Da Kaba, the Bambara appear to have developed an interest in the Black Volta region to their south. In an obscure passage Mungo Park drew attention to a late-eighteenth-century clash of

161 I. Wilks, 'The position of Muslims in metropolitan Ashanti in the early nineteenth century', *Islam in Tropical Africa*, ed. Lewis.
162 Hutchison, in Bowdich, *op. cit.*, pp. 396–7 and 401–2.
163 Bowdich, *op. cit.*, p. 179. Robertson, *op. cit.*, pp. 179–81.
164 Skinner, *The Mossi of Upper Volta*, Oxford, 1964, p. 97.
165 See e.g. Bowdich, *op. cit.*, p. 320–1. Dupuis, *op. cit.*, p. xxxix. Reindorf, *op. cit.*, p. 140, suggests that a revolt against Asante occurred *temp.* Osei Kwadwo, but other evidence of this is lacking.
166 Davies, 'History and Organisation of the Kambonse in Dagomba', MS in the National Archives of Ghana, Tamale, n.d.
167 Bowdich, *op. cit.*, pp. 181–2.
168 Goody, Introduction to *Ashanti and the North-West*, pp. 29–35. Wilks, *The Northern Factor in Ashanti History*, pp. 22–3.
169 Tauxier, *Nouvelles Notes sur le Mossi et le Gourounsi*, Paris, 1924, ch. 3; *Histoire des Bambara*, Paris, 1942, pp. 88 *et seq.*

arms between Segu and 'Gotto', presumably Ghutugu as Bonduku is known in the Western Sudan,[170] a reference which might be dismissed as erroneous were it not for other evidence of a Bambara expedition in 1817–18 against Bole in western Gonja, Mango and Buna, the people of which latter town sought refuge in Asante.[171] In the present state of knowledge it is impossible to determine the extent of Segu involvement in the turbulent situation in the Asante north-west, but, in the event, any major confrontation between the Asante and Bambara was averted by the collapse of the latter power before the armies of Shehu Ahmadu Lobbo of Massina in or about 1818.

170 Mungo Park, *Travels in the Interior Districts of Africa*, London, 1799, pp. 216–17.
171 *Royal Gazette and Sierra Leone Advertiser*, 16 October 1824.

Note. I have been grateful to Phyllis Ferguson of Newnham College, Cambridge, for comments on this paper, and for material relating especially to Dagomba.

CHAPTER 11

The Western Atlantic coast 1600–1800

J. SURET-CANALE

THE GEOGRAPHICAL FRAMEWORK

The area to be discussed here corresponds approximately to the present-day territories of the Republic of Senegal, Gambia, Portuguese Guinea (or Guinea-Bissau) and part of the Republic of Guinea, consisting of two of its natural regions, coastal Guinea or Lower Guinea and Futa Jallon or Central Guinea. The Sudanese zone and forest lands of the present Republic of Guinea fall into different natural and historical divisions and are outside the area under consideration. The River Senegal in the north and the Kolente in the south form the natural boundaries of this area, enclosed inland by the eastern foothills of the Futa Jallon massif; the Atlantic side belongs to that part of the African coastline which faces directly west.

THE IMPACT OF EUROPEAN CONTACT

The integration of the Sudan into the Islamic world during the Middle Ages opened the frontiers of Africa on the Sahara side, along the Sahel. Since the sailing techniques of the time made sea routes to and from West Africa impracticable[1] contact with the outside world was maintained by means of cross-country routes through the Sahara. For this reason Futa-Toro, the 'Tekrur', made an early appearance in written history, almost at the same time as Ghana.

The Portuguese discovery of Africa completely upset this long-established state of affairs. Suddenly, trading centres sprang up and went into operation along the Atlantic coast, dealing in goods which had always—till then—come directly from the Maghreb and selling them at a very much lower price.

At first the western sector of the Atlantic coast was the most strongly affected by these great changes. The Portuguese settled all along this coast during the second half of the fifteenth century and from the island of

1 R. Mauny, *Les Navigations médiévales sur les côtes sahariennes antérieures à la découverte portugaise (1434)*, Lisbon, Centro de estudos historicos ultramarinos, 1960.

Arguin to the river of Sierra Leone, set up a close-packed and continuous chain of establishments not found further along the coast except on the Gold Coast. Gold from Bambuk and Bouré was from now onwards directed towards the coast instead of being sent up to the Sahel. It was taken from Bambuk by the Senegal, but more especially by the most direct route which involved a very limited amount of travelling by land, ending up in Gambia, which was still a remarkably active centre for the gold trade at the beginning of the seventeenth century.[2] The gold from Bouré came across the Futa-Jallon to the present-day 'Rivières du Sud'. After Elmina, the western Atlantic coast seems to have been the second largest supplier of African gold. Until the middle of the sixteenth century, the traffic in gold was on the same vast scale as that of America.[3] Besides gold, ivory and Guinea pepper (*malaguette*) were of some importance in the African trade—but it was the slave trade which showed the most startling developments. This traffic started more or less as soon as the Portuguese began their exploration, directed in the first instance towards Portugal, but from 1510 onwards travelling towards Spanish America.

As a result of this trade, the influence of Portuguese settlement was considerable. At the end of the sixteenth century, Alvares d'Almada commented that all along the coastline, there were small pockets of Negroes 'dressed as Europeans and speaking Portuguese',[4] descendants of half-breeds or of the servants of early Portuguese settlers. At some date which old Portuguese records could doubtless provide, this particular section of the population managed to settle in the very centre of the Bambuk gold-producing area and take control of the entire neighbourhood. Their power was shortlived and their greedy extortions turned the local natives against them: one single day of revolt and massacre saw them disappear. This

2 Cf. Richard Jobson, *The Golden Trade or a Discovery of the River Gambia*, London, Nicholas Oke, 1623.

3 Ad. Soetbeer ('Edelmetallproduktion seit der Entdeckung Amerikas', *Petermanns Mitteilungen*, Ergänzungsheft 57, Gotha, 1879, pp. 107-10) gives the following estimates for the sources of gold used in Europe (in Kilos):

From 1493-1520	African gold	3,000
	European gold	2,000
	American gold	800
From 1521-1544	African gold	2,400
	European gold	1,500
	American gold	3,260
From 1545-1560	African gold	2,000
	European gold	1,000
	American gold	5,400
From 1561-1580	African gold	2,000
	European gold	1,000
	American gold	3,840

4 Alvares d'Almada, *Tratado breve dos Rios de Guiné do Cabo Verde*, 1594 (Reed Porto 1841) p. 60.

probably happened at some time in the sixteenth century[5] and it was still remembered at the end of the eighteenth. Proper diplomatic relations existed between the King of Portugal and the rulers of the interior: there were links with the Damel of Cayor[6] and, moving still further inland, with the Mansa of Mali to whom João III sent an ambassador, Pero Fernandez, in 1534.

The western Atlantic coast, however, was not as deeply influenced culturally as the Congo. Portuguese settlements stayed closely linked to regular ports of call. It is certain though that the growth of trade between local chiefs throughout the territory contributed to economic, social and political evolution in the sense that a new form of social differentiation developed: this was based on the acquisition of imported goods and these included items which, like guns and horses, were of great value in capturing slaves: it must not be forgotten that slaves were themselves a most valuable means of acquiring even greater wealth. Everything contributed to a consolidation of the old hierarchies based on the Mande pattern.

The Portuguese never achieved in Africa the same thorough colonisation that they accomplished in Brazil.[7] There were excellent reasons for this. First, there was the situation in Portugal itself where the incompetence and corruption common abroad became a basic feature of everyday life in the home country. The reign of João III (1521–57) saw Portugal become steadily weaker and in 1580 came the final degradation: Portugal passed to the Spanish crown. At the same time there was serious trading competition from Holland and England in areas where Portugal had held a virtual monopoly for many years. In 1602 the Dutch East India Company was formed and took over a large number of Portugal's most important trading centres. In 1640 João IV of Braganza won back his country's independence and in order to strengthen this was obliged to make further sacrifices in the colonies: the treaty which he signed with the Dutch on 12 June 1641 conceded to them, in exchange for military and naval aid, not only the territories they had already conquered but also those which they might acquire in the course of the following year. It needed a war of revenge (1651–69) for the Portuguese to retrieve part of their lost Empire - Brazil, São Tomé, Luanda - but Arguin and Elmina were lost forever to Portugal. In 1588 Queen Elizabeth I had granted a group of English merchants the right to trade for ten years on the Senegal and the Gambia, as well as at the ports of

5 Golberry, *Fragmens d'un voyage en Afrique fait pendant les années 1785, 1786 et 1787*, Paris, Treutel and Würtz, 1802, 1, pp. 401–3. The author points out as traces of Portuguese occupation the ruins of a few forts and the survival in the local vocabulary of a few words of Portuguese origin.

6. Cf. Jean Boulègue and Benjamin Pinto-Bull, 'Les relations du Cayor avec le Portugal dans la première moitié du XVIème siècle d'après deux documents nouveaux', *Bulletin de l'Institut Français de l'Afrique Noire*, ser. B, xxviii, 3–4, 1966, pp. 663–7.

7 'L'Afrique noire entre hier et aujourd'hui', Un colloque. *Annales—Economies, Sociétés, Civilisations*—1958, i, pp. 64–6.

Rio Fresco (Rufisque) Portudal and Joal; this charter was renewed in 1598 and a further extension was granted by James I in 1618. A company of merchants from Dieppe and Rouen was formed in 1626 to trade with this part of the coast, and in 1633 its members got a licence from Richelieu for the commerce of Senegal and Gambia. In 1635 another company won the monopoly of various regions in this area—from Arguin to Senegal and from the Gambia to Sierra Leone. In 1651 even the Duke of Courland established a settlement in Gambia, on the Island of St André, and this was maintained until 1660.

One thing must be mentioned at this point. Arguin and Gorée were lost irrevocably, but in the other territories on the West Atlantic seaboard the Portuguese were supplanted rather than driven out. The area was left in the hands of individual slave traders: the Portuguese more or less gave up and willingly went away. When they returned to Africa and started new settlements all along the coast of present-day Portuguese Guinea, they were really re-establishing contact rather than starting a process of reconquest. Reconquest was technically restricted to territory beyond Sierra Leone.

This sums up the crux of the matter. Even before 1580, the West African coast had ceased to be the vital feature in the Portuguese colonisation of Africa, because gold, ivory and malaguette had become less and less important in the African trade. The slave trade to America formed the basic part of all business speculation and the main sources of supply lay on the other side of Sierra Leone (Angola, Congo, the Gabon, Benin, the Gold Coast). The western Atlantic coast was not considered specially useful as a source of black manpower: evidence supporting this is found in the terms of the Franco-Spanish treaty which in 1701 gave France the monopoly of the Asiento—the supplying of slaves to Spanish America: the 48,000 'head' to be supplied for the Indies over the next ten years were not to include Negroes taken from this part of the coast, since slaves from these particular territories were not suitable for work in the West Indies.[8]

In spite of being only a secondary source of supply, the western Atlantic coast was nonetheless deeply involved in the slave trade and it was this more than anything else which helped mould the developing relations between Europe and Africa in the sixteenth century. All plans for proper colonisation were abandoned: Africa was not to be a new Brazil. The slave trade took its final shape during the seventeenth and eighteenth centuries; in the event, it closed rather than opened the continent. This arrangement did not greatly disturb Europeans.

A great complex of historical factors led to the development of this paradoxical system whereby manpower had to be brought from the African continent to ensure the profitable functioning of tropical plantations on the other side of the Atlantic. Direct control of the African territories for their

8 Quoted by R. Cornevin, *Histoire de l'Afrique*, Paris, Payot, 1966, ii, p. 345.

fullest economic exploitation soon proved to be difficult, if not impracticable. The social and political organisation of the African countries opposed such an enterprise: their chiefdoms and military kingdoms were based on a patriarchal hierarchy and were totally opposed to the idea of collective slavery—they were soon supplied with firearms and were well able to organise guerrilla manoeuvres from deep in the interior.

Nevertheless many self-governing groups and states, with a few notable exceptions, accepted and even sought out commercial relations, on condition that Europeans restricted themselves to operations on the coast, leaving the profitable monopoly of internal trade as the local inhabitants' prerogative. Trade in gold, ivory or malaguette offered small prospects for increased production, but the slave trade had infinite possibilities—especially now that European firearms could be brought to bear on those less fortunate adversaries who fought back with only bows and arrows. Enslavement by conquest had been a well-established institution in African societies for a very long time. When the captured slave was not integrated by adoption into the conquering patriarchal family—which conferred certain rights and guarantees on him as a sort of 'house prisoner'—he remained at the mercy of the victor and could be killed, sometimes eaten (ritual cannibalism, rather than dietary preference), or else he could be sold. This last possibility depended on the existence of an outside market. During the sixteenth century the beginnings of colonisation in America had resulted in the extermination of the original indigenous population of the Caribbean and had caused a marked fall in population on the continent of America.[9] There was no formalised social and political situation to hinder commercial exploitation, but a local labour force was lacking. Europeans were not suitable for work on the plantations, less for reasons of climate (for some settled down comfortably even in truly tropical climates) than for reasons of their technical incompetence: agriculture in the temperate zones is far different from that in the damp and steamy tropics. Negroes, on the other hand, were completely used to the work and to the practical methods of tropical agriculture. Torn away from their own social environment and set down in isolation on the plantations, they were the ideal and indispensable instrument for colonial development. It cost hardly anything to acquire them—a few inferior and shoddy goods, cheap items made of base metal, cloth, firearms and gunpowder, tobacco and poor quality liquor—this more than compensated for the expenses and the risks involved in the sea passage.

This system was the dominating feature of African history throughout the seventeenth and eighteenth centuries, the end of the fifteenth and the sixteenth centuries being only the beginning of it all. This was the real era of the slave trade, even though there had always been a certain amount of trans-Sahara traffic in slaves: the vast scale of this European-controlled

9 For Mexico, cf. Pierre Chaunu, 'La population de l'Amérique indienne', *Revue historique*, 1964, pp. 111–18.

phenomenon is of quite another order,[10] and its economic implications are completely different. The outcome—the establishment of a Negro population in America—indicates the scope of this great demographic movement, and this can be further appreciated if one realises that as far as Africa was concerned the population did not reach its former size until the end of the eighteenth century. By this time a rise in the birthrate seems to have adjusted the natural balance. Of course the number of slaves taken varied from region to region. In the area which forms part of this study where the supply was not highly thought of, it was relatively modest. But it was nowhere without some economic and social side-effects, not so much from the point of view of the actual capture of the slaves (although this in itself, robbing the tribe as it did of its strongest and most vigorous members, was bound to have repercussions on the labour force and its productivity level) as from its indirect consequences: the unfairness of the exchange (a labour force in return for shoddy goods of negligible value); the development of the manhunt as a basic means of acquiring wealth and power, all to the detriment of productive activity. The consequences for Africa were by no means inconsiderable.

CENTRALISED STATES

The whole of this area was deeply influenced by the Mandé civilisation, its social as well as its political structures. The influence was of course strongest in the group of territories which were most directly affected by the Mali Empire: namely, the present-day territories of Senegal, Gambia and the hinterland of Portuguese Guinea. These states were in existence before 1600 and, apart from a few minor losses of territory and changes of boundary, changed little externally and internally till the end of the eighteenth century and in some cases well into the nineteenth. They all had a hierarchic social structure which operated a system of state control: this was in direct contrast to the segmentary nature of the tribes living along the Guinea coast.

The Djoloff empire and its disintegration

According to tradition, the founder of this kingdom was Ndiadiane N'Diaye who seems to have reigned at the end of the twelfth century or the beginning of the thirteenth.[11]

In this legendary account of the empire's early days, it is difficult to distinguish what is really historical. It is generally agreed that the formation

10 Arguments against accepting the expression 'the era of the slave trade', 'L'historien devant l'Afrique moderne', *The Historian in Tropical Africa*, Oxford University Press, 1964, p. 27; its effects queried in H. Brunschwig, 'Histoire, passé et frustation en Afrique noire', *Annales E.S.C.* (cf. note 20), 1962, pp. 873–84. Arguments in support of the expression in J. Suret-Canale, 'Contexte et conséquences sociales de la traite africaine', *Présence Africaine*, 2nd edn 1964, pp. 127–50.

11 Amadou Wade, 'Chronique du Walo sénégalais', pub. and annotated by V. Monteil, *Bull. I.F.A.N.*, ser. B, xxvi, 3–4, 1964, pp. 440–98, gives as dates of the reign 1186–1202; Sall Boubou suggests 1215 as the first year of the reign; Yoro Diao, who makes the reign last forty years (sixteen years according to Wade), places it from 1212 to 1256.

of the Djoloff state could not possibly antedate the fourteenth century and it is certain that when the Portuguese arrived in Africa it stretched from Senegal in the north to Gambia in the south.[12] On the eastern side near Futa-Toro, it also encompassed Dimar and a part of Bambuk at one time.[13]

At the time of the 'Great Djoloff', the Bourba selected or installed the *lamane* for each province, *lamane* being the Serer term for a local chief, though in the Sine and Salum he seems always to have borne the title of *Bour* (King). The lamanes of the provinces outside Djoloff territory (Walo, Cayor, Baol, Sine, Salum) owed the Bourba a tribute levied four times a year on the occasion of traditional pagan ceremonies, which were later Islamised (Tabaski, Kori, Gamou, Tamkharete).

This tribute consisted of two hundred loincloths, two fine horses, a young male captive (a groom) and a young female captive (a cook). Besides this, the vassal kingdoms had to observe certain obligations relating to their particular resources: sweet-smelling hay from Salum, baobab bark from Baol, and from Cayor white sand for the courtyards of the Bourba's palace and baobab bark for plaiting halter ropes for his horses.

By the beginning of the seventeenth century all this grandeur belonged to the past. Alvares d'Almada (1594) noted that the Bourba, this emperor-figure to whom other kings owed obedience and paid tribute, had lost his power and was even obliged to pay tribute to the neighbouring king of Futa-Toro.[14]

The five vassal kingdoms all had access to the sea. Walo which consisted basically of the Lower Senegal region (the delta), but with occasional extra territories varying throughout history,[15] was a coastal country. Cayor occupied the sandy plain which stretches along the Atlantic coast from Lower Senegal to the Cape Verde peninsula: the local ports were Bezeguiche (Gorée) and Rio Fresco (Rufisque). Baol, kingdom of 'Ale' mentioned in the sixteenth- and seventeenth-century chronicles, had access to the Atlantic through Portudal (Porto d'Ale). Sine had Joal as its port; Salum reached the ocean via the Salum estuary and the port of Joar on the right bank of the Gambia.[16]

12 Duarte Pacheco Pereira, *Esmeraldo de Situ Orbis*, ed. R. Mauny, Centro de Estudos da Guiné portuguesa. Memorias no. 19, Bissau, 1956, pp. 49–51. Valentim Fernandes, *Description de la côte occidentale d'Afrique* (du Sénégal au Cap de Monte, Archipel), Centro de Estudos da Guiné portugesa, Memorias no. 11, Bissau, 1951, pp. 5–7: 'The River Çanaga separates the Azenegue Moors (Sanhadja) from the province of Geloffa (Joloff) which starts on the other side. . . . The kingdom of Gyloffa starts at this river and goes up as far as the river of Gambia . . .'.

13 V. Monteil, 'Le Dyoloff et Albouri N'Diaye', *Bull. I.F.A.N.*, ser. B., xxviii, 3–4, 1966, pp. 595–637.

14 Alvares d'Almada, Tratado breve . . . , p. 3.

15 'Walo' means an area liable to be flooded as compared with 'Dieri', high land always beyond the reach of flooding.

16 J. B. Labat, *Nouvelle relation de l'Afrique occidentale*, Paris, Cavelier, 1738, iv, p. 131. Information on the 'customs' to be paid to the coastal sovereigns or their representatives in John Barbot, *A Description of the Coasts of North and South Guinea* . . . , London, 1746.

There must inevitably be some link between the empire's downfall and the arrival of the Portuguese on this coast: the vassal provinces and kingdoms, all sea-going nations, had gained much benefit from the new developments in European trade. The Djoloff empire, on the other hand, was cut off from the sea by its completely landlocked position. The acquisition of wealth and independent means led their vassals to reject a sovereignty that had always been somewhat weak, based more on the moral authority of the Bourba than on the mechanism of a state with all the proper apparatus of authority.

In this connection Father Labat comments:

> The ruler of the country at present known as the kingdom of Cayor was the first to revolt against his sovereign, taking up arms and having himself acknowledged as King of the country of which he was in fact only the governor. Others followed his example and their legitimate sovereign found himself reduced to the possession of only the smallest part of his territories, the worst and the furthest away from all trade.[17]

If, as is probable, the arrival of the Portuguese was contemporary with the attack of Koli Tenguella (at the end of the fifteenth century) which deprived the Djoloff of part of its lands in the interior, the downfall of the empire is even easier to understand.

It was during the reign of the Bourba, Lele Foul i Fak, that the rupture between Cayor and Djoloff must have taken place, in 1549 (according to Yoro Diao) or in 1566 (according to R. P. Labat from information gathered by André Brue or La Courbe). Walo ceased to pay tribute in 1630; the kingdoms of Sine and Salum, cut off from Djoloff by the independent Cayor and Baol, (these two provinces or kingdoms being closely linked), probably achieved their independence at some date in the sixteenth century.

17 The traditional capitals of Djoloff were Tieng and Ouarkhokhe, residences of the king and the court, largely occupied by the royal slaves. The electoral assemblies were held at Dediguedje. In the seventeenth century the capital of Walo was Ndiourbel on the right bank. Moorish invasions caused it to be abandoned in about 1705. The capital was then transferred to Ndiangué directly opposite on the left bank until 1782, and then to Khouma, upstream from the delta, still on the left bank, facing the Torobe of the Futa. In the nineteenth century, however, the capital was taken to Nder, on the western shore of Lake Guiers, more protected from the attacks of the Moors and the Futankobe. The assembly of Seg ag Baor was first held at Touguene, residence of Diogomaye, then was transferred in about 1705 to Ndiangué. In Cayor, Amari Ngone Sobel (second half of the sixteenth century) transferred the capital from Mpalene-Dedd to Bardial, then to Nguiguis and finally to Mboul, which remained the royal seat until the end of the eighteenth century. The Damel-Tegne (uniting the two crowns of Cayor and Baol)—from the reign of Lat Soucabe onwards (end of the seventeenth century) lived in Mekhe, from where they were easily able to supervise the two kingdoms. The electoral assembly of Cayor was held at Diamatile. The capital of Baol was Lambaye: the enthronement took place there (the ritual bathing—by sprinkling—was performed at Dâf, on the outskirts of Lambaye, on a sacred stone). The electoral assemblies were held at Mekhe. The capital of Sine was Mbissel, then Diakhao. The capital of Salum was Kahone.

Social organisation. As in all tropical Africa, the social organisation of the Djoloff empire was based on the patriarchal system, having the great family as a fundamental unit of society, this unit being considered a fraction of a clan, matrilinear or patrilinear. It was called a 'Keur' in Wolof and this was the equivalent of the Peul or Tucolor 'Gallé'. The matrilinear system seems to have predominated, but it gradually gave an increasingly large place to patrilinear organisation though the principle of matriliny 'was carefully preserved in the most powerful families which still based their political rights and heritages on its observance.'[18]

In general, patrilinear organisation, which can be recognised by the passage of a clan name from father to son (*Sant*), became predominant; for the Serer and the Lebu, however, the matrilinear organisation continued unchanged. For the princely families, the system was combined with that of the matrilinear clans (*khète*) which were themselves divided into matri-lineages (*mène*). They played a vital part in the selection of the ruling set except for in the Djoloff, where the king had always to be taken from the N'Diaye patrilinear clan.

High in the social hierarchy came the princely families (*garmi*) which were eligible for the throne. In the Djoloff empire, these families were the mènes of Sangome and Djilor (very closely related but short-lived) and of Ugane and Diagasumbe.[19] It was always the patrilinear clan of the N'Diaye which was the most important.

In Walo, the king (*Brak*) had to belong to the patrilinear clan of the Mbodje as well as to one of the three rival mènes: Loggar, Dyeus and Tedyek. In Cayor, there were seven garmi mènes: Muïoy, Wagadu, Dorobe, Guedj, Guelowar, Sogno and Bey, and the king also had to belong to the *guegno* Fall. In Sine and Salum, only the Guelowar matriliny of Malinke origin counted. The *tagne* from the royal mène were the princely nobility, but they were excluded from the throne because of their paternal line; in Sine and Salum were the Dom-i-Bour with a Guelowar father but a commoner for mother.

The non-royal nobility comprised free men (Guêr), families of district chiefs (Kangame) or of certain village headmen. The Serer aristocracy of district chiefs in Sine and Salum (Diambour-Boureye: great free men) is similar to this, apart from the vassal dynasty of the Bour Ganieck; they had no particular political functions. The 'free men' were usually ordinary peasants (Badolo), rather like the European villeins in the Middle Ages.

Below the free men came people belonging to various castes (*nyênyo*) which comprised the Teug (blacksmiths and jewellers), the Wudé (tanners

18 H. Gaden, 'Légendes et coutumes sénégalaises (Cahiers de Yoro Diao)', *Revue d'ethnologie et de sociologie*, Paris, Leroux, 1912, pp. 119–37, 191–202.
19 According to Rousseau, and based on Yoro Diao, 'Etudes sur le Cayor', *Bulletin du Comité d'Etudes historiques et scientifiques de l'A.O.F.*, 1933, pp. 237–98; but Monteil, *loc. cit.*, notes ten royal matrilineages.

and shoemakers), the Mabubé (tailors), the Laobé and Sègnes (makers of wooden utensils), four categories of Sab-Leck (musicians) and finally the *griots* (*guewel*).

The caste system, of Mande origin, was established in the Futa-Toro at an early date and was observed with great strictness; it may be an indication of peoples of different ethnic origin fixed in endogamous groups by division of labour. The caste names are almost all of Fula origin (Tucolor) and Yoro Diao suggests that these caste-based workers would probably have come from Futa-Toro to Cayor during the reign of Lat-Soucabé (end of the seventeenth—beginning of the eighteenth century). In any event, there were griots at Cayor as early as the fifteenth century; the Portuguese described them exactly and referred to them as 'Jews'.

At the bottom of the social scale came the slaves (*diam*). There were the slaves for trading (bought and liable to be resold: *diam-sayor*) and house slaves (born into the family, in theory not likely to be sold and enjoying certain rights: *diam-dyoudyou*). The legal inferiority of the slaves' social status sometimes masked a surprising fact: apart from ordinary house slaves and field-workers, there were slaves belonging to noble families and especially to the crown who could be given functions to perform which endowed them with an authority which in practice placed them far above the free men, for example those who had certain duties to perform at court or who were responsible for collecting customs dues and above all those who formed the king's personal bodyguard, the *tiedos*. In spite of their humble origin, the tiedos became in time a regular military aristocracy from whom the kings sought support in their resistance to the rival princes, who constantly tried to establish themselves as possible candidates for the throne. There came an interesting change in meaning: the term *diambour*, which really means 'king's captive', came to mean nobleman or man of influence. These slaves could themselves have slaves, *diam-i-diam*, who could in turn have their own slaves, *diam-diamat-i-diam*.

To summarise: on the economic basis of the 'Keur'—the unit corresponding to the patriarchal family—families joined themselves together by a network of bonds, sometimes on the grounds of the division of labour (between free men and the caste-based workers) but without fail with a hierarchical significance. The royal household and the princely households (designated by the same term, 'Keur') were based on the same general principle. They were by and large far too cumbersome, being overloaded with dependents and slaves. These were not simply superimposed on the basic structure but actually cut across it (dependents and slaves belonging to these powerful households had in turn their own households and often put on a show of aristocracy). In the political field dominated by the princely families and noble lords with bands of armed retainers on one hand and the powerful tiedos on the other, a place must be kept for the marabouts. Portuguese chroniclers record the Wolof as being Muslims, though they added that the bulk of the population made little attempt to follow the precepts of Islam and that the kings and chiefs were only slightly more assiduous, frequently having Moorish or local-born marabouts[20] in their entourage.

Accounts from the end of the eighteenth century and the beginning of the nineteenth give the impression of a movement away from Islam among the Wolofs, especially in the royal courts, where there was often open hostility to the Muslim religion in spite of its being firmly established in the nearby Futa-Toro since the eleventh century.

This did not, however, mean that Islam had been wiped out. Among the Wolofs in the sixteenth century, Islam seems to have been only a court religion, represented by a few marabouts, often of foreign extraction (Moors) living under the protection of the sovereign and giving him the benefit of their religious, or, even better, magic powers (making charms out of written extracts from the Qur'ān). It seems that during the seventeenth and eighteenth centuries an indigenous Muslim group grew up, under the guidance of Wolof marabouts, political in intent and acting as a focus for the discontent of a section of the peasant masses (the *badolos*) who were victims of more and more exacting demands on the part of princes and tiedos. This led to an anti-Muslim reaction from the traditional aristocracies, a reaction which—unlike that prevalent among various neighbouring countries such as Futa-Toro—successfully undermined Muslim influence up to the nineteenth century.

Political structures. As mentioned above, succession to royalty was by election on the condition of belonging to a certain number of matrilineages or to a predetermined patrilineage. According to Mande traditions, royalty remained both religious and military in character, throughout this period. Embodying at a higher level the traditional attributes of those responsible for the land (or the water) and of war leaders,[21] the king (the Bour-ba-Djoloff, the Brak in Walo, the Damel in Cayor, the Tègne in Baol, Bour-Sine and Bour-Salum) was regarded as a sort of talisman, a sacred being responsible for the prosperity of the community, a plentiful catch at sea (in Walo) and a fine harvest.

The ritual of enthronement symbolised this responsibility: a sacred bathing ceremony (in memory of Ndiadiane N'Diaye who first appeared

20 Fernandes, *Description*, p. 7: 'The king and all his nobles and dignitaries of the province of Giloffa are mahometans and have white "bischerijs" (marabouts) who are priests and preachers of Mahomet and can read and write.' In the same way, Lemaire, in the seventeenth century, remarks that the Muslim religion 'is extremely badly observed by the ordinary people who are only slightly touched by it. The important people are in closer contact with it, normally having a Moorish marabout about them' (*Voyages du sieur Lemaire aux îles Canaries, Cap Vert, Sénégal et Gambie*, Paris, Jacques Colombet, 1695, pp. 143–4).

21 The colonial term chief or master is not altogether correct: 'those responsible' would be more exact.

to his subjects emerging from the waters of the Senegal); rites of fertility and abundance (in the Djoloff seeds from the local crops were planted in the hole filled with water where the sacred bath had taken place: the subsequent development of the plants was taken as a forecast for the reign); in Walo, when the Brak was taking his sacred bath, he had to seize a live fish with his right hand—discreetly helped by a courtier; in Walo and Cayor, as a part of the enthronement ceremony, the king was given a vase containing seeds from all types of crops cultivated in the country. In Cayor, it is evident that Muslim elements were introduced into the pagan ritual in that the sacred bathing, the Khouli-khouli, was presided over by the descendant of a Moorish marabout and a turban had been added as a sign of royalty.

The king was also the war leader; he was given arms in Walo and a turban in Cayor, as well as the traditional seeds. His military strength rested on the royal slaves who had become professional soldiers, the tiedos.

The king was surrounded by numerous dignitaries, of noble birth or crown slaves (certain duties, originally assigned to slaves, seem to have passed at a later date to the nobility). In the Djoloff empire, these dignitaries included the *Great Diaraf*, a sort of prime minister, president of the electoral Assembly, attended by the *Diaraf Satlé*, the electors' spokesman to the Bourba; the *Great Farba* (a Malinke title meaning chief of the royal slaves) who announced the decisions of the assembly; then came the chiefs responsible for various other groups of apparently foreign origin (Fulbe, Moors, various castes); finally the king's vassal 'governors', each governing a particular area; the *toubé*, viceroy, who replaced the king when he was indisposed, the *Boumi*, formerly the crown prince, who lived at Mouille, the *bargam* who stayed at Ngapp, and a dozen *kangame*, head of provinces: the most important (the Beur Lap and the Fara Bakal) protected the southern borders.

In Walo the duties which fell to the Grand Diaraf of Wolof were shared among the 'three great men' of the kingdom: the *diogomaye* (lord of the water) who conducted the royal audiences, the *diaoudine* (lord of the land) and the *malô* (treasurer) who was a later addition to the two original 'masters'.

In Cayor, the two highest chiefs were the *Lamane Diamatile*, formerly the president of the electoral college of the Lamane Cayor before the country's independence, now downgraded to second rank by the *Diaourigne Mboul*, a post created at the time of independence. This person, fulfilling the rôle of prime minister, had probably been at the outset the chief of the royal slaves (a post later taken by the Diaourigne Mboul Gala). The Tialaw Diambanyane held the position of treasurer. We also find again the Boumi, the appointed successor. Among high-ranking feudatories, a few bear titles of Muslim 'marabout' origin: Elimane Mbal, Serigne Cobé.

In Baol, less well known, a *Diaraf Baol* performed the same functions as his namesake in the Djoloff, assisted by two vassal governors bearing the title of *Sandigné*. The *Tialaw* is the crown prince (the same as the Boumi).

In Sine and Salum, Serer countries ruled by an aristocracy of Malinke origin (Guelowars) but having Wolof elements in the north and the east, the general character of all political and social institutions was basically Wolof.[22] Among the high dignitaries, the most important was the Great Diaraf (*Diaraf Boundao*). He was appointed by the Bour, but only at the representation of the provincial chiefs (the Sakh-Sakh or 'little' Bours commanding the frontier regions); they could have him removed from office if they wished. He had to be a free man but must on no account have a commoner mother; this automatically excluded him from all claim to the throne. The Great Diaraf was the free men's representative to the king and had considerable powers: it was he who presided over the electoral assembly and proposed the candidature or abdication of the king; he fulfilled the rôle of regent during interregnum periods. He alone had the right to pronounce the death sentence (the Bour holding the right of pardon). The *great Farba* was the chief of the royal slaves and was himself a slave; he was also the leader of the army (chief of the tiedos).

The *farba birkeur*, also a slave, was chief of the domestic slaves; he ran the palace, collected taxes and fines and was responsible for any dirty deeds that were to be done. On that account, he was greatly feared. The *diaraf beukenek* was a sort of lord chamberlain of the royal household attending to the household management, supervising the king's meals and tasting the dishes, keeping his accounts and receiving petitioners. The provincial chiefs (the equivalent of the kangame in the Djoloff) were called *sakh-sakh*; some of them (the chiefs of the border provinces) bore the title of bour ('little' bours) or Mâd (the Serer equivalent of the Wolof term 'bour'). In Salum, the Bour N'Gaye was always the boumi, or heir to the throne. Each village had a chief (*diaraf*) and a *saltigué* (wise man/soothsayer, sometimes consulted by the king, responsible for the foretelling of good harvests or disasters). The *dialigué* were the royal slaves, chiefs of slave villages or else were responsible for administering foreign settlements (Fulbe villages or Fulbe quarters, for example).

In all the Wolof or Serer kingdoms an important part was played by two women, the *Linguère* (mother, sister or maternal cousin of the king from the same matrilineage, except in the Djoloff where she was a female relation of the patrilineage, that is of the clan of N'Diaye) and the *awo* (first wife); both women held fiefs and had a court of their own, playing an active part in political life, especially in Walo as well as in Sine and Salum (countries where the matrilineage played an essential rôle).

The king was everywhere elected and overseen by an electoral assembly

22 To the sources quoted in n. 35 on p. 406, add for the Serer kingdoms: L. Aujas, 'la région du Sine-Saloum', *Bull. Com. Etud. hist. scient. A.O.F.*, 1929, pp. 92–132; 'les Sérères du Sénégal' *ibid.*, 1931, pp. 293–333; J. Bourgeau, 'Coutumes des Sérères du Sine et du Saloum', *ibid.*, 1933, pp. 1–65; and Pathé Diagne, 'Les royaumes Sérères', *Presence africaine*, liv, 2e trimestre 1965, pp. 142–72.

(the *Ndyenki* in the Djoloff; the *Seg ag Baor* in Walo; the *Wa-Rew*: 'those of the country' in Cayor). In Walo, the Seg ag Baor nominated the Brak, dismissed him, advised him, controlled him; it had the right, like the Brak himself, to one third of all booty accumulated during the year, brought in by the 'Kangame' on the occasion of the festival of Gamou (the last third of the booty meeting the costs of the festival). The powers of this assembly were so wide that Walo was more of a republic or oligarchy than a monarchy. Conversely, in Sine the prerogatives of the Assembly were limited and the Bour enjoyed greater freedom of action. It is none too clear how these assemblies were composed, but it seems likely that they comprised various groups, each consulted as and when it was appropriate.

The Seg ag Baor seems sometimes to have been no more than a committee of three high dignitaries (diogomaye, diaoudine, malô), but at other times it seems to have included representatives of the three royal matrilineages, occasionally even the provincial chiefs (kangame) and the representatives of the free men.

Yoro Diao explains that the Serer bours and especially the Sine bour enjoyed great authority because the electoral assemblies included many dignitaries of slave origin, more submissive than electors of princely descent in the other states.

Conflicts between kingdoms—Conflicts between clans—The war of the marabouts

The history of the seventeenth and eighteenth centuries is basically a struggle for supremacy between the various kingdoms, especially between Djoloff, Cayor and Walo—the Moors and the Futa-Toro offering some external interference. The truly internal problems—often inextricably involved with external ones—were concerned with clashes between the different princely households (in Walo) and the political endeavours of the Muslim party (in Cayor).

Djoloff. According to tradition, two attempts were made by different Bourba to reconquer Cayor in 1593–4 and 1695–7. Both were unsuccessful.

In 1759 came the only successful—but shortlived reconquest: the Bourba Birayamb Ma Djiguene Ndaw N'Diaye defeated and routed the Damel—who took refuge in Walo—and annexed Cayor. One year later, the vanquished Damel, Maissa Bigué, returned to the attack supported by troops provided by the Brak of Walo and the Moorish emir of Trarza; the Bourba was defeated and killed.

The end of the eighteenth century was marked by the long reign of Mba Compasse (1763–96 according to Oumar N'Diaye Leyti), deposed without bloodshed by the dignitaries and replaced by Mba-Bouri (1797–1829?) whose reign was equally peaceful, except for one unsuccessful raid from the Futa-Toro led by the Almamy Bokar.[23]

23 Oumar N'Diaye Leyti, 'Le Djoloff et ses Bourbas', *Bull. I.F.A.N.*, ser. B, xxviii, 3–4, 1966, pp. 966–1008.

Walo. The history of Walo, more perhaps than that of the other states which emerged from the breaking up of the Djoloff Empire, was particularly unsettled. The reasons for this can be seen first in its quasi-republican or oligarchic constitution with the consequent clashes between the Brak and the Seg ag Baor and the rivalries between the three royal matrilineages, each one with its own chiefs and armed following. The other main cause was its geographical position from which resulted the constant intervention of neighbouring peoples into the internal affairs of the country, encouraging civil strife. The Cayor, but more especially the Moors and the Tucolor, were troublesome neighbours, always on the point of invasion.

Beur Tiaka, the Brak from 1630 to 1670 (?)[24], came up against the hostility of his paternal nephews whom he had dismissed in favour of his maternal nephews. In the end, he had to go into exile himself and died trying to win back his kingdom with the aid of the Tucolor.

From 1645 to 1660, the Brak had to pay tribute to his Moorish neighbours. The Damel of Cayor, Madior I, took advantage of this situation by annexing Diambour from Walo; the Brak had to recognise this in 1650. In 1660, the war between Hassani warriors and Berber marabouts in Mauritania allowed Walo, the Hassanis' ally, to cast off Moorish protection. But the defeat of the marabouts (1674) resulted in the renewal of Moorish oppression, obliging the Brak to abandon Ndiourbel at the end of the century.

Walo had then to pay tribute to the sovereign of Futa-Toro, the powerful Silatigui. According to Labat, writing at the beginning of the eighteenth century, 'the King Brac, and the leaders of the Oual kingdom are his vassals' and every four years had to pay him a tribute of forty-three captives and a large amount of cattle. From 1714 onwards the Brak refused to pay this tribute: the Silatigui sent out bands of Moors and Moroccans against him but the united Wolof front of the Brak and the Bourba—backed by Cayor and Baol—made them retreat.[25]

The reigns of Ndiack Aram Bakar and Natago Aram Bakar[26] were

24 According to Wade, 'Chronique du Walo . . .', 1576–1640. We follow here the more probable chronology of Brigaud, *Histoire traditionnelle du Sénégal* (Etudes Sénégalaises, no. 9), St Louis du Sénégal, 1962, p. 73.

25 Labat, *op. cit.*, i, p. 196, and Delcourt, *La France et les établissements français au Sénégal entre 1713 et 1763*, Dakar, Bull. I.F.A.N., 1952, pp. 154–6.

26 Brigaud ends the reign of Ndiack Aram Bakar in 1736. Wade (*op. cit.*) puts the reign of Ndiak after that of his brother Natago, and not before. This is not the only question raised by this uncertain chronology, which stretches over almost a century (in Brigaud as in Wade) the reign of the three sons of Aram Bakar, sister of Beur Tiaka. Here are the respective chronologies:

Wade		*Brigaud*	
Beur Tiaka	1576–1640		1630–1670
Yerim Mbagnick	1640–1674		1670–1703
Natago	1674–1708	Ndiack	1703–1736
Ndiack	1708–1733	Natago	1736–1769

These chronologies certainly place the reign of Yerim Mbagnick too early since, on the evidence of the French colonial archives, he was still Brak in 1717—the date in which he had a quarrel with André Brüe (cf. Delcourt, *op. cit.*, pp. 154–6).

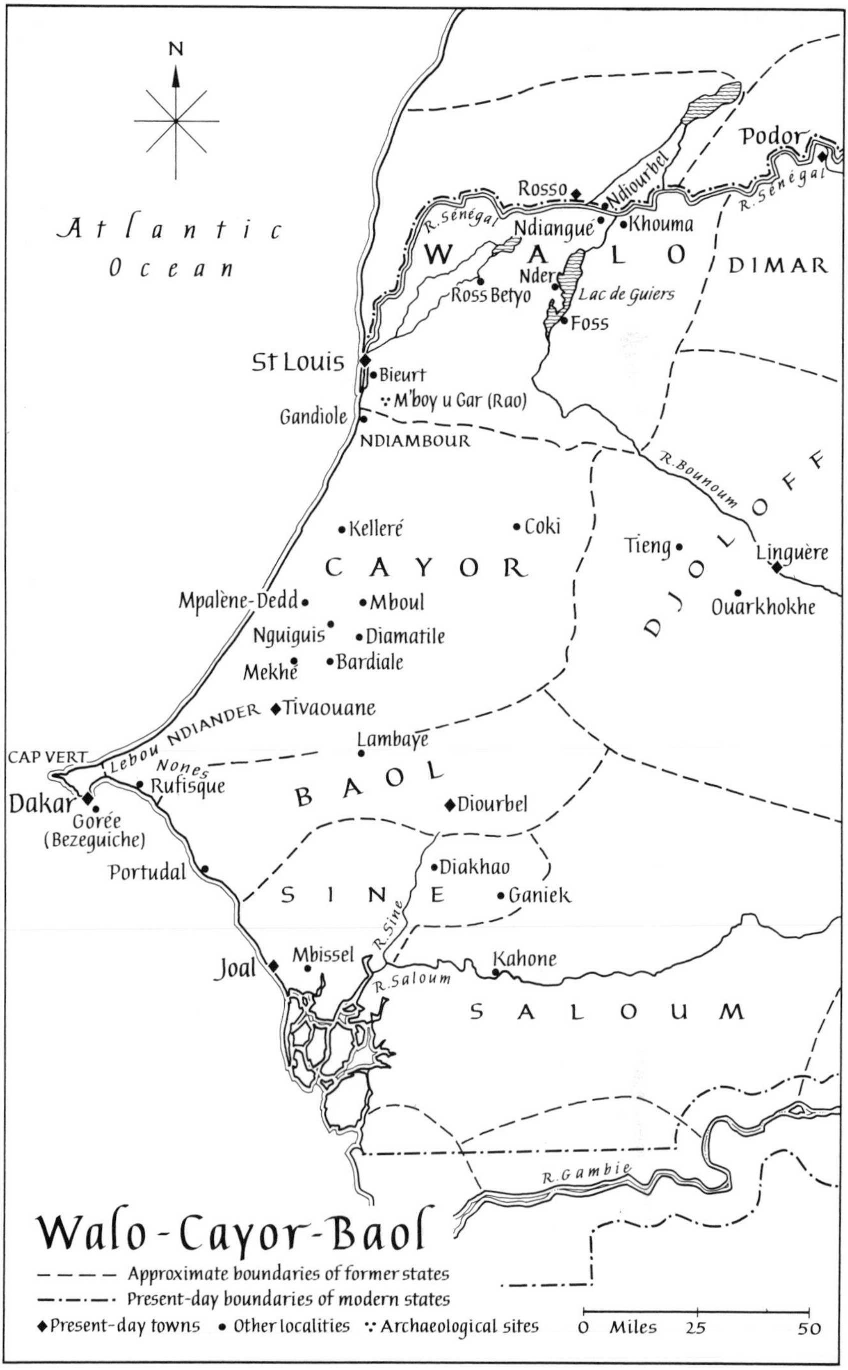
N
Atlantic
Ocean
Podor
R. Sénégal
Rosso
Ndiourbel
Ndiangué
Khouma
W A L O
DIMAR
Nder
Ross Betyo
Lac de Guiers
Foss
St Louis
Bieurt
M'boy u Gar (Rao)
Gandiole
NDIAMBOUR
R. Bounoum
D J O L O F F
Kelleré
Coki
Tieng
Linguère
C A Y O R
Ouarkhokhe
Mpalène-Dedd
Mboul
Nguiguis
Diamatile
Mekhé
Bardiale
Tivaouane
Lebou NDIANDER
Lambaye
CAP VERT
Nones
Rufisque
B A O L
Dakar
Gorée
(Bezeguiche)
Diourbel
Portudal
Diakhao
S I N E
Ganiek
R. Sine
Joal
Mbissel
Kahone
R. Saloum
S A L O U M
R. Gambie
Walo-Cayor-Baol
Approximate boundaries of former states
Present-day boundaries of modern states
Present-day towns
Other localities
Archaeological sites
0 Miles 25 50

11:1

notable for their various attempts at intervention in Cayor, ending in this country's being handed over to Macodou, the Tegne of Baol. He remained in Cayor from 1766 to 1777, much to the detriment of Walo from whom he captured the territories of Gandiole, Ndiol, Mouit and Djelene, in revolt against the Brak since about 1769. The outcome of Walo intervention in Cayor thus seems to have ended fairly disastrously in spite of promising beginnings.

The death of Natago (1769) 'marked the beginning of a period of wars which lasted twenty-nine years, destroyed the supremacy of Walo and diverted the Braks from their former desire to bring Cayor to its knees.'[27] The ferocious civil wars between the Dyeus and Têdyek clans allowed the Moors and then the Tucolors to intervene in the internal affairs of Walo.

Fara Penda Tègne Rel (1788–97), the ally of the Almamy Abdoul Kader, helped him to defeat and kill the emir of Trarza, but afterwards turned against him. The subsequent battle was indecisive and was followed by a truce: the Seg ag Baor advised the Brak to feign conversion to Islam to lull the Almamy's suspicions. But when the Almamy called him to fight against the Damel, the Brak warned the king of Cayor and changed sides in the middle of the battle, thereby ensuring the Almamy's defeat. At the beginning of the nineteenth century, in spite of pressure from the Almamys, the Braks again refused to embrace Islam: 'The Brak will never be converted' replied the nobles chosen to negotiate with the Almamy by the Brak Amar Fati Mborso (1812–21) father of Queen (Linguere) Guimbotte (Dieumbeut), the last but one sovereign of independent Walo.[28] Ravaged by wars against the Moors, by the first half of the nineteenth century Walo was no more than a ruined and depopulated country, the shadow of its former self.

Cayor. The history of Cayor is fairly well known to us, although the chronology is as uncertain as for the neighbouring kingdoms. The last lamane, Dithié Fou Ndiogou, died accidentally during festivities organised to celebrate the country's independence. His son, Amari Ngoné Sobel, the victor of Danki (the battle or, according to the Djoloff version, the ambush, where the Bourba had been defeated and killed), was the first real independent damel.

The important event of the reign of Amari Ngoné Sobel (1549–93) was the union with Baol. Three days after his second victory over the Djoloff, the death of his uncle, the Tegne Gnokhor Ndiaye, led him to claim this crown which indeed was offered to him by the electors. He therefore became Damel-Tègne.[29] Time and time again, Cayor and Baol were to be united

27 Rousseau, 'Etudes sur le Oualo . . .', *loc. cit.*, p. 147.
28 From 1830 to 1855, the power was held by the two 'queens' (*lingueres*) Guimbotte and Ndete-Yalla, under the nominal authority of the Brak 'ghosts', to use an expression borrowed from General Faidherbe, who annexed Walo.
29 Tradition explains this new title as a derivation from the word 'dam': to smash or break. But this title is much earlier than 1549 since we find it under the form Budomel (Bour-Damel) as early as 1455–7 in Ca da Mosto.

under one sovereign without either country ever losing its internal autonomy.

The succession of Amari Ngoné Sobel gave rise to a curious situation. In order to keep the kingship in his mother's family (the Wagadu mène), he managed by a clever ruse to marry his own son, Massamba Tako, to the boy's aunt—half-sister of Amari Ngoné Sobel on his mother's side and the linguere of Baol. The son born of this union, Mamalick Thioro[30] inherited only Baol and not Cayor where Massamba Tako succeeded his father, only to be attacked and killed by Mamalick, his own son, who had then to renounce Cayor which passed to his brothers on his father's side.[31]

The reigns of Ma Khouredia Kouli (1600-10) and Biram Mbanga (1610-40) are said to have been happy reigns with neither wars nor raiding. Daou Demba (1640-47) always appears as an immoderate and cruel prince. He persecuted the Mouyoi mène, the maternal clan of his nephew, Madior, who had to go into exile; he surrounded himself with young people, dismissed the elders, and had the chief of the royal slaves executed. He joined battle with the wise Kotche Barma, Lamane Diamatile, who had him deposed by the electors at the annual Assembly of the Tabaski. He took refuge in Walo where the Brak allowed him to settle.

Madior I, who succeeded him (1647-64) and gave his name to the dynasty (Fall-Madior), 'reigned seventeen years without one rifle-shot being fired in Cayor'.[32] Tradition ascribes the wisdom of his government to his councillor, Kotche Barma. During his reign, Ndiambour passed by treaty from the Walo fief to the control of Cayor (1650).

The 'war of the marabouts' (1681-83) marks the failure of an Islamic bid for supremacy, a fascinating foretaste of moves to come in the following century—all equally doomed to failure in the domain of the ancient Wolof empire.

The widow of Madior I had been appointed linguère by her son Biram Yacine Boubou (1664-1681)—whose reign was distinguished only by a

30 This is probably the Amad Malique mentioned by Alvares d'Almada, of the 'race of the "Budumels"' living in Lambaye (capital of Baol).

31 List and chronology of the Damels of the Fall Madior dynasty (part of the patrilinear clan of the Fall which kept the throne during the whole of the seventeenth century, and received this name in honour of Madior 1st), according to Yoro Diao.

Massamba Tako	1593-1600
Makhouredia Kouli	1600-1610
Biram Mbanga	1610-1640
Daou Demba	1640-1647
Madior I	1647-1664
Biram Yacine Boubou	1664-1681
Detie Maram	1681-1683
Ma Fali	1683-1684
Makhouredia Coumba Diodio	1684-1691
Biram Mbenda Tilor	1691-1693
De Tialao	1693-1697

32 Yoro Diao, according to Rousseau, 'Etudes sur le Cayor'.

fruitless attempt to seize control of Baol. Biram's successor, Dithié ou Maram (1681–83), removed her in favour of his own mother. The ex-linguère Yacine Boubou then made an alliance with the marabout party, giving her daughter, Anta, in marriage to its chief, the Qadi of Cayor, N'Diaye Sall. At the battle of Kellere, rebels from the Muslim faction defied and killed the Damel Dithié ou Maram (1683) and replaced him with their own candidate, Ma Fali. The tiedos were obliged to accept conversion to Islam. But six months later, the new Damel, caught by the talibes in the act of drinking brandy, was executed by order of the qadi. The angry Yacine Boubou appealed to the Bour Saloum Ma Khourédia Coumba Diodio Diouf (son of Madior I, born during his exile in Salum to the guelowar Coumba Diodio Diouf); the tiedos renounced Islam and changed sides. The qadi was beaten at the second battle of Kellere and was killed. Lemaire mentions this episode, but in a different version. He says that the Damel's power was usurped by a marabout who incited the people to revolt, promising them harvests without work. As a result the fields were left untilled and there was general famine. The people rose against him and he fled the country.[33] Ma Khouredia reigned for seven years (1684–91), uniting Cayor and Salum for the first time under his rule.

Dé Tialaw (1693–97), who came to the throne at the general wish of the people, became blind after reigning for two years. Thanks to his entourage, he managed to disguise this infirmity for the next two years, but of course blindness was incompatible with his royal function of talisman. In spite of his popularity, he had to abdicate. He was replaced by the Tègne Lat Soucabé (1697–1719) who once more united Cayor and Baol under one government and successfully resisted an attack from the Bourba-Djoloff. His reign marks the establishment of a new dynasty, that of the Fall Tié Yacine (1697–1763). This period was distinguished by the misfortunes of Maissa Bigué, three times Damel; he was driven out in 1749 by an attack from Walo, then in 1759 by one from Wolof, but each time he managed to win back the throne. Twice more, under Maissa Tende (1719–48) and under Mahoua (1749–57), Cayor and Baol were united under the rule of the same Damel-Tègne. With Madior II (1763–6) the Fall Madior branch returned to power but he was driven out by the Brak Natago Aram Bakar, on whom he had unwisely declared war. The crown was given to the Tègne Macodou (1766–77) who once more united Cayor with Baol and established yet a new branch of the dynasty—that of the Fall Tié Ndella.[34]

During the reign of Amari Ngoné Ndella Coumba (1790–1809), Damel-Tègne, there were various repercussions in Cayor from the Muslim revolutions at the end of the eighteenth century. An internal rising of

33 *Voyages du sieur Lemaire. . . .*

34 List and chronology of the Damels from 1697–1809 (from Brigaud, who follows the chronology of Yoro Diao, *op. cit.*, pp. 105 and 109): *(continued overleaf)*

Muslims was crushed but the rebels took refuge in the Cape Verde peninsula where together with the local Lebu population they formed the independent Republic of Cape Verde.

Two or three months later, the Damel had to fight the Almamy of Futa, Abdoul Kader, who, as we have seen, was conquered when his Walo allies abandoned him. Taken prisoner, he was treated magnanimously and freed by the Damel.

Baol. In spite of its political unity, Baol had a mixed population, part Wolof, part Serer. Very little is known about its history, however, much less than about Cayor,[35] but since Baol and Cayor were so frequently united under one ruler, the reasonably good documentation on Cayor allows some account to emerge. It was apparently under the seventh tègne (Bouré Fara Kap) that Baol managed to establish that its rulers would no longer be chosen by the Bourba but elected instead by an assembly of local dignitaries, under the chairmanship of the Diaraf Baol (probably during the fifteenth century). The eighteenth tègne was Gnokhor N'Diaye, uncle of Amari Ngoné Sobel.

Sine and Salum. The mass of the indigenous population of the Sine and the Salum are Serer. Originally from the north, the Serer seem to have driven out or else assimilated the previous occupants, the *Socés* (Malinke), who moved on to the south, near to Gambia.

The Guelowar aristocracy (of Malinke origin) seems to have settled after the Serer migration. They were probably a group of warriors,

(34 *continued*)

Fall Tié Yacine (1697–1763)	
Lat Soucabe	1697–1719
Maissa Tende	1719–1748
Maissa Bigue	1748–1749
Mahoua	1749–1757
Biram Codou	1757–1758
Maissa Bigue	1758–1759
Maissa Bigue	1760–1763
Madior II (Fall Madior)	1763–1766
Macodou (Fall Tié Ndella)	1766–1777
Birahim Fatim Penda (")	1777–1790
Amari Ngone Ndella Coumba (Fall Tié Yacine)	1790–1809

35 Alvares d'Almada, *op. cit.*, 1594, situates this kingdom between the Cayor and Joal; Lemaire (*op. cit.*, 1695) mentions the 'King of Portugady' (Portudal) and comments 'Jain (Tegne) is the name of his rank' (p. 86). The name of Baol seems to appear for the first time in O. Dapper (*Description de l'Afrique*, texte français—Amsterdam, 1686) which mentions it as different from the 'Kingdom of Ale'; no conclusion can be drawn from this (the author, without realising, must have found the two names in different sources and written them down, one after the other). Labat (*op. cit.*, iv, pp. 129–40) mentions only the Baol between Cayor and Boursin (Sine). Some details on the Baol in Gaden, 'Légendes et coutumes sénégalaises . . .' *op. cit.*, and Rousseau, 'Etudes sur le Cayor' *op. cit.*, 1933, pp. 283–4 (using an unpublished monograph on the circle of Thiès).

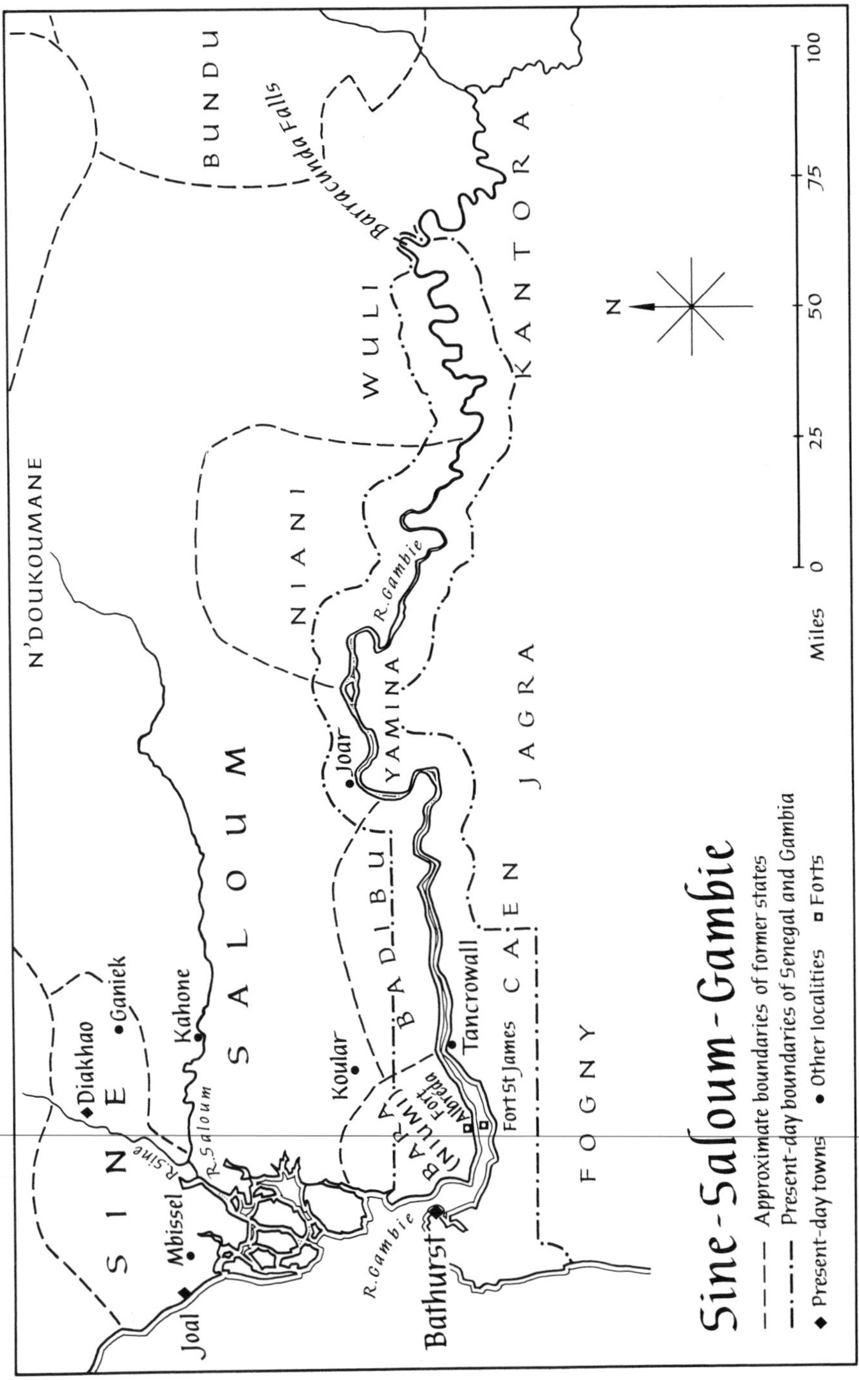
Sine-Saloum-Gambie
Approximate boundaries of former states
Present-day boundaries of Senegal and Gambia
Present-day towns
Other localities
Forts
Miles
0
25
50
75
100
N
N'DOUKOUMANE
BUNDU
Barracunda Falls
WULI
KANTORA
NIANI
R. Gambie
YAMINA
Joar
JAGRA
SALOUM
BADIBU
CAEN
FOGNY
SINE
Diakhao
Ganiek
Kahone
Koular
Tancrowall
Fort St James
Fort Albreda
BARA (NIUMI)
R. Saloum
R. Sine
Mbissel
Joal
Bathurst
R. Gambie

11:2

emigrating from Gabu after some local trouble. The Guelowar apparently crossed the Casamance, then the Gambia, and settled in the village of Koular (fourteenth century?); then, after crossing over into Salum, they seized control of the village of Mbissel which became their first capital.

According to tradition—and this is possibly quite true—the Serer country was in a state of anarchy (indeed, the country of the Serer Nones remained so until the colonial period). A local aristocracy of wealthy tribal chiefs had begun to emerge but it was not yet powerful enough to assert its authority. Its chief, the Lamane Pangay Yai Sar, surrendered to the conquering Guelowar whose chief, Maissa Wali Dione, recognised the authority of the Serer lamane over the land. The descendants of the Serer lamane became his vassals with the title of Bour Ganieck while their sovereign, taking the title of Bour Sine (king of Sine) finally set up his capital further inland, at Diakhao.[36]

The conquest of Salum came later. It was the work of Mbegane Ndour, conqueror of the Tucolor marabout, Eli Bana, who had settled at Kahone. Tucolor tradition also mentions him and makes him a contemporary of Koli Tenguella. From the royal list of the Bours Salum (which relates the number of years of each reign to the number of rainy seasons) we can establish that the reign of Mbegane Ndour covered the years 1494–1514.[37] It should be noted that the term Broçalo (Bour Salum) used by Portuguese writers to indicate the Salum estuary, did not appear before the beginning of the sixteenth century.[38]

Practically nothing is known of the history of Salum and Sine in the seventeenth and eighteenth centuries, apart from lists of dynasties, handed down by oral tradition.[39] The Salum list which gives the number of years each king reigned may be considered accurate because three items can be satisfactorily cross-checked: the Lagatir Balhana, father of the reigning Salum Bour, mentioned by Alvares d'Almada in 1566, would be Lat Tilor Badiane (1551–60); Haman Seaca, the former Salum Bour who abdicated

36 Diakhao must have been founded by the eighth Bour Sine, Diengatj. (Brigaud, *op. cit.*, p. 159).

37 cf. Brigaud, *op. cit.*, p. 161.

38 Fernandes (1506–7), *op. cit.*, pp. 27 ff, shows that 'the Sereos (Serer) and the Barbacijs (deriving from Bourba Sine: subjects of the King of Sine) were not subject to the King of Çanagaa (Emperor of Djoloff) and have no king or special overlord'. These people were 'great idolaters' who used poisoned arrows and hid in the bushes and the woods. In vain the King of Çanagaa undertook expeditions to subdue the country: he was defeated each time.

Fernandes nowhere mentions the existence of organised states in Serer country. But it is possible that his description applied only to the Serer Nones, who remained independent until the end of the nineteenth century within the confines of Cayor, Baol and Sine. The use of the terms Barbacijs, Broçalo, Borjoniq—transcriptions of 'Bour Sine, Bour Salum, Bour Ganieck'—to indicate the branches of Salum, and for the first of these terms, to indicate the Serer population, presupposes the existence of sovereigns with these names.

Alvares d'Almada (1594) mentions the kingdoms of the Barbacins and Borçalo.

39 Brigaud, *op. cit.*, pp. 159–62.

in favour of his brother and was seen in 1731 by Francis Moore, would be Ama Siga Seck (1730–2) and the Sandéné Bour, mentioned by Golberry as the one who signed the treaty with Repentigny in 1785, would be Sandéné Codou Bigué Dao (1779–88). The dates more or less agree.[40]

The Lebu community of Cape Verde.[41] The Lebu population of the Cape Verde peninsula, who have the distinction of being fishermen rather than farmers, seem to have resulted from a mixture of Serer and Wolof strains. Tradition suggests that they came from the Mauritanian Hodh which they left in order to move towards the lower Senegal, then to Cayor, and finally to end up in the seventeenth century in the N'Diander region.

In 1790, the marabouts of Cayor who had defied the Damel, took refuge in the peninsula. The Lebu leader was Dial Diop, son of a marabout from Coki (Cayor); his father had settled in the area and had married the daughter of a Lebu village chief. The Lebu, joining forces with the marabout refugees, turned against the tiedos of the Damel and built a series of trenches across the isthmus to protect themselves. The successor to Amari Ngoné Birahim Fatma Tioub had to recognise their independence in 1812.

The Fula state of Futa-Toro: the Denianke monarchy

The Futa-Toro or Senegalese Futa extends along all the central valley of Senegal from Bakel up the river and down as far as the delta. It is a sort of oasis between the semi-desert region of Mauritania to the north and the Ferlo to the south, an area which is deprived of water throughout the dry season. The area of land under cultivation stretches from the *fondé*, a ridge of land along the low water line sometimes covered by the floodwaters, to the *diéri*, a similar ridge of dry land at high level: the area between is called the *walo* and is covered by floodwaters every year. The population is mixed, though mainly Tucolor. There are still many Fulbe (20 to 30 per cent of the population). With the exception of the Fulbe, the population is divided in a large number of endogamous castes: Torobé ('those who pray'), a caste descended from the Muslim faction which triumphed at the end of the eighteenth century; Sebbe (plural of Tiedo), farmers and fishermen, probably descended from royal slaves who had been warriors in the service of the ancient Denianke kings; Soubalbé, fishermen of Serer or Wolof descent who are thought to have lived in the valley from the earliest times; Diawambe, marabouts, part of the chiefs' households; artisan castes similar to those established in the Djoloff (indeed most of them are thought to have originated in the Futa): mabube (weavers), sakebe (shoemakers), laobe (craftsmen in wood), blacksmiths, griot

40 Jean Boulègue, 'Contribution à la chronologie du royaume du Saloum', *Bull. I.F.A.N.*, ser. B, xxviii, 3–4, 1966, pp. 657–67.

41 Cf. C. Michael, 'L'organisation Coutumière de la collectivité Leboue de Dakar', *Bull. Com. Etud. Hist. Scient. A.O.F.*, 1934, pp. 510–24.

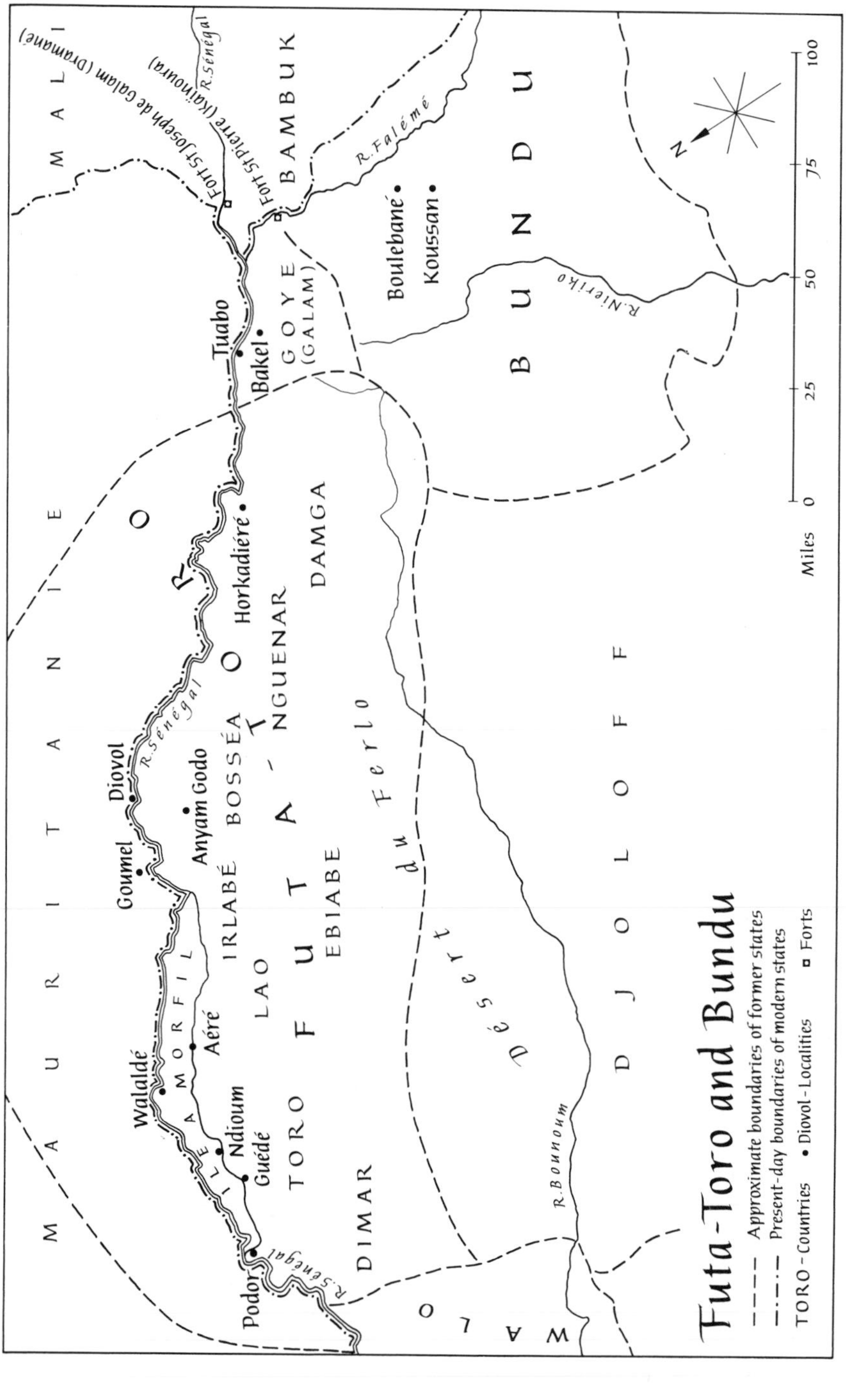

Futa-Toro and Bundu
Approximate boundaries of former states
Present-day boundaries of modern states
TORO - Countries
• Diovol - Localities
▫ Forts
Miles
0
25
50
75
100
N
M A U R I T A N I E
M A L I
B A M B U K
B U N D U
GOYE
(GALAM)
F U T A - T O R O
TORO
DIMAR
LAO
IRLABÉ
EBIABE
BOSSÉA
NGUENAR
DAMGA
W A L O
D J O L O F F
Désert du Ferlo
ILE A MORFIL
R. Sénégal
R. Falémé
R. Nieriko
R. Bounoum
Fort St Joseph de Galam (Dramane)
Fort St Pierre (Kaïnoura)
Podor
Guédé
Ndioum
Walaldé
Aéré
Goumel
Diovol
Anyam Godo
Horkadiéré
Tuabo
Bakel
Boulebané
Koussan

II:3

musicians, griots responsible for the memorising and reciting of vital traditions and, of course, slaves.

At the beginning of the sixteenth century, the Futa-Toro fell under the control of the dynasty founded by the war leader Koli Tenguella (the Denianke dynasty). He established his warrior bands there: they were probably men of diverse origins, though most of them were Fulbe or Malinke (the 'Koliagbé'). Like Koli Tenguella, his successors bore the Malinke title *Silatigui* (leader of the way—written wrongly as 'Siratique' by French writers in the seventeenth and eighteenth centuries).

The state of the Silatigui was very powerful, thanks to its resources (the rich valley of the Senegal, kept fertile by annual floods), its direct contacts with Europeans (the Portuguese, and later on, the French, came up the Senegal and established direct commercial relations), and finally its military organisation, inherited from Koli.[42]

Institutions based on Malinke patterns absorbed the administrative structures that existed prior to the conquest: the vassal chiefs of the provinces bore the most varied titles, going back to the time of the *Faren* of Anyam Godo, vassals of Diara: *Farba*, a Malinke title; *Lam* or *Ardo*, Tucolor or Fulani titles; *Silatigui*, as the ruler was called; also Muslim titles, like *Thierno*, *Elimane*, and others. One of these vassals, the Kamalinkou (whom Labat called Camalingue) was, like the Boumi, the appointed successor, or Crown Prince, brother or nephew on the mother's side, according to Labat. Among the officials, Labat mentions the 'Bouquenet', 'grand master of the Siratic household': this is the same name and the same function as the 'Diaraf Beukeneg' of Sine and Salum, the 'Beukneg Ndiourbel' of the Walo, chief of the royal slaves.[43]

The list of the early successors of Koli (up until 1650) which the Tarikh-Es-Soudan provided is a good crosscheck for that of Sire Abbas-Soh and the dates put forward by Delafosse are perfectly possible. In the Tarikh, al-Saʿdi tells us that Gueladyo-Tabara (1593–1603?) had a reputation for justice equalled only by that of the Mansa of Mali, Kanku-Musa and his eighteenth-century successors.

The 'Siratic Siré' who, according to Labat was 'Roi des Foules' (King of the Fulbe) in 1700 is the Sire-Sawa-Lamu of tradition (1683–1702 according to Delafosse). He wanted to ensure his son's succession and made him Kamalinkou by dismissing his nephew and legitimate successor, Sambaboe (Samba Boyi) from his position. Lemaire (end of the seventeenth century) said that this Silatigui 'never drank either wine or spirits, observing the law of Muhammed more scrupulously than the other Negroes'.[44] He was much influenced by the Moors who formed his army,

42 For the Portuguese, Pereira (1506–8), *op. cit.*, p. 53 supplies details of commerce with the kingdom of Tucurol and the navigation of the Sénégal as far as the falls of the Felou.

43 'Beukneg' originally meant 'one who was circumcised at the same time', i.e. a person belonging to the same age or initiation group: in modern terms, it could mean 'class-mate'.

44 Lemaire, *op. cit.*, pp. 84–5.

and especially by a Moorish marabout. On his death, Samba Boyi took power and expelled the Moors. But his nephew and successor, Samba Dondé (Sawa Dondé) or Demba Dumbé was beaten and killed by his brother Boubacar Siré (Bôkar-Siré-Sawa-Lamu) who enlisted the services of a band of Moors and Moroccans led by Salé renegades. He was finally driven out by the Kamalinkou Guelangaye (Gueladyo Yegui) in 1725.[45]

The most famous of his successors was Soule Ndiaye (1740–8 according to Delafosse; he was in power when the French set up at Podor).[46] Siré Abbas Soh was unstinting in his praises and insisted that he was the only Silatigui of the eighteenth century to be a good Muslim. Soule Ndiaye was the first to organise a property-owning system, trying to consolidate his own financial position by granting lands in return for ground rent (diôwré—sing. diowouré, possessions administered by the descendant of the ancestor of the older branch of the family who acted as local chief). Apparently he restricted himself to handing over territories that were either unassigned or else newly won back from rebels without actually suppressing any existing grants based on the rights of the first pioneers or going back to allocations made before the sixteenth century by Lam Termes or distributed by Koli and the other Silatigui to their companions in arms.

The diagarafs, who collected taxes on a percentage basis, also collected rents from the sovereign's lands and rapidly became the equivalent of the other 'concessionnaires' on the estates where they carried out their duties.

After four fairly short reigns, Soulé Ndiaye II (or the Younger) had to deal with the rebellion of his vassal, the Silatigui of Dekle, whose lands were in the north of the country and who had the support of the Moors. He suppressed the rebellion and killed its leader (1760–9 according to Delafosse).[47]

In spite of the reforms of Soulé N'Diaye I, the Denianke did not manage to set their state's administration on a very firm basis:

> The Denianke Kings [Vidal observes] passed their time battling against rebels from the interior and attacks from outside; their only resources

45 Sources: *Tarikh-Es-Soudan*, re-ed. Paris. Adrien-Maisonneuve, 1964, p. 128; Labat, *op. cit.*, pp. 198–9; Delcourt, *op. cit.*, pp. 155–8. The chronology of Delafosse (in Siré Abbas Soh, *Chroniques du Fouta sénégalais*, trans. M. Delafosse and H. Gaden, Paris, 1913) agrees with the information given by Labat, but is contradicted by the colonial archives used by Delcourt. This chronology makes Boubacar Siré reign from 1709–10 while Delcourt's information seems to set this reign between 1718 and 1724 (with, as from 1721, a series of clashes with a rival called Baba Moussa, not mentioned in Delafosse's list unless it was, in fact, Boubou Moussa: 1727–33 according to this list).

46 Cf. Brigaud, *op. cit.*, p. 21. Vidal attributes him with a reign of forty years (M. Vidal, 'Etude sur la tenure des terres indigènes au Fouta', *Bull. Com. Etud. Hist. Scient. A.O.F.*, 1935, pp. 415–48) following the information given by Siré Abbas Soh, *op. cit.*, pp. 32–6.

47 Kane Abdoulaye (*Histoire et origine des familles du Fouta-Toro*, Annuaire et Memoires, Com. Etud. Hist. Scient. A.O.F., 1916) says he reigned for only two years.

came from plunder, from raids ordered on the most futile pretexts against villages or settlements suspected of political indifference and above all from tributes of natural produce which they levied for the needs of their warrior bands or else stole from the peasant farmers and cattle breeders as their fancy took them.

This state of anarchy and insecurity lasted for almost two centuries.[48]

This situation left the Futa-Toro at the mercy of attacks from other countries.

At the end of the eighteenth century the problem of pressure from the Moors was all-important in the history of the Futa-Toro (as it was in that of Walo). Accounts from the seventeenth and beginning of the eighteenth century say that the possessions of the Silatigui covered a wide area on the right bank of the river.[49]

It was in the name of the struggle against the Moors, allies of the Silatigui of Dekle, that the marabout Souleymane Bal mobilised his Muslims and gave the signal for the Islamic revolution which marked the end of the dynasty.

The Muslim party called on everyone for help, whatever their origin: for this reason, it attracted those who found traditional society oppressive and it took on a revolutionary character.

Soulé-Boubou (1769–76), the last of the Denianke, set up his headquarters first at Horkadiere, then moved on to the village of Wali Diantan on the right bank in his struggle against the Muslim rebels. Three times he drove back and defeated the Almamy Abdoul Kader, but the fourth expedition saw his defeat and death.[50]

Mandinka Kingdoms and Chieftainships from the Gambia to the Faleme

Portuguese explorers left accounts showing that some sort of Mali sovereignty, even if only theoretical, still extended to the regions between the Gambia and the River Geba[51] as late as the mid-fifteenth century. Basically, however, central authority had been broken up into a multitude of tiny chieftainships.

48 Vidal, *op. cit.*

49 Lemaire, *op. cit.*, p. 83, says that the states of Cheyratick extended along the two banks of the Sénégal; Labat, *op. cit.*, ii, p. 195, that the kingdom of the Foulles or of Siratique 'extended a long way along the two sides of the river'; moreover, its capital Goumel was on the right bank.

50 Siré Abbas Soh, *op. cit.*

51 The informants of Diogo Gomes (end of the fifteenth century) at Cantor (Gambia) declared that 'the whole region on the right side of the river was under his rule', but gave him as residence Quioquia (Koukia, the old capital of Songhai?). Provided there has been no confusion on the part of the author, the conclusion might be drawn that in the minds of the Mandinka of Gambia, the capital of Songhai, then at the height of its powers, had taken the place of Niani, the true capital of Mali, then in a state of decadence. The sovereignty of Mansa might therefore be entirely theoretical. (Diogo Gomes, *De la première decouverte de la Guinée*, Bissau, Centro de Estudos da Guiné portuguesa, 1959; Memorias no. 21, p. 38 and notes 64 and 65).

There is a fairly large amount of information on those of the Gambia which remained largely unchanged from the time of the first Portuguese explorers to the eighteenth century. These were the kingdoms of Niumi (or of Bara) and Badibu on the right bank of the river near its mouth and of Niani, Wuli and Cantor upstream. Other less important ones occupied the left bank.[52] The creation of these states (or at any rate the creation of Wuli) is attributed to Sire Birama Berete, lieutenant of Sundiata.[53]

Further inland according to V. Fernandes, there were three Mandinka states in the sixteenth century: Gabu, to the east of the River Geba, was the oldest and most important. It was from here that the Guelowar set off to conquer Sine and Salum. To the west of the Geba were the two kingdoms of Oio and Braço (the sovereign of Braço bearing the Malinke title of *Faren* or *Farim*, a name which the Portuguese later gave to a river port).

The foundation of the states of Gabu (thirteenth century?) is attributed either to one of Soundiata's lieutenants, Tira Makhan (according to Moreira) or to Sama Coli, great-grandson of Soundiata, on the female line (according to Caroço).[54] Gabu was made up of three provinces (Pathiana, Djimara, Sama) whose princes took it in turn to rule the whole country; the capital was Kansala.[55]

There is no definite information about the history of these states. Koli's incursion does not seem to have affected Mandinka supremacy but it seems to have encouraged the settlement of numerous Fulbe who had until then been nomadic, politically disorganised and paying tribute to the

52 Cf. Gomes, *op. cit.*, pp. 30-6. Nome Mains (Niumi Mansa) is situated on the right bank at the mouth of the river; Ulimaüs or Ollimansa (Wuli Mansa), and Animaüs (Niani Mansa) corresponding to the countries of Wuli and Niani. Batti-Mansa according to A. Teixeira da Mota, was a king of the country of Vintang on the left bank; but Diogo Gomes seems possibly wrongly to put the chief Forisangul (Fara Sani Koli?), vassal of the Mansa of Mali, on the right bank; it is perhaps really a question here of the chief of Badibu, on the right bank. For the political geography of the eighteenth century—practically unchanged—see Francis Moore, *Travels into Inland Parts of Africa*, London, E. Cave, 1738. D. Westermann refers to R. W. Macklin's monograph which gives an interesting table of the institutions of the Niumi kingdom. The Mansa was assisted by a prime minister (Alkaito: this Arab term, coming via Portuguese, probably represents a native title)—the chief of the royal village (Alkali), a Sila-Tio (Silatigui or Satigui), the leader of the army and an executioner. The council of elders was drawn from the nobility (the Kanda). The king had a bodyguard made up of slaves. There is a remarkable similarity with the nearby kingdoms of Sine and Salum, both of Mandinka origin. According to D. Westermann (*Geschichte Afrikas*, Cologne, Greven Verlag, 1952, pp. 86-7) the monograph includes a list of seventy kings—queens at the outset—divided into three branches comprising respectively 2, 3 and 2 royal lines. Unfortunately it has not been possible to consult the actual monograph for the purpose of this study.

53 Dr Rançon, *Dans la Haute-Gambie*, Paris, Societé d'Editions scientifiques, 1894.

54 Jose Mendes Moreira, *Fulas do Gabu*, Memorias . . . no. 6, Bissau, 1948. Jorge Velez Caroço, *Monjur-O Gabu e a Sua historia*, no. 8, Bissau, 1948. Sama Koli, first king of Gabu, is said to be the son of Ufara who was the daughter of Tenemba, herself daughter of Soundiata. See also Antonio Carreira, *Mandingas da Guine portuguesa*, Memorias . . ., no. 4, Bissau, 1947.

55 J. Girard, 'Notes sur l'histoire traditionnelle de la Haute-Casamance', *Bull. I.F.A.N.*, ser. B, xxviii, 1-2, 1966, pp. 540-54.

Malinke chiefs. The Fulacunda, who settled in this region, probably arrived there later on (at the end of the seventeenth century or during the eighteenth), migrating from Macina.

It should be noted that in the nineteenth century the chiefdoms of Niani, Wuli and Cantor were recorded as being ruled by Malinke from Bambuk, driven from their country by the Almamys of Bundu.[56]

It is probable that the relative stability enjoyed by the Malinke states until the great Fula advances of the mid-nineteenth century was related to some extent to successive migration of Fulbe and Malinke peoples into the region.

There is little to say on the settlements and scattered chiefdoms of Upper Gambia. There were still a few remaining groups living in comfortable disunity in spite of attacks from the Futa-Dialonke. There were people of the Tenda group—Coniagui, Bassari, Badyaranke and the Dialonke from Sangalan to the north of Gambia who had never been conquered in spite of incessant attacks but were incapable of forming a cohesive unit.[57]

Finally, there was a scattering of Malinke chiefdoms under the general name of Bambuk, with three main kingdoms: Bambuk itself (its capital, Farabana, on the Faleme, governed by the Niakhate); Beledugu or Sirimana (probably the 'Samarina' of Coste d'Arnobat) where the Sissoko from Bambuk ruled over the Sumaré (Soninke) who seem to have left Khasso and Guidimaka to settle in this kingdom before the arrival of the Sissoko, but who nevertheless owned the land and remained 'masters of the gold'; Satadougou or Bafé, in the present-day republic of Mali, ruled by the Seydicora (Diula). To these may be added Dantila where the Damfaka, who claimed descent from the legendary hero, Samakhoto, ruled over the indigenous Samoura (Dialonke) and Badon, where the Keita from Manding territory ruled the Damfaka and the Sadiogo (possibly Malinke-assimilated Bassari?).[58]

Coste d'Arnobat stresses the feebleness of the authority of the Bambuk kings:

> The power of these princes is, however, so slight that one scarcely notices that they are kings; they have no other prerogatives over their subjects than those which normally accompany age—which Negroes greatly respect. . . . None of these kings would dare to make the smallest demand on his subjects. Everything (business) is passed to the council,

56 Rançon, *op. cit.*

57 Cf. G. Vieillard, *Notes sur les Peuls du Fouta-Djalon, Bull. I.F.A.N.*, ii, 1940, p. 106. Mungo Park, crossing this region (or that of Dinguiraye where the population was also Dialonke), observed: 'The "Jallonkas", like the Mandinke, are governed by a small number of petty chiefs who are for the majority independent of each other, and in fact these chiefs are rarely sufficiently united among themselves to help each other, even in time of war' (*Voyage dans l'interieur de l'Afrique fait en 1795, 1796 et 1797*, ii, p. 120).

58 Cf. Brigaud, *op. cit.*, p. 197–9 and A. Aubert, 'Légendes historiques et traditions orales recueillies en Haute-Gambie', *Bull. Com. Etud. Hist. Scient. A.O.F.*, 1923, pp. 348–428.

> that is to say that all the men, young and old alike, assemble at a place called Bentaba.[59] There, each carefully listens to what the King has to propose and they then consider what they should do. The voice of the prince was no more authoritative than that of others.[60]

They were elected by the village chiefs (*farims*), and were almost independent, though their subjects could always depose them. It is easy to see why Golberry considers this constitution 'almost republican'. According to him, after the Portuguese conquest (sixteenth century ?) a marabout conspiracy against the kings ended in the massacre of the marabouts, and from then onwards they were not allowed in the country.[61] Under these conditions, the vague Mohammedanism professed by the Malinke of Bambuk was more or less forgotten until they even forgot how to pray.[62]

THE FULA-ISLAMIC REVOLUTIONS OF THE EIGHTEENTH CENTURY

The rise of the Fulbe-Tucolor hegemonies[63]

This is not the place to discuss the details of the ethnic characteristics and the history of the Fulbe. The origins of these nomadic herdsmen with their light skin and tall slender bodies has aroused great interest among historians and ethnologists.

Over the last century a great deal has been written on this subject, much of it fanciful rather than factual; a substantial part of the literature has sought to give the Fulbe a white ancestry, this being more in keeping with their rôle of empire-builders, according to the colonial point of view.[64] Islam-inspired traditions suggest an Arab origin, possibly Yemenite if not from the family of the Prophet himself, and Delafosse thought they might possibly be what he called 'Judaeo-Arabs'.

More recently it has been suggested by the work of Lhote, and supported by A. Hampaté Ba and G. Dieterlen, that the herdsmen found in the Sahara rock-paintings could be the ancestors of the Fulbe.[65] They could have come from the area around the Nile valley and they certainly bear

59 *Bentaba*: place of public meetings, generally in the shade of a silk-cotton tree (benta in Malinke).
60 Coste d'Arnobat, *Voyage au pays de Bambouk*, Brussels, Dujardin, 1789, pp. 14–15.
61 Golberry, *op. cit.*, vol. i.
62 Coste d'Arnobat, *op. cit.*, p. 46.
63 See Richard-Molard, *l'Afrique occidentale francaise*, Paris, Berger-Levrault, 1948 (3rd edn, 1956), pp. 93–100, and J. Suret-Canale, 'Zur historischen und sozialen Bedeutung der Fulbe-Hegemonie' in *Geschichte und Geschichtsbild Afrikas*, Berlin, Akademie Verlag (Academic Press), 1960, pp. 29–59. French text: *Essai sur la signification historique et sociale des hégémonies peules*, Paris, Cahiers du C.E.R.M. (polygraph copies) n.d. (1964).
64 Cf. Tauxier, *Histoire des Peuls*, Paris, Payot, 1937, provides a good summary of all this literature, accompanied by a few personal conclusions.
65 Lhote, 'L'extraordinaire aventure des Peuls', *Présence africaine*, xxii, Oct.-Nov., 1958, pp. 48–57: 'Les peintures pariétales d'époque bovidienne du Tassili. Eléments sur la magie et la religion', *Journal de la société des Africanistes*, xxxvi, 1966, pp. 7–28 and A. Hampaté Ba and G. Dieterlen: 'Les fresques d'époque bovidienne du Tassili N'Ajjer et les traditions des Peuls: hypothèses d'interprétation', *ibid*, pp. 141–57.

some physical resemblance with the 'Ethiopian' or Nilotic peoples of East Africa.

Specialisation in certain herds, and the consequent nomadic existence, is what sets the Fulbe apart in West Africa. The association with cattle became so close that the animals were integrated into Fula society and were actually given clan names.

In their primitive state, these herdsmen were far from propagating a superior culture of Hebrew or Arab origin. They were ordinary, typical primitive folk. They borrowed most of their cultural and social institutions from neighbouring peoples, notably the Soninke and the Mande. Their division into four clans (Ba, Diallo, Bari and Sow), characteristic of the West African Fulbe, may also be borrowed from the Mande social structure.

From Termès (in southern Mauritania, where there are still many of them) several groups moved to the Futa-Toro. The earliest migrations towards Ferlo, Upper Gambia and Futa-Jallon probably date back to at least the thirteenth and fourteenth centuries.

Tradition and genealogical data support Tauxier in his suggestion that the second wave of migration came in the second half of the seventeenth century though from Macina rather than Termès. But it is possible that they started moving at an earlier date.

The living conditions of the Fulbe obliged them to stay in very small groups, or 'households' which in practice comprised very often no more than the parents and their own children. These small inoffensive groups were usually tolerated reasonably well by the farmers on whom they depended for water and pastureland in the dry season. They were occasionally harassed and bullied, to which they usually reacted by running away. At the beginning of the seventeenth century, Jobson compared the Fulbe nomads of Gambia to European gypsies emphasising that 'these people lived in great subjection to the Mandingo'.[66]

It seems scarcely possible that these primitive people with their rudimentary culture and ardent animism could change into aristocratic warriors, founders of empires, a sword in one hand and the Qur'ān in the other.

The Fulbe from Macina, who started the seventeenth century migrations, had for a long time, like the Tucolors, been associated with both the rural and urban civilisation of states based on Mande tradition, in the Niger valley as well as in the valley of the Senegal. They had been in contact with the more developed civilisation and knew about Islam though they were rarely converted and even then they frequently relapsed into animism. The Fula chiefdoms of Macina appeared in the fifteenth century, followed eventually by the formation of the Denianke state. Although the states were pagan, they were not unaware of Islam. It was these Fulbe from Macina who emigrated to the Futa-Jallon and the Tucolor from the

66 R. Jobson, *op. cit.*, p. 44.

Senegal valley who were deeply involved in the Islamic revolutions. The revolutions of the eighteenth and nineteenth centuries did not in any event affect the whole ethnic group. Among the older settlements founded after the wave of migrations to Futa-Jallon and right up to the colonial conquest in Ferlo, there were many pagan Fulbe who remained faithful to the primitive way of life and fiercely opposed Islam.[67] On the other hand, these revolutions swept a number of ethnic groups other than the Fulbe into conversion to Islam; the 'Torobe' movement of the Tucolor is much more like the marabout party in Cayor in a peasant context than the Fula movement in the Futa-Jallon. In the event it was a 'war of marabouts' which was successful.

These revolutions cannot be explained simply within the framework of ethnic groups. Politico-religious movements started up by the Fulbe found support among malcontents and dissidents of other ethnic groups, to say nothing of the Tucolor movement where a different ethnic group was involved and where the movement was, moreover, directed against the ruling Fula aristocracy of the Denianke.

These reservations apart, the privileged position of the Fulbe must be acknowledged. Moreover, their position was not due to chance alone. There was clearly a link between the revolutions and their gradual renunciation of the nomadic way of life, as cattle-breeding made them even richer.

Against the background of general impoverishment, trade promoted some developments in the system of exchange and a sharpening of social distinctions. These circumstances led the privileged classes to seek a form of wealth which was both easy to keep and easy to convert. In a country where metal coinage was not in use and where privately owned and transferable landed property did not exist, cattle seemed to be the best form of wealth. It did not deteriorate and it reproduced itself freely; it was easily changed from collective ownership into private property. In ancient times, before the Romans adopted metal currency, they used cattle as the symbol and the means of preserving wealth: the word for money, *pecunia*, derives from *pecus* meaning herd and the first bronze ingots to be used for money bore the imprint of a bull.

Wealth did not mean capital in the modern sense of the word. The concept of productive capital increasing in value, ceaselessly creating extra capital apparently all by itself (though more precisely by its use of paid workers), is a notion foreign to pre-industrial societies. This was forgotten by J. Richard-Molard when he left his extremely shrewd observations to wonder at the 'cattle mania' (*boomanie*) of the Fulbe, what he called 'their overriding passion for useless cattle'. He wrote that 'for the Mediterranean and the West, *pecus* = *pecunia*, *cheptel* (livestock) = capital...

67 Mollien (*Découverte des sources du Sénégal et de la Gambie en 1818*, re-ed. Paris, Delagrave, p. 110), notes concerning the Fulbe of Djoloff (Ferlo): 'They are all pagan and have a violent hatred for the Mahometans.'

but nothing like this occurred to the Pullo as yet untouched by "civilisation". The horned beast is of no use to him.'[68]

This needs some qualification. First of all, cattle—or rather the cow—certainly is of some use to him: he lives on it. It is clotted milk from the cow which is his basic food and which he gives to the farmer in exchange for the millet he needs. But at the same time the sheer utility of the cow is matched by its undeniable value as a means of accumulating and displaying wealth.[69]

Certain Fulbe groups gave up the purely nomadic life for a relatively regular change of pasturage and settled in one region where they established a proper understanding with the non-nomadic Negro farmers on whose lands they settled during the dry season. They bartered their dairy products for rice or millet. The farmers willingly agreed to let the skilled Pullo herdsman take charge of the cattle which represented their life's savings.

At this point, the Fulbe found themselves in a special position; not only were they the acknowledged experts in the care of cattle, the accepted form of wealth in the country, but they were also in sole charge of this desirable commodity. They were not slow to appreciate the possible advantages of the situation and besides, they were less and less willing to be treated as vassals, harried and oppressed as though they were slaves.

A confused desire to reverse the social order gradually formed in their minds, but the way they lived—small family units meeting only occasionally for simple religious ceremonies based on the old animist beliefs—was in no way suitable for such an aim. It was Islam which offered them the framework within which they could operate the change, gave them the ideological bond to hold their small units together, warmed them with the fire of revolt.

Naturally, one should not underestimate the rôle of the religion itself. The part played by the Moorish marabouts and Fula-speaking Muslim Tucolors who had held high the torch of Islam under Denianke rule was not negligible. But they were less the cause of what happened than the opportunity for it. They were social catalysts providing a social movement which had its own causes with the political and ideological form necessary for its expression.

The result was nothing like that of earlier 'Islamisations'. Hitherto there had been an urban Islam (in the towns of the Niger valley)—a merchant Islam—a court Islam which often had a superficial character, aroused superstition rather than faith, always subject to backsliding and degradation.

The Fulbe expressed a militant rural Islam which had appeared only once before under the Almoravides. The whole cultural heritage of animism was by no means obliterated. Some traces of it still remained, but it was necessarily hidden beneath a Muslim guise. The extent of this Islamisation is

68 Richard-Molard, *op. cit.*, pp. 95–6.
69 On the rôle of stock breeding as a means of accumulating property cf. Lucien Febvre, *La Terre et l'évolution humaine*, Paris, Albin-Michel, 1922, pp. 350–3.

shown by the universal teaching of the Qur'ān; it was probably taught fairly mechanically, but at the beginning of the nineteenth century, 60 per cent of the population of the Futa-Jallon and the Bundu could read and write Arabic script and eventually used it for transcribing their maternal tongue, the Fula language. Compared with the past or with other places in the region, this was indeed a cultural revolution.

The formation of the Fula State of Futa-Jallon

At first the Futa-Jallon seems to have been both refuge and an obstacle. The population mainly comprised Dialonke, Susu and Malinke, who were of Mande origin; but, especially in the north-west, these people lived with a variety of groups which have by now been pushed back towards the plains in the north and west—Tenda, Landuma-Tyapi (or Kokoli), Baga, etc.

These tribes were mainly hunters and farmers and had come down the valleys to occupy the glens and the plains. The Fulbe had reached the highlands at an early date; here the grassy plateaux of the heights offered them fine pastures, and they lived there in easy harmony with the Negro farmers.

In the fifteenth century when the Wururbe (Ba) of Koli Tengella came from Termes and founded the nucleus of a State under Fula rule (strongly linked with the Malinke elements and including various local ethnic groups), they probably integrated with Fulbe groups who were already living in the region. By the second half of the sixteenth century, they were all over the mountains, right up to the frontier of Sierra-Leone.

In the seventeenth century, these Fulbe who were ancestors of the present-day 'Pullis' or 'Fulbé Bururé' were pagans; the only Muslims were a branch of the Denianke (descendants of Yayé), who had some Malinke blood, and a few Diula (Malinke) merchants.

According to tradition, it was during Koli's lifetime that a new wave of immigrants under the leadership of Ilo Dialali came from Macina to join the original Fula population. Arcin and Tauxier may be right in saying that it was at the end of the seventeenth century (1654–94?) that the greatest wave of immigration from Macina took place.

The Daebe (Bari) were closely linked and intermarried with the Malinke (local Muslim merchants with whom they formed an alliance, or comrades in arms: ten Malinke for every twelve Fulbe, said tradition).[70] They settled high up in the valleys of the Bafing and the Tene, chiefly in the 'between rivers' area which was to become the main centre of the Fula State.

They lived side by side with the Dialonke. They subdivided into two main branches, descendants of Seri (Seriyanke), who settled in the valley

70 Other facts quoted in support of this by G. Vieillard ('Notes sur les Peuls du Fouta-Djalon', *Bull. I.F.A.N.*, ii, 1–2, 1940, p. 102): the slave chiefs of the between-rivers area bear the Malinke title of 'satigui'; elsewhere they have the Susu-Dialonke name of 'manga' (chief). Cf. Paul Marty, *L'Islam en Guinée*, Paris, Leroux, 1921. Military terms are generally Malinke.

of the Tene around Fougoumba, and descendants of Saidi or Sedi (Sedyanke), who settled in the valley of Bafing around Timbo. They were joined by the Yirlabe (Diallo) who became the Sedyankes' auxiliaries, especially in Timbo—generals, councillors and spokesmen for earlier arrivals. The third successor of Saidi of Timbo (Nouhou) was the first to be converted to Islam and he persuaded the members of his group and their Yirlabe allies to be converted along with him.

In the Upper Futa, the noble families were principally Elayabe, and according to Koin tradition were descended from the first influx of Wururbe; they were converted by one of themselves, Thierno Saliou Ba, an emigrant from Macina, who became a marabout and came back to his country to win it over to Islam.[71] In the Labe region, the noble branch was that of Kalidouyabe, who were Yirlabe (Diallo) from Khasso; Kalidou, founder of the Fula village of Labe, was not a Muslim but seemed to be well disposed to the Muslims.

It seems that clashes between these new arrivals and the Dialonke masters of the land became increasingly violent; the resident farmers demanded the payment of a tithe on incoming herds as damages for the ravaging of their crops. The Fulbe who were already settled took the Dialonke side. Conversion to Islam represented a sort of protest and act of resistance on the part of the new immigrants. This at least was how it was interpreted by the local Dialonke who fought back with persecution and a ban on public prayer.

It was at this point that Alfa Ibrahima Sambegou (or Moussa Ibrahima) son of Nouhou, subsequently honoured by the religious title of 'Karamoko Alfa' called for a revolt, backed by the Yirlabe Modi Maka Maoudo, chief of the council of elders of Timbo. Secret contact was established with the different Muslim groups and finally an Assembly was held on the banks of a sacred stream in 1727–28 (1140 A.H.).

According to tradition, it was the young nephew of Karamoko Alfa, Ibrahima Yoro Pate (later given the name Ibrahima Sori) who gave the signal for the holy war by smashing the war drums of the pagans of Timbo.[72]

The conspirators had gathered around them armed bands comprising 'numerous Dialonke or Malinke, young people living on the fringe of society, escaped or freed slaves given to pillage and murder'.[73]

It seems that there had been some previous mobilisation here and there but Dialonke and Pullis were incapable of achieving any unity of command. The confederates made a surprise attack on the villages of Timbo and

71 Saint-Père, 'La creátion du royaume du Fouta-Djalon', *Bull. Com. Etud. Hist. Scient. A.O.F.*, 1929, pp. 484–55.

72 This point seems unlikely to Arcin (*Histoire de la Guinée française*, Paris, 1911); according to him, Ibrahima Sori died in 1813 and could not have been of an age to fight in 1726. In fact if, as we think, Ibrahima Sori died in 1793, an octogenarian, he could have been between seventeen and twenty years old in 1727–8.

73 Arcin, *op. cit.*, p. 88.

Fougoumba, killing one of the principal chiefs, Dian Yéro of Kebali.

This opened the long period of the holy war; we know little of its chronology.[74] The resistance was led by the Dialonke and the Pullis with allies from the Susu, Baga, Fulacunda, as well as from the Malinke of Sankaran and the Wassulunke. But their enemies, the Futa-Dialonke, concluded an alliance with the Dialonke kingdom of Sulimana, then ruled by Ayina Yella (1730–50).

The Pullis were taken by surprise at Talansan near Sokotoro and were totally defeated. Their Dialonke allies were crushed first at Tiayé and then at Bantinyel.

The conquered Dialonke, Susu and Pullis were reduced to slavery (except for their earliest allies who managed to keep their lands and the last-minute converts who lost their land but kept their freedom). Those who could escape began to move towards the border territories, the Susu towards the coast, the Dialonke eastwards. It was probably at this moment that the assembly gathered to prepare the Constitution of the Futa-Djallon (Timbi-Touni, 1160 A.H.). The nine chiefs of the Muslim groups which were to be the nine provinces (*diwé*), probably accompanied by the most important family chiefs, founded the Futa-Djallon confederation (indicating by this term the union of the Fulbe and Dialonke elements). In spite of opposition from the chiefs of Kollade and Labe, the combined influence of the Yirlabe of Timbo and the other chiefs gave the leadership of the confederation to Karamoko Alfa. The chief of the Labe, Mamadou Cellou, had a better reputation as war leader but 'the Yirlabe bourgeoisie, although they were closely related to the Dialo of the Labe, preferred a less authoritarian man'.[75]

Meanwhile the war continued, but constantly on the offensive; their allies, the Sulimana, joined them in campaigns against Sankaran and Gabu and laid siege to Farabana on the upper Falémé (1754) during the reign of Yella-Dansa (king of Sulimana from 1750 to 1754). During the reign of his successor, Tahabaire, Farabana was attacked again (1755). In 1755–56 there was a general uprising of slaves: some of them managed to resist attacks from the 'great' Fulbe and the Dialonke of Sulimana and fled to the borders of Bundu, where they set up the fortified village of Koundie. The remainder were cruelly dealt with: the old were beheaded, the young condemned to a hundred lashes. A new assembly was summoned to deal with the revolt.

74 The soundest chronological basis (used by Arcin, then by Tauxier) is indirectly provided by the facts relating to the Dialonke kingdom of Sulimana, gathered together by Gordon Laing at the beginning of the nineteenth century (Gordon Laing, *Voyage dans le Timanni, le Kouranko et le Soulimana*, French translation, Paris, Arthus-Bertrand, 1826). This information should be cross-checked with that of the tarikhs, which is dated according to the Mohammedan calendar, but these tarikhs have not yet been translated or systematically collated. An attempt to use a nineteenth century tarikh is found in Jose Moreira, *op. cit.*; unfortunately the author converted the dates incorrectly.

75 Arcin, *op. cit.*, p. 87. The Timbi-Touni assembly seems to have given Ibrahima Sambégou only the title of 'Alfa'. If he was in fact called 'Almamy', it must have been at a later date, unless the title was held for the first time by his successor Ibrahima Sori.

After further joint expeditions, the last campaign of the Fulbe and Dialonke allies in Sankaran took place in 1762: this time they came up against a military chief of the highest order, Konde Birama, who inflicted a shattering defeat on them at Balia as they were retreating (1762). The Dialonke took advantage of this defeat to withdraw their support from the Fulbe who swiftly retaliated by beheading all the Dialonke chiefs of Sulimana who were in the Futa. The future king, Assana Ayira, then a fellow-student of the future Almamy Abdoul Kader in Labe, managed to escape to his own country. This reversal of alliances exposed the Futa to joint attacks from Konde Birama and Tahabaire, thereafter allies: they marched on Timbo which was taken and burned (1763). Then they came every year to loot and burn the villages of the Futa.

In the meantime, Karamoko Alfa, who had always been more of a mystic than a war leader, had gone completely mad. The Assembly met this hopeless situation by going into the mountains to choose a new leader. The son of Karamoko Alfa was judged to be too young, the Assembly preferring Ibrahima Yoro Pate, cousin and disciple of the first Almamy (1766?).

In 1767 Tahabaire experienced his first failure when he attacked Fougoumba: he was driven back and to make up for his failure pillaged the country of Limba as he retreated taking three thousand five hundred prisoners, all of which he sold to the River Pongo slave-traders. In 1768 the Dialonke of Sulimana built a fortified capital, Falaba, to protect themselves against possible raids. The wars continued for another ten years, but the Futa-Jalonke answered raids from the outside with a fierce offensive; in 1776, while the Dialonke were plundering the Futa, they captured Falaba which had been left practically undefended.

In 1778 Konde Birama and Tahabaire launched a huge expedition against the Futa in the hope of bringing the war to a close. It ended in disaster: at the Sirakouré river near Fougoumba, their army was destroyed and both leaders killed in the fighting. Assana Ayira, Tahabaire's successor, abandoned all hope of attacking the Fulbe in open country.

There were no further invasions of the Futa until the colonial conquest. The independent Dialonke and Susu who had managed to survive in the outer limits of the nine provinces were converted or driven out; Ibrahima Sori attacked and defeated the last Pullis at Hore Bougou, and led a campaign into Wassulu, and in the upper Gambia. Fula influence extended far beyond the boundaries of the Futa; many chiefs in lower Guinea, as well as the chief of Bundu, had to accept the overlordship of the Almamy, profess Islam and accept investiture by the turban.

According to Arcin, it is possible that Ibrahima Sori received the title of Almamy only after the country's military recovery; the title was confirmed by the Yirlabe of Timbo who made him the temporal and spiritual chief of the Confederation. However, his power aroused the jealousy of the great council of Fougoumba. When he was ordered to appear before it, Sori

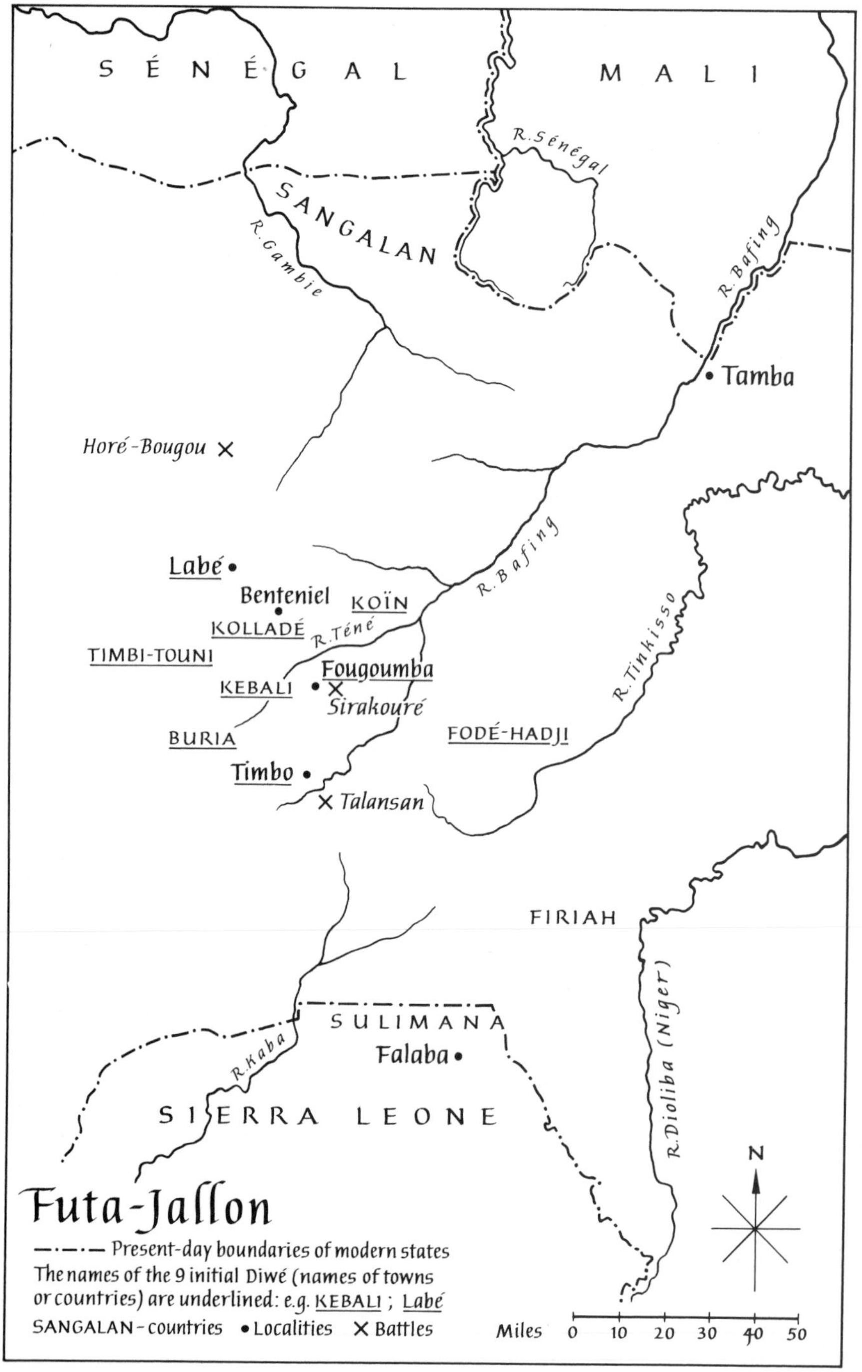
SÉNÉGAL
MALI
R. Sénégal
SANGALAN
R. Gambie
R. Bafing
Tamba
Horé-Bougou
R. Bafing
Labé
Benteniel
KOÏN
KOLLADÉ
R. Téné
TIMBI-TOUNI
R. Tinkisso
Fougoumba
KEBALI
Sirakouré
BURIA
FODÉ-HADJI
Timbo
Talansan
FIRIAH
SULIMANA
R. Kaba
Falaba
R. Dioliba (Niger)
SIERRA LEONE
N
Futa-Jallon
Present-day boundaries of modern states
The names of the 9 initial Diwé (names of towns or countries) are underlined: e.g. KEBALI ; Labé
SANGALAN - countries • Localities X Battles
Miles 0 10 20 30 40 50

11:4

arrived with an armed escort which seized the members of the council and executed them.[76]

Ibrahima Sori had a new council elected and this set up its headquarters near him at Timbo. Fougoumba remained the seat of the general Assembly and the place of investiture where the Karamoko chief of the dîwal had the honour of bestowing on the elected Almamy the nine successive turbans (one for each province). It was then that Sori was given the name 'Maoudo' (the Great) (1780?).

Ibrahima Sori stayed in power till his death in 1793; he knew how to combine firmness (the execution episode at Fougoumba is proof of this) with diplomatic skill; he handled the son of Karamoko Alfa, Alfa Salihou, and his family extremely well, lavishing signs of esteem on them. The Fulbe complained that he placed too much reliance on his soldiers, converted Malinke, Bambara and Dialonke.

Ibrahima Sori was succeeded by his son Sâdou, but he was murdered five years later by men of the Alfaya party (descendant of Karomoko Alfa). Salihou, Karamoko's son, was so angry that he refused to succeed and it was his brother, Abdoulaye Bademba, who took power (1798–99).

Structure and organisation of the Fula state of the Futa-Jallon

The history of the Futa-Jallon during the eighteenth century is adequate explanation for the peculiarities of its social structure, which had become particularly hierarchical. At the top was the aristocracy of the 'Great Fulbe', descendants of the families who had taken part in the holy war, with the addition of various allies, dependents and vassals. They lived on the work their slaves did, on the rents they collected in the territories they administered and, of course, on what they got from the various raids they made over their frontiers and sometimes even inside their own borders. In the Labé, this aristocracy was made up of comparatively pure-blooded Fulbe, but in the 'between rivers' area the strain was a mixture of Fulbe and Malinke, and there the aristocrats looked more like the African Negro, typical Fula features being more easily found among the vassals.

Lower down the scale come the Fulbé Bururé—the bush Fulbe—descendants of Pullis who were converted relatively late. They were

76 According to the traditions collected by Saint-Père and Guebhard, this episode comes at the end of a long rivalry between the partisans of Karamoko Alfa and his sons on the one hand, and Sori on the other. In Saint-Père (*op. cit.*) before Karamoko Alfa went mad, he shared his power with his nephew, who had become popular through his military successes. But when Sori replaced several provincial chiefs with his own men, discontentment from the opposing side drove him away from the Futa, leaving his uncle as temporary governor, while he led a campaign against Konde Birama. According to Guebhard, it was when Konde Birama and Tahabaire attacked that the Council of Elders and its president Modi Maka rallied round to the Alfaya side, and replaced him by one of the sons of Karamoko. He acquiesced and left Timbo; but the growing anarchy and the enemy raids forced the Council to call him back; the victory of Heriko sealed his return to power. Was this the same episode or were there two successive episodes? Or was this a justification on the part of tradition of the strength of the diarchy in the nineteenth century? Arcin does not mention these episodes at all.

vassals of the Great Fulbe and had never abandoned their pastoral activities, still content to keep the herds of the aristocracy.

Right at the bottom came the slaves, the *matyoubé*, descended from the original Susu and Dyalonké inhabitants. By the nineteenth century they were almost completely assimilated with their masters from the linguistic point of view: they spoke Fula and claimed to be Fulbe, practising Mohammedanism with the same fervour as their masters.

On the fringes of society were foreigners: Diawambé, Tucolor griots, Dioula merchants, Diakhanké (Soninké) marabouts, and so on.

By the end of the eighteenth century the Futa was a fortress, not a place of refuge. It was no longer a fastness under constant siege, but the starting point for endless sorties into the surrounding countryside. This helped to keep the slave trade going. In exchange for slaves and for gold brought down from the Bouré (which stood in a more or less vassal position to the Futa), the Futa-Jalonké got what they needed from the Rivières du Sud: imported goods from Europe, mainly gunpowder and firearms. The Karamoko of Kankalabe had little opportunity for capturing slaves so was given a sort of compensation: he was allowed to pardon any criminal or wrongdoer escaping from the powers of justice who managed to take refuge in his territories. This was possibly not the ideal form of retribution, but it furnished him with a useful means of income.

Not all the captives taken were sold; many were allowed to settle in farming villages (*roundés*) in underpopulated areas and this is undoubtedly one of the reasons why the present-day Futa is comparatively overpopulated. This section of the community assured the subsistence of the State and its leaders by means of a system of levies, organised in a proper form, but not always collected in accordance with the rules.

The slaves worked exclusively for their masters, only two days a week—Thursday and Friday—being left to them for rest and for their own agricultural work. Revenue also came from death duties, collected by the chief of the dîwal who passed on the part reserved for the sovereign. The families of the aristocracy were exempt from this, except that they had to make a gift to the Almamy when they notified him of a death. All subjects paid the *farilla*, a tithe on harvests (gradually confused with the *zakat* of the Qur'ān). This tithe went into a special reserve which was used in case of famine as well as when the Almamy gave alms or entertained. In fact, it was used more and more for the maintenance of the Almamy's entourage—his personal supporters, armed retainers and griots.

The population was fairly scattered. The residential hamlet, the *foulasso* of the masters, and the *roundé* of the slaves, lacked the cohesion of the large Malinke village, with some exceptions. The parish (*misîde*) was a political and religious district, within which all the inhabitants had to join in prayer every Friday in one consecrated place or mosque. Within the framework of the parish, large families were grouped in 'quarters', sociological units rather than geographical locations: one family occupied the position of leader with one, two or three—rarely more than four—subordinate families around it. This particular form of social grouping was known as *tekun*, a Dialonke word used for classification by age, that is to say, a horizontal grouping whereby in any particular territory people from different families or clans had a special social association.

The parishes formed the province (*dîwal*: plural *diwe*). First of all there were the nine original ones whose spiritual leaders composed the Assembly of 1727–28: Timbo, Fodé-Hadji in the low countries (Ley Pelle); Fougoumba, Kebali, Bouria in the 'between the rivers' (Hakkunde Mâdye); Labé, Timbi, Kolladé (Kankalabe), Koin in the highlands (Dow Pelle: the top of the mountains).

Other provinces were added to these later on, both for administrative convenience and for the better control of the growing immigrant settlements in the border regions: Kolen, Bomboli, Bruwal-Tapé, Benteniel, Timbi Madina (repeating the name of the first Timbi, which had become Timbi Touni), Kebou, Mali.

The relative stability of the state was accompanied, paradoxically enough, by a semi-permanent state of internal anarchy which in time became a basic part of the establishment.

The assemblies were the most important section of the state: first the Council of Elders (*Kautital Maoube*) established at Timbo by Ibrahima Sori. This was elected by the representatives of the four tekun of Timbo, two Sedyanke tekun and two Yirlabe tekun. It was this council which formed the great electoral assembly which chose the Almamys, deposed them where necessary and decided on peace or war. Its president, who belonged to the Yirlabe, was the 'great Fulbe spokesman'.[77]

For important matters, assemblies of a wider range could be called and these incorporated the free men. There were two stages in such an assembly: first, at Timbo two assemblies met, the first comprising delegates from the dîwal of Timbo, the second the delegates of the other three diwe of the 'between rivers' (Fougoumba, Kebali and Bouria); then came the second stage when the delegates from all the diwe met at Fougoumba.[78]

The election of the Almamy took place at Timbo and his investiture at Fougoumba. The rites of enthronement involved giving the Almamy the nine turbans symbolising the nine provinces: after this the Almamy gave the chiefs of the diwe the turban which symbolised their authority. But the rites also included survivals of the pre-*jihād* days—a retreat of seven days in a hut where the ground was strewn with all the different kinds of grain and

77 The original council, sitting at Fougoumba, comprised thirteen members, elected in two states by the village chiefs, the number of delegates being proportionate to the number of warriors for each dîwal represented. (Cf. Arcin, *op. cit.*, and Hecquard, *Voyage sur la côte et dans l'intérieur de l'Afrique occidentale*, Paris, Benard & Cie, 1853.)

78 Marty, *op. cit.*, 1921.

tubers grown in the nine diwe. As the location of the general assemblies and the enthronement, the dîwal of Fougoumba enjoyed the privilege of neutrality (not always respected) in the event of civil war; preparation for fighting was forbidden there.

Each dîwal and misîde chief was attended by a council of elders; occasionally dîwal and misîde served as the framework for general assemblies of free men.

Here, as in other traditional states, were the same sort of institutions: the bodies of representatives (essentially oligarchic) alongside the ruler, who was the chief talisman figure (in this case the imam who directed the prayers of the faithful), the war leader (here, the successor to the Caliphs, leader of the holy war). To the permanent bodies of guards, made up of slaves or mercenaries was added, in case of danger or an important expedition, the national army. Each province provided a contingent from among its free men, and this could number as many as twelve thousand men. The Almamy was also the great judge: after the placing of the turban, he promised to maintain justice; the president of the council of the Elders would reply: 'Futa is balanced on your head like a pot of fresh milk. Do not stumble, or else the milk will spill.'[79]

But he did not balance the Futa. The Yirlabe and Sedyanke of Timbo, who provided the Almamy with men to act as his messengers in each province as well as the delegates of each dîwal at Timbo, the heads of the great families and, most of all, the powerful *Alfa Mo Labe*, were able to make and break the Almamys, all the more readily because each candidature and enthronement was an occasion for them to receive substantial gifts.

The rivalry which existed between the descendants of Karamoko Alfa and Ibrahima Sori—the Alfaya and Soriya—for accession to the dignity of Almamy increased the opportunity for such intrigues.

Certain traditions trace back to this rivalry of Karamoko Alfa and Ibrahima Sori the establishment of the rule of alternative succession between the two families,[80] but historical facts do not support this assertion. Marty suggests that the rule enforcing alternation every two years between an Almamy Alfaya and an Almamy Soriya was adopted by arbitration, around 1840, and this seems more likely. The same system was also established at the level of the provincial chiefs. The rule was almost never respected, for the Almamy in power rarely consented to give up his place to his colleague and rival of his own free will.

Civil wars, anarchy, perpetual robbery and violence lasted for over a century and still the state of Futa-Jallon stood firm. Its system of vassalage and the rights and dues which pertained to it kept the country functioning on a reasonably firm basis. The Muslim faith and a strong feeling of ethnic

79 Vieillard, *op. cit.*, p. 128.
80 Note particularly Paul Guebhard, *Au Fouta Djalon*, Paris, Comité de l'Afrique française, 1910.

pride gave its inhabitants the confidence to offer to the outside world all the solidarity and inner superiority of those who have subjected the land 'of the palm tree of Kakandé (Boké) to the silk-cotton tree of Sareya (Kouroussa), the realm of salt water to the Dioliba (Niger)'.[81]

The revolution of the Torobe and the creation of the theocratic state of Futa Toro. The inability of the Silatigui Denianke to defend the river valley against Moorish invasions, and the constant pillaging of their tiedos contributed equally to the formation of a Muslim party among the Tucolor population, a party which, led by the marabout Souleymane Bal, took up the fight against the Moors. The Torobe led the fight, as much against the Denianke as against the Moors. United by their faith, the Torobe belonged to all sorts of classes and were often of humble extraction. The Denianke observed with contempt that it was enough for a slave to learn to read the Qur'ān to become a 'Torodo', 'Torobe' and slave coming to mean the same thing. The Torobe offered the sovereignty of the state they planned to build to Souleymane Bal, who refused the offer and suggested they approach the marabout Abdoul Kader from Ape. It was only after Soulemayne had been killed in a campaign against the Moors, that Abdoul Kader accepted their offer and took the title of Almamy, religious and political head of the new Islamic community. He managed, not without some difficulty, to defeat and kill the last Silatigui (1776).

The new state preserved the existing framework of the Denianke kingdom. The social measures adopted during the revolution, especially the enfranchisement of literate slaves able to read the Qur'ān, were soon abandoned and a stable system operating in favour of the victorious Torobe was pursued. Islam became the state religion everywhere, but the old vassal kingdoms maintained their existing systems—Lam, Ardo, Farba, Silatigui, Diom, Kamalinkou—and, of course, so did Elimane and Thierno. Converted Denianke were integrated with the new aristocracy.

Abdoul Kader's most far-reaching reform related to land tenure. This was the *Fetiere Futa* (the dividing of the Futa) which can be dated to about 1790. The land holdings which went back to the Silatigui or even earlier, or those based on the right of first settlement, were maintained in most cases, but sometimes they were reduced in size. Opponents of the régime lost their lands and these territories were given by the Almamy to his victorious warrior chiefs and marabouts. In this way the Denianke aristocracy was supplanted by the new aristocracy of the Torobe who even today still constitute the 'landed gentry', owning the larger part of the valley lands. From this time onwards the Almamy was chosen from their ranks.

Abdoul Kader had mosques built in every village and sent his representatives to them, either as village chiefs or as religious chiefs (elimane—el imam). In return for these duties, the representatives were awarded grants

81 Vieillard, *op. cit.*, p.

of land taken from those who had refused to surrender and also a part of the assakal (Zakat)—a Muslim tithe on the crops of family lands—or of the ndyoldi—the right to rent state lands, *leydi bayti*. Elsewhere the rents from the state holdings went on being collected by *diagarafs* whose payment was a certain percentage of the dues; this was the old Denianke system. Besides the ndyoldi there was the tyoggou, collected every three years from tree plantations and every seven years on grassland, and finally a conveyance tax to be paid by the heirs to a landholding whenever an incumbent died. This ensured the payment of usufruct to the state.[82]

Once the Futa had been conquered and reorganised, Abdoul Kader's deep sense of religious mission led him to try and convert his neighbours by force of arms. He attacked Walo and here the Brak on advice of the Seg ag Baor, pretended to accept conversion. He attacked Cayor, was defeated and made prisoner by the Damel who later released him and sent him away honourably in answer to the prayers of the inhabitants of Futa, according to certain versions, or, according to others, because they feared his religious powers. A complaint from an imam led him to have the king of Bundu Sega put to death. He replaced him with the dead man's cousin, Amadi Pate.

The fall of the old aristocracy was not a great advantage for the Futa, for the Torobe who took their place were greedy for gain and power. The Almamy pursued an adventurous foreign policy and at home was constantly rigorous in his application of Muslim law and practice;[83] this possibly kept alive the early crusading spirit and the feeling of popular revolution, but it ended in opposition and sedition from the new aristocracy. There are two versions of the Almamy's fate: Siré Abbas Soh says that he was persuaded by his adversaries to lead an expedition against the Bambara, their idea being to trap him in an ambush; Gray and Dochard[84] say that he was obliged to flee to the Guidimaka to escape from them. Whatever the truth, he was murdered at the age of eighty-one in 1804.

The death of Abdoul Kader, the first and only real head of state of Futa Toro, led the country into what Mollien called a 'theocratic oligarchy in which the people (for which we may read "torodo aristocracy") exerted a great influence'.[85]

From then onwards, the new Almamys were chosen and sometimes also deposed by an electoral body of seven. Only three central provinces out of

82 Cf. H. Gaden, 'Du régime des terres de la vallée du Sénégal au Fouta antérieurement à l'occupation française', *Bull. Com. Etud. Hist. Scient. A.O.F.*, 1935, p. 403–4; M. Vidal, 'Etude sur la tenure des terres indigènes au Fouta', *ibid.*, 1935, pp. 415–48 and Abdou Salam Kane, 'Du régime des terres chez les populations du Fouta sénégalais', *ibid.*, 1935, pp. 449–61.

83 Abdoulaye, *op. cit.*

84 Gray and Dochard, *Voyage dans l'Afrique occidentale pendant les années 1818, 1819, 1820, et 1821*, French trans., Paris, Avril de Gastel, 1826.

85 Mollien, *op. cit.*, p. 169.

six—Guena, Bossea, Lao—were represented in this body, the other provinces—Damga to the east, Toro and Dimar to the west—were considered outer dependencies. Furthermore, the delegates from Bossea had voting rights which assured them of the majority. The election took place as follows: the electoral body of seven, comprising delegates from the following tribes or groups: Irlabe, Bosseyabe, Diofann, Ebiabe, Lao, Denianke and Fulbe (the first two playing an essential rôle) elected the candidates by acclaim; then the final choice was entrusted to a council of five delegates (Ebiabe, Diofann, Fulbe and Bosseyabe, the last of whom had two majority votes).[86] For these reasons the authority of the Almamy was rarely recognised in the outer provinces. Lam Toro, in particular, was quick to declare its independence. Even in the central provinces, his authority was nominal. 'After the Almamy Abdoul Kader, his successors on the throne of the Futa were there in name only, the absolute power belonging to the principal dignitaries, who had the right to name or revoke an Almamy, according to their fancy.'[87] Each reign was invariably very short, rarely exceeding two years—there were more than fifty Almamys between 1804 and 1881; nineteenth-century travellers all commented on the inadequacy of their powers.

The formation of the state of Bundu

The formation of the third Fula imamate of Bundu is generally placed at the end of the eighteenth century. Little attention has been devoted to its origins, but these appear to have been quite different from those of the earlier states. The Almamys of Bundu are in fact descended from an old dynasty and their extremely centralised monarchic government is very different from the chaotic oligarchies of the Futa-Jallon and the Futa Toro.

It is even possible that Bundu may have been the very first Muslim state of this type, for tradition has it that the founder of Bundu was the Tucolor marabout Malick Sy from Souïma, near Podor. He is said to have made the pilgrimage to Mecca, spending some time in the service of the king of Diara. Then he came and settled in Goye (referred to as Galam by European writers), a little Soninke kingdom founded at the beginning of the seventeenth century by Silman Khassa, chief of the Bathily dynasty.[88] This ruler lived at Tuabo and bore the Soninke title of *Tounka*. Malick Sy did not manage to convert the Tounka but was allowed to have Bundu, then practically a wilderness, managing by a ruse to increase the size of the area he had been granted. Malick Sy (and probably his successors after him) made Bundu a sanctuary to which refugees, mostly Fulbe and Tucolors, came from all over the west. Bundu grew at the expense of its neighbours, the

86 Cf. Mollien, *op. cit.*, and Anne Raffenel, *Voyage dans l'Afrique occidentale*, Paris, Arthus-Bertrand, 1846, pp. 260–8.
87 Abdoulaye, *op. cit.*
88 Eleven generations of Silman Khassa up to the present generation (1960).

Malinke of Bambuk, who were driven back onto the right bank of the Faleme or else forced to migrate to Gambia.[89]

It is difficult to fit these events into a chronological framework. The genealogical list by generations, which is given by F. Brigaud, shows that seven generations separate Malick Sy and the last Almamy. If one allocates a span of thirty years to each generation, then Malick Sy would have lived at the end of the seventeenth and the beginning of the eighteenth century. This attempt at a proper chronology is supported by the dating for the generation of the Almamys Sega and Amadi; Brigaud sets them between 1785 and 1815, and this corresponds to accurate historical evidence.[90] Documents from the end of the seventeenth century and the beginning of the eighteenth which give considerable information on Bambuk seem to ignore Bundu completely.[91] Does this mean that Bundu was not the first Muslim state? Contemporary evidence stands in the way of such an interpretation. Adanson's map (1756) calls this country 'Republic of Bundu' and gives its ruler the Malinke title of *Farim*, which suggests that its political structures were therefore similar to those of its neighbours. Tradition maintains that the first Sissibe (sovereigns of the Sy family) bore the Muslim title of *Elimane*. This is not necessarily a contradiction in terms for many chiefs who were in no way Muslim bore this honorary title.[92] What is certain is that the ruler even if he descended from a family of marabout origin, was no longer Muslim at the time of Abdoul Kader. Houghton (1790) and Mungo Park (1795) record that in spite of being a non-believer, the king had taken the title of Almamy.

King Sega was assassinated by order of Abdoul Kader who replaced him with a nephew, Amadi Pate. But the brother of the dead king, Amadi Isata, won back the throne and made an alliance against Abdoul Kader with the

89 Brigaud, *op. cit.*, pp. 208–23. See also G. Adam, *Légendes historiques du pays de Nioro (Sahel)*, Paris, Challamel, 1904, pp. 47–55.

90 Gray and Dochard, *op. cit.*, point out the Sega was assassinated about 1780 and that Amadi was still Almamy in 1817.

91 According to Pere Labat, who got his information from La Courbe and Compagnon; the map of Senegal by Delisle (1726) reproduced by Brigaud, *op. cit.*, also leaves it out, unless the locality named 'Bonda' on the left bank of the Faleme is in fact designating this country.

92 M. Adanson, *Histoire naturelle du Sénégal* . . . with the abridged account of a journey made in this country during the years 1749–53. Paris, Bauche, 1757. The title of 'Farim' is the one used by the village chiefs of Bambuk. Cf. Coste d'Arnobat, *op. cit.*, and Golberry, *Fragmens d'un voyage en Afrique* made during the years 1785–7 (*op. cit.*, vol. i). But Labat, *op. cit.*, iv, chap. 2, points out that the village chiefs of Bambuk carry the title of Farim or Elimane.

According to tradition, it was the grandson of Malick Sy and the third representative of the Maka Djiba dynasty (1747–78 according to Lamartiny) who took the title of Elimane. Local tradition in the Futa Djallon says that it was the Almamy Ibrahima Sori who obliged him to accept conversion and pay tribute. If this superficial and somewhat temporary conversion actually took place, it does not seem to have had any special consequences (cf. Lamartiny, *Le Bondou et le Bambouk*, Paris, Société de géographie commerciale 72 p., and Capitaine Roux, *Notice historique sur le Bondou*, St-Louis, Sénégal. Imprimerie du gouvernement, 1893, 15 p.).

(pagan) Bambara king of Kaarta whose vassal he then became.[93] He also formed an alliance with the chiefs of the Futa Toro who were hostile to Abdoul Kader: Gray and Dochard say that it was Amadi Isata who pursued and killed him in Guidimaka to revenge the death of his brother.

Houghton notes that Bundu, like Wuli and Bambuk, was divided between Muslims and pagans (1790). Mungo Park, a few years later, tells us that the government of Bundu differed from that of the Mandinke, 'primarily in that it is more under the influence of Muslim law. With the exception of the king, all the men of importance and most of the inhabitants of Bundu are Muslims.'[94] He attributes this religious development to the tolerance of the Muslims, backed by active propaganda and the increased numbers of Qur'ānic schools, soon present in 'all the towns' (or rather villages). Amadi Isata must have finally decided to profess Islam officially since Gray and Dochard date the conversion of Bundu from his reign, though they attribute him with essentially political motives.

'When the Almamy Amady embraced this false religion, he consulted only his personal interest and his desire to attract to him the peoples of the Futa Toro and the Jallon.'[95] A few years later, Islam became the 'only religion',[96] and Raffenel adds that 'the Muhammadan religion is practised at Bundu with greater fidelity and true belief than in the Futa'.[97]

The influence of the Muslim revolutions in the Futa Jallon and the Futa Toro on Bundu is indisputable—except that in Bundu there was no revolution; religious propaganda gradually brought a religious conformity in no way promoted by the kings—indeed, they seem to have been the last to be converted—although they became reconciled to the idea and used it for their own ends.

The transformation of small local chiefs, constantly fighting and robbing one another, into Muslim heads of state seems to have been encouraged by the growing commercial rôle of Bundu, which lay on the route which led from gold-producing Bambuk to the European trading posts of the Gambia, the same route used to transport slaves from the Sudan to the sea in return for trading goods and imported salt. The collection of tithes and fairly high dues on merchandise (a certain amount of the European merchandise per donkey-load) brought the Almamy a substantial revenue. 'Because of these taxes, the King of Bundu was well provided with arms and ammunition,

---

93 Gray and Dochard, *op. cit.*, and Tauxier, *Histoire des Bambara*, Paris, Larose, 1942. According to Gray and Dochard, he paid the king of Kaarta a tribute of a 'moulo' of gold. About 1815, he refused to pay this tribute any longer and had the envoys from Kaarta put to death. The Bambara, by way of reprisal, twice invaded Bundu and laid waste to it (1817 and 1818). According to the genealogical table published by Brigaud (*op. cit.*, p. 221), Amadi Isata was a second cousin, not a brother of Sega.

94 Mungo Park, *op. cit.*, i, p. 91.

95 Gray and Dochard, *op. cit.*, p. 178.

96 Hecquard, *op. cit.* (voyage en 1850–51).

97 Raffenel, *op. cit.*, p. 269 (voyage en 1843–44).

which made him a formidable opponent for all his neighbours.'[98] This trade also encouraged production and because the population was comprised of more or less equal numbers of Fulbe and Malinke, stock-raising and agriculture were fairly well balanced.

The royal family, the Sissibe, lived in two large villages, Boulebane and Koussan, which were designated capital in turns. The hereditary royal title passed from brother to brother, down the male line, in the Sissibe family.

All observers stress the absolute authority of the king and the profound difference between the political institutions here and in the two Futa countries. There was no council with the power to obstruct the will of the king: only a minister, spokesman for the Almamy and responsible for his finance (collecting tributes and giving hospitality to strangers). The village chiefs were appointed and dismissed by the Almamy.

Houghton, who was robbed by the king, had good reason to complain of his absolute power, but most other travellers judged the regime of Bundu, which assured relative safety and justice, preferable to the anarchy reigning in both the Futa regions.[99]

COASTAL PEOPLES OF THE RIVIÈRES DU SUD

Seaboard peoples of the Casamance and Guinea rivers

The location of the ethnic groups scattered over this portion of the coastline has changed little since the days of the first Portuguese explorers.

Although these peoples today live in a predominantly segmentary society, in the fifteenth century they were part of the empire of Mali and their society was made up of small kingdoms and chieftainships on Mande models.[100] It seems that the seventeenth and eighteenth centuries saw a tendency towards the break-up of these small political units into a much more segmentary social order.

The Diola of the right bank of the Casamance (Diola of Fogny, Bliss-Karone, Djougout) were even more strongly influenced than their brothers on the left bank (Floupes, Diamat, Bayottes) who resisted any kind of formal political organisation. V. Fernandes, however, mentions a 'Mansa Falup' (King of the Floupes) who had the power of life or death over his subjects; today there are only chiefs with little or no influence. The Bainouks (especially their Cassangue branch), now gradually dying out, were driven back by the Diolas to the west and by the Balantes in the south, and set up a small kingdom similar to the Mandinka kingdoms of the Gambia. Their king, Kassa-Mansa, gave his name to the river. His capital was Birkama, on

98 Mungo Park, *op. cit.*, i, p. 91. According to Gray and Dochard, *op. cit.*, the army of the Almamy consisted of about five to six hundred cavalrymen, two to three hundred foot-soldiers.

99 Mollien, *op. cit.*, p. 193.

100 According to Fernandes, *op. cit.*, the Mandimansa 'is the Emperor of all these kings and they obey him completely'. In fact, this sovereignty was entirely theoretical, in so far as Mandinka chieftainships of the interior were concerned. But it did exert an indisputable influence on various cultural features. On these peoples, see A. Teixeira da Mota, *Guine Portuguesa*, Lisbon, 1954 (2 vols), and by the same author *Inquérito etnográfico*, Bissau, 1947.

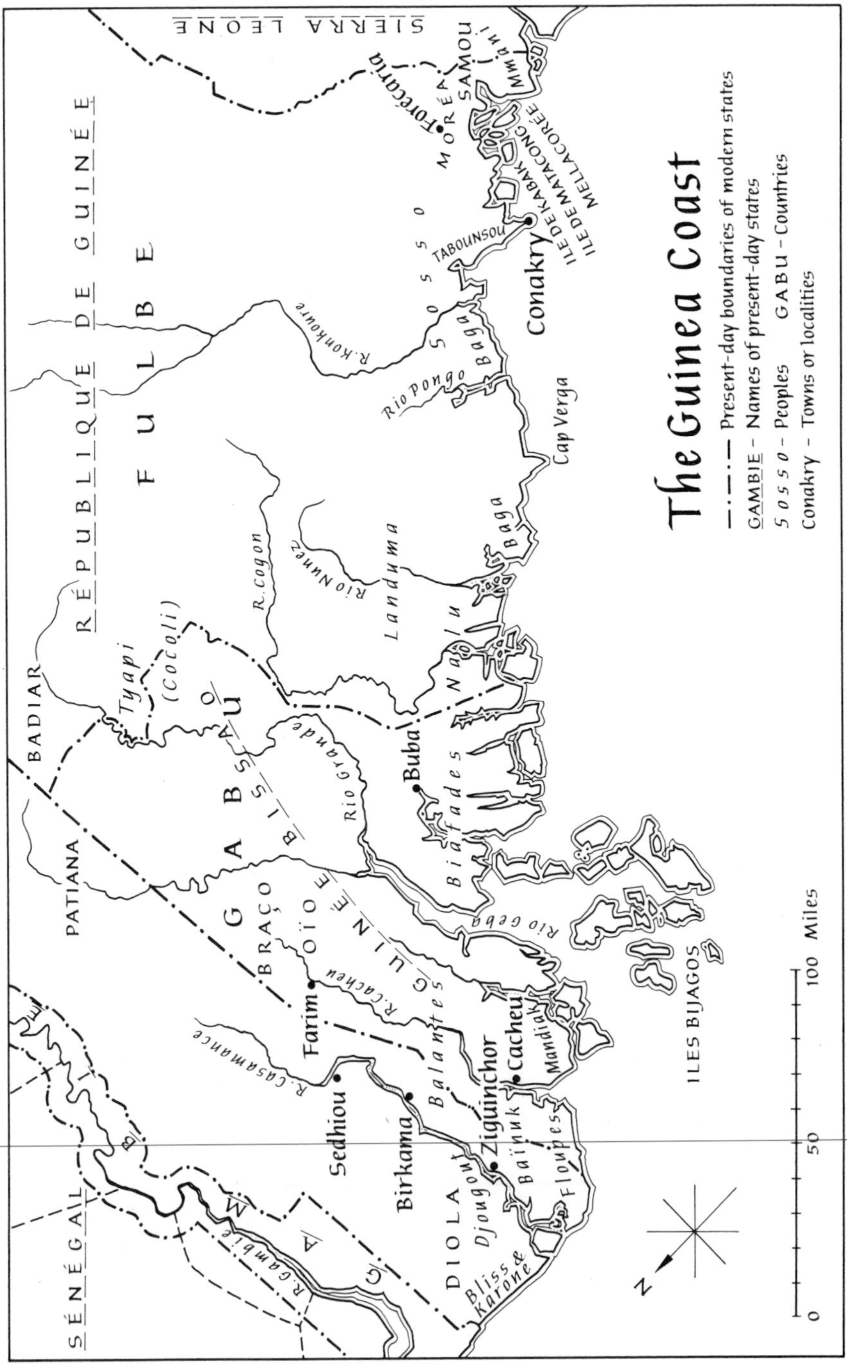
The Guinea Coast
Present-day boundaries of modern states
GAMBIE - Names of present-day states
S o s s o - Peoples
GABU - Countries
Conakry - Towns or localities
SÉNÉGAL
RÉPUBLIQUE DE GUINÉE
SIERRA LEONE
GUINÉE BISSAU
GAMBIE
FULBE
GABU
BRAÇO
OIO
DIOLA
BADIAR
PATIANA
Tyapi
(Cocoli)
Landuma
Nalu
Baga
Sosso
MOREA
SAMOU
Biafades
Balantes
Baïnuk
Floupes
Djougout
Bliss & Karone
Mandiak
Conakry
TaboUnsou
Forecaria
Buba
Farim
Sedhiou
Birkama
Ziguinchor
Cacheu
R. Gambie
R. Casamance
R. Cacheu
Rio Geba
Rio Grande
Rio Nunez
R. Cogon
Rio Pongo
R. Konkouré
Mmani
Cap Verga
ILE DE KABAKONG
ILE DE MATACORÉE
ILE DE MELLACORÉE
ILES BIJAGOS
N
0
50
100 Miles

11:5

the left bank. In the nineteenth century the golden sceptre of the ancient kings was still preserved at Diagnou and the sacred stones used as a throne for the coronation ceremony were still to be seen at the edge of the river. According to local legend, the last king, too powerful for the liking of his subjects, was murdered by them. It is possible that these kings were not local inhabitants, but members of a victorious Mandinka aristocracy.

At the beginning of the sixteenth century, it seems that all the coastline of present-day Guinea and part of the Futa-Jallon were occupied by the Landuma-Tyapi (Cocoli)-Baga-Timné ethnic groups whose languages were closely related and whose cultures (religious rites, secret societies) had many features in common.[101]

At the beginning of the sixteenth century, the Portuguese found the Cocoli living at the mouth of the Rio Geba, alongside the Nalus: these Cocoli are the present-day Landuma-Tyapi who have moved slightly towards the south (the Tyapi from the interior, whose name is a nickname of Fula origin, still call themselves Cocoli).

This proves that Arcin's suggestion that the 'Sapes' mentioned by Alvares d'Almada are really the Tyapi is based on a basically faulty etymology.

The Portuguese writers says that 'the kingdom of the Sapes' covered the coastline from Cape Verga to Sierra Leone and that its important men were called 'Solategis' (Silatigui).[102] This suggests that the state had a Malinke origin. Alvares d'Almada goes on to say that the Baga and Cocoli were dressed like the Sapes and spoke languages as similar as Portuguese is to Spanish. We also know that the place names all along the coast from Kaloum to Sierra Leone are Baga, though the Bagas themselves seem never to have lived in that area.[103] This is readily understandable if the Sapes are a people from the Baga-Cocoli-Temné group, probably particularly closely related to the Temné. V. Fernandes says that the King of the Sapes lived on the Casse river (Scarcie) at the beginning of the sixteenth century and was known as the Obe Vrig (Bey meant king in Temné). The other ethnic groups which live in the area at the present time were living in the area even then—Baga, Boulom, Temné, Limba, Susu, Dialonke. The Dialonke were already settling down close to the Fulbe in the interior. The Sapes kingdom was wiped out in the middle of the sixteenth century by an invasion of Sumba warriors 'who called themselves Manes'[104] and who were said to look and speak like Mandinka. Who were these mysterious Manes? M. Houis chose to think that they were the Mmani (Mandenyi in Susu) who occupied the seaboard between Kaloum and Scarcie in the seventeenth and eighteenth

101 M. Houis, 'Les minorités ethniques de la Guinée côtière', *Etudes guinéennes*, no. 4, pp. 25–48.
102 Fernandes, *op. cit.*, p. 77, makes them come from the Rio Grande (Geba) but specifies that they are 'mixed with other races'.
103 M. Houis, *op. cit.*
104 Alvares d'Almada, *op. cit.*, p. 81; Dapper, *op. cit.*, p. 249, dates the invasion of Sumba as 1515.

centuries. M. Yves Person has a grave objection to this interpretation: Portuguese documents categorically state that the Sumba invasion came from the south-east, crossing Sierra Leone before reaching Guinea. Now the first home of the Mmani—today reduced to a few last remaining groups in the Samou area—was in the mountainous interior near the Benna Mountains and the upper Tamisso; today the inhabitants are Susu but the place names are all Mmani. M. Person thinks that the 'Manes' of Alvares d'Almada must have been Mande warriors coming from the Toma country, possibly Kamara from Konian who formed the ruling aristocracy of the coast after the conquest (especially in the Temné country). When the Sape kingdom collapsed after the Sumba invasion, the Mmani could have infiltrated into the seaboard area, possibly settling down in chiefdoms under the control of the Mane-Sumba aristocracy.[105] We know in any case that the Mmani kingdom had its period of greatness in the eighteenth century. At the beginning of that century, Kandé Kalla extended his kingdom from Rio Pongo to Sierra Leone (his vassal Fatima ruling over the territory between Rio Pongo and Mellacoree).[106] This could be the 'Younkala' we know from tradition, but is it the name of a person or of a dynasty?

It was probably about 1760 that Susu from Kanea led by Soumba Toumane overran the Baga chiefdoms of Tabounsou and Bagatai. The chiefdom of Toumania was alternately under the control of the Soumah (Susu descendants of the conqueror) and the local Bangoura (Baga).

At the end of the eighteenth century Matthews noted that the region in the south of the Island of Matacong was occupied by Mohammedan 'Mandinka' and rice-growers, the northern zone as far as Tumbo (Conkary) being occupied by the Susu.[107]

These 'Mandinka' seem more likely to be Malinke from Futa-Jallon (Yattara and Youla) than the Mmani who had been pushed towards the Samou and the Kabak island.

Matthews explains that the Almamy of the Futa-Jallon (King of the Fulbe) had imposed his rule on the Mandinka and the Susu; the Baga, the Temné and the Bullom, on the other hand, refused to acknowledge all authority other than that of their own chiefs. In 1785 these Mandinka were

105 Y. Person, 'Les Kissi et leurs statuettes de pierre dans le cadre de l'histoire ouest africaine', *Bull. I.F.A.N.*, ser. B, xxiii, 1–2, 1961, pp. 1–59, and 'En quête d'une chronologie ivoirienne' (in *History in tropical Africa*, *op. cit.*, p. 326).

The Mmani, as well as the Bullom, Sherbro, Krim, constituted an ethnic group related to the Kissi, but cut off from these by the Mende invasion from the south-east.

106 Cf. Arcin, *op. cit.*, pp. 71–2, and N. Moity, 'Notes sur les Mani', *Bull. I.F.A.N.*, xix, 1–2, 1957, pp. 302–7.

107 John Matthews, *Voyage à la rivière de Sierra Leone sur la côte d'Afrique*, French trans., Paris, Hautbout l'aîné, An.V. It seems likely that as from the period of the 'Sape' kingdom, Malinke-Dioula elements were incorporated into the local aristocracy, coming from the Kankan region and following the main trading route leading from this town to Sierra Leone and the nearby 'Rivières'. In the nineteenth century the Touré in this same region (south of Kaloum), Almamys of Moréah, claimed to be Malinke originating from Kankan.

the victims of a general uprising of their slaves; their masters had gone on a war party when the slaves massacred those remaining in the villages, and burned their stores of rice. They set up their own fortifications, cut off the roads and finally obliged their masters to come to terms with them. In 1821 Gordon Laing mentions the civil war between Amara, 'Almamy or King of the Mandinke', who had his capital at Forecariah, and his vassal, Sannassi, who was defeated through the intervention of Yarredi, the *Kelle Mansa* (general, war leader) of the Dialonke king of Sulimana, Assana Ayira. In the nineteenth century the Susu element had absorbed almost all the populations of the coastal area right up to the frontier of Sierra Leone.

The gradual infiltration of the Susu was clearly related to the formation of the state of Futa-Jallon. They were driven back from the mountains with the Baga, and settled down with their brothers on the coast. Rio Pongo tradition has preserved the memory of the arrival of the Dialonke after the holy war during the eighteenth century. The Susu allowed them to settle, but they were scattered in small groups throughout their villages so as to avoid the formation of a rival ethnic block, and so were rapidly assimilated.[108]

CONCLUSION

If one endeavours to isolate the development characteristics of this region of Africa in the course of the seventeenth and eighteenth centuries, one is left with the impression of contradiction. Its development was slow—particularly when it is compared to changes typical of Europe at the same time—but it was indisputable. Some of the development factors were in the realm of progress. Trade, for instance, even though less considerable here than elsewhere, gave an undeniable impetus to the process of social differentiation within African society, concentrating wealth and capital at one end of the scale and poverty at the other.

Inland, this differentiation brought the establishment of Fula-Islamic rule in the Futa-Toro, Bundu and the Futa-Jallon. There were certain original features about each of these states: in the Futa-Jallon, it was a section of the newly settled immigrants which seized control of the country, with the help of adventurers and local allies, reducing the former masters of the soil to dependence or servitude: in Bundu, a country with a scattered population, immigrants from almost everywhere sought first a refuge, then the security of the trade route so that the original occupants were either integrated or

108 M. Houis writes: 'Historically, it is likely that the Susu and Dialonke were of the same ethnic group. The actual difference in terminology should not mislead. The Dialonke of Guinea and Sierra Leone were sporadic groups, separated from the main body of their ethnic group in the course of fighting against the Fulbe when they were founding the State of Futa-Dialo' (*Etude descriptive de la langue Susu*, Dakar, *I.F.A.N.*, 1963, p. 2). They were obviously closely related, but one should note the distinction drawn by the Portuguese who mentioned the 'Jaalungas' (Dialonke) and the 'Suzes' (Susu) as two different people. This episode brings supplementary evidence of an awareness of this difference.

driven elsewhere. In the Futa Toro it was among the indigenous population that a revolutionary group was formed to act against a minority ruling aristocracy, at once oppressive and weak, and incapable of defending the country against the encroachments of the Moors.

But, apart from the Islamic and Fula-speaking character of the movement, social trends common to all three states emerge: they all rejected the framework of the tribal pagan kingdom where the royal authority took to itself all the traditional functions of both *chefs de terre* and war leaders, relying for much of its authority on small bands of slaves who belonged to the royal household and who served as professional soldiers.

The state was no longer simply a royal household, an inflated version of the extended family, superimposed over others. It was now a community of believers, the *Umma*, which replaced units based on blood ties alone. In Arabia the Prophet himself had altered traditional society in the same way. The theocratic and oligarchic republic replaced the tribal monarchy.

There was not too great a contradiction, in fact. In the states with a Mande tradition, the princely families with a claim to the throne and the royal slaves constituted a *de facto* oligarchy; the social structure had already taken on a feudal aspect. For this reason the new states were easily able to integrate the old structures rather than destroy them.

Bundu seems to be an exception to the rule: but this was a state created out of nothing—a state which was established to give a unity to peoples of various ethnic groups and which retained the simple structure of a dynastic house maintained by a band of warriors, which eventually found in Islam a basis of ideological authority.

The progress—or the increasing complexity—of social and political structures was accompanied by unmistakable cultural progress, even if this involved the denial and on occasion the destruction of former cultural values: one cannot consider the spread of writing as a feature of no importance.

Conversely, this same process resulted in actual regression in other regions. The medieval kingdoms seemed powerful when judged by the extent of their dominion, but they were really only a fragile and superficial edifice. The authority of the Mansa of Mali or of the Bour-ba-Djoloff was all the more easily recognised because it demanded little and had little to ask for. The attraction of European merchandise and the means it afforded to those who were sufficiently well placed to obtain it brought about the collapse of these weak states, encouraged small political units and on occasion a return to a segmentary society. This happened all along the coast.[109]

109 'Does there not exist on the coast of Africa, in the last quarter of the seventeenth century, a close correlation between anarchy or political collapse and the vast supplies of slaves, the latter in turn fostering a state of war?' (Abdoulaye Ly, 'La Compagnie du Sénégal, *Presence Africaine* (Paris), 1958, pp. 290–1.)

This contradictory process is again found in the context of production. Without exaggerating the effects of the slave trade, there is no doubt that the hunting and capturing of slaves had a negative effect on agricultural work both indirectly and directly (losses in man-power and in crops, lack of security). Conversely, the introduction from the sixteenth century onwards of seeds and plants brought from America, depending on their importance in agriculture, had a positive effect by replacing indigenous species with a low yield. Did the one balance out the other? It is difficult to say.

It is most probable that the effects of contact with Europeans which restrained and in some cases even stopped the existing course of development in African societies, helped to accentuate the disparity both at the level of technical achievement and in social and political organisation, a disparity which was to come to its logical conclusion in the nineteenth century: the exploration and conquest of Africa.

CHAPTER 12

The Western Sudan from the Moroccan invasion (1591) to the death of Al-Mukhtar Al-Kunti (1811)

JOHN RALPH WILLIS

The Moroccan invasion of 1591 constitutes a watershed in the history of the Western Sudan in so far as it brought to an end the greatest of a series of large Sudanic states, and ushered in a new period of political intervention in the Sudan from the north. It has been argued that the period 1600 to 1800 was a 'time of troubles' characterised by political instability, large-scale dislocation of peoples, and chronic famine. It has been further asserted that these two hundred years witnessed a sharp decline in Islamic learning and a dimunition of economic prosperity in the Middle Niger region. One of the main tasks of this chapter will be to ascertain to what extent these long-held contentions can be substantiated.

THE MIDDLE NIGER, 1591–1737: THE PERIOD OF RUMA ASCENDANCY

The Moroccan invasion

The Moroccan invasion of the Middle Niger region was yet another manifestation of al-Manṣūr's designs on the universal Caliphate. Aḥmad al-Manṣūr al-Dhahabī, sixth sovereign of the Moroccan Saʿdid dynasty, like his dynastic predecessors, laid claim to the titles *Khalīfa* and *Amīr al-Mu'minīn* by virtue of his alleged sharifian descent through Ḥasan, son of ʿAlī by Fāṭima.[1] These *sharīfs*—self-ordained champions of Islam against

1 For an introduction to Saʿdid history, one might usefully begin with the *Nuzhat al-hādī bi-akhbār mulūk al-qarn al-ḥādī* of Muḥammad al-Ṣaghīr al-Wafrānī (*c.* 1669–1738), translated by O. Houdas as *Nozhet el Hadi: Histoire de la Dynastie Saadienne au Maroc (1511–1670)*, (French translation, 1889, Arabic text, 1888), the major source for the period. Cf. E. Lévi-Provençal, *Les Historiens des Chorfa: Essai sur la Littérature Historique et Biographique au Maroc du XVIe au XXe Siècle*, Paris, 1922; Henri Terrasse, *Histoire du Maroc*, 2 vols, Casablanca, 1949–1950; and E. Mercier, *Histoire de l'Afrique Septentrionale (Berbérie)*, 3 vols, Paris, 1888–91; and Ch.-André Julien, *Histoire de l'Afrique du Nord*, 2 vols, Paris, 1952, cf. also B. A. Mojuetan, *The Rise of the Alawi Dynasty in Morocco, 1631–1672*, Ph.D. thesis, S.O.A.S., 1969. This was completed after this chapter was written.

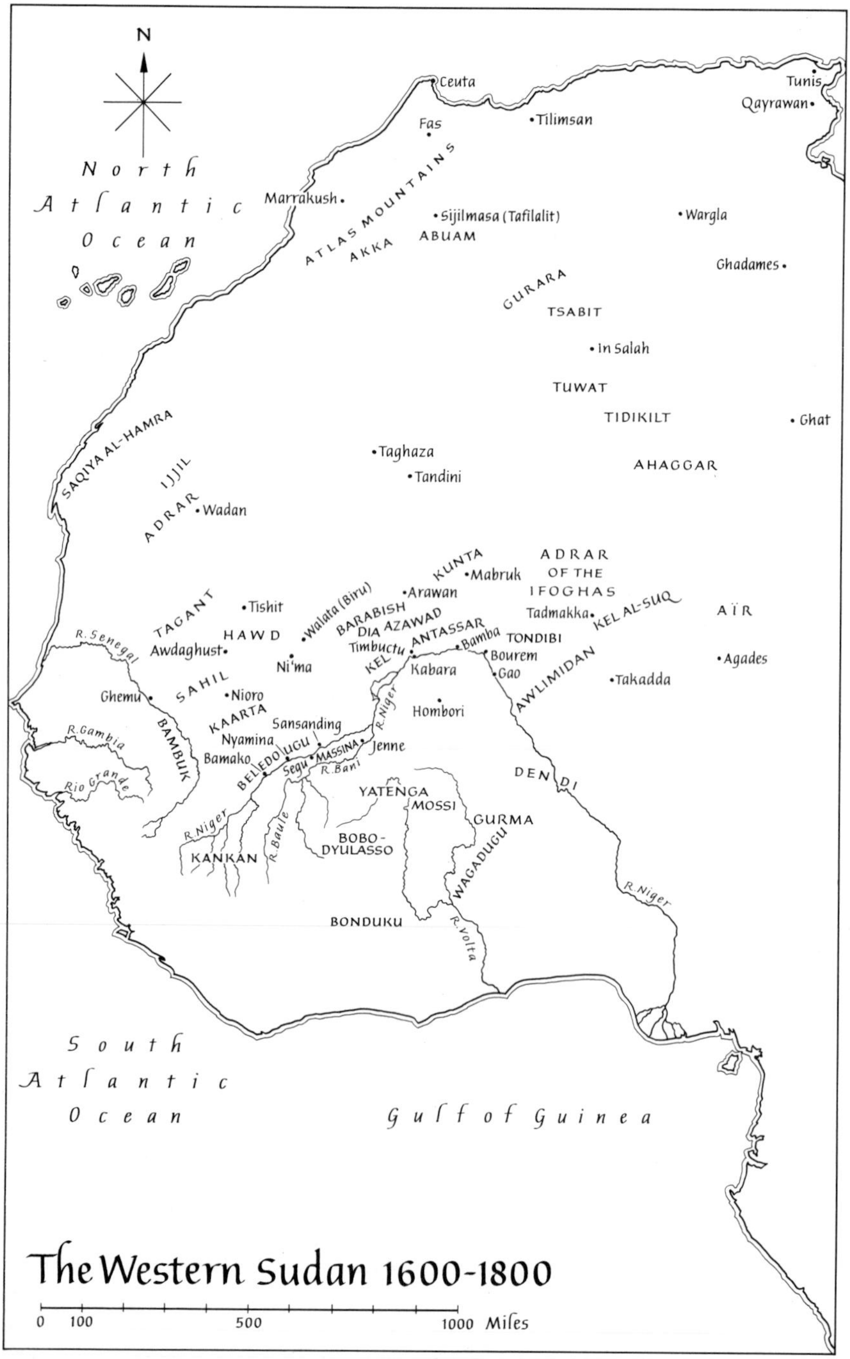
N
North Atlantic Ocean
Ceuta
Tunis
Qayrawan
Fas
Tilimsan
ATLAS MOUNTAINS
Marrakush
Sijilmasa (Tafilalit)
AKKA
ABUAM
Wargla
Ghadames
GURARA
TSABIT
In Salah
TUWAT
TIDIKILT
Ghat
SAQIYA AL-HAMRA
IJJIL
ADRAR
Wadan
Taghaza
Tandini
AHAGGAR
KUNTA
Mabruk
ADRAR OF THE IFOGHAS
TAGANT
Tishit
Walata (Biru)
Arawan
BARABISH
DIA
AZAWAD
Tadmakka
KEL AL-SUQ
AÏR
HAWD
Awdaghust
Ni'ma
Timbuctu
KEL ANTASSAR
Bamba
TONDIBI
Bourem
Gao
Agades
R. Senegal
SAHIL
Kabara
AWLIMIDAN
Takadda
Ghemu
Nioro
KAARTA
Hombori
BAMBUK
R. Gambia
Sansanding
Nyamina
R. Niger
Bamako
BELEDOUGU
Segu
MASSINA
Jenne
R. Bani
Rio Grande
DENDI
YATENGA
MOSSI
GURMA
R. Niger
KANKAN
R. Baule
BOBO-DYULASSO
WAGADUGU
R. Niger
BONDUKU
R. Volta
South Atlantic Ocean
Gulf of Guinea
The Western Sudan 1600-1800
0
100
500
1000 Miles

12:1

the usurpation of the Turks[2] and the encroachments of the Portuguese (whom they dislodged from Agadir in 1541 and ejected from Safi and Azemmour)—proclaimed *jihād* against usurper and infidel alike, soliciting support and recognition from Muslim communities in the Maghrib and the Sudan.

When Askia Isḥāq II refused to accept the levy imposed by al-Manṣūr over the salt from Taghaza, Manṣūr convoked an emergency assembly of his religious advisers. The Askia, he contended, had left him no alternative —an attack on Songhay was necessary in order to 'reunite in one and the same opinion all the forces of Islam'.[3] Furthermore, the Sudan was a very rich country—capable of furnishing the Muslim armies with enormous revenues. In any case, in al-Manṣūr's opinion the ruler of Songhay had forfeited his functions, as he did not 'belong to the family of the Quraysh' and did not satisfy any of the other legal requirements essential for the exercise of caliphal authority.

Finally, he argued persuasively that it would be more advantageous to make war against the Sudan than to renew the effort against the Turks. Ifrīqiya was less affluent than the Sudan, and a conflict against the Turks would occasion a great struggle with little profit accruing from victory.[4]

Thus it was with the unanimous assent of his advisers that Aḥmad al-Manṣūr initiated the Moroccan invasion of the Middle Niger.

The establishment of Moroccan rule in the Middle Niger

The Moroccan occupation of Timbuctū was met by considerable hostility —especially from the influential quarters of religious scholars (*ʿulamā'*) and merchants. Both had been traditionally opposed to any political upheaval, and the merchants were especially apprehensive of any activity which might disrupt trade. Hence the Moroccan intervention was initially an unwelcomed event. It is true, however, that neither ʿulamā' nor merchants had been entirely pleased with the Songhay administration. One manifestation of this discontent was seen in the alleged recognition by the ʿulamā' of Tunis and not Gao as the capital seat of Islam in the Maghrib and Western Sudan.[5] The closing years of Isḥāq's reign had been unremarkable, if one excepts the increasing tendency toward tyranny and arbitrariness. Indeed al-Saʿdi preferred to interpret the Moroccan takeover as 'an

2 The Turks were regarded as usurpers because they were not from the Prophet's group, the Quraysh, and because they seized the Caliphate by intrigue and force. (Julien, *Histoire*, ii, p. 207.)

3 al-Wafrānī, *Nuzhat al-ḥādī*, trans., p. 159.

4 *Ibid.*, p. 152.

5 Mercier, *Histoire*, vii, 162. The Hafsids were a Berber (Sanhaja) dynasty which held sway in Tunis from 1224 until 1574. The authority for Mercier's statement is unidentified, and it would seem improbable that the *ʿulamā'* of Timbuctū would recognise the claims of non-Arabs to the universal Caliphate—even in face of the threat from Morocco. For the Hafsids see R. Brunschvig, *La Berbérie orientale sous les Hafsides*, 2 vols, Paris, 1940–47.

act of Allah' inflicted upon Songhay as punishment for the Askias' decadence. By the time of the Moroccan arrival, he claimed,

> the faith had been transformed into infidelity; there had not been a single act forbidden by Allah that was not practiced overtly. Some were given to wine drinking; others indulged in sodomy; and as for adultery —it had become so commonplace that its practice would have seemed licit. And they could neither be glorified nor adorned, unless by virtue of it—so much so that some of the children of the rulers performed it with their sisters.[6]

Yet notwithstanding these reservations, there were few in Timbuctū who could not fail to recognise the distinct advantages of Songhay administration as exemplified by the relative prosperity achieved through constant vigilance over the vital arteries of trade. The Askias, for the most part, had not maintained an overtly oppressive administration, and they had brought about a considerable period of peace and stability.[7] Hence a reasonably efficient though progressively decadent master was to be preferred to an unfamiliar and seemingly opportunist one.

As if to justify these misgivings, the Moroccans clamped down harshly on all sectors of discontent. The ʿulamā' of Timbuctū were among the first to incur the wrath of the victors, intent on undercutting the influence of those who had opposed them. Among those arrested was the celebrated Muslim jurist, Aḥmad Bābā, who, together with all the members of his family, was placed in chains and led captive to Marrākush, deprived of his books and other possessions. But what was done for political expediency should not be mistaken for religious persecution.[8] Indeed Manṣūr himself was an accomplished Islamic scholar. He had brought to his court some of the most brilliant minds in Western Islam. His secretary, ʿAbd al-ʿAzīz al-Fishtalī, was highly esteemed as poet, writer, and scholar. It is against this background that the capture of Aḥmad Bābā and his colleagues must be understood.[9]

Once these dissident voices had been silenced, opposition to Moroccan rule came to a virtual standstill in Timbuctū. But such was not the case in Jenne, where resistance continued unabated. Unlike their counterparts in Timbuctū, the Jenne scholars and merchants preferred peaceful capitulation to resistance. Several minority groups, however—notably Fulbe and Tuareg—were reluctant to cooperate with the Moroccans, and often found themselves in concert with the Jenne-kay and the Askias of Dendi against the Moroccan régime.[10]

6 Al-Saʿdi, *Taʾrīkh al-Sūdān*, trans., p. 224.
7 *Ibid.*, p. 222.
8 Al-Wafrānī, *Nuzhat al-ḥādī*, trans., p. 169.
9 *Ibid.*, trans., p. 164.
10 Charles Monteil, *Une Cité Soudanaise: Djénné*, Paris, 1932, p. 48.

The military contingent sent to conquer Songhay consisted of some 3,000 troops, most of which were enslaved mercenaries from Andalusia. Others originated from Marrākush, Fās, and Tāfīlālit. These troops contracted marital and concubinal unions with Songhay women, and it was the offspring of these unions which came to be called by the name *Ruma* or *Arma*.[11] The early Ruma were from the outset responsible to the sovereign of Morocco. They were required to remit a specified percentage of the income acquired from the newly conquered salt mines and from the lucrative trade of such cities as Jenne, Timbuctū, and Gao. This they did faithfully in the beginning; and it is a tribute to their loyalty that the early Ruma, faced with the considerable administrative task of overseeing a large geographical area, maintained contact with the metropole, and for the most part did what was required of them, despite serious difficulties of communication.[12]

The Moroccans selected Timbuctū as their administrative capital. Their effective authority extended as far north as Marrākush and Fās (the key cities of the Saʿdid dynasty), as far south as Jenne; south-east to the limits of Mossi; west to the confines of Māssina; and east to Gao. In Gao and Timbuctū the early Ruma established a system of indirect rule in which, in return for investiture of traditional officials who swore loyalty to them, they wisely refrained from interference with the previous political, judicial, and religious structure.

Yet these various local officials had no authority over the Moroccan populations which resided among them. A unique and independent administrative structure was created for their benefit. The *ahl al-Makhzan* (as they are known in the texts) came under the supervision of their own government or *Makhzan*. The *Makhazani* included: the hereditary *corps d'élite* which consisted of all members of the Moroccan army, and the various public officials in the employ of the Makhzan. They lived in their own separate quarters, maintained their own judicial courts, and benefited from several privileges as members of the ruling class. At the summit of the Makhzan hierarchy was the *bāshā*—a military governor accountable only to the ruler of Morocco. This office was to rotate between the three major divisions of the governing élite: the division of Fās, that of Marrākush, and that of Sharaqa—all originally military contingents of the invading army. Next in importance was the *amīn*, one of the *khalīfa's* agents and closest confidants, responsible for fiscal or economic matters—especially in the realm of tax collection. He also seems to have carried some powers in the appointment of district governors on behalf of the khalīfa. A minor

11 (Captaine) Péfontan, 'Les Armas', *Bulletin du Comité d'Etudes historiques et scientifiques de l'A.O.F.*, ix, 1926, pp. 153–80, p. 154. The word 'Arma' was a local corruption of the Arabic, *Ruma*, meaning *tireurs* or *fusileurs*, according to Paul Marty, *Etudes sur l'Islam et les tribus du Soudan*, 4 vols, Paris, 1918–21, ii, p. 7.
12 Houdas, introduction, al-Saʿdi, *op. cit.*, trans., p. vii.

official, the *ḥākim*, a kind of magistrate with limited judicial and executive powers, presided over each district. He was customarily, but not always, chosen from among the ahl al-Makhzan.[13]

The newly established ruling class made no attempt to discard its original military character. The ahl al-Makhzan were above all professional soldiers bred on provisions of booty. There were few intellectuals and trained bureaucrats among them—and this, perhaps more than any other factor, helps to explain some of their shortcomings. The bāshā himself was a rather weak *primus inter pares*—a fact which would seem to underscore the major weakness of the chief office of state. The real power in the *Makhzan* continued to rest with the military leaders (or *qā'ids*) of the divisions of Fās, Marrākush, and Sharaqa. The Moroccan community also contained an important class of traders and ʿulamā'—called sharīfs because they traced their lineage to the Prophet's group. At times they appeared to perform the rôle of intermediaries (frequently with and without invitation) in the disputes between the three divisions. But their influence was always unofficial and unpredictable.[14]

Ruma independence and decline

Had it not been for two unfortunate events and one underlying imperial defect there is little reason why the Middle Niger valley should not have continued to flourish under Moroccan auspices. The recall of Jawdhar in 1599—needed in Marrākush to quell a civil disturbance—deprived the Ruma of a gifted leader; and the unexpected death of Khalīfa Mawlay Aḥmad in 1603 precipitated a succession crisis that threatened to dismantle the state. Gripped in a period of interregnum and internecine strife, Morocco was forced to distract its attention from the Niger provinces.[15]

By 1608, when the Saʿdid dynasty had regained its balance, fundamental defects in the imperial policy were all too evident. What had been of little moment for the Askias conveniently situated at Gao, had become insuperable for the Moroccans remotely isolated in Marrākush; Saʿdid imperial rule collapsed—incapacitated by insoluble difficulties inherent in the administration of an overextended empire. Distance had become the enemy of effective administration. Six months were necessary to obtain the simplest confirmation, but often exigency could not await the prolonged deliberation of an administration petrified by problems of communication. Even if one discounts the difficulties of communication, the efficacy of the imperial system itself must be brought in question. As has been indicated,

13 For a description of the offices *amīn* and *ḥākim*, see al-Wafrānī, *Tadhkirat al-Nisyān*, French trans. and Arabic text ed. O. Houdas as *Tedzkiret en-Nisian*, Paris, 1899–1901, pp. 281 and 295 respectively.

14 Al-Saʿdi, *op. cit.*, trans., p. 318 *et seq.* For Jawdhar's official periods of governorship see al-Wafrānī, *Tadhkirat*, trans., p. 364.

15 Cf. Terrasse, *Maroc* ii, p. 209, and Julien, *Histoire* ii, p. 217.

the bāshā was no more than a weak *primus inter pares*. And when internal disorder arose among competing factions of the army of occupation, the over-facile solution of two bāshās—one civil and one military—was proposed as a panacea for breaking the deadlock. Hence what had once been a weak authority was now no authority at all. Moreover, the situation was exacerbated by the constant intervensions of the Khalīfa's amīn who appeared to be at odds with both bāshās over a variety of issues.[16]

Thus it would seem that the consequent usurpation by bāshās beginning with Jawdhar, was perhaps due more to the persistence of grave matters warranting immediate action than to any caprice. In any case, the army's appointment of an independent bāshā in 1612[17] finally eliminated the nuisance of justifying unapproved actions in long and apologetic dispatches. By 1632 virtually all semblance of adherence to Moroccan imperial authority had vanished, as the amīn—the one remaining link with the metropole—was appointed by the bāshā himself.[18] Thus, independent and free of the encumbrances of a vigilant amīn, in 1660 the bāshā could remove the name of the reigning Moroccan Khalīfa from the Friday *khuṭba* and substitute his own with complete impunity.[19]

The initial restraint which the Ruma had so admirably displayed in local affairs soon gave way to varying degrees of direct interference. It is possible to estimate the degree of Ruma interference in indigenous religious and political affairs by taking cognisance of the circumstances surrounding appointments to religious and political office. By comparing the circumstances of appointment together with the known period certain officials remained in office, it is also possible to arrive at the relative stability of political as opposed to religious offices. Initially no effort was made to interfere with the appointment of local religious officials. It was not until the end of Bāshā Maḥmūd's reign (*c.* 1598) that the Makhzan designated its first *qā'ḍī* of Timbuctū.[20] Similar religious appointments were made in other principal centres under Makhzan control. Whatever the quality of these appointments, their stability of tenure cannot be denied. Of the twelve qā'ḍīs appointed for Timbuctū between *c.* 1599 and 1750, all are known to have died in office after long periods of administration. The same can be said of those religious figures appointed *imāms* of the chief mosque of Timbuctū and of those appointed to religious offices in Jenne. This would suggest that the chief religious officials of Jenne and Timbuctū were not exploited for political purposes—that they had not become part of the patronage system which obtained in the political sphere of administration.

In contrast to the stability which characterised these religious offices,

16 See Houdas, introduction, al-Saʿdi, *op. cit.*, p. vii.
17 Al-Saʿdi, *op. cit.*, trans., p. 307.
18 *Ibid.*, p. 377.
19 Al-Wafrānī, *Tadhkirat al-Nisyān*, trans., p. 145.
20 *Ibid.*, p. 466.

political offices at virtually all levels seemed to have succumbed to the shortcomings of a system increasingly victimised by the venal aspects of patronage. The period of Ruma ascendancy in Jenne began inauspiciously. On the death of Abū Bakr b. Muḥammad, the Jenne-kay for thirty-six years (1556–92),[21] the Ruma unwisely appointed a replacement who was not from the traditional ruling family.[22] As a consequence, they immediately alienated the ruling élite and their followers, who were in any case reluctant to swear loyalty to the Makhzan. Realising their mistake, the Ruma sought to accommodate the dissidents by restoring the élite to power in 1597.[23] But this attempt at a *modus vivendi* seems to have been to no avail, as the Jenne-kay persisted in their disloyalty. Hence in 1620 the Makhzan again resorted to the appointment of Abū Bakr b. ʿAbdallāh, a Jenne-kay from a non-traditional family. This became necessary after the appointments of two Jenne-kay were revoked for unrepentant participation in subversion against the Makhzan. Abū Bakr b. ʿAbdallāh remained in office until his death in 1627.[24] After this period, until 1653, the Ruma sought unsuccessfully to effect a *rapprochement* with the traditional élite. But the Jenne-kay, with their Massina and Dendi allies, were simply too strong to be subjugated by the Ruma though too weak to oust the Ruma themselves. By 1653, when the Jenne-kay had finally taken refuge in Foromana, on the left bank of the Bani, the Makhzan troops of Jenne were themselves virtually independent of Timbuctū and the Jenne-kay.[25]

The office of *askia,* while lacking the stability of the office of imām and qā'ḍī, does reflect some degree of stability during the Makhzan period, as only eighteen askias were appointed between 1591 and 1750. Six had reigns of more than ten years, and of these two were able to maintain themselves in office for nineteen years. Despite this relative stability, the office was at times a sinecure of the patronage system, mirroring to some extent the high rate of instability which always characterised the office of bāshā. Thirteen askias were dismissed from office, and only three actually died while executing their functions; one disappeared; and the reigning askia in 1750 was in danger of being revoked. The chief explanation for dismissal would seem to lie in the nature of the patronage system. Some were appointed in return for the military support which they promised a new bāshā. Although the office was at the disposal of the bashalik, bāshās cultivated good relations with Songhay dignitaries by sometimes merely confirming and investing an askia nominated by the community's leaders. Though there can be little doubt that the askia was almost completely devoid of political power, a shrewd officeholder was able to exert some

21 Monteil, *Djénné*, pp. 44 and 48.
22 *Ibid.*, p. 56.
23 *Ibid.*, p. 62.
24 *Ibid.*, p. 70.
25 *Ibid.*, p. 79.

sort of influence through his position as traditional representative of the Songhay people, from whom a not inconsiderable number of troops were drawn, and on whom devolved a major part of the responsibility for maintaining order. Another indication that the office was not entirely without its usefulness is seen by the number of times bāshās had recourse to the mediating services of an askia against the independent askia of Dendi and his followers.[26]

The most ineffective and unstable office under Makhzan control was the office of bāshā; and herein lies the main explanation for Ruma inability to evolve a stable form of administration. The inordinate influence of the military precluded any transition from military rule to civilian forms of government. The Makhzan period was characterised by rivalries which tended to weaken the state and maintain the bāshā in a position of almost perpetual prostration. There were rivalries between and within divisions;[27] and competitions between bāshās and chiefs of divisions who were often more powerful and more influential than the bāshā himself.[28] Theoretically, the chief office of state was to rotate between the three major divisions—each electing a bāshā for a specified period of tenure. Yet, because rivalry between divisions was so intense, this formal arrangement does not seem to have been implemented with any degree of consistency. The ultimate determinant of tenure appears to have been the power of the division which waxed strongest at any given moment. Although the office was elective, bāshās could be easily deposed if they failed to gain a vote of confidence over a particular issue. An incumbent bāshā found it necessary to be for ever on his guard against the renewed claims of a deposed one. The administration of the bashalik was further weakened by the lack of continuity in lesser offices. The succession of nearly every bāshā prompted a reshuffle of lesser offices at his disposal. New bāshās felt constrained to remove military chiefs of the main divisions, as well as the ḥākim and *Kabara-farma*, replacing them with confidants whose loyalties could be assured.[29]

The Makhzan's main function seems to have been that of maintaining order and securing the vital trade routes. Since the Makhzan's wealth, like that of the merchants, depended on the safe-keeping of these commercial arteries, there was no basic conflict of interest between the two groups. Indeed trade was so fundamental to the economic well-being of the Middle Niger, that the Ruma—far from exploiting the merchants—sought to become their patrons and guardians. Conversely, groups of merchants

26 Cf. al-Saʿdi, *op. cit.*, trans., pp. 463 and 470. It should be noted that after the capture of Timbuctū in 1591, the ruling dynasty of Songhay (the askias) fled to Dendi, where they continued to oppose Ruma administration. The Ruma, however, continued to appoint askias of their own choice over Songhay peoples within their sphere of influence.

27 Cf. al-Saʿdi, *op. cit.*, trans., p. 48.

28 Al-Wafrānī, *Tadhkirat*, trans., pp. 101 and 144.

29 *Ibid.*, trans., p. 237.

affiliated themselves with one of the three divisions which constituted the Makhzan, thus creating a relationship of mutual confidence and interest.[30] Merchants were periodically required to underwrite the cost of military expeditions in reprisal against various pillaging groups which obstructed commercial traffic. This they did in the form of 'contributions' *maks* (sometimes misleadingly termed 'tribute'), which were collected for payment of troops undertaking the expeditions.[31] The sums collected would seem relatively modest in comparison to the unquestionable affluence of the traders—especially those who resided in Timbuctū and Jenne. Often no more than one thousand *mithqāls* were collected, a sum which (when levied upon hundreds of traders) must have been of only nominal economic consequence to any individual merchant. It is true that sometimes the sum collected was misappropriated, but such misbehaviour appears to have been more to the detriment of reigning bāshās (who were responsible for the distribution) than to the traders who were defrauded.

Makhzan rule does not appear to have been oppressive. On the contrary, the Ruma seemed to have been on the whole quite sensitive to the complaints of various interest groups; traders, cultivators, and ʿulamā' all had their means of exerting pressure when vital interests were at stake, and not unsuccessfully. This is not to say that oppression was non-existent during the Makhzan period, but it should be appreciated that oppression was not ordinarily forthcoming from the government, but rather from disseminators of discontent who manifested opposition to the government, or from quarters which demonstrated an overt contempt for law and order. Ambitious military leaders, casting envious eyes upon the office of bāshā, were apt to indulge in a host of rebellious activities in quests for power, leaving economic and political disorder in their wake. Uninhibited slaves of irresponsible soldiers were inclined to unleash their appetites for booty and adventure on defenceless citizens. If acts of brigandage and pillage were not normally tolerated by the Makhzan, and if suppression of such acts was not entirely dependent on Makhzan response to pressures of irate traders or cultivators, it cannot be denied that the frequency of pillage, brigandage, and rebellion reflected the political and administrative weakness of the Ruma.

Divided by disputes, weakened by administrative ineptitude, the Ruma were forced to abdicate traditional responsibilities. Traders were constrained to look elsewhere for protectors; citizens were compelled to organise themselves in defensive units or endure the dire consequences of non-protection. In 1664 the people of Timbuctū seized the initiative and attempted to arrest the Qāʾid Ahmad and his troops, who had confiscated goods to the value of 37,000 mithqāls.[32] In 1718 recalcitrant slaves of Bāshā

30 Al-Wafrānī, *Tadhkirat*, trans., p. 147.
31 *Ibid.*, trans., p. 126.
32 *Ibid.*, trans., p. 149.

al-Manṣūr nearly succeeded in gaining control of Kabara and paralysing its commercial traffic. In 1719 an uprising against al-Manṣūr himself took place because no security had been provided against the devastating attacks of Legha from within and Tuareg from without.[33] By 1728 the situation had grown intolerable; for the next four years Timbuctū was to witness a period of interregnum unparalleled since the reign of Bāshā Jawdhar.[34]

But it was the increasing dependence on mercenaries—summoned to suppress or sustain these wanton acts of lawlessness or to defend the state against external penetration—that accelerated the pace of Ruma decline. Reliance on mercenaries seems to have reached the critical point during the reign of Bāshā al-Manṣūr (1716–19). Even as early as 1712, when Manṣūr briefly held the bashalik, there were unmistakable signs of a radical shift in the power alignment; Arab, Berber, Fulbe and Tuareg mercenaries filled the ranks of the army, and personal slaves were beginning to displace army regulars in the chief administrative offices of state.[35] Such a revolutionary experiment was apparently pursued by al-Manṣūr in order to ensure loyalties to himself rather than to divisions or divisional commanders. A black slave was appointed Kabara-farma—a post previously occupied by the Ruma. The canonical *kharaj*, and *diyya* (the millet tithe) as well as taxes paid in dried fish, were remitted directly to these slaves. The Legha, however, grew infamous for their lack of tact and for their high-handed extortionist methods which ignited a popular rebellion against al-Manṣūr.[36]

In 1717 al-Manṣūr resorted to the Tadmakkat Tuareg in an unsuccessful bid to maintain himself in power. His opponents, led by the Qāʿid ʿAbdallāh, had recourse to the Bambara—well known throughout the Western Sudan for their mercenary services which seemed always available to the highest bidder. Moreover, Arab, Tuareg and Berber mercenaries were frequently employed in external raids against other Arab, Tuareg and Berber groups who gained their livelihood through pillage and extortion. The deployment of ethnic groups against each other was not without its diplomatic advantages. Al-Manṣūr, as a matter of policy, retained a majority of 'stranger' elements (Fulbe, Bambara and Tuareg especially) among his regulars. If the expedition proved successful, credit could always be given to the Ruma officers; if it were to fail, the mercenaries could be held responsible.[37] In 1720 al-Manṣūr summoned still another group of mercenaries, the Aulimadan Tuareg, to assist him against an *ad*

33 *Ibid.*, trans., pp. 26 and 226. The *Legha* were the personal black slaves of the bāshā, al-Manṣūr. It is quite possible that al-Manṣūr created the legha corps as a means of seizing power and stabilising the administration.

34 *Ibid.*, trans., p. 87.

35 Richer, *Les Ouillimenden*, p. 85.

36 Al-Wafrānī, *Tadhkirat*, trans., p. 29.

37 Richer, *op. cit.*, p. 85.

hoc army led by the new bāshā, Ba-Haddu. Further conflicts ensued in 1723 and 1724.[38]

By 1734 there could be no doubt that the experiment had been an abysmal failure. Reliance on mercenaries as a means of gaining the edge in Ruma disputes, far from achieving this purpose, had shown itself self-defeating. Indeed, in the classic pattern, it was the mercenaries who proved ultimate victors over the Ruma. From 1734 until 1737 Timbuctū was subjected to an almost endless series of pillaging raids by various groups of Tuareg and Berbers. In 1737 the Ruma suffered a humiliating defeat at the hands of the Tadmakkat who imposed upon them a sizeable tribute. Henceforth the future of the Middle Niger was in control of the Tuareg and their allies who now ravaged at will and without risk.[39]

THE NIGER-BANI REGION, *c.* 1600–1800: THE EMERGENCE OF BAMBARA POWER

Bambara and Fulbe settlement

While the Middle Niger region was witnessing the far-ranging impact of the Moroccan invasion, the Niger-Bani area was reaching the culmination of a radical transformation in its ethnic composition. This process was initiated as early as the seventh century when Bozo fishermen, the first of several Mande-speaking groups, came to inhabit Segu. The Bozo migration was followed shortly after by the appearance of large groups of Bambara cultivators and Mande traders who developed communities alongside their Bozo predecessors, between the ninth and eleventh centuries. In the twelfth century Soso peoples effected a suzerainty over the area only to find themselves politically displaced by more powerful Mande groups in the thirteenth century. From this period, until the beginning of the eighteenth century, these Mande-speakers retained some semblance of superiority over other ethnic groups.[40]

38 *Ibid.*, p. 86.
39 *Ibid.*, p. 89.
40 Louis Tauxier, *Histoire des Bambara*, Paris, 1942, p. 54. The most useful older works concerning Bambara history and culture are: A. Raffenel, *Nouveau voyage au pays des nègres*, 2 vols, Paris, 1856; Mungo Park, *Second Voyage in the Interior of Africa during the year 1805*, London, 1816; Gallieni, *Voyage au Soudan Français. Haut-Niger et pays de Segou, 1880–1883*, Paris, 1885; L. G. Binger, *Du Niger au Golfe de Guinée*, 2 vols, Paris, 1892; Perignon, *Haut-Sénégal et Moyen-Niger, Kita et Segou*, Paris, 1901; Robert Arnaud, 'La Singulière légende des Soninkés', *L'Islam et la politique française en Afrique Occidentale Française*, Paris, 1912; L. Le Barbier, *Les Bambaras, coutumes, religions*, Paris, 1918; Charles Monteil, *Les Bambaras de Ségou et du Kaarta*, Paris, 1924; L. Tauxier, *La Réligion Bambara*, Paris, 1927; and M. Delafosse, *Haut-Sénégal-Niger*, 3 vols, Paris, 1912; Adam, *Légendes historiques du pays de Nioro (Sahel)*, Paris, 1904; and M. Delafosse, *Traditions historiques et légendaires du Soudan Occidental*, Paris, 1913. To these must be added the more recent studies of Z. Ligers, *Les Sorko (Bozo) maîtres du Niger*, 3 vols, Paris, 1966; André Bîme, *Ségou, veille capitale,* Angoulême, 1952; and several works by Robert Pageard: *Notes sur l'histoire de Bambara de Ségu*, Clichy, 1957: 'Une Tradition musulmane relative à l'histoire

(*continued opposite*)

At the start of the seventeenth century, slave-owning Fulbe nomads, possibly uprooted by the unrest caused by the Moroccan conquest of Songhay, made their first significant settlements in the area of Segu. By 1625 Fulbe intermarriage with Berber, Bambara, and other Mande women had produced a (Massassi) dynasty, of which the Kouloubali constituted the leading family.[41] The Kouloubali had expanded from the region of Segu and Baiko through a series of pillaging expeditions; another branch of the Massassi predominated in Beledougu.[42] An ephemeral state was established by Kaladian Kouloubali (1652–82), who was able to effect a temporary suzerainty over several villages on both banks of the Niger in the Segu region. The raiding activities of these warrior-cultivators were continued by his successors, Danfassari (1682–97) and Souma (1697–1712).

Bambara community and clan organisation

By the beginning of the eighteenth century Bambara state organisation had begun to crystallise. All the diverse peoples of the Segu area appear to have been organised in similar family, community and clan units. The clan unit (or *ton*) had evolved from the close association of several families coalescing to form larger village or community units called *dugu*, and still larger provincial units called *kafu*. Each dugu was presided over by a custodian elected by the representatives of member communities. The Bambara community was cemented by ancestral ties, but common interests in cultivation also served as a binding factor. Mande traders, the most affluent group in the Segu area, were also organised on a community basis, attracted by similar commercial and religious interests.[43]

Each unit, irrespective of size, consisted of four principal classes of people, differentiated according to birth, occupation, and political status.[44] Free people occupied the highest echelons of society. They could be further distinguished according to affluence and influence.[45] The lower strata of society were occupied by people who had lost caste—who had forfeited their rights and as a consequence had become excluded from citizenship in the community. If their indignity was associated with a particular trade

(40 *continued*)
de Ségou', *Notes Africaines,* no. 101, janvier 1964, pp. 24–6; 'Notes sur les Somonos', *Notes Africaines*, janvier 1961, pp. 17–18; 'Notes sur le rapport de "Senankouya" en Soudan français particulièremont dans les cercles de Ségou et de Macina,' *Bull. I.F.A.N.*, sér B, 1958, pp. 123–41; 'Ségou', *Ann. Africaines*, 1958, pp. 293–304; 'Notes sur les Diawambé ou Diakorame', *Journal Soc. Africaines*, xxix, 1959, pp. 238–60.

41 Louis Tauxier, *Histoire des Bambara*, p. 60; cf. Pageard, *Notes sur l'histoire des Bambaras de Ségou*, p. 7, for a tradition which presents the Kouloubali as a branch of the Keita, the dynastic family of Mali.

42 *Ibid.*, p. 67.

43 Monteil, *Les Bambara*, p. 287 ff.

44 *Ibid.*, p. 158.

45 *Ibid.*, p. 161 ff.

regarded by society as degrading, they fell into the category termed *nyama-ka-la (gens de caste)*, and because of their inferior rank were relegated to the fringe of society. Despite the fact that they remained technically 'free', gens de caste were in practice placed under the tutelage of non-caste peoples. Although they were usually to be distinguished by their occupation, it is clear that their caste was affirmed by their loss of social standing rather than their occupation. Gens de caste tended to be blacksmiths (associated with certain magical practices); pottery workers (usually women); coppersmiths; leather workers; woodcarvers; and hunters. On a slightly higher scale were to be found the Bozo and Somono fishers and colporteurs. The lowest of the gens de caste were the *dyeli* or domestics, though some of these were not without distinction as keepers of family oral traditions. Gens de caste captured in battle ordinarily entered into a kind of client relationship with free persons, but were allowed to pursue their habitual modes of occupation.[46]

The third important class of people to be found in each unit were the slaves. These people were excluded from membership in the community. Some individuals seemed to fall into this classification by birth, others by virtue of their activity in war, failure to clear debts, or commission of certain crimes. In rare cases, slaves could purchase their freedom, but during the reign of Biton Kouloubali it would appear that many free men of low status actually sought to sell themselves into slavery. Slaves were not precluded from owning other slaves.[47] If passage into slavery status and eventual emancipation did not preclude re-entry into the community, removal of the stigma of slavery was a virtual impossibility even for those who rose to the highest stations of society.[48]

The last distinguishable category of persons were those in some sort of tributary relationship *vis à vis* the community or clan. Tributaries were normally sedentary peoples—traders or cultivators—who either purchased protection from stronger nomadic groups (notably various Berber factions) or had it forced upon them, as was the case with the Fulbe who came to predominate over certain Mande-peoples in Segu and Baiko. Gens de caste could also be said to have been in client or tribute relationship to various groups of free people.

The administration of community and clan units rested in the hands of a custodian who sought advice and consent from an assembly of elders. Certain duties devolved upon the custodian and reciprocal duties were incumbent on ordinary members of the unit. He was under obligation to ensure that goods were distributed equitably; he might obtain the bride-

46 *Ibid.*, pp. 24 and 221. Pageard, 'Notes sur les Somonos', claims that the view that the Somonos are *gens de caste* is a mistaken one. He himself refers to them as a 'professional community', p. 17.
47 Monteil, *Les Bambara*, p. 190.
48 *Ibid.*, p. 221.

price for a youth without means; he was also required to ransom members who had fallen into slavery and acquit the debts incurred by members acting on behalf of the community. In return for these services, members were required to contribute their labour towards the general welfare of the communal or clan unit. If they were physically unable to work, they were required to send a son or slave in substitution. Citizens laboured five days a week for community benefit and two days for their own profit. Wealthy and influential members were expected to direct and control the work; free people of penurial status might very well find themselves working much harder than certain classes of slaves. It was not unknown for affluent communities to employ an entire force of slaves to cultivate their territorial units.[49] The wealth of the patrimony (for example gold, beasts, cereals, agricultural products, industrial and commercial goods) was, at least theoretically, equally shared by all members. Property and even habitations belonged to the communal unit, and individual landownership was non-existent.[50]

All this is indicative of a fairly fluid and loosely stratified society—a society with specified classes of citizens and non-citizens, yet one which allowed for a considerable degree of social mobility for those with and without caste—even for those with and without freedom. Indeed the meteoric rise to power of Biton Mamari Kouloubali, the son of a relatively poor cultivator, affirmed the underlying, though admittedly qualified, egalitarianism of this Bambara-dominated social system.

Biton Mamari Kouloubali and the emergence of Segu

It would seem implicit in the oral traditions available for the period before 1712 that the Kouloubali family lost whatever prestige it held during the reign of Kaladian (1652–82). Since its influence after 1682 seems to have been restricted to only a few villages, the power and authority of Souma Kouloubali would appear to have been no more than a mere shadow of that possessed by Kaladian. In the region of Segu the Marka, and especially the Boirey family, had apparently recouped most of the political power usurped by the Bambara-Massassi. Nevertheless, there remained a good deal of cooperation between the two groups. Before 1712 Marka traders and Bambara cultivators were often to be found in the same dugu—each ton presumably fulfilling the needs of the other. The relationship, however, seems to have become considerably strained as the Marka Muslims considered themselves culturally superior to the Bambara animists. Moreover conflicts were intensified by the wealth of the Marka—totally disproportionate to their relatively small numbers, and contrasting sharply with the comparatively impoverished state of the Bambara majority.[51]

49 *Ibid.*, p. 185 ff.
50 *Ibid.*, p. 187.
51 *Ibid.*, pp. 29 and 289.

That the raids of Souma were perhaps not as successful as some chronicles would suggest is further evident from the unquestionably reduced status of his immediate progeny. His son, Fa Sine, had three children, and it is said that the marriage of Fa Sine's daughter to a wealthy and powerful leader of Dina 'brought a certain notoriety to the family'.[52] Furthermore, Fa Sine's son, Mamari Kouloubali, is described in the traditions as the son of a poor cultivator and a pious Marka Muslim woman.[53] Mamari, at the appropriate age, affiliated himself with a Bambara-Marka youth association composed of 'lesser worthies' (primarily Bambara engaged in cultivation). This age group was separate from another youth association comprising the sons of what is called the aristocracy of the ton. Almost constant friction existed between the Bambara and some of the Marka members of the age group. The traditions assert that Mamari distinguished himself among his peers through his bravery and expertise in occultism, to such an extent that he was elected leader of the association. Yet his election seems to have alienated a significant faction of the Marka youth which was reluctant to accept his leadership, even to the point of allying themselves with the Mande of Kong (*c.* 1725).[54] The perpetual feuding and intrigue between the two groups came to the notice of the clan elders, who sought to ameliorate the situation by splitting the association into two youth groups—one Bambara, led by Mamari, and one Marka.[55]

Mamari's age group subsisted on hunting and raiding expeditions, which attracted the displeasure of the elders, who repeatedly reprimanded the youths for their indiscipline and illicit behaviour. Instead of defending himself and his followers, Mamari opted to disentangle the age group from the elders' supervision, establishing himself in an independent residence. Once free from the elders' authority, the association renewed its pillaging activities, and a considerable amount of booty accrued to its treasury.[56] Supported by these funds, Mamari set about increasing the numerical strength of the association by purchasing men who had fallen into captivity. When a fine was imposed on a criminal unable to satisfy his obligations, Mamari advanced the amount on condition that the man become his personal slave. If a man was condemned to death, Mamari purchased his pardon on the same condition. Similarly, if one of the group failed to contribute taxes levied upon him by its members, Mamari contributed the sum in return for the man's enslavement; if the man was aged, he was allowed to substitute a son in his place. Others, fleeing the persecution of superiors, voluntarily sold their freedom to Mamari. All these newly

52 *Ibid.*, p. 28.
53 Cf. Pageard, 'Notes sur l'histoire de Bambara de Ségou', and 'La marche orientale du Mali (Ségou-Djénné) en 1644 d'après le *Tarikh es-Soudan*', *J. Soc. Afr.*, xxxi, 1, 1961, pp. 75–90, especially p. 89.
54 Cf. Tauxier, *Histoire des Bambara*, p. 72 and Monteil, *Les Bambara*, pp. 28 ff and p. 293.
55 Monteil, *Les Bambara*, pp. 30 and 293.
56 *Ibid.*, p. 293.

acquired slaves agreed to work only for the age group association, taking the name *ton-dyon*—that is 'slaves of the ton'. Members of the association, called *ton-den* (affiliates of the ton), though distinguished from these slaves (who could never aspire to ton membership), also agreed to labour exclusively on behalf of the ton, usually in the cultivation of millet fields.[57]

The growing wealth of Mamari's association led to a deterioration of relations with the Marka, who saw their once unassailed position deteriorating. Several attempts to reunite the two groups ended in failure. Finally, in an open conflict, Mamari decisively defeated the Marka at their capital Kirango[58] (1740). Encouraged by this victory, Mamari next summoned to his capital the leaders of the various clans whom he invited as personal advisers. The leaders, however, appeared more insulted than enticed by this invitation, rejecting it out of hand. At this point, Mamari must have perceived the necessity for ridding himself of such obstinate obstructors of his ambitious schemes—he had them all murdered.

Mamari was now in complete control of his own affairs. Unchallenged and uninhibited, he turned on the only remaining free men of his community, the ton-den. He issued an edict forcing them to don the raiment of the ton-dyon; thus in one act of emasculation, he had revolutionised the character of the clan members. From the status of free men with recognised rights and privileges they were transformed into the personal slaves of an absolute dictator.

Mamari Kouloubali next set about the augmentation and expansion of his newly constituted community. He persuaded his allies to turn over their armed warriors, whom he incorporated among the ton-dyon.[59] Somono fishers and colporteurs, as well as various groups of pastoralists, were given some sort of associate though subservient status with respect to the clan. Mamari realised the potential wealth to the community which could accrue from exploitation of the Niger banks, then under Somono control. He effected a kind of hegemony over the Somono, who were experts in the transportation of goods and people along the Niger. The Somono were further required to contribute a tax in kind in the form of dried fish, but they were not disturbed in their traditional observances.[60] In return, they were protected by the clan, and their leaders often benefited from the largesse bestowed on them by Mamari and his successors. Sometimes they reaped a not inconsiderable share of the distributions of booty. They were sent a sizeable contingent of slaves from the clan, whom they trained in fishing and in the construction of rivercraft. These slaves were well treated, but in exchange for their relatively privileged status they were compelled to pay tax in cowries; to contribute a contingent to the clan army; and to

57 Cf. Tauxier, *Histoire des Bambara*, p. 77, and Monteil, *Les Bambara*, p. 294.
58 Tauxier, *Histoire des Bambara*, p. 77.
59 Monteil, *Les Bambara*, p. 297.
60 *Ibid.*, p. 323.

construct and maintain the walls of fortified villages. They were also employed as clan couriers and as conveyors of military personnel over the Niger. But the greatest benefit which the Somono derived from their alliance with the Bambara was an uncontested and protected monopoly of Niger fishing and transportation. Indeed many of them grew wealthy from porterage transport taxes which Mamari allowed them to retain. The Somono, despite their enviable economic position, remained a caste apart. Yet scores of individuals of diverse origins saw the obvious advantages of attaching themselves to various Somono groups. Some of the slaves sent by Mamari did so with his permission, and their offspring became Somono by right of birth.[61]

The successors of Biton Mamari Kouloubali, 1755–1808

The death of Biton Mamari Kouloubali in 1755 marked the end of an era. He had transformed the modest legacy of his predecessors into a powerful edifice solid in its foundations, but much too dependent on the skilful manipulations of one man. His less fortunate successors were unable to rule absolutely or wisely, and fell victim to his most significant creation—the corps d'élite of ton-dyon. Dekoro (1755–7) had his brief but turbulent reign terminated by assassination provoked by his incalculable cruelties.[62] The reign of his brother, Bakari, was still shorter (fifteen days) but perhaps more interesting. Converted to Islam, and educated at Timbuctū under the renowned Mukhtār al-Kuntī, ʿAlī, as he is sometimes called, demonstrated considerable valour, but little wisdom in what proved a premature introduction of an uncompromising variety of Islam. He quickly incurred the displeasure of the ton-dyon who violently objected to his insistence on abstinence from fermented drinks and eradication of pagan superstitions. He too met with assassination at the hands of the ton-dyon, as indeed did practically the entire Kouloubali family. This act signalled the resurgence of the ton-dyon as the dominating political force in Segu.[63]

For most of the ensuing decade (1757–67), Segu struggled to regain the equilibrium which obtained under Mamari Kouloubali. This period of ton-dyon rule initiated by the Diara family who replaced the Kouloubali, was characterised by internal struggles in which powerful warriors unsuccessfully attempted to establish themselves over the community. All three military leaders who reigned between 1757 and 1766 were assassinated.[64] In 1766 Ngolo Diara's assumption of power began a new era of relative stability.

61 *Ibid.*, p. 324.

62 Tauxier, *Histoire des Bambara*, p. 80.

63 *Ibid.*, pp. 82–3. There is some disagreement among authorities as to whether ʿAlī (Bakari) or Dekoro succeeded Biton Mamari Koloubali. Cf. Pageard, 'Une tradition musulmane relative à l'histoire de Ségou', p. 25; and P. Marty, ed., 'Les chroniques de Oualata et de Nema', *Revue des Etudes Islamiques*, 1927, iii et iv, p. 569.

64 Tauxier, *Histoire des Bambara*, pp. 84–8.

By the time of his death in 1790 Ngolo Diara had firmly entrenched the Diara dynasty as the hereditary rulers of the Segu state. The succession fell to his son, Mansong (1790–1808), notwithstanding a prolonged period of internecine struggle. Mansong's notable achievement was the extension of Segu control over the Massassis of Kaarta, who had supported his brother's claim to the succession. By the end of his reign, the Segu state had reached its greatest territorial extent. Nearly all the large communities to its immediate west—Dedougou, Kaarta, Beledougou and Fouladougou—capitulated before an unrelenting assault.[65]

After the death of Mamari Kouloubali (1755), Bambara clan organisation underwent several important revisions, some of which have already been noted. The assassination of Mamari's son, Dekoro, had ended the evolution of absolute power in the hands of Mamari's progeny. Indeed the rebellion against Dekoro was as much a reaction against the kind of absolute power usurped by Mamari as it was a revolt against the severe injustices of Dekoro himself. The assassination made possible a return to the essential egalitarianism of the community.

The Massassis and the emergence of Kaarta

North of Segu, in the Marka inhabited savannah region of northern Beledougou, the Kouloubali-Massassi sustained a small settlement of warrior-cultivators. From *c.* 1600 until 1754, the community enjoyed a relative prosperity derived from booty and slaves apprehended at the expense of less-powerful neighbours. In 1753 the Massassis entered into a disastrous altercation with Biton Mamari Kouloubali of Segu, the details of which have become distorted by myth and legend. Whatever the nature of the dispute, its outcome unmistakably led to the dislodgement, and indeed near extinction, of the Massassis in Beledougou. The surviving members of the Massassis clan moved farther westward, finding a not inhospitable reception among the Diawara branch of Mande who resided in the region of Kaarta.[66]

It would appear that between 1754 and 1777 Massassi and Diawara lived in comparative amicability. Towards the end of this period however, traditions speak of an increasing intervention of the Massassis in the internal affairs of their Diawara neighbours. These intrusions, at least initially, were not unsolicited.[67]

Indeed by the reign of Sira Bo (1761–88), it had become quite clear that the pattern of relationships which had evolved between Massassi and Diawara was one of protector and client. Massassi power had become considerably augmented in the intervening years between their defeat at the hands of Biton Mamari and the succession of Sira Bo. His predecessor,

65 *Ibid.*, p. 98.
66 Cf. Tauxier, *Histoire des Bambara*, p. 112, and Monteil, *Les Bambara*, p. 104 ff.
67 Tauxier, *Histoire des Bambara*, p. 125; cf. Raffenel, *Nouveau Voyage*, i, p. 425.

Desse Babo (1758–61), is said to have seized three hundred villages in Bakhunou, Benko and Bambuk. Tradition says that Desse Babo abandoned the traditional sedentary mode of existence in favour of the nomadic life based on pillaging. The Massassi at this time had no permanent capital. They depended on supplies captured from conquered villages, which they successively occupied; when supplies became exhausted, they moved on to still another village where the pattern was repeated.[68] Hence the establishment by Sira Bo of a capital at Guemou, south-west of Nioro, marked a new departure in the evolution of Massassi society. It was Sira Bo as well who was responsible for transforming the protector-client relationship (which had for so long obtained between Massassi and Marka) into one of overlord and tributary. The continued Marka dependence on Massassi military power was soon proved counterproductive. The expulsion of the Dabora faction in 1777, after a prolonged period of quarrels with the Sagone faction, accomplished with the assistance of the Massassi, elevated the latter to an unchallenged position of supremacy. The Diawara were required to pay the Massassi tribute, though the amount involved is said to have been no more than that required of free men, and the military contingent with which they were to supply the Massassi was said to be the only real restriction on their collective liberty. The Diawara were given the northern province of Kaarta, where they maintained a precarious existence between the Massassi to their west and the Awlad Mbarak Arabs to their east.[69]

During the reign of Desse Koro (1788–99), the Kaarta Massassi sought to capitalise upon the reigning chaos in Segu which followed closely upon the death of Ngolo Diara. In 1792 they razed Nyamina to the ground. Four years later, however, a revitalised Segu under the firm leadership of Mansong retaliated by destroying Guemou, the long-standing capital of Kaarta, and by recapturing nearly all the territory conquered by Sira Bo. The fall of Kaarta had two important consequences. It released the Diawara from Massassi domination, but had the effect of placing them at the mercy of the Awlad Mbarak, their former protectors and adversaries. Hence the Diawara were forced to shift their tributary relationship to these Arabs, who agreed to protect them against the Massassi.[70]

Although the Massassi had been severely weakened by the attacks of Segu, they were able to regain some of their lost power by seizing 2,500 slaves owned by Dyula merchants who passed through their new capital at Dioka.[71] With this added strength they were able to reconstitute under their suzerainty much of the territory seized by Sira Bo. But rather than risk further confrontations against the Diawara and their Arab protectors,

68 Tauxier, *Histoire des Bambara*, p. 121.
69 *Ibid.*, p. 126. For Sira Bo, see pp. 124 ff.
70 *Ibid.*, p. 127, 129.
71 *Ibid.*, p. 128.

they redirected their energies westwards toward the Khasso, where they achieved some sort of political predominance. Thus it was not until the beginning of the nineteenth century that the Massassi of Kaarta were able to approximate the military strength and political influence wielded by their ethnic counterparts in Segu.[72]

The Central Niger Delta: Fulbe communities in Massina

The eastern confines of Massina from the fifteenth century onwards became a focal point of Fulbe settlement and rediffusion. Bozo fishers, Mande cultivator-traders (Zaghrana),[73] and Berber nomads had preceded the Fulbe as inhabitants of Massina. Semi-nomadic Fulbe pastoralists from Fittaja came to settle among these predominantly sedentary peoples at the beginning of the fifteenth century. They brought with them their herds of cattle and sheep, as well as serfs (largely the product of Fulbe fathers and Negroid mothers),[74] whom they employed in various servile occupations. The more intelligent and ambitious of these *hommes de caste* gained places of distinction in the community as affluent cattle-merchants or as counsellors to important personages. Others of these *diavambe*, as they were called, acted as intermediaries, emissaries, and functionaries to all social groups separated by traditional conventions.[75] Next in order of importance were the *rimaibe* or cultivators. Many of them were to obtain an elevation in status by virtue of their exemption from agricultural labour, which they turned over to offspring who replaced them in the fields.[76] Other rimaibe were able to obtain this exemption by payment of an agreed amount. Such persons were placed under the

72 *Ibid.*, p. 67.
73 Tauxier, *Moeurs et Histoire des Peuls*, Paris, 1937, p. 157. There is no satisfactory monograph on Massina for this period. A substantial amount of unpublished material can be found in the Bibliothèque Nationale, Paris, and the Institut Fondamental d'Afrique Noire, Dakar. Cf. Georges Vajda, *Index Général des Manuscrits Arabes Musulmans de la Bibliothèque National de Paris*, Paris, 1953; E. Blochet, *Catalogue des Manuscrits Arabes des Nouvelles Acquisitions* (1884–1924), Paris, 1925; and T. Diallo, Mame Bara M'Backe, Mirjana Trikovic, and Boubacar Barry, *Catalogue des Manuscrits de l'I.F.A.N.*, Dakar, I.F.A.N., Catalogues et Documents no. xx, 1966 (see especially Fonds Vieillard, Masina; Fonds Gaden, Masina; and Fonds Brévié, Masina). The Institut de France holdings are very poorly and misleadingly catalogued, but cf. J. O. Hunwick and H. Gwarzo, 'Another look at the de Gironcourt papers', *Centre of Arabic Documentation Research Bulletin*, iii, no. 2, 1967, pp. 74–100; and H. F. C. Smith, 'Source material for the history of the Western Sudan', *J.H.S.N.*, i, no. 3, 1958, pp. 238–48; D. P. de Pedrals, *L'Archaeologie de l'Afrique noire*, Paris, 1950, pp. 69–74; de Gironcourt, 'Répertoire des manuscripts rapportés du Soudan par la mission de Gironcourt', *Missions de Gironcourt en Afrique Occidentale, 1908–1909, 1911–1912*, Paris, 1920, pp. 358–69; M. Bouteron, and A. Tremblot, *Catalogue générale des manuscripts des Bibliothèques publiques de France: Bibliothèque de l'Institut ancien et nouveau fonds*, Paris, 1928.
74 Tauxier, *Moeurs et Histoire des Peuls*, p. 143.
75 *Ibid.*, p. 140. See also Fonds Vieillard, Masina, *Documents historiques*, cahier no. 2, 'Notes sur la nation peule au Masina', texte français 28 f, and Pageard, 'Notes sur les Diawambé ou Diakoramé', p. 252.
76 Monteil, *Djénné*, p. 55.

protection of a patron to whom they became allies. Further down the hierarchy of this caste system were to be found still other gens de caste, not unlike those described in Segu: butchers, blacksmiths, jewellers, wood-workers (or joiners—often regarded as magicians),[77] leather-workers, tanners, weavers, and cobblers.[78] These caste groups rarely formed separate villages, though groups of griots existed at Guyey and communities of courtiers long inhabited Sokoura. They were normally assimilated into Fulbe communities distinguished largely by their trade and perhaps their ethnic origin.

During this early period of settlement, the Fulbe seem to have been divided into several independent clans, each under the direction of a camp master or *ardo*.[79] Tradition recounts that the Diallo clan was the first Fulbe group to settle in Massina. The Diallo ardo and his followers are said to have received investiture from the representatives of the ruler of Mali, who resided in Bagana, but later came within the Songhay sphere of influence.[80] Fulbe existence was characteristically transhumant. When beasts and people became sufficiently numerous, offshoots occurred and secondary groups of Fulbe emerged, each with its own camp master. Each clan contained a segment of warriors or ardo which constituted itself as a kind of ruling aristocracy.[81] In a subsequent period another Fulbe group, the Bari clan, joined the Diallo, bringing with them a considerable number of gens de caste, particularly diavambe.[82]

The Mande society of Massina into which these Fulbe groups incorporated themselves was apparently structurally quite similar to that which obtained in Segu and Kaarta. Besides Marka and Bozo peoples, groups of Tuareg and Berbers came to reside in Massina, each with its own slaves; each depending on a traditional livelihood rooted in the breeding of she-camels and goats; and on caravan trafficking, pillaging and extortion.[83] Again, not dissimilar to that pattern of relationships which evolved elsewhere in the Upper and Middle Niger regions, these nomadic and semi-nomadic groups of Berber, Tuareg, and Fulbe effected alliances with various sedentary groups of Mande-speaking peoples with whom they often fell into conflict. Although the Fulbe do not appear to have exercised any tight political control over these various Mande-speaking groups, that is with the exception of those serfs which they obtained by various means and assimiliated into their society, they did constitute by the end of the sixteenth century the most important single ethnic group.

The Fulbe communities struggled to maintain an autonomy with

77 Tauxier, *Moeurs*, p. 140.
78 *Ibid.*, p. 9, and Fonds Vieillard, Masina, *Documents historiques*, cahier no. 2.
79 Fonds Vieillard, Masina, *Documents historiques*, cahier no. 2.
80 Tauxier, *Moeurs*, pp. 69 and 157.
81 Fonds Vieillard, Masina, *Documents historiques*, cahier no. 2.
82 Tauxier, *Moeurs*, p. 69.
83 Fonds Vieillard, Masina, *Documents historiques*, cahier no. 2.

respect to the more powerful states which encircled them. They fell intermittently under the political influence of Mali, Songhay, the Ruma of Timbuctū, and Segu (*c.* 1750). After 1750, much of northern Massina became subjected to Tuareg domination.[84] The pressure of a rather precarious existence within the shadow of these greater powers seems to have given added impetus to the continuing Fulbe diaspora. A massive rediffusion occurred in *c.* 1675 as Fulbe migrated from Massina to Futa Jallon. In the eighteenth century Fulbe groups left Massina in order to settle in the Mossi hinterland.[85] In the beginning of the nineteenth century numerous groups of Fulbe settled in the region of Ansongo, where they found suitable land for pasturing their large herds.[86] Yet despite these external pressures, the Fulbe communities of Massina survived and indeed continued to grow and prosper, though the crystallisation of their state formation would have to await the appearance of Seku Aḥmadu, who in the first decade of the nineteenth century succeeded for the first time in unifying the Massinankobé.

THE MIDDLE NIGER 1737–1811, THE ERA OF TUAREG DOMINATION

Berber and Arab settlements in the Middle Niger

The fertile banks of the Middle Niger presented an unending attraction to nomadic Berber and Tuareg groups driven from desiccated homelands or uprooted by political disorders.[87]

The period 1600 to 1800 was one of active Tuareg dispersion along both banks of the Niger. The ancient Adrar massif of the southern Sahara gave birth to two large and closely associated confederations—one dominated by the Kel Tadmakka, and the other by the Aulimadan. Other Tuareg groups to be found along the Niger between Timbuctū and Bourem were

84 Tauxier, *Moeurs*, p. 162.

85 *Ibid.*, pp. 15 and 281.

86 Richer, *Les Oulliminden*, p. 98.

87 F. de la Chapelle, 'Esquisse d'une histoire du sahara occidental', *Hespéris*, xi, 1930, pp. 35–95, esp. p. 84. The most useful monograph for Tuareg activities in the Middle Niger is Richer's *Les Oulliminden*, but the following should also be consulted: P. Marty, *Tribus*; A. G. P. Martin, *Les Oases Sahariennes*, Paris, 1908; and *Quatre Siècles d'Histoire marocaine*, Paris, 1923 (the first volume covers the period to 1504, and the second concerns the Sahara, 1504–1902, and Morocco, 1894–1912); P. de La Martinière, and N. La Croix, *Documents pour servir à l'étude du nord-ouest Africain*, 5 vols, Gouvernement Général de l'Algérie, service des Affaires indigènes, 1897; P. Marty (ed. and trans.), 'Les chroniques de Oualata et de Nema (Soudan Français)'. *Révue des Etudes Islamiques*, iii et iv, 1927, pp. 355–575; Maurice Cortier, *D'Une rive à l'autre du Sahara*, Paris, 1908; Ismael Hamet, 'Les Kounta', *Revue du Monde Musulman*, xv, 1911, pp. 302–18 (cf. Maurice Cortier, *Mission Cortier 1908, 1909–1910*, p. 263 for translation of a 'Tarikh Kounta' by Hamet); Ismael Hamet, 'Littérature Arabe Saharienne', *Révue du Monde Musulman*, xii, 1910, pp. 194–213, and pp. 380–405 (these two articles contain a summary of the *Kitāb al-ṭarā'if wa'-l-Talā'id bi-Karamāt al-shaykhayn al-wālida wa-wālid*, which constitutes a key source for the biography of Sīdī al-Mukhtār al-Kuntī as written by his son Muḥammad); Ismael Hamet, *Chroniques de la Mauritanie Sénégalaise*, Paris, 1911. H. T. Norris, 'Sanhaja Scholars of Timbuctu', *B.S.O.A.S.*, xxx, 3, 1967, pp. 634–41.

the Idnanes, Immadadran, and the Ouadalen, all of whom after the fall of Gao were forced into some sort of tributary relationship with the Ruma who invested their leaders in office. East of Gao (in Agadès) the Kel Aïr organised another strong Tuareg confederation—but one with an increasingly southerly orientation after the fall of Gao. Indeed the conquest of the Middle Niger in 1591 marked the nascence of Berber ethnic consciousness. Once released from Songhay control, Berbers and Tuareg began to appreciate the strength of their own numbers and perceived the advantages of large-scale organisations.[88]

In 1653 a dispute erupted between Tadmakka and Aulimadan over the nature of the confederation's leadership. The severity of the disagreement was such that the Tadmakka were forced out of the Adrar. They gravitated toward the right bank of the Niger, where they successfully sought permission to settle from the Ruma representative. With an authority uncontested in the Adrar, the Aulimadan easily subjected the remaining Tuareg groups to their leadership.[89]

The Aulimaden and their allies were not unnaturally attracted by the richly appointed Ruma garrisons at Gao and Bamba. Situated within convenient striking distance of these fortresses, they initiated a series of pillaging raids, each of which terminated in swift retirement to a natural protection afforded by the Adrar massif. These raids also seem to have given encouragement to certain independent Tuareg groups in the Gao-Bamba area.[90] From 1650 to 1655 a series of revolts against Ruma authority emanated from these sources. By 1680 what had begun as a menace to the area's stability had developed into a direct threat to continued Ruma control. Aided by these dissident and sympathetic clansmen, who must have constituted something of a 'fifth column', the Aulimadan struck heavily upon Gao and wrested control from the Ruma. They controlled the region for eight years, once again relinquishing it to the Makhzan in 1688.

The recapture of Gao forced the Aulimadan to rethink their relationship with the Ruma. From a policy of wilful obstruction and permanent hostility they turned to one of peaceful coexistence. It was no accident that this change of tactics coincided with an equally significant shift of residence. Confronted with an ever-encroaching desert, in 1690 the Aulimadan abandoned the Adrar and moved southwards, progressively installing themselves along the river to the east of Gao. But to the Songhay peoples among whom they resided the Aulimadan settlement was an unwelcome intrusion. These sedentary cultivators had an inherent fear of nomadic peoples, acquired after years of exploitation, and their fears of the Aulimadan were justified. Upon their installation in the Niger region, the

88 Richer, *Les Oulliminden*, p. 70.
89 *Ibid.*, p. 73.
90 *Ibid.*, p. 81.

Aulimadan wasted little time in seeking official Ruma approval for this action. In doing so, they voluntarily accepted a kind of nominal suzerainty of the Ruma bāshās of Timbuctū. Their shrewd and cautious leader, Kari Denna, received investiture at the hands of Bāshā Ḥamad b. ʿAlī, an act which, after the Moroccan conquest of Timbuctū, had actually been imposed on other Tuareg leaders. The custom was voluntarily conserved by Kari Denna's successors, whose installations were sanctioned by Ruma bāshās in 1715 and 1741.[91]

Yet bv lending official sanction to the Aulimadan installation, the Ruma unwittingly appeared to support Tuareg acts of brigandage against weaker Songhay populations. Indeed they forfeited effective control of the Niger's left bank (from Ansongo to Bamba), and were unable to forestall extension of Aulimadan influence to the confines of Timbuctū itself. Indirectly assisted by internal weaknesses of the Makhzan, the Aulimadan experienced little difficulty in reasserting their former dominance over lesser Tuareg groups in the area. But they seemed content to arrest their expansion before the gates of Timbuctū.[92]

If the Ruma had achieved a precarious *modus vivendi* with the Aulimadan —albeit at Songhay expense, and to a large extent their own—they had failed to contain the Tadmakka. As a result of the tactical errors they committed by involving Tuareg mercenaries in their internal difficulties, the Ruma had initiated the crystallisation of Tuareg power in the Middle Niger. The folly of their policy plunged them into an insoluble dilemma. They were apparently incapable of perceiving the incongruities and dangers of a policy which on the one hand sought to diminish their adversaries, and on the other to employ them as allies. The Aulimadan restrained themselves for the moment, but the Tadmakka proceeded to inflict a resounding defeat upon the Ruma in 1737, an act which ushered in the era of Tuareg domination over the Middle Niger.[93]

Al-Mukhtār al-Kuntī and the realignment of powers in the Middle Niger

The eclipse of the Ruma had left the Middle Niger virtually in control of two powerful Tuareg confederations. The Tadmakka had slowly regained strength after their expulsion from the Adrar. They forged a confederation of considerable power among the Iguadaran, a section of Immadadran, and a group of Igallad residing in the region west of Timbuctū. They seemed destined to inherit the commanding rôle relinquished by the Ruma —that is, until the death of their brilliant leader, Oghmor, in 1755.[94] The passing of Oghmor plunged the Tadmakka into serious internal disputes and brought about a crisis within the confederation from which they never

91 *Ibid.*, p. 82.
92 *Ibid.*, p. 83.
93 *Ibid.*, p. 89; cf. al-Wafrānī, *Tadhkirat*, trans., p. 181.
94 Richer, *Les Oulliminden*, p. 91.

fully recovered. At the same time as the Tadmakka were experiencing succession difficulties, two other Berber groups, the Aulimadan and the Kunta, were in the beginning stages of an alliance which was to place the Tadmakka alongside the Ruma as a minor political force in the region.

Before *c.* 1770 the Kunta exercised no major influence in the political life of the Middle Niger. Relative newcomers, they were considered a group of only secondary political significance, as their efforts were largely confined to commercial and religious activities. They were most active in the Azawad area, where in 1720 they established at Mabruk a small fortified village, 150 kilometres north of the Niger.[95] From this base they launched an unprecedented programme of religious proselytisation which had a revolutionary impact on both the Middle and Upper Niger regions. This activity, which had its political aspect, seems largely due to the efforts of one man, Sīdī al-Mukhtār b. Aḥmad b. Abī Bakr al-Kuntī.

The Kunta were primarily a *zawāyā* group—that is, they had renounced the use of arms and the pillaging activities which characterised the life of so many other Berber groups. Unlike most zawāyā (who would seem to have sacrificed a good deal of political autonomy in return for their dependence upon a protector), the Kunta managed to achieve parity with their various protectors, and indeed by clever diplomacy gained the upper hand spiritually and politically. This outstanding achievement was by no means easily attained. For years the Kunta had been geographically divided into two feuding religious groups—one occupying the west (Hawd) and the other the east (Azawad). A split took place after the death of the Qādirī shaykh, Sīdī ʿUmar al-Shaykh (*c.* 1460–1552/3), a contemporary and disciple of Muḥammad b. ʿAbd al-Karīm al-Maghīlī.

The task of reuniting these disparate Qādirī factions under one spiritual leadership was skilfully accomplished by Sīdī al-Mukhtār.[96] It was at the helm of a united Kunta, and as the religious master of a powerful brotherhood, that he appears to have brought about a complete realignment of political relationships in the Middle Niger.

Al-Mukhtār al-Kuntī's diverse diplomatic activities involved the safeguarding of Kunta commercial interests, the preservation of their political autonomy, and above all the expansion of Kunta religious influence over Arabs, Berbers and Sudanis of the Western Sudan. His chief political rôle was that of a peacemaker—a supreme arbiter in the endless feuds between groups and subgroups. One of his first diplomatic achievements

95 *Ibid.*, p. 92.
96 Hamet, 'Littérature Arabe', p. 209; cf. Marty, *Tribus* i, p. 136. Marty's material on Sīdī al-Mukhtar is based on the *Kitāb al-ṭarāʾ if,* and the *Fatḥ al-Shakūr fī maʿrifat aʿyān ʿulamāʾ al-Takrūr,* by Muḥammad ʿAbd Allāh b. Abī Bakr al-Bartilī (cf. Smith, 'Source materials', p. 244; and J. O. Hunwick, 'A new source for the biography of Aḥmad Bābā al-Tinbuktī (1556–1627)', *B.S.O.A.S.*, xxvii, no. 3, 1964, pp. 568–93, p. 19. An index to the *Fatḥ al-Shakūr* has been published in the *Centre of Arabic Documentation Bulletin*, i, no. 1, 1964).

was to bring about a cessation of hostilities between the Kunta and the Kel-Hoggar.[97] He is said to have negotiated successfully all disputes which broke out between Kunta and Barabish during the second half of the eighteenth century. This alliance with the Barabish safeguarded Kunta commercial interests, which had been threatened by the pillaging activities of the Awlad Mulad.

Sīdī al-Mukhtār appears also to have maintained reasonably good relations with the leaders of Walata and the nomadic Berber groups of the Saharan west. These groups eagerly sought out his *baraka* (religious blessing) through which he seems to have exercised considerable religious influence.[98]

Al-Mukhtār al-Kuntī's relationship with the stronger powers—Aulimadan, Tadmakka, and Ruma—though notably strained at first, rapidly improved as he gained a certain respect and proved himself an indispensable and impartial mediator to whom all could turn with relative confidence. But his impartiality would appear to have stemmed from arrogance and feelings of intellectual and moral superiority when confronted with these lesser worthies who to him appeared unfit to rule, much less to lead.[99]

But Sīdī al-Mukhtār was able to apply some degree of restraint to the expanding authority of Tuareg, and especially to the Aulimadan, with whom he became allied. He became the chief religious adviser to the Aulimadan *amenokal* (sovereign) and to the Tadmakka as well.[100] If he failed to check the rapid development of Tuareg power in the Middle Niger, by virtue of his mediating and religious rôle he seems to have been instrumental in establishing a *modus vivendi* between Ruma and Tadmakka, and between Tadmakka and Aulimadan. By 1770 the Aulimadan were firmly entrenched at Gao; in 1787 they imposed a heavy indemnity upon the Ruma of Timbuctū.[101] From this period onwards their power spread throughout the region from Timbuctū to Tillabery, gaining varying degrees of ascendancy over all Songhay and Tuareg peoples in the process.[102] At the beginning of the nineteenth century the Aulimadan and their Tuareg allies had eclipsed the authority of the Ruma, but at the same time had allowed themselves to become subjected to the religious authority of the Kunta. Yet with the initiation of Seku Aḥmadu's revivalist movement in the first quarter of the century, Kunta religious authority would become reinforced at the same time that the political power of the Tuareg would begin to give way to that of the Fulbe of Massina.

97 Marty, *Tribus*, i, p. 42.
98 *Ibid.*, p. 54.
99 Hamet, 'Littérature Arabe', p. 386.
100 Marty, *Tribus*, i, pp. 43 and 53; cf. Hamet, 'Littérature Arabe', p. 381.
101 Richer, *Les Oulliminden*, p. 96.
102 Martin, *Quatre Siècles*, p. 55.

THE EXPANSION OF ISLAM IN THE WESTERN SUDAN[103]

Islamic diffusion in the Upper and Middle Niger

There is little evidence to support the contention that Islamic learning and diffusion underwent a marked decline in the Western Sudan during the period 1600 to 1800. Indeed this period—especially after 1750—witnessed a vigorous expansion of Islam into areas relatively untouched. Moreover, the diffusion of Islam and the development of Islamic learning must be looked upon as a continuous process.

It is possible to identify two major processes of Islamic diffusion. What might be called 'quietist' Islam spread largely through the work of the religious confraternities—notably the Qadiriyya. This essentially peaceful method of expansion also took place as a by-product of the commercial activities of Muslim traders.

The second major process of Islamic diffusion was generated by means of what might be called 'militant' Islam. In contrast to quietist Islam, militant Islam had conversion as its principal aim.[104] Traders and holy men (the leading cultivators of Islam by peaceful means) often had trade as their major objective, and were rarely willing to afford the disruptions risked by militant methods of diffusion—commerce thrives best in a peaceful environment. But during the period 1600 to 1800, militant Islam of the *jihādist* variety was not the dominant technique of Islamic propagation.

The Zawāyā and the expansion of Islam

From the fifteenth century onwards, out of the complex jigsaw of ethnic movements and conflicts, emerged a pattern of religious proselytisation which was to characterise the expansion of Islam for the next four centuries. In the western Sahara, with the influx of large numbers of nomadic Arab groups, a process of Arabisation was initiated. In the oases just north of the Middle Niger, the reverse process took place. Here Arab groups and factions came into contact with Berber groups, commencing a process of Berberisation. In both instances Berbers and Arabs respectively became culturally emasculated—in the western Sahara Berber groups adopted the language, customs, and institutions of their new conquerors; in the Middle Niger, Arabs became politically subjected to Berbers and Tuareg, settled amongst them, and adopted their manners and ways. Moreover Arabisation of Berbers led indirectly to their conversion to Islam. Significantly

103 There have been no thorough studies of the diffusion of Islam during the seventeenth and eighteenth centuries, but the most useful of older studies are: A. Le Chatelier, *L'Islam dans l'Afrique occidentale*, Paris, 1899; A. Quellien, *La Politique Musulmane dans l'Afrique Occidentale*, Paris, 1910; L. Binger, *Le Péril de l'Islam* (esp., p. 42 ff.); Monteil, *Bambara* (p. 336 ff.); Marty, *Tribus*; and Delafosse, *Haut-Sénégal-Niger*.

104 See John Ralph Willis, '*Jihād fi sabīl Allāh*—Its doctrinal basis in Islam and some aspects of its evolution in nineteenth-century West Africa', *J.A.H.*, viii, no. 3, 1967, pp. 395–415, esp. p. 398.

Berberisation of Arabs led also to the Islamisation of nearly all Berber communities in the Middle Niger.

In each case the main instruments of Islamic diffusion were the so-called zawāyā peoples. When the Arab Banū Hassan conquered the western Sahara, largely populated with Berbers of the Sanhaja confederation, they forbade the use of arms and reduced the Sanhaja to a servile status—indeed the term itself later became synonymous with servitude.[105] As if in compensation for their loss of political status, some of these Berber groups turned to purely religious pursuits—forging themselves into an Islamic clerisy which pitted the religious influence of Islam against the more worldly interests of the warrior peoples to whom they became attached. From the Mauritanian Adrar, the Banū Hassan nomadised towards the Sudanic fringe; and from the Hawd some of their number infiltrated the Azawad. It was undoubtedly at this time that they established among Berber peoples the social hierarchy which has persisted into modern times. At the summit were the 'warrior' descendants of the Banū Hassan; next in rank came the zawāyā, a clerisy of Sanhaja origin; then followed the non-zawāyā descendants of Sanhaja who were in varying degrees of tribute to the Banū Hassan. At the base of the hierarchy could be found the black-smiths of Jewish origin; and lastly, the *ḥarāṭin*—a sedentary people of mixed descent attached to the preceding groups.[106]

In the Middle Niger three zawāyā groups were particularly notable for their dominant rôles in the dissemination of Islam: the Kel al-Sūq, Kel Antassar, and the Kunta. The Kel al-Sūq (the clerisy wing of the Kel Tadmakka), before their displacement by the Kunta, appear to have been the traditional religious advisers and teachers of the Tadmakka and Aulimadan Tuareg.[107] They derived their name from their association with the region of Tadmakka—later called *al-Sūq* (the market)—because it was the only commercial centre in the central Sahara, and the meeting point of caravans from Tripoli and Tuwat en route to Gao. The centre was established by Muslim Berbers from Ifrīqiya who came to preach Islam and who belonged to the Islamic clerisy called *Iforhass*. Upon the conquest of Tadmakka by the Aulimadan, the Kel al-Sūq are said to have fled with other zawāyā groups and settled in the Adrar of the Iforhass where they continued their active proselytisation.[108]

The Kel Antassar belonged to the Igallad group of semi-nomads. Their traditions attempt to establish an Arab genealogy and an eastern origin.

105 'Sanhaja' and its variants (zanaja, znaga, zenaga, zanaga) all seem to have assumed the connotation of tributary, cf. J. Spencer Trimingham, *Islam in West Africa*, London, 1962, p. 136; Marty, *Tribus*, i, p. 15; H. Barth, *Travels and Discoveries in North and Central Africa*, 5 vols, London, 1855, v, p. 525; and Chapelle, 'Esquisse', p. 86.
106 Chapelle, 'Esquisse', p. 68.
107 Richer, *Les Oulliminden*, p. 10.
108 Cf. Delafosse, *Haut-Sénégal-Niger*, i, p. 194; 'Note presentée au Congres au nom de la Delegation Espagnole', *Hespéris*, xi, 1930, p. 28; and Richer, *Les Oulliminden*, p. 47.

They are said to have migrated from Fas to the Ahaggar (thirteenth century), and later to Bamba and Burem, finally settling in the Adrar region north of Timbuctū (*c.* 1550). Here they gradually became Berberised through contact with the Tuareg Idnanes.[109] At the beginning of the seventeenth century they had established several small encampments which became commercially prosperous. During this period their leader was a certain Muḥammad Quṭuba, to whom tradition credits the dramatic religious and constitutional transformation of the group structure. While defending the necessity to bear arms, Muḥammad Quṭuba commended the group to the pastoral life of sheep-raising, and whenever the situation allowed, to a life devoted to commerce, religious study, and prayer. Muḥammad Quṭuba is said to have been the first active cultivator of Islam in this region, and was responsible for the conversion of several Tuareg communities.[110] His immediate successors continued this dual concentration upon commerce and religious proselytisation. The Kel Antassar produced several eminent jurists, scholars, and holy men who were sought out by their politically stronger neighbours. They became the religious advisers of the Kel Tadmakka, and especially of the Tengueredief. When the need arose, they offered their spiritual services to these groups and provided them with charms and amulets upon demand.[111]

But like their sister zawāyā group, the Kel al-Sūq, the Kel Antassar were soon eclipsed commercially and religiously by the Kunta. The remarkable rise to ascendancy of this ethnic group witnessed the introduction of a new element in the diffusion of Islam in the Western Sudan—that of the religious confraternity (*ṭarīqa*). Neither the Kel al-Sūq nor the Kel Antassar[112] appear to have belonged to any ṭarīqa. Yet Kunta affiliation to the Qādiriyya ṭarīqa would seem to date from the fourteenth century. Zawāyā methods of religious proselytisation (which achieved maximum refinement with the Kunta) also appear to have markedly departed from those used by Maghribian cultivators of Islam. In the Maghrib Islamic diffusion issued principally from fixed religious centres. But Islamic diffusion in the Western Sudan emanated largely from the highly mobile activities of itinerant zawāyā traders and holy men (and their Sudanese opposites) who used the *ribāṭ* and zāwiya as bases of operation and points of departure.

Al-Mukhtār al-Kuntī and the recrudescence of quietist Islam

During the intervening years between the death of Sīdī ʿUmar al-Shaykh and the emergence of Sīdī Mukhtār al-Kuntī as the outstanding Islamic figure of the Western Sudan, Islam won over practically all the Berber

109 Richer, *Les Oulliminden*, p. 41.
110 Marty, *Tribus*, i, p. 258.
111 *Ibid.*, p. 252.
112 *Ibid.*, p. 319.

peoples of the Middle Niger and penetrated deeply into the Sudanic heartlands. There is even evidence to suggest that the Moroccan invasion, far from stifling this religious activity, might have accentuated the movement of scholars and traders southwards.[113] Yet if the majority of Tuareg and Berber groups had become Islamised, conversion had done very little to mellow their belligerent ways. Indeed, as questions of belief and unbelief were to dominate doctrinal discussions of a later era, the subject of Tuareg affinity to brigandage and what to do about it was to become the burning issue among peaceful Muslims of the eighteenth century. Al-Mukhtār al-Kabīr al-Kuntī was in the forefront of those who denounced the Tuareg for their unlawful expropriation of the Muslims' wealth, comparing them with the disorderly Meccan brigands of the Prophet's day.[114]

Yet the intensity of the Kunta-Kel Antassar rivalry for commercial and religious supremacy in the Azawad clearly illustrates that the zawāyā were themselves not always in a position to set the example for warrior groups who revelled in brigandage. Before the arrival of large numbers of Kunta from the Hawd (*c.* 1690–1775), the water holes in the Azawad region were in the complete control of the Kel Antassar. The Kel Antassar also seem to have exercised considerable religious influence over the various Berber groups in the Azawad.[115] But after 1750 this influence was seriously challenged by the Kunta. Indeed the steady rise of al-Mukhtār al-Kuntī to a position of religious pre-eminence parallels the gradual decline of Kel Antassar authority in religious matters. Sīdī al-Mukhtār launched a spiritual jihād in order to remove accretions which had polluted the Islamic religion. His preaching and teaching seemed particularly directed against various superstitious practices which appear to have been survivals of pagan Berber and Sudanic culture.

The impact of al-Mukhtār al-Kuntī's spiritual jihād on the Muslims of the Middle and Upper Niger was revolutionary. The fervour of his preaching and the extent of his literary output[116] gave impetus to a renewed interest in mystical studies and restored dignity to Islamic piety.[117] Moreover, for the first time in nearly two hundred years the estranged branches of the Qādiriyya order merged under a dynamic spiritual leadership. There is some evidence to suggest that ʿUthmān b. Fūdī and Seku Aḥmadu Lobbo, both of whom retained spiritual links with the Qādiriyya ṭarīqa, drew considerable moral inspiration for their revivalist movements from

113 *Ibid.*, p. 2.

114 Bibliothèque Nationale, Paris, MS. Arabe 5259, fols. 37–39 (Letter from Sidi al-Mukhtār al-Kuntī), f. 37.

115 Hamet, 'Littérature Arabe', p. 403; cf. Marty, *Tribus*, i, p. 302.

116 Sīdī al-Mukhtār is credited by some authors with over three hundred books and treatises. Cf. *Fatḥ al-Shakūr* (MS Arabe 118, de Gironcourt Papers, Bibliothèque de l'Institut de France, Paris, f. 22); Marty, *Tribus*, i, p. 41; and William A. Brown, 'The Bakkā'iyya Books of Timbuctū', Centre of Arabic Documentation (Ibadan), *Research Bulletin*, iii, 1, 1967, pp. 40–5.

117 Marty, *Tribus*, i, p. 141.

Sidi al-Mukhtār.[118] The jihād's influence upon the pagan peoples of the Middle and Upper Niger regions was no less important. The Kunta *shaykh* received students from all over the Western and Central Sudan, many of whom were inspired to foster the cultivation of Islam amongst their own people.[119]

The evolution of Islam in the Upper Niger region

Contrary to previous impressions, there would seem little evidence to support the contention that the overwhelmingly pagan populations of the Upper Niger valley manifested inherent opposition to the gradual implantation of Islamic beliefs within their societies. Nor would there appear sufficient support for the view that Muslims who resided amongst them were regarded with resentment or inhibited in the practice of their religion. Indeed there is every indication that during the seventeenth and eighteenth centuries significant numbers of pagans in the large trading centres—Sansanding, Segu, Nyamina, Kankan and Nioro—had reached the embryonic stages of a syncretist process of religious evolution. A salient feature of Islamic expansion during this period was the decisive rôle assumed by certain Muslim commercial families, who became active in these large urban centres in which the interests of religion and commerce tended to converge and become almost imperceptibly integrated. If the zawāyā became catalysts of Islamic diffusion from the Middle to the Upper Niger, their protegés—the Mande, Bozo and Somono clerisies—emerged as the veritable agents of that diffusion.

In Segu, as early as the beginning of the seventeenth century, several Somono families—notably the Kane, Dyire and Tyero—had acquired reputations as conscientious cultivators of a syncretist version of Islam. The commercial links which the Kane, Dyire and Tyero retained with Dia, their place of origin and the chief centre in the Middle Niger valley for the fabrication of charms and amulets, largely but not entirely explains the preponderance of their religious influence in Segu and Kaarta.[120] For they performed an equally vital function in these societies as arbiters in internal disputes between members of leading families. In other instances of internal discord and crisis, advice was sought from various Muslims because of their integrity or recognised proficiency in occultism. Yet if they could number among their most important 'converts' the leaders and notables among the Kouloubali and Diara, they could make no claim to having won their unqualified allegiance. For these leaders and notables had not been attracted to Islam as an alternative religious system, but rather by what they perceived as its magical qualities—Islamic 'magic' provided a new

118 Hamet, 'Littérature Arabe', p. 402; Cf. ʿAbd Allāh ibn Muḥammad, M. Hiskett, ed. and trans., *Tazyin al-Waraqāt*, Ibadan, 1963, p. 108; and Barth, *Travels*, iv, p. 629.
119 Marty, *Tribus*, iv, p. 47.
120 Monteil, *Les Bambara*, pp. 338–9.

dimension to the complex rituals of animist sorcery. Thus they indulged in that variety of geomantic divination to which Sīdī al-Mukhtār expressed especial aversion.[121] Ironically, the very Mande traders who prided themselves as followers of the Kunta shaykh appear responsible for the persistence of this deviation. The joint participation of Muslims and pagans in the purveyance of magical paraphernalia—charms, amulets, and gris-gris—underlines an essential characteristic of the early development of Islam in this region, namely the intimate contact of Islam and paganism at the level of sorcery and divination. Moreover, the great men in these societies were initiated into things Islamic coincident with their introduction to the occult rituals of animist religion. Yet they perceived no contradiction in the retention of pagan practices alongside the newly acquired Islamic ones.

The delicate balance in dualistic belief was sustained in every situation which demanded occult knowledge.[122] During the Muslim feast of *Bairam*, attended by the prominent members of the Kouloubali family, as well as minor clan leaders; their parents, and allies; the principal leaders among slaves; and other pagan dignitaries, the rituals of this distinctly Muslim celebration were merged with cultural offerings to *Nyana*, the spiritual protector of the Massassi clan. It was apparently the custom of some of the Mande ʿulamā' to offer prayers during the feast for the continued vitality of the sovereign and prolonged prosperity of his reign. In return, the sovereign was known to bestow riches upon these religious leaders, as a sign of favour and gratitude. Thus on the one hand could be seen the celebrations of Bairam terminating the Muslim fast of Ramadan (*ʿId al-Fiṭr*) and, on the other, participation in the Islamic sacrificial feast (*ʿId al-Aḍḥā*) syncretised with the pagan ceremonies which involved renewal of the oath of allegiance to the pagan idol, Nyana. Similarly during the Muslim feast of *Tabaski (ʿId al-Kabīr)*, presided over by the Mande clerisy, the Bambara masses joined in full participation—even to the point of sacrificing sheep in observance of this ancient Islamic custom. Despite such syncretism, however, and notwithstanding the fact that according to one observer one half of the Bambara army was composed of 'Muslims', and that the Bambara apparently distinguished amongst themselves 'faithful' and 'infidel', and indeed that the Kouloubali would have in fact considered themselves Muslims, it should not be overlooked that acceptance of Islam in Bambara did not go unqualified. Whenever promotion of Islamic interests threatened to mitigate the essential interests of the clan—as was the case with the unfortunate Bakari, and later with Touro-Koro Mari who sided with al-Ḥājj ʿUmar against his own clansmen—the delicate balance which obtained between Islam and paganism was apt to be severely disrupted; hence such action was strongly resisted as political deviation. The Bambara in general, and the Kouloubali in particular, were

121 *Ibid.*, pp. 333–4.
122 *Ibid.*, p. 331.

content to adopt the superficial formalism of Islamic adherence, while at the same time demonstrating a distinct reluctance to abandon their traditional polytheism—Allah simply took his place among other supernatural beings within the Bambara pantheon of deities.[123]

The Kunta-inspired Kane, Dyire and Tyero families also became the chief confereres of the Qādirī *wird* among the peoples of the right bank of the Niger. Other religious families of the Qādirī persuasion launched an equally vigorous proselytisation on the Niger's left bank: Karamoko Ousman Dyari at Nyamina; and the Khoma and Diakhate at Sansanding. Also at Sansanding could be found a number of sharīfs, notably Sharīf Ismāʿīl, who actively proselytised among the local peoples.[124]

One of the chief focal points of Islamic dissemination further west was the great Dyula commercial centre of Kankan, a principal source of the wealth of Segu and Timbuctū.[125] Kankan appears to have been first settled toward the end of the seventeenth century by Mande mixed with Kunta.[126] The settlement would seem a direct outgrowth of the dynastic struggles within the Bambara communities of Segu which apparently prompted the migration of large numbers of Mande seeking a more congenial environment.[127] These Mande belonged to the Kunta by virtue of marriage alliances through which they were able to claim a sharifian origin.[128] Their descendants became zealous apostles of Sīdī al-Mukhtār al-Kuntī, and were responsible for the dissemination of the Qādirī wird in the areas surrounding Kankan. Many had received their education in the Qādirī zāwiyas of the north, from which they returned to promulgate the teachings of the Kunta shaykh and his predecessors in the order.[129] The Kaba and Sakho families were among the leading exponents of Qādirī Islam, and the latter became especially known for the efficacy of their amulets and their rôles as 'magicians'. The most prominent Muslim family, however, would appear to have been the Diakhanke, formed from the Diakha of the Middle Niger.[130]

Credit for converting the large number of Fulbe who came to settle in Futa Jallon must also be given to these Qādirī Mande. During the early phase of these migrations, one of the outstanding leaders of the Sakho Mande was the Qādirī shaykh, Sanounou, who succeeded in converting the Fulbe clan leader Alipha Ba. Although it appears that other clan leaders

123 *Ibid.*, pp. 334–5, p. 337.
124 *Ibid.*, p. 340.
125 G. Mollien, *Travels in the Interior of Africa to the sources of the Senegal and Gambia*, London, 1820, p. 301.
126 Chatelier, *Islam*, p. 149.
127 *Ibid.*, p. 166.
128 *Ibid.*, p. 149.
129 *Ibid.*, p. 162.
130 André Arcin, *Histoire de la Guinée Française, Rivières du Sud, Fouta-Dialo, Région sud du Soudan*, Paris, 1911, p. 80.

had embraced Islam prior to Alipha Ba's conversion, notably Alfa Foukoumba, his action seems to have been instrumental in winning over to Islam Alfa Omar Labbe, Alfa Bouria, Tierno Balla, Tierno Makolade, Alfa Sire, and their followers. The result was a widespread acceptance of Islam among the remaining clans of Futa Jallon Fulbe, who proceeded (with the exception of the Houbous) to coalesce around the leadership of Alipha Ba.[131]

During the course of the eighteenth century Kankan became the major foyer for the expansion of Islam southwards. Emigrants from Kankan established a new Muslim colony in Musardu (Liberia) and its hinterland; the numerous villages which bear Islamic names are a surviving testimony to their pioneering endeavours: Medina, Musardu, Billallah, Mohammedou, Ballallah, and Dhakirallah—all of which reveal an Islamic origin.[132]

THE DEVELOPMENT OF TRADE IN THE UPPER AND MIDDLE NIGER

Principal commercial centres

There can be little doubt that the caravan traffic between the Maghrib and the Western Sudan remained active during the seventeenth and eighteenth centuries.[133] If the decline of Songhay brought about a reconstitution of political power in the Upper and Middle Niger, it would seem to have had a relatively insignificant impact on the economic life of this region—business was carried on as usual. To affirm the continuance of commercial vitality, however, is not to dismiss the periodically damaging effect of natural disasters—floods, epidemics, and famines—nor to underestimate the perpetual threat of pillaging, particularly from nomadic Tuareg groups. Nevertheless, only forty years of this period were characterised by the chronic famine and pestilence which has been so erroneously applied to the entire era between 1600 and 1800.

One of the most striking developments of this period is seen in the way in which two relative newcomers to the area—the Barabish and the Kunta—seized almost complete control of the economic lifelines of the Middle Niger. The former seemed to have gained *de facto* control of the vital Taghaza-Timbuctū route about the middle of the seventeenth century. No trade could be safely conducted without their consent, and

131 Le Chatelier, *Islam*, p. 149 ff.

132 *Ibid.*, p. 162.

133 The economic history of the Upper and Middle Niger regions during this period has been neglected by historians. Readers may benefit, however, from relevant material in the following: E. W. Bovill, *Caravans of the Old Sahara* (first published in 1935, a new edition of a later version of this work (i.e. *The Golden Trade of the Moors*) has been prepared by Mr Robin Hallett); N. R. Laurent, 'The economic history of the Songhai Empire, 1465-1591', a dissertation submitted as part of the requirements for the Diploma in African Studies of the University of Birmingham, 1965, 49 pages; and Sekene-Mody Cissokho, 'Famines et Epidémies à Tombouctou et dans la Boucle du Niger du XVIe au XVIIIe Siècle', a paper submitted to the Second Congress of Africanists, Dakar, Senegal, 11-20 December 1967, 20 pages.

as the tradition says, 'those who paid were protected, and those who did not were pillaged. . . .'[134] The rapprochement which the Kunta shaykh, al-Mukhtār al-Kuntī, established with the Barabish Walad Suliman after the death of their uncompromising leader, Muḥammad b. Raḥḥal, was instrumental in stabilising trade in the Middle Niger region, and in substantially increasing the economic wealth of the Kunta. In return for a monopoly of taxes derived from the tobacco trade, ʿAlī, the son of Muḥammad b. Raḥhal, placed himself under the spiritual protection, and hence influence of Sīdi al-Mukhtār.[135]

Although the Ruma still maintained a qāʿid at Taodeni, their rôle seems to have become somewhat negligible by the middle of the eighteenth century.

The principal means of carrying the salt from Taghaza and Taodeni to the Sudan was still the *azalai*, or large caravan of sometimes several thousand camels. Even before the time of al-Mukhtār al-Kuntī, the Kunta middlemen had achieved a dominant rôle in the salt traffic southwards. The enterprising Kunta (non-resident owners of the mines) provided the business acumen for organising the caravans, but the Barabish and other nomads were contracted to ṭransport the salt to Timbuctū, Bamba, and other settlements in the Middle Niger.[136]

Before the beginning of the seventeenth century the bulk of the caravan traffic passed from Taghaza through Walata (Biru), the successor to Ghana as the dominant commercial and religious centre of the Hawd. After the turn of the century, however, Walata was eclipsed culturally and commercially by Timbuctū, and large-scale migration led to a consequent desiccation and further decline of the village. Caravans no longer proceeded westwards through Walata, but travelled directly to Timbuctū through Arawan, situated some 250 kilometres north of Timbuctū.[137] This important watering point established during the course of the fifteenth century[138] was closely guarded by Makhzan troops, but seems to have later fallen into Barabish hands. Before the arrival of the Barabish and the Kunta, the Kel al-Sūq seem to have held the dominant commercial and religious position in the village, and their members occupied the most important religious posts of imām and chief qāʿḍi.[139] Around the middle of the eighteenth century, the Barabish established a village just outside Arawan at Bou Djebiha,[140] the region of which was also initially inhabited by Kel al-Sūq.

134 'Ceux qui payèrent furent protégés et ceux qui s'y refusèrent furent pillés . . .'. Martin, *Quatre Siècles*, p. 55. Cf. Marty, *Tribus*, i, p. 247.

135 Hamet, 'Littérature Arabe', p. 385.

136 Marty, *Tribus*, i, p. 247.

137 *Ibid.*, p. 324 ff.

138 *Ibid.*, p. 239.

139 *Ibid.*, p. 241.

140 *Ibid.*, p. 244.

An important northern market, Tsabit, part of the group of Gourara oases, served as an entrepôt for the commerce passing between the Mediterranean region and the Sudan. In the middle of the seventeenth century (*c.* 1663), it received great quantities of cloth from Timbuctū and was a key dispersal point for Moroccan goods such as dromedaries, cloth, and silk en route to the Sudan.[141] Caravans from Tsabit also stopped over at Tuwat, the capital of which was In Salah. Tuwat was the meeting point of caravans from Agadès, Timbuctū, and other regions of the Sudan. Al-Ayashi, a seventeenth-century traveller, observed that goods coming from these areas were to be found in abundance, and that items of Maghibian origin—such as horses, cloth and silk—were more costly than those derived from the Sudan.[142]

Timbuctū was the southern terminus of three important overland routes which began farther north: the Mauritanian route from Wadi Nun through Ijjil, Wadan, and Tishit; the Taghaza route southwards; and the road proceeding from In Salah and passing through Arawan. Ijjil was the source of salt which subsequently was transported through Tishit, Kaarta, Walata, and Timbuctū and exchanged for cotton goods, grain and slaves.[143] The city was also the destination of merchants travelling by water from regions in the Upper Niger. Kabara, the port of Timbuctū, and hence the point of entry for these commodities, was heavily guarded by Makhzan troops who sought to keep the traffic flowing at all costs. At one time (*c.* 1736), when the fortunes of the Makhzan reached their nadir, it became necessary, as a protection against the marauding activities of the Tuareg, to provide armed escorts for the donkeys which carried daily provisions from Kabara to Timbuctū.[144] In 1694, during another crisis, thirty-seven boats were recaptured, seventeen of which were charged with salt from the Saharan mines, seventeen containing various commodities from Jenne and appreciable amounts of gold. The value of this cargo was estimated at 37,000 mithqāls (£17,500), which indicates the considerable volume of trade which passed through Timbuctū.[145] Another incident which gives some indication of the extent of commercial wealth in Timbuctū is seen in the amount recovered in 1700 from the bāshā, who had been accused of embezzlement. It is said that the bāshā hoarded 12,000 mithqāls (£6,000), when no other person possessed more than 4,000.[146] It is significant to note that the period 1694 to 1696 was a specially difficult one, and it is reasonable to expect that the volume of trade might have been somewhat lower than usual.

It should be understood, however, that Timbuctū was essentially the

141 La Martinière et La Croix, *Documents*, iv, p. 393.
142 Martin, *Quatre Siècles*, p. 57.
143 Henri Schirmer, *Le Sahara*, Paris, 1893, p. 347.
144 Al-Wafrānī, *Tadhkirat*, trans., p. 164.
145 *Ibid.*, trans., p. 149.
146 *Ibid.*, trans., p. 33.

entrepôt for commercial traffic converging from far north and far south. Its destiny was almost inextricably linked with Jenne, its sister commercial centre. The marshes of Jenne, which constituted a natural barrier against outside invasion, allowed it to maintain a precarious autonomy in face of attacks by the Fulbe of Massina, the Makhzan, and the Bambara. Jenne received the salt which came from the northern routes in exchange for rice and millet coming from the commercial centres of the Upper Niger. Commercial agents from Jenne retained sub-agents and residences in Timbuctū. Merchants travelling by camel from the north did not ordinarily venture beyond Timbuctū, where they could obtain payment for their goods, despite the fact that at Jenne they might have obtained these commodities at a considerable reduction.[147] Jenne was also the northern terminus for the important route originating in Ashanti and the forest states. The cherished kola nuts (a luxury item with ritual significance), gold and slaves were transported from Ashanti through Begho, Bonduku, Kong, and Bobo-Dyulasso to Jenne, where they were exchanged for the brassware and cloth of the Maghrib.[148]

Segu (*c.* 1785), one of the great riverain cities of the Niger-Bani region, seems to have been the principal source of slaves exported by the French merchants of Senegal and Gambia.[149] Indeed slaves appear to have been the major commodity exported by the Bambara of Segu. The trade was conducted by Dyula merchants who escorted the caravans to the Atlantic coast.[150] Segu also must have been one of the chief sources of grain for the regions of the Upper and Middle Niger. Its position on the right bank of the Niger allowed it to attract trade from Kong and Futa Jallon.[151]

Two other market towns, Sansanding and Kankan, became vital commercial centres during the period 1600 to 1800. Sansanding, (situated fifty-five kilometres downstream from Segu-Sikoro), on the left bank of the Niger, occupied a prominent position as an exchange centre for a variety of commercial items. The river's sudden twisting northwards made it a point of convergence for Saharan trading routes, and the natural exchange market between the peoples of the Savanna and those of the Sudan.[152] Berber traders from the Hawd frequented Sansanding in the dry season, attracted by its enormous quantities of millet. Mungo Park (*c.* 1805) has left an excellent description of the market, which he said was

147 Dubois, *Timbuctū the Mysterious*, London, 1896, p. 171.
148 Cf. three articles by Ivor Wilks: 'A medieval trade route from the Niger to the Gulf of Guinea', *J.A.H.*, iii, no. 2, pp. 337–43; 'The northern factor in Ashanti history', Institute of African Studies, University of Ghana, 46 pages, see p. 2; and 'The position of Muslims in metropolitan Ashanti in the early nineteenth century', in I. M. Lewis, ed., *Islam in Tropical Africa*, London, 1966, p. 321.
149 Tauxier, *Histoire des Bambara*, p. 29.
150 *Ibid.*, p. 57.
151 Elisée Reclus, *Nouvelle Géographie Universelle* (vol. xii, *L'Afrique Occidentale*), Paris, 1887, p. 557.
152 *Ibid.*, p. 559.

crowded with people from morning to night: some of the stalls contain nothing but beads; others, indigo in balls; others wood-ashes in balls; others Houssa and Jinnie cloth. I observed one stall with nothing but antimony in small bits; another with sulphur, and a third with copper and silver rings and bracelets. In the houses fronting the square is sold, scarlet, amber, silks from Morocco, and tobacco, which looks like Levant tobacco, and comes by way of Tombuctoo. Adjoining this is the salt market, part of which occupies one corner of the square. A slab of salt is sold commonly for 800 cowries (£1.15.0).[153]

The Mande merchants of Kankan, situated on the Milo, an eastern affluent of the Niger, sent caravans as far as Freetown in the west, and as far as the Saharan salt mines of Tishit in the north-west, where they exchanged slaves and other commodities of the south. They also pursued an active trade with Segu and Timbuctū.[154]

The economy of the Western Sudan: currency and currency fluctuations

Commercial transactions in the Upper and Middle Niger were effected by means of two major currencies: cowry shells and gold coins (mithqāls). Cowry shells seem to have been the most convenient means of conducting small market transactions, whereas gold coins were reserved for transactions involving substantial sums of money. The use of these two major currencies appears to have been restricted to the principal commercial centres situated along the main caravan routes.[155] Outside these trading establishments, barter arrangements appear to have characterised the daily economic life of rural villages.

The value of cowry shells was fixed in relation to gold coins. The mithqāl was minted in the Maghrib from gold dust traditionally imported in considerable quantities from the Western Sudan.[156] The rate of exchange between the cowry and gold mithqāl fluctuated during the seventeenth and eighteenth centuries, but at the same time manifested a remarkable constancy. Discounting periods of economic abnormality, which are discussed below, the rate of exchange levelled at 3,000 cowries to one mithqāl of gold.[157]

Both natural and man-made disasters tended periodically to upset the economic stability of the Upper and Middle Niger regions. The most serious natural disasters which caused havoc in the region were inundations of the Niger; infrequent droughts and epidemics; and attacks by waves of locust which struck down upon cultivated areas. Man-made disasters, brought on by political instability and the raids of predatory nomads on cultivators

153 Mungo Park, *Travels*, 1805, p. 157.
154 Reclus, *Géographie*, p. 549.
155 Cf. H. Miner, *The Primitive City of Timbuctu*, p. 48; and Caillie, *Travels*, ii. p. 30.
156 Martin, *Quatre Siècles*, p. 13.
157 Monteil, *Djénné*, p. 280.

and merchants, sometimes tended to upset the ecological balance and to exacerbate conditions otherwise due to natural phenomena. The region from Jenne in the central delta of the Niger, to Arawan in the Sahil, was susceptible to severe climatic changes which had an adverse effect on the economy. The irregularity and paucity of rainfall were factors which led to periods of intense dryness or flooding, depending on circumstances.[158] The most serious scourge to the inhabitants of these regions was famine, brought on essentially by intense periods of drought. In cases of partial drought, the harvest in cereals was lessened in volume, leading to a scarcity which intensified from November to April. Conversely, during periods of complete drought, harvests were extremely meagre and hence famine occurred as early as November. Drought in the region of Jenne, the economic hub of the Middle Niger, had a dominoe effect on the rest of the villages in the region of the Niger's buckle. Inundation of the Niger also brought on famine. Each time the river overflowed, it tended to destroy cultivation in the adjoining valleys and provoked a scarcity, initially of limited effect, but with dire consequences the following year when it was followed by any drought. A third factor which brought about varying degrees of scarcity was the presence of hoards of locust, which ravaged the planted areas.[159] Prolonged famine was invariably accompanied by an actual epidemic or widespread outbreaks of Yellow Fever, cholera, smallpox, or cerebro-spinal meningitis.[160]

During these periods of economic abnormality the rate of exchange between cowries and gold coins was subject to fluctuations. In times of scarcity, the value of cereals and other materials of prime necessity showed a sudden upturn in relation to cowries, as did the value of cowries in relation to gold. During difficult times the rate of exchange fell from a normal 3,000 cowries to one mithqāl, to as low as 700, or even 500 cowries to the mithqāl. The sharp fall in the exchange rate has been attributed to the diminution of the quantity of gold in circulation—or rather to the amount of gold available to the indigenous population.[161] Nevertheless, the relative constancy of the value of cowries with respect to gold during the seventeenth and eighteenth centuries strongly indicates that the period was in fact one of considerable economic stability.

CONCLUSIONS: PROBLEMS FOR FUTURE RESEARCH

The absence of historical monographs on the Western Sudan during the seventeenth and eighteenth centuries can be attributed more to scholarly disinterest than to lack of materials. Historians of West Africa have tended to revel in the glories of Songhay, and dismiss the period 1600 to 1800 as

158 Cissokho, 'Famines et epidémies', p. 3.
159 *Ibid.*, p. 7.
160 *Ibid.*, p. 8.
161 Monteil, *Djénné*, p. 280.

one of 'Islamic stagnation', economic decline, and political instability. With almost indecent haste they have then proceeded to discuss the nineteenth century in terms of 'Islamic revival', Islamic 'resistance' to European penetration, and the establishment of imperial rule.[162] Such cursory treatment of a vital two centuries has resulted in a variety of misinterpretations of the period itself, and in some misunderstanding of its relationship to previous and subsequent periods of Western Sudanese historical development.

A closer consideration of available sources demonstrates the unjustifiability of many previous impressions of this era. The period of Ruma ascendancy in the Middle Niger was not nearly as chaotic as has been believed. Indeed from 1591 until the late 1720s, the Ruma maintained a not insignificant degree of political and economic stability, which in any case contrasts favourably with the ineptitude of the closing decades of Songhay rule. The administrative deficiencies of the Ruma—who admittedly after 1730 had shown themselves untutored in the politics of stability—largely explain their failure to cope effectively with the Tuareg menace. Yet even at this point a certain balance was restored after 1750 when the political skill exerted by al-Mukhtār al-Kuntī somewhat offset the administrative collapse of the Makhzan.

Nor were the Niger-Bani states of Segu and Kaarta without their merits or achievements. The Bambara state under Biton Mamari Kouloubali, for the most part, was a successful experiment in ethnic cohesion. Bambara warrior-cultivators, Mande merchants, and Somono and Bozo fishers, though not without their differences, were closely linked in alliance, and all shared in the benefits of Bambara imperial expansion. Historically underprivileged caste groups perceived in the newly forged society an opportunity for social mobility previously denied them.

There are, moreover, few signs of 'Islamic stagnation'. On the contrary, the period 1600 to 1800 witnessed an acceleration in the pace of Islamic diffusion. The Moroccan invasion quite possibly increased commercial and religious contacts with the Maghrib; and the steady influx of sharīfs from the north affirms the maintenance of strong religious links with North Africa.[163] Nor does there appear to have been any 'pagan reaction' to the gradual encroachment of this quietist variety of Islam. The privileged positions which Muslim traders and holy men enjoyed at the courts of pagan rulers allowed them to initiate the process of syncretism, and hence gain acceptance and respect for many Islamic beliefs.

It is also difficult to support the widely held contention that the Moroccan invasion ushered in an era of economic decline. There is no substantial evidence to suggest that the wealth of Middle Niger diminished. Similarly, much of the denigration of the Ruma in the economic sphere would seem

162 See for example J. Spencer Trimingham, *A History of Islam in West Africa*.
163 Marty, *Tribus*, i, pp. 2 and 136.

undeserved. The merchants within the Ruma sphere of economic influence were protected—and indeed patronised—by the Makhzan, which depended upon them for its material well-being.

Major problems for future research

Certain aspects of Western Sudanese history during the seventeenth and eighteenth centuries remain problematical. We are, for example, very poorly informed about the region of Massina during this period. An understanding of the social, religious, and political conditions prevailing in Massina before the rise of Seku Aḥmadu Lobbo would seem essential for any useful assessment of his movement.[164] The inspirational rôle of Sidi al-Mukhtār al-Kuntī, a seriously neglected figure, in the *jihāds* of ʿUthmān b. Fūdī and Seku Aḥmadu remains obscure and almost totally unexplored. A considerable body of correspondence written by al-Mukhtār al-Kuntī and his son Muḥammad exists; and a detailed analysis of extant letters exchanged between the Kunta shaykhs and Muḥammad Bello, Seku Aḥmadu, and Usuman dan Fodio, should prove invaluable in uncovering the nature of relationship between these individuals.

The fiscal and administrative institutions of the Ruma warrant further investigation. Very little is known about the nature of the taxation system which obtained in Muslim and non-Muslim areas under Ruma control. Was the fiscal system which evolved canonical—that is to say, did the Ruma attempt to develop and execute measures which corresponded to the requirements of Islamic law? To what extent was the law applied equitably? Did it, for example, apply in the same way to all classes of people—to all classes of merchants?

Another interesting problem which awaits further research concerns the 'caste' systems which evolved in the Middle and Upper Niger regions. A comparative study of the caste system should be a fruitful addition to our knowledge of the social history of these areas. One important question impinging on this problem immediately comes to mind. To what extent, for example, can Tauxier's hypothesis that the caste system was in origin a distinctly Fulbe phenomenon be upheld? He observed that it was

> très important chez les Peuls et ce sont eux, on peut le supposer, qui l'ont propagé dans l'ouest Africain nègre tout entier, car il n'est nulle part aussi développé que chez les Peuls et, au contraire, chez les nègres du sud et de la forêt (non contaminés par les Peuls), il n'existe pas, même chez des nègres aussi développés sous d'autres rapports que les

164 Several scholars are presently concerned with various aspects of this problem: Mr ʿAbd al-ʿAzīz Batran (University of Birmingham), al-Mukhtār al-Kuntī; Mr N. R. Laurent (University of London), the 'Songhay Bāshālik'; Mr William Brown (University of Wisconsin), Massina; and Mr Charles Stewart (Oxford University), with the spread of the Qādiriyya *ṭarīqa*.

nègres Agni.[165]

Finally, considerably more information is needed on the agents, methods, and nature of Islamic diffusion during the seventeenth and eighteenth centuries. Some studies of the Kunta, and the dissemination of Islam by the Qādiriyya, have already been undertaken.[166] Yet the activities of other *zawāyā* clerisy groups such as the Kel al-Sūq and Kel Antassar remain obscure.[167] Detailed studies of the proselytising Mande families of Kankan and Sansanding, to mention only two prominent centres, might also shed light on this problem.[168]

165 Tauxier, *Moeurs*, p. 140. The present writer is investigating the historical evolution of the West African Artisan estate.
166 e.g. Batran and Stewart.
167 Unpublished material for the Kel al-Sūq and Kel Antassar can be found in the Bibliothèque de l'Institut de France, Paris, de Gironcourt Papers.
168 C. Meillassoux (University of the Sorbonne, Paris), is presently working on the Mande.

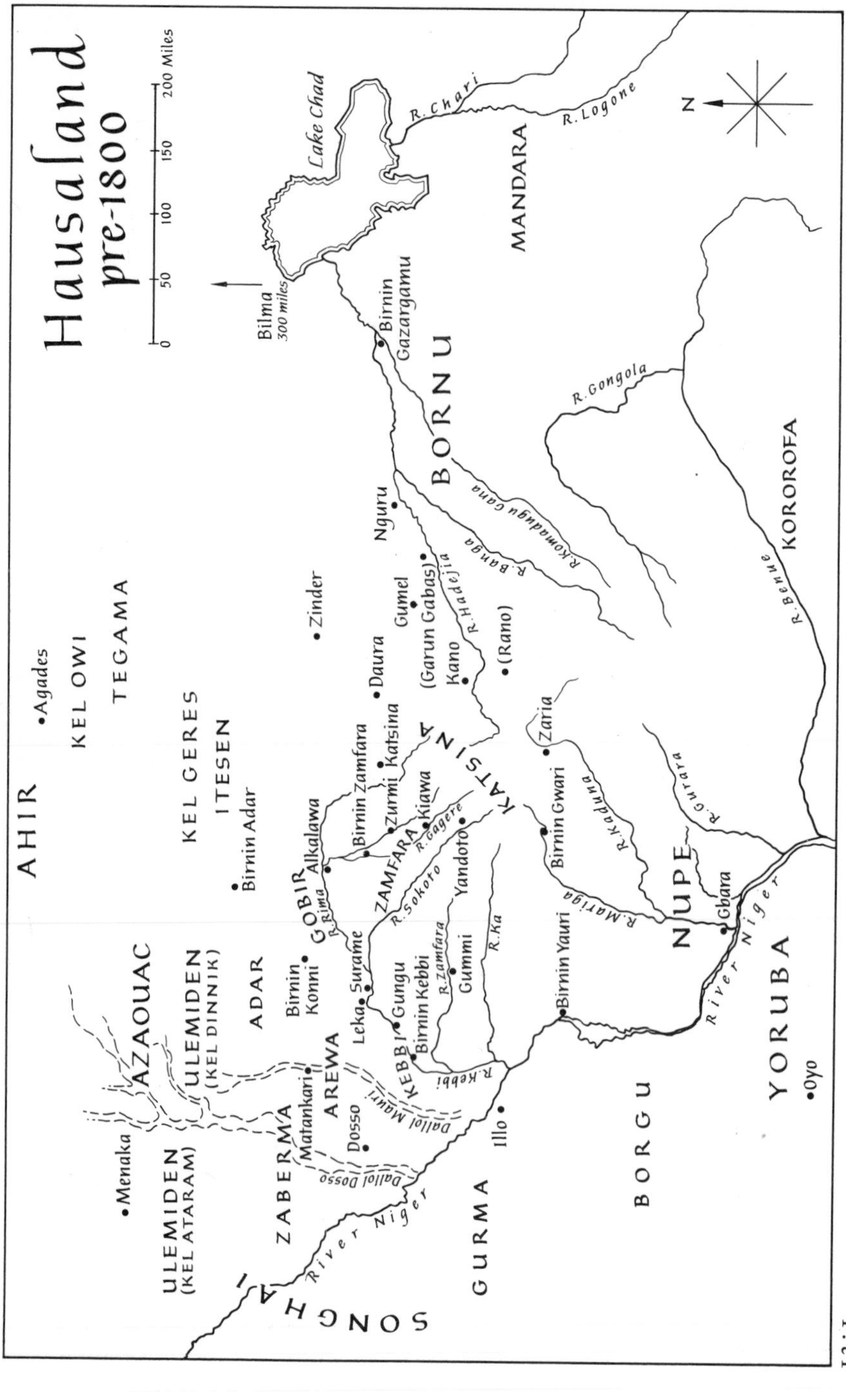
Hausaland
pre-1800
0 50 100 150 200 Miles
Bilma
300 miles
Lake Chad
R. Chari
R. Logone
N
MANDARA
BORNU
Birnin Gazargamu
R. Gongola
KOROROFA
R. Benue
R. Komadugu Gana
R. Banga
R. Hadejia
Nguru
Gumel
(Garun Gabas)
Zinder
Kano
(Rano)
Daura
Katsina
KATSINA
Zaria
AHIR
Agades
KEL OWI
TEGAMA
KEL GERES
ITESEN
Birnin Adar
Alkalawa
Birnin Zamfara
Zurmi
Kiawa
ZAMFARA
R. Gagere
GOBIR
R. Rima
Yandoto
R. Sokoto
Birnin Gwari
R. Kaduna
R. Gurara
NUPE
Gbara
R. Mariga
River Niger
YORUBA
Oyo
Birnin Yauri
R. Ka
Gummi
R. Zamfara
Surame
Gungu
Leka
Birnin Kebbi
KEBBI
R. Kebbi
Birnin Konni
ADAR
ULEMIDEN
(KEL DINNIK)
AZAOUAC
AREWA
Matankari
Dosso
Dallol Mauri
Dallol Dosso
ZABERMA
Menaka
ULEMIDEN
(KEL ATARAM)
SONGHAI
GURMA
Illo
BORGU

13:1

CHAPTER 13

Hausaland and Bornu 1600–1800

R. A. ADELẸYẸ

At the beginning of the seventeenth century, Bornu, west of the Lake Chad, had newly emerged as a well established empire after a century of strife and chaos followed by one of gradual reconstruction, expansion and consolidation. The latter processes touched the highest peak of realisation under the redoubtable mai, Idrīs Aloma. At this period, Kebbi was the leading power in Hausaland. The political intervention of the Songhay empire had just received a firm and final check by having fallen to Moroccan invasion. Kano and Katsina, with a long tradition of mutual conflict, growth and expansion behind them, were still locked in mutually destructive rivalry. The other Hausa states and principalities followed behind Kano and Katsina at various stages of political maturation. In a wider perspective, the histories of Hausaland and Bornu had been, and were to remain, closely interwoven. Furthermore both regions had interacted, and were to continue to do so, with Tuaregland to their north. To the west their past was closely linked with the rise and fall of the Mali and Songhay empires. These interactions at various levels determined the nature and direction of change in this area.

Continuity of theme in the history of Hausaland and Bornu is a question to which scant attention has been given. The student of the history of the area in the seventeenth and eighteenth centuries is seriously handicapped by a dearth of material. The kinglists, fragments of chronicles and histories which are available, are only too apt to give the impression that historical development in the area was fragmented, the lines of demarcation following with close fidelity the vague boundaries of the known states and principalities. Up to a point, the fact that a coherent and meaningful pattern is difficult to establish in the activities of the states and pseudo-state organisations arises not only from the scrappy nature of the information which can be gleaned from the sources. It is also to some extent a reflection of the political and socio-economic condition of the area. Yet when these are brought together and studied in ensemble, some pattern does emerge.

The surviving sources are replete with reports of wars and conflicts, with references to trade routes and trade, and to the growth and impact of a foreign religion—Islam—all providing clear symptoms of the predicaments and triumphs of an emergent society and polities perennially engaged in an intensive search for a foundation on which to base socio-political organisation and allegiance. In this endeavour many factors, foreign and local, economic and religious, had their significance. In a politically disparate society, the common goal of political and economic well-being and self-sufficiency—as just ends of all governments—were seen and pursued through the parochial views of the numerous polities. The conflict implicit in this situation meant that the dominant theme of the history of Hausaland and Bornu was the movement towards larger and larger political units. This study, therefore, attempts an appraisal of the dynamics of larger-units state formation and state building. It is scarcely possible, given the state of knowledge, to discuss intelligibly or to understand clearly the history of this process through an analysis which begins abruptly in 1600. The history of the area in the seventeenth and eighteenth centuries is essentially a continuation of its history in previous centuries—notably from about the fifteenth. At the risk of some repetition of points already discussed in previous chapters, the broad outlines of the earlier period must be restated here.

Attention must be drawn firstly to the fact that in the wider context of the Western Sudan, Hausaland, which forms the geographical link between the West and the Central Sudan, remained a relatively isolated area of historical development down to about the fourteenth century. The political influence of Mali to the west in its early heyday did not extend to Hausaland in a sufficiently powerful form to break this isolation. To the east, the centre of the Kanem empire still lay east of the Chad. To the north were the fragmented Tuareg groups among whom the emergence of state or pseudo-state organisations postdated such developments in Hausaland.

The argument that large-scale political organisation must depend solely on outside influences cannot be sustained in respect of Hausaland. Were this the case the Tuareg groups, open for centuries to the North African world and the benefits of the trans-Saharan trade, should have produced such a feature. While foreign influence can speed up the development of states actual establishment must usually be a response to local geographical environmental factors, not least of which is the human ecology and economic culture of the people. Thus the Tuareg groups, nomadic and living in semidesert, sometimes mountainous or wholly desert, conditions, did not have the same impetus towards state-building as the sedentary predominantly agricultural Hausa inhabiting fertile rolling savannah country. The Tuareg country screened Hausaland from the salutary effects of the trans-Saharan trade and contact up to about the fourteenth century. The trans-Saharan trade routes up to this period sidetracked Hausaland on their ways to Mali and Songhay as well as to Kanem-Bornu. The economic and ideological impetus which these empires derived therefrom were therefore denied to Hausaland. In their isolation the Hausa states do not seem to have developed political and economic organisations on a scale sufficiently large, coherent and powerful to attract outside attention as a region of worthwhile commercial possibilities.

Kano provides an example of the pattern of growth which the Hausa city states seem to have undergone. The chronicle shows clearly that from about the eleventh century to the fourteenth, the city underwent a process of internal consolidation and gradual territorial expansion based on a corresponding building up of its military power and improvements in weapons and organisation. Thus the building of the city walls is said to have begun at the turn of the eleventh and twelfth centuries.[1] During the reign of Yusa, son of Gijimansu (*c.* 1136–94), shields (*garkwa*) were introduced and further territorial expansion was accomplished. Yusa's son, Naguji (*c.* 1194–1247) was faced with revolts of subjected peoples.[2] The expansion was to a large measure dependent on the ability of the ruler to apply adequate military sanctions whenever occasion demanded. Early fourteenth-century Kano witnessed a reorganisation of the army, apparently involving some training. A sort of general staff including a *madawaki*, a *makama* and a *jarmai*, was established under Sarki Tsamia, son of Shekarau.[3] The appointment of a madawaki—chief cavalry officer—as Commander of the Kano forces, a position which grew in importance through subsequent centuries, indicates that horses were available in substantial numbers and that they were being used as the backbone of the army to revolutionalise warfare.

The institution of a cadre of professional top-ranking military men meant that such men also occupied positions of eminence in the political and administratrative hierarchy. With the new organisation of the army and with a range of weapons comprising bows, arrows, spears and swords, Kano underwent a military technological revolution suited to territorial expansion on a larger scale than hitherto. Thus the fourteenth century witnessed a southward expansion and the subjugation of the Warji of the Bauchi plateau and even the distant Kwararafa. Kanajeji b. Yaji (*c.* 1390–1410) was reportedly so constantly at war that he hardly lived in Kano. Although many of the Kano wars, particularly against Bauchi plateau tribes, were unsuccessful, Kano domains were expanded and further improvements in the armour of the Kano soldiers were introduced, notably the *lifidi*, iron helmets and coats of mail. With these developments Kano occupied a pre-eminent position among the Hausa city states. Indeed the conquests and expansion of the fourteenth century almost

1 H. R. Palmer, *Sudanese Memoirs*, iii, Lagos, 1928, *Kano Chronicle*, p. 101.
2 *K.C.*, p. 101.
3 *Ibid.*, p. 103.

amounted to the creation, though ephemeral, of a sort of empire of Kano.

Little is known of the other Hausa states before the fourteenth century. It is, however, pertinent to suggest that the inability of Kano to impose its overlordship on them without difficulty in subsequent centuries indicates, at least, that development in these states followed a similar pattern to that in Kano although they did not attain the same level.

It is well known that Kano and Katsina formed the core of fourteenth-century Hausaland. Immediately behind, or perhaps on a comparative level of development with Kano and Katsina, was Zaria. Situated on the southern frontiers of Hausaland with many heterogeneous groups, Zaria's development must have been characterised by high tension. This probably accounts, at least partially, for the numerous movements of capitals. Birnin Zaria was the sixth capital of the state.[4] The exploits of the legendary Queen Amina in the early fifteenth century seem to indicate that Zaria was reasonably well consolidated by the preceding century.[5] Rano, Daura and Biram ta Gabas (Garun Gabas) seem to have been, politically, in the backwaters of Hausa society, while Gobir was yet to be pushed southwards from its original Ahir home. The founding of Kebbi and Zamfara by Kanawa and Katsinawa Hausa respectively as yet lay in the future. The small principalities of Shira, Auyo, Teshena and—no doubt—numerous village-states, remained for long inconsequential.

Towards the end of the fourteenth century, the centre of the Kanem empire had to be moved from east to west of the Chad as a consequence of conflict between the Seifawa Mais and their Bulala neighbours. Already, in their Kanem home, the Seifawa Mais had developed a machinery of state organisation suitable for holding together heterogenous ethnic groups under one political authority. East as well as west of the Chad, the Kanem-Bornu empire was an expanding state by reason of its superior military might. By the end of the fifteenth century the new Bornu empire had secured a firm foothold in the Kanuri country. Birnin Gazargamo, their capital, had been built. The So and other recalcitrant groups had been brought under some form of subjection sufficient to permit the Mais to embark on a career of westward expansion into Hausaland and to secure mastery over the predatory Tuareg and other groups—the confederation of Ahir, the kel-Geres of Damerghou as well as the Teda immediately north of the Chad.

The gradual decline of Mali from the fourteenth century was followed by the rise and expansion of Songhay contemporaneously with the firm

4 A. E. J. Arnett, *Gazetteer of Zaria Province,* London, 1920, p. 9. Other capitals were Kawuri, Kikochi, Wuchicheri, Turunku and Kufena.

5 The Wangarawa migration led by Abdulrahman Zaite was not focused only on Kano and Katsina. Groups of the immigrants are said to have settled in various other places (Gobir, Kebbi, etc.); see trans. of a chronicle of this migration by M. Al-ḥajj, 'A seventeenth century chronicle on the origins and missionary activities of the Wangarawa', *Kano Studies,* i, no. 4, 1968, pp. 7–16.

consolidation of Seifawa rule west of the Chad by the late fifteenth century. These events meant that Hausaland was hemmed in, east and west, by two powerful, expanding and competing powers. The founding of the sultanate of Ahir in the fifteenth century and the establishment of Agades as its capital later in the same century resulted in the southward movement of the Gobirawa from Ahir into a territory where they necessarily impinged on Kebbi and Katsina spheres of influence. These momentous events were to have far-reaching consequences on the historical developments of Hausaland and Bornu in subsequent centuries. Indeed, they provided important background to political, economic and social relations in the area.

The existence of the powerful empires to its east and west meant that Hausaland's isolation could not have been total. The horses used by the Kano cavalry force in the early fourteenth century and the *lifidi*, iron helmets and coats of mail introduced at the end of that century, were presumably obtained through contact between Hausaland and one or both of the Kanem and Mali empires. Before any establishment of political relations between Kanem-Bornu and Mali-Songhay with Hausaland, migrants from the west and east had travelled to or settled in Hausaland. These contacts had introduced Islam into Hausaland by the fourteenth and fifteenth centuries to which period the conversion to Islam of the *sarakuna* of Kano and Katsina is dated.[6] The conversion of Sarkin Kano, ʿAlī Yaji b. Tsamia (*c.* 1349–85), was accomplished in the wake of substantial migration of Wangarawa devouts and clerics from the Mali empire. It was accompanied by the establishment of a hierarchy of Muslim religious offices alongside the traditional hierarchy of the state's administration.[7]

The Islamic penetration came with the beginning of a thoroughgoing opening of Hausaland to an east-west communication within West Africa in which Hausa traders became an active element. With this expansion of communication, Hausaland was becoming a buffer, not only militarily and politically but also in terms of gradual absorption of Islamic culture. Politically, economically and culturally, the absorption of Hausaland into the wider West African and Muslim worlds marks a turning point in Hausa history. Through the ensuing admixture between the universalist Islamic culture and the particularist world view of the indigenous Hausa culture a gradual polarisation of society along the lines of two often conflicting religio-political ideologies had begun. As yet, and for centuries thereafter, Islam coexisted with the indigenous culture, conditioning it only marginally. This aspect will receive fuller attention below.

In the absence of serious natural barriers, Hausaland and the Tuareg country north of it constituted obvious areas into which Songhay and Bornu would direct their expansion. The buffer position of Hausaland in

6 *Ibid.*
7 *Ibid.*, also *K.C.*, p. 105.

the new wider world in which it found itself would have underlined the urgency for each state to take firm security precautions to ensure its survival and independence. It is also reasonable to suggest that the leading Hausa states had reached such a stage of expansion from their city-state nuclei that in terms of territorial claims they were beginning to tread on one another's toes. Even then, the external stimulus provided by the rise of Songhay and Bornu cannot be discounted as it must at least have speeded up political and economic development of the Hausa city-states. The fifteenth and sixteenth centuries witnessed a more rapid military build-up among the Hausa states than hitherto. Thenceforth efforts to resolve the clash of territorial ambitions and other associated competing interests which expansion had brought to the fore dominated Hausa history. Thus, in the fifteenth and sixteenth centuries, we hear of frequent wars between the leading states—Kano, Katsina and Zaria.

Following Kano's immoderate expansion in the fourteenth century, Zaria enjoyed a brief period of efflorescence during the fifteenth century. The legendary Queen Amina of Zaria was said to have ruled from the Kwararafa state to Nupe, subjugated Bauchi and exacted tribute from Kano and Katsina.[8] Her conquests and achievements may have been exaggerated but the basic fact remains that she exercised such a wide sway that she stands in history as the first Hausa empire builder. Her name is associated with a widely dispersed activity of wall building all over the Hausa states and beyond. Though not all the city walls referred to as *Ganuwar Amina* could possibly be credited to her, such associations underline her imperial achievements; they also mark the fifteenth century as one of intensive activity, amounting to a revolution, in the defence arrangements of the Hausa states in the face of pressing threats to their security. An aspect of this threat undoubtedly consisted in the conflicts arising from the expansion of individual Hausa states. Shorn of legendary accretions, Amina emerges as a historical personage, and the exploits of Zaria credited to her must be seen as based on historical fact.[9] During Amina's ascendancy the products of the south found their way to the Hausa market. She received eunuchs and kola nuts as 'tribute' from Nupe. 'She first had eunuchs and kola nuts

8 *Ibid.*, p. 109. According to Muḥammad Bello, Zaria (Zakzak or Zazzau) comprised also the Gwari states, the Gwandara, Koto, Kwararafa; see Muḥammad Bello, *Infāq al-Maisūr fī Tarīkh bilād al-Takrūr*, ed., C. W. J. Whitting, London, 1951, pp. 18–19; also *Saurauniyar Amina*, Gaskiya Corporation, Zaria (n.d.).

9 *Kano Chronicle*, p. 109. Muḥammad Bello (*op. cit.*, p. 18) says that Queen Amina of Zazzau (Zaria) was the first to whom power was given over the Hausa states. According to *The Kano Chronicle*, p. 109, she was a contemporary of Sarki Dauda son of Kanajeji (*c.* 1421–38). Although it is common to suppose that Amina reigned during the sixteenth century. the exploits credited to her could not have been possible in the context of that century. With Zaria, Kano and Katsina under the sway of Songhay and then Kebbi as well as Bornu, Zaria was in no position to assert the dominance credited to Amina. It is important to note that Amina surprisingly escapes mention in Songhay and Bornu sources—the powers with which she would have clashed had she lived in the sixteenth century. Evidence, therefore, points to Amina as a fifteenth century personage.

in Hausaland', and during her reign goods from the west also came to Hausaland.[10] Hausaland was becoming an open market in east-west as well as south-north Sudanese trading relations.

Added to the conflicting political and economic interests among the Hausa states were the competing imperialisms of Songhay and Bornu during the sixteenth century. These have been discussed in chapter 6 above. Bornu was first in the field of foreign expansion into Hausaland. As early as between *c.* 1438–52 Kano had had to acknowledge the superior might of Bornu. Sarkin Kano ʿAbdullāh Burja was the first Hausa king to pay 'tribute' to Bornu, followed very shortly by other Hausa states.[11] The degree of Bornuan control over Hausaland appears to have been very slight. We read of no sustained Bornu expeditions into Hausaland at this time, nor of any Bornuan influence besides the single reference in the Kano chronicle.

Although Bornu had its grave problems of consolidation to face at home, the rapidly expanding and developing Hausa states were a great temptation though also a potential challenge to its expansionist ambitions. The desire to contain threats from Ahir and other central Sudan Tuareg groups would have further attracted Bornu to Hausaland and the country to the north of it. Hausaland, divided against itself, fell prey to Bornu whose overlordship the states acknowledged. With the opening of the sixteenth century, Bornu's worst period of precarious sway over the numerous non-Kanuri west and south of the Chad was over. Mai Idrīs b. ʿAlī Katagarmabe (*c.* 1503–26) was therefore free to deal with the Ahirawa and to assert Bornu domination over Hausaland on a basis firmer and surer than ever before.[12] The position of Ahir as a major staging post along the important commercial highway from the Western Sudan to North Africa may have made it a tempting prize to a conqueror establishing his control over Hausaland.

As Idrīs Katagarmabe was pursuing his exploits in Hausaland and Ahir, the Songhay empire reached its apogee under Askia Al-Ḥajj Muḥammad Ture b. Abī Bakr. Songhay, like Mali before her, was deriving much wealth from trade along the Gao–Takedda–Ahir–North African caravan highway. With the western expansion of Bornu, it must have become even more urgent for Songhay to control this route.

Meanwhile developments in the Hausa country had been rapid. During the fifteenth century Agades had supplanted Takedda as a major caravan centre. It served Hausaland directly. Katsina had already begun to nourish a trans-Saharan trading connection and contact. The city developed as

10 *Kano Chronicle*, p. 109.

11 *Ibid.*, pp. 109–10. This payment may not have followed necessarily on conquest. It could have been paid in pursuit of a strong desire to open Bornu to Kano trade and that of other Hausa states. There is no known evidence of Bornu's direct military intervention in Hausaland at this time.

12 H. R. Palmer, *Bornu, Sahara and Sudan*, London, 1936, pp. 226–7.

the terminus of the trans-Saharan caravan route and the entrepôt for the whole of Hausaland. The route from Katsina passed through present-day Tessawa to Agades. By the fifteenth century Katsina was a main feeder to Agades. As Agades grew, a colony of Katsinawa developed in the city, so influential that it is said to have had some say in the installation of the Sultan. Gobir also enjoyed connection with the caravan route through Takedda. With its newly acquired prosperity, Katsina expanded southwestwards into Yauri during the reign of Aliyu Karia-Giwa (*c.* 1419–31) and maintained its dominance there until the rise of Kebbi.[13] Towards the end of the century Katsina was sufficiently powerful to ward off Kano attacks, even though it could not shake off the yoke of Bornu. The *Kano Chronicle* records the coming of traders from Gwanja to Katsina during the fifteenth century.

In Kano, Sarki ʿAbdullāh Burja is said to have opened routes to Gwanja and Bornu, and the establishment of colonies of Bornawa (in substantial numbers) and Arabs (i.e. North Africans) in Katsina and Kano shortly after is on record. Horses were being traded with Nupe in exchange for slaves. By the end of the fifteenth century the impact of these wider commercial connections is reflected in the pomp and luxurious living with which the pious Sarki Muḥammad Rimfa (*c.* 1463–99) surrounded himself. The power of the king, and thus of the state, is reflected in the 'twelve innovations of Rimfa'. These indicate an intensification of the Islamic influence as well as vast expansion in the king's household establishment, the building of a new palace, the extension of Kano Walls and the institution of an inner Council of state.[14] The foreign influence and the direction it came from are preserved in the sobriquet applied to Rimfa: 'The Arab Sarki of wide sway.' Katsina was foremost in commercial connections, enjoying advantages in this regard which Kano lacked. The mutual expansion of both states, not surprisingly, brought them to blows for the first time at the turn of the fifteenth and sixteenth centuries.

The newly acquired wealth and power of these states explain further the attraction to them of both Bornu and Songhay. Outside the two empires, the country occupied by Kano, Katsina, Zaria—the last as gate to the rich products of the south—and Ahir had become a centre of intensive political, economic and even intellectual developments which made it a rich prize and a strategic advantage for the aspiring conquerors. The overall effect of the rivalry of Songhay and Bornu over Hausaland in the sixteenth century, analysed earlier in this book in detail, was to speed up the developments already noted. The result was that Hausaland became fully integrated into the commercial and ideological nexus which linked the Western Sudan societies together as well as with the wider Islamic World.

13 Tilho, *Documents Scientifiques de la Mission Tilho*, Paris, 1911, ii, pp. 154, 156, 157, 165, 235–6.

14 *K.C.*, pp. 109, 111–120.

The foregoing developments underline the main trends in the history of Hausaland and Bornu to the end of the fifteenth century and the fundamental forces which were to be at work in the subsequent period to the beginning of the nineteenth. The general theme of the history of Hausaland in the sixteenth century was one of overlapping imperialisms, while Bornu rose to its peak of power. Both Songhay and Bornu rivalry in Hausaland at the beginning of the century seems to have been shortlived. It did not issue in effective control by either power. The explanation of this phenomenon must be sought in the rise of Kebbi under Kanta Kotal as an imperial power on a scale comparable to other Sudanese empires known in history. The defiance of Songhay by the Kanta and his imposition of some degree of overlordship over the Hausa states put paid to Songhay enterprise in these states. Kebbi became a bulwark against Songhay encroachment on the Hausa country. The isolated and abortive Songhay attack on Katsina in 1554 was the end of the former's serious imperial tentatives in Hausaland.[15] The Kebbi bulwark was an effective check to Songhay even north of Hausaland. Important as was Ahir to Songhay-North African trading connections, Kebbi's power seems to have counted far more politically in Agades than Songhay overlordship. Hence, when the yoke of Kebbi became too irksome it was to Garzargamo rather than to Gao that Agades turned for assistance.[16] The failure of the Bornu attack on Surame, capital of Kebbi, about the mid-century demonstrated the former's ineffectiveness as protector of Ahir.[17]

The pre-eminence of Kebbi among the leading Hausa states during the first half of the sixteenth century is not open to doubt. However, Kebbi does not appear to have evolved an administrative machinery for a thorough integration of its 'dependencies' with its metropolitan province. Rather, it was enough that vassal states acknowledged Kebbi's overlordship and paid their tribute to the Kanta. In administrative organisation it could not compare with the high degree of centralisation in Askia Muḥammad Ture's Songhay. After Kanta Kotal's death the southern dependencies of Kebbi—Zaria, Nupe and others—regained their independence.[18] The precise nature and degree of control exercised by Kebbi over the northern Hausa states is unknown, but varying degrees of Kebbi influence were noticeable there down to the middle of the seventeenth century.

As the Hausa states continued to enjoy a near-complete autonomy under Kebbi they carried on pretty much as was their wont in the preceeding

15 See above, ch. 6.
16 Muḥammad Bello, *op. cit.*, p. 20.
17 *Ibid.*, also 'Abd al-Qādir b. Al-Muṣtafa, *Rauḍāt al-Afkār*, University of Ibadan Library 82/18, f. 3b.
18 P. G. Harris, *Sokoto Provincial Gazetteer* (mimeographed). It is said that the payment of tribute stopped during the reign of Maliki b. Ibrahima (*c.* 1644–57) see also R. M. East, *Labarun Hausawa da Makwabtansu*, Zaria, 1932, i, p. 38, and Y. Urvoy, *Histoire des populations du Soudan Central*, Paris, 1936, p. 250.

centuries. The century which opened with Kano victory over Katsina and Zaria and then Kano's capitulation before a Bornu expeditionary force was to reveal clearly that no Hausa state tolerated the yoke of imperialism either from their neighbours or from complete foreigners. Within the larger compass of the Kebbi empire, Sarkin Kano Muḥammad Kisoki (*c.* 1509–65) was described as ruling over Hausaland, 'east and west and south and north'.[19] The earlier capitulation to Bornu had no memorable sequel. Kano in the first half of the sixteenth century carried expansion and war to the western marcher provinces of Bornu without the latter being able to bring her to heel. The first half of the century after the far-flung exploits of Katagarmabe seems to have witnessed a Bornu sufficiently encumbered with internal problems of consolidation to be deprived of the capacity to intervene effectively abroad. It was during this half century that Kano's eastward expansion was backed up by the building of stockades round many of the towns in that direction.[20] These stockades had to be reduced by Idrīs Aloma's forces before Kano could be attacked.

Kano's pre-eminence over Katsina was shortlived. The latter had accepted the overlordship of Songhay and Kebbi grudgingly. It was at the hands of Katsinawa rebels that Kanta Kotal had died of a poisoned arrow wound in 1555. Mention has already been made of the disastrous rout of a small Songhay expeditionary force by Katsina cavalrymen in 1554. In the half-century that preceded the seventeenth, Katsina asserted its superior might over Kano. During the reign of Sarkin Kano Abubakar dan Rimfa (*c.* 1565–73) Katsinawa forces launched a heavy offensive against Kano, coming to the very gates of the city and exciting a panic among the Kanawa that led to a scattering of the inhabitants in search of refuge. Pressing home their initial victory, the Katsinawa did not abate their pressure on Kano for the rest of the century.[21]

At the end of the century Kano was under severe Katsinawa pressure which bade fair to engulf its territory. To the east the power of Idrīs Aloma had risen in Bornu. His army, well drilled and confident, with a core of Turkish musketeers, dealt swiftly with new Kano offensives on Bornu's western marches. The numerous stockaded towns which Kano had erected on its eastern frontiers, from which they used to make swiftly executed raids into Bornu, were reduced one after the other.[22] Against the fire-power of muskets and the disciplined Bornu forces, Kano poisoned arrows availed nothing. Stockaded settlements that were not directly attacked were deserted with, no doubt, the attendant problems of population displacements.

19 *K.C.*, pp. 112–13.
20 Aḥmad b. Fartua, *History of the first 12 years of the reign of Idris Aloma*, trans. H. R. Palmer, Lagos, 1938, p. 11.
21 *K.C.*, pp. 112–16.
22 Aḥmad b. Fartua, *op. cit.*, pp. 11, 30–1.

As if to complete Kano's woes, the Kwararafa came into their own. Having been building up their power in the Gongola valley for several centuries, and having been at one time or other subjected to Kano and Zaria, by the end of the sixteenth century they had developed into a strong militarist state. Very little else is known about their rise and their internal organisation. In the seventeenth century their military force was capable of striking effectively over long distances, far away from their home base: this must imply a complex efficient administrative organisation. For most of the seventeenth century they harassed first Kano and then the other Hausa states, as well as Bornu. Kano was the first to suffer Kwararafa attack towards the very end of the sixteenth or the beginning of the seventeenth century.[23] Kano was thus under fire from Katsina, Bornu and the Kwararafa.

In their first onslaught the Kwararafa ravaged Kano territory, and many dwellers in the city fled to Daura for refuge. As the chronicler puts it: 'Kano became very weak.'[24] The effect of the three-sided invasion on Kano commercial life, not to mention its military might, must have been devastating. As yet Katsina was untouched by the Kwararafa invasion. As the Kwararafa invasions were provoked neither by Bornu nor any of the Hausa states, who at this time had their hands full with other preoccupations, it can only be surmised that the invasions were aimed at obtaining an active share in the trans-Saharan commercial prosperity enjoyed by the northern states. They may also have been a natural expansion by an overgrown power. After the fall of Songhay to Moroccan invasion, Katsina's position as a commercial emporium was enormously enhanced. Its pre-eminent position among the other Hausa states well into the second half of the seventeenth century must, it appears, be ascribed to its wealth and power.

On the west and north-western frontiers of Hausaland the decline and fall of Songhay had not led to the strengthening of Kebbi's hold over the Hausa states as might have been expected. Power in these regions was undergoing a process of diffusion among Kebbi and a number of neighbouring states which were rising to prominence. These neighbours were Zamfara and Gobir. To the north of Gobir was the sultanate of Ahir, which became a dominant factor in deciding political relations between Gobir, Kebbi, Zamfara, Katsina and even Kano during the seventeenth century.

In seventeenth century Hausaland, therefore, the rise of these new powers to prominence prevented the emergence of what might have become a Katsina empire. The new powers shared commercial prosperity with Katsina, though not to the same degree, and it may be surmised that endeavour to have an increasing share of the growing economic prosperity

23 *K.C.*, p. 116.
24 *Ibid.*

in Hausaland lay at the root of the rivalries between the states.

Zamfara, which lies to the south of Gobir and east and south-east of Kebbi, had been consolidating its power and expanding its territory throughout the sixteenth century. Under their king Burum Burun, who reigned during the second quarter of the sixteenth century, Zamfara exerted influence on Yauri and carried war as far as the banks of the Niger. During the mid-century Zamfarawa expansionist wars were directed to Zaberma with some measure of success, albeit with no permanent tangible results. From this time, shortly after the death of the first Kanta, Zamfara had begun to challenge the might of Kebbi by war.[25] This is understandable in the light of succession disputes among the sons of Kanta Kotal following his death. For the rest of the century Zamfara was gradually consolidating its strength until by the beginning of the seventeenth century its position as a power to be reckoned with in north-western Hausaland was assured. Indeed at the end of the sixteenth century Zamfara appears to have become well established. It was also seeking expansion eastwards, or at any rate, it was viewed by Katsina as a threat to its own interests and power. Between *c.* 1595 and 1609 there was war between Zamfara and Katsina.[26] During the first quarter of the seventeenth century, Zaudai, king of Zamfara, cast aside traditional friendship and attacked Katsina. Only the opposition of his notables, who appear to have set greater store on friendship with Katsina, postponed further conflicts between the two states. As yet enmity with Kebbi and Ahir, which states constituted barriers between Zamfara and the main artery of commerce from North Africa, weighed most heavily in Zamfarawa counsels. The problem of Zamfara, and perhaps its main incentive to expansion, was that it was hemmed in on all sides, except on the relatively less important southern frontier, by powerful states—Kebbi, Ahir, Gobir, Katsina and Kano. Situated in a rich agricultural area, its economy needed easy contact with the outside world to give it the incentive necessary for development.

Kebbi, though still powerful, was on the downgrade during the sixteenth century, after the first Kanta's death. Hamadu, Kanta's son, had to share the throne with his brother for some time after their father's death until he liquidated his brother.[27] Nonetheless, during the first half of the seventeenth century Kebbi remained a threat, though no longer a scourge, to the neighbouring states of Gobir, Ahir and the rising Zamfara. Unlike Kebbi, Gobir was on the upgrade during the sixteenth century. Having been pushed southwards from its original home in Ahir with the rise of the sultanate of Agades, it found a home hedged in by Konni, Kebbi, Adar and

25 K. Krieger, *Geschichte von Zamfara* (which includes *Tarihin Zamfara* and other sources); Baesler Archiv—Beitrage zur Volkerkunde; Neue Folge, Beiheft, i (Berlin, 1959), pp. 33, 35.

26 *Tarihin Zamfara, loc. cit.*, p. 37.

27 Rauḍāt al-Afkār, Harris, *op. cit.*, p. 241.

Katsina, on whose territories it was encroaching. The position of Gobir on the eve of the seventeenth century therefore necessarily implied conflict with these neighbouring states. To the north of Gobir was Ahir, founded in the fifteenth century. Its first century of existence having been marked by considerable instability reflected in assassinations, depositions and very short reigns.[28] Ahir enjoyed relative quiescence during the Songhay century and underwent rapid economic development based on its favourable location as a commercial link between North and West Africa. Sixteenth-century reigns of Agades sultans were very long and, with the exception of the deposition of Muḥammad b. Talazu in 1556 by his successor al-ʿAdīl, the throne was stable.[29] With the fall of Songhay and the subsequent decline of Kebbi, Ahir was well established to play a notable, often decisive, rôle in the politics of the south.

The situation in Hausaland at the beginning of the seventeenth century may be seen therefore from the political standpoint as resolved into two power groups. There was the Kano–Katsina axis to the east, while in the west the dominance of Kebbi was being effectively threatened and undermined by new and powerful neighbouring states. These two groups were to interact with each other during the following two centuries to bring about new political arrangements eliciting unstable alignments in the whole of Hausaland. During the same period Bornu was to act as a conditioning force in Hausa political relations and to maintain an uncertain suzerainty, which however was not ignored by the disparate Hausa states. The threat of the Kwararafa in the 1670s was applicable to Bornu as well as to eastern Hausaland. Bornu formed a third axis of political relations within our area of study during this period. As a 'separate' political unit it interacted with the two Hausa axes just mentioned. It is convenient first to examine Bornu.

BORNU UNDER IDRĪS ALOMA: *c.* 1571–1603

While interstate rivalry, which Kebbi could not contain, tore Hausaland apart, Bornu attained its apogee under Idrīs Aloma (1571–1603). The achievements of Idrīs Aloma have been studied in detail in chapter 6. A few salient points in his career must be recapitulated here as background to Bornu's political history. The most outstanding contribution of Idrīs Aloma to the Bornu empire was that he carried through Bornu's expansion to its limits; he imposed Bornu control over the numerous factious ethnic groups that had before his time defied the central authority with impunity and plagued the empire with chronic, and indeed endemic, revolts. He achieved a final and durable, though not unchallenged, settlement of the Bulala question by effecting a boundary demarcation between Bornu and

28 Y. Urvoy, 'Chroniques d'Agades', *J. Soc. Afr.*, 1934, iv, Document A, p. 151; the fifteenth century was marked by short reigns which were the result of assassination and deposition of rulers.
29 *Ibid.*, p. 152.

Kanem and granting the latter a full measure of home rule within the empire.[30] His wars secured the trade routes to the north.[31] With the decline and fall of Songhay, he asserted Bornu's hegemony over Hausaland, particularly over Kano, and reduced Ahir and the Tuareg groups of the Damerghou lowlands to pliable compliance if not to subjection.

Idrīs Aloma's achievements were made possible not merely by adroit political manoeuvres and through his administrative genius but mainly through a profound military technological revolution which ranks him as a thoroughgoing modernist. In this regard attention must be drawn to his acquisition of Turkish muskets and musketeers, which proved fatal to resistance based on bows and arrows. The power of Bornu depended on the economic prosperity of the kingdom, which in turn rested on strong commercial ties with Tripoli and the Turkish empire. In his dependence on North Africa Idrīs Aloma was merely following an age-old Bornu tradition. But it is clear from the reply of Murad III of Turkey, sent through Mai Aloma's ambassador, that he secured friendly commercial relations with the Turkish empire[32]—perhaps the leading world power of those times. Idrīs Aloma also sent an appeal to the sultan of Morocco requesting help in the form of troops and of muskets and cannon.[33] Although the negotiations with Morocco produced neither tangible nor lasting results, they demonstrate the wide ramifications of Idrīs Aloma's diplomatic relations, all geared to his effort to strengthen his kingdom. Far more successful were his friendly relations with the Pasha of Tripoli. In 1578 he sent an embassy to the Pasha of Tripoli, Jaʿfar Agha, which was warmly received. Shortly after Jaʿfar reciprocated by sending an ambassador with a gift of some horses and firearms to Idrīs Aloma.[34] It was on such a thoroughgoing organisation of international trade, assiduously cultivated, that the power of Bornu rested.

The adoption of firearms, as amply demonstrated by history, does not in itself automatically lead to an enhancement of military effectiveness. The Mamlukes of Egypt for instance had fallen easily to Ottoman conquest

30 Palmer, *S.M.*, i, pp. 22, 30, 67–9.

31 Aḥmad b. Fartua, *op. cit.*, pp. 31–2, 34–5. The Tuareg, who were the main obstacle on the northern routes, were subjugated.

32 Murad III to Idris Aloma, 21 March 1577. Bashbahanlik Arsivi, Istanbul, Muhimme Deftere, 30/213/494. Photocopy with Northern Nigerian Historical Research Scheme Zaria. I am grateful to Professor H. F. C. Smith for a copy of the English translation done by him.

33 Abū al-Abbās Aḥmad b. Khālid al-Naṣirī, *Kitāb al-Istiqsā Lī Akhbār Duwāl al-Maghrib al-Aqsa*, ed. Jaʿfar al-Naṣirī and Muḥammad al-Naṣirī (Dar al-Kitāb, Casablanca, 1955, vol. v, part i.). I am grateful to Professor H. F. C. Smith for a copy of the translation of a report on transactions between Idris Aloma and Sultan ạl-Manṣūr—contained in pp. 104–11 of this book.

34 *Histoire chronologique de Royaume de Tripoli de Barbarie*, Fonds Français, 12219. Bibliothèque nationale, Paris, *c.* 1685, folio, 151. It is also stated: 'Le Commerce continuoit [*sic*] toujours entre les Tripolins et ceux de Bornou avec une égale satisfaction des uns et des autres.'

because, among other things, their adoption of firearms was not coupled with the military drill and strategy essential thereto. The struggle of Africans against European invaders in the nineteenth and twentieth centuries revealed that lack of skill in the use of firearms and divorcement from the drill and strategy which go with them can have fatal consequences. Idrīs Aloma achieved military pre-eminence in West Africa because his firearms were backed with appropriate drill and strategy. Even though he did not abandon traditional dependence on feudal levies and did not therefore depend solely on his standing army, it is clear that in the very early years of his reign, drill and organisational superiority, rather than reliance on muskets, was the secret of his successful campaigns. His well known scorched-earth policy reduced enemies to impotence. During the siege of Amsaka in Mandara great reliance was placed on improvisations to fill the ditches round the walls and for scaling these walls. Detailed preparations preceded attack as exemplified by his wars against the Ngafata So of the western Chad and the Tatala So.[35] One of his defensive methods was the building of *Ribāṭs* on difficult frontiers as against the Ngafata and Tatala. Commissariat problems were given detailed attention. After the season's campaigns, 'he ordered his army to disperse to their homes after he had given them advice about the journey and good counsel about transport, arms and stores necessary for warlike expeditions in the future'.[36] After detailed instructions concerning provisions, fighters returned to their villages: nor were they negligent or idle but exerted themselves industriously in finding animals for the journey, as well as spears, shields, horses and provisions for general use.[37] On expeditions the army was divided into two; an attacking force and a rear command, which could come to the assistance of the advance guard in difficulty or join in completing the rout of the enemy. The musketeers were mounted. They were storm-troopers who apparently advanced first, while other mailed cavalrymen and footmen armed with conventional weapons came after to ensure utter defeat of the enemy forces already 'softened' by the gun-men. For convenience of mobility in waterless terrain camels were used as transport animals instead of oxen and donkeys.[38] Large boats replaced small ones for the quick crossing of the big rivers. Free women and slave maidens played their part in the wars as cooks. Spies were extensively used to detect enemy positions prior to the advance of the main force. Above all, the musketeers were trained in the use of firearms. Aḥmad b. Fartua records that among the benefits bestowed by God was Aloma's acquisition of 'Turkish musketeers and numerous household slaves who became skilled in firing muskets'.[39]

35 Aḥmad b. Fartua, *op. cit.*, pp. 15–16, 24 and 25.
36 Palmer, *S.M.*, i, p. 37.
37 *Ibid.*, p. 46.
38 Aḥmad b. Fartua, *op. cit.*, p. 34.
39 *S.M.*, i, p. 11.

In his internal administration, Aloma relied on his big fiefholders whose loyalty was ensured by the justice of his administration. The notables shared with their ruler a common adherence to Islam and reliance on its law and precepts as basis of government. The *ʿulamāʾ*, from whose ranks the wazirs and judges were recruited, dispensed justice. His chronicler records that in his time 'truth and right came into their own, and shone in the land of Bornu. Evil went and hid herself and the path of righteousness was plainly established without let or hinderance, or deviation, so that all the notable people became Muslims except the atheists and hypocrites and malevolent persons.'[40]

To such an extent was government built on the *sharīʿa* that Ibn Fartua must be regarded as justified in describing Aloma as Amīr al-Muʾminīn. The Muslim Law, more than ever before, governed political and economic relations in peace and war. This does not mean that traditional religion was wholly destroyed, but he established an independent Muslim theocracy, a Bornu Caliphate. Having evolved order out of chaos, Idrīs Aloma laid a sure foundation for a prosperous and powerful Bornu. At the beginning of the seventeenth century, therefore, Bornu was well prepared for a career of splendour. However, after his death, Bornu withdrew into its own shell. Its enterprise in, and relations with, the Hausa states and Tuareg groups settled down to relative normalcy. Occasional strains in these relations necessitated expeditions, but the éclat which had characterised Bornu's involvement with Hausaland lapsed. It is therefore necessary at this point to see Bornu's history basically as a separate entity.

BORNU: 1603–1800

Very few details of Bornu history in this period have come down to us. It is perhaps as a result of this that historians have taken the view which suggests that nothing much of note happened. From this deduction arises the general view that Bornu entered a period of decline and degeneracy following the death of Idrīs Aloma. Yves Urvoy aptly sums up the prevailing view of Bornu's history in the seventeenth and eighteenth centuries when he wrote: 'Les successeurs d'Idris semblent bien falot; il y a encore quelques années de bonace, mais le Bornou s'affaisse bientôt rapidement sous les poids de princes aveulis, des attaques extérieures et de famines.'[41] Urvoy concedes, however, that under the first three successors of Idrīs, who reigned till *c.* 1644, the empire was still thriving on anterior conquests and glories. Other writers, such as Landeroin and H. R. Palmer, put the decline of Bornu at about 1750. In considering Bornu history or that of the West and Central Sudan generally, it must always be remembered that we depend for sources on chronicles which deal primarily with wars and with religious matters.

40 *Ibid.*, i, p. 188.
41 Y. Urvoy, *Histoire de l'Empire du Bornou*, Paris, 1949, p. 85.

The conquests of Idrīs Aloma, because they resulted in the effective subjugation of recalcitrant groups within the empire under a well ordered government, meant that his successor in the seventeenth century did not have to engage in as many wars. Revolts ceased to be chronic and when they did occur they did not demand mobilisation of forces on scales which different and graver circumstances had imposed not only on Idrīs Aloma but also on his predecessors. Because of this reduction in warfare the chronicles place more emphasis on the religious life of the successors of Idrīs Aloma and their *ʿulamāʾ*.

Another important consideration is that with the fall of Songhay it might be expected that Bornu would automatically inherit its imperial dominance in the West-Central Sudan. Bornu, however, was under the constant threat of the Kwararafa from the reign of Idrīs Aloma. Indeed this threat became a major preoccupation of the Bornu empire and the eastern Hausa states for the better part of the seventeenth century. Judging by the somewhat meagre memories of Kwararafa incursions which have come down to us, the conclusion must be that, until the second half of the century, Bornu was able to withstand the threat.[42] Nonetheless the Kwararafa depredations in Kano, Zaria and Katsina would mean that Bornu's scope of effective intervention to maintain its imperial dominance over Hausaland was thereby limited. Yet the suzerainty of Bornu over the Hausa states, though challenged and shaken by the Kwararafa, was not destroyed.

Another factor influencing the external activities of Bornu in the seventeenth century was the rise in the power of its Hausa vassals and the emergence of Zamfara and Gobir into prominence. This meant that the rulers of Bornu had more powerful vassals to deal with than Idrīs Aloma, and therefore could not have pushed a policy of belligerency as far as he could. Added to the increase in the power of the Hausa states was the increasing bellicosity of the Tuareg. The Sultanate of Ahir rose to its apogee during the seventeenth century and under el-Mubārak (*c.* 1654–87) and his son, Ag-Abba (Agaba), that state vehemently challenged Bornu's suzerainty. Ahir and the Tuareg of Damerghou, notably the Imakiten, now consolidating themselves more coherently than ever before, conducted regular raids into Bornu territory. Against these new dimensions in West-Central Sudan political relations Bornu maintained its core intact and continued to command acknowledgement of its suzerainty by its vassal states to the west.

ʿAbd al-Qādir ibn al-Muṣṭafā in his *Rauḍāt al-Afkār* maintains that the Hausa states continued to send tribute to Bornu through Sarkin Daura. This position was not successfully challenged until the late eighteenth century, when Sarkin Gobir Bawa jan Gwarzo stopped payment of tribute by his state.[43] Indeed during the early years of the Sokoto *jihād* (*c.* 1805) it

42 See below, p. 523.
43 *Rauḍāt al-Afkār*, ff. 4b, 7b.

was to Bornu, their suzerain, that the Hausa states of Katsina, Kano and Daura appealed against the scourge of the *mujāhidūn*. It is therefore not easy to fix a dateline for the decline of Bornu, nor can it be accepted uncritically that decline set in during the seventeenth century, once the momentum generated by Idrīs Aloma had spent its force.

The peace and stability conferred on Bornu apart, the successors of Idrīs Aloma were not mere ciphers. The first three were his sons. It is reported that peace prevailed under Mai Muḥammad b. Idrīs *c.* 1603–18. The chief attribute of the mai which is stressed in a Bornu *dīwān* was his patience and endurance as a consequence of which 'no discord was heard of in his prosperous days'.[44] Peace under Muḥammad b. Idrīs did not imply a state of inactivity. He is reported to have died fighting a *jihād*; perhaps against external enemies. From *c.* 1618–25, under Mai Ibrāhīm b. Idrīs, Bornu enjoyed great prosperity. From a dissolute career in his early days Ibrāhīm, alive to the challenges and responsibilities which ruling imposed on him, soon grew into a pious man and a notable warrior. He fought ten big battles in a reign of eight years and was involved in thirty skirmishes.[45] Evidence of the continued strength of the Bornu army in his days can be inferred from the song to the Queen Mother, Amina, who is eulogised as 'owner of a thousand thrones and five hundred gunmen'. Her fiefs were extensive along the Komadugu-Yobe and also included Maradi town. The last son of Idrīs Aloma, Ḥājj ʿUmar (Ḥājj ʿUmar b. Idrīs *c.* 1625–44) was noted for his piety. He went on pilgrimage in *c.* 1634. Already sixty at his succession, we do not hear of any wars in his time. But he did not abandon the strengthening of Bornu's power.

During the reigns of the first three mais of the seventeenth century, Bornu kept alive its strong trading connections with North Africa, notably Tripoli. Sometime between 1612 and 1614 the ambassadors of Mai Muḥammad b. Idrīs received a magnificent welcome from the Pasha of Tripoli.[46] The mission, which involved an exchange of rich presents (including several firearms from Tripoli) between the two rulers, was undertaken primarily to express the gratitude of the mai for the diverse merchandise of Europe which were reaching Bornu through her commercial link with Tripoli. A similar mission was sent to Tripoli during the last year of the reign of Ibrāhīm b. Idrīs.[47] Under Mai Hājj ʿUmar b. Idrīs (*c.* 1625–44) the trade with Bornu was so lucrative that the Pasha of Tripoli was anxious to secure a personal monopoly of it. To this end he dispatched ambassadors to the mai's court—laden with rich presents of leaf-copper, imitation Venetian pearls and cloth.[48] The Pasha was to

44 Palmer, *Bornu, Sahara and Sudan*, p. 244.
45 *Ibid.*
46 *Histoire chronologique du royaume de Tripoli de Barbarie*, 12219 f. 171.
47 *Ibid.*; H. Barth, *Travels and discoveries in North and Central Africa*, London, 1857, vol. ii, Appendix v, p. 659.
48 *Histoire chronologique . . .*, 12220 f. 198.

assume close surveillance over the Bornu trade ensuring that none of his subjects engaged in it without his consent. All the goods for the Bornu trade were to be bought up by the Pasha's officers. The terms were acceptable to Bornu and in 1637 the first caravan under the new arrangements arrived at Birnin Gazargamo. They returned with gold dust in exchange for their merchandise. In 1638 a Bornuan ambassadorial mission arrived at Tripoli to cement the commercial relations. They carried presents comprising thirty eunuchs, a hundred young negroes, fifty maidens and a golden tortoise, among many other items. In return the mai received 200 choice horses, fifteen young European renegades, several muskets and swords.[49]

Besides Tripoli, Bornu also had trading connections with merchants from Cairo.[50] There may have been other similar connections of which we have no knowledge. In view of the foregoing, it seems clear that the prosperity of the court was such as could keep up the glory of the kingdom as established by Idrīs Aloma. The early seventeenth century kings based their position on solid achievements of which they were the architects. They were not dependent merely on the momentum generated by their father, Aloma, to sustain the power of the kingdom. Because of the supreme importance to Bornu's power of commercial connections with the north, keeping the caravan routes open remained a cardinal aspect of Bornu's external policy down to the nineteenth century.

After the death of ʿUmar, the Tuareg and the Kwararafa were menacing Bornu, as they were Hausaland. During the long reign of his son, Ḥājj ʿAlī, who went on pilgrimage in the years *c.* 1648, *c.* 1656 and *c.* 1667,[51] Tuareg and Kwararafa incursions increased. ʿAlī's reign coincided with that of Muḥammad el-Mubārak of Agades (1654–87), under whom the sultanate of Ahir embarked on a highly successful expansionist career. The Kwararafa invasion of Hausaland also reached its peak of intensity during this time. The fact that, in spite of this, Mai ʿAlī was able to perform the Ḥajj thrice during his reign speaks much for the stability and prosperity of the period and leads us to draw the conclusion that the external invasions constituted more of a nuisance value than any real threat of conquest. That Bornu was in a firm position to deal with this threat is confirmed by the defeat of a simultaneous attack in *c.* 1668 on Birnin Gazargamo by the Kwararafa from the south and Ahir forces from the north.[52] Mai ʿAlī contrived to deal separately with the attackers. Bornu's victory was complete and was celebrated in a song to the praise of Mai ʿAlī by the learned

49 *Ibid.*
50 *Ibid.*, f. 201.
51 'Chronologie des Rois de Bornou de 1512 à 1677', by a French slave in Tripoli. Photocopy supplied by Mr J. Lavers of Abdullahi Bayero College of Aḥmadu Bello University.
52 *Ibid.*, also H. Palmer, *Bornu, Sahara and Sudan*, p. 246.

Dan Marina of Katsina.[53] ʿAlī's victory and rout of the powerful Kwararafa army put an end to the latter's raid of Bornu territory.

Besides these exploits, ʿAlī led expeditions to Mandara, again in revolt during his reign, as well as to Tuareg country.[54] Songs to important notables[55] such as the Yerima (commander of the north) indicate that Ahir failed to throw off the Bornu yoke. Moreover, it seems clear that Mai ʿAlī was engaged in constant warfare on a scale which would have done credit even to the renowned Idrīs Aloma. The songs composed during his reign, records of which have survived, show that the tradition of using musketeers in warfare persisted very strongly.

Since the time of Idrīs Aloma, no king in Bornu history down to the jihādists' invasion of the early nineteenth century seems to have distinguished himself in war or wielded as much unrivalled power within the empire as Ḥājj ʿAlī. The last four years of his life, *c.* 1680–4, were spent almost entirely away from the capital. His son and successor, Idrīs, acted as regent during those four years. His grip on power and on the country was sure from the beginning of his reign. When Kashim Birri, his brother, who acted as regent during the early part of his reign whenever he was away on pilgrimage, attempted to seize the throne, ʿAlī dealt with him summarily by blinding and exiling him.[56] Perhaps as a result of instability, the consequence of constant warfare, the first of a series of severe famines in Bornu was recorded during his reign. These famines were to become a recurrent theme of Bornu history thereafter. To what extent these famines must be ascribed to evidence of warfare or to other unknown factors is unclear. It seems, however, simplistic to see them as due essentially to political decline.

During ʿAlī's reign another recurrent theme of Bornu history, the piety of the rulers and the rise of the *ʿulamā'* to dominance, pervades the records of the chroniclers. This demonstrates the continuous development of Islam as a state religion, given a vigorous fillip by Idrīs Aloma. Gazargamo from the mid-seventeenth century became the foremost centre of Islamic learning and education for Bornu and Hausaland. In an account of the city written by Muḥammad Ṣāliḥ b. Ishāq in 1658, the highly intellectual and religious atmosphere of the mai's court is vividly portrayed.[57] At the court were numerous *ʿulamā'* who indulged constantly in learned disputations in which Mai ʿAlī took an active part. Regard was paid to fine points and

53 *Bornu, Sahara and Sudan*, p. 246. In celebration of the Mai's victory (victory of an earlier date?). Muḥammad Ibn al-Sabaghī (Dan Marina) of Katsina composed a poem, part of which in translation is as follows: '. . . in praise of Amir al-Mu'minin ʿAlī Sultan of Bornu, and in censure of the Kwararafa. Has he brought us succour? Verily but for him our hearts had never ceased from dread of the unbelievers. Narrow had become to us the earth pressed by the foe, Till Ali saved our children and their children yet unborn . . .'

54 Palmer, *Bornu, Sahara and Sudan*, pp. 246–50.

55 See e.g. *ibid.*—To the Yerima, p. 249; to the Zakama, p. 250.

56 *Ibid.*, p. 248.

57 *Ibid.*, pp. 33–5.

details of the *sharīʿa*. In Gazargamo alone, which had grown into a large city with a labyrinth of roads, there were four Friday mosques each with its own Imām, and several thousand worshippers.

There can be no doubt that the Ḥajj ʿAlī had to face so much opposition from the Tuareg because they too wanted to control the caravan trade with North Africa which, as noted earlier, had become unprecedentedly profitable. ʿAlī, for unknown reasons, discounted the Tripoli connections at the beginning of his reign, perhaps out of a jealous regard for the independence of his kingdom. A diplomatic rumpus followed in 1648. However, in 1653 he sent an embassy to the Pasha of Tripoli with a letter and rich presents to reopen amicable relations.[58] Active commercial relations were thereafter maintained with Tripoli to the end of ʿAlī's life. ʿAlī, renowned as 'a great warrior and traveller', died in Tibesti.[59]

From his death to the mid-eighteenth century there were recurrent famines. One such lasted seven years during the reign of Mai Dunama b. ʿAlī (*c.* 1699–1717); another, called ʿAlī Shu',[60] lasted two years during the reign of Mai Muḥammad b. Hamdūn (*c.* 1731–47) and seems to have continued into the next reign (*c.* 1747–50) which is noted for yet another severe famine. Against the background of these famines, which are separated one from the other by many years, the Bornu chronicles record prevailing peace. This peace had to be worked for. Mai Dunama b. ʿAlī, noted as a great warrior, is celebrated for his firmness in stamping out evil deeds, particularly highway robbery. Mai Muḥammad b. Ḥājj Ḥamdūn (*c.* 1731–47) another great warrior, laid siege to Kano for a period of seven months during the reign of Sarkin Kano Kumbari b. Sharefa (*c.* 1731–43).[61] It appears, therefore, that there was sufficient security at home to justify or encourage foreign adventure. Peace at home was achieved through the mai's military exertions. In a song celebrating Mai Muḥammad's achievements, constant reference is made to his successful wars against pagans while the ethnic heterogeneity of the subjects of his empire with the diversity of their cultures is alluded to in the lines: 'Of those who wear turbans, and those who wear only loin cloths, you are the chief. You are the ruler alike of men who have a leather loin cloth tied between their legs and of those who ride on fine horses.'[62] The same source refers to the mai's firm hold on Kanem.

Although Bornu's military exploits did not attain the same scale as in the period up to the end of the sixteenth century, it seems that one reason for this was that Bornu had not the same necessity to engage in large-scale warfare in the last two centuries of the mais as in the earlier period. Whenever the need for war did arise the mais of Bornu down to the

58 *Chronologie des rois de Bornou.*
59 Palmer, *Bornu, Sahara and Sudan*, p. 248.
60 *Ibid.*, p. 252.
61 *Ibid.*, p. 253; *Kano Chronicle*, p. 124.
62 Palmer, *Bornu, Sahara and Sudan*, p. 253.

middle of the eighteenth century, and indeed for several decades after, usually rose to the occasion. Ruling over a well-secured empire they had the opportunity denied their forebears to cultivate diligently the art of peace.

In the relative calm of the seventeenth and eighteenth centuries after the storm of the earlier period, Bornu rulers, though they did not and could not abandon paying attention to the army, slipped from the standards of Idrīs Aloma. After the seventeenth century the chronicles and praise songs make no single reference to the use of firearms. No reference is made to the use of firearms in Bornu's resistance to the attacks of the Fulani *Mujahidūn* at the beginning of the nineteenth century. It is well known that in the early days the jihād fighters did not use firearms. Had the Bornu army employed firearms on any large scale, therefore, they would presumably have proved superior to the attackers. Even the Kanembu followers of Muḥammad el-Amīn el-Kānemī were reputed as spearmen not as musketeers.

The Bornu rulers of the eighteenth century had clearly not kept alive the tradition of importing firearms on the same scale as their predecessors. Bornu was therefore apparently armed in a similar manner to her enemies and vassal states. These states, as noted earlier, had grown enormously in their military strength from their pre-seventeenth-century positions. Bornu's decline in military superiority was definitely a factor of decline in the state. There is, however, no reason to suppose that while basing itself on traditional weapons its military organisation along those lines had equally deteriorated. During the long reign of ʿAlī b. Ḥājj Ḥamdūn (*c.* 1750–91) the Bornu army kept at bay Tuareg attacks which had become fiercer than ever before. The new element in Ahir and other Tuareg rivalries with Bornu was control over the salt mines of Bilma in Kawar, which had become a central factor in the trans-Saharan caravan trade. Over and above but tied up with this was control of the trans-Saharan trade routes. A determined onslaught of the Ahirawa on Bornu in 1759 did not result in a clear victory for the mai's forces. Bornu had to grant to Ahir undisturbed participation in the Bilma trade.[63] Bornu's suzerainty over Ahir had, for all practical purposes, been terminated. Keeping Ahir at bay did not mean the exercise of control over it. With its favourable location on the trade routes from Hausaland to the north, the sultanate of Ahir was strongly placed to compete with Bornu in wealth and power. Down to the cataclysm of the early nineteenth century, which disrupted Bornu and released centrifugal forces latent within its body politic, the Seifawa successfully maintained their dominance, though always disputed by the Tuareg, over the trans-Saharan routes to the north.

The centuries old problem of Mandara revolts was a different matter. Mandara, grown more powerful through centuries of resistance to Bornu,

63 F. J. Rennell Rodd, *People of the Veil*, London, 1926, p. 415.

was most ungovernable in the eighteenth century. Mai ʿAlī b. Ḥājj Ḥamdūn sent several expeditions to quell Mandara rebellion. The successful resistance of the Mandarawa gradually sapped the strength of the Bornu army until it was routed in *c.* 1781. This rout spelt disaster for the Bornu army from which it did not recover until it was engulfed by the deluge of the *jihād*. The last mai before the *jihād*, Aḥmad b. ʿAlī (1791–1808), was apparently a feeble and blind old man who had virtually abdicated to his son about six months before the first jihādists' attack on his capital city.[64] The weakness of Aḥmad did not improve the fortunes of Bornu in her baffling predicament. The *jihād* delivered the blow to the Seifawa empire which sent it tottering to its collapse.

The Islamic factor which for over seven centuries had been a mainstay of the Bornu monarchy proved its undoing in the end. From the time of Idrīs Aloma Islam had become a state religion, determining, to a large extent, the law which ruled the state. The mais were styled *Amīr al muʾminīn*, signifying that they ruled over a Muslim state. The Bornu rulers of our period are, almost without exception, renowned for their piety and the majority of them performed the *ḥājj*. Though described as indolent, Ḥājj Ḥamdūn b. Dunama (*c.* 1726–38) was remarkable for his piety and learning. Such was the priority he accorded to learning that his reign has been described as the age of the domination of the *ʿulamā'*.[65] The long reign of ʿAlī b. Ḥājj Dunama (*c.* 1750–91) was also said to have been completely dominated by the learned class. On this evidence Bornu ought not to have been the object of a *jihād*. However, like Hausaland, the basin of the Gongola and the Upper Benue region, the Fulani had settled in large numbers in Bornu, since the fifteenth and sixteenth centuries.

As in other parts of the Western Sudan the Bornu Fulani suffered the disabilities of second-class citizens in their adopted countries. Albeit, there were to be found among their members a large number of learned men, and the incidence of Islamisation was highest among them as an ethnic group. I have discussed the Fulani position and their grievances elsewhere.[66] Suffice it here to say that the most important consequence of Fulani isolation was a common bond of Pan-Fulanism. With their unity of view induced by their separateness, coupled with a close identification with Islam as a national badge, their scattered groups in their different localities nursed deep feelings of resentment against existing governments. Whatever religious motivation lay behind Fulani revolt against Bornu authority, the prevailing circumstances of their time were such as to excite their spirit of revolt. Further evidence of Fulani restiveness is shown by the fact that prior to the *jihād* the Fulani of Gombe and future Adamawa had

64 Palmer, *Bornu, Sahara and Sudan*, pp. 255, 259.
65 Y. Urvoy, *L'Empire du Bornou*, p. 85.
66 R. A. Adeleye, *Power and Diplomacy in Northern Nigeria 1804–1906*, London, 1971, pp. 19–22.

attempted revolts against their liege-lords. The early successes of the Sokoto *jihād*, which spread like wildfire throughout the West-Central Sudan under Fulani leadership, was a signal the temptation of which the Fulani in Bornu could not resist. Their *jihād* was the outburst of a latent spirit of revolt. Although they could marshall arguments of oppression, tyranny and anti-Islamic practices against the Bornu empire, which the learned El-Kānemī could not but confirm, it is correct to see their revolt, in a large measure, as an expression of their 'Fulaniness'.

A final point about Bornu's Islam and the *jihād* is that in so far as el-Kānemī confirmed the Sokoto *mujāddidūn's* charges of corruption, bribery to pervert justice, oppressive and tyrannical rule and the worshipping of idols in places called Kubara and Kakaua (which was plain polytheism—*shirk*—the most virulent antithesis of Islam) Bornu Islam had not moved very far outside the court circles. It does not appear to have been the religion of the masses, at least, away from the big towns like Gazargamo and mallam settlements, and the Kanuri core of the empire. In fine, attack on Bornu was legitimised by the Sokoto *mujāddidūn* on the ground not of general sins against Islam or polytheism but on the fact that by giving aid to the *Sarakuna* (chiefs) and other refugees of Kano, Katsina and Daura—'heathens'—the mai had confessed himself a heathen. Yet, in supporting the Sarakuna of Hausaland the mai was only carrying out an obligation to his vassals. This was the last act of Bornu intervention in its wider imperial domains of Hausaland before the deluge.[67]

The *jihād* invasion apart, the Bornu empire had shrunk in size by the end of the eighteenth century. Hegemony over the Hausa states had worn very thin in virtually everything but name. Kanem's attachment had also become tenuous while Baghirmi was virtually independent.[68] Yet, in the core of Bornu as we know it today the process of Kanurisation had been going on for centuries, and by the end of the eighteenth century 'the kingdom . . . had developed from a highly diversified province ruled by a beleaguered dynasty in the late fifteenth century to a relatively homogeneous nation ruled by a powerful aristocracy.[69]

KANO-KATSINA RIVALRY AND KWARARAFA INVASIONS IN THE SEVENTEENTH CENTURY

Despite Katsina's rise to pre-eminence in the last half of the sixteenth century, developments in Kano were also rapid. In spite of external threats mentioned above Kano was growing in wealth and power and was therefore able to reduce the struggle with Katsina to a stalemate during the first half of the seventeenth century. As will be seen below, Katsina was

67 Muḥammad Bello, *op. cit.*, pp. 121–2. The Sarkin Daura, Sarkin Katsina and Sarkin Kano appealed to Bornu.
68 Louis Brenner, 'The Shehus of Kukawa: A history of the Al-Kānemī dynasty of Bornu', unpublished Ph.D. thesis, 1968, p. 22.
69 *Ibid.*, p. 19.

not without urgent problems to grapple with in directions other than Kano. A phenomenon of Kano's development during the seventeenth century was the rise of overmighty subjects, mostly military chieftains. During the reign of Muḥammad Nazaki b. Zaki, the Wombai, ʿAbdullāh, a slave official, had acquired so much wealth and power that he was able to undertake the expansion of Kano city walls at staggering expense to himself. An indication of his wealth is provided by a gift of 100 horses, all mailed, which he gave to his king on the latter's return from a war. The Wombai, subsequently installed at Karayi, near Katsina frontier, became the bulwark against Katsina attacks. The next ruler had to depose him as a security measure against possible revolt by him on account of his overgrown power. Yet Nazaki's son and successor, Kutumbi (Muḥammad Alwali) also had similarly unduly powerful lieutenants. One of them, Dawaki Kwashi, had to be placated to dissuade him from rebellion which, it was feared, would have carried the majority of the chief men of Kano to his camp.[70] Al-Ḥājj, son of Kutumbi (*c.* 1648–9) was deposed. Kukuna, son of al-Ḥājj, was turned off his throne by his Madawaki who proceeded to appoint his sister's (i.e. Kukuna's) son, Soyaki, as sarki. Kukuna fled to Zaria. Kano's military predicaments appear to have brought the top echelons of the military hierarchy into unprecedented peaks of power which tempted them to dominate the political life of the state. The Madawaki's action divided the Kano nobility into two camps—those of the Madawaki and Kukuna. This resulted in civil war which culminated in the restoration of Kukuna in 1652, and the arrest and humiliation of the Madawaki. Military commanders multiplied by leaps and bounds during the seventeenth century and well into the eighteenth. From a recorded number of eight war captains under Muḥammad Kisoki in *c.* 1582–1618, the number had climbed to fifty-two by the mid-eighteenth century.[71]

We do not possess information on the internal affairs of Katsina in these years. But so powerful and menacing had the state become by the beginning of the seventeenth century that Sarkin Kano Muḥammad Kisoki, *c.* 1582–1618, trembled under the fear of Katsinawa ravages of his territory. The main fear was that Katsina might absorb Kano. In a determined effort which apparently involved the total mobilisation of the state's resources, including the initiation of the *Dirki* talisman as well as charms prepared by a leading Maghrībī savant resident in Kano, the king scored an important victory against Katsina towards the end of the sixteenth or beginning of the seventeenth century.[72] Kano's victory was indecisive and the struggle continued. The pressure of Katsina on Kano had apparently become aggravated during the second decade of the seventeenth century. With his ascension to the throne, Sarkin Kano Muḥammad Zaki (*c.* 1618–23) sent

70 *K.C.*, pp. 117, 118.
71 *Ibid.*, pp. 117, 125.
72 *Ibid.*, pp. 116–18; Urvoy, *Histoire des populations du Soudan Central*, p. 242.

envoys to arrange peace with Katsina. The latter, apparently confident in their strength, not only refused the offer of peace but invaded Kano forthwith. The Kano source maintains that the invaders were defeated at Karayi in this encounter. Two major expeditions in which Kano took the offensive against Katsina are reported during the long reign of Sarkin Kano, Kutumbi (*c.* 1623–48). In the first the Kano army laid a nine-month siege to Katsina and during the second expedition in *c.* 1648 the Kano army camped close to the western gate of Katsina. According to the *Kano Chronicle*, Kano was victorious in the first expedition but was decisively defeated in the second. Kutumbi died from wounds sustained in the battle. Under Sarki Uban Yari (*c.* 1626–38?) Katsina was very powerful. The protracted struggle with Kano had issued in a stalemate. Apparently weary of war and having other urgent threats to their power to face, Kano and Katsina concluded a treaty of peace in perpetuity, *c.* 1649–51.[73] The pact was not broken thereafter.

The Kwararafa attack at about the end of the sixteenth century in which Kano territory was devastated and the population thrown into panic and confusion has been mentioned. We have no record thereafter of similar Kwararafa invasions until the middle of the seventeenth century. Nevertheless, the threat from the Kwararafa conditioned the external policy of Kano as much as did constant warfare with Katsina. It was, no doubt, in response to the threat from Katsina and the Kwararafa that the expansion of Kano city was undertaken by the Womban (Wombai) Kano between *c.* 1618 and 1623. While the expansion of the city was under way, the sarki with his army was fighting in the future Gombe region at Kalam. Defending the southern frontiers (from which came the Kwararafa) by offensive action became a regular Kano policy or military strategy for the greater part of the seventeenth century. Through this policy Kano's sphere of influence, if not empire, was pushed into Bauchi and present-day Gombe regions. Thus Kano and Zaria had direct boundaries with the Kwararafa empire. It was from these exploits that the kings of Kano and their warlords captured numerous slaves.[74] This must have greatly strengthened Kano economy and external commercial relations. The leading city of the Gombe region was actually sacked by Sarki Kutumbi. The accumulation of domestic slaves must have raised new social and perhaps political problems. So numerous were the slaves in Kano that a new titled chief, *Sarkin Samari*, was created to handle the affairs of slaves in their prime. The Fulani of Gombe and Kano were first made to pay *jangali*—cattle tax—by Kutumbi. Wealth derived from exploits in the south was apparently applied to strengthening the army. The vast increase in the number of warlords during the century was a reflection of the growth in the size of the army and of territorial expansion as well as the buoyancy of the economy.

73 *K.C.*, p. 120.
74 *Ibid.*, p. 119.

Horses and mail-coats came more into use among a substantial proportion of the army.

By its incursions to the south Kano constituted a bulwark against the Kwararafa. But by the middle of the century, the latter embarked on a major offensive not only against Zaria and Kano but also Katsina. It was doubtless partly in appreciation of the odds which they both had to face in the Kwararafa invasions that peace between Kano and Katsina, elusive for one and a half centuries, now became possible. Civil dissension within Kano, which began in *c.* 1649 and culminated in war in *c.* 1652, must have predisposed Kano to peace.

The civil war which had split the ranks of the notables into two factions made Kano particularly vulnerable to foreign invasion. In *c.* 1653 the Kwararafa attacked Kano. The sarki, Muḥammad Kukuna, was away on a grand tour of his subject districts to the east.[75] His tour took him as far as Auyo in present Hadejia emirate—then also claimed by Bornu. The same year the Kwararafa forces led by their chief Adashu ravaged Katsina territory until they laid siege to the city itself.[76] Once they succeeded in entering the city they set it on fire. In the midst of the panic which gripped the city the sarki (Muḥammad Kabiya b. Usman, *c.* 1648–57) appealed to the pious and learned poet and commentator, Dan Marina (i.e. Muḥammad al-Kashinawī b. al-Sabbagh) who is said to have saved the city by his prayers. As the Kwararafa retreated they are said to have lost their chief and his first minister together with many of their great men.[77]

The two cities of Kano and Katsina suffered another Kwararafa attack in 1671. All the forces of Kano—physical and spiritual, Islamic and traditional—were thrown into the struggle. The old gods, Chibiri and Bundun, were revived, the mallams came out in full strength, the soldiers put up a valiant resistance. All was to no avail.[78] The Kwararafa did great slaughtering; much of the cream of Kano society among the warriors and the learned men perished in the battle inside the city. The inhabitants were scattered, the sarki fled to Daura for refuge. Katsina was also sacked by the Kwararafa. Great slaughtering was done there too. Oral traditions emphasising the brutality of the invaders claim that many of the inhabitants were cast alive into a pit still known as the *Giwa Baka* (*sic*).[79]

No records or any other indication point to subsequent Kwararafa invasions of Hausaland after the 1671 expedition. The Kwararafa withdrew to their kingdom as suddenly as they had burst upon the Hausa and Bornu scenes towards the end of the preceding century. The explanation lies, perhaps, in the internal affairs of their kingdom, records and memories of which appear lost to history. The Kwararafa invasions had important

75 *Ibid.*, p. 121.
76 East, *op. cit.*, i, p. 41; F. Daniel, *History of Katsina* (mimeographed), 1937, p. 10.
77 East, i, p. 41.
78 Urvoy, *Histoire des populations . . .*, p. 242; *K.C.*, p. 122.
79 Daniel, *loc. cit.*

consequences for Kano in that it weakened it considerably. During the rest of the century the spirit of revolt was abroad in its eastern districts. Sarkin Gaya revolted and paid for rebellion with his life. A deliberate policy of tightening Kano's hold on the eastern districts was pursued. The chief military officer, Sarkin Dawaki, was installed at a place called Aujera to watch over Miga, Dutsi and Gaya between Kano and present-day Hadejia.[80]

During the eighteenth century Kano had to face the challenge of the power of Zamfara and then of Gobir. Katsina had been drawn into conflict with Kebbi, Zamfara and Gobir from the seventeenth century. Thus Kano and Katsina after many centuries of relative political isolation from western Hausaland were, by the end of the seventeenth century, integrated into the system of political relations with the rest of the Hausa states. Now we must return to western Hausaland.

WESTERN HAUSALAND IN THE SEVENTEENTH CENTURY

For the greater part of the seventeenth century Kebbi was the centre around which political developments in western Hausaland revolved. There are no grounds to doubt Muḥammad Bello's assertion that Kebbi's power endured for about 100 years after the death of the first Kanta.[81] However, Kebbi's pre-eminence was threatened by military challenge from its neighbours. Zamfara, one of its vassal states, initiated an independence movement about the end of the sixteenth century which also launched it on the path of imperial expansion.[82] The attack on Kebbi, begun by Sarkin Zamfara, Zartai, at this time, was continued by his successors with varying degrees of success. Kebbi was also the common target of raids by the Tuareg of Ahir and the Gobirawa. Ahir considered as part of its territory Adar, another vassal of Kebbi lying southwards and south-westwards of Ahir; this caused tension and actual conflict with Kebbi. To the west of Gobir were Adar and Konni, the latter also a Kebbi vassal.

By the seventeenth century Gobir was expanding not only westwards but at the same time southwards away from the area to which it had been pushed by the rise of Ahir in the fifteenth century.[83] This Gobirawa expansion involved conflict with Kebbi over Konni, with Ahir over Adar and with Katsina on its south-eastern frontiers. Kebbi's attempts to expand westwards to Zaberma and Gurma as well as southwards towards the Niger clashed with the extension of Zamfara's influence in these directions. The foregoing underlines the position of isolation to which political developments around its frontiers were forcing Kebbi during the seventeenth century. Unlike its neighbours, though still powerful, Kebbi lacked the drive of a rising power. Moreover its isolation also constituted a delicate diplomatic problem. A forward policy against its adversaries might con-

80 *K.C.*, pp. 122–3.
81 Muḥammad Bello, *op. cit.*, p. 20; *Rauḍāt al-Afkār*, f. 5a.
82 Krieger, *op. cit.*, p. 35.
83 Urvoy, *Histoire des populations . . .*, p. 244.

ceivably call forth an alliance, be it one of convenience, against it. As yet, for the better part of the century, Kebbi's enemies were yet to consolidate their power.

Zamfara was not only strengthening its independence movement: it was also attempting to expand westwards, eastwards and northwards with raids into Zaberma, Katsina, Kano and Adar. The eastward push was apparently successful. Zamfara sources claim that during the third quarter of the seventeenth century, their Sarki Abdu Na Bawanka successfully attacked Kano close to the city killing and capturing many Kanawa.[84] Similarly, his son attacked Kano during the 1670s. There is no mention of these Zamfarawa attacks in Kano sources. This is not, however, to discount them. The victories recorded were more significant and more glorious for a rising power. They may even have been exaggerated. But compared with the contemporaneous ravages of Kano by the Kwararafa, the Zamfarawa raids would not have inspired the same awe or claimed as strong a place in Kanawa memories as the menace of the Kwararafa. Furthermore the relative weakness of Kano resulting from Kwararafa attacks following on the protracted Kano-Katsina struggles may have rendered Kano a tempting target of attack by Zamfara. In these circumstances, the reported Zamfara enterprise in Kano seems not unlikely.

Perhaps as a reflection of Zamfara's mounting status among its neighbours, an intensive conversion to, and propagation of, Islam in the state is said to have taken place during the second quarter of the century. Sarki Aliyu, described as a redoubtable warrior, is said to have built mosques in Birnin Zamfara and in the villages. The introduction of Islam and its active propagation suggests, perhaps, an influx of foreigners—as mallams, merchants, or both—to a state which was developing fast and becoming militarily, commercially and economically important. Zamfara's period of relative isolation as a second-rate power was drawing to a close. Decline in Kebbi may have contributed to Zamfara's new-found importance. It is instructive to note that Sarki Abdu dan Suleiman had to undertake a vast expansion of the walls of Birnin Zamfara towards the end of the century.[85]

As noted above the other rising power of the west was Gobir, under their sarki Muḥammad Mai Guitti. Their southward and westward expansion met with great success. Mai Guitti established his capital at Birnin Naya on the present site of Chibiri (Tsibiri) during the second half of the seventeenth century.[86] For a long time, he was engaged in war with Shagarana IV of Katsina on whose territory he was encroaching.[87] Gobir's westward expansion into Adar and Konni resulted in constant conflict between her, Kebbi and Ahir. The Asbenawa (i.e. Ahirawa) were pushing

84 Krieger, *op. cit.*, pp. 37–9.
85 *Ibid.*, p. 43.
86 Tilho, *Documents scientifiques de la mission Tilho*, p. 470.
87 *Ibid.*, also Urvoy, *Histoire des populations . . .*, p. 237.

southwards to the richer and well-watered territories to the south, while Gobir was also attempting to push into the fertile region of the Zamfara-Rima river system. Moreover, besides Ahir expansion into Adar, Gobir lay across the Ahir-Kebbi caravan route.

The interstate raids and skirmishes in western Hausaland during the first half of the century set the stage for the more bitter struggles which characterised the second half. Zamfara, Gobir and Ahir had in the meantime waxed stronger. Suleiman dan Abdu Na Bawanka, who appears to have reigned in the 1660s and early 1670s is said to have scored a notable victory over a Kebbi force comprised of several thousand horses and Adarawa allies.[88] Suleiman's successor, Muḥammad Na Makake, continued the war with Kebbi in the 1670s and 80s. He also raided Zaberma.

During the reign of Muḥammad el-Mubārak (1654–87) Ahir attained its peak of power. This factor probably more than any other determined the character of interstate political relations in western Hausaland. It had the effect of heightening tension and deepening the intensity of military conflicts. While Gobir was immersed in its perennial wars with Katsina and Kebbi, and Zamfara-Kebbi hostilities dragged on, Ahir was left with a free hand to profit from the troubles. In *c.* 1674 the Ahir Sultan, Muḥammad el-Mubārak, sent a strong force of his kingdom into Kebbi territory. Adar was decisively conquered. In the same year, and perhaps as part of the same expedition, the army of Ahir led by his son, Ag-Abba (Agaba), routed the Kebbi army, killed Sarkin Kebbi and destroyed a number of Kebbi villagers.[89] The conquest of Adar, followed by the appointment of Ag-Abba as its ruler, not only meant the permanent excision of Adar from Kebbi[90] vassalage; it also placed Ahir in a stronger position to realise its further ambitions in the south.

In *c.* 1685 Ag-Abba moved his residence to Adar. For Gobir, Zamfara and Kebbi the Ahirawa establishment in Adar was far too close to be tolerated. After the defeat of Kebbi in *c.* 1674, the initiative for repelling the southward push of the Asbenawa from Adar was in the hands of Zamfara and Gobir but not Kebbi. In 1685 the Sarkin Zamfara and his troops fell on a large party (said to be about 700) of Kel-Owi Tuareg and killed them. During the same year (Rabi'l-awāl 996 A.H.) Sultan Muḥammad el-Mubārak, bent on vengeance, collected a formidable army comprising all Tuareg forces, Itesen, kel-Owi and kel-Geres, under the supreme command of Muḥammad b. Al-ḥājj Ibrāhīm (Amma Fatim). He was assisted by a large number of nobles. In the ensuing encounter the Zamfara army was routed. Ahir's resounding victory is reflected in the report that the Zamfarawa left 1,000 killed on the battle field. The following year, yet another expedition comprising all Tuareg groups under El-Mubārak's influence

88 Krieger, *op. cit.*, p. 40.
89 Urvoy, *Journal Société . . .*, *op. cit.*, p. 170.
90 *Ibid.*, p. 156.

launched a second attack on Zamfara. The chronicler's graphic description claims that Zamfara lost all her best and leading men—all the flower of their state. The Tuareg, too, are said to have lost some of their nobles in this battle.[91]

An epidemic which ravaged Agades for two years after this expedition carried El-Mubārak away in 1687. His son Ag-Abba, who succeeded him, had to undertake an expedition against Gobir in 1689.[92] The Gobirawa had attacked, under cover of night, a party of Tuareg led by sons of Sultan el-Mubārak. They were deprived of their horses and camels, and other property. The Tuareg escaped singly to Adar to tell the story. The revenge expedition fell on the unsuspecting Gobirawa. Gobir villages were sacked while numerous Gobirawa were captured. Some of the children were reported sold into slavery in Tuat and some to Fezzan. So crushing was Gobir's defeat that it had to sue for a truce, which Sarkin Ahir granted.

For the rest of the century the Ahir throne was unstable. Succession disputes did not set in until the eighteenth century but in the meantime there were internecine conflicts between the various Tuareg groups. From *c.* 1696–7 there were severe wars between the Kel-Owi and Itesen Tuareg. A prolonged draught accompanied by severe famine and a steep price rise coincided with the Kel-Owi-Itesen dissension. For the last quarter of the century nothing more is heard of Kebbi, which had been forced to the background while Gobir and Zamfara occupied the forestage. The seventeenth was, *par excellence*, a century of warfare for western Hausaland. It had also been a century of rapid power build-up. The power of the newly consolidated Hausa states of the west had implications not only for western Hausaland but also, in more than a marginal sense, for the rest of Hausaland in the eighteenth century.

HAUSALAND IN THE EIGHTEENTH CENTURY

While Kebbi—a declining power—succumbed to the buffetings from her neighbours and Ahir, Gobir—a rising power—consolidated its strength in the face of new challenges. By the beginning of the eighteenth century Gobir had seized the opportunity of Kebbi's weakened position to assume control over Konni and to push further south between Adar and Zamfara territories.[93] Expansion into Katsina territory was more difficult. Indeed, the founding of a new capital at Goran Rami[94] early in the eighteenth century was probably a result of the defeat suffered by Gobir at the hands of Katsina warriors, who sacked Birnin Naya and are said to have carried away its iron gates. Wars waged against Katsina from the new capital during the first half of the eighteenth century were unsuccessful. Zamfara

91 *Ibid.*, pp. 160, 171–2.
92 *Ibid.*, p. 174.
93 Urvoy, *Histoire des populations . . .*, p. 246.
94 *Mission Tilho*, p. 471.

was to be the dominant power in western Hausaland during the first half of the eighteenth century. When the century opened, its capital city was at Dutsi, a short distance north-west of Zurmi. Its territory extended roughly from Sabon Birni in the north to Kwiambana to the south; Muniya and Rubu to the east and Gindi to the west.[95] Its rise to pre-eminence followed the fall of Kebbi as a major power.

The use of dates ascribed to reigning kings in available kinglists seems highly unreliable in many cases but all indications point to the fact that Kebbi most probably fell during the last decade of the seventeenth century or possibly during the early years of the eighteenth. The sources are agreed on the fact that Kebbi was the victim of a concerted attack by the Sarkin Zamfara Babba,[96] Chiroma, Sarkin Gobir, and Ag-Abba, Sultan of Ahir. It is not certain whether the armies of the three states made a combined attack or whether they attacked separately from different frontiers. In the upshot the major Kebbi cities of Surame (the capital) Gungu and Leka fell to Zamfara.[97] Gobir forces captured the king of Kebbi and a number of his chiefs who were then put in confinement. Kebbi was not thereby extinguished as a state, it merely became a second-class power in the context of eighteenth century power-politics in Hausaland. Its survival was later proved by its valiant and successful resistance to the jihādists throughout the nineteenth century. After the fall of Surame a new capital was founded at Birnin Kebbi.

Zamfara's tenure as the leading power in western Hausaland was uneasy and precarious. In the end it proved transient. It did not result in the founding of an empire. The power of the future—Gobir—was at the heels of Zamfara from the beginning. Ahir, even though it was torn internally by succession disputes in which the throne changed hands with astounding frequency from the 1720s to the mid-century, had time and energy enough to spare to engage Zamfara in many conflicts. Situated in an arid region and without any important mineral wealth, the position of Agades (on which its prosperity had depended for centuries) was that of a middleman in the trans-Saharan trade. With the decline and extinction of the Gao-Agades-North African route, the Agades-Gobir-Kebbi route had supervened. The salt trade with Bilma in Kawar was sustained by the grain from Hausaland and other products from south of it. Keeping these routes open bred conflicts between Zamfara and Gobir—the two powers guarding the routes to the south—and Ahir. From the fall of Kebbi down to the 1770s, therefore, there were many Ahir expeditions against Zamfara and Gobir.[98] As Ahir was also engaged in a bitter struggle with Bornu over the control of the trade routes to the north, its power to wage successful

95 Urvoy, *Histoire des populations* . . ., p. 246.
96 Muḥammad Bello says Yaʿqūb b. Babba q.v. *Infāq*, p. 19.
97 *Ibid.*, also *Rauḍāt al-Afkār*; f. 5a–5b; Krieger, *op. cit.*, pp. 44–7.
98 Urvoy, *Journal de la Société* . . ., pp. 161–7.

attacks on its neighbours to the south was much reduced.

Zamfara continued to defend its newly won independence as well as attempting, though unsuccessfully, to expand, particularly eastwards into Katsina and Kano, which states had risen to peaks of prosperity hitherto unknown in their history. Under Sarkin Zamfara Faskare (Falkare?) who ruled in the 1720s, war was in the forefront of Zamfara policy. Both internal and external policies are said to have come under the surveillance of the military chiefs. Attempts to subjugate Kano apparently achieved military victories but no tangible political advantages for Zamfara. During the reign of Sarkin Kano, Muḥammad Sharefa dan Dadi (*c.* 1703–31), a Zamfara expedition led by Sarki Yaʿqūb dan Babba advanced on Kano. The rout of the Kanawa turned to a *melée*. Sarkin Kano was deserted by the bulk of his soldiers. Fear that Zamfarawa raids might be extended to eastern Kano and other districts seems to have compelled the Sarki to order his vassal chiefs to build walls round their towns.[99] Zamfarawa raids into Katsina territory made no devastating impact.

From the achievement of independence by Zamfara, the phenomenal rise and expansion of Gobir was ominous for its future expansion and its very survival. Immediately after the joint spoliation of Kebbi, Gobir undertook wars of expansion in Zaberma, Gurma and Katsina; the same regions into which Zamfara desired to expand.[100] For seven years Sarkin Gobir Soba, son of Muḥammad Chiroma, harassed Maradi, an important town on the eastern branch of the trade route from Agades leading to Katsina. Between *c.* 1731 and 1743, covering the reign of Kumbari dan Sharefa in Kano, Sarkin Gobir Soba is reported to have launched several undecisive attacks on Kano. 'If the Gobirawa defeated the Kanawa one day, the Kanawa defeated them the next. This state of affairs continued for a long time.'[101] The significance of Gobirawa enterprises for Zamfarawa ambitions is emphasised by the fact that from the 1730s we hear no more of any major Zamfarawa push against either Katsina or Kano. In the north Soba lost his life fighting against Ahir forces during the late 1730s.

Zamfara was an empire that might have been. Its growth was stunted by the rise of Gobir before it could realise its potentialities. During the 1730s a steady immigration of the Gobirawa into Zamfara territory began. Having been reluctantly allowed by Sarkin Zamfara Yaʿqūb dan Faskare to settle on the fief of the Alkali (*Al-Qāḍī*) as peaceful farmers, they had become sufficiently numerous during the 1740s to constitute a direct threat to the state of their adoption.

The sources are silent on the reason which impelled the immigration of the Gobirawa. Threat from Ahir may, however, be suggested. At first

99 *Kano Chronicle*, p. 123; the Sarkin Zamfara is referred to as Dan Mazura.
100 *Rauḍāt al-Afkār*, f. 6a. Soba fought in Zaberma for about three years and against Maradi for seven years.
101 *Kano Chronicle*, p. 124.

they showed themselves loyal subjects of Zamfara. But from the 1740s, when they seem to have become hungry for more land, they waxed virulently truculent and started raiding Zamfara villages. Their raiding bands rapidly became very efficient, and harassed Kebbi and Adar with great economic profit to themselves.[102] When Sarkin Kebbi, Malu, died in *c.* 1748,[103] the settlers seized the opportunity of the succession dispute which set in before the appointment of the next sarki to break away from Zamfarawa allegiance.[104] In *c.* 1750 they defeated Kebbi in battle. Thereafter they directed attack on Zamfara itself. The latter's army proved incapable of containing the threat.

The rise of Gobir to its peak of power is the story of the reign of Babari (1741–69). Leader of the Gobirawa immigrants in Zamfara, he had acceded to the throne after a short period of high instability of the Gobir kingship.[105] Four kings reigned in Gobir within a very short spell which followed the death in battle of Soba, his son and a daughter—the Magajiya of Gobir. The last of these kings, Dan Ashi, was deposed. The deposed Sarki allied with Katsina against Gobir. The allies were repelled. Although Gobir forces failed to take Katsina city,[106] the traditional hostility between Gobir and Katsina was thereby deepened. During the early part of his reign (1743–53) Babari fought many wars with Kano in which the latter came off worse.[107] In the end the wars were inconclusive. The chronicler sums up the chronic nature of these wars: 'No record can be kept of the fighting between them in Kabe's time'[108] (1743–53). Beyond Kano, Babari raided as far as Shira in Bornu territory.[109] The farflung exploits of Gobir at the height of its power, apart from the temporary setback which this involved for its adversaries, did not produce any lasting consequences for political relations in Hausaland generally. But the weight of Gobir's might was keenly felt by its immediate neighbours, particularly Zamfara and Katsina.

The revolt of the Gobirawa immigrants in Zamfara and their early wars against that state took place under Babari's leadership. Thereafter Gobirawa onslaught against Zamfara persisted. The struggle was protracted and fierce.[110] The Zamfara threw all into their war effort. But in *c.* 1762[111]

102 Krieger, *op. cit.*, pp. 57–8.
103 *Ibid.*, also *Rauḍāt al-Afkār*, f. 7a.
104 Krieger, *op. cit.*, p. 63. The Gobirawa installed one of themselves as Sarki.
105 *Rauḍāt al-Afkār*, 6b.
106 *Ibid.*
107 *Ibid.*, f. 7a; *Kano Chronicle*, p. 125.
108 *Ibid.*, p. 125.
109 *Rauḍāt al-Afkār*, f. 7a.
110 Krieger, *op. cit.*, p. 65.
111 1764 has usually been suggested as the correct date. But reckoning by the dates in *Rauḍāt al-Afkār* 1762 would be more acceptable. The defeat of Dan Gudi by the Ahirawa was in 1771, which agrees with the *Rauḍāt*. That Dan Gudi is known to have reigned for two years and Barbari died seven years after the sack of Birnin Zamfara fixes the date of this latter event at 1762.

Birnin Zamfara was sacked. The Sarki Mairoki escaped to Kiawa where, allied with Katsina, the wars continued until the 1780s. Bawa jan Gwarzo, Sarkin Gobir *c.* 1771–89, is said to have warred against the Zamfarawa at their refuge in Kiawa and the Katsinawa for fifteen years, until the death of Sarkin Zamfara, Mairoki.[112]

Following the fall of Birnin Zamfara, Babari fortified Alkalawa which became the capital of Gobir. His son, Dan Gudi (1769–71), apparently still preoccupied with an insecure northern frontier, died fighting against the Tuareg. Under Bawa jan Gwarzo, the Gobirawa pressure was directed mainly against Katsina, not just as an ally of the Zamfarawa but as an enemy in their own right. Sarkin Katsina, feeling the pinch, appealed to Gobir for peace but received only deceitful friendship. The Gobirawa did a great deal of plundering and ravaging in Katsina territory but at the end of Bawa's life they suffered a heavy reverse at Dan Kashe. Bawa died very shortly after the battle. His successor, Yaʿqūb dan Bawa, also carried war to Shira as well as continuing the struggle against Katsina. He died in battle in *c.* 1795, fighting against an allied army of Katsina and Kiawa at Kiawa.[113] This brought war between Katsina and Gobir in the eighteenth century to an end. Nafata, Yaʿqūb's successor (1795–1802) diverted his attention to Zamfara. But his wars yielded no permanent results. A new age was dawning in Hausaland. Very soon the perennial conflicts among the Hausa states would be swept away by the Muslim reformers' revolution for a new political arrangement, and a new basis for conflicts.

Meanwhile other developments had taken place in Katsina and Kano. Despite attacks, first from Kebbi, then from Zamfara and lastly from Gobir, Katsina appears to have risen to its peak of prosperity in the course of the eighteenth century. It also attained its pre-*jihād* territorial limits. In the north it included Tessawa and Maradi; it was bounded on the north-west by Gobir and on the west by Zamfara. To the east it had boundaries with Damagaram and Daura and to the south-east with Kazaure and Kano.[114] Its southern boundary was with Birnin Gwari and Zazzau. That Katsina had been able to maintain its territory intact against Gobir onslaughts attests to its power in the seventeenth and eighteenth centuries. Indeed Katsina had proved unconquerable by Kano, Zamfara and Gobir in succession. With the exception of the victory over Maradi by Babari, Gobir, powerful and feared as it was, did not record a single major victory over Katsinawa forces.

No doubt the basis of this strength was Katsina's wealth. We may not doubt Barth's judgment that Katsina in the seventeenth and eighteenth centuries seems to have been the major town of commercial as well as

112 Krieger, *op. cit.*, p. 65, and *Rauḍāt al-Afkār*, f. 7a.
113 *Ibid.*, *Rauḍāt*, ff. 7b, 8b.
114 Daniel, *op. cit.*, p. 10; also *Mission Tilho*, pp. 460–1.

political importance 'in this part of negroland'.[115] In Katsina city there were several foreigners' quarters, including Tudun Mele and a Wangarawa quarter for merchants—people and mallams from the west in the region of old Mali and neighbouring peoples. There were Tuareg and Arab quarters as well as separate quarters for Hausa from other states such as the Kebbawa and the Kogoyawa from Kogo in Katsina Laka.[116] During the second half of the eighteenth century, there seems to have been a large influx of Tuareg from Ahir to Tessawa, Maradi and Katsina.[117] These foreigners were involved in the commercial and religious life of the city. Katsina, as noted earlier, was better placed than Kano for the trans-Saharan trade. It was connected with Agades through Tessawa and with Nupe through Birnin Gwari, with probably a branch route to Zaria from Birnin Gwari.

Since the seventeenth century, following the decline of the Gao-Ahir route, Agades traders had concentrated on trade with Bilma. Every October caravans set out for Bilma laden with grains and diverse articles, some being re-exports, from Hausaland. These caravans returned with Bilma salt and other merchandise.[118] The other route into Hausaland from Agades ran through Gobir and Kebbi to the south. However, it would seem that with the constant wars in the Gobir-Kebbi-Zamfara region, the Agades-Katsina branch of the caravan route was the more peaceful and therefore more heavily used.

During the reign of Kumbari dan Sharefa in Kano (1731-43) Arabs are said to have left Kano, following disturbances there, for Katsina.[119] The existence of a Wangarawa quarter must indicate that Katsina was still involved in the Gwanja-Hausaland trade. The southward extension of Katsina territory between Daura, Kazaure and Kano to the east and south-east, and Zamfara to the west may be seen as having been determined by a policy of protecting the trade route to the south. Having guaranteed its boundaries to ensure the security of its trading connection, Katsina was apparently satisfied with maintaining its territorial integrity without embarking on adventures of expansion during the eighteenth century. It was able to, and did, uphold this policy throughout the eighteenth century.

Kano contrasted sharply with Katsina during this period. Like Katsina, its wars with Gobir may have strained its resources but they had no lasting adverse political consequences. For Kano the century was one of wars. Between 1731 and 1743, during the reign of Kumbari dan Sharefa, Kano was attacked, with no significant success, by a Bornuan army.[120] With the southward movement of the Tuareg Kano was attacked by the Kel-Owi in *c.* 1761. Yet another source of attack from outside came from the

115 H. Barth, *op. cit.*, ii, pp. 79-80.
116 Daniel, *op. cit.*, p. 12.
117 Rennell Rodd, *op. cit.*, p. 411.
118 Urvoy, *Histoire des populations . . .*, p. 187.
119 *K.C.*, p. 124.
120 *Ibid.*, also Rennell Rodd, *op. cit.*, p. 413.

Sosebaki states of Miria, Washa and Dungas.[121] These states, of basic Kano Hausa population, had broken away from Kano allegiance and placed themselves under Bornu during the late seventeenth century. By the eighteenth century they had federated, with a capital at Babaye. From about the mid-century the Sosebaki had asserted their independence of Bornu and embarked unsuccessfully on attacks on Kano.[122] Sosebaki revolt and subsequent attacks on Kano were symptomatic of what appears as general unrest within Kano provinces dating from the late seventeenth century. A recurrent theme of Kano history in the eighteenth century was the constant wars against rebellious districts.[123] It seems that during the late seventeenth and eighteenth centuries the vast expanse of territory under Kano raised problems of effective control from the centre of pseudo-states at a time when Kano's power, though not inconsiderable, was not in the ascendant. The bitter struggles of seventeenth-century Kano against foreign enemies had induced a weakness which may have encouraged secessionist revolts.

For Kano the strain on the state's resources in trying to stem external war and contain internal rebellion is reflected in the rise of taxation imposed by its eighteenth century rulers. Mohamma Sharefa dan Dadi (1703–31) is reported to have introduced seven practices for raising revenue, 'all of which were robbery'.[124] These were *karo*, *rinsua*, *matafada*, *yan dawaki*, *kuaru*, tax on maidens at marriage and tax on the main market—Kurmi. Of him the chronicler writes: 'He invented many other methods of extortion.' His successor, Kumbari, is said to have almost killed Kurmi market by his excessive taxation. He taxed even learned men—mallams—and it was on account of his extortions that there were disturbances in Kano, leading to the departure of Arabs from the city for Katsina.

Kano remained a prosperous commercial centre. There were, as in Katsina, wards of foreign merchants from North Africa, Bornu and other parts of West Africa, including an Ogbomọshọ Yoruba community which settled in the city during the eighteenth century. Kano's connection with the south was through Zaria and Nupe. From the reign of Kumbari (1731–43) imports from Nupe included shields and guns. The latter were probably re-exports of Nupe from its trade with Europeans on the Dahomean coast. Nonetheless, Kano's resources were hardly sufficient to tide over a period of internal and external political problems which put the central power in rather straitened circumstances. Hard pressed, the rulers seem to have attempted to concentrate power in their own hands as the century wore on, not only to ensure firm direction of policy but also to obtain revenue. Baba Zaki dan Yaji (*c.* 1768–76) is said to have compelled

121 *Mission Tilho*, pp. 425–6.
122 *Ibid.*, pp. 427, 429.
123 *K.C.* pp. 123–5.
124 *Ibid.*, p. 123.

the nobility not only to fight in wars against their judgment but also to give 'gifts' to him against their wish.[125]

To the south of Katsina and Kano was Zazzau, about which very little pertinent to our period is known. However, it appears that its hegemony over territories to the south had persisted to the eighteenth century. Its area of authority would have been reduced by the increase in Nupe power during the seventeenth and eighteenth centuries. But at the southern frontiers of metropolitan Zazzau, districts such as the Katab, Morwa, Kajuru, Kauru, Karigi, Kaje and Kagoro had come under some forms of the overlordship of Sarkin Zazzau.[126] They paid tribute to Zaria. Away from these frontier districts, the claims of Zazzau were extensive but apprently tenuous.

The history of Hausaland in the seventeenth and eighteenth centuries was a direct continuation of the process of state-formation and state-building which the present writer sees as the dominant theme not only of the history of the area under study but also of the greater part of sub-Saharan Africa. It may be contended that such a process would normally dominate political and economic thinking in any region comprising primarily small states and a diversity of ethnic groups with similar and therefore competing economic cultures and relations. This thesis would be correct granting, as with Hausaland, the absence of any agreed code of inter-state or international relations. Good and peaceful neighbourliness becomes a philosophy of convenience. In this context, power politics is *Real-politik*. Thus in Hausaland historical ethnic consaguinity was of marginal, if any, relevance to political relations. The attempt to realise boundaries most conducive to political and economic survival as well as prosperity and power was the perennial source of conflict and wars. The possession of superior military power was apparently a temptation to use it against neighbouring states.

In the seventeenth and eighteenth centuries in Hausaland, Kano, Katsina, Kebbi, Zamfara and Gobir had emerged as the dominant states. Daura, Rano and Biram, late developers among the traditional seven, were of necessity out of the contest. Thus, they remained in the backwaters of political and economic development. Zazzau, with a field of expansion to the south only limited by her ability to expand was relatively isolated from the rivalry of its sister states to the north. Moreover Zazzau as the gateway to the rich countries of the south was during our period immune from the antagonism of its northern neighbours.

None of the competing Hausa states ever possessed the power to impose its hegemony effectively over the others. As the technology of warfare was not advanced and the difference between the power of one state and another

125 *Ibid.*, p. 126.
126 C. K. Meek, *The Northern Tribes of Nigeria*, Oxford, 1925, ii, pp. 1–2.

was one of degree rather than of absolute superiority in sophisticated weapons and military strategy, total defeat essential for the absorption of one state by another was out of the question. Hence a recurrent theme of the history of Hausaland was frequent wars leading either to a stalemate or very transient dominance of one state over another. More often than not victory in a war resulted in the acquisition of booty and mere boundary adjustments. Some such adjustments could be major. The encroachment of Gobir, Zamfara and Ahir on Kebbi territory as well as the seizure of part of Zamfara territory by Gobir in the early second half of the eighteenth century aptly illustrate this situation. Both Kebbi and Zamfara survived not only to the nineteenth century but beyond. The inability of one state to impose its rule over the others is shown by the careers of Zaria, Kebbi and Gobir in the fifteenth to the eighteenth century. Apart from their military incapacity to continue to ensure acceptance of conquest by the conquered, these states had not the resources, either human or economic, to turn their victories into permanent gains.

Tributary states honoured their subservient positions only so long as they had to. It is said that the Hausa states continued to pay tribute to Bornu right up to the end of the eighteenth century, with the exception of Gobir whose king, Bawa jan Gwarzo, abrogated this relationship late in that century. How regular compliance was among the Hausa states is a matter for conjecture. Available evidence suggests that Kano, which had to be invaded by Bornu during the first half of the eighteenth century, was probably irregular in meeting its tributary obligations to Bornu. The continued rendering of tribute to Bornu was probably sustained for so long among the Hausa states because Bornu remained the dominant power in these parts, a power which no state could challenge effectively on its own. Further, the internecine conflicts between the Hausa states ruled out combination against an external power. Fear of the dominant position of Bornu, rather than any effective Bornuan control over the affairs of the Hausa states, seems to have kept alive the tradition of payment of tribute. There was always the chance that Bornu might, as it could, visit dissent with an expedition. Such indeed appears to have been the grounds which sustained even the ephemeral dominance of one Hausa state over some of the others. With regard again to Bornu it may be assumed that payment of tribute over several centuries engendered a habit which no one thought of breaking. 'Empire' in our area came to mean recognition by vassal polities of the remote sovereignty of a power that counted for little if anything in the ordering of their states, their administration and security problems. The imperial power, in reality, hardly exercised sovereign powers.

Still on Hausaland, a division was made earlier between western and eastern Hausaland up to the seventeenth century on the grounds of political relations. The rise of Zamfara and Gobir in the eighteenth century tended in a sense to involve Hausaland as a whole in a common political experience. This was not an experience in cooperative building but an indication of accentuation of interstate political conflict—a direct result of the rise of the said two powers. Kano and Katsina fought Zamfara and Gobir in turn, in self-defence. During the seventeenth and eighteenth centuries they (Kano and Katsina) were concerned with preserving what they held. That their powers had attained great heights is proved by the inability of either Zamfara or even more notably Gobir to subdue them. Indeed, Katsina on the whole had the upper hand in its resistance to Gobir onslaughts. The immoderate expansion of Gobir was already, by the end of the eighteenth century, pushing it down the path of decline. The Hausa states were probably not far from achieving a balance of power essential to the maintenance of stable interstate relations.

Another aspect of Hausa history was the involvement of the states in wide commercial relations: east-west and south-north. Internally there were commercial relations between the states. Before our period opens the trading connections with the wider world of east, west, south and north had become well established. Reference has already been made at various points to the fact that many of the political conflicts between states had part of their origins in the desire to control the highways of commerce.

The Hausa states, as well as Bornu, were organised to promote exchange. Trade routes were strictly protected by armed patrols located at stage-posts about ten to fifteen miles apart.[127] The capital cities had become centres of congregation for foreign merchants from other parts of West Africa as well as from North Africa. Hausa trading communities during our period were to be found widely dispersed throughout West Africa. Hausa agricultural products found a place in sustaining these wide commercial connections not only by providing sustenance for the foreign merchant communities but also as exports. In return for manufactured wares, salt, dates and other merchandise from other parts—notably North Africa—Hausaland supplied grains, leather products, woven cloths and various other manufactured goods. The cities had become centres of artificers. Besides, Hausaland and Bornu, straddling the savannah and scrubland belt south of the Sahara, occupied a middleman's position in the exchange of complementary commercial articles between North Africa, (and indirectly Europe) with the peoples of the forest belt. Europeans trading on the Guinea coast did not seriously undermine the transcontinental trade though they did supplement it. It was on this extensively wide contact with the outside world that the economic prosperity not only of Hausaland but of all the savannah Sudanic states depended. With the successive decline of Ghana, Mali and Songhay, Hausaland and Bornu became the main centres of this trade during the seventeenth and eighteenth centuries.

127 M. G. Smith, 'Exchange and marketing among the Hausa', in G. Dalton and P. Bohannan, *Markets in Africa*, N.W. University, 1961.

One of the most important commodities of the trans-Saharan trade was slaves. They were largely the products of the frequent wars, and the need to keep up their supply may have motivated many of the wars. The capture and sale of slaves was an amoral act not different from the acquisition of any other economic product. Slaves seem to have supplied the lifeblood of commerce. They were central to the economic life of the states. As domestic slaves they supplied manpower for generating profit. They were employed for agriculture as well as in war. They were in themselves an international currency as well as a means of earning currency. The institution of slavery and the organisation of the slave trade must have had profound implications for Hausa political, economic and social structures.

While one may see the dominant theme of Hausa and Bornu history as tied up with the problems of state-building and the guarantee of security for individual polities, it is important to note, even if it cannot now be thoroughly studied, that economic activities and considerations for promoting these lay at the root of each state's power and organisation as well as its political relations with its neighbours. Other factors, such as religion, groups and subcultures within the states, must have had far-reaching effects on political, social and other forms of organisation. Details regarding most of these factors appear largely lost to history. But of them, the introduction and spread of Islam and the immigration of the Fulani in large numbers into various parts of Hausaland and Bornu have had the most far-reaching consequences for historical developments.

During the first decade of the nineteenth century, the Hausa states and their kings were swept away by the well known *jihād* of ʿUthmān dan Fodiye. Adherents of this movement assailed Bornu, shook it to its roots and thus touched off a chain of events which led ultimately to the fall of the Seifawa dynasty and the substitution of the Shehus in their place. Consideration of the causes of the *jihād* are outside the scope of this chapter. It may only be noted that the enthronement of Islamic values as the dominant ideology of ordering society, of which the *jihād* was the instrument, was the end-point of an undercurrent of Islamic acculturation which had been running largely parallel with, but often marginally undercutting, traditional values through centuries of symbiotic coexistence. The acceptance of Islam by the kings of Bornu from the eleventh century and those of Hausaland from the fourteenth as imperial cults for obvious political and economic advantages is a familiar theme in the history of these states.

By the seventeenth century Islam had not only 'invaded' the courts but had made important incursions into the ranks of the general masses. A more important development during our period was that the storm-troopers of Islamic expansion had long ceased to be mainly foreign savants or foreign merchants selling the faith with their wares but were indigenous men who had not only learned but were themselves teachers of Islamic sciences. Such men were to be found in the state capitals as well as scattered throughout the major settlements.[128] Birnin Gazargamo held primacy of place among such centres and was followed by Katsina and Kano. There were also numerous settlements (villages) which grew around famous savants. These became strong outposts of Islamic learning to which zealots from far and wide resorted. The consequent emergence of a widening circle of Islamic pundits was, the present writer suggests, the most crucial factor in the Islamisation of Hausaland and Bornu. It also marks the point at which a definite move was made in the direction of the enthronement of Islamic values as those which would dominate society and determine its corporate organisation. The immediate effect of the expansion of Islamic education was the spread among neophytes of an awareness of the fundamental bases of the faith beyond the simple acceptance of the five pillars.

The intellectual awareness, as distinct from irrational belief, lent crucial vigour to the spirit of questioning which cut at the root of traditional religions, values and customs, and the whole moorings of the existing societies in so far as they affected the life of the Muslim man *per se*. Similar questions had indeed been raised in the courts in preceding centuries and there had been aspiring reformist rulers in Hausaland and Bornu.[129] But these were operating in situations in which Islam, despite royal support, was a fifth wheel in the state. Its base was too narrow successfully to challenge prevailing traditions and attitudes. With the spread of education and the growth in depth of intellectual awareness, by the eighteenth century the time was ripe for a revolution. Religious educational propaganda began seriously to be pursued through the medium of writing during the seventeenth century in Hausaland, and no doubt before then in Bornu. Aḥmad b. Fartua, whose historical writings have come down to us, and the graphic description of the court at Gazargamo in the seventeenth century with its learned disputations are reliable pointers to the level of intellectual development in that kingdom.[130] Bivar and Hiskett have drawn attention to a number of seventeenth-century authors of northern Nigeria.[131] Among these were the famous scholar Muḥammad al-Kashīnawī al-Sabbagh, better known to history as Dan Marina, and his pupil Abū ʿAbdullāh Muḥammad b. Masanih who became a celebrity in his own right. To both of them eleven works on various subjects have been credited. Some six authors are mentioned by the same writers for the eighteenth century.

During the first half of the eighteenth century Al-Imām Muḥammad b. Al-Ḥājj ʿAbd al-Raḥmān al-Barnawī composed his treatise in verse called

128 Muḥammad Bello gives a long list of learned men in Hausaland and Bornu, see *Infāq al-Maisūr*, pp. 5–14 and pp. 22–9 from Baghirmi through Bornu and Hausaland.
129 Muḥammad Korau of Katsina, Muḥammad Rimfa of Kano (*c*. 1463–99), Idris Aloma (1571–1603).
130 See above, pp. 504–5.
131 M. Hiskett and A. D. H. Bivar, 'The Arabic literature of Northern Nigeria to 1804, a provisional account', *B.S.O.A.S.*, xxv, pp. 104–48.

Shurb al-Zulāl[132] (the drinking of the sweet)—'a didactic *fiqh* poem'. It deals with the distinction between what is permissible (*ḥalāl*) and what is forbidden (*ḥarām*) according to the *sharīʿa*. Concerned principally with what is legal or illegal for Muslims to eat, it lashes out against various aberrations of the times which would compromise the Muslim. Oblique criticisms are launched against illegal taxations, perfidious gains, perversion of justice and other illegalities, significantly foreshadowing the criticisms later levied against contemporary governments by ʿUthmān dan Fodiye. It is important to observe that the *Shurb al-Zulāl* is addressed to confessing Muslims.

From about the second half of the eighteenth century social criticism was receiving unprecedented impetus. It was directed at Muslims, exhorting them to follow the path of truth as individuals. The number of practising savants had increased, as also had the general awareness of the stipulations of the *sharīʿa*. Muslim savants travelled from one place to another with their sermons (*waʿẓ*). Students moved from the feet of one master to another to learn their specialities. Itinerant preaching was for many savants a full-time profession. Proliferation of learned men must have initiated a rivalry between them[133] which urged each to strive to deepen his learning as a prerequisite to success. The direct result of this development would be not only the deepening of the ordinary Muslim's faith but also his increasing alienation from the existing social and political order. The embracing of Islam had become a revolutionary fountain in the state which in time drew new converts into the fold of the faith. Reform had become a movement. Each learned man of note had his own community of adherents around him. This development was widespread throughout Hausaland and beyond.

Leadership of Islamisation in the state had by the eighteenth century shifted from the kings to the religious savants. The kings had themselves been left behind by the impetus which learning had lent to the movement. Their ancestors, in embracing the faith, had merely borrowed from its law and its culture such aspects as would augment their power and the economic wellbeing of their states. Beyond this they had made no basic departures from the traditional religious, political and social structuring of their states in the direction of Islam. Therefore by the late eighteenth century they belonged to a world in which Islam was marginally and ceremonially conditioning traditional cultures. That such was the case could be easily demonstrated by the Muslim leaders. The familiar departures from the *sharīʿa*, such as those detailed out in the *Kitāb al-Farq* of ʿUthmān dan Fodiye, needed only pointing out to be recognized by the Believer not only as anti-Islamic but unjust.

132 *Ibid.*, pp. 119–29 (text and translation).

133 Such rivalry is exemplified by the hostility of many mallams to 'Uthmān dan Fodiye during his preaching career. This is discussed by F. H. El-Masri, 'A critical edition of Dan Fodio's Bayān Wujub al-hijra ʿala 'l-ʿibad; with introduction, English translation and Commentary', unpublished Ph.D. thesis, Ibadan, 1968, pp. 4–5.

Sarkin Kano Kumbari dan Sharefa (*c.* 1731–43) is said to have levied illegal taxes in the Kurmi market as well as imposing *jizya* on learned men. Baba Zaki (1768–76) was noted for oppression of his subjects, including the notables whom he exploited in every way and compelled to fight his battles,[134] thus giving validity to the criticisms of *Kitāb al-Farq*. Hausa kings were also charged with practising or condoning polytheism (*shirk*) the most antithetical stand to Islam. The *Dirki*—the Qur'ān turned into a fetish to which sacrifices of cattle were offered—was not destroyed in Kano until the reign of Al-Wali (1781–1807).[135] A Katsina talisman, similar to the sacred Mune of Bornu in the belief attached to it as guardian of state security, was reportedly opened only towards the end of the eighteenth century. These actions were not in deference to Islam. They were popularly regarded merely as presaging the end of the kingdom. Besides, Hausas had many deities such as *Uwandowa,* goddess of hunting, and *Uwargona,* goddess of agriculture. Although Hausas seem not to have made graven images they did offer sacrifices to their gods. Certain communities also believed in a water-spirit—*Sarkin Rafi*—sacrifice to whom seems to have required a virgin girl.[136] A similar practice prevailed in Bornu as an annual event at the advent of the floods of the Komadugu Yobe. Other communities had their totems. There was widespread belief in divination, conjuring and 'black magic'.[137] It was circumstances such as these to which Muslims were radically opposed that brought about the tension in society which precipitated the *jihād.*

The growth of Islamic acculturation had reached a stage wherein the old order had either to ally or come to grips with it. A particularly vocal section of the states—the Muslim leaders and their followers—were demanding reforms in consonance with their conception of a just society. Their demands are understandable since they could not be true Muslims while they were subjected to anti-Muslim laws. Reform of the religion could not stop at the level of the individual or sectional groups. From being fifth wheels in the state in earlier centuries the Muslims had become fifth columnists by the late eighteenth century. Rather than seeing the *jihād* as something consciously planned and executed by a group, one must view it as a clash, natural enough, resulting from an attempt to resolve a basic ideological contradiction in the states represented by the guardians of the old order on one hand and the protagonists of a new age on the other.

The enthronement of Islam as a state religion and as the fountain head of society's values lay in the womb of the Hausa states and Bornu, granting the nature of their historical development up to the eighteenth century. The

134 See above, pp. 521–2.
135 *Kano Chronicle*, p. 127.
136 A. J. N. Tremearne, *Hausa superstitions and customs: an introduction to the folk-lore and the folk*, London, 1913, pp. 111–19.
137 *Ibid.*, p. 169 f.

process of its development had hitherto been one of gradual evolution. It need not have become a revolution. But its phenomenal intellectual development during the latter part of the eighteenth century quickened the pace of change to a revolution and swelled the ranks of Muslims. During a visit to Bawa in 1788/89 ʿUthmān dan Fodiye is said to have had 1,000 mallams on his side.[138] Yet his was only one of many Muslim *jamāʿas*, albeit the most distinguished and the most powerful.

Other factors, which may seem to belong more to accidents or subsidiary flows of history rather than to its main currents, aided the precipitation of a revolution. Existing governments whose political ideology had been outstripped by the intellectual development among Muslims left wide scope for just criticisms which made Islam by contrast an alluring attraction to those who felt the rigours of state authority. Those who were most open to this allurement were the Fulani. Politically they had remained aliens in Hausaland and Bornu, yet after a sojourn of about four centuries they had no other homes. Fulanis did serve in the governments of many if not all the states, sometimes in very high offices, not in their right as representatives of Fulani groups but on individual merits usually related to scholarship. However, being the most highly Islamised and learned group in these states they naturally assumed leadership of the cause of Islam.

In short the piety and learning of numerous Fulani put them at the vanguard of the rising force of change. Their critical insight into existing conditions as Muslims was not hampered since they had no vested interest in contemporary governments from which they were excluded. They were therefore unfettered as the leaders of the new movement. The isolation of the Fulani as a group had, moreover, created a cohesion among them which seems to have contributed to the widespread following which ʿUthmān dan Fodiye enjoyed and which in the end ensured the success of the *jihād* over a wide area. Having common grievances Fulani groups had a community of interests which crystallised in Islamic terms. This argument has no direct bearing on the ethnic motivation of the *jihād*, with which this study does not concern itself.

One of the most crucial factors which precipitated the revolution, particularly at the time it occurred, was the personality of ʿUthmān dan Fodiye. A learned theologian and a pious *Ṣufi*, heir to a centuries-old tradition of learning and social respectability in his family, he had all the makings of a successful charismatic leader. Even though a Fulani, it was his towering personality that called into coordinated existence the many scattered *jamāʿas* of Hausaland and beyond it. The phenomenal growth of his *jamāʿa* in Gobir produced the political tension between his group and established authority which exploded in military conflict. His success in Gobir and the authority he gave to mallam leaders elsewhere supplied the

138 D. M. Last, *The Sokoto Caliphate*, London, 1968, p. 7.

enthusiasm and the leadership which carried other movements to success. As far as we know events which led to the *jihād* in other places had not followed the same pattern of gradual development through various stages and negotiations, ending in a clash which had become inevitable. The Gobir *jihād* had therefore forced the pace which led to the outbreak of conflict in many future emirates of the Sokoto Caliphate.

The above summary of the background of the *jihād* draws attention to the social dynamics in the Hausa states which had been at work as an undercurrent of decisive change. While through their interstate conflicts, Hausa rulers had for centuries searched in vain for arrangements which would guarantee political order and stability, the *jihād* by enthroning Islam supplied these states and their neighbours with a supra-state ideology for integration.

Index

Index

Baoule region, 76
Bara province, 228, 239; *see also* Niumi kingdom
Barabara people, found Gonja kingdom, 346
Barabish people, 467; and trade routes, 475-6
Barbados, 250, 251, 265; slave imports, 259
Barbarossa brothers, corsairs, 209
Barbot, J., 276n, 286, 287, 293, 294n, 295, 296, 297, 300n, 302n, 314n, 318n, 358n, 370, 393n
Barbushe, Kano chief, 193
Bardial, city, 394n
Barendson, G. W., 47n, 69n
Bari, Fulbe clan, 417, 420, 462
Bariba region, 312, 340; wars with Ọyọ, 316, 341
barley, climatic barrier, 65
Barmandana, King of Mali, 154
Barros, J. de, 347, 360n, 362n, 365n
Barth, H., 167n, 175n, 220n, 221n, 353n, 469n, 502n, 519, 520n
Baru, Sunni of Songhay, 227-8
Basden, G. T., 297n, 298n
bāshās, Ruma state, 445, 449
Baṣọrun, Ọyọ chief, 316
Bassa people, 81
Bassambiri kingdom, 283
Bassan people, 293; traders, 294
Bassari people, 345, 415
Bathily dynasty, 431
Batran, Abd al-ʿAzīz, 482n, 483n
Bauchi district, 26, 490, 510
Baumana, *see* Bambara
Bawa jan Gwarzo, Sarkin Gobir, 501, 519, 523
Bawo, Hausa founder dynast, 20, 191
Bayajidda (Bayejida), ancestor of the Hausa, 20, 191-2
Bayotte people, 434
Bazilio, J., 327n, 328, 332n
bead trade, 295
Begho, town, 212, 478
Bekri, El, geographer, 14n
Bekwai, town, 372, 373
Beledugu (Sirimana) chiefdom, 415
Beledugu (Beledougou), 131, 453, 459; Massassis clan in, 459-61
Beletiema, village, 289
Bende market, 29
Benga (or Bangu) province, 228, 347
Benin empire, 23, 76, 273-4, 300, 302-3; bronzes, 273-4; dynasties, 119; political role in Delta states, 273-4; in succession disputes, 302; trade with Gold Coast, 295
Benko region, 460
Benteniel province, 427
Bentia region, 142, 143
Benue-Congo languages, 273
Benue River, 9
Benue Valley, 49
Beʿo, *see* Bighu
Berbers, 19, 26, 464; 'Arabisation', 468-9; and the Fulani, 104; and the Hausas, 183; Islamisation, 124, 470-1; in Massina, 472; Songhay empire, 140-1, 143; trade with Phoenicians, 72; and trans-Saharan trade, 120-1, 152; *see also* Ṣanhāja, Tuareg
Bernard, E. A., 39n
Bernus, E., 382n
Bertho, J., 306n, 308n, 309
Beur Tiaka, Brak of Walo, 401
Bezeguiche (Goree), 390, 393
Bight of Biafra, source of slaves, 262, 267
Bight of Benin, source of slaves, 262, 267
Bighu (Beʿo, Begho, Bitu) state, 355-6, 362, 375; town, 139; Dyula settlement, 355-6
Bilad al-Takrur, Western Sudan, 135
Bile, town, 282, 283, 290
Bilma, town, 170, 171, 520; salt mines, 506, 516
Bîme, A., 452n
Binger, L. G., 353n, 452n, 468n
Biobaku, S. O., 311n, 341n
Birahim Fatma Tioub, Damel of Cayor, 409
Biram, Hausa founder dynast, 191
Biram, Hausa state, 20, 522
Biram Mbanga, Damel of Cayor, 404
Biram ta Gabas (Garun Gabas) state, 488
Biram Yacine Boubou, Damel of Cayor, 404-5
Birayamb Ma Djiguene Ndaw N'Diaye, Bourba of Djloff, 400
Biri, Mai of the Sefawa, 172
Birifor people, 94
Birkama, town, 434
birni (birane), Hausa cities, 185-8
Birni Gazargamu (Gazargamo), Bornu, *see* Ngazargamu
Birnin-Dare, 191

South Carolina, 250, 262
Southall, A., 119
Southern Akan kingdoms, 364–72; gold industry, 371; military developments, 371–2; slave trade, 371; *see also* Asante
Sow, Fulbe clan, 417
Soyaki, Sarkin Kano, 509
Spain, 245; contacts with Songhay, 144
Spanish America, slave imports, 259, 260; *see also* Americas
spatial and social distance, 86–8; village system, 98
spy system, Bornu, 499; Dahomey, 324
Stamp, L. D., 8n
state formation, 109–19
stateless societies, agriculturalists, 82–104; approach to history of, 78–80; definition, 78; distribution, 80–2; dispersed, territorially defined communities (Type III), 93–7; gods and outsiders, 106–9; large compact village system (Type II), 97–104; and Mossi kingdoms, 345–6; and origins of states, 109–19; pastoralists, 104–6; population, 81; segmentary lineage system (Type I), 84–93
Stebbing, E. P., 7n, 8n
steles, Songhay royal family, 144
Stenning, D., 105n, 106n
Stewart, C., 482n, 483n
Stone Age, African terminology, 44; persistence, 75; Earlier Stone Age, 45–8; First Intermediate, 48–50; Middle Stone Age, 50–53; Second Intermediate, 53; Later Stone Age, 53–64
Stone Bowl culture, 65
stone implements, 37–8, 41, 44, 46, 63; Middle Stone Age, 50–3; periods, 42; Sangoan, 43, 48–50
stone working techniques, 50, 51
Studer, E. F. S. de, 261n
Sudan, 'alien' dynasties, 121–2; consequences of Islamisation, 387; savannah, 5; *see also* Central Sudan, Western Sudan and the individual states
sugar trade, 250; Brazil, 248–9; development, 247–8; and maritime revolution, 246; plantations, 245; slavery in the, 243–4; *see also* plantation system
Suhuyini, Mossi princess, 348
Sulaymān, Mansā of Mali, 134, 147, 155
Sulayman Dandi, *see* Sonni Sulayman Dandi
Suleiman dan Abdu Na Bawanka, Sarkin Zamfara, 514
Sulimana kingdom, 422
Sumaa, town, 372
Sumanguru Kante, King of Sosso, 131, 133
Sumba people, 436
Summers, R., 71n
Sundjata (Sundiata), founder of Mali empire, 131, 132–3, 154–5
Sunnī (Shi) dynasty, *see* Sonni dynasty
Suntreso, 372, 392n, 416n
Surame, city, 222, 223, 493, 516
Susu (Sosso) people, 420, 422, 436, 438; kingdom overthrown by Sundjata, 133, 452
Suyuti, al-, 213, 220
swamp forest, 3

taboos, 218
Tabounsou chiefdom, 437
Tadmakka (Tadmekka), Berber town, 135, 144, 150
Tadmakka confederation, 451, 464, 465–6, 467, 469, 470
Tado kingdom, 308
Tafo, town, 365, 371, 373
Tagant, 121
Taghaza (Tagaza), town, 139, 140, 443, 476, 477; salt mine, 150, 235–8, 443, 476, 477
Tahabaire, King of Sulimana, 422, 423
Tahert, state, 143
Tait, D., 96n, 348n, 349n, 350n, 351n, 381n
Takārir, *see* Takrūr
Takedda, 491
Takoradi, harbour at, 11
Takrūr (Tekrur, Takārir), kingdom, 122, 127, 135–7; Islamisation, 136, 153; trading centre, 122
Takyiman state, 357, 359, 375
talakawa, Hausa common people, 189
Talansan, battle, 422
Talbot, P. A., 288n
Tallensi people, 345
Tamakloe, E. F., 348, 349n, 353n
Tampolensi people, 363
Tankondibo, battle at, 238
Tao(u)deni, 476; salt workings, 14